The Essentials of American History

Y0-AUZ-107

Richard N. Current University of North Carolina at Greensboro

T. Harry Williams late of Louisiana State University

Frank Freidel Harvard University

W. Elliot Brownlee University of California, Santa Barbara

The Essentials of American History

Fourth Edition

ALFRED A. KNOPF   **New York**

THIS IS A BORZOI BOOK PUBLISHED BY ALFRED A. KNOPF, INC.

Fourth Edition
987654321
Copyright © 1976, 1980, 1986 by Alfred A. Knopf, Inc.
 © 1959, 1961, 1964, 1966, 1971, 1972 by Richard Current,
  T. Harry Williams, and Frank Freidel

All rights reserved under International and Pan-American Copyright Conventions. No part of this book may be reproduced in any form or by any means, electronic or mechanical, including photocopying, without permission in writing from the publisher. All inquiries should be addressed to Alfred A. Knopf, Inc., 201 East 50th Street, New York, N.Y. 10022. Published in the United States by Alfred A. Knopf, Inc., New York, and simultaneously in Canada by Random House of Canada Limited, Toronto. Distributed by Random House, Inc., New York.

Library of Congress Cataloging in Publication Data

Main entry under title:

The Essentials of American history.

  Includes bibliographies and index.
  1. United States—History.   I. Current,
Richard Nelson.
E178.1.E79   1986b   973   85-18073
ISBN 0-394-35491-5

Manufactured in the United States of America

Cover: "The Cranberry Harvest, Island of Nantucket," by Eastman Johnson, 1880. Courtesy of the Putnam Foundation Collection, Timken Art Gallery, San Diego, California.
Cover Design: Marsha Cohen

To the Memory of William Best Hesseltine (1902–1963)

Preface

The six years since the third edition of this book appeared have witnessed a swift torrent of historical scholarship and an even more rapid flow of national events. In revising *The Essentials of American History* we have sought to bring the book up to date in terms of both recent scholarship and current history. As part of that effort, we have revised the historiographical essays, "Where Historians Disagree," and updated the treatment of various topics, including the history of women and the history of Reconstruction.

In this revision we have attempted to make *The Essentials of American History* even more useful as a brief textbook by reducing significantly both the length of the text and the number of chapters. We have also made the lists of readings more selective.

The Essentials of American History provides the main themes of American history while omitting much of the factual and illustrative material commonly found in longer texts. The organization — with chapters grouped in chronological units and with an introduction for each period — is intended to make the overall structure quite clear and at the same time to allow a good deal of flexibility in assignments. The brief historiographical essays included in the text introduce the student to several of the most serious conflicts of historical interpretation and thus, it is hoped, help the student understand that the study of history involves far more than merely collecting and memorizing "facts."

In preparing this revision, we have profited from the expertise of the editors at Alfred A. Knopf, Inc. We shall be grateful for any suggestions regarding improvements to be made in future reprintings and revisions of this text.

R.N.C.
F.F.
W.E.B.

Contents

to 1783 • PART ONE
English Colonists Become Americans and Gain Their Independence   **1**

Chapter 1
ENGLAND TRANSPLANTED:
THE SEVENTEENTH CENTURY   **3**

Interest in Colonization	3
The Wilderness Setting	3
The Woods Indians	4
European Rivals	5
Virginia and Maryland	5
Plymouth and Massachusetts Bay	7
The Puritan Way of Life	7
Expansion of New England	8
Carolina	9
New York	9
The Quaker Colonies	10
The "Glorious Revolution"	11

Chapter 2
PROVINCIAL AMERICANS,
1700–1763   **13**

The Scarcity of Labor	13
Population Growth	14
Agriculture	15
Industries	17
Money and Commerce	18
The Class Structure	18
Home and Family	19
The Pattern of Religions	20
The Great Awakening	21

Reading and Writing	22
The Higher Learning	22

Chapter 3
THE EMPIRE UNDER STRAIN   **24**

Toward Self-Government	24
New France	25
Anglo-French Conflict	25
The Great War for the Empire	26
Burdens of Victory	27
The New Imperialism	28
Colonial Self-Interest	29
The Stamp Act Crisis	30
The Townshend Program	31
The Philosophy of Revolt	32
The Tea Excitement	33

Chapter 4
THE AMERICAN REVOLUTION   **35**

Lexington and Concord	35
Declaration of Independence	36
State Governments	36
The Confederation	37
Mobilizing for War	38
The Fighting, to 1777	40
Foreign Friends	41
Victory at Yorktown	42
Winning the Peace	43

Selected Readings   **44**

1783–1823 • PART TWO
**The Young Republic Makes a Successful Start Under a New
Constitution**   **45**

Chapter 5
A MORE PERFECT UNION   **47**

Failures in Foreign Affairs   47
The Needs of the West   48
Debts, Taxes, and Daniel Shays   48
Advocates of Centralization   50
A Divided Convention   50
Differences Compromised   51
The Constitution of 1787   52
Federalists, Antifederalists   54
Filling in the Gaps   55

Chapter 6
FEDERALIST FOUNDATIONS   **57**

Hamilton's Financial Plans   57
Enacting the Program   58
Rise of Political Parties   59
Securing the Frontier   59
Maintaining Neutrality   60
Jay's Treaty   61
Election of 1796   62
Quasi-War with France   62

Repression and Protest   63
The Republicans Win   64

Chapter 7
THE REPUBLICAN ERA   **65**

Jefferson in Power   65
Conflict with the Courts   65
Dollars and Ships   66
The Louisiana Purchase   67
The Burr Conspiracy   68
Freedom of the Seas   69
Indians and Western Lands   70
The War of 1812   71
The Peace Settlement   72
Banks, Tariffs, Roads   72
"Era of Good Feelings"   73
Florida and the Far West   73
The Great Migration   74
The Missouri Compromise   75
Marshall and the Court   77
Origin of the Monroe Doctrine   78

Selected Readings   **79**

1823–1848 • PART THREE
Sectionalism Contends with Nationalism as the Country Expands   **81**

Chapter 8
**TOWARD A NATIONAL
ECONOMY**   **83**

Industrialization Emerges   83
Transportation: Oceans and Roads   84
The Canal Age   85
Railroads and the Telegraph   86
The Northeast: Farms and Labor   88
The Northwest   90
King Cotton's Country   91
The "Peculiar Institution"   93
The Population   94

Chapter 9
FREEDOM'S FERMENT   **96**

Democracy and Civilization   96
Spirit of Social Reform   97
Advancing Education   98
Remedying Society's Ills   100
The Movement for Women's Rights   100
The Nativist Movement   102
North of Slavery   103
The White Abolitionists   103
The Campaign for Liberation   104
The Slave's Response   105
The Proslavery Reaction   106

Chapter 10
JACKSONIAN DEMOCRACY   **109**

More and More Voters   *109*
"Corrupt Bargain"   *109*
The Second President Adams   *110*
The Common Man's President   *111*
The Nullification Theory   *111*
Removing the Indians   *112*
South Carolina Interposes   *113*
The Bank War   *114*
Whigs Against Democrats   *115*
Parties and Ethnicity   *115*
Van Buren and Hard Times   *116*
The Log Cabin Campaign   *116*

Chapter 11
MANIFEST DESTINY   **118**

Frustration of the Whigs   *118*
Webster's Diplomacy   *119*
Election of Polk   *119*
Partitioning of Oregon   *120*
Annexation of Texas   *121*
Lands Beyond Texas   *122*
"American Blood"   *124*
War with Mexico   *124*
Settlers in the Far West   *126*
Wartime and Postwar Politics   *127*

Selected Readings   **128**

1848–1877 • PART FOUR
North and South Separate, Fight, and Rejoin, While the Slaves
Gain Partial Freedom   **131**

Chapter 12
THE ROAD TO DISUNION   **133**

Taylor and the Territories   *133*
The Compromise of 1850   *134*
Renewed Agitation   *136*
Latin American Ambitions   *137*
The Kansas-Nebraska Act   *137*
Republican Ideology   *139*
"Bleeding Kansas"   *139*
Buchanan and Sectional Politics   *140*
The Dred Scott Case   *141*
Kansas Again   *141*
Lincoln Against Douglas   *142*
John Brown's Raid   *143*

Chapter 13
THE NATION DIVIDED   **144**

The Great Decision of 1860   *144*
The Secession of the South   *145*
War Potential, North and South   *146*
The North's Economic Program   *146*
Mobilizing the Union Armies   *148*
Northern Politics, to 1862   *150*
Emancipation   *151*
The Confederate Government   *152*
Southern Money and the Draft   *152*
Confederate Politics   *154*

Chapter 14
THE CIVIL WAR   **155**

The Commanders in Chief   *155*
The Role of Sea Power   *155*
Europe and the Disunited States   *156*
The Opening Battles   1861   *157*
The Western Theater   1862   *158*
The Virginia Front   1862   *159*
Year of Decision   1863   *160*
The Ending   1864–1865   *161*
The War's Aftermath   *164*
Presidential Reconstruction: Lincoln   *164*
Presidential Reconstruction: Johnson   *166*

Chapter 15
RADICAL RECONSTRUCTION   **167**

Congress Takes Over   *167*
The President Impeached   *170*
The Reconstructed States   *171*
A Soldier in the White House   *171*
Successes in Foreign Affairs   *173*
The Evils of "Grantism"   *174*
The Greenback Question   *175*
Southern Republicans Lose   *175*
The Compromise of 1877   *176*

Selected Readings   **178**

Contents

1865–1917 · PART FIVE
Modern America Emerges   **179**

Chapter 16
ECONOMIC LIFE, 1865–1917   **182**

Industrialization	182
Railroads	182
The Rise of Big Business	183
Bigness in Specific Industries	184
The Automobile	185
Distribution of Wealth	186
Labor Organizes	186
Rise of the AFL	187
Major Strikes	188
Unionization Slows	189
The Last West	190
The Western Indians	191
The Farmers' Grievances	192

Rise of the Populists	206
Harrison and Then Cleveland Again	207
The Choice of 1896	209
Origins of Progressivism	210
Social Justice	212
Reform in the Cities	212
Statewide Reforms	213
Women's Causes	214
T. R. and the Trusts	215
Government and Labor	216
Regulation and Conservation	217
Taft and the Progressives	217
A Rift in Republican Ranks	218
Woodrow Wilson Wins	219
Enacting the New Freedom	219

Chapter 17
SOCIETY AND CULTURE IN THE
INDUSTRIAL ERA, 1865–1917   **194**

Population	194
The Newer Immigrants	194
The Urban Scene	195
Women: Outside the Home	196
Women and Family Life	196
Black Americans	197
Toward Universal Schooling	199
New Uses of Leisure	200
The Publishing Business	200
Reflections in Literature	201
Business Philosophy and Its Critics	201

Chapter 19
EMERGENCE OF A WORLD
POWER, 1865–1917   **222**

The New Manifest Destiny	222
Hawaii and the Pacific	222
Controversy over Cuba	223
The "Splendid Little War"	224
Decision for Imperialism	224
The Colonial Empire	225
The Open Door	226
T. R. and World Politics	227
The Asian Balance	227
The Panama Canal	228
The "Roosevelt Corollary"	228
Taft and Dollar Diplomacy	229
Wilsonian Intervention	229
Making Mexico Behave	230
War in Europe	230
Neutral Trade and Neutral Rights	231
The Preparedness Program	232
Leading the People to War	233

Chapter 18
POLITICS, 1865–1917   **204**

The Politics of Complacency	204
Return of the Democrats	205
Ethnic Politics	205

Selected Readings   **234**

1917–1941 • PART SIX
From Total War Through Depression   237

Chapter 20
THE WAR TO END WAR AND
ITS AFTERMATH, 1917–1920   239

Mobilizing Labor and Resources	239
Mobilizing Opinion	240
The AEF in France	240
Preparing for Peace	242
Wilson at Versailles	242
Opposition to the League	243
The Versailles Treaty	243
Defeat in the Senate	243
Demobilization	244
"Red" Scare and Reaction	245
Progressivism Turns Sour	246
Harding's Election	247

Chapter 21
FROM NORMALCY TO
DEPRESSION, 1920–1933   248

The Tragedy of Harding	248
Keeping Cool with Coolidge	248
Business Is Business	249
Consumers and Workers	250
Thunder from the Farm Belt	250
The United States and the World	251
The Jazz Age	251
Hoover Follows Coolidge	253
Repeal of Prohibition	253
The Wall Street Crash	254
Hoover Faces the Depression	254
The People in Hard Times	255
The Election of 1932	256
The Interregnum	257

Chapter 22
THE NEW DEAL   258

F. D. R. Takes Command	258
The Bank Holiday	258
Emergency Relief	259
The First AAA	259
The NRA	261
TVA and Conservation	262
Money and Banking	263
Expression and Escape	263
Thunder from the Left	264
The Second New Deal	265
AFL and CIO	266
Mandate from the People	267
Storm over the Court	267
Recovery and Recession	268
A Discriminatory Deal	269

Chapter 23
FROM ISOLATION TO
INTERVENTION   271

American Ambivalence	271
Seeking Friends and Customers	271
The New Neutrality	272
Japan's "New Order"	273
War in Europe	274
Aiding the Allies	274
Isolationists vs. Interventionists	275
Election of 1940	275
The Lend-Lease Act	276
Toward Belligerency	276
Pearl Harbor	277

Selected Readings   279

1941–1960 • PART SEVEN
Another Foreign Crusade with Mixed Results   281

Chapter 24
THE SECOND WORLD WAR   283

Mobilizing for Defense	283

Mobilization of Labor	284
Scientists Against the Axis	285
Freedoms Abroad and at Home	285
Wartime Politics	286

The American War Strategy   286
On the Defensive   1941–1942   287
The Mediterranean Offensive   287
The Liberation of Europe   289
The Pacific Offensive   289
Atomic Triumph over Japan   291
The Dangerous Alliance   291
The Yalta Conference   292

Chapter 25
POSTWAR READJUSTMENTS
AND THE START OF THE
COLD WAR   295

The Postwar Military Program   295
The "Fair Deal"   295
Truman Beats Dewey   297
Beginnings of Containment   297
The North Atlantic Alliance   299
The Chinese Revolution   300
The Japanese Ally   300
Conflict in Korea   300
Founding the United Nations   293

Delayed Peacemaking   293
Trumanism and McCarthyism   303
A Troubled Electorate   303

Chapter 26
THE EISENHOWER YEARS   305

Eisenhower Elected   305
John Foster Dulles   305
A Truce in Korea   305
"Massive Retaliation"   306
Involvement in Vietnam   306
The Geneva Spirit   308
Menace in the Middle East   308
The Rocket Race   309
Disgruntled Neighbors   310
"Eisenhower Prosperity"   311
Decline of McCarthyism   311
Desegregation Begins   312
A Second Term for Ike   312

Selected Readings   313

Since 1960 · PART EIGHT
Hope in Space, Persistent Problems on Earth   315

Chapter 27
THE AFFLUENT SOCIETY   317

The Promise of Technology and Science   317
The Crowding Country   318
Rise of the Megalopolis   319
Abundance and Its Costs   320
The Energy Crisis   321
Distribution of Wealth   322
Education   323
The Role of Television   324

Chapter 28
SEEKING THE "GREAT
SOCIETY"   326

The "New Frontier"   326
The Kennedy Economic Program   327
Kennedy and Civil Rights   327
"Let Us Continue"   328
Commitment to Equality   328

"One Man, One Vote"   329
Johnson Thrashes Goldwater   329
The Johnson Program   330
Black Power   331
The Spanish-Speaking Minority   332
The Pan-Indian Movement   333
Women's Liberation   333

Chapter 29
THE POLITICS OF LOWERED
EXPECTATIONS, 1968–1985   335

Election of 1968   335
The Imperial Presidency   336
Law and Order   336
The Nixon Economy   337
A Triumphant Reelection   338
Watergate   339
A President Resigns   340
The Ford Administration   341
The Great Recession   342

Election of 1976   *342*
Economic Dilemmas   *343*
Energy Policy   *344*
Women's Rights   *344*
Election of 1980   *345*
The Reagan Revolution   *346*
Election of 1984   *347*

Chapter 30
THE BALANCE OF TERROR,
1961–1985   **349**

Diversified Defense   *349*
Heightening Tension   *349*
Cuba: The Missile Crisis   *350*
Loosening of Alliances   *351*
Deeper Involvement in Vietnam   *351*
Escalating the War   *353*
Deescalation Begins   *354*
Nixon-Kissinger Foreign Policy   *354*
Vietnamization   1969–1972   *355*
Rapprochement with China   *356*
Détente with Russia   *357*
Exit from Indochina   *358*
Trouble in the Middle East   *359*
Kissinger-Ford Diplomacy   *360*
Carter Tries New Directions   *361*
The Year of the Hostages   *362*
Reagan and the World   *363*

Selected Readings   **365**

APPENDICES

The Declaration of Independence   *i*
The Constitution of the United
   States of America   *iv*
Admission of States to the Union   *xvii*
Presidential Elections   *xviii*

INDEX   **xxiii**

MAPS

North American Empires   *26*
The War in the North   1775   *41*
British Campaigns   *42*
Road to Yorktown   *43*
Boundary Settlements   1818–1819   *74*
The Missouri Compromise   1820   *76*
American Expansion in Oregon   *121*
American Expansion into the Southwest   *123*
The Mexican War   *125*
Slave and Free Territory   1850   *134*
The War in the West   1861–1862   *158*
Virginia Campaigns   *162*
Sherman's March through the
   Confederacy   1864–1865   *163*
U.S. Participation in Allied
   Offensives   1918   *241*
The Normandy Landings   *288*
The War in the Pacific   *290*
The Korean War   1950–1953   *301*
Vietnam   *352*

WHERE HISTORIANS DISAGREE:

The American Revolution   *39*
Background of the Constitution   *53*
Sources of Economic Growth   *87*
The Slave's Response to Slavery   *107*
The Causes of the Civil War   *149*
The Nature of Reconstruction   *172*
Leaders of Big Business   *184*
The Nature of Progressivism   *211*
The Nature of the New Deal   *260*
The Background of Pearl Harbor   *278*
Origins of the Cold War   *298*

The Essentials of American History

English Colonists Become Americans and Gain Their Independence

The history of the United States from its colonial beginnings is fairly short. It covers a period of less than 400 years, a period that can be spanned by the overlapping lifetimes of a mere half-dozen men. Yet the roots of American civilization go deep into the human past.

There is no evidence that human life originated in the New World. No bones or fossils of the ape-like ancestors of our species, such as those unearthed on other continents, have ever been found in either North or South America. The earliest remains of humanity so far discovered here are, at the most, only about 30,000 years old.

The American continents were peopled as a result of two long-continuing immigration movements, the first from Asia, the second from Europe and Africa. Probably the first began thousands of years ago when Siberian tribes, in search of new hunting grounds or of refuge from pursuing enemies, crossed over the Bering Strait to Alaska. From Alaska the newcomers and their descendants fanned out to populate both the continents. By 1492 there were at least a million people north of Mexico, 3 million in Mexico and Central America, and 6 million (some estimates run higher) in South America.

The Stone Age forefathers of these people brought little with them from Asia. Over the centuries the first Americans developed for themselves such tools and customs as they possessed when the Europeans arrived. At that time the aboriginal cultures ranged from the simple to the complex, from those of primitive, acorn-gathering

tribes to that of the Aztecs, the inheritors of the Mayas, who before A.D. 1000 had created in Central America one of the most brilliant civilizations then existing anywhere in the world.

The second peopling of the Americas began with the expansion of Europe at the end of the medieval and the start of the modern period. The history of the United States is an extension of European and particularly English history. The new Americans had much to learn from those already here, and they were to be influenced a good deal by the wilderness environment they found, but their way of life was to be based mainly on the European traditions they brought with them.

The colonists who came to English America in the seventeenth century were transplanted Englishmen. They had no desire to lose their Englishness. Rather, they hoped to build in the New World a better England, one that would be free from the imperfections of their native land.

Even the first arrivals, however, began to depart from many of their accustomed ways. As new generations grew up in America they developed a more and more distinctive character. In the course of the eighteenth century they became provincial "Americans" — a term that had been applied to them even before 1700 but did not come into general use until after 1750.

There were three main reasons for the divergence between the culture of the colonies and that of the homeland. First, English society was not transplanted as a whole. The people who left for Amercia were not entirely typical of England:

usually they were the more discontented or the more adventurous; they were themselves in some degree "different." Second, they found in the New World an unfamiliar environment with its own challenges and opportunities. Certain elements of the English inheritance flourished and were adapted to the strange surroundings, while others withered or never took root at all. Third, some of the early colonists (the Dutch, for example) had come from countries other than England, and during the eighteenth century new arrivals in much larger numbers came from other places — Scotland and Ireland, the European continent, and Africa. Hence, in America, there was a mixture of peoples and cultures, though the English continued to predominate.

In the developing American society there were variations from colony to colony and from region to region. The New England colonies had much in common with one another, less in common with the middle colonies (Pennsylvania, New Jersey, New York), and still less in common with the southern colonies. These last fell into two subgroups with important differences between the two: the tobacco colonies (Maryland, Virginia, and North Carolina) and the others (South Carolina and Georgia).

From the perspective of two centuries later, it is easy enough to see that the people of the thirteen colonies, for all their diversity, had come to share some distinctive characteristics by the middle of the eighteenth century. As yet, however, few of the colonists thought of themselves as Americans. Their "country," as they saw it, was first of all their particular colony, and then perhaps their region (at least in the case of the Southerners and the New Englanders), and finally the British Empire.

As of 1763 the Empire appeared to be an imposing success, having just disposed of its last great imperial rival in North America — France. Yet it was about to prove a failure, at least so far as its ability to hold the thirteen colonies was concerned. After the great victory over the French, the policy makers in London undertook to bind the outlying provinces more closely than ever to the metropolitan center. Instead of consolidating the Empire, however, its rulers unwittingly prepared the way for its early disruption.

The colonies by then had long been used to a large measure of self-rule, and to preserve this they resisted the imperial program of George III's government. Resistance came in consequence of a clash of interests, economic and political, between the groups dominant in England and those dominant in the colonies. In the course of resistance, Americans developed a new sense of common cause and new forms of political cooperation. They were not yet conscious of belonging to, or of desiring to create, a separate country, but they eventually found themselves engaged in the first battles of a war that was to lead to independence.

The actual fighting seems insignificant in comparison with more recent wars. Battle deaths on the American side totaled less than 5,000. Yet the war as the Patriots fought it had one feature that made it new and revolutionary in itself. In previous wars the battles had been fought by comparatively small numbers of professional soldiers, serving only for pay. In this one the people on the American side took up arms in their own cause. Though their armies seldom numbered more than a few thousand at any one time, a total of almost 400,000 men enlisted (most of them for short terms) during the eight years (1775–1783) that the war lasted.

Its consequences also were revolutionary. The first of the modern wars against colonialism, it brought into being a new nation which was eventually to grow into one of the greatest powers of all time. The ideals the war aroused provided inspiration for future generations not only in the United States but also in other countries. One of the leading revolutionaries of 1776, Thomas Paine, averred that the war "contributed more to enlighten the world, and diffuse a spirit of freedom and liberality among mankind, than any human event . . . that ever preceded it."

Chapter I

England Transplanted: The Seventeenth Century

Interest in Colonization

The innovative and powerful merchants who led in the development of the English interest in colonization were part of a rising class of merchant capitalists who prospered from the expansion of foreign trade. Their relentless search for new markets for English cloth and for new sources of fish to feed Catholic Europe led them to sail to North American shores by the end of the fifteenth century and to plant permanent colonies there by the beginning of the seventeenth century.

To further their profitable trade, spokesmen for the merchant capitalists developed a set of ideas about the proper relation of government and business — ideas supporting the argument that the whole nation benefited from the activities of the overseas traders. The trade of England as a whole, it was said, was basically like that of any individual or firm: transactions were worthwhile if sales exceeded purchases in value. The difference in value would have to be paid in money (gold and silver), and the inflow of money into England would stimulate business and strengthen the national economy by raising commodity prices and lowering interest rates. According to their theory, the government should act to encourage a "favorable" balance of trade — that is, an excess of exports over imports. This economic philosophy came to be known as "mercantilism." It guided the economic policies not only of England but also of Spain, France, and other nation-states.

Colonies could fit well into this mercantilist program by providing an additional market for English manufacturers and supplying products for which England previously had depended upon foreigners — products such as lumber, naval stores, furs, and above all, silver and gold.

There was yet another reason for the growing interest in colonies. The Church of England, in the form it took under Queen Elizabeth, by no means satisfied all English subjects. It was much too Protestant to suit those of the English who held onto the Roman Catholic faith, and at the same time it seemed too "popish" to many who opposed the ways and influence of Rome. Among these were the Puritans, who, affected in varying degrees by the teachings of John Calvin, wished to "purify" the Church. Religious nonconformists began to look for places of refuge outside the kingdom.

The Wilderness Setting

The fate of the English colonies — their success or failure, the kind of development they took — was to depend largely upon the environment in which they were planted along the Atlantic seaboard of North America.

The geographical fact that most distinguished the new from the old country and most influenced the economic development of the colonies was sheer space. Not that all the land was readily accessible. The need for clearing the forest, the presence of hostile tribes, the dependence upon water transport, and ultimately the difficulty of crossing the mountain barrier — all these considerations hindered the actual occupation of the land, and increasingly so in proportion to the re-

3

moteness from seaports. Hence the English settlements, scattered though they might seem, remained on the whole fairly compact throughout the colonial period, at least in comparison with the Spanish and French settlements in the New World, though not in comparison with the crowded towns and countryside of the Old World. There populations teemed and lacked sufficient room. Here land was plentiful and people relatively scarce.

The Woods Indians

The North American Indians had the general features of their Mongoloid ancestors — yellow or brown skin, straight and coarse black hair, and high cheekbones — but there were minor variations in physical appearance among the numerous tribes. There were greater differences in modes of living and ways of speaking. Hundreds of languages were spoken, but most of them belonged to one or another of about a dozen linguistic stocks. People of different tribes with related languages could not always understand each other, any more than the French could understand the Spanish, nor were such tribes necessarily alike in their cultural patterns.

European diseases preceded European colonies to American shores. The native population lacked immunity to European childhood diseases, such as measles and mumps. Whenever the Indians encountered the first wave of European traders and fishermen, they were attacked by these diseases, as well as smallpox and syphilis, with fatal results. Death swept ahead of settlement and cleared the Atlantic seaboard of much of the native people. By 1600 a native population of about 125,000 — perhaps only half the number in 1500 — remained along the coast south of the St. Lawrence River. The meeting of Europeans and Indians produced a demographic crisis of catastrophic proportions for the Indian populations.

Concentrated in southern New England and around Chesapeake Bay, most of the Indian tribes carried on a primitive form of agriculture. They made clearings by cutting into trees to kill them and by setting fires in the forest. Among the dead and blackened trunks they planted pumpkins, squash, beans, and corn — crops they had learned

of indirectly from the Indians of Mexico and South America. A tribe abandoned its clearing and made a new one when the yields fell or when the accumulated filth of the village became too deep to endure. The Indian "old fields," especially in New England, and the sites abandoned by tribes decimated by disease attracted incoming settlers as convenient places to begin settlement. The newcomers eagerly adopted the cultivation of native crops, above all corn. Without the clearings and the crops that the Indians provided, the English would have had much greater difficulty than they did in getting a start in the New World.

To the colonists the Indians were of interest as customers for English goods and as suppliers of woodland commodities, especially hides and skins. Trade brought the white and red peoples together. It was a disadvantage to the Indians, for while they obtained guns, knives, blankets, and iron pots, they also became increasingly dependent upon whites, their commerce and their culture.

None of the Indians of the eastern woodlands (or, for that matter, of the entire continent north of Mexico) had developed political organizations comparable in sophistication to those of the Aztecs or the Incas. The most elaborate organization was the Iroquois league of five nations, centered in New York. Other tribes had their own separate and rudimentary governments and were often at war with one another or with the Iroquois. From time to time they made alliances or temporary confederations.

The primitive tribal system offered both advantages and disadvantages for the invading English. On the one hand, the divisions and rivalries among the Indians made it easier for whites to deal with them than would otherwise have been the case. If the Indians had been united, they could possibly have driven out the invaders. On the other hand, the disunity of the tribes prevented the English from making such a quick and easy conquest as the Spaniards had made when they won control of Mexico and Peru by killing or capturing the native imperial rulers. Even though they aided the first European arrivals, the Indians attempted to obstruct the expansion of white settlement, and life on the frontier derived many of its peculiarly "American" qualities from the Indian danger and the Indian wars.

European Rivals

In the wilderness the English were to encounter threats not only from the Indians but also from rival Europeans. To the south and southwest were scattered the outposts of the Spaniards, who, despite a peace that Spain and England made in 1604, continued to look upon the English as intruders. The English in their settlements along the coast could not for many years feel entirely safe from attack by Spanish ships.

On the north and northwest were beginning to appear the outposts of another and eventually even more dangerous rival, France. The French founded their first permanent settlement in America at Quebec in 1608, less than a year after the English had started their first at Jamestown. New France grew in population very slowly. Few Roman Catholics felt any inclination to leave their beloved homeland, and the discontented Protestants who desired to emigrate were excluded from the colony. To the English in America, however, the French presented a danger disproportionate to their numbers, largely because of their influence upon the Algonquin Indians, who became dependent upon French fur traders.

Besides the Spanish and the French, the English were soon to find in the New World another European rival, the Dutch. Shortly after the planting of the first two English colonies, at Jamestown and Plymouth, the Dutch began to wedge themselves in between when the Dutch West India Company established posts on the Hudson, Delaware, and Connecticut rivers.

Virginia and Maryland

Virginia was the name that — in honor of Elizabeth, the Virgin Queen — had been given to an indefinite stretch of the North American mainland bordering the Atlantic coast. In 1606 a company of London merchants obtained from King James I a charter giving them the right to start a colony in Virginia. They intended to found not an agricultural settlement but a trading post. To it they expected to send English manufactures for barter with the Indians, and from it they hoped to bring back American commodities procured in exchange or produced by the labor of their own employees.

Their first expedition, about 100 men, sailed into Chesapeake Bay and up the James River in the spring of 1607. The colonists ran into serious difficulties from the moment they landed and began to build the palisaded settlement of Jamestown. Though beautiful to look at, the site was low and swampy and unhealthful. It was surrounded by thick woods, which were hard to clear for cultivation, and it was threatened by hostile Indians under the imperial chief Powhatan.

By January 1608, when ships appeared with additional men and supplies, all but thirty-eight of the first arrivals were dead. The winter of 1609–1610 turned into a "starving time" worse than anything before. While Indians killed off the livestock in the woods and kept the settlers within the palisade, these unfortunates were reduced to eating "dogs, cats, rats, snakes, toadstools, horsehides," and even the "corpses of dead men," as one survivor recalled.

The basis of Virginia's future prosperity was laid when one of the planters, John Rolfe, experimented successfully with the growing and curing of tobacco. And a truce with the Indians was cemented when Rolfe married Powhatan's daughter Pocahontas, who afterward was entertained as a princess on a visit to England, where she died. But Powhatan's brother and successor, Opechancanough, broke the peace with a massacre of more than 350 unsuspecting Virginians.

The lack of adequate defenses in the colony, the general mismanagement of the Virginia Company, and the bickerings among its directors led James I, in 1624, to revoke the charter and take the government of Virginia into his own hands. As a profit-making venture for its investors the colony was a failure, yet in a larger sense it was a success, for it demonstrated that English men and women could survive and prosper in America.

One of the stockholders of the Virginia Company, George Calvert, Lord Baltimore, conceived the idea of undertaking a new colony on his own. Himself a convert to the Roman Catholic faith, Calvert had in mind primarily a gigantic speculation in real estate and incidentally the establishment of a refuge for Roman Catholics, victims of political discrimination in England. From Charles I he obtained a patent to a wedge of Virginia's territory which lay north of the Potomac and east of Chesapeake Bay, and which the King now christened Maryland in honor of his Roman Catholic wife, the Frenchwoman Henrietta Maria.

Spending a large part of the family fortune in the development of their American possessions, the Calverts had to attract many thousands of settlers if their venture was to pay. They encouraged the immigration of Protestants as well as Roman Catholics, and since relatively few of the latter were inclined to leave England, the Protestant settlers soon far outnumbered them. In both Maryland and Virginia, Anglicans predominated.

Tobacco growing quickly spread throughout the Chesapeake settlements — in both Maryland and Virginia — as England and English merchants welcomed the opportunity to reduce their imports of tobacco from the Spanish empire. Tobacco shaped the society that developed in the region in a variety of ways. One way was that in taking up land along the bay and navigable streams, the early settlers acquired extensive tracts. Thus most of the people came to be widely scattered, living on isolated farms. Villages or towns were few.

Even if a man owned a thousand acres or more, he actually farmed only a small part of his land, because of the difficulty of clearing it. He worked in his fields alongside his boys and his servants or slaves — if he had any. His servants might have come with him from England. Or they might have come later, binding themselves to their master in return for their passage over. Some were sold into servitude against their will. Upon completing his term (usually four or five years) the servant was entitled to certain benefits — clothing, tools, and occasionally land — in addition to his freedom and the privilege, if he could afford it, of acquiring servants of his own.

In Jamestown John Rolfe had recorded in 1619: "About the last of August came in a Dutch man of war that sold us twenty negars." These black men were bought not as slaves but as servants to be held for a term of years and then freed, like the white servants with whom the planters already were familiar. The number of black workers on the tobacco farms increased rather slowly. In Vir-

ginia there were fewer than 300 blacks in 1640, and only about 2,000 in 1670, when the total population of the colony had reached 40,000. By that time blacks were being treated as permanent slaves and no longer as temporary servants. But the day of the great tobacco plantation, with its labor force consisting almost entirely of black slaves, still lay in the future.

On July 30, 1619, in the Jamestown church, delegates from the various communities met as the House of Burgesses to consider, along with the governor and his council, the enactment of laws for the Virginia colony. This was the first meeting of an elected legislature, a representative assembly, within what was to become the United States. The members of this House of Burgesses were chosen in county elections in which all men aged seventeen or older were entitled to vote. When, five years later, the King took over the government of the province, he allowed the burgesses to continue to meet. From then on, however, Virginia was a "royal" colony, and the King rather than the Virginia Company was responsible for the appointment of the governor and the governor's council.

As Virginia grew in population, the House of Burgesses became less democratic than it had been in the beginning. Each county continued to have only two representatives, even though some of the new counties of the back country contained many more people than the old ones of the tidewater area; hence the more recent settlers on the frontier were underrepresented. After 1670 the vote was restricted to landowners, and elections were seldom held, the same burgesses remaining in office year after year. One long-serving governor, Sir William Berkeley, corrupted the council and the burgesses and made himself an autocrat.

Discontent with the Berkeley regime flared into violence in 1676. The frontier followers of Nathaniel Bacon, exasperated at the governor's neglect of Indian defenses, marched on Jamestown, attacked and defeated the governor's troops, and set fire to the place. After Bacon died of fever, the rebellion came to a sudden end. Berkeley took a bloody revenge, seeing to the execution of thirty-seven of the leading rebels.

In the aftermath of Bacon's Rebellion, Virginia's political leaders made certain that all members of the planter elite felt represented in government. Further, they supported a more vigorous taking of Indian lands to satisfy western interests. And Virginia's planters committed themselves more heavily to the use of African slaves, partly in order to avoid future revolts by unruly indentured servants, who had supported Bacon.

Plymouth and Massachusetts Bay

New England from the 1620s to the 1670s took its character as a colony in part from the Pilgrims who settled at Plymouth, but in a much larger measure from the Puritans who later landed at nearby Massachusetts Bay and then spread out from there. These Puritans would have liked to remake the institutions of England, but they faced too much opposition there. In the wilderness of America they saw an opportunity to create society anew and to set an example for the Old World.

Slipping away a few at a time, the members of a congregation that wished to separate from the Church of England had crossed the English Channel and begun their lives anew in Holland. Some of them decided to move again and won permission from the Virginia Company to settle as an independent community on its land.

From Plymouth, England, the *Mayflower* took its 102 passengers to Plymouth in New England, where on a bleak December day in 1620 they disembarked, though they had not reached their intended destination. During the first winter half of them died from scurvy and exposure, but the rest managed to put their colony on its feet. As citizens of a virtually independent republic they went their way for over seventy years, until Plymouth was annexed to the much larger colony of Massachusetts Bay.

The English were first attracted to Massachusetts Bay by its fisheries. From these a plan developed for establishing a permanent fishing and trading station and then a missionary outpost at Salem. A corporation, formed to raise funds for putting the struggling colony on a sounder basis, was reorganized in 1629 as the Massachusetts Bay Company, with a royal charter that granted a strip of land between the Charles River and the Merrimack.

Some members of the company, alarmed by the pro-Anglican and anti-Parliament attitudes of the new King, Charles I, were beginning to look upon the colony less as a business venture and more as a Puritan refuge. Some were eager to migrate themselves if they could do so and still control the company. They arranged to buy the stock of those who preferred to stay at home. Then, in 1630, they sailed under the lead of the company's governor, John Winthrop, a gentleman of means, with a university education, a deep but narrow piety, a cool and calculating way, and a remarkably forceful and stubborn character. The expedition, with 17 ships and 1,000 people, was the largest of its kind in the seventeenth century. These colonists founded a number of new towns, among them Boston, which was to be both the company's headquarters and the colony's capital. During the 1630s, while Charles I ruled England without a Parliament, Puritans escaping from his tyranny migrated in such numbers that by 1643 the colony had a population of about 15,000.

The Puritan Way of Life

The Massachusetts Bay Company soon was transformed into the Massachusetts colonial government. Governor Winthrop brought with him the company charter. According to its terms, the "freemen" (the stockholders) were to meet as a General Court to choose officers and adopt rules for the corporation. After their arrival in America the freemen proceeded to elect officials and pass laws for the colony.

To be a freeman, to take any part in the colonial government, a man had to be a member of the Puritan (Congregational) Church. This was not easy. The Puritans in England (and the Pilgrims in Plymouth) had required for church membership only that a person profess the faith, sign the covenant, and live an upright life. The Puritans in Massachusetts, however, soon began to limit membership to the "visible saints," that is, to those who could demonstrate that they had experienced God's saving grace and hence belonged to the elect, the group whom He had chosen for eventual salvation.

Winthrop and the other Massachusetts founders saw themselves as starting a holy commonwealth, a model for the corrupt world to see. The problem was to keep it holy. In this effort the preachers and the politicians worked together.

The ministers did not run the government, but they supported it, and they exerted great influence upon the church members who alone could vote or hold public office. The government in turn protected the ministers, taxed the people (members and nonmembers alike) to support the Church, and enforced the law requiring attendance at services. In this Puritan oligarchy the dissidents had no more freedom of worship than the Puritans themselves had had in England.

The early settlers almost always took up land in groups. A congregation arriving from England received from the General Court the grant of a town (township), an area of twenty-five square miles or so. Its distribution was left to the leaders of the new settlement. They laid out a village, in which they set aside a "common" as pasture and timberland, chose a site for a meeting house (church) and for a fort, and assigned each family a strip of land as a home lot on either side of the one village street. They also divided up the outlying fields in the town, the size of a field and the desirability of its location depending on the family's numbers, wealth, and social standing. Wherever he went to work his fields, the typical seventeenth-century New Englander lived not in a lonely farmhouse but in a village with neighbors close by, and he maintained a strong sense of community.

Coastal towns developed an overseas trade through fishing, shipping, shipbuilding, and related enterprises. With the growth of commerce, the colonial shipowning merchants came to dominate the New England economy. These rich businessmen might be good Puritans — though many were not — and yet their way to wealth inevitably created tensions within Puritan society. The Puritan oligarchy gradually lost some of its political power and the ministers lost some of their authority, while the merchants gained in influence.

As the first generation of American Puritans passed away, the number of church members declined, for few of the second generation could show the saving grace that church membership required. Eventually in most communities the Congregational Church came to include all who cared to join and could profess the faith. As the number of church members rose, so did the number of men who could take part in colonial politics as voters and officeholders.

Expansion of New England

Meanwhile, an outpouring from Massachusetts Bay to various parts of New England (and to other places in English America) had begun. This exodus was motivated by several considerations: the unproductiveness of the stony soil around Boston, the intolerance of established Puritan communities, and the oppressiveness of the Massachusetts government.

By the early 1630s a few of the English had already moved to the fertile meadows of the Connecticut Valley, 100 miles beyond the settled frontier. The settlers of Hartford, Windsor, and Wethersfield on the Connecticut River decided to set up a colonial government of their own in 1639. A separate colony had grown up around New Haven on the Connecticut coast. Eventually the governor of Connecticut obtained a royal charter (1662) that not only authorized his colony but also extended its jurisdiction over the New Haven settlements.

Rhode Island had its origin in the religious dissent of Roger Williams, a young minister of Massachusetts Bay. Williams was an extreme Separatist who at first advocated not religious freedom but rather a church made even more pure and strict. Making friends with the neighboring Indians, he concluded that the land belonged to them and not to the King or to the Massachusetts Bay Company. The colonial government, considering Williams a dangerous man, decided to deport him, but he escaped. He took refuge with the Narragansett tribe during a bitter winter, then bought a tract of land from them and in 1636, with a few of his friends, created the town of Providence on it.

Anne Hutchinson, the charming and strong-minded wife of a substantial Bostonian, attracted many more followers than Williams with her heretical doctrine that the Holy Spirit dwelled within and guided every true believer. If this were so, the Bible would have no more authority than anyone's personal revelation, and both the church and the government would be exposed to anarchy, or so it seemed to Governor Winthrop and his associates. In 1638 she was convicted of sedition and banished as "a woman not fit for our society." With her family and some of her followers she moved to a point on Narragansett Bay not far from Providence.

In time other communities of dissidents arose in that vicinity. In 1644 Williams got from Parliament a charter authorizing a government for the combined settlements. The government, though based on the Massachusetts pattern, did not restrict the vote to church members, nor did it tax the people for church support. A royal charter of 1663 confirmed the existing arrangement and added a guarantee of "liberty in religious concernments."

As New England spread, the settlers ran into trouble with the Indians. With a few exceptions, like Roger Williams, the Puritans viewed the redmen as "pernicious creatures" who deserved extermination unless they would adopt the ways of whites. In 1637 the exasperated Pequots went on the warpath in the Connecticut Valley. The Connecticut frontiersmen marched against a palisaded Pequot stronghold and set it afire. About 500 Pequots were burned to death or massacred when trying to escape, and most of the survivors were hunted down, captured, and sold as slaves. The Pequot tribe was almost wiped out.

To provide frontier protection, Massachusetts, Plymouth, Connecticut, and New Haven joined (in 1643) in "The Confederation of the United Colonies of New England." By 1675 the New England Confederation had deteriorated so much that it could no longer be relied on for organizing frontier defense. In that year war broke out between Massachusetts towns and the Wampanoag Indians, who lived by Narragansett Bay and were led by King Philip. During the three years of King Philip's War the Indians were able to destroy completely twelve towns, to damage half of the towns in New England, and to kill one out of every sixteen New England men of military age.

These brutal confrontations lowered the moral standards of both peoples. Native Americans renounced their traditions of limited and symbolic forms of warfare. Puritans likewise adopted total warfare, calling for complete annihilation of their tribal enemies.

Carolina

Carolina, partly taken like Maryland from the Virginia grant, was awarded by Charles II to a group of eight of his favorites, including the Virginia governor, Sir William Berkeley. They ex-pected to profit as landlords and land speculators, reserving tremendous estates for their own development, selling or giving away the rest in smaller tracts, and collecting fixed annual rents — called quitrents — from the settlers. The proprietors, four of whom had investments in the African slave trade, also intended to introduce slaves into the colony so as to profit both from selling them and from using their labor. Early settlers were offered a bonus of extra land for every black bondsman or woman they brought in.

The northern part of Carolina, the first part to be settled, suffered from geographical handicaps — the coastal region being isolated by the Dismal Swamp, by the southeastwardly flow of the rivers, and by the lack of natural harbors usable for ocean-going ships. As a Carolina proprietor, Virginia's Governor Berkeley worked hard to induce Virginians to take up land on the other side of the colonial boundary, and gradually the Albemarle settlements grew. Most of the settlers were poor tobacco-growing farmers who could afford few roads, churches, schools — or slaves.

The southern part of Carolina was favored with an excellent harbor at the point where the Ashley and Cooper rivers joined. Here in 1670 a fleet brought colonists, and in 1680 the city of Charleston was laid out. It soon had wharves, fortifications, and fine houses. Settlers took up land along the two rivers, down which they began to send large quantities of corn, lumber, cattle, pork, and (in the 1690s) some rice to Charleston, for shipment to Barbados in the British West Indies. To Charleston also came furs, hides, and Indian slaves obtained by traders who were advancing farther and farther into the interior, around the southern end of the Appalachians, to deal with the southwestern tribes. The wealthy planters and merchants, centering in Charleston, dominated the region's economy, social life, and politics.

Already there were in fact two Carolinas, each having a distinctive way of life, long before the colony was formally divided (1729) into North and South Carolina, with completely separate governments.

New York

The year after making his Carolina grant, Charles II bestowed (1664) upon his brother, the

Duke of York, all the territory lying between the Connecticut and Delaware rivers. The whole region was claimed by the Dutch, who occupied strategic points within it.

The Dutch republic, after winning independence from Spain in 1648, had launched upon its own career of overseas trading and empire building in Asia, Africa, and America. On the basis of Henry Hudson's explorations, the Dutch staked an American claim and proceeded promptly to exploit it with a busy trade in furs. To add permanence to the business, the Dutch West India Company began to encourage settlement, offering vast feudal estates to "patroons" who would bring over immigrants to work the land. So developed the colony of New Netherland. It centered around New Amsterdam with its blockhouse on Manhattan Island and included thinly scattered settlements on the Hudson, the Delaware, and the Connecticut rivers. In 1655 the Dutch extended their sway over the few Swedes and Finns settled along the lower Delaware.

Three Anglo-Dutch wars arose from the commercial and colonial rivalry of England and the Netherlands throughout the world and particularly in America. The Dutch dominated the lucrative trade with the Caribbean Spanish empire and competed effectively (and illegally) with English merchants in the trade with the English West Indian colonies. The ambitious English wished to reduce the power of the Dutch. They viewed the New Amsterdam colony as a dangerous stronghold that posed a military threat to their northern and southern mainland colonies; the colony also supported Dutch commerce, particularly smuggling with English colonies. In 1664 troop-carrying vessels of the English navy put in at New Amsterdam and extracted a surrender from the arbitrary and unpopular governor, the peg-legged Peter Stuyvesant.

New York, formerly New Netherland, already the property of the Duke of York and renamed by him, was his to rule as virtually an absolute monarch. The Duke confirmed the Dutch patroonships already in existence, the most notable of them being Rensselaerswyck with its 700,000 acres around Albany, and he gave comparable estates to Englishmen in order to create a class of influential landowners loyal to him. Wealthy English and Dutch landlords, shipowners, and fur traders, along with the Duke's political appointees, dominated the colonial government.

The Quaker Colonies

The Society of Friends originated in mid-seventeenth-century England in response to the preachings of George Fox, a Nottingham shoemaker, whose followers came to be known as Quakers from his admonition to them to "tremble at the name of the Lord." The essence of Fox's teachings was the doctrine of the Inner Light, the illumination from God within each soul, the divine conscience, which when rightly heeded could guide human beings along the paths of righteousness.

Like the Puritans earlier, Fox and his followers looked to America for asylum. As the head of a sect despised in England, however, he could not get the necessary colonial grant without the aid of someone influential at the court. Fortunately for his cause, his teachings had struck the hearts of a number of wealthy and prominent men, including William Penn.

New Jersey had been given by the Duke of York to two of the Carolina proprietors, one of whom sold his half-interest to two Quakers. The colony received Penn's attention when he was asked to assist the two Quakers with their debts. In their behalf he helped to see to the division of the province into East and West Jersey, one of the original proprietors keeping the East, and the Quakers the West. West Jersey soon began to fill up with Friends from England while East Jersey was being populated mostly by Puritans from New England. Before long Penn together with other wealthy Quakers purchased the eastern property (1682), and eventually the two Jerseys were reunited as one colony (1702), second in Quaker population only to Pennsylvania itself.

Pennsylvania was based on the King's grant of 1681. Penn had inherited Irish lands from his father and also a claim to a small fortune owed by the King. Charles II, possessing more real estate than ready cash, paid the debt with a grant of territory larger than England and Wales combined.

Penn undertook in Pennsylvania what he called a Holy Experiment. Colonies, he said, were the "seeds of nations," and he proposed to plant the seeds of brotherly love. Closely supervising the planting, he devised a liberal Frame of Government with a representative assembly. He personally voyaged to Pennsylvania (1682) to oversee the laying-out, between the Delaware and Schuylkill rivers, of the city he appropriately named Philadelphia ("Brotherly Love"). Penn believed, as had Roger Williams, that the land belonged to the Indians, and he was careful to see that they were reimbursed for it. With the Indians, who honored him as a rarity, an honest white man, his colony had no trouble during his lifetime. It prospered from the outset, partly too because of the mildness of the climate and the fertility of the soil.

The "Glorious Revolution"

The colonies, for the most part, had originated as quite separate projects and had grown up in rather independent ways, with little thought for a long time that they belonged, or ought to belong, to a unified empire. Beginning in the 1660s, however, England took steps to tighten the bonds of empire and enforce the mercantile system.

Hence in 1660 Parliament began to pass the Navigation Acts, which were aimed at excluding the Dutch from American trade. These acts closed the colonies to all trade except that carried in English ships, which were defined as ships built in England or the colonies and manned by sailors of whom three-fourths were Englishmen or colonists. This law also required that certain enumerated items, among them tobacco, be exported from the colonies only to England or to an English possession. Another act (1663) provided that all goods sent from Europe to the colonies had to go by way of England and that taxes could be put on the goods during their transshipment. If the Navigation Acts were to be strictly enforced, the King would have to get more direct control over the colonial governments than he had.

Only in Virginia, a "royal colony" since 1624, did the King as yet have the right to appoint the governor. In Massachusetts, a "corporate colony," the people elected their own governor, as they also did in Plymouth. In Maryland, a "proprietary colony," the appointing power had been delegated to the proprietor. When Charles II created other proprietary colonies — Carolina, New York, New Jersey, Pennsylvania — he himself followed the Maryland example. And when he gave royal charters to Connecticut and Rhode Island, he accepted these two as "corporate colonies" by allowing them to go on choosing their officials. Moreover, he and his predecessors had permitted the development of an assembly representing the people (or some of the people) in each of the colonies — royal, corporate, or proprietary. And the assemblies were claiming more and more power for themselves.

Massachusetts, the worst offender, behaved practically like an independent republic. In 1679 Charles II started legal proceedings that led, in 1684, to the revocation of Massachusetts' corporate charter. His brother and successor, James II, went much further when he came to the throne in 1685. He combined Massachusetts and the rest of the New England colonies into one Dominion of New England, and later he added the Middle Atlantic colonies of New York and New Jersey to it. Within this dominion he eliminated the existing assemblies, and over it he placed a single governor, Sir Edmund Andros, with headquarters in Boston. An able but stern and tactless administrator, Andros thoroughly antagonized the people as he proceeded to levy taxes and enforce the Navigation Acts.

Soon after the Bostonians heard of the 1688 movement to overthrow James II in England, they determined to overthrow his viceroy in New England. A mob set out after Andros and other royal officials: he escaped but later surrendered and was imprisoned.

The Massachusetts leaders now hoped to get back their old corporate charter, but the new sovereigns, William and Mary, combined Plymouth with Massachusetts and claimed the land as a royal colony (1691). Under the new charter, they themselves appointed the governor, but they restored the General Court with its elected lower house and allowed the General Court to choose the members of the upper house. This charter also did away with the religious test for voting and officeholding. Though there remained a property requirement, the great majority of Massachusetts men could meet it.

Andros had been ruling New York through a lieutenant governor, Captain Francis Nicholson, who enjoyed the support of the wealthy merchants and fur traders of the province. The groups that were excluded from a fair share in the government — farmers, mechanics, small traders, and shopkeepers — already had a long accumulation of grievances when news came of James' fall and Andros' arrest. Rebellious militiamen promptly seized the New York City fort, and Lieutenant Governor Nicholson sailed away to England.

The leadership of the New York rebels fell to Jacob Leisler, who had come from Germany, succeeded as a merchant, and married into a prominent Dutch family, but had never gained acceptance as one of the colony's ruling class. Leisler's followers proclaimed him commander in chief, and he declared his loyalty to William and Mary. These sovereigns finally appointed a new governor, who was given authority to call an elected assembly. When, ahead of the new governor, a British officer appeared with a contingent of troops, Leisler refused to surrender the fort to him. Leisler afterward yielded, but the delay gave his political enemies, soon back in power, a pretext for charging him with treason. He and a son-in-law were hanged, drawn, and quartered.

Thus the Glorious Revolution of 1688 in England touched off revolutions, mostly bloodless, in the colonies. Under the new regime the representative assemblies that had been abolished were revived, but not the scheme for colonial unification from above. Several of the provinces, however, were now royal colonies in which the King appointed the governor, and over which he potentially had greater direct control than he once had had.

Chapter 2

Provincial Americans, 1700–1763

The Scarcity of Labor

The transplanted Europeans discovered an abundance of land in North America but faced an acute shortage of labor, which was necessary to unlock the continent's vast wealth. However, the wide availability of land proved to be a powerful attraction for European immigrants; it also provided a need for importing Africans. Immigration and the high rate at which the established population multiplied led to a rate of growth in the population and the labor force far greater than that of contemporary England and Europe.

After 1700 few European immigrants went to either New England or to the South. The largest numbers went to Pennsylvania, where opportunities were more attractive than in stony, intolerant New England or in the slave South. At least half of these people arrived not as free persons, but in various states of voluntary servitude. Conditions were most difficult for the "redemptioners" who gave their indentures to the captain of the ship they boarded. He auctioned off their contracts after putting in at an American port, and each buyer then claimed his servants.

Although the terms under which the redemptioners labored were very poor, they were flexible and lenient compared to those the African slaves were subjected to. The slaves found themselves almost completely under the control of their owners. Identifiable by their color, black slaves could not run away and merge themselves with the mass of free humanity as white servants could. Nor could slaves rise out of their bondage to compete with their masters for wealth and political influence as the servants sometimes did. It was, of course, this total control of labor that made slavery increasingly attractive to southern planters. Planters in Virginia and Maryland had developed a highly marketable crop in tobacco, but they discovered that few Englishmen would willingly contract to provide the needed labor. Tobacco planters thus turned to African slaves, in spite of the tendency of the wealthier sugar planters in the West Indies to drive up the price of slaves. By 1700 blacks accounted for as much as 15 percent of the population of the southern colonies.

During the eighteenth century, tobacco planters became even more committed to slavery, especially after European demand for their product increased dramatically during the 1720s. In 1720 only 25 percent of the planters in the Chesapeake were slaveholders, but by 1770 over half owned slaves. By the time of the Revolution the slave population amounted to well over one-third of the total population of the South, as the exceptionally heavy demands of Carolina rice planters for unskilled labor came to reinforce the needs of the tobacco growers. At the same time, the number of slaves supplied by American and European traders increased rapidly.

The slave trade was dominated by ships owned in England but was shared by others owned in New England. The latter often followed a "triangular" route. That is, a ship took rum and other items from a New England port to the Guinea Coast of Africa, slaves from Africa to the West Indies, and sugar and molasses as well as specie and bills from the West Indies to the home port. There some of the cargo would be distilled into rum for another voyage of the same kind. On the African coast the slave marts were kept supplied by native chieftains who made a business of capturing enemy tribesmen in warfare and bringing them, tied together in long lines known as "coffles," out of the jungle. Then, after some haggling on the seashore, came the horrors of the "middle passage" — so called because it was the second of the three legs of the voyage — during which the slaves were packed in the dark and stinking hold, with no sanitary facilities, no room to stand up, and scarcely air enough to breathe. Those who died en route were thrown overboard, and the losses from disease were generally high. Those who survived were "seasoned" for a time in the West Indies before being shipped on to the mainland.

Economic conditions throughout much of North America appeared conducive to the spread of slavery. The combination of very cheap land and very expensive labor existed not only in the southern colonies. Yet, while men owned slaves in all the colonies, only 20 percent of the slave population lived in New England and the middle colonies in 1763 (45,000 out of 230,000 slaves). Slavery spread extensively only in the South. The higher costs of clothing and sheltering slaves in the more northerly colonies and the less expansive condition of agriculture in the North placed even the wealthiest northern landowners at a disadvantage in bidding for slaves.

Population Growth

Besides the Africans, other non-English peoples came in large numbers to the colonies after the end of the seventeenth century, while immigration from England itself fell off. Recovering from a prolonged depression in the 1630s, England thereafter began to develop more and more industries which demanded workers, so that the talk of overpopulation ceased to be heard. Instead of encouraging emigration from its own shores, the government tried to check the loss of English labor by prohibiting the departure of skilled artisans, while continuing to unload the unemployable or the undesirable upon the colonies.

Although during the eighteenth century the colonies received relatively few newcomers from England, the populations of several of them were swelled by vast numbers of arrivals from France, Germany, Switzerland, Ireland, and Scotland.

Of these immigrants the earliest though not the most numerous were the French Calvinists, or Huguenots. Under the Edict of Nantes (1598) they had enjoyed liberties and privileges that enabled them to constitute practically a state within the state in Roman Catholic France. In 1685 the edict was revoked, and singly and in groups the Huguenots took the first opportunity to leave the country, until a total of about 300,000 had left for England, the Netherlands, America, and elsewhere, only a small minority of them going to the English colonies.

Like the French Protestants, many German Protestants suffered under arbitrary rulers, and German Catholics as well as Protestants suffered even more from the devastating wars of the Sun King of France, Louis XIV. The Rhineland of southwestern Germany, the area known as the Palatinate, was especially exposed to the slaughter of its people and the ruin of its farms. For the Palatine Germans, the unusually cold winter of 1708–1709 came as the last straw, and more than 12,000 of them sought refuge in England. The Catholics among them were shipped back to Germany and the rest were resettled in England, Ireland, or the colonies. Pennsylvania was the usual destination of Germans, who sailed for America in growing numbers, to form the largest body of eighteenth-century white immigrants except for the Scotch-Irish.

The Scotch-Irish, the most numerous of the newcomers, were not Irishmen at all, though coming from Ireland, and they were distinct from the Scots who came to America directly from Scotland. In the early 1600s King James I, to further the conquest of Ireland, had seen to the peopling of the northern county of Ulster with his subjects from the Scottish Lowlands, who as good Presbyterians might be relied upon to hold their ground against the Irish Catholics. These Ulster colonists — the Scotch-Irish — eventually prospered despite the handicap of a barren soil and border fighting with the Irish tribes. Then, after about a century, the English government destroyed their prosperity by prohibiting the export of their woolens and other products, and at the same time threatened their religion by virtually outlawing it and insisting upon conformity with the Anglican Church. As the long-term leases of the Scotch-Irish terminated, in the years after 1710, the English landlords doubled and even tripled the rents. Rather than sign new leases, thousands upon thousands of the ill-used tenants embarked in successive waves of emigration. Understandably a cantankerous and troublesome lot, these people often were coldly received at the colonial ports, and most of them pushed out to the edge of the American wilderness.

The Scots and the Irish, as migrants to America, had no connection with the Scotch-Irish. Scottish Highlanders, some of them Roman Catholics frustrated in the rebellions of 1715 and 1745, went with their tartans and kilts and bagpipes to more than one of the colonies, but mostly to North Carolina. Presbyterian Lowlanders, afflicted with high rents in the country and unemployment in town, left in largest numbers shortly before the American Revolution. The Irish had migrated in trickles over a long period and, by the time of the Revolution, were about as numerous as the Scots, though less conspicuous, many of them having lost their Roman Catholic religion and their identity as Irishmen.

All these various immigrants contributed to the remarkable growth of the colonies. In 1700 the colonial population totaled a quarter of a million or less; by 1775 it was nearly ten times as large, more than two million. Its rate of growth was more than twice that common in Europe during the same period. Important as the continuing immigration was, the rapid growth of the colonial population was mainly due to natural increase, to the excess of births over deaths. As a consequence, only about one-tenth of the white population alive at the end of the colonial period had been born abroad. Contributing to the high rate of natural increase was the fact that colonists married earlier and had more children. The abundance of land and opportunity made it possible for young couples to set up households and follow the Biblical advice: "Be ye fruitful and multiply." Even more important for rapid population growth was a mortality rate that was low everywhere except around the malarial swamps of the Chesapeake

and the South Carolina coast. In an average year, the American mortality rate was about one-half of that prevailing in Europe. Crops were more abundant, sharply reducing periods of famine, and although the winters were harsher in much of America, families were better able to protect themselves because of the great availability of wood for building of houses and for heating and cooking fuel. The infant mortality rate, in particular, was lower, because pregnant and nursing women were better able to sustain their own health.

The colonial population was surprisingly mobile; New Englanders resettled in New Jersey and other colonies to the south, and Pennsylvanians (Scotch-Irish and Germans) swarmed up the Shenandoah Valley to people the back country of the Carolinas. In all the colonies men and women pushed upstream toward the unsettled wilderness, until with Daniel Boone leading the way into Kentucky (1769) they began even to occupy the land beyond the mountains.

Along the seacoast a number of villages grew into small cities. For more than a century after its founding, Boston remained the largest town, but eventually it was overtaken by Philadelphia. After 1700 these and other colonial towns increased more rapidly than most English cities. Indeed, by 1775 Philadelphia, with its 40,000 inhabitants, had become larger than any English city with the exception of London. Eight out of 100 Americans lived in towns in 1720. The rest of the people — the overwhelming majority throughout the colonial period — were scattered over the countryside and lived on farms of one description or another.

Agriculture

In the shaping of the provincial economy — that is, in the determination of the ways the colonists made their living — four forces were especially important. One of these was the policy of the British government, which discouraged certain occupations, such as iron finishing, and encouraged others, such as shipbuilding, in accordance with mercantilist principles. A second and more important influence derived from the geographical conditions in America, which favored some lines of activity, such as wheat farming, and made others, such as growing sugar cane, impracticable. A third consisted of the aims and energies of the individual settlers, who brought with them from the British Isles and the European continent (and, in the case of the slaves, from Africa) their own skills and habits and aspirations for personal success, including the desire for a higher standard of living. A fourth was the rapidly growing demand of European and West Indian consumers for a wide variety of products. As a result of these diverse factors, there flourished in the eighteenth century a variety of agricultural, industrial, and commercial pursuits, not all of which conformed to the broad mercantilist plan.

In George Washington's time the tools and methods of farming were not much advanced beyond what they had been in the day of the pharaohs, and in provincial America there was even less care of the soil than there had been in ancient Egypt. Most of the colonists gave little thought to conserving their land by rotating crops, applying fertilizers, or checking erosion. Their attitude was reasonable enough in their circumstances: it paid them to economize on labor and capital, not on land.

Near the frontier — that ever-expanding arc from Maine to Georgia, which bounded the area of settlement — subsistence farming was the rule. The frontiersman planted his corn and beans amid the stumps in patches he had incompletely reclaimed from the forest, and with his crops and his catch of wild game he fed himself and his family. Eventually some of the backwoodsmen went in for cattle raising on a fairly large scale, especially in Pennsylvania and the Carolinas.

In New England — where farmers once had lived on village lots, shared the "commons" as pasture and timberland, and tilled outlying fields — the system of landholding gradually changed. After 1700 the commons were partly divided into private property, and the fields were consolidated into separate farms. The typical farm became one that was small enough to be worked by the farmer, his sons, and perhaps an occasional hired hand, with the aid of neighbors at harvests and at house or barn raisings. It was bounded by fences made of stones that had been laboriously cleared off the fields. A fairly self-sufficient unit, producing mainly for use rather than for sale, it contained a variety of livestock, apple and other orchards, and fields devoted chiefly to hay and corn, the prevalence of the "blast" or black-stem rust having discouraged the cultivation of wheat.

In New York, despite the abundance of excellent soil, agricultural productivity lagged because of the engrossment of the land in great estates, running to thousands and even hundreds of thousands of acres, on which few people were willing to work as tenants when they could get farms of their own in other colonies. In Pennsylvania, of all the colonies the most favored by nature for farming, the Germans applied the intensive cultivation they had learned in the old country. In both New York and Pennsylvania the farmers concentrated on the production of staples to be sold abroad and at home. After ceasing to produce enough food to feed all its own people, particularly those living in the port cities, New England depended upon these "bread colonies" for its wheat. The most important demand for wheat was that of the West Indian planters, who specialized heavily in sugar production. By 1763 exports of wheat exceeded those of any crop except tobacco.

In the Chesapeake region there still existed tobacco farms as small as 100 acres, cultivated by the owners, their families, and perhaps a servant or a slave or two. Such farms, however, had come to be overshadowed by large plantations with thousands of acres and dozens or even hundreds of blacks. On the tobacco plantations slave labor was easily adapted to the simple and repetitive round of tasks that the crop required — sowing, transplanting, weeding, worming, picking, curing, stripping, and packing.

Slave labor was also fairly well suited to rice culture along the Georgia and Carolina coasts. Here dikes and ditches leading from the tidal rivers permitted the necessary flooding and draining of the paddies, while care was taken to see that no salt water reached the rice with the incoming tide. To cultivate the growing rice, men had to stand knee-deep in mud, their bare backs exposed to malarial mosquitoes and to the broiling sun. Since white men could not be hired to do it, slaves were compelled to perform this torturing and unhealthful work.

Indigo supplemented rice after the successful

cultivation of the dye plant (1743) by Eliza Lucas, the daughter of a West Indian planter. Grown on high ground, the indigo did not get in the way of the rice on the river bottoms, and it occupied the slaves at times when they were not busy with the rice. They tended the indigo fields, cut the leaves, soaked them in vats, and extracted the residue as a blue powder. Glad for a chance to be freed from foreign sources of the dye, Parliament granted a bounty of sixpence a pound.

The British government tried to encourage the production of other crops that would meet the needs of mercantilism. It gave bounties for hemp, and a little was grown in the colonies, particularly in North Carolina, but not enough to make the experiment pay. The government also attempted to force the growth of grapes for wine and of mulberry trees for silk, but had even less success with these than with hemp. Too much skilled labor was required for such products. Obstinately the colonial farmers and planters stuck to those lines of production in which they had a comparative advantage over producers elsewhere in the world. In some cases, as with tobacco and indigo, the colonial products happened to supplement those grown in England and thus fit the mercantilist pattern. In other cases, as with wheat, the produce of the colonies competed with that of the mother country, conflicting with the mercantile system.

Industries

In the 1700s, as in earlier times, most families produced nearly all their necessities within the household, but an increasing quantity of goods was manufactured outside the home, in shops. In the rising towns artisans of many kinds appeared — carpenters, chandlers (candlemakers), coopers (barrelmakers), cordwainers (shoemakers), weavers, tailors, wheelwrights, and dozens of others. In such lines as millinery and dressmaking, women artisans were common and often a widow took over her husband's work and succeeded as a cobbler, tinworker, or even blacksmith. By 1750 almost a third of the people of Philadelphia owed their living to a craft of some kind.

Colonial artisanship became notable for quantity as well as quality. As late as 1700 all but a

tiny fraction of the manufactures that the colonists bought were made in England. Before the Revolution, most of the manufactures were made in America. The rise of the provincial artisan was watched with concern by those in London who took the doctrines of mercantilism seriously.

Water power was widely used in various kinds of colonial mills. At the rapids of streams small enough to be easily dammed, grist and fulling mills were set up to take some of the heavier labor out of the household, grinding grain and fulling cloth (shrinking and tightening the weave by a process of soaking and pounding) for the farmers in the area. The mill owner was usually a farmer himself in his spare time. He frequently used his water wheel to power a sawmill for cutting his neighbors' logs.

Like lumbering, the fur trade and the fisheries were extractive industries, depending closely upon the resources provided by nature. Both fishing and fur trading became big businesses employing what were, by colonial standards, large amounts of capital. The fisheries led to shipbuilding, the first colonial-built ships being put together on the New England coast for the use of fishermen, and the abundance of timber and naval stores enabled the industry in the provinces to expand to the point of outdoing that of England itself. So cheap and yet so seaworthy were the materials that, despite the high wages of colonial labor, excellent ships could be produced at as little as half the cost of those built in English yards. By the Revolution almost one-third of all British-owned ships were of colonial construction.

From the beginning of colonization, the home government encouraged the colonial production of iron in a crude form, as a raw material for English mills and foundries. When provincial iron makers began to produce more than merely the crude metal, their competitors in England induced Parliament to pass the Iron Act of 1750, which removed the English duty on pig and bar iron but forbade the colonists to erect new mills for the secondary processing of iron or steel. This prohibition was in line with other acts intended to limit the rise of advanced manufactures in America. The Woolen Act (1699) prohibited the export of wool or woolens from a colony to any place outside its boundaries, and the Hat Act

(1732) similarly prohibited the export of hats, which could be cheaply made in America because of the availability of beaver skins. But the colonists usually disregarded such legislation when it was in their interest to do so, and by the Revolution colonial iron makers produced 15 percent of the world's iron.

Money and Commerce

Though the colonists produced most of what they consumed, they by no means achieved economic self-sufficiency. The colonies as a whole could not supply their entire wants from their own agriculture and industry. To maintain and raise their living standards the mainland colonists had to have the benefits of trade with one another and with people overseas.

The central problem in the overseas commerce of the colonies was to find the means of payment for the increasing imports. Such payment had to be in the form of exports of colonial goods or of specie. The colonies had to sell abroad in order to buy from abroad, but British policy attempted to limit and control their selling opportunities.

Though the tobacco planters had an abundant staple for export, they were not allowed to dispose of it to the highest bidder in the markets of the world. According to the Navigation Acts, tobacco was one of the "enumerated items" that must be exported only to the British Isles, whence more than half of it was reexported to other places.

A typical planter sold his annual crop to an English merchant (or after the 1720s to a Scottish merchant) either directly or through a middleman in the colonies, and the merchant credited him with its value, after deducting charges for shipping, insurance, and a merchant's commission. Through the merchant he bought slaves and manufactured goods, and the merchant deducted the cost of these from the planter's credit on the books. After tobacco prices had begun to fall, the planter often found at the end of a year that his crop did not pay for all the goods he had ordered in return. The merchant then carried him until the next year and charged interest on the extension of credit. As the years went by, the planter went more and more deeply into debt, eventually leaving his indebtedness to his heirs.

The colonial merchant in such ports as Boston, New York, and Philadelphia did not have the same difficulties as the tobacco planter, though he had others of his own. He was favored by the Navigation Acts, passed in 1650 and after, which excluded foreign ships from practically all the colonial carrying trade. And he found a market in England for the furs, timber, naval stores, and vessels produced in the northern colonies. But he could not profitably sell in England all the fish, flour, wheat, and meat that the colonies produced for export. He had to find other markets for these commodities if he was to obtain adequate means of paying for his imports from England.

In the English island colonies of the West Indies the colonial merchant found a ready outlet for mainland foodstuffs and livestock. In the French, Dutch, and Spanish islands of the Caribbean he also got eager customers — and often better prices. Responding to pressure from English sugar planters, who wished to monopolize the growing mainland sugar market, Parliament in the Molasses Act of 1733 put a high duty on foreign sugar taken to the continental colonies. The molasses duty was intended to discourage commerce with the foreign islands. But the northern merchant could evade the tax by smuggling, and he often did.

To and from England, to and from the West Indies — these were much the most important routes of trade for the northern merchant. He also worked out a number of routes of indirect trade with the mother country; some of them complex and frequently changing, others fairly stable and somewhat "triangular" in their simplicity. Thus he might direct his ships to Catholic southern Europe with fish, then to England with wine and other proceeds in cash or bills of exchange, and then back home with manufactured goods.

The Class Structure

In provincial America the generous economic basis of life supported a society in which the benefits of physical well-being were more widely diffused than anywhere else in the world. It was a comparatively open society, in which people had more opportunity than elsewhere to rise in economic and social status. Yet it was also a society with great inequalities, one that offered only hardship and poverty to many of its members and especially to those of African descent.

In the colonies the English class arrangement was not reproduced. Few or none of the nobility became colonists, though some of them were colonial enterprisers. A relatively small number of untitled gentlemen and a great many members of the middle and lower orders migrated to Virginia, Massachusetts, and other colonies. Some of these arrivals doubtless hoped to reconstruct in America something like the social system they had known in England, only here they hoped to occupy the higher levels themselves. A fortunate few did acquire extensive landholdings and proceeded to mimic the aristocrats back home, but no true aristocracy was transplanted to the colonies.

A colonial class system nevertheless grew up. Once social differentiation was well developed, as it was by the middle of the eighteenth century, the upper classes in the colonies consisted of the royal officials, the proprietary families, the great landholders in the North and the planters in the South, and the leading merchants with their investments mostly in forms of property other than land. The middle classes included most of the landowning farmers and, in the towns, the lesser merchants, shopkeepers, ship captains, professionals, and self-employed artisans. The lower classes comprised the indentured servants and the poorest farmers, together with the comparatively small number of wage earners, including farm hands, sailors, and fishermen. Forming a separate class or caste, though often working in the fields alongside white servants and even alongside members of the master class, were the black slaves, the lowest of all.

All except the slaves could aspire to a higher place for themselves or at least for their children. The colonists, believing in enterprise and material success, honored the self-made man. Afterward his descendants were inclined to forget the humble and even grubby origins of the family fortune and to think of themselves as thoroughgo-

ing aristocrats. For example, one of the "first families" of eighteenth-century Virginia, the Byrds, enjoyed a fortune that William Byrd I had put together in the seventeenth century by selling pots, pans, guns, and rum to the Indians in exchange for furs and hides, as well as by dealing in Indian and African slaves.

As some of the rich grew richer, some of the poor became more impoverished. There was a widening of extremes. If many of the early indentured servants acquired valuable land and respectable status after completing their servitude, many of the later ones either took up subsistence farming on the frontier or sank to the level of the "poor whites" on worn-out lands in the neighborhood of the planters. Yet, especially in New England and Pennsylvania, the majority of the people came to form a property-owning middle class.

The institution of slavery grew more and more rigid, with slave codes that were increasingly severe. This was especially true in South Carolina, where whites had reason to fear the blacks, who greatly outnumbered them. There, slave conspiracies or mere rumors of them brought savage retribution and further tightening of the already strict laws governing slavery. Near Charleston several slaves accused of conspiring to revolt were burned to death in 1720. In the city itself fifty were hanged in 1740, and when a disastrous fire followed, two more were executed for arson.

Such events were not confined to the South. In New York City an insurrection of blacks led in 1712 to the execution of twenty-one participants, three of whom were burned at the stake while another was chained up without food or drink until he died. Again, in 1741, 101 blacks were convicted of plotting with poor whites to burn the city; eighteen of the blacks were hanged, thirteen burned alive, and the rest banished; four whites, two of them women, went to the gallows.

Home and Family

From the beginning, the family shelters of the colonists were fairly close imitations of those already familiar to them; yet houses were altered by Americanizing trends. The first English pioneers built thatched huts rather than log cabins of the kind now considered peculiarly American. Introduced by the early Swedish settlers along the Delaware, the log cabin did not become the typical frontier dwelling until the eighteenth century. By that time a variety of building materials and architectural styles had appeared in the older settled areas. Though a higher proportion of colonial than of English houses were built of wood, a considerable number were built of stone or brick, some of which was imported. In New England a common type of farmhouse was the "salt-box," two stories high in front and one in back, and sided with unpainted clapboards. In the middle colonies the red-brick house with a Dutch gambrel roof and the substantial farmhouse of native stone were characteristic. In the South the more prosperous planters erected Georgian mansions, which as a rule were copies of English models, reduced in size and simplified in ornament.

Crowded into the generally small houses were comparatively large families, at least in the early years of settlement. The family often included not only numerous children but also a varying number of dependent relatives, such as elderly grandparents or unmarried aunts. The household was further enlarged in many cases by the presence of servants, domestic slaves, or hired hands living under the same roof.

As head of the household, the father traditionally wielded strong authority over its members. He was entitled to whatever property his wife had owned before her marriage to him, but he was responsible also for her debts. A woman's place in society was as an obedient daughter to her father and as a "helpmeet" to her husband. Women concentrated on the diverse and demanding tasks of farm life and child rearing. Most women who grew up in Puritan communities learned to read and write, but elsewhere only a minority did so. And women had virtually no opportunities to participate in social life outside the family. Even in churches, with a few exceptions, they could not vote or become ministers.

In the life of the colonial family there was much more than congeniality and companionship to hold a married couple together. The family as a unit performed many functions that have since been taken over by business enterprises or by the state. It had economic functions as the producer of most of what its members consumed. It performed educational services, many children learning their ABCs at their mother's knee from the family Bible. The family served as a welfare agency in caring for the aged, the unemployable, and the sick. It was even a defense organization, at least on the frontier, where the lonely farmstead became a fortress to be defended by the whole family at the sound of the war whoop. Having all these forces of cohesion, families were rarely broken, except by death. Divorces were seldom sought and, except in New England, were difficult or impossible to obtain. Occasionally, it is true, husbands deserted or wives absconded, as advertisements in contemporary newspapers reveal.

Nevertheless, the patriarchal family, with its enlarged household, proved difficult to maintain under the conditions of life in eighteenth-century America. Here, where land was so much more abundant and labor so much scarcer than in England, separate and smaller families could manage to survive much more easily. Dependents increasingly left the patriarchal household, setting up their own.

The Pattern of Religions

Though originating abroad, religions developed a new and distinctive pattern in America. With the immigration of diverse sectarians from several countries, the colonies became an ecclesiastical patchwork made up of a great variety of churches. Toleration flourished to a degree remarkable for the time, not because it was deliberately sought but because conditions favored its growth. No single religious establishment predominated in the colonies as the Church of England did in the British Isles and as other state churches, Lutheran or Roman Catholic, did in Western Europe.

By law, the Church of England was established in Virginia, Maryland, New York, the Carolinas, and Georgia. In these colonies everyone regardless of belief or affiliation was supposed to be taxed for the support of the Church. Actually, except in Virginia and Maryland, the Church of England succeeded in maintaining its position as the established church only in certain localities.

Protestants extended toleration to one another more readily than to Roman Catholics. To strict Puritans the Pope seemed no less than Antichrist. Their border enemies in New France, being "papists," seemed agents of the devil bent on frustrating the divine mission of the wilderness Zion in New England. In most of the English colonies, however, the Roman Catholics were far too small a minority to occasion serious conflict. They were most numerous in Maryland, and even there they numbered no more than 3,000. Ironically, they suffered their worst persecution in that colony, which had been founded as a refuge for them and had been distinguished by its Toleration Act of 1649. According to Maryland laws passed after 1691, Catholics not only were deprived of political rights but also were forbidden to hold religious services except in private houses.

Even fewer than the Catholics, the Jews in provincial America totaled no more than about 2,000 at any time. There was relatively little social discrimination against the Jews, but there was political discrimination: in no colony could they vote or hold office.

The Great Awakening

During the early 1700s the pious outlook gave way more and more to a worldly view. With the westward movement and the wide scattering of the colonial population, many of the frontier settlers lost touch with organized religion. With the rise of towns and the multiplication of material comforts, the inhabitants of the more densely settled areas were inclined toward an increasingly secular outlook. With the appearance of numerous and diverse sects, some people were tempted to doubt whether any particular denomination, even their own, possessed a monopoly of truth and grace. And with the progress of science and free thought in Europe, at least a few Americans began to adopt a rational and skeptical philosophy.

For thousands of the colonists, the trend away from religion was reversed by a revival movement known as the Great Awakening, which reached a climax in the 1740s. Wandering exhorters from abroad did much to stimulate the revivalistic spirit. John and Charles Wesley, founders of Methodism, which began as a reform movement within the Church of England, visited southern colonies in the 1730s with the intention of revitalizing religion and converting Indians and blacks. George Whitefield, a powerful open-air preacher from England and for a time an associate of the Wesleys, made several evangelizing tours through the colonies.

Yet the outstanding preacher of the Great Awakening in New England was Jonathan Edwards — one of the most profound theologians in the history of American religious thought. From his pulpit in Northampton, Massachusetts, Edwards attacked the new doctrines of easy salvation for all. He called upon his people to return to the faith of their fathers. He preached afresh the old Puritan ideas of the absolute sovereignty of God, the depravity of man, predestination, the necessity of experiencing a sense of election, and election by God's grace alone. Describing hell as vividly as if he had been there, he brought his listeners to their knees in terror of divine wrath. Day after day the agonized sinners crowded his parsonage to seek his aid; at least one committed suicide.

The Great Awakening spread over the colonies like a religious epidemic. It was most contagious in frontier areas and among the comparatively poor and uneducated folk, especially in the South. It led to the division of existing congregations and the founding of schools for the preparation of ministers. To some extent, too, it aroused a spirit of humanitarianism, a concern for the physical as well as the spiritual welfare of the poor and oppressed. The widely preached doctrine of salvation for all — of equal opportunity to share in God's grace — encouraged the notion of equal rights to share also in the good things on earth. Thus it stimulated feelings of democracy.

Though the Great Awakening had these important and lasting consequences, many of the converted soon backslid, and by the end of the colonial period English America contained fewer church members for its population than did any other Christian country of the time, and fewer than the United States has today.

Reading and Writing

As an American variant of English culture developed in the colonies, it was reflected in the partial Americanization of the English language. After 1700 English travelers in America began to notice a strangeness in accent as well as vocabulary, and in 1756 the great lexicographer Dr. Samuel Johnson mentioned the existence of an "American dialect."

Dr. Johnson thought of Americans as barbarians, and some no doubt were, but from the beginning many had been concerned lest civilization be lost in the wilderness. They continued to provide schooling for their children as best they could, particularly in New England. In various colonies the advancement of religion being one motive for education, the Quakers and other sects operated church schools. Here and there a widow or an unmarried woman conducted a "dame school," holding private classes in her home. In some of the cities master craftsmen set up evening schools for their apprentices, at least 100 such schools appearing between 1723 and 1770. Far more people learned to read than ever attended school, and by the time of the Revolution perhaps a majority of Americans could read.

Founded in 1704, the first regular newspaper in the colonies was the weekly Boston *News-Letter*, a small folded sheet of four pages with two columns to a page. By the 1760s one or more weekly papers were being published in each of the colonies except New Jersey and Delaware, both of which were well enough supplied by the presses of New York and Philadelphia. Several monthly magazines, notably the *American Magazine* of Philadelphia, were started after about 1750, with hopes of wide circulation. One after another they appeared for a year or two and then expired. More successful and more widely read were the yearly almanacs. Originally mere collections of weather data, these turned into small magazines of a sort, containing a great variety of literary fare. *Poor Richard's Almanac*, now well remembered, was only one of many, though a superior one.

Its publisher, Benjamin Franklin, was one of a few colonial-born men of letters who wrote works of lasting literary merit. As a rule, provincial authors had no time for belles-lettres, for fiction, poetry, drama, and the like. Writers concentrated upon sermons, religious tracts, and subjects of urgent, practical concern.

The Higher Learning

Of the six colleges in actual operation in 1763, all but two were founded by religious groups primarily for the training of preachers. Harvard (1636) was established by Congregationalists, William and Mary (1693) by Anglicans, and Yale (1701) by conservative Congregationalists who were dissatisfied with the growing religious liberalism of Harvard. The College of New Jersey (1746), later known as Princeton, was set up by Presbyterians in response to the Great Awakening. At any of these institutions a student with secular interests could derive something of a liberal education from the prevailing curricula, which included logic, ethics, physics, geometry, astronomy, rhetoric, Latin, Hebrew, and Greek. From the beginning Harvard was intended not only to provide an educated ministry but also to "advance learning and perpetuate it to posterity." King's College (1754), afterward Columbia, had no theological faculty and was interdenominational from the start. The Academy and College of Philadelphia (1755), which grew into the University of Pennsylvania, was a completely secular institution, founded by a group of laymen under the inspiration of Benjamin Franklin. It offered courses in utilitarian subjects as well as the liberal arts — in mechanics, chemistry, agriculture, government, commerce, and modern languages.

In the provincial colleges, considerable attention was given to scientific subjects. Chairs in "natural philosophy," or physical science, were endowed at William and Mary and at Harvard. The most advanced scientific thought of Europe — Copernican astronomy and Newtonian physics — eventually made its way into American teaching. But scientific speculation and experiment were not the exclusively academic, professional occupations that they later became.

Jonathan Edwards and many other ministers, merchants, and planters in America were active as amateur scientists. The Royal Society of London, founded in 1662 for the advancement of science, honored a number of them by electing them as fellows. To this society the American members and nonmember correspondents sent samples and descriptions of plants, animals, and remarkable phenomena. By means of their contributions the colonial amateurs added a good deal to the accumulation of data upon which later scientific progress was to be based. They also sent in plans for mechanical inventions and helped to start the reputation of Americans as a mechanically ingenious people.

Though women were excluded from the colleges and the professions, a few of them gained the equivalent of a higher education through their own exertions. Notable examples were Abigail Smith (who married John Adams) and Mercy Otis, both of whom belonged to learned, book-loving Massachusetts families. Relying on traditional cures and Indian remedies, most women served as nurses and, to some extent, even as doctors within their own households. At least one woman, Hannah Williams of South Carolina, emulated the men who were making modest contributions to science. As early as 1705 she was collecting specimens of "some of our vipers and several sorts of snakes, scorpions, and lizards," besides insects, wild bees' nests, and various native plants.

The greatest of colonial scientists and inventors, Benjamin Franklin, gained world-wide fame with his kite experiment (1752), which demonstrated that lightning and electricity were one and the same. He interested himself in countless subjects besides electricity, and he was a theoretical or "philosophical" scientist as well as a practical one. He also was a promoter of science. In 1727 he and his Philadelphia friends organized the Junto, a club for the discussion of intellectual and practical matters of mutual interest. In 1744 he led in the founding of the American Philosophical Society, the first learned society in America.

Chapter 3

The Empire Under Strain

Toward Self-Government

After England's Glorious Revolution of 1688 and the collapse of the Dominion of New England, the English government (or the British government after 1707, when Great Britain was created by the union of England and Scotland) made no serious or sustained effort for more than seventy years to tighten its control over the colonies. During that time, it is true, additions were made to the list of royal colonies (New Jersey, 1702; North and South Carolina, 1729; Georgia, 1754) until they numbered eight, in all of which the King had the power of appointing governors and other colonial officials. During that time, also, Parliament passed new laws supplementing the original Navigation Acts and elaborating on the mercantilist program — laws restricting colonial manufactures, limiting paper currency, and regulating trade. Nevertheless, the British government itself remained uncertain and divided about the extent to which it ought to interfere in colonial affairs. The colonies were left, within broad limits, to go their separate ways, and they were able to assert fairly extensive rights of self-government.

Resistance to imperial authority centered in the colonial assemblies. By the 1750s they had established the right to levy taxes, make appropriations, approve appointments, and pass laws for their respective colonies. Their legislation was subject to veto by the governor and to disallowance by the Privy Council (the central administrative agency in England), but they could often sway the governor by means of their money powers, and they could get around the Privy Council by repassing disallowed laws in slightly altered form. The assemblies came to look upon themselves as little parliaments, each practically as powerful within its colony as Parliament itself was in England.

Meanwhile some developments were laying a basis for the eventual growth of a sense of intercolonial community. The increase of population, which produced an almost continuous line of settlement along the seacoast, brought the people of the various colonies into closer and closer contact, as did the gradual construction of roads, the rise of intercolonial trade, and the improvement of the colonial post office.

Still, the colonists were loath to cooperate even when, in 1754, they faced a new threat from old and dreaded enemies, the French and their Indian allies. A conference of colonial leaders — with delegates on hand from Pennsylvania, Maryland, New York, and the New England colonies — was meeting in Albany to negotiate a treaty with the Iroquois. The delegates stayed on to talk about forming a colonial federation for defense. Benjamin Franklin proposed to his fellow delegates a plan by which Parliament would set up in America "one general government" for all the colonies, each of which would "retain its present constitution" except for the powers given to the general government. The King would appoint a President-General, and the colonial assemblies would elect representatives to a Grand Council. The President-General in consultation with the Council would take charge of all relations with the Indians; the Council, subject to his veto, would make laws and levy taxes for raising troops, building forts, waging war, and carrying on other Indian affairs.

War with the French and Indians was already beginning when this Albany Plan was presented to the colonial assemblies for their consideration. Yet none of them approved it, and none except the Massachusetts assembly even gave it very serious attention. "Everyone cries, a union is necessary," Franklin wrote to the Massachusetts governor, "but when they come to the manner and form of the union, their weak noddles are perfectly distracted."

New France

The French had founded a string of widely separated communities, strategically located fortresses, and far-flung missions and trading posts. On Cape Breton Island they established Fort Louisbourg, one of the most redoubtable strongholds in all the New World, to guard the approach to the Gulf of St. Lawrence. On a high bluff above the river stood Quebec, the pride of the French empire in America. Farther up the river was Montreal, even more "provincial" and less sophisticated than Quebec. Hundreds of miles to the northwest, near the juncture of Lake Superior with Lakes Michigan and Huron, was the tiny outpost of Sault Sainte Marie. Hundreds of miles to the southwest, at the juncture of Lakes Huron and Erie, was the well-fortified Detroit. Still farther in the same direction, along the Mississippi between the Missouri and the Ohio, was a cluster of hamlets — Cahokia, Kaskaskia, Fort Chartres, Sainte Genevieve — each with its outlying common fields of black earth under cultivation. Over on the Wabash was the fifth tiny settlement of the Illinois country, Vincennes.

On the lower Mississippi were plantations much like those in the southern colonies of English America, plantations worked by black slaves and supporting a race-conscious class of "Creoles." Founded in 1718, New Orleans soon grew into a city comparable in size with some of those on the Atlantic seaboard but quainter than most, with its houses built of cypress logs and bark roofs and set upon stilts above the swampy ground. To the east of New Orleans, along the Gulf of Mexico, were the towns of Biloxi (founded 1699) and Mobile (1702), completing the string of mainland settlements which stretched all the way around from Fort Louisbourg.

Anglo-French Conflict

Spacious though it was, the continent of North America seemed too small to contain both the English and the French. The English, as Protestants, and the French, as Roman Catholics, eyed each other with suspicion and fear. As fishermen and fur traders they competed for the profits of the forest and the sea. Each national group began ultimately to feel that its very survival in America depended upon the elimination of the other's influence. No serious trouble between English and French colonists occurred, however, so long as their homelands remained at peace.

Eventually two wars spread from Europe to America, where they were known to the English colonists as King William's War (1689–1697) and Queen Anne's War (1701–1713). The first, which involved few of the colonists except in northern New England, led to no decisive result. The second, which entailed border fighting with the Spaniards in the south as well as the French and their Indian allies in the north, ended in one of the great and far-reaching international settlements of modern history — the Treaty of Utrecht (1713). At Utrecht the English were awarded some sizable territorial gains in North America at the expense of the French: Acadia (Nova Scotia), Newfoundland, and the shores of Hudson Bay.

After about a quarter of a century of European and American peace, England went to war with Spain over the question of English trading rights in the Spanish colonies. The Anglo-Spanish conflict soon merged in a general European war. Again New England and New France were involved in the hostilities — in what the English colonists referred to as King George's War (1744–1748). New Englanders captured the French bastion at Louisbourg on Cape Breton Island, but to their bitter disappointment they had to abandon it in accordance with the peace treaty, which provided for the mutual restoration of conquered territory.

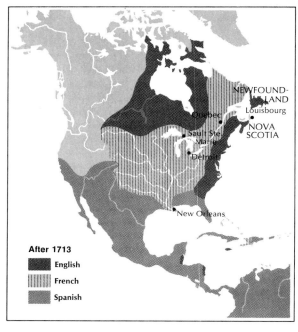

North American Empires

The next conflict was different. Known to the colonists as the French and Indian War, it was in fact a "Great War for the Empire." Unlike the preliminaries, this climactic struggle originated in the interior of North America.

The Great War for the Empire

Within the American wilderness a number of border disputes arose, but the most serious of them concerned the ownership of the Ohio Valley. The French, desiring to control this direct route between Canada and its southern settlements began to build a chain of fortifications to make good their claim. Pennsylvania fur traders and Virginia land speculators (the latter organized as the Ohio Company) looked to the country across the Alleghenies as a profitable field for their operations, and the British government, aroused to the defense of its territorial rights, gave instructions to the colonial governors to resist French encroachments.

Acting on these instructions, the governor of Virginia sent George Washington, then only twenty-one, to protest to the commanders of the French forts newly built between Lake Erie and the Allegheny River, but these commanders politely replied that the land was French. While Washington was on his fruitless mission, a band of Virginians tried to forestall the French by erecting a fort of their own at the strategic key to the Ohio Valley — the forks of the Ohio, where the Allegheny and Monongahela rivers join. A stronger band of Canadians drove the Virginians away, completed the work, and named it Fort Duquesne. Arriving with the advance guard of a relief force from Virginia, Washington met a French detachment in a brief but bloody skirmish. He then fell back to a hastily constructed stockade, Fort Necessity, where he was overwhelmed by troops from Fort Duquesne and compelled to surrender (July 4, 1754). The first shots of the French and Indian War had been fired.

At first the overall direction of British strategy

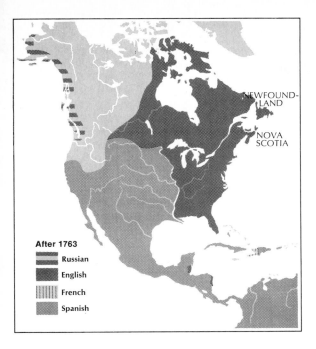

After 1763

Russian

English

French

Spanish

French territory east of the Mississippi, except the island of New Orleans, to Great Britain, and New Orleans and the French claims west of the Mississippi to Spain. Thus the French gave up all their title to the mainland of North America.

Burdens of Victory

So strong had grown the colonial feeling against direct legislation by Parliament that, during the French and Indian War, the English government did not attempt to tax or draft the colonists directly but called upon the assemblies to provide quotas of soldiers and supplies. This requisition system, itself a concession to provincial prejudice, heightened the self-importance of the assemblies, and most of them further asserted their autonomy by complying in a slow and niggardly way. Some of them, unwilling to be taxed by Parliament, also refused to tax themselves; they issued paper money instead.

In Virginia the legislature not only issued paper money but, when the price of tobacco rose, also passed a law to deprive the Anglican clergy (who were paid in tobacco) of the benefits of the price rise. When this law was disallowed (1759), one of the ministers sued his vestrymen for his full pay. At the trial of the "parson's cause" the young lawyer Patrick Henry, defending the vestrymen, denounced the Privy Council for its tyranny and told his fellow Virginians to ignore its action. Roused by Henry's oratory, the jurors awarded the parson damages of only one penny. Thus did they defy the authority of the British government.

Massachusetts merchants disregarded the laws of the Empire even more flagrantly than did the Virginia planters. Throughout the war these merchants persisted in trading with the enemy in Canada and in the French West Indies. British officials resorted to general search warrants — "writs of assistance" — for discovering smuggled goods and stamping out the illegal and unpatriotic trade. As attorney for the Massachusetts merchants, James Otis maintained that these searches violated the ancient rights of Englishmen and that the law of Parliament authorizing the warrants was therefore null and void. With eloquence as stirring as Henry's, Otis

was weak. Then, in 1757, William Pitt, as prime minister, was allowed to act as practically a wartime dictator of the Empire. With Pitt as organizer, the British regulars in America, together with colonial troops, proceeded to take one French stronghold after another, including Fort Duquesne in 1758. The next year, after a siege of Quebec, supposedly impregnable atop its towering cliff, the army of General James Wolfe struggled up a hidden ravine, surprised the larger forces of the Marquis de Montcalm, and defeated them in a battle in which both commanders were slain. The fall of Quebec marked the climax of the American phase of the war.

Peace finally came after the accession of the peace-minded George III and the resignation of Pitt, who disagreed with the new King and wished to continue hostilities. Yet Pitt's aims were pretty well realized in the treaty signed at Paris in 1763. By its terms the French ceded to Great Britain some of their West Indian islands and all their colonies in India except two. The French also transferred Canada and all other

insisted that Parliament had only a limited power in legislating for the colonies.

Believing in a kind of commercial imperialism, most English merchants opposed the acquisition of territory for its own sake. But some English and American citizens began to believe that land itself should be acquired for the Empire because of the population the land would support, the demand for English manufactures and the taxes it would produce, and the sense of imperial greatness it would confer. Both William Pitt and Benjamin Franklin were among the advocates of this new territorial imperialism. Franklin wrote powerfully upon the future greatness of the British Empire in America, stressing the need for vast spaces to accommodate the rapid and limitless growth of the American people. Old-fashioned mercantilists, however, continued to think of trade and the importation of raw materials as the essences of empire, and of island and coastal possessions as bases for trade and centers of agricultural production.

The issue came to a head with the peace making at the end of the French and Indian War. Commercial imperialists urged that Canada be returned to France in exchange for the most valuable of its sugar islands, Guadeloupe. Territorial imperialists, Franklin among them, and English sugar planters in the West Indies argued in favor of keeping Canada and leaving Guadeloupe in French hands. The decision to retain Canada marked a change in the emphasis of imperial policy.

With the acquisition of Canada and the other fruits of war in 1763, the area of the British Empire was more than doubled, and the problems of governing it were made many times more complex. The war had left the British government with a staggering burden of debt, and English landlords and merchants objected violently to increased taxes. The rather half-hearted war effort of the colonists had shown the cumulative evils of the Empire's rather loose administration. And, by giving Great Britain undisputed title to the territory east of the Mississippi as well as Canada, the peace had brought new problems of administration and defense. British statesmen feared that France, by no means crushed, might soon launch an attack somewhere in America for the recovery of its lost territories and prestige.

The New Imperialism

As the war ended, the London policy makers faced a dilemma, though they were not fully aware of it. On the one hand, they could revert to the old colonial system with its half-hearted enforcement of the mercantilist program, but that would mean virtual independence for the colonies. On the other hand, the policy makers in London could renew their efforts to reform the Empire and enforce the laws, but that would lead to revolt and absolute independence. The problem was further complicated by both the costs and the rewards of the war — the debts and the territory that it brought.

Responsibility for the solution of these postwar problems fell to the young monarch George III. More immediately responsible was George Grenville, whom the King made prime minister in 1763. Grenville, a brother-in-law of William Pitt, did not share Pitt's sympathy with the colonial point of view. He agreed with the prevailing British opinion that the colonists should be compelled to obey the laws and to pay a part of the cost of defending and administering the Empire. Promptly he undertook to impose system upon what had been a rather unsystematic aggregation of colonial possessions in America.

The Western problem was the most urgent. With the repulse of the French, frontier settlers from the English colonies had begun promptly to move over the mountains and into the upper Ohio Valley. Objecting to this intrusion, an alliance of Indian tribes, under the remarkable Ottawa chieftain Pontiac, raised the war cry. As an emergency measure the British government issued a proclamation forbidding settlers to advance beyond a line drawn along the mountain divide between the Atlantic and the interior.

Though the emergency passed, the principle of the Proclamation Line of 1763 remained — the principle of controlling the westward movement of population. This was something new. Earlier the government had encouraged the rapid peopling of the frontier for reasons of both defense and trade. In time the official attitude had begun to change, because of a fear that the interior might draw away so many people as to weaken markets and investments nearer the coast, and because of a desire to reserve land-speculating and fur-trading opportunities for English rather than colonial enterprisers. Then, having tentatively announced a new policy in 1763, the government soon extended and elaborated it. A definite Indian boundary was to be located, and from time to time relocated, in agreement with the various tribes. Western lands were to be opened for occupation gradually, and settlement was to be carefully supervised to see that it proceeded in a compact and orderly way.

To provide further for the defense of the colonies, and to raise revenue and enforce imperial law within them, the Grenville ministry with the cooperation of Parliament meanwhile instituted a series of measures, some of which were familiar in principle and others fairly novel. Regular troops were now to be stationed permanently in the provinces, and the colonists were called upon to assist in provisioning and maintaining the army. Ships of the navy were assigned to patrol American waters and look out for smugglers. The customs service was reorganized and enlarged, and vice-admiralty courts were set up in America to try accused smugglers without the benefit of sympathetic local juries. The Sugar Act (1764), designed in part to eliminate the illegal trade between the continental colonies and the foreign West Indies, lowered the high molasses duty of the Molasses Act of 1733 but imposed new duties on a number of items and made provision for more effective collection. The Currency Act (1764) drastically restricted the ability of colonial assemblies to create paper money. Most momentous of all, the Stamp Act (1765) imposed a tax to be paid on every legal document in the colonies, every newspaper, almanac, or pamphlet, and every deck of cards or pair of dice.

Thus the new imperial program with its reapplication of old mercantilist principles began to be put into effect. In a sense it proved highly effective. British officials soon were collecting more than ten times as much annual revenue in America as before 1763. But the new policy was not a lasting success.

Colonial Self-Interest

The colonists still had much to gain by remaining within the Empire and enjoying its many benefits. They still held grievances against one another as well as against the authorities in London. In 1763, for example, a band of Pennsylvania frontiersmen known as the Paxton Boys descended on Philadelphia to demand defense money and changes in the tax laws, and bloodshed was averted only by concessions from the colonial government.

In 1771 a small-scale civil war broke out as a consequence of the Regulator movement in North Carolina. The Regulators were farmers of the Carolina upcountry who organized to oppose the extortionate taxes that the sheriffs collected. These sheriffs, along with other local officials, were appointed by the governor. At first the Regulators tried to redress their grievances peaceably, by electing their leaders to the colonial assembly. The western counties were badly underrepresented in the assembly, and the Regulators were unable to get control of it. They finally armed themselves and undertook to resist tax collections by force. To suppress the revolt, Governor William Tryon raised an army of militiamen, mostly from the eastern counties. The militiamen met and defeated the Regulators, some 2,000 strong, in the Battle of Alamance, in which nine on each side were killed and many others wounded. Afterward, six Regulators were hanged for treason.

Though such bloodshed was exceptional, the people of the colonies were divided by numerous conflicts of interest. After 1763, however, the policies of the British government increasingly offset the divisive tendencies within the colonies and caused Americans to look at the disadvantages of empire more closely than at its benefits. These policies threatened, in some degree or other, the well-being of nearly all classes in America.

Northern merchants would suffer from the various restraints upon their commerce, from the closing of the West to their ventures in land speculation and fur trading, from the denial of opportunities in manufacturing, and from the increased load of taxation. Southern planters, already burdened with debts to English merchants, would not only have to pay additional taxes but would also be deprived of the chance to lessen their debts by selling Western land, in which George Washington and others were much interested. Professionals — preachers, lawyers, and professors — considered the interests of merchants and planters to be identical with their own. Small farmers, clearly the largest group in the colonies, stood to lose as a result of reduced markets and hence lower prices for their crops, together with an increase in their taxes and other costs. Town workers faced the prospect of narrowing opportunities, particularly because of the restraints on manufacturing.

At the end of the French and Indian War, the colonists already were beginning to feel the pinch of a postwar depression. If all the government's measures should be strictly enforced, the immediate effect would be to aggravate the hard times. The long-run effect would be to confine the enterprising spirit of the colonists and condemn them to a fixed or even a declining level of living.

Grievous as were the economic consequences of George III's program, its political consequences would be as bad or worse. While colonial democracy was far from all-inclusive, the colonists were used to a remarkably wide latitude in self-government. Nowhere else in the world at that time did so large a proportion of the people take an active interest in public affairs. The chief centers of American political activity were the provincial assemblies, and here the people (through their elected representatives) were able to assert themselves because the assemblies had established the right to give or withhold appropriations for the costs of government within the colonies. If, now, the British authorities should succeed in raising extensive revenues directly from America, the colonial voters and their representatives would lose control over public finance, and without such control their participation in politics would be very nearly meaningless.

Home rule was not something new and different that these Americans were striving to get. It was something old and familiar that they desired to keep. They would lose it if the London authorities were allowed to carry out the program of raising revenues from colonial taxation and providing unconditional salaries for royal officials. The discontented Americans eventually prepared themselves to lay down their lives for a movement that was both democratic and conservative — a movement to conserve the liberties they already possessed.

The Stamp Act Crisis

The experience of the French and Indian War, while convincing prominent Englishmen of the need for tighter imperial control, had exerted an opposite effect on the attitude of colonials. The French threat having been removed from the frontier forest, many of the colonists felt a new surge of expansive energy and daring. In short, they concluded that they needed not more but rather less of imperial guidance and protection than they had previously received.

If Prime Minister Grenville had wished deliberately to antagonize and unify some of the most influential groups in the colonies (which, of course, he did not), he could have chosen no means more effective than the Stamp Act. The tax fell upon all Americans, of whatever section, colony, or class. In particular, the stamps required for ship's papers and legal documents offended merchants and lawyers. Tavern owners, often the political oracles of their neighborhoods, now were supposed to buy stamps for their licenses; and printers, for their newspapers and other publications. Thus the tax antagonized those who could play most effectively upon public opinion.

Nevertheless, it occurred to few colonists that they could do more than grumble and buy the stamps, until the Virginia House of Burgesses sounded a "trumpet of sedition" that aroused Americans to action almost everywhere. Patrick Henry, ambitious to enlarge the fame he had gained in the "parson's cause," made a fiery speech in the House (May 1765), concluding with a hint that George III like earlier tyrants might lose his head. There were shocked cries of "Treason!" and, according to a man who was present, Henry apologized, though many years afterward he was quoted as having made the defiant reply: "If *this* be treason, make the most of it." In any case, he proceeded to introduce a set of resolutions declaring that Americans possessed all the rights of Englishmen, especially the right to be taxed only by their own representatives.

Stirred by these Virginia Resolves, mobs in various places began to take the law into their own hands, and during the summer of 1765 riots broke out in various places, the worst of them in Boston. Men belonging to the newly organized "Sons of

Liberty" went about terrorizing stamp agents and burning the stamps.

At about the time that Patrick Henry presented his resolutions to the Virginia assembly, James Otis proposed to his fellow legislators in Massachusetts that they call an intercolonial congress for concerted action against the new tax. In October 1765 the Stamp Act Congress met in New York, with delegates from nine of the colonies present. The delegates decided to petition both the King and the two houses of Parliament. Though admitting that Americans owed to Parliament "all due subordination," the congress denied that colonists could rightfully be taxed except by their provincial assemblies.

If the British government had tried to enforce the Stamp Act, possibly the Revolutionary War would have begun ten years earlier than it actually did. The government was not deterred by resolves, riots, and petitions, but the Americans also used something more persuasive than any of these — economic pressure. Already, in response to the Sugar Act of 1764, many New Englanders had quit buying English goods. Now the colonial boycott spread, and the Sons of Liberty intimidated those colonists who were reluctant to participate in it. The merchants of England, feeling the loss of much of their colonial market, begged Parliament to repeal the Stamp Act, while stories of unemployment, poverty, and discontent arose from English seaports and manufacturing towns.

King George III himself finally was convinced that the act must be repealed. Opponents of repeal, and they were strong and vociferous, insisted that unless the colonists were compelled to obey the Stamp Act, they would soon cease to obey any laws of Parliament. So Parliament passed the Declaratory Act, asserting parliamentary authority over the colonies in "all cases whatsoever," and then repealed the Stamp Act (1766).

The Townshend Program

A new chancellor of the exchequer, Charles Townshend, had to deal with imperial problems and colonial grievances left over from the Grenville ministry. By the Townshend Act (1767), duties were laid upon colonial imports of glass, lead, paint, paper, and tea. Townshend reasoned that the colonists could not logically object to taxation of this kind. For Benjamin Franklin, as a colonial agent in London trying to prevent the passage of the Stamp Act, had drawn a distinction between "internal" and "external" taxes and had denounced the stamp duties as internal taxation. The Townshend duties were to be collected externally.

Townshend also took steps to enforce commercial regulations in the colonies. The most fateful of these steps was the establishment of a board of customs commissioners in America. The commissioners, with headquarters in Boston, virtually ended the smuggling at that place.

Naturally the Boston merchants were the most indignant, and they took the lead in organizing another boycott. In 1768 the merchants of Philadelphia and New York joined those of Boston in a nonimportation agreement, and later some of the southern merchants and planters also agreed to cooperate. Throughout the colonies, crude American homespun became suddenly fashionable, while English luxuries were frowned upon.

Before the consequences of his program were fully apparent, Townshend died, leaving the question of revising his import duties to his successor, Lord North. Hoping to break the nonimportation agreement and divide the colonists, Lord North secured the repeal (1770) of all the Townshend duties except the tea tax.

Meanwhile the presence of the customs commissioners in Boston led to violence. The terrified officials were driven to take refuge in Castle William, out in the harbor. So that they could return safely to their duties, the British government placed four regiments within the city. The presence of the redcoats antagonized the Boston radical Samuel Adams and his followers. While his men ragged the soldiers and engaged them in brawls, Adams filled the newspapers with imaginary stories of rapes and other atrocities committed by the troops, and he spread throughout Boston a rumor that the soldiers were preparing for a concerted attack upon the citizens. On the night of March 5, 1770, a mob of dockworkers and other "liberty boys" fell upon the sentry at the custom house. Hastily a British captain lined up several of his men in front of the building to protect it. There was some scuffling, and one of the soldiers was knocked down. Other soldiers then fired into the crowd, killing five of its members.

These events quickly became known as the "Boston Massacre" through the efforts of Samuel Adams and his adherents, who published an account bearing the title *Innocent Blood Crying to God from the Streets of Boston* and giving the impression that the dead were victims of a deliberate plot. The soldiers, tried before a jury of Bostonians and defended by Samuel Adams' cousin John Adams, were found guilty of no more than manslaughter and were given only a token punishment.

The Philosophy of Revolt

Though America quieted down for a while after 1770, Americans did not abandon their principles, and these principles were revolutionary, at least in implication. Very few of the people thought of outright independence, but many desired autonomy within the Empire. They argued that the English constitution, correctly interpreted, supported their claims to individual liberty and colonial self-rule, and that the laws of nature and of God justified them in resisting infringements upon their rights.

Of these rights the most fundamental, according to the colonists, was the right to be taxed only with their own consent. When Townshend levied his "external" duties, the Philadelphia lawyer John Dickinson maintained in the *Letters of a Pennsylvania Farmer* that even external taxation was legal only when designed to regulate trade and not to raise revenue. But Americans did not like trade regulations, either, when the regulations began to be enforced. Eventually the discontented colonists took an unqualified stand upon the slogan "No taxation without representation."

This clamor about "representation" made little sense to the English. Only about one in twenty-five of them was entitled to vote for members of Parliament, and some populous boroughs in England had no representatives at all. According to the prevailing English theory, however, Parliament did not represent individuals or geographic areas. Instead, it represented the interests of the whole nation and indeed the whole Empire, no

matter where the members happened to come from. The unenfranchised urban boroughs of England, the whole of Ireland, and the colonies 3,000 miles away — all were represented in the Parliament at London.

That was the theory of "virtual" representation, but Americans believed in actual representation. They felt they could be represented in Parliament only if they sent their quota of members to it. Some of them, even James Otis, considered proposals for electing American representatives, but most of the colonists realized that if they should participate in the action of Parliament they would be bound by that action, even though they were outnumbered and outvoted. So they reverted to the argument that they could be fairly represented only in their own colonial assemblies.

According to the American view of the Empire, and according to actual fact, these assemblies were little parliaments, as competent to legislate for their respective colonies as Parliament was for England. The Empire was a sort of federation of commonwealths, each with its own legislative body, all tied together by common loyalty to the King (much as in the later British Commonwealth of Nations). This being their conception of the Empire, the Americans protested bitterly against the pretensions of Parliament but had nothing except kind words for George III — until they decided to cut their imperial ties completely and declare for independence. According to the English view, the Empire was a single, undivided unit, and everywhere within it the King and Parliament together were supreme.

The American doctrine of resistance to unconstitutional and tyrannical laws was based heavily upon the writings of John Locke. Locke (1632–1704) would probably have been shocked if he had lived to see the use that Americans made of his doctrines. In his *Two Treatises of Government* (1690) he had attempted to justify the English revolution of 1688 by which Parliament had won supremacy over the King. According to Locke's theory, people originally lived in a state of nature and enjoyed complete liberty, then agreed to a "compact" by which they set up a government to protect their "natural rights," especially their right to the ownership and enjoyment of private property. The government was limited by the terms of the compact and by "natural law." It was contrary to natural law for a government to take property without the consent of the owners. And, according to Locke, if a government should persist in exceeding its rightful powers, the people would be released from their obligation to obey it. What was more, they would have the right to make a new compact and establish another government.

Also influential in developing revolutionary thought were the works of English radical publicists, such as John Trenchard and Thomas Gordon who joined to write the widely read and quoted *Cato's Letters* (1720). They argued that the English revolution had established a constitution that created a balance among the monarchy, the aristocracy, and the common people that could protect the English against the abuses of absolute power. A continual battle to contain power was required to protect the rights that the English won in 1688. These publicists maintained that this battle ought to be regarded as a natural part of the political order, and while the struggle ordinarily would be peaceful, it might require force to check the most absolute and corrupt form of power — the tyranny enforced by a standing army.

The Tea Excitement

A dispute over the importation of tea broke the relative calm that had descended over Anglo-American politics during the early 1770s. The East India Company, with a large stock of unsalable tea on hand, was nearly bankrupt, and Lord North induced Parliament to go to the company's relief with the Tea Act of 1773. This law permitted the company to export its product to America without paying any of the usual taxes except the tea tax still remaining from the original Townshend duties. With these privileges the company could undersell American merchants who bought their tea supplies in England.

With strong public support, leaders in various colonies made plans to prevent the East India Company from landing its cargoes in colonial ports. In Philadelphia and New York determined men kept the tea from leaving the company's ships, and in Charleston they stored it away in a public warehouse. In Boston, having failed to turn

back the three ships in the harbor, the followers of Samuel Adams staged a spectacular drama. On the evening of December 16, 1773, three companies of fifty men each, masquerading as "Mohawks," passed between the protecting links of a tremendous crowd of spectators, went aboard, broke open the tea chests, and heaved them into the water. As the electrifying news of the Boston "tea party" spread, other seaports followed the example and held tea parties of their own.

When the Bostonians refused to pay for the property they had destroyed, George III and Lord North decided upon a policy of coercion, to be applied not against all the colonies but only against Massachusetts — the chief center of resistance. In four acts of 1774 Parliament proceeded to put this policy into effect. One of the laws closed the port of Boston, another drastically reduced the local and provincial powers of self-government in Massachusetts, still another permitted royal officers to be tried in other colonies or in England when accused of crimes, and the last provided for the quartering of troops in the colonists' barns and empty houses.

These Coercive Acts were followed by the Quebec Act, which was separate from them in origin and quite different in purpose. Its object was to provide a civil government for the French-speaking, Roman Catholic inhabitants of Canada and the Illinois country. The law extended the boundaries of Quebec to include the French communities between the Ohio and Mississippi rivers. It also granted political rights to Roman Catholics and recognized the legality of the Roman Catholic Church within the enlarged province. In many ways it was a liberal and much-needed piece of legislation.

To many Protestants in the thirteen colonies, however, the Quebec Act was anathema. They were already alarmed by rumors that the Church of England schemed to appoint a bishop for America with the intention of enforcing Anglican authority upon all the various sects. To them the line between the Church of England and the Church of Rome always had seemed dangerously thin. When Catholics ceased to be actively persecuted in the mother country, alarmists in the colonies began to fear that Catholicism and Anglicanism were about to merge, and at the passage of the Quebec Act they became convinced that a plot was afoot in London for subjecting Americans to the tyranny of the Pope. Moreover, those interested in Western lands believed that the act, by extending the boundaries of Quebec, would reinforce the land policy of the Proclamation Line of 1763 and put an additional obstacle in the way of westward progress.

Had it not been for the Quebec Act, Lord North might have come close to succeeding in his effort to divide and rule the colonies by isolating Massachusetts. As it was, the colonists generally lumped the Quebec law with the Massachusetts measures as the fifth in a set of "Intolerable Acts." From New Hampshire to South Carolina the people prepared to take a united stand.

Chapter 4

The American Revolution

Lexington and Concord

From 1765 on, colonial leaders had provided a variety of organizations for converting popular discontent into action, organizations which in time formed the basis for an independent government. The most famous and most effective were the committees of correspondence. Massachusetts took the lead (1772) with such committees on the local level, a network of them connecting Boston with the rural towns, but Virginia was the first to establish committees of correspondence on an intercolonial basis. These made possible cooperation among the colonies in a more continuous way than had the Stamp Act Congress, the first effort at intercolonial union for resistance against imperial authority. Virginia took the greatest step of all toward united action in 1774 when, the governor having dissolved the assembly, a rump session met in Williamsburg, declared that the Intolerable Acts menaced the liberties of every colony, and issued a call for a Continental Congress.

Variously elected by the assemblies or by extralegal meetings, delegates from all the thirteen colonies except Georgia were present when, in September 1774, the Continental Congress convened in Philadelphia. The delegates drew up a somewhat self-contradictory statement of grievances, conceding to Parliament the right to regulate colonial trade but demanding the elimination of all oppressive legislation passed since 1763. They agreed to nonimportation, nonexportation, and nonconsumption as means of stopping all trade with Great Britain, and they formed a "Continental Association" to see that these agreements were carried out. They also approved

a series of resolutions from a Suffolk County (Massachusetts) convention recommending that military preparations be made for defense against possible attack by the British troops in Boston.

For months the farmers and townspeople of Massachusetts had been gathering arms and ammunition and training as "minutemen," ready to fight on a minute's notice. The Continental Congress having approved preparations for a defensive war, these citizen-soldiers only waited for an aggressive move by the British regulars.

In Boston, General Thomas Gage, commanding the British garrison, knew of the warlike bustle throughout the countryside but thought his army too small to do anything until reinforcements should arrive. But when he heard that the minutemen had stored a large supply of gunpowder in Concord (eighteen miles from Boston), he at last decided to act. On the night of April 18, 1775, he sent a detachment of about 1,000 men out from Boston on the road to Lexington and Concord. He intended to surprise the colonials with a bloodless coup.

But during the night the hard-riding horsemen William Dawes and Paul Revere warned the villages and farms, and when the redcoats arrived in Lexington the next day, several dozen minutemen awaited them on the common. Shots were fired and some of the minutemen fell, eight of them killed and ten more wounded. Advancing to Concord, the British burned what was left of the powder supply after the Americans hastily had removed most of it to safety. On the road from

Concord back to Boston the 1,000 troops, along with 1,500 more who met them at Lexington, were harassed by the continual gunfire of farmers hiding behind trees, rocks, and stone fences.

A war was on, and most Americans believed the enemy had started it.

Declaration of Independence

Three weeks after the battles of Lexington and Concord, when the Second Continental Congress met in Philadelphia, the delegates adopted a Declaration of the Causes and Necessity of Taking up Arms, announcing that the British government had left the American people with only two alternatives, "unconditional submission to the tyranny of irritated ministers or resistance by force," and that the people had decided to resist.

For the first year of the war, the Americans were fighting for a redress of grievances within the British Empire, not for independence. During that year, however, many of them began to change their minds, for various reasons. For one thing, they soon were making sacrifices so great that their original war aims seemed incommensurate with the cost. For another thing, they lost much of their lingering affection for the mother country when Britain prepared to use Indians, slaves, and foreign mercenaries (the hated "Hessians") against them. And, most important, they felt that they were being forced into independence when the British government closed the colonies to all overseas trade and made no concession except an offer of pardon to repentant rebels. The Americans desperately needed military supplies to continue the war, and now they could get them from abroad in adequate amounts only if they broke completely with Great Britain and proceeded to behave in all respects as if they comprised a sovereign nation.

These feelings in America were not caused, but were clarified and crystallized, by the publication, in January 1776, of the pamphlet *Common Sense*. Its author, unmentioned on the title page, was Thomas Paine, who with letters of introduction from Benjamin Franklin had emigrated from England to America less than two years before. Though long a failure in various trades, Paine now proved a brilliant success as a revolutionary propagandist. In his pamphlet he argued with

flashing phrases that it was plain common sense for Americans to separate from an England rotten with the corrupt monarchy of George III, brutal as an unnatural parent toward its colonies, responsible for dragging them in to fight its wars in the past, and no more fit as an island kingdom to rule the American continent than a satellite was fit to rule the sun.

Despite the persuasion of *Common Sense*, the American people were far from unanimous, and they entered upon a bitter debate over the merits of dependence and independence. While the debate raged, the Continental Congress advanced step by step toward a final break. Congress opened the ports of America to all the world except Great Britain, entered into communication with foreign powers, and recommended to the various colonies that they establish governments without the authority of the Empire, as in fact they already were doing. On July 2, 1776, Congress adopted a resolution "That these United Colonies are, and, of right, ought to be, free and independent states. . . ." Two days later Congress approved the Declaration of Independence, which gave reasons for the action already taken.

The thirty-three-year-old Virginian Thomas Jefferson wrote the Declaration. In it he restated the familiar contract theory of John Locke, who had held that governments were formed to protect the rights of life, liberty, and property, but Jefferson gave the theory a more humane twist by referring instead to the rights of "life, liberty and the pursuit of happiness" and by adding the democratic principle that "all men are created equal."

Some people in America had disapproved of the war from the beginning, and others had been willing to support it only so long as its aims did not conflict with their basic loyalty to the King. These people, numerous but in the minority, refused to cross the new line that had been drawn. Either openly or secretly they remained Loyalists, as they chose to call themselves, or Tories, as they were known to the Whig or Patriot majority.

State Governments

While waging war, the Patriots also busied themselves with providing a government for the new nation. With the outbreak of war they set up

provisional governments based upon existing assemblies or emergency conventions as the royal
officials fled from their positions in one colony
after another. When the colonies became states,
the Patriots formed permanent governments with
written constitutions. The constitution-making
procedure varied from state to state. In Rhode Island and Connecticut the legislatures merely revised the old colonial charters, and in most of the
other states the legislatures, though not elected
for that purpose, took it upon themselves to draft
new constitutions. Thomas Jefferson, for one, insisted that the fundamental law should come from
the people of each state, who should elect constitutional conventions and then vote on ratification. Actually, conventions were held in only
three states, referendums in only five, and both a
convention and a referendum in only one — Massachusetts.

The new constitutions, all pretty much alike in
general outline though different in detail, were
both conservative and democratic. They were
conservative in retaining essentially the same
structure as the old colonial governments. Except
in Georgia and Pennsylvania, both of which experimented with a unicameral legislature, each
constitution provided for a two-house legislature,
with an elected senate taking the place of the former governor's council. All the constitutions except Pennsylvania's continued the office of governor, though most of them denied the holder of
this position the bulk of the executive powers he
had enjoyed in colonial days. All the new documents confirmed and extended the ideas of popular rule that long had been put into practice;
seven had fully fledged bills of rights, and some
had preambles stating that sovereignty (the ultimate power of government) resided in the people.
To vote in any state a man had to own only a
modest amount of property, in some states just
enough so that he could qualify as a taxpayer. To
hold office he had to meet a somewhat higher
property requirement, essentially as in pre-Revolutionary times. Only in New Jersey were women
allowed to vote, and eventually they were deprived of the suffrage even there. But, considering
the widespread ownership of property, something
approaching universal manhood suffrage existed
from the beginning in all the states.

Once in operation, the new states proceeded to
make advances in social as well as political de-

mocracy. New York and the southern states, in
which the Church of England had been tax-supported, soon saw to its complete disestablishment,
and the New England states stripped the Congregational Church of some of its privileges. Virginia, in its Declaration of Rights, boldly announced the principle of complete toleration and,
in 1786, enacted the principle in the Statute of
Religious Liberty, which Jefferson long had
championed.

The new states took steps toward personal as
well as religious freedom. All of them except
South Carolina and Georgia prohibited the importation of slaves, and even South Carolina laid
temporary wartime bans on the slave trade. After
the first antislavery society in America (founded
in 1775) began its agitation, and prominent
southerners including Jefferson and Washington
declared their opposition to slavery, Virginia and
other southern states changed their laws so as to
encourage manumission; Pennsylvania passed a
gradual-emancipation act (1780), and Massachusetts through a decision of its highest court (1783)
held that the state's bill of rights outlawed the
ownership of slaves. Besides all this, five of the
new states put provisions into their constitutions
for the establishment of public schools, and
all soon began to revise their criminal codes so
as to make the punishment more nearly fit the
crime.

The Confederation

While the separate states were fashioning constitutions and recasting their legal systems, the
Second Continental Congress tried to create a
written form of government for the states as a
whole. No sooner had the Congress appointed a
committee to draft a declaration of independence
than it appointed another to draft a plan of union,
and after much debate and many revisions the
Congress, in November 1777, adopted the committee's plan, the Articles of Confederation.

The Articles of Confederation provided for a
central government very similar to the one already in actual operation, though it increased the
powers of Congress somewhat. Congress was to
have the powers of conducting war, carrying on
foreign relations, and appropriating, borrowing,
and issuing money, but not the powers of regulat-

ing trade, levying taxes, or drafting troops. For troops and taxes it would have to petition the states. There was to be no separate, single, strong executive (the "President of the United States" was to be merely the presiding officer at the sessions of Congress), but Congress itself was to see to the execution of the laws through an executive committee of thirteen, made up of one member from each state, through ad hoc and standing committees for specific functions, and through such administrative departments as it might choose to create. There were to be no Confederation courts, except for courts of admiralty, but disputes between the states were to be settled by a complicated system of arbitration. The states were to retain their individual sovereignty, each of the legislatures electing and paying the salaries of two to seven delegates to Congress, and each delegation, no matter how numerous, having only one vote. At least nine of the states (through their delegations) would have to approve any important measure, such as a treaty, before Congress could pass it, and all thirteen state legislatures would have to approve before the Articles could be ratified or amended.

Ratification was delayed by differences of opinion about the proposed plan. Some Americans were willing enough to accept a relatively weak central government, but others preferred to see it strengthened. Above all, the states claiming lands in the West wished to keep them, but the rest of the states demanded that the whole territory be turned over to the Confederation government. Except for New York, the "landed" states, among which Virginia had the largest and best claim, founded their claims upon colonial charters. The "landless" states, particularly Maryland, maintained that as the fruit of common sacrifices in war the Western land had become the rightful property of all the states. At last New York gave up its rather hazy claim, based upon a protectorate over the Iroquois Indians, and Virginia made a qualified offer to cede its lands to Congress. Then Maryland, the only state still holding out against ratification, approved the Articles of Confederation, and they went into effect in 1781.

The Confederation government came into being in time to conclude the war and make the peace. Meanwhile, during the years of fighting from 1775 to 1781, the Second Continental Con-

gress served as the agency for directing and coordinating the war effort of the people of the thirteen states.

Mobilizing for War

Congress and the states faced enormous tasks in raising and organizing armies, providing the necessary supplies and equipment, and paying the costs of war.

Some of the states offered bounties for the encouragement of manufactures, especially for the production of guns and powder, and Congress in 1777 established a government arsenal at Springfield, Massachusetts. Even so, the Americans themselves managed to manufacture only a small fraction of the equipment they used. They got most of their war materials through importations from Europe, particularly from France.

In trying to meet the expenses of war, Congress had no power to tax the people, and the states had little inclination to do so. Indeed, cash was scarce in the country, as it always had been. When Congress requisitioned the states for money, none of them contributed more than a tiny part of its share. At first Congress hesitated to requisition goods directly from the people but finally allowed army purchasing agents to take supplies from farmers and pay with certificates of indebtedness.

Congress could not raise much money by floating long-term loans at home, since few Americans could afford war bonds and those few usually preferred to invest their funds in more profitable wartime ventures, such as privateering. So Congress had no choice but to issue paper money, and Continental currency came from the printing presses in large and repeated batches. The states added sizable currency issues of their own.

With goods and coin so scarce and paper money so plentiful, prices rose to fantastic heights and the value of paper money fell proportionately. Eventually, in 1780, Congress decided that the states should accept Continental currency from taxpayers at the rate of forty paper dollars to one silver dollar, then send it to Congress to be destroyed.

The states added to their financial resources by seizing lands belonging to the Crown and to colo-

The American Revolution

How revolutionary was the American Revolution? The pioneer American historian George Bancroft wrote in 1876 that it "was most radical in its character, yet achieved with such benign tranquility that even conservatism hesitated to censure." Its aim, Bancroft believed, was to "preserve liberty" against the threat of British tyranny.

The revolutionary effort, however, was not directed only against the British, or so Carl Becker maintained in his *History of Political Parties in the Province of New York, 1760–1776* (1909). At least in New York, Becker said, there was a movement for both independence and democracy. Not one but two questions were involved. "The first was the question of home rule; the second was the question, if we may so put it, of who should rule at home." What occurred, then, was partly a kind of civil war, a contest for power between radicals and conservatives, one that led to the "democratization of American politics and society."

After prevailing for several decades, this interpretation came under strong attack. In *Middle-Class Democracy and the Revolution in Massachusetts, 1691–1780* (1955), Robert E. Brown contended that long before 1776 Massachusetts was "very close to a complete democracy," with practically all men enjoying the right to vote. Brown agreed more nearly with Bancroft than with Becker, and so did E. S. Morgan, who, in *The Birth of the Republic, 1763–1789* (1956), argued that most Americans of the period held the same political principles. Morgan emphasized ideas; he took seriously the rhetoric of the Revolution. Another who did so was Bernard Bailyn. After reading hundreds of Revolutionary pamphlets, Bailyn said in *Ideological Origins of the American Revolution* (1967): "Study of the pamphlets confirmed my rather old-fashioned view that the American Revolution was above all else an ideological, constitutional, political struggle and not primarily a controversy between social groups undertaken to force changes in the organization of the society or the economy."

At the same time Bailyn wrote, other historians were forwarding an economic interpretation of the Revolution, stressing the significance of domestic class conflict. Jesse Lemisch, for example, emphasized the role of mobs in colonial cities in providing radical leadership. Joseph Ernst found significant economic pressures on colonial merchants. And Gary B. Nash, in *The Urban Crucible* (1979), argued that increasing economic stress in colonial cities fostered a revolutionary ideology. "Everyone," Nash wrote, "has economic interests; and everyone . . . has an ideology." Historians are now trying to determine the exact relationship between ideology and economic self-interest in the American Revolution.

nial proprietors. In 1777 Congress recommended that the states also confiscate and sell the property of Loyalists active in the British cause, then lend the proceeds to the central government. The states were eager enough to expropriate the Loyalist property, though not to make the requested loan. Around 100,000 of the Loyalists, either voluntarily or because of banishment, left the country during the course of the war, the most numerous group going to Quebec and laying the foundations of English-speaking Canada.

As for the Patriots, only a small proportion of

them were willing to volunteer for the American armies once the first surge of patriotism at the start of the war had passed. The states had to resort to persuasion and force, to bounties and the draft, the bounties being commonly in the form of land scrip, since land was an asset with which the states were well supplied. Thus recruited, militiamen remained under the control of their respective states.

Foreseeing some of the disadvantages of separately organized militias, Congress called upon the states (while they were still colonies) to raise troops for a regular force, the Continental army, and agreed that it should have a single commander in chief. George Washington, forty-three years old, sober and responsible by nature, possessed more command experience than any other American-born officer available. And he had political as well as military qualifications. An early advocate of independence, he was admired and trusted by nearly all the Patriots. A Virginian, he had the support not only of southerners but also of northerners who feared that the appointment of a New Englander might jeopardize sectional harmony. As the unanimous choice of the delegates, he took command in June 1775.

The Fighting, to 1777

For about the first year of the fighting (1775–1776) the colonial armed forces took the offensive. After the British retreat from Concord and Lexington, the Americans besieged the British garrison in Boston, and though suffering severe casualties in the Battle of Bunker Hill (June 17, 1775), they inflicted even greater losses upon the enemy and thereafter they continued to tighten the siege. Finally the British gave up their attempt to hold Boston and departed with hundreds of Loyalist refugees (March 17, 1776) for Halifax. Within a year from the firing of the first shots, the enemy had been driven from American soil.

The British soon returned, however, to put the Americans on the strategic defensive for the remainder of the war. During the summer of 1776, in the weeks immediately following the Declaration of Independence, the waters around the city of New York became filled with the most formidable military force Great Britain ever had sent

abroad. Here were hundreds of men-of-war and troopships and a host of 32,000 disciplined soldiers under the command of the tall and affable Sir William Howe. Having no grudge against the Americans, Howe would rather awe them into submission than shoot them, and he believed that most of them, if given a chance, would show that they were at heart loyal to the King. In a parley with commissioners from Congress he offered the alternatives of submission with royal pardon or battle against overwhelming odds.

To oppose Howe's awesome array, Washington could muster only about 19,000 poorly armed and trained soldiers, including both Continentals and state troops, and he had no navy at all. Yet without hesitation the Americans chose continued war, which meant inevitably a succession of defeats. The British pushed the defenders off Long Island, compelled them to abandon Manhattan Island, and drove them in slow retreat over the plains of New Jersey, across the Delaware River, and into Pennsylvania.

For the campaign of 1777 the British devised a strategy that, if Howe had stuck to it, might have cut the United States in two and prepared the way for final victory by Great Britain. According to this plan, Howe would move from New York up the Hudson to Albany, while another force, in a gigantic pincers movement, would come down from Canada to meet him. One of Howe's ambitious younger officers, the dashing John Burgoyne, "Gentleman Johnny," secured command of this northern force and elaborated upon the plan by preparing for a two-pronged attack along both the Mohawk and the upper Hudson approaches to Albany.

Then, fortunately for the United States, Howe adopted a different plan for himself, intending to dispirit the Patriots and rally the Loyalists by seizing the rebel capital, Philadelphia.

Up north, Burgoyne was left to carry out his twofold campaign without aid from Howe. He got off to a flying start, easily taking Fort Ticonderoga and an enormous store of powder and supplies, and causing such consternation that Congress removed General Philip Schuyler from command in the north and replaced him with Horatio Gates, in response to the demands of New Englanders.

By the time Gates took command, Burgoyne al-

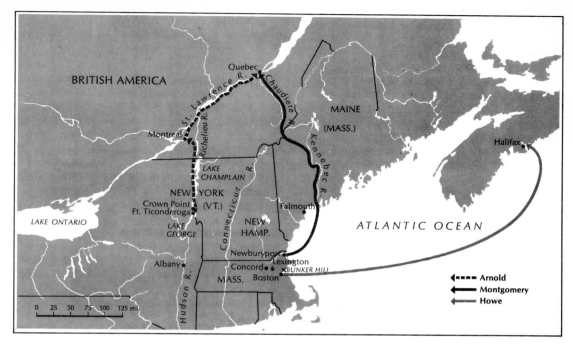

The War in the North 1775

ready faced a sudden reversal of his military fortunes in consequence of two staggering defeats. Short of materials, with all help cut off, Burgoyne withdrew to Saratoga, where Gates surrounded him. Burgoyne was through, and he knew it. On October 17, 1777, he ordered what was left of his army, nearly 5,000 men, to lay down their arms.

Not only the United States but also Europe took note of the amazing news from the woods of upstate New York, and France in particular was impressed. The British surrender at Saratoga, a great turning point in the war, led directly to an alliance between the United States and France.

Foreign Friends

Of all the possible foreign friends of the United States, the most promising and most powerful was France, which still resented its defeat at the hands of Great Britain in 1763. France had an astute and determined foreign minister in the Count de Vergennes, an expert practitioner of Machiavellian principles, thoroughly trained in the cutthroat diplomacy of eighteenth-century Europe. Vergennes soon saw that France had a vital interest in the outcome of the American war. If the colonies should assert and maintain their independence, the power of Great Britain would be seriously weakened by the loss of a good part of its empire, and the power of France would be correspondingly increased.

Early in the war the King of France and the King of Spain financed the shipment of large quantities of munitions to America through a fictitious trading firm. Whether this assistance was a gift or a loan became a question of bitter dispute.

After the Declaration of Independence, Benjamin Franklin went to France to get further aid and outright recognition of the United States. A natural diplomat, the equal if not the superior of the world's best at that time, Franklin immediately captivated Frenchmen of all classes — and Frenchwomen too. But Vergennes hesitated. At the first news of the American Declaration, he was inclined to make a treaty recognizing United

States independence, but he did not wish to act without Spain; and when reports came of Washington's defeat on Long Island he decided to wait and watch the military developments in America. If and when the Americans should show that they had a real chance of winning, then France would intervene. Meanwhile Vergennes was willing to go on financing the American war. He initiated a series of subsidies which in time amounted to nearly $62 million and a series of loans which totaled over $6 million.

The news that Vergennes and Franklin were waiting for — the news from Saratoga — arrived in Paris on December 4, 1777. Without waiting for Spain to go along with France, Vergennes on February 6, 1778, signed two treaties, one of commerce and amity, and the other of alliance. France (for its own reasons, of course) was the true friend in need of the Americans. Not only did it furnish them most of their money and munitions, but it also provided a navy and an expeditionary force that, with Washington's army, made possible the decisive victory at Yorktown.

Victory at Yorktown

During the final two years of fighting, all the significant action occurred in the South.

Sir Henry Clinton, who had replaced General Howe, planned a southern offensive that was supposed to end the American will to resist, but he put the command of the operation in the hands of Lord Cornwallis, an able general but one as rash as Clinton himself was cautious. Clinton and Cornwallis based their strategy on assumptions that were not to prove facts. They assumed that sea power would enable them to move their troops from point to point along the coast with ease, that the difficulties of overland travel would make American counteraction ineffectual, and that Loyalists would rise en masse to welcome and assist the redcoats as liberators. With the conquered South as a base, Clinton and Cornwallis thought they could dispose of the rest of the country at their leisure.

The British succeeded in taking Savannah (December 29, 1778) and Charleston (May 20, 1780), inspiring many Loyalists to take up arms, and advancing far into the interior. At every turn they were harassed, however, by Patriot guerrillas.

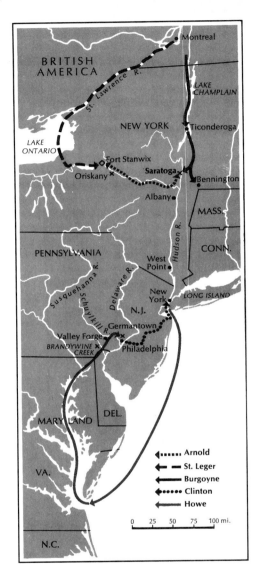

British Campaigns

Penetrating to Camden, well up the Wateree River in South Carolina, Cornwallis met and crushed (August 16, 1780) a combined force of militiamen and Continentals under Horatio Gates, who did not quite deserve his fame as the hero of Saratoga. Congress recalled Gates, and Washington gave the southern command to Nathanael Greene, a former Quaker blacksmith of Rhode Island and probably the ablest of all the

Road to Yorktown

land and sea. After a few shows of resistance, he asked for terms on October 17, 1781, four years to the day after the capitulation of Burgoyne, and two days later he surrendered his whole army of more than 7,000.

The fighting was over, but the war was not quite won. The United States continued to be something of an occupied country, with British forces holding the seaports of Savannah, Charleston, Wilmington, and New York. Before long a British fleet met and defeated Admiral de Grasse's fleet in the West Indies, ending Washington's hopes for further sea power assistance. So far as the naval and military situation was concerned, the British still held the upper hand in America. And peace was yet to be made.

Winning the Peace

When, in 1779, Spain in the role of mediator proposed a peace conference, Congress promptly named John Adams as the American delegate and sent him instructions to enter into no negotiations unless Great Britain first recognized the United States as "sovereign, free, and independent." Later Congress replaced the single delegate with a whole delegation, including Franklin and John Jay as well as Adams, and told the prospective peacemakers to keep in close touch with the French government, tell it everything, and follow its advice. Thus the United States was put into the hands of Vergennes by the time (1781) Austria and Russia made their joint mediation offer that led eventually to a general peace settlement.

Then the victory at Yorktown, by giving the Americans new bargaining power, rescued them from their dependence upon Vergennes. In England, Cornwallis' defeat provoked outcries against continuing the war and demands for cultivating American friendship as an asset in international politics. British emissaries appeared in France to talk informally with Franklin. He suggested what he called "necessary" terms of peace, including independence and the establishment of the Mississippi as the western boundary of the United States, and "desirable" terms including the cession of Canada for the purpose of "reconciliation," a "sweet word," as he said. But John Jay, recently arrived from his fruitless mission to Spain, where he had acquired reason to be suspi-

American generals of the time next to Washington himself.

Greene combined all his forces and arranged to meet the British on ground of his own choosing at Guilford Court House, North Carolina. After a hard-fought battle (March 15, 1781) Greene was driven from the field, but Cornwallis lost so many men that he decided at last to abandon the Carolina campaign.

Cornwallis retreated to the peninsula between the York and James rivers and began to build fortifications at Yorktown. While Clinton worried about Cornwallis' moves, Washington made plans with the Count de Rochambeau, commander of the French expeditionary force in America, and with Admiral de Grasse, commander of a French fleet in American waters, for trapping Cornwallis. Washington and Rochambeau marched a Franco-American army from the New York vicinity to join Lafayette in Virginia while de Grasse sailed with additional troops for Chesapeake Bay and the York River. These joint operations, perfectly timed and executed, caught Cornwallis between

cious of Spaniards and all Europeans, objected to continuing the negotiations on the grounds that the Americans were addressed not as plenipotentiaries of a sovereign nation but as "persons" from "colonies or plantations." The negotiations were delayed until Jay was satisfied.

The final treaty was signed September 3, 1783, when Spain as well as France agreed to end hostilities. It included a number of provisions that Franklin, Jay, and Adams had opposed, and some of these were to lead to serious friction with Great Britain and Spain in the years ahead. Yet it also included essentially the "necessary" terms that Franklin originally had indicated, though not his "desirable" ones such as the cession of Can-

ada. On the whole the peace was remarkably favorable to the United States in granting a clear-cut recognition of independence and a generous, though ambiguous, delimitation of territory — from the southern boundary of Canada to the northern boundary of Florida and from the Atlantic to the Mississippi. Indeed, by playing off the powers of Europe against one another, Franklin and his colleagues had achieved the greatest diplomatic success in the history of the United States. Wtih good reason the American people celebrated as the last of the British occupation forces embarked from New York and General Washington at the head of his troops rode triumphantly in.

Selected Readings

For a general account of colonial life and culture see Clarence L. Ver Steeg, *The Formative Years, 1607–1763* (1964). On seventeenth-century developments in New England see E. S. Morgan, *The Puritan Dilemma: The Story of John Winthrop* (1958), and Perry Miller, *The New England Mind: The Seventeenth Century* (1939).

Aspects of life in the expanding settlements of the eighteenth century are treated in the following: R. B. Morris, *Government and Labor in Early America* (1946); W. D. Jordan, *White over Black: American Attitudes Toward the Negro, 1550–1812* (1968); Eugene Genovese, *The World the Slaveholders Made* (1970); E. S. Morgan, *American Slavery, American Freedom* (1975); J. T. Lemon, *The Best Poor Man's Country* (1972); and W. R. Jacobs, *Dispossessing the American Indian* (1972).

Backgrounds of the American Revolution are discussed in J. C. Miller, *Origins of the American Revolution* (1957); L. H. Gipson, *The Coming of the Revolution, 1763–1775* (1954); A. M. Schlesinger, *The Colonial Merchants and the American Revolution 1763–1776* (1917); R. E. Brown, *Middle-Class Democracy and the Revolution in Massachusetts, 1691–1780* (1955); E. S. and H. M. Morgan, *The Stamp Act Crisis* (1953); John Shy, *Toward Lexington: The Role of the British Army in the Coming of the American Revolution* (1965); Bernard Bailyn, *Ideological Origin of the American Revolution* (1967); Gary Wills, *Inventing America* (1978); and Gary Nash, *The Urban Crucible: Social Change, Political Consciousness, and the Origins of the American Revolution* (1979).

*Titles available in paperback.

The Young Republic
Makes a Successful Start
Under a New Constitution

William E. Gladstone, a nineteenth-century British statesman, once described the Constitution of the United States as the "most wonderful work ever struck off at a given time by the brain and purpose of man." Actually, the Constitution was not the result of a sudden stroke of genius. It was the product of generations of experience with colonial and state governments and with the Articles of Confederation. It took form in the heat of political controversy and was adopted in the face of bitter opposition. Yet, though far from flawless, it was indeed a wonderful work. Certainly it created, as it was intended to do, a "more perfect union" than existed at the time it was written.

From the beginning the Constitution took on some of the characteristics of a sacred writing, a holy mystery of the Americans. Among its virtues was its brevity (only about 7,000 words), but the defect of that virtue was a considerable ambiguity, which left room at certain points for a variety of interpretations. Political differences, no matter what the interests that underlay them, came to be expressed in constitutional terms. In discussing a governmental policy, men asked not only whether it was to their particular advantage, or whether it contributed to the public good, but also whether it was in accord with the Constitution. Those who had opposed the adoption of the Constitution joined in the discussion instead of advocating repeal. All were willing to obey the fundamental law, but not all agreed on what it permitted.

Two basic lines of interpretation quickly ap-peared. Acording to one, the words of the document were to be broadly construed, so as to give the new government "implied powers" beyond those literally specified. According to the other, the words were to be strictly followed, so as to leave to the states all powers not plainly delegated to the central government. Alexander Hamilton was the first great exponent of liberal or loose construction, and Thomas Jefferson of strict construction and state rights.

The party followers of Hamilton — the Federalists — controlled the Presidency during the first dozen years under the Constitution. The Federalists infused vigor into the federal government, putting it on a sound financial basis, and they set the young republic on the path of neutrality and diplomatic independence. In their grasp for power, however, they overreached themselves. They faced the dilemma of all rulers in a government that depends upon the will of the people — the dilemma of choosing between governmental strength and individual freedom — and they made their choice in favor of strong government at the expense of popular liberty and popular support. The Federalists never won another presidential election after 1796, yet their main achievements endured.

Once Jefferson and his party followers were in control, after 1801, they had to deal with situations that seemed to demand strong, unfettered action. Soon the Jeffersonian Republicans were going even farther, in some respects, than the

Federalists in the exercise of federal authority. If Jefferson appeared to be inconsistent, so did many of his opponents, for they now adopted the theory of state rights and turned his former arguments against him. Some even objected to his greatest achievement as President, when he doubled the territory of the United States by acquiring Louisiana, which then consisted roughly of the entire Mississippi Valley to the west of the great river, plus the New Orleans area to the east of it.

A European war, which had begun in 1793 and was renewed in 1803, jeopardized the policy proclaimed by President Washington and endorsed by President Jefferson — the policy of neutrality and peace. Twice the United States got involved in the European struggle: the first time with France (1798), the second time with Great Britain (1812). The War of 1812, though avowedly waged for free seas and sailors' rights, was resisted by the group most directly interested in seagoing commerce, the New England merchants, who sneeringly referred to it as "Mr. Madison's war." The war ended in what was at best a draw. Yet it had important consequences. It broke the Indian barriers that had blocked northwest and southwest expansion. It gave a boost to the spirit of nationalism, which discredited the antiwar party and helped overcome the divisive force of postwar sectionalism. And it stimulated the growth of manufactures, thus accelerating the progress of the nation toward industrial greatness.

The westward movement of population led to a sectional crisis (1819–1821). The specific question was whether Missouri, which had been organized out of a part of the Louisiana Purchase, should be admitted as a slaveholding state, but also at stake was the larger question of whether the North or the South should dominate the rising West. The Missouri controversy was settled by a compromise, and the ideal of a strong national government was vigorously reasserted in the Supreme Court decisions of Chief Justice John Marshall and in the foreign policies of President James Monroe.

The year the war ended, 1815, marks a turning point in the relations of the United States with the rest of the world. Previously, this country had become involved again and again in the broils of Europe, and much of the time the requirements of diplomacy had dictated domestic policies. Afterward, for almost a century, domestic politics held a clear priority over foreign affairs as the country entered upon a period of comparative "isolation."

Chapter 5

A More Perfect Union

Failures in Foreign Affairs

The peace treaty of 1783 recognized the independence of the United States and granted the new nation a vast domain — on paper — but Americans found it hard to exercise their full sovereignty in fact. At once they ran into serious conflict with both Great Britain and Spain, yet they could not count on the support of France even though France remained technically America's ally.

Despite the treaty provision calling upon the British to evacuate American soil, British forces continued to occupy a string of frontier posts along the Great Lakes within the United States. The Spaniards claimed that their territory of Florida extended farther north than the boundary the United States and Great Britain had agreed upon. Possessing Louisiana as well as Florida and thus occupying both banks of the lower Mississippi, Spain had lawful power to close the river to American navigation, and did so in 1784.

Though commerce now flourished in new directions, most American trade persisted as much as possible in the old, prewar patterns. In the United States the bulk of imports continued to come from British sources, for Americans were used to British goods, and British merchants knew and catered to American tastes, offered attractive prices, and extended long and easy credit. To earn the British funds needed to pay for these imports, Americans desired free access to more British markets than were open to them after the war.

In 1784 Congress sent John Adams as minister to London with instructions to get a commercial treaty and speed up the evacuation of the frontier posts. Taunted by queries about whether he represented one nation or thirteen, Minister Adams made no headway in England, partly because Congress had no power to retaliate against the kind of commercial warfare that Great Britain was pursuing against the United States. Throughout the 1780s the British government refused even to return the courtesy of sending a minister to the American capital.

The Spanish government, by contrast, was willing to negotiate its differences with the United States, and in 1785 its representative, Don Diego de Gardoqui, arrived in New York (where Congress had moved from Philadelphia) to deal with the secretary for foreign affairs, John Jay. After months of the most friendly conversations, Jay and Gardoqui initialed a treaty (1786). By its terms, the Spanish government would have granted Americans the right to trade with Spain but not with its colonies; would have conceded the American interpretation of the Florida boundary; and (in a secret article) would have joined in an alliance to protect American soil from British encroachments. The United States, besides guaranteeing Spanish possessions in America, would have agreed to "forbear" the navigation of the Mississippi for twenty years, though not to abandon the right of navigation. Jay found it hopeless, however, to secure the necessary nine state votes for the ratification of his treaty by Congress, since the delegates from the five Southern states objected bitterly and correctly that the interests of Southerners in Mississippi navigation were being sacrificed to the interests of Northerners in Spanish trade.

47

The Needs of the West

Into the areas of postwar border conflict with Great Britain and Spain moved an unprecedented horde of American settlers during and after the Revolution. When the war began, only a few thousand lived west of the Appalachian divide; by 1790 their numbers had increased to 120,000. These frontier settlers needed protection from the Indians, access to outside markets for surplus crops, and courts with orderly processes of law. In dealing with the West, Congress inherited responsibilities that formerly had baffled King and Parliament.

With Virginia's cession in 1781, the landed states had begun to yield their Western claims to the Confederation. Congress soon began to make policy for the national domain. The most momentous decision was that settlements in the territory should not be held in permanent subjection as colonies but should be transformed ultimately into states equal with the original thirteen.

The Ordinance of 1785 provided a system of land survey and sale. The land to the north of the Ohio was to be surveyed and marked off in a rectangular pattern before any of it was sold. This land ordinance provided for east-west base lines, north-south "ranges," and townships with sides paralleling the ranges and base lines. Each township was to contain thirty-six square-mile sections. In every township four sections were to be set aside for the United States and one for the support of schools. The rest of the sections were to be sold at auction for not less than $1 an acre. Since there were 640 acres in a section, the prospective buyer of government land had to have at least $640 in ready cash or in United States certificates of indebtedness. These terms favored large speculators over the actual settlers. The Ordinance of 1787 provided for territorial government. This famous "Northwest Ordinance" established one Northwest Territory for the time being; provided for its subsequent division into several territories, not fewer than three nor more than five; and laid out three stages for the evolution of each territory into a state. In the first stage, Congress-appointed officials would govern the territory; in the second an elected legislature would share power with them; and in the third, when the people numbered 60,000 or more, they might frame a constitution and apply for statehood. These two ordinances constituted the Confederation's greatest accomplishment — the institution of enlightened management of western territory.

The Indian policy of Congress fell short of the requirements of land speculators as well as frontier settlers. In 1785 and 1786 congressional commissioners made treaties with representatives of the Iroquois and other tribes, who thereby surrendered their claims to a stretch of land north of the Ohio in return for comparatively worthless trinkets. Feeling betrayed by the treaties, many of the tribes went on the warpath. Congress vainly instructed Colonel Josiah Harmar, commanding the federal troops in the Ohio country, to drive the Indians back, then in desperation called upon the aging hero George Rogers Clark. While the campaign against the Indians in the Northwest faltered, a new threat arose in the Southwest, where the Creeks under the half-breed Alexander McGillivray formed an alliance with the Spaniards to resist the advance of American settlers.

Some of the frontier leaders in the Southwest, instead of fighting the Spaniards, turned to collaborating with them. These leaders and their followers thought for a time that they saw advantages for themselves in the possible creation of a Southwestern confederacy under Spanish tutelage. They might thus get what the United States seemed unable to give them — protection from the Indians, cheap or free land, and an outlet to Eastern and foreign markets through the navigation of the Mississippi. At the same time another underground separatist movement was afoot on the far northern frontier. The aspirations of Vermont for statehood having been frustrated by the rival claims of New York and New Hampshire to its soil, some Vermonters intrigued with British agents for returning the Green Mountain country to the British Empire.

Debts, Taxes, and Daniel Shays

At the end of the war foreign ships crowded into American seaports with cargoes of all kinds, and the American people bought extravagantly with cash or credit. In consequence the wartime accumulations of specie were drained out of the country, consumer indebtedness to importing merchants was multiplied, and a postwar depression lasting from 1784 to 1787 was made worse than it might otherwise have been. The depression, with its money scarcity, bore heavily upon both public and private debtors, complicating the financial problems of many citizens and of the Confederation and state governments.

The Confederation government had canceled most of its war debt to Americans by repudiating hundreds of millions of dollars in Continental currency. Yet it still owed a large domestic debt; and through continued borrowings from abroad, mostly from the Netherlands, its foreign debt increased. During the 1780s the government had to make do with uncertain and fluctuating revenues. It could only make requisitions on the states, and they paid an average of only about one-sixth of the total that was requested. This was barely enough to meet the government's ordinary operating expenses. To pay the interest on the foreign debt, Secretary of the Treasury Robert Morris used the proceeds from the new loans. Thus he maintained an excellent credit rating with Dutch and other foreign bankers. But he could not keep up with the domestic obligations, and the government lost credit at home. At a fraction of the face value, shrewd speculators bought up Confederation certificates of indebtedness from former Revolutionary soldiers and others who lost hope of payment from Congress and who needed ready cash.

The states, too, came out of the war with large debts, and one by one they added to their obligations by taking over parts of the Confederation debt owed to their respective citizens. Taxable resources varied a good deal from state to state. The chief reliance everywhere was upon the direct tax on land and its improvements.

Suffering from the postwar deflation and from the tax burden upon their land, the debtor farmers of the country demanded relief in the form of paper money, and seven of the states responded by issuing such currency. The other six states refused to yield to the advocates of inflation and pursued policies of unrelieved taxation to support their public debts. To the state creditors — that is, the bondholders — all this was sound and honest public finance. But it seemed like robbery and tyranny to many to the poverty-stricken farmers,

especially in New England, who felt that money was being extorted from them to swell the riches of the wealthy bondholders in Boston and other towns. At a time when cash was not to be had, these farmers were called upon to pay in specie not only state tax collectors but also mortgage holders and other private creditors. Moreover, falling prices meant that their debts, as measured in real terms, were growing in size. When debtors failed to pay, they found their mortgages foreclosed and their property seized, and sometimes they found themselves in jail.

Mobs of distressed farmers rioted in various parts of New England but caused the most serious trouble in Massachusetts. There the malcontents of the Connecticut Valley and the Berkshire Hills, many of them Revolutionary veterans, found a leader in Daniel Shays, himself a former captain in the Continental army. Organizing and drilling his followers, Shays put forth a program of demands including paper money, tax relief, a moratorium on debts, the removal of the state capital from Boston to the interior, and the abolition of imprisonment for debt. During the summer of 1786 the Shaysites concentrated upon the immediate task of preventing the collection of debts, private or public, and went in armed bands from place to place to break up court sittings and sheriffs' sales. In Boston, members of the legislature, including Samuel Adams, denounced Shays and his men as rebels and traitors. When winter came these rebels, instead of laying down their arms, advanced upon Springfield to get more of them from the arsenal there. From Boston approached an army of state militiamen financed by a loan from wealthy merchants who feared a new revolution. In January 1787, this army met Shays' ragged troops, killed several of them, captured many more, and scattered the rest to the hills in a blinding snowstorm.

As a military enterprise, Shays' Rebellion was a fiasco, yet it had important consequences for the future of the United States. In Massachusetts it resulted in a few immediate gains for the discontented groups. Shays and his lieutenants, at first sentenced to death, were soon pardoned, and some concessions to Shays' earlier demands were granted in the way of tax relief and the postponement of debt payments. Far more significant, the rebellion also affected the country as a whole by giving added urgency to the movement for a new Constitution.

Advocates of Centralization

Weak though the Confederation government was, it satisfied a great many — probably a majority — of the people. They did not want a strong central government. Having just fought the Revolutionary War to avert the danger of remote and, to them, tyrannical authority, they desired to keep the centers of political power close to home in the thirteen states.

Others, however, either disliked the Articles of Confederation from the outset or came eventually to desire something different. Disgruntled at the refusal of Congress to grant them half pay for life, some of the military men through their exclusive and hereditary Society of the Cincinnati hoped to control and to invigorate the government, some of them even aspiring to a kind of army dictatorship. Artisans or "mechanics," the manufacturers of the time, preferred a uniformly high national tariff to the varying state tariffs so that they could more effectively shut out British goods. Merchants and shippers preferred a single and effective commercial policy to thirteen different and ineffective ones. Land speculators wished to see the "Indian menace" finally removed from their Western tracts, and creditors desired to stop the state issues of paper money. Investors in Confederation securities hoped to have the Confederation debt made good and the value of their securities enhanced. Large property owners in general looked for a reliable means of safety from the threat of mobs and noted that the Confederation had lacked any authority to intervene in Shays' Rebellion.

The issue was not whether the Confederation should be changed but how drastic the changes should be. Even its defenders reluctantly came to agree that the government needed strengthening at its weakest point — its lack of power to tax. To save the Articles of Confederation, its friends backed the important amendment of 1782, which would have authorized Congress to levy customs duties. All the states ratified the amendment except Rhode Island, whose single veto was enough to kill it. The next year a similar amendment was

accepted by Rhode Island but defeated by New York. Later the state-rights advocates proposed that the states make to Congress a temporary and qualified grant of taxing authority (not an amendment to the Articles), but most of the centralizers had begun to lose interest in such remedies. They insisted upon a much more thoroughgoing change.

The most resourceful of the reformers was the political genius, New York lawyer, one-time military aide to George Washington, and illegitimate son of a Scottish merchant in the West Indies — Alexander Hamilton. From the beginning he had been dissatisfied with the Articles of Confederation, had seen little to be gained by piecemeal amendments, and had urged the holding of a national convention to overhaul the entire document. To achieve his aim he took advantage of a movement for interstate cooperation which began in 1785 when a group of Marylanders and Virginians met in Alexandria to settle differences between their two states.

One of the Virginians, James Madison, who was as eager as Hamilton to see a stronger government, induced the Virginia legislature to invite all the states to send delegates to a larger conference on commercial questions. This group met at Annapolis in 1786, but representatives from only five states appeared at the meeting. Hamilton, a delegate from New York, took satisfaction in seeing the conference adopt his report and send copies to the state legislatures and to Congress. His report recommended that Congress call a convention of special delegates from all the states to gather in Philadelphia the next year and consider ways to "render the constitution of the Federal government adequate to the exigencies of the union."

A Divided Convention

Fifty-five men, representing all the states except Rhode Island, attended one or more sessions of the convention that sat in the Philadelphia State House from May to September 1787. Practically all of them represented, both directly and indirectly, the great property interests of the country. Many feared what one of them called the "turbulence and follies" of democracy. Most agreed that the United States needed a stronger central government. There were differences of opinion, however, as to how much stronger the government should be, what specific powers it should have, and what structure it should be given. There were differences, in particular, over the relative influence the large and small states should exert in the new system.

The Virginians took the initiative from the moment the convention began. Washington was easily elected to preside, and then a resolution was passed to keep the proceedings absolutely secret. Next, Edmund Randolph of Virginia proposed that "a *national* government ought to be established, consisting of a *supreme* Legislative, Executive, and Judiciary." This being approved, Randolph introduced the plan that Madison already had worked out. The Virginia Plan, if adopted, would give the larger influence to the richer and more populous states. It would also mean abandoning the Articles of Confederation and building the government anew.

But the existing Congress had called the convention "for the sole and express purpose of revising the Articles of Confederation," and the states in commissioning their "deputies" had authorized them to do no more than revise the Articles. Some of the delegates — especially those from the smaller states — now raised doubts whether the convention properly could entertain such proposals as were embodied in the Virginia Plan. At first, however, these men had nothing to offer in its stead. After some delay, William Paterson of New Jersey submitted an alternative scheme for a "federal" as opposed to a "national" government. The New Jersey Plan was intended only to revise and strengthen the Articles.

The stage was now set for a full debate between large-state and small-state delegates. To the latter, one of the worst features of the Virginia Plan was the system of representation in the proposed two-house legislature. In the lower house, the states were to be represented in proportion to their population, and so the largest state (Virginia) would have about ten times as many representatives as the smallest (Delaware). In the upper house, the members were to be elected by the lower house, and some of the smaller states at any given time might have no members at all!

To the small-state delegates the Congress of the Articles of Confederation, as well as the Congress of the New Jersey Plan, at least had the merit of equal representation for all the states, regardless of size. But the New Jersey Plan gained the support of only a minority in the convention and, after much argument, was tabled.

The Virginia Plan was left as the basis for discussion. Its proponents realized that they would have to make concessions to the small-state men if the convention were ever to reach a general agreement. The majority soon conceded an important point by consenting that the members of the upper house should be elected by the state legislatures rather than by the lower house of the national legislature. Thus each state would be sure of always having at least one member in the upper house, but there remained the question of how many members each state should have.

There remained also the question of the number of representatives each state should have in the lower house. If the number was to depend upon population, were slaves to be included in the population figure? The delegates from the states where slavery seemed a permanent institution — especially those from South Carolina — insisted that slaves should be counted as persons (though not, of course, entitled to vote) in determining a state's representation. But these delegates argued that slaves ought to be considered as property, not as persons, when it was proposed that the new legislature be allowed to levy a direct tax (such as a land or poll tax) on each state in proportion to its population. Men who came from states where slavery had disappeared or was expected to disappear argued that slaves should be included in calculating taxation but not representation. Thus an issue between slave and free states was added to the one between large and small states.

Differences Compromised

On these and other matters, the delegates bickered day after day. By the end of June, as both temperature and tempers rose to uncomfortable heights, the convention seemed in danger of breaking up, with nothing accomplished. If this should happen, the men at Philadelphia would "become a reproach and byword down to future ages," said the venerable Franklin, the voice of calmness and conciliation throughout the summer. "And what is worse, mankind may hereafter, from this unfortunate instance, despair of establishing governments by human wisdom, and leave it to chance, war and conquest."

Through the calming influence of Franklin and others, especially Oliver Ellsworth of Connecticut, the delegates managed to settle the most serious of their disputes and go on with their work. A committee of twelve, with one member from each state, brought in a report that culminated in what afterward was known as the "Great Compromise" (adopted on July 16, 1787). One part of this report provided that the states should be represented in the lower house in proportion to their population and that three-fifths of the slaves should be included in determining the basis for both representation and direct taxation. The three-fifths formula was based on the dubious assumption that the slave, on the average, produced goods at only three-fifths of the rate of a free person. Another part of the Great Compromise provided that in the upper house, the states should be represented equally with two members apiece.

In the ensuing weeks, while committees busied themselves with various parts of the document that was beginning to take shape, the convention as a whole effected another compromise, this one having to do with the legislative power to impose tariffs and regulate commerce. The men from some of the Southern states feared that this power might be used for levying export duties on their crops, interfering with the slave trade, and making commercial agreements (as in the recent Jay-Gardoqui treaty) that would sacrifice the interests of rice and tobacco growers. The South Carolinians proposed that a two-thirds vote in the legislature be required not only to approve commercial treaties but also to pass commercial laws. Though not accepting that proposal, the convention made concessions by forbidding the legislature to levy a tax on exports, to put a duty of more than ten dollars a head on imported slaves, or to prohibit slave importations until twenty years had elapsed.

The convention was unable to reconcile some differences of opinion, and it disposed of them by

evasion or omission. One of these concerned the question whether the new courts or some special agency should be empowered to review legislative acts and set them aside. The "council of revision," a part of the original Virginia Plan, was dropped, and no provision was added to confer the power of judicial review explicitly upon the courts.

The Constitution, as it finally took form at the end of the summer in 1787, though an outgrowth of the Virginia Plan, was in some respects so different that Randolph himself refused to sign it. Yet it differed even more from the New Jersey Plan, and several refused on that account to give it their approval. Indeed, the completed document did not entirely satisfy any of the delegates. Nevertheless, thirty-nine of them affixed their signatures to it, doubtless with much the same feeling that Franklin expressed. "Thus I consent, Sir, to this Constitution," he said, *"because I expect no better, and because I am not sure that it is not the best."*

The Constitution of 1787

Madison, who was responsible for most of the actual drafting, observed that it was, "in strictness, neither a national nor a federal Constitution, but a composition of both."

Certainly it possessed some strongly national features. The Constitution and all laws and treaties made under it were to be the "supreme law" of the land, regardless of anything to the contrary in the constitution or laws of any state. Broad powers were granted to the central government, including the congressional powers of taxation, regulation of commerce, control of money, and the passage of laws "necessary and proper" for carrying out its specific powers. At the same time, the individual states were deprived of a number of the powers — such as the issuance of money and the passage of laws "impairing the obligation of contracts," for example, laws postponing the payment of debts — which the states had been free to exercise under the Articles of Confederation. Now all state officials were to be required to take an oath of allegiance to the Constitution, and the state militias were to be made available, upon call, for enforcing the new "supreme law." No-

Background of the Constitution

The 1780s once seemed to historians like a "critical period," one of impending collapse and chaos from which the newly independent republic was rescued only by the timely adoption of the Constitution. This was the theme of a widely read book that John Fiske, a popularizer of both science and history, wrote a century afterward (1888). Fiske and other writers emphasized the difficulties and failures of the 1780s — the business depression, the weaknesses of the central government under the Articles of Confederation, the threats to American territory from Great Britain and Spain, the debts of the Confederation and of the states, the interstate jealousies and barriers to trade, the widespread resort to paper-money inflation, and the disorders and lawlessness culminating in Shays' Rebellion. All this, according to Fiske and those who followed him, represented the darkness before dawn.

One of the greatest of American historians, Charles A. Beard, challenged the prevailing view in an arresting and controversial work, *An Economic Interpretation of the Constitution of the United States* (1913). Beard maintained that the 1780s had been a "critical period" only for certain business interests, not for the people as a whole. According to him, these interests desired a central government strong enough to promote industry and trade, safeguard private property, and make good the public debt. Many of the delegates to the constitutional convention, he said, stood to gain directly as well as indirectly from their efforts, for they had bought up the Confederation's "certificates of indebtedness" cheaply, and these would rise in value if a strong central government were set up. He added that the advocates of the Constitution succeeded in obtaining its ratification despite the indifference or opposition of a majority of the people. In a later book (1927) Beard suggested that the Articles of Confederation might still be serving quite satisfactorily as our twentieth-century frame of government if a comparatively small group of impatient and determined men had not managed to bring about a drastic change in 1787–1788.

Most historians promptly adopted Beard's conclusions, and some proceeded to elaborate upon his work. Merrill Jensen, for one, in *The Articles of Confederation* (1940) and *The New Nation* (1950), produced additional evidence to show that the 1780s were a time of hopeful striving rather than black despair, of economic recovery and not persisting depression, of governmental progress under the Articles despite temporary failures. Other historians disagreed with Beard, however, and in recent years the dissenters, notably Robert E. Brown and Forrest McDonald, have criticized his methods and findings with increasing effectiveness. Today, few if any historians accept the Beard thesis without qualification. And some, like Gordon S. Wood in his *The Creation of the American Republic, 1776–1787* (1969), find that the 1780s were important primarily for the resolution of intellectual and constitutional issues; they see the writing of the Constitution as the orderly culmination of the Revolution.

where were the former claims of the states to individual sovereignty recognized. Gone was the stipulation of the Articles that "each State shall retain every power, jurisdiction, and right not *expressly* delegated to the United States in Congress assembled." Lacking was any bill of rights to limit the central government as the state bills limited the state governments.

On the other hand, the Constitution was federal in setting up a government that presupposed the existence of separate states and left wide powers to them. For instance, the states were to be represented as separate and equal entities in one of the two branches of the new legislature.

Within the allotted sphere of its powers, the new government was authorized to act directly upon the people of the United States. It would not have to act upon them solely through the member states, as the previous Confederation government, and indeed all confederation governments of the past, had done. Here, then, was something new and unique, something for which old terms were hardly adequate. It was a combination of two kinds of government, state and central, with each of them intended to be supreme within its respective sphere.

Next to the distinctive federal arrangement (the "division of powers"), the most striking feature of the new system was the complex organization and operation of the central government itself, with its checks and balances among the legislative, executive, and judicial branches (the "separation of powers").

This complicated structure resulted from accident — that is, from the compromising of contradictory views — as much as from deliberate planning. Nevertheless, the complexity was such as to give the founders hope that no single group or combination of groups in the country could ever gain absolute and unchecked power. A government so divided against itself ought to frustrate tyranny from whatever source. When the founders spoke of tyranny, they usually had in mind the rule of mobs and demagogues — the threat of such leaders as Daniel Shays.

Federalists, Antifederalists

Since the delegates at Philadelphia had exceeded their instructions from Congress and the states, they had reason to doubt whether the Constitution would ever be ratified if they followed the procedures laid down in the Articles of Confederation, which required *all* of the state *legislatures* to approve alterations in the form of the government. So the convention changed the rules, specifying in the Constitution that the new government should go into effect among the ratifying states when only *nine* of the thirteen had ratified, and recommending to Congress that the Constitution be submitted to specially called state *conventions* rather than to the legislatures of the states.

The Congress in New York, completely overshadowed by the convention in Philadelphia, accepted the latter's work and submitted it to the states for their approval or disapproval. The state legislatures, again with the exception of Rhode Island, arranged for the election of delegates to ratifying conventions, and sooner or later each of these conventions got down to business. Meanwhile, from the fall of 1787 to the summer of 1788, the merits and demerits of the new Constitution were debated in the legislatures, in mass meetings, and in the columns of newspapers, as well as in the convention halls.

Since the idea of a strongly national government was thought to be unpopular, the advocates of the new Constitution chose to call themselves "Federalists" and to call their opponents "Antifederalists." These misnomers stuck, despite the insistence of opponents of ratification that they were "Federal Republicans," the true federalists of the time.

Among the Federalists were some of the most profound political philosophers of any period or place, including Hamilton, Madison, and Jay, who under the joint pseudonym "Publius" wrote a long series of newspaper essays expounding the meaning and virtues of the Constitution. Afterward published in book form as *The Federalist*, these papers have been considered as the most authoritative of all constitutional commentaries and, indeed, as one of the greatest of all treatises on political science.

The opponents of ratification produced no comparable set of Antifederalist papers, yet these men too were able and sincere, and they made a vigorous case for themselves in their own speeches and newspaper propaganda. Necessarily, the Antifederalists resorted mainly to negative argument. The Constitution, they protested, was illegal — as indeed it was if judged by the Articles of Confederation, the existing fundamental law. The new government would increase taxes, obliterate the states, wield dictatorial powers, favor the "well-born" over the common people, and put an end to individual liberty, the Antifederalists added. Of all their specific criticisms the most compelling was this: the Constitution lacked a bill of rights.

For all the efforts of the Antifederalists, ratification proceeded during the winter of 1787–1788. Delaware, the first to act, did so unanimously, as did two others of the smallest states, New Jersey and Georgia. In the large states of Pennsylvania and Massachusetts the Antifederalists put up a determined struggle but lost in the final vote. By June 1788, when the New Hampshire convention at last made up its mind, nine of the states had ratified and thus had made it possible for the Constitution to go into effect among themselves.

A new government could hardly hope to succeed, however, without the participation of Virginia and New York, whose conventions remained closely divided. Before the end of the month Virginia and then New York consented to the Constitution by rather narrow votes. The New York convention yielded to expediency — even some of the most staunchly Antifederalist delegates feared that the state's commercial interests would suffer if, once the other states had got together under the "New Roof," New York were to remain outside. Massachusetts, Virginia, and New York all ratified on the assumption, though not on the express condition, that certain desired amendments would be added to the Constitution, above all a bill of rights. Deciding to wait and see what became of these hopes for amendment, the North Carolina convention adjourned without taking action. Rhode Island, for the time being, did not even call a convention to consider ratification.

Filling in the Gaps

When the first elections under the Constitution were held, in the early months of 1789, the results showed that the new government was to be in the hands of its friends. Few if any of the newly elected congressmen and senators had been ex-

treme Antifederalists; almost all had favored ratification, and many had served as delegates to the Philadelphia convention. The President-elect, George Washington, had presided at the convention; many who had favored ratification did so because they expected him to preside over the new government also. He received the votes of all the presidential electors whom the states, either by legislative action or by popular election, had named. John Adams, a firm Federalist, though not a member of the convention, received the next highest number of electoral votes and hence was to be Vice President.

By filling certain gaps in the Constitution, the first Congress served almost as a continuation of the constitutional convention. The work of the convention had been incomplete in various respects, especially in that it had omitted a bill of rights. Dozens of amendments intended to make up for this lack had been proposed in the state ratifying conventions, and Congress now undertook the task of sorting these, reducing them to a manageable number, and sending them to the states for ratification. Of the twelve sent out, ten were ratified, and these took effect in 1791. The first nine of them limited Congress by forbidding it to infringe upon certain basic rights, such as freedom of religion, of speech, and of the press, immunity from arbitrary arrest, and trial by jury. The Tenth Amendment, reserving to the states all powers except those specifically withheld from them or delegated to the federal government, bolstered state rights and changed the emphasis of the Constitution from nationalism to federalism.

In regard to the structure of the federal courts, the Constitution had only this to say: "The judicial power of the United States shall be vested in one Supreme Court, and in such inferior courts as the Congress may from time to time ordain and establish." Thus the convention had left up to Congress the number of Supreme Court judges to be appointed and the kinds of lower courts to be organized. In the Judiciary Act of 1789 Congress provided for a Supreme Court of six members, with one chief justice and five associate justices; for thirteen district courts with one judge apiece; and for three circuit courts, each to consist of one of the district judges sitting with two of the Supreme Court justices. In the same act, Congress gave the Supreme Court the power to make the final decision in cases involving the constitutionality of state laws. If the Constitution was in fact to be the "supreme law of the land," the various state courts could not be left to decide for themselves whether the state legislatures were violating that supreme law.

As for executive departments, the Constitution referred indirectly to them but did not specify what or how many they should be. The first Congress created three such departments — state, treasury, and war — and also the offices of attorney general and postmaster general.

In appointing department heads and other high officials, President Washington selected men who were qualified by character and experience, who were well disposed toward the Constitution (no Antifederalists), and who as a group would pro-vide a balanced representation of the different sections of the country. To the office of secretary of the treasury he appointed Alexander Hamilton of New York, who had taken the lead in calling the constitutional convention and who, though only thirty-two, was an expert in public finance. For secretary of war he chose the Massachusetts Federalist General Henry Knox. As attorney general he named Edmund Randolph of Virginia, sponsor of the plan upon which the Constitution had been based. He picked as secretary of state another Virginian, Thomas Jefferson, who had not opposed the Constitution though he had had nothing to do with its framing or adoption, having been away from the country as minister to France.

Chapter 6

Federalist Foundations

Hamilton's Financial Plans

As President, George Washington thought it his duty to see that the laws of Congress, if constitutional, were faithfully carried out. A man of strong will, he was the master of his own administration, but (unlike later Presidents such as Andrew Jackson and Franklin D. Roosevelt) he did not conceive of himself as a popular leader who should find out the will of the people and then see that Congress enacted it into law. One of his department heads, Secretary of the Treasury Alexander Hamilton, provided the legislative leadership that Washington himself lacked.

Hamilton thought the new government could be strengthened and made to succeed if the support of the wealthy people of the country could be brought to it. And, believing that all people are motivated by self-interest, he assumed that the way to gain the support of the wealthy was to give them a stake in the success of the new government. He therefore planned a program of financial legislation which, among other things, was intended to cause the propertied classes to look to the federal government for profitable investments and for the protection and promotion of their property interests.

If people of means were to have faith in the government, then the government must keep faith with them by paying its debts and establishing its credit on a sound basis. Therefore, Hamilton first of all proposed that the existing public debt be "funded," or in other words that the miscellaneous, uncertain, depreciated certificates of indebtedness that the old Congress had issued during and since the Revolution be called in and

exchanged for uniform, interest-bearing bonds, payable at definite dates. Next he recommended that the Revolutionary state debts be "assumed" or taken over by the United States, his object being to cause the state as well as the federal bondholders to look to the central government for eventual payment. His plan was not to pay off and thus eliminate the debt, either state or federal, but just the opposite: to create a large and permanent public debt, new bonds being issued as old ones were paid off.

Hamilton also planned the establishment of a national bank. At the time, there were only a few banks in the country, located in Boston, Philadelphia, and New York. A new, national bank would serve several purposes. It would aid business by providing loans and currency — in the form of bank notes, which in those days were used instead of checks. It would aid the government by making a safe place available for the deposit of federal funds, by facilitating the collection of taxes and the disbursement of the government's expenditures, and by keeping up the price of government bonds through judicious bond purchases.

The funding and assumption of the debts, together with the payment of regular interest on them, would cost a great deal of money, and so Hamilton had to find adequate sources of revenue. He thought the government should depend mainly upon two kinds of taxes (in addition to the receipts to be anticipated from the sales of public land). One of these was an excise to be paid by distillers of alcoholic liquors. This tax would hit most heavily the whiskey distillers of the back country, especially in Pennsylvania, Virginia, and North Carolina. These were small farmers who converted part of their corn and rye crop into whiskey, so as to have a concentrated and valuable product that they could conveniently take to market by horseback or muleback over poor mountain roads.

The other tax upon which Hamilton relied was the tariff on imports. Such a tax would not only raise a revenue, but also protect and encourage American manufactures by raising the price of competing manufactured goods brought in from abroad. In the old Articles of Confederation, according to its defenders as well as its critics, the worst defect had been Congress' lack of power to levy customs duties. One of the first acts of the new Congress, in 1789, was the passage of a tariff law designed to foster industries while raising a revenue, but the average level of duties under this law was extremely low. Hamilton advocated a higher and more decidedly protective tariff. In his Report on Manufactures he glowingly set forth the advantages, as he saw them, of stimulating the growth of industry in the United States. Factories, he said, would make the nation more nearly self-sufficient in wartime, would increase prosperity by creating a home market for the produce of the farms, and would make possible the fuller utilization of all kinds of labor, including the labor of women and children, even those (to quote Hamilton himself) of "tender years."

Enacting the Program

Between 1789 and 1792 Hamilton succeeded in persuading Congress to pass the necessary laws for erecting his financial system — but only after a bitter struggle with a rising opposition group.

His assumption bill ran into special difficulty. Its opponents had a very good case, for if the federal government took over the state debts, the people of one state would have to pay federal taxes for servicing the debts of other states, and some of these debts, such as that of Massachusetts, were much larger than others, such as that of Virginia. Naturally, Virginians did not think it fair for them to have to pay a share of the large Massachusetts debt, and their representatives in Congress balked at the assumption bill.

Finally the bill got the support of some of them and so managed to pass, but only because of a log-rolling deal. The Virginians wanted the national capital to be permanently located near them in the South. After Jefferson's return from France, Hamilton appealed to him, and Jefferson held a dinner at which arrangements were made to barter Virginia votes for the assumption bill in return for Northern votes for a Southern location of the capital. In 1790 the capital was changed from New York back to Philadelphia for a ten-year period, and after that a new capital city was to be built on the banks of the Potomac River, on land to be selected by Washington himself.

When Hamilton's bank bill was introduced into Congress, Madison and others opposed it on the grounds that it was unconstitutional, and though a majority voted for it, President Washington himself had his doubts. He therefore asked his official advisers for written opinions on the subject. In Hamilton's opinion the establishment of a bank was a fitting exercise of the powers of Congress, though the Constitution nowhere explicitly gave Congress the right. But Jefferson, with the support of his fellow Virginian Thomas Randolph, argued that the Constitution should be construed in a strict sense and that Congress should be allowed no powers not clearly given to it. Washington found Hamilton's case more convincing, and he signed the bank bill when it came to him. The Bank of the United States began operations in 1791, under a charter that granted it the right to continue in business for twenty years.

Once enacted, Hamilton's program worked as he had intended. The public credit quickly was restored; the bonds of the United States were soon selling at home and abroad at prices even above their par value.

At the same time, speculators got rich and corruption was rife. Many congressmen had bought up large amounts of the old certificates of indebtedness, and these men profited by their own legislation in funding the debt at par. Directly or indirectly, properly or improperly, thousands of wealthy merchants in the seaports also gained from the Hamilton program.

The mass of the people — the farmers scattered over the countryside — profited much less. While these people shared some of the benefit of national strength and prosperity, they bore most of the burden of paying for it. The financial program required taxes, and these came mostly from the farmers, who had to pay not only land taxes to their state and local governments but also the excise and, indirectly, the tariff to the federal government. The feeling grew that the Washington administration was not treating all the people fairly, and out of this feeling an organized political opposition arose.

Rise of Political Parties

The Constitution made no reference to political parties, and the founders, George Washington in particular, believed that such organizations were evil and should be avoided. Yet parties soon arose from a division between the followers of Hamilton and those of Madison and Jefferson.

Jefferson and Madison were such close collaborators that it is sometimes difficult to separate the contributions of the two. To describe the political philosophy of one is, in the main, to describe the political philosophy of both. Jefferson, himself a farmer, believed that farmers were God's chosen people and that an ideal republic would consist of sturdy citizens tilling their own soil. Though an aristocrat by birth, his mother belonging to one of the first families of Virginia, the Randolphs, he had faith in the good intentions of such farmer-citizens and thought that, if properly educated, they could be trusted to govern themselves through the election of able and qualified representatives. But, in the 1790s, he feared city mobs as "sores upon the body politic." He then opposed the development of extensive manufactures because they would lead to the growth of cities packed with propertyless workers. While Hamilton emphasized the need for order and stability, Jefferson stressed the importance of individual freedom.

The two secretaries continued to work against each other, and each began to organize a following in Congress and in the country at large. Hamilton's followers came to be known as Federalists, Jefferson's as Republicans. Republicans and Federalists differed in their social philosophies as well as in their economic interests and their constitutional views. Their differences in social outlook are seen in their reactions to the progress of the revolution in France. When that revolution began, as a rather mild movement in favor of constitutional monarchy and human rights, practically all Americans hailed it as a step in the right direction. But when the revolution went to radical extremes, with attacks on organized religion, the overthrow of the monarchy, and eventually the guillotining of the King and Queen, Americans adopted different views about the events in France, the Federalists denouncing and the Republicans applauding them. The Republicans believed that American interests would best be served by maintaining close relations with France, while Hamilton and the Federalists believed that friendship with Great Britain was essential for the success of the United States.

When the time came for the election of 1792, the Republicans had no candidate to put up against Washington. Jefferson as well as Hamilton urged him to run for a second term, and the President consented for the good of the country.

Securing the Frontier

The Washington administration made the power of the federal government felt even on the farthest reaches of the frontier.

The federal authority was challenged when, in 1794, the farmers of western Pennsylvania refused to pay the whiskey excise and terrorized the would-be tax collectors, much as the colonists had done throughout America at the time of the Stamp Act. The so-called Whiskey Rebellion was not left to the authorities of Pennsylvania as Shays' Rebellion had been left to the authorities of Massachusetts. Urged on by Hamilton, Washington took drastic steps. Calling out the militia of three states, he raised an army of nearly 15,000, a larger force than he had commanded against the British during most of the Revolution, and he personally accompanied this army as far as the town of Bedford. At the approach of the militiamen, the farmers around Pittsburgh, where the rebellion centered, either ran for cover or stayed home and professed to be law-abiding citizens. The rebellion quickly collapsed.

While the whiskey rebels were intimidated into obedience, other frontier settlers were made loyal to the government by its acceptance of new states as members of the Union. First to be admitted were two of the original thirteen, North Carolina (1789) and Rhode Island (1790), both of which had ratified the Constitution when they found that a bill of rights was definitely to be added and that they could not conveniently go on as independent commonwealths. Then Vermont, which had had its own state government since the Revolution, was accepted as the fourteenth state (1791) after New York and New Hampshire finally agreed to give up their claims to sovereignty over the Green Mountain country. Next came Kentucky (1792) with the consent of Virginia, which previously had governed the Kentucky counties as its own. After North Carolina finally ceded its Western lands to the Union, these were given a territorial government similar to that of the Northwest Territory and after six years became the state of Tennessee (1796). With the admission of these frontier states, the schemes for separating Vermont, Kentucky, and Tennessee from the Union soon came to an end.

In the more remote areas of the Northwest and the Southwest, meanwhile, the government had to contend with the Indians and their foreign allies, British and Spanish, in order to get a firm grasp upon all the territory belonging to the United States. In 1790 President Washington tried to buy peace with the Southwestern Indians, but the Indians continued to accept subsidies from the Spanish and to raid American settlements along the border. At last, in 1793–1794, the Tennesseans went on the warpath themselves, their militia invading the Indian country and making the Southwestern frontier safe for white settlers.

In the Northwest the government pursued a policy of force against the Indians, even at some risk of becoming involved in hostilities with their protector and ally, Great Britain. Two expeditions failed before a third one finally succeeded in the conquest of the Ohio country. General "Mad Anthony" Wayne, in the summer of 1794, met and decisively defeated the Indians in the Battle of Fallen Timbers. Next summer the Indians agreed in the Treaty of Greenville to abandon to the whites most of what afterward became the state of Ohio.

Before the government could be sure of its hold upon the border areas, it had to bring to terms the foreign powers that persisted in exerting influence there — Great Britain and Spain. In its diplomacy the Washington administration, by taking advantage of the opportunities that arose from the accidents of international politics, managed to reassert American independence and redeem the West.

Maintaining Neutrality

A crisis in foreign affairs faced the Washington administration when the French revolutionary government, after guillotining King Louis XVI, went to war in 1793 with Great Britain and its allies. Should the United States recognize the radical government of France by accepting a diplomatic representative from it? Was the United States obligated by the alliance of 1778 to go to war on the side of France? Washington decided to recognize the French government and to issue a proclamation announcing the determination of the United States to remain at peace. The proclamation (1793), though it did not mention the word "neutrality," was generally interpreted as a neutrality statement, which it actually was. In the next year Congress passed a Neutrality Act, forbidding American citizens to participate in the war and prohibiting the use of American soil as a base of operations for either side.

The first challenge to American neutrality came from France. A newly arrived minister from that country, the youthful and brash Edmond Genêt, made plans for using American ports to outfit French warships, authorized American shipowners to serve as French privateers, and proposed to send a band of Americans on an overland expedition against the territory of Spain, which at the moment was an ally of Great Britain and an enemy of France. In all these steps Genêt brazenly disregarded American neutrality. At last Washington demanded that the French government recall him, but by that time Genêt's party, the Girondins, were out of power in France and the still more extreme Jacobins in control, so it would not have been safe for him to return. Generously the President granted him political asylum in the United States, and he settled down to live to a ripe old age with his American wife on a Long Island farm.

The second challenge, an even greater one, came from Great Britain. Early in 1794 the Royal Navy suddenly seized hundreds of American ships engaged in trade in the French West Indies. The pretext for these seizures was a British interpretation of international law — known as the Rule of 1756 — which held that a trade prohibited in peacetime (as American trade between France and the French overseas possessions had been) could not be legally opened in time of war. With peace thus endangered, Hamilton grew concerned, for war would mean an end to imports from England, and most of the revenue for maintaining his financial system came from duties on those imports.

Jay's Treaty

To Hamilton and to other Federalists it seemed that this was no time for ordinary diplomacy. Jefferson had resigned in 1793 to devote himself to organizing a political opposition, and the State Department was now in the hands of an even more ardently pro-French Virginian, Edmund Randolph. Bypassing the State Department, Washington named as a special commissioner to England the staunch New York Federalist, former Secretary for Foreign Affairs under the old Confederation and current Chief Justice of the Supreme Court John Jay. Jay was instructed to secure damages for the recent spoliations, withdrawal of British forces from the frontier posts, and a satisfactory commercial treaty, without violating the terms of the existing treaty of amity and commerce with France, signed at the time of the alliance in 1778.

The treaty that Jay negotiated (1794) was a long and complex document, dealing with frontier posts, boundaries, debts, commerce, ship seizures, and neutral rights. It yielded more to Great Britain and obtained less for the United States than Jay had been authorized to give or instructed to get. When the terms were published in the United States, the treaty was denounced more than any treaty before or since, and Jay himself was burned in effigy in various parts of the coun-

try. The Republicans were unanimous in decrying it; they said it was a departure from neutrality, favoring Great Britain and unfair to France. Even some of the Federalists were outraged by its terms, those in the South objecting to its provision for the payment of the pre-Revolutionary debts. Opponents of the treaty went to extraordinary lengths to defeat it in the Senate, and French agents aided them and cheered them on. The American minister to France, James Monroe, and even the secretary of state, Edmund Randolph, cooperated closely with the French in a desperate attempt to prevent ratification. Nevertheless, after amending the treaty a bit, the Senate gave its consent.

There was much to be said for Jay's Treaty, despite its very real shortcomings. By means of it the United States gained valuable time for continued peaceful development, obtained undisputed sovereignty over all the Northwest, and secured a reasonably satisfactory commercial agreement with the nation whose trade was most important. More than that, the treaty led immediately to a settlement of the worst of the outstanding differences with Spain.

In Madrid the Spanish foreign minister feared that the understanding between Great Britain and the United States might prove a prelude to joint operations between those two countries against Spain's possessions in North America. Spain was about to change sides in the European war, abandoning Great Britain for France, and it was therefore to Spain's interest to appease the United States. The relentless pressure of American frontier settlers advancing toward the Southwest made it doubtful whether Spain could long hold its borderlands in any event. And so, when Thomas Pinckney arrived in Spain as a special negotiator, he had no difficulty in gaining practically everything that the United States had sought from the Spanish for over a decade. Pinckney's Treaty (1795) recognized the right of Americans to navigate the Mississippi to its mouth and to deposit goods at New Orleans for reloading on ocean-going ships; fixed the northern boundary of Florida where Americans always had insisted it should be, along the thirty-first parallel; and bound the Spanish authorities to prevent the Indians in Florida from raiding across the border.

Thus, before Washington had completed his second term in office, the United States had freed itself from the encroachments of both Great Britain and Spain.

Election of 1796

As the time approached for the election of 1796, some of the party friends of Washington urged him to run again. Already twice elected without a single vote cast against him in the electoral college, he could be counted upon to hold the Federalist party together and carry it to a third great victory. But Washington, weary of the burdens of the presidential office, disgusted with the partisan abuse that was being heaped upon him, longed to retire to his beloved home, Mount Vernon. Though he did not object to a third term in principle, he did not desire one for himself. To make his determination clear, he composed, with Hamilton's assistance, a long letter to the American people and had it published in a Philadelphia newspaper.

When Washington in this "Farewell Address" referred to the "insidious wiles of foreign influence," he was not writing merely for rhetorical effect. He had certain real evils in mind. Lately he had dismissed the secretary of state, Edmund Randolph, and had recalled the minister to France, James Monroe, for working hand in hand with the French to defeat Jay's Treaty. The French were still interfering in American politics with the hope of defeating the Federalists in the forthcoming presidential election.

There was no doubt that Jefferson would be the candidate of the Republicans. With Washington out of the running, there was some question as to who the Federalist candidate would be. Hamilton, the very personification of Federalism, was not "available" because his forthright views had aroused too many enemies. John Adams, who as Vice President was directly associated with none of the Federalist measures, finally won the nomination for President at a caucus of the Federalists in Congress. The Federalists elected a majority of their presidential electors, despite the electioneering tactics of the French government, whose efforts may have boomeranged and helped the Federalists. But when the electors balloted in the various states, some of the Adams men declined to vote for his running mate, Thomas Pinckney, so Pinckney received fewer votes than Jefferson. The next President was to be a Federalist, but the Vice President was to be a Republican.

By virtue of his diplomatic services during the Revolution, his writings as a conservative political philosopher, and his devotion to the public weal as he saw it, "Honest John" Adams ranks as one of the greatest American statesmen. Like most prominent members of the illustrious Adams family afterward, however, he lacked the politician's touch essential for successful leadership in a republican society. Even Washington, remote and austere as he sometimes seems to have been, was fairly adept at conciliating factions and maintaining party harmony. Unwisely, the new President chose to continue Washington's department heads in office. Most of them were friends of Hamilton, and they looked to him for advice, though he held no official post.

Quasi-War with France

As American relations with Great Britain and Spain improved in consequence of Jay's and Pinckney's treaties, relations with France, now under the government of the Directory, went from bad to worse. The French, asserting that they were applying the same principles of neutral rights as the United States and Great Britain had adopted in Jay's Treaty, continued to capture American ships on the high seas and, in many cases, to imprison the crews. The French declined to receive the new minister whom Adams sent to replace Monroe.

War seemed likely unless the Adams administration could settle the difficulties with France. Adams appointed a bipartisan commission of three to approach the Directory. In France, in 1797, the three Americans were met by three agents of the Directory's foreign minister, Prince Talleyrand, who had a reputation as the wizard of European diplomacy but who did not understand the psychology of Americans, even though he had lived for a time in the United States. Talleyrand's agents demanded a loan for France and a bribe for French officials before they would deal with Adams' commissioners.

When Adams received the commissioners' report, he sent a message to Congress in which he urged readiness for war, denounced the French for their insulting treatment of the United States, and vowed he would not appoint another minister to France until he knew the minister would be "received, respected and honored as the representative of a great, free, powerful and independent nation." The Republicans, doubting the President's charge that the United States had been insulted, asked for proof. Adams then turned the commissioners' report over to Congress, after deleting the names of the three Frenchmen and designating them only as Messrs. X., Y., and Z. When the report was published, the "X. Y. Z. Affair" provoked even more of a reaction than Adams had bargained for. It aroused the martial spirit of most Americans, made the Federalists more popular than ever as the party of patriotism, and led to a limited and undeclared war with France (1798–1800).

With the cooperation of Congress, which quickly passed the necessary laws, Adams cut off all trade with France, abrogated the treaties of 1778, and authorized public and private vessels of the United States to capture French armed ships on the high seas. Congress set up a Department of the Navy (1798) and appropriated money for the construction of warships. The new United States Navy soon gave a good account of itself. Its warships won a number of duels with French vessels of their own class and captured a total of eighty-five ships including armed merchantmen. Talleyrand finally began to see the wisdom of an accommodation with the Americans.

When, in 1800, Adams' new three-man commission arrived in France, Napoleon Bonaparte was in power as First Consul. The Americans requested that France terminate the treaties of 1778 and pay damages for seizures of American ships. Napoleon replied that, if the United States had any claim to damages, the claim must rest upon the treaties, and if the treaties were ended, the claim must be abandoned. Napoleon had his way. The Americans agreed to a new treaty that canceled the old ones, arranged for reciprocity in commerce, and ignored the question of damages. When Adams submitted this treaty to the Senate, the extreme Federalists raised so many objections

that its final ratification was delayed until after he had left office. Nevertheless, the "quasi-war" had come to an honorable end, and the United States at last had freed itself from the entanglements and embarrassments of the "perpetual" alliance with France.

Repression and Protest

The outbreak of hostilities in 1798 had given the Federalists an advantage over the political opposition, and in the congressional elections of that year they increased their majorities in both houses. Meanwhile their new-found power went to their heads. Some of them schemed to go on winning elections by passing laws to weaken and to silence the opposition. They had as an excuse the supposed necessity of protecting the nation from dangerous foreign influence in the midst of the undeclared war.

Since many Republican critics of the administration were foreigners by birth, especially Irish or French, the Federalists in Congress thought it desirable to limit the political rights of aliens and make it more difficult for them to become citizens of the United States. The Federalists struck at the civil liberties of both native Americans and the foreign-born in a series of laws commonly known as the Alien and Sedition Acts. These extended the residence requirement for naturalization from five to fourteen years, authorized the deportation of enemy aliens, and provided punishment for persons criticizing the government.

President Adams did not invoke the Alien Act nor deport any aliens, but this law together with the Naturalization Act doubtless had some effect in discouraging immigration and encouraging many foreigners already here to leave. The administration did enforce the Sedition Acts, arresting about two dozen men and convicting ten of them.

The Republicans had no reason to look to the Supreme Court for protection of their civil rights. Indeed, the Court never yet had declared an act of Congress unconstitutional, and the Republicans denied that it had the power to do so. They believed, however, that the recent Federalist legislation, particularly the Sedition Act, was unconstitutional, for the First Amendment stated that

Congress should pass no law abridging freedom of speech or of the press.

What agency of government should decide the question of constitutionality? The Republican leaders Jefferson and Madison concluded that the state legislatures should decide. They ably expressed their view in two sets of resolutions, one written (anonymously) by Jefferson and adopted by the Kentucky legislature (1798, 1799), and the other drafted by Madison and approved by the Virginia legislature (1798). These Kentucky and Virginia resolutions asserted the following doctrines. The federal government had been formed by a "compact" or contract among the states. It was a limited government, possessing only certain delegated powers. Whenever it exercised any additional and undelegated powers, its acts were "unauthoritative, void, and of no force." The parties to the contract, the states, must decide for themselves when and whether the central government exceeded its powers. And "nullification" by the states was the "rightful remedy" whenever the general government went too far. The resolutions urged all the states to join in declaring the Alien and Sedition Acts null and void and in requesting their repeal at the next session of Congress, but none of the others went along with Virginia and Kentucky.

The Republicans Win

In the election of 1800 Thomas Jefferson and Aaron Burr, representing the alliance of Virginia and New York, were again the Republican candidates. Adams was running for reelection on the Federalist ticket.

During the nearly twelve years of Federalist rule, the party had created numerous political enemies in consequence of Hamilton's financial program, the suppression of the Whiskey Rebellion, Jay's Treaty, and the Alien and Sedition Acts. Denouncing these measures, and especially the last of them, the Republicans made state rights and constitutional liberties the main issues of their campaign in 1800. They pictured Adams as a tyrant and a man who wanted to be King.

The Federalists, on the other hand, described Jefferson as a dangerous radical and his followers as wild men who, if they got into power, would bring on a reign of terror comparable to that of the French Revolution at its worst.

When the state electors cast their votes, Adams received a total of 65, but Jefferson got 73 and so did Burr. The election was not yet over: in accordance with the Constitution the decision between the two highest — between Burr and Jefferson — was up to the House of Representatives, with the delegation from each state casting a single vote.

Since the Federalists controlled a majority of the states' votes in the existing Congress, they had the privilege of deciding which of their opponents was to be the next President, though the Republicans, in making their nominations, had clearly intended for Jefferson to have the first place on their ticket. During the winter of 1800–1801 the House balloted again and again without mustering a majority for either candidate. Finally, only a few weeks before inauguration day, the tie was broken, and Jefferson was named as President, Burr as Vice President.

In addition to winning a majority of the presidential electors in 1800, the Republicans also won a majority of the seats in both houses of the next Congress. The only branch of the government left in Federalist hands was the judiciary, and Adams and his fellow partisans during his last months in office took steps to make their hold upon the courts secure.

By the Judiciary Act of 1801 the Federalists succeeded in greatly increasing the number of federal judgeships. To these newly created positions Adams proceeded to appoint deserving Federalists. It was said that he stayed up until midnight on his last day in office, March 3, 1801, in order to complete the signing of the judges' commissions, and so these officeholders were known as his "midnight appointments." Since federal judges held office for life — that is, with good behavior — Jefferson as the incoming President would be powerless to remove Adams' appointees. Or so the Federalists assumed.

Chapter 7

The Republican Era

Jefferson in Power

Long afterward, Jefferson referred to his party's victory as "the revolution of 1800," but in his inaugural address of 1801, trying to sweeten the bitterness of the recent campaign, he emphasized the common principles of the two parties while restating the principles of his own. Noting that the country was separated by a wide ocean from the "devastating havoc" of the European war, he recommended a foreign policy of "peace, commerce, and honest friendship with all nations, entangling alliances with none" — much as George Washington had done in his Farewell Address. With respect to domestic affairs, Jefferson proposed a "wise and frugal government" that would leave men free to "regulate their own pursuits of industry." Yet he also favored the "encouragement of agriculture and of commerce as its handmaid."

Jefferson was a strong executive, but neither his principles nor his nature inclined him to dictate to Congress. Yet Jefferson, as party leader, gave direction to his fellow partisans among the senators and representatives, by quiet and sometimes by rather devious means.

The Twelfth Amendment, added to the Constitution in 1804 before the election of that year, was intended to prevent another embarrassing tie vote like that of 1800. By implication, the amendment recognized the function of political parties; it stipulated that the electors should vote for President and Vice President as separate and distinct candidates. Burr had no chance to run on the ticket with Jefferson a second time. In place of Burr, the congressional caucus of Republicans nominated his New York factional foe, George Clinton. The popular Jefferson carried even the New England states, except Connecticut, and was reelected by the overwhelming electoral majority of 162 to 14, while the Republican membership of both houses of Congress was increased.

Jefferson refused to consider a third term for himself, for he was opposed to it in principle, unlike Washington. James Madison was nominated for the Presidency in 1808. Jefferson's refusal established a tradition against a third term for any President, a tradition that remained unbroken until Franklin D. Roosevelt was elected for a third time in 1940 (and then for a fourth time in 1944).

Conflict with the Courts

The Federalists had used the courts as a means of strengthening their party and persecuting the opposition, or so it seemed to the Republicans, and soon after Jefferson's first inauguration his followers in Congress launched a counterattack against the Federalist-dominated judiciary. They repealed the Naturalization Act, changing the residence period for citizenship of foreigners from fourteen to five years, and they allowed the hated Alien and Sedition Acts to expire. Then they repealed the Judiciary Act of 1801, abolishing the new judgeships that the Federalists had created and that President Adams had filled with his "midnight appointments."

In the debate on the Judiciary Act of 1801 the Federalists maintained that the Supreme Court had the power of reviewing acts of Congress and disallowing those that conflicted with the Constitution. The Constitution itself said nothing about such a power of judicial review, but Hamilton in one of *The Federalist* papers had argued that the Supreme Court should have the power, and the Court actually had exercised it as early as 1796, though upholding the law of Congress then in question. In 1803, in the case of *Marbury* v. *Madison*, the Court for the first time declared a congressional act, or part of one, unconstitutional. (Not for more than half a century, in the Dred Scott case of 1857, did the Court do so a second time.)

William Marbury, one of President Adams' "midnight appointments," had been named as a justice of the peace in the District of Columbia, but his commission, though duly signed and sealed, had not been delivered to him at the time Adams left the Presidency. Madison, as Jefferson's secretary of state, refused to hand over the commission, and so Marbury applied to the Supreme Court for an order (writ of mandamus) directing Madison to perform his official duty.

The chief justice of the United States was John Marshall, a leading Federalist and prominent lawyer of Virginia, whom President Adams had appointed in 1801. (For the remainder of Adams' term, Marshall had continued to serve also as secretary of state. It was he himself who, in that capacity, had neglected to see that Marbury's commission was delivered.) Marshall, as chief justice, did his best to give the government unity and strength.

In the case of *Marbury* v. *Madison*, Marshall decided that Marbury had a right to the commission but that the Court had no power to issue the order. True, the original Judiciary Act of 1789 had conferred such a power upon the Court, but, said Marshall, the powers of the Court had been defined in the Constitution itself, and Congress could not rightfully enlarge them. Thus, Marshall cleverly established a precedent of judicial review without placing the Court in the embarrassing position of having to enforce its ruling and thereby reveal its weakness.

Dollars and Ships

According to the Republicans, the administrations of Washington and Adams had been extravagant. Yearly expenditures had risen so much that by 1800 they were almost three times as high as they had been in 1793, and the public debt also had grown, though not so fast, since revenues had increased considerably. A part of these revenues came from internal taxation, including the hated whiskey excise. In 1802 the Republicans in Congress abolished the whole system of internal taxes, leaving customs duties and land sales as practically the only sources of revenue. The Jefferson administration sought to reduce the public debt by economizing on federal expenses. Secretary of the Treasury Albert Gallatin proceeded to carry out a drastic retrenchment plan, scrimping as much as possible on expenditures for the ordinary operations of the government and effecting what Jefferson called a "chaste reformation" in the army and the navy. The tiny army of 4,000 men was reduced to only 2,500. The navy was pared down from twenty-five ships in commission to seven, and the number of officers and men was cut accordingly.

But Jefferson was compelled to reverse his small-navy policy and build up the fleet because of trouble with pirates in the Mediterranean that jeopardized the profitable grain trade with ports in France and Italy. For years the Barbary states of North Africa — Morocco, Algiers, Tunis, and Tripoli — had made piracy a national enterprise. They demanded protection money from all nations whose ships sailed the Mediterranean. "Tribute or war is the usual alternative of these Barbary pirates," he said. "Why not build a navy and decide on war?" The decision was not left to him. In 1801 the Pasha of Tripoli, dissatisfied with the American response to his extortionate demands, had the flagpole of the American consulate chopped down, that being his way of declaring war on the United States. Jefferson concluded that, as President, he had a constitutional right to defend the United States without a war declaration by Congress, and he sent a squadron to the relief of the ships already at the scene. In 1805 the Pasha, by threatening to kill captive Americans, compelled the United States to agree to a peace that ended the payment of tribute but exacted a large ransom ($60,000) for the release of the prisoners.

Though the war in Tripoli cost money, Secretary Gallatin pressed on with his plan for diminishing the public debt. He was aided by an unex-

pected surge in trade, which increased tariff revenues. By the time Jefferson left office, the debt
had been cut almost in half (from $83 million
to $45 million), despite the expenditure of $15
million to buy Louisiana from Napoleon Bonaparte.

The Louisiana Purchase

In the year that Jefferson was elected President
of the United States, Napoleon made himself dictator of France with the title of First Consul, and
in the year that Jefferson was reelected, Napoleon
assumed the name and authority of Emperor.
These two men, the democrat and the dictator,
had little in common, yet they were good friends
in international politics until Napoleon's ambitions leaped from Europe to America and brought
about an estrangement.

Jefferson began to reappraise Franco-American
relations when he heard rumors of the secret re-
trocession of Louisiana from Spain to France. "It
completely reverses all the political relations of
the U.S.," he wrote to Minister Livingston (April
18, 1802). Always before, we had looked to
France as our "natural friend." But there was on
the earth "one single spot" the possessor of which
was "our natural and habitual enemy." That spot
was New Orleans, the outlet through which the
produce of the fast-growing West was shipped to
the markets of the world. If France should actually take and hold New Orleans, Jefferson said,
then "we must marry ourselves to the British fleet
and nation."

There was possibly a way out of the dilemma,
and that was to purchase from Napoleon the port
so indispensable to the United States. Jefferson
sent a special envoy to work with the American
minister, Robert R. Livingston, in persuading the
French to sell. For this extraordinary mission he
chose James Monroe, who was well remembered
in France. While Monroe's coach was on its way
to Paris, Napoleon suddenly made up his mind to
dispose of the entire Louisiana Territory. Napoleon then was expecting a renewal of the European war, and he feared that he would not be able
to hold Louisiana if the British, with their superior naval power, should attempt to take it. He
also realized that, quite apart from the British
threat, there was danger from the United States:

he could not prevent the Americans, who were
pushing steadily into the Mississippi Valley, from
sooner or later overrunning Louisiana.

Livingston and Monroe, after the latter's arrival in Paris, had to decide first of all whether
they should even consider making a treaty for the
purchase of the entire Louisiana Territory, since
they had not been authorized by their government to do so. They dared not wait until they
could get new instructions from home, for Napoleon in the meantime might change his mind as
suddenly as he had made it up. They decided to
go ahead, realizing that Jefferson could reject
their treaty if he disapproved what they had
done.

By the terms of the treaty (April 30, 1803), the
United States was to pay 60,000,000 francs
directly to the French government and up to
20,000,000 more to American citizens who held
claims against France for ship seizures in the
past — or a total of approximately $15,000,000.
The United States was to incorporate the people
of Louisiana into the Union and grant them as
soon as possible the same rights and privileges
as other citizens. This seemed to imply that the
Louisiana inhabitants were to have the benefits of statehood in the near future. The boundaries were not defined, Louisiana being transferred to the United States simply with the "same
extent" as when owned by France and earlier by
Spain.

In Washington, the President was both pleased
and embarrassed when he received the treaty. He
was glad to get such a bargain, but, according to
his oft-repeated views on the Constitution, the
United States lacked the constitutional power to
accept the bargain. In the past he had always insisted that the federal government could rightfully exercise only those powers assigned to it in
so many words, and nowhere did the Constitution
say anything about the acquisition of new territory. Now he thought, at first, that an amendment
should be adopted to give the government the
specific right to buy additional land; he even went
so far as to draft a suitable amendment. But his
advisers cautioned him that ratification might be
long delayed or possibly defeated, and they argued that the President with the consent of the
Senate could make treaties, and the treaty-mak-
ing power would justify the purchase of Louisiana. Years afterward (in 1828) the Supreme Court

upheld this view, but Jefferson continued to have doubts about it. Finally he gave in, trusting, as he said, "that the good sense of our country will correct the evil of loose construction when it shall produce ill effects." Thus, by implication, he left the question of constitutional interpretation to public opinion, and he cut the ground from under his doctrine of state rights.

Meanwhile the geography of the far-flung territory was revealed by a series of explorations. In 1803, before Napoleon's offer to sell Louisiana, Jefferson planned an expedition that was to cross all the way to the Pacific Ocean and gather not only geographical facts but also information about the prospects for Indian trade. Congress having secretly provided the necessary funds, Jefferson named as leader of the expedition his private secretary and Virginia neighbor, the thirty-two-year-old Meriwether Lewis, who as a veteran of Indian wars was skilled in wilderness ways. Lewis chose as a colleague the twenty-eight-year-old William Clark, also an experienced frontiersman and Indian fighter.

Lewis and Clark, with a chosen company of four dozen hardy men, set up winter quarters in St. Louis at about the time the United States took formal possession of Louisiana. In the spring of 1804 they started up the Missouri River and eventually crossed the Rocky Mountains, descended the Snake and the Columbia rivers, and in the late autumn of 1805 encamped on the Pacific coast. In September 1806 they were back again in St. Louis, bringing with them carefully kept records of what they had observed along the way. No longer was the Far West a completely unknown country.

While Lewis and Clark were on their epic journey, Jefferson sent out Lieutenant Zebulon Montgomery Pike to fill in the picture of the Louisiana Territory. In the fall of 1805, then only twenty-six, Pike led an expedition from St. Louis up the Mississippi River in search of its source, and though he did not find it, he learned a good deal about the upper Mississippi Valley. However, his account of his Western travels left the impression that the land between the Missouri and the Rockies was a desert that American farmers could never cultivate and that ought to be left forever to the nomadic Indian tribes.

The Burr Conspiracy

In the long run the Louisiana Purchase prepared the way for the growth of the United States as a great continental power. Immediately, however, the Purchase provoked reactions that threatened or seemed to threaten the very existence of the Union. From both the Northeast and the Southwest there soon arose rumors of secession plots.

Most of the American people heartily approved the acquisition of the new territory, as they indicated by their overwhelming reelection of Jefferson in 1804, but some of the New England Federalists raged against it. Their feelings were understandable enough. Both their party and their section stood to lose in importance with the growth of the West. A group of the most extreme of these men, known as the Essex Junto, concluded that the only recourse for New England was to secede from the Union and form a separate "Northern Confederacy." They justified such action by means of state-rights arguments similar to those Jefferson had used only about five years earlier in opposition to the Alien and Sedition Acts.

If a Northern Confederacy were to have any hope for lasting success as a separate nation, it would have to include New York as well as New England. But the prominent New York Federalist Alexander Hamilton had no sympathy with the secessionist scheme. His New York Republican rival, Aaron Burr, agreed to run for governor with Federalist support in 1804. Rumor had it that he was implicated in the disunion plot and that, if elected, he would lead the state into secession along with New England. Hamilton accused Burr of plotting treason and cast slurs upon his personal character. Burr lost the election, then challenged Hamilton to a duel. And so the two men with their seconds met at Weehawken, New Jersey, across the Hudson River from New York City, on a July morning in 1804. Hamilton was mortally wounded; he died the next day. New Jersey and New York indicted Burr for murder and then later dropped the charges.

Burr presided over the United States Senate the following winter and then, at the end of his term as Vice President, busied himself with mysterious affairs in the Southwest. Some people believed (and some historians still believe) that he intended to separate the Southwest from the Union and rule it as an empire of his own. His ultimate aim most probably was the conquest of Spanish territory beyond the boundaries of Louisiana rather than the division of the United States. In the fall of 1806 his armed followers started by boat down the Ohio River, Burr himself joining them after they were well under way. Jefferson soon issued a proclamation calling for the arrest of Burr and his men as traitors. Eventually Burr was captured and brought to Richmond for trial.

Chief Justice Marshall, presiding over the case on circuit duty (1807–1808), applied quite literally the clause of the Constitution that says no one shall be convicted of treason except upon the testimony of at least two witnesses to the same "overt act." He excluded all evidence not bearing directly upon such an act, and so the jury had little choice but to acquit Burr, since not even one witness had actually seen him waging war against the United States or giving aid and comfort to its enemies. Though freed, Burr gained lasting notoriety as a traitor; after exiling himself abroad for a few years, he returned and lived long enough to hail the Texas revolution (1836) as the fruition of the same sort of movement that he had hoped to start.

Freedom of the Seas

In the early 1800s the warring nations of Europe found it impossible to take care of their own shipping needs. American shipowners prospered as, year after year, they engrossed a larger and larger proportion of the carrying trade between Europe and the West Indies. Farmers shared in the prosperity, for exports from the United States to the West Indies and Europe also increased prodigiously.

Powerless to invade the British Isles, Napoleon devised a scheme, known as the Continental System, which he hoped would bring the British to terms. In a series of decrees beginning with those of Berlin (1806) and Milan (1807), he proclaimed that British ships and neutral ships touching at British ports were not to land their cargoes at any European port controlled by France or its allies.

The British government replied to Napoleon's decrees with a succession of orders-in-council.

These announced an unusual kind of blockade of the European coast. The blockade was intended not to keep goods out of Napoleon's Europe but only to see that the goods were carried either in British vessels or in neutral vessels stopping at a British port and paying for a special license.

Caught between Napoleon's decrees and Britain's orders, American vessels sailing directly for Europe took the chance of capture by the British, and those going by way of a British port ran the risk of seizure by the French.

American ships also risked being stopped and searched by the British Navy, which claimed the right to impress (force) into service naturalized Americans born on British soil. According to the laws of England a true-born subject could never give up allegiance to the King: once an Englishman, always an Englishman.

In the summer of 1807, in the *Chesapeake-Leopard* incident, the British went to an outrageous extreme. The *Chesapeake* was a public and not a private vessel, a frigate of the United States Navy and not an ordinary merchantman. Sailing from Norfolk, with several alleged deserters from the British Navy among the crew, the *Chesapeake* was hailed by His Majesty's Ship *Leopard*, which had been lying in wait off Cape Henry, at the entrance to Chesapeake Bay. Commodore James Barron refused to allow the *Chesapeake* to be searched, and so the *Leopard* opened fire and compelled him, unprepared for action as he was, to strike his colors. A boarding party from the *Leopard* dragged four men off the American frigate.

This was an attack upon the United States, and most of the people cried for a war of revenge. Jefferson and Madison, however, believed that, if worse came to worst, the United States could bring Great Britain to terms, and France as well, through the use of economic pressure instead of military or naval force.

Hence Jefferson hastily drafted an embargo bill, Madison revised it, and both the House and the Senate promptly enacted it into law. The embargo prohibited American ships from leaving this country for any port in the world.

The embargo brought on a serious depression. Though the Northeastern merchants disliked impressment, the orders-in-council, and Napoleon's decrees, they hated Jefferson's embargo much more; they lost money every day their ships idled at the wharves. Again, as at the time of the Louisiana Purchase, Jefferson seemed to have violated the Constitution (as indeed he had — if judged by the principles he had advocated before becoming President). A few days before going out of office, Jefferson approved a bill terminating his and Madison's first experiment with what he called "peaceable coercion." But Jefferson's succession by Madison meant no basic change in policy.

Meanwhile, a border conflict developed between the British Empire and the expanding American frontier.

Indians and Western Lands

Receiving from Jefferson an appointment as governor of Indiana Territory, William Henry Harrison devoted himself to carrying out Jefferson's policy of Indian removal. According to the Jeffersonian program, the Indians must give up their claims to tribal lands and either convert themselves into settled farmers or migrate west of the Mississippi. Playing off one tribe against another, and using whatever tactics suited the occasion — threats, bribes, trickery — Harrison made treaty after treaty with the separate tribes of the Northwest. By 1807 the United States claimed treaty rights to eastern Michigan, southern Indiana, and most of Illinois. Meanwhile, in the Southwest, millions of acres were taken from other tribes in the states of Georgia and Tennessee and in Mississippi Territory. Having been forced off their traditional hunting grounds, the Indians throughout the Mississippi Valley seethed with discontent.

For years the British authorities in Canada had neglected their Indian friends across the border to the south. Then came the *Chesapeake* incident and the surge of anti-British feeling throughout the United States. Now the Canadian authorities, expecting war and an attempted invasion of Canada, began to renew friendship with the Indians and provide them with increased supplies.

Also intensifying this conflict was the rise of a remarkable native leader, one of the most admirable and heroic in Indian history. Tecumseh, "The Shooting Star," chief of the Shawnees, aimed to unite all the tribes of the Mississippi Valley, resist the advance of white settlement, and recover the whole Northwest, making the Ohio River the boundary between the United States and the Indian country. He maintained that Harrison and others, by negotiating with individual tribes, had obtained no real title to land in the various treaties, since the land belonged to all the tribes and none of them could rightfully cede any of it without the consent of the rest.

In his plans for a united front, Tecumseh was aided by his brother, a one-eyed, epileptic medicine-man known as the Prophet. The Prophet, visiting the Great Spirit from time to time in trances, inspired a religious revival that spread through numerous tribes and helped bring them together. The Prophet's town, at the confluence of Tippecanoe Creek and the Wabash River, became the center of spiritual power as well as the headquarters of Tecumseh's confederacy. Leaving his brother there after instructing him to avoid war for the time being, Tecumseh journeyed down the Mississippi in 1811 to bring the Indians to the south into his alliance.

During Tecumseh's absence, Governor Harrison saw a chance to destroy the growing influence of the two Indian leaders. With 1,000 soldiers he camped near the Prophet's town, provoked an attack (November 7, 1811), and though suffering losses as heavy as those of the enemy, succeeded in driving off the Indians and burning the town. Tecumseh returned to find his confederacy shattered, yet there were still plenty of warriors eager for the warpath.

Westerners blamed Great Britain for providing the guns and supplies that enabled the Indians to attack. To Harrison and most of the frontier settlers, there seemed only one way to make the West safe for white Americans. That was to drive the British out of Canada and annex that province to the United States.

While frontier settlers in the North demanded the conquest of Canada, those in the South looked to the acquisition of Florida. In Spanish hands, that territory was a perpetual nuisance, with slaves escaping across the line in one direction and Indians raiding across it in the other. In 1810 American settlers in West Florida took matters into their own hands, fell upon the Spanish fort at

Baton Rouge, and requested that the territory be annexed to the United States. President Madison unhesitatingly proclaimed its annexation, then schemed to get the rest of Florida too. Spain was Britain's ally, and a war with Britain would give the settlers an excuse for taking Spanish as well as British territory.

Three days before the Battle of Tippecanoe a new Congress met in Washington for the session of 1811–1812. Of the newly elected congressmen and senators, the great majority were warlike Republicans, and after the news of Tippecanoe they became more eager than ever for a showdown with the power that seemed to threaten both the security of the frontier and the freedom of the seas.

These "war hawks" got control of both the House and the Senate. As Speaker of the House, Henry Clay of Kentucky held a position of influence then second only to that of the President himself. Clay filled the committees with the friends of force, appointing John C. Calhoun of South Carolina to the crucial Committee on Foreign Affairs, and launched a drive toward war for the conquest of Canada.

While Congress debated, President Madison moved reluctantly toward the conclusion that war was necessary. In May 1812 the war faction took the lead in the caucus of Republican congressmen who renominated him for the Presidency, and on June 1 he sent his war message to Congress. The close vote on the declaration, 19 to 13 in the Senate and 79 to 49 in the House, showed how badly the American people were divided.

The War of 1812

The conquest of Canada, supposedly a "mere matter of marching," as Jefferson himself put it, soon proved to be an exercise in frustration. A three-pronged invasion failed in 1812. While British sea power dominated the ocean, American fleets arose to control the Great Lakes. This made possible, at last, an invasion of Canada by way of Detroit. Harrison's troops now pushed up the River Thames, won a victory (October 5, 1813), and killed Tecumseh, whom the British had com-

missioned as a brigadier general. The Battle of the Thames resulted in no lasting occupation of Canadian soil, but it disheartened the Indians of the Northwest.

While Harrison was harrying the tribes of the Northwest, another Indian fighter was striking an even harder blow at the Creeks in the Southwest. The Creeks, aroused by Tecumseh on his Southern visit, received supplies from the Spanish in Florida. These Indians had fallen upon Fort Mims, on the Alabama River just north of the Florida border, and had killed the frontier families taking shelter within its stockade. Andrew Jackson, Tennessee planter and militia general, turning from his plans for invading Florida, tracked down the Creeks. In the Battle of Horseshoe Bend (March 27, 1814) Jackson's men took frightful vengeance, slaughtering Indian women and children along with warriors. Then Jackson went into Florida and seized the Spanish fort at Pensacola.

After the battles of the Thames and Horseshoe Bend, the Indians were of little use to the British. But, with the surrender of Napoleon in Europe, the British could send their veterans of the European war to dispose of the "dirty shirts," the unkempt Americans. In 1814 the British prepared to invade the United States by three approaches — Chesapeake Bay, Lake Champlain (the historic route of Burgoyne), and the mouth of the Mississippi.

The British marched into Washington (August 24, 1814), putting the government to flight. Then they deliberately burned the public buildings, including the White House. Leaving Washington in partial ruins, the invading army reembarked and proceeded up the bay, toward Baltimore. But Baltimore, guarded by Fort McHenry, was ready. From a distance the British bombarded the fort (September 12, 1814), then withdrew. Meanwhile the invasion force descending upon northern New York met defeat in the Battle of Plattsburg (September 11, 1814) and returned to Canada.

In December 1814, a formidable array of battle-hardened veterans, fresh from the Duke of Wellington's Peninsular campaign against the French in Spain, landed below New Orleans. Neither the British nor the American forces knew that a treaty of peace between their governments had been signed in faraway Belgium on December 24. Awaiting the British advance up the Mississippi was Andrew Jackson with a motley collection of Tennesseans, Kentuckians, Creoles, blacks, and pirates drawn up behind breastworks. For all their drill and bravery, the redcoats advancing through the open (January 8, 1815) were no match for Jackson's well-protected men. Finally the British retreated, leaving behind 700 dead, 1,400 wounded, and 500 other prisoners. Jackson's losses: 8 killed, 13 wounded.

The Peace Settlement

With notable exceptions, such as the Battle of New Orleans, the military operations of the United States, 1812–1815, were rather badly bungled. The government was woefully unprepared for the war at the outset and faced increasing popular opposition as the contest dragged on. The opposition centered in New England, and it went to remarkable extremes. Some of the Federalists there celebrated British victories, sabotaged their own country's war effort, and even plotted disunion and a separate peace.

On December 15, 1814, while the British were beginning their invasion by way of New Orleans, delegates from the New England states met in Hartford, Connecticut, to consider the grievances of their section against the Madison administration. The would-be seceders were overruled by the comparatively moderate men who were in the overwhelming majority at the Hartford Convention. The convention's report reasserted the right of nullification but only hinted at secession, observing that "the severance of the Union by one or more States, against the will of the rest, and especially in time of war, can be justified only by absolute necessity." But the report proposed seven essential amendments to the Constitution, presumably as the condition of New England's remaining in the Union.

The Federalists, apparently in a strong bargaining position, assumed that the Republicans would have to give in to the Hartford Convention terms, since the government was in such dire extremity. Soon after the convention adjourned, however, the news of Jackson's smashing victory

at New Orleans reached the cities of the Northeast. While most Americans rejoiced, the Federalists were plunged into gloom. A day or two later came tidings from abroad concerning the conclusion of a treaty of peace.

The Treaty of Ghent did not even mention the original war aims of eliminating impressment and acquiring Canada. It merely provided for peace on the basis of the status quo, which meant a return to things as they had been before the fighting began. Each of the belligerents was to restore its wartime conquests to the other. Four commissions with both American and British members were to be appointed to agree upon disputed or undetermined segments of the boundary between Canada and the United States.

Banks, Tariffs, Roads

The War of 1812 led to chaos in shipping and banking, stimulated the growth of manufactures, and exposed dramatically the inadequacy of the existing transportation system. Hence arose the postwar issues of reestablishing the Bank of the United States, protecting the new industries, and providing a nationwide network of roads. On these issues the former war hawks Clay and Calhoun became the leading advocates of the national as opposed to the local or sectional point of view. The party of Jefferson now sponsored measures of a kind once championed by the party of Hamilton.

After the first Bank's charter expired (1811), a large number of state banks sprang up. These issued vast quantities of bank notes and did not always bother to keep a large enough reserve of gold or silver to redeem the notes on demand. The notes passed from hand to hand more or less as money, but their actual value depended upon the reputation of the bank that issued them, and the variety of issues was so confusing as to make honest business difficult and counterfeiting easy.

Congress struck at the currency evil not by prohibiting state bank notes but by chartering a second Bank of the United States in 1816. Though its potentialities were not realized until the 1820s, this national bank possessed the power to control the state banks by presenting their notes from time to time and demanding payment either in cash or in its own notes, which were as good as gold. The state banks would have to stay on a specie-paying basis or risk being forced out of business.

During the war, manufacturers had prospered as foreign competition almost disappeared in consequence of the embargoes and the blockade. As the war came to an end, the manufacturing prospects of the United States were suddenly dimmed. British ships swarmed alongside American wharves and began to unload their cargoes of manufactured goods at cut prices, even selling below cost. As Lord Brougham explained to Parliament, it was "well worth while to incur a loss upon the first exportation, in order, by the glut, to stifle in the cradle those rising manufactures in the United States, which war had forced into existence, contrary to the natural course of things."

The "infant industries" needed protection if they were to survive and grow strong enough to stand upon their own feet against foreign competition. So the friends of industry maintained, reviving the old arguments of Hamilton. In 1816 the protectionists brought about the passage of a tariff law with rates high enough to be definitely protective, especially on cotton cloth.

The War of 1812 had demonstrated that the nation lacked a system of transportation adequate to meet the needs of national defense. In 1815 President Madison called the attention of Congress to the "great importance of establishing throughout our country the roads and canals which can be best executed under the national authority," and he suggested that a constitutional amendment would resolve any doubts about the authority of Congress to provide for the construction of canals and roads. Representative Calhoun promptly espoused a bill by which the moneys due the government from the Bank of the United States would be devoted to internal improvements.

Congress passed the bill, but President Madison, on his last day in office (March 3, 1817), returned it with his veto. While he approved its purpose, he still believed that a constitutional amendment was necessary.

"Era of Good Feelings"

After 1800 the Presidency seemed to have become the special possession of Virginians, who passed it from one to another in unvarying sequence. After two terms in office Jefferson named his secretary of state, James Madison, to succeed him, and after two more terms Madison secured the nomination of *his* secretary of state, James Monroe. Many in the North already were muttering against this succession of Virginians, the so-called "Virginia Dynasty," yet the Republicans had no difficulty in electing their candidate in the rather listless campaign of 1816.

Soon after his inauguration Monroe did what no other President since Washington had done: he made a goodwill tour through the country, eastward to New England, westward as far as Detroit. In New England, so recently the scene of rabid Federalist discontent, he was greeted everywhere with enthusiastic demonstrations. The *Columbian Centinel*, a Federalist newspaper of Boston, commenting on the "Presidential Jubilee" in that city, observed that an "era of good feelings" had arrived. This phrase soon became popular, and eventually it came to be almost synonymous with the Presidency of Monroe. He was reelected in 1820 with the nearest thing to a unanimous electoral vote that any presidential candidate, with the exception of George Washington, has ever had.

Florida and the Far West

The first big problem facing John Quincy Adams as secretary of state in the Monroe administration was that of Florida. Already the United States had annexed West Florida, but Spain still claimed the whole of the province, East and West, and actually held most of it, though with a grasp too feeble to solve the problems about which Americans long had complained — the escape of slaves across the border in one direction, the marauding of Indians across it in the other. In 1817 Adams began negotiations with the Spanish minister, Don Luis de Onís, for acquiring all of Florida.

Andrew Jackson, in command of American

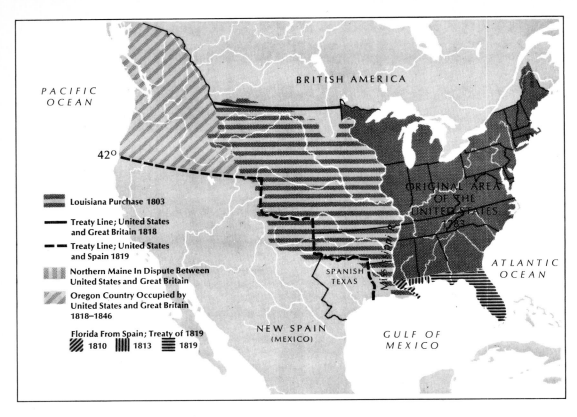

Boundary Settlements 1818–1819

troops along the Florida frontier, had orders from Secretary of War Calhoun to "adopt the necessary measures" to end the border troubles. Jackson also had an unofficial hint — or so he afterward claimed — that the administration would not mind if he undertook a punitive expedition into Spanish territory. At any rate he invaded Florida, seized the Spanish forts at St. Marks and Pensacola, and ordered the hanging of two British subjects on the charge of supplying the Indians and inciting them to hostilities.

Jackson's raid demonstrated that the United States, if it tried, could easily take Florida by force. Unable to obtain British support, Spain had little choice but to come to terms. In the treaty of 1819 it was agreed that the King of Spain should cede "all the territories which belong to him situated to the eastward of the Mississippi and known by the name of East and West Florida." In return

the United States assumed the claims of its citizens against the Spanish government to the amount of $5,000,000. The United States gave up its claims to Texas, while Spain gave up its claims to territory north of the forty-second parallel from the Rockies to the Pacific. Thus a line was drawn from the Gulf of Mexico northwestward across the continent delimiting the Spanish empire and transferring to the United States the Spanish title to the West Coast north of California. Adams and Onís had concluded something more than a Florida agreement: it was a "transcontinental treaty."

The Great Migration

A sudden surge of population, greater than any preceding it, swept westward during the boom years that followed the War of 1812. "Old America seems to be breaking up and moving westward," remarked an Englishman who joined the throng heading for the woodlands and prairies of the Old Northwest, particularly southern Ohio, Indiana, and Illinois. Some were restless spirits from Kentucky and Tennessee who had begun to feel crowded as their states became increasingly populous. Others were small farmers from the back country of Virginia and the Carolinas who fled the encroachment of slavery and the plantation system. Still others came from the middle states, New England, and foreign countries, but the great majority were Southerners. Whatever the starting point, the Ohio River was for most of the migrants the main route, the "grand track," until the completion of the Erie Canal in 1825.

To the Southwest moved people from Kentucky, fron Tennessee, and from as far away as New England. Most numerous among the settlers on the Southern frontier, however, were farmers and planters from the South Atlantic states, especially from the foothills of Georgia and the Carolinas. Their motive for migrating was, in a word, cotton. With the spread of cotton cultivation throughout the uplands of the older South, the soil there lost much of its natural fertility from repeated croppings or washed away as torrential rains gullied the hillsides. Seeking fresh soil with a climate suitable for cotton, the planters naturally looked to the Southwest, around the end of the Appalachian range, where there stretched a broad zone within which cotton could thrive. Included in this zone was the Black Belt of central Alabama and Mississippi, a prairie with a fabulously productive soil of rotted limestone.

Though by 1819 settlers already were pushing beyond the Mississippi, much of the area to the east of the river, around the Great Lakes and along the Gulf of Mexico, was yet to be occupied. Despite the gaps in settlement, the population of the Mississippi Valley had increased far more rapidly than that of the nation as a whole. The census of 1810 indicated that only one American in seven lived to the west of the Appalachian Mountains; the census of 1820, almost one in four. During the immediate postwar years four new states were created in this region — Indiana (1816), Mississippi (1817), Illinois (1818), and Alabama (1819). Meanwhile Missouri had grown populous enough

for statehood. For the time being, however, the westward movement was slowed down by the onset of the depression following the Panic of 1819.

Rising prices for farm produce had stimulated a land boom in the United States, particularly in the West. After the war the government land offices did a bigger business than ever before; not for twenty years were they to do as good a business again. Neither the settlers not the speculators needed hard cash to buy government land: they could borrow from the state banks and pay the government with bank notes. And, under the law of 1800, they could buy on credit, with a down payment of one-fourth and the rest in three yearly installments.

In 1819 the United States Bank suddenly began to tighten up credit. It called in loans and foreclosed mortgages, acquiring thousands of acres of mortgaged land in the West. It gathered up state bank notes and presented them to the state banks for payment in cash. Having little money on hand, many of these banks closed their doors. Most of the rest soon had to follow suit, for they were beset by depositors with notes to be cashed. A financial panic was on.

Six years of depression followed. Prices rapidly fell. With the prices of farm products so low, those settlers buying land on credit could not hope to keep up their payments. Some stood to lose everything — their land, their improvements on it, their homes. They demanded relief from their congressmen, and Congress responded with the land law of 1820 and the relief act of 1821. By the new land law the credit system was abolished but the minimum price was lowered from $2.00 (as set in 1796) to $1.25 and the minimum tract from 160 (as set in 1800) to 80 acres. Hereafter purchasers would have to buy their farms outright, but they could get one for as little as $100. The relief act allowed a previous buyer to pay off debt at the reduced price, to accept the reduced acreage and apply the payments to it, and to have an extension of time in meeting installments.

The Missouri Compromise

When Missouri applied for admission as a state, slavery already was well established there. Repre-

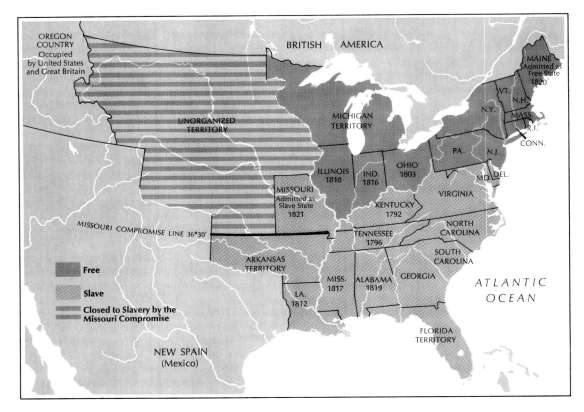

OREGON
COUNTRY
Occupied
by United States
and Great Britain

BRITISH   AMERICA

MAINE
Admitted as
Free State
1820

VT.   N.H.

N.Y.

MASS.
R.I.
CONN.

UNORGANIZED
TERRITORY

MICHIGAN
TERRITORY

PA.   N.J.

ILLINOIS
1818   IND.
1816   OHIO
1803

MD. DEL.

MISSOURI
Admitted as
Slave State
1821

KENTUCKY
1792

VIRGINIA

MISSOURI COMPROMISE LINE 36°30'

TENNESSEE
1796

NORTH
CAROLINA

ARKANSAS
TERRITORY

SOUTH
CAROLINA

Free

Slave

Closed to Slavery by the
Missouri Compromise

MISS.
1817   ALABAMA
1819   GEORGIA

ATLANTIC
OCEAN

LA.
1812

NEW SPAIN
(Mexico)

FLORIDA
TERRITORY

The Missouri Compromise 1820

sentative James Tallmadge, Jr., of New York, moved to amend the enabling bill so as to prohibit the further introduction of slaves into Missouri and to provide for the gradual emancipation of those already there. This Tallmadge amendment provoked a controversy that was to rage for the next two years.

Though the issue arose suddenly, waking and terrifying Thomas Jefferson like "a fire bell in the night," as he said, sectional jealousies that produced it had been accumulating for a long time. Already the concept of a balance of power between the Northern and Southern states was well developed. From the beginning, partly by chance and partly by design, new states had come into the Union more or less in pairs, one from the North, another from the South. With the admission of Alabama in 1819, the Union contained an equal number of free and slave states, eleven of each. Thus the free and slave states were evenly

balanced in the Senate, though the free states with their more rapidly growing population had a majority in the House. If Missouri should be admitted as a slave state, the existing sectional balance would be upset. Northerners, in particular the Federalists, never tired in their denunciations of the Virginia Dynasty and the three-fifths clause which, they charged, gave the Southern states a disproportionate weight in national politics.

The Missouri question soon was complicated by the application of Maine for admission as a state. Massachusetts had consented to the separation of the northern part of the Commonwealth but only on the condition that Maine be granted statehood before March 4, 1820. The Speaker of the House, Henry Clay, informed Northerners that if they refused to consent to Missouri's becoming a slave state Southerners would deny the application of Maine.

A way out of the impasse opened when the

Senate combined the Maine and Missouri bills, without prohibiting slavery in Missouri. Then, to make the package more acceptable to the House, Senator Jesse B. Thomas of Illinois proposed an amendment prohibiting slavery in all the rest of the Louisiana Purchase territory north of the southern boundary of Missouri (latitude 36° 30′). The Senate adopted the Thomas amendment, and Speaker Clay undertook to guide the amended Maine-Missouri bill through the House. Eventually, after the measure had been broken up into three separate bills, he succeeded.

The first Missouri Compromise (1820) did not end the dispute; a second compromise was necessary. In 1820 Maine was actually admitted as a state, but Missouri was only authorized to form a constitution and a government. When the Missouri constitution was completed, it contained a clause forbidding free blacks or mulattoes to enter the state. Several of the existing states, denying the right of citizenship to "free persons of color," already had laws against their immigration. Other states, among them New York, recognized non-white persons as citizens. According to the federal Constitution, "The citizens of each State shall be entitled to all privileges and immunities of citizens in the several States." This meant that a citizen of such a state as New York, whether white or black, was entitled to all the privileges of a citizen of Missouri, including of course the privilege of traveling or residing in the state. The antiblack clause was clearly unconstitutional, and a majority in the House of Representatives threatened to exclude Missouri until it was eliminated. Finally Clay offered a resolution that Missouri should be admitted to the Union on the condition that the clause should never be construed in such a way as to deny to any citizen of any state the privileges and immunities to which he or she was entitled under the Constitution of the United States. In the circumstances, this resolution was meaningless, yet it made possible the admission of Missouri as a state in 1821.

Marshall and the Court

John Marshall remained as chief justice for almost thirty-five years, from 1801 to 1835. During these years Republican Presidents filled vacancies with Republican justices, one after another,

and yet Marshall continued to carry a majority with him in most of the Court's decisions. The net effect of the hundreds of opinions delivered by the Marshall Court was to strengthen the judicial branch at the expense of the other two branches of the government; increase the power of the United States and lessen that of the states themselves; and advance the interests of the propertied classes, especially those engaged in commerce.

For example, in *McCulloch* v. *Maryland* (1819), Marshall confirmed the "implied powers" of Congress by upholding the constitutionality of the Bank of the United States. The Bank, with headquarters in Philadelphia and branches in various cities throughout the country, had become so unpopular that several of the states tried to drive the branches out of business by outright prohibition or by prohibitory taxes. Maryland, for one, laid a heavy tax on the Baltimore branch. This case presented two constitutional questions to the Supreme Court: could Congress charter a bank and, if so, could one of the states thus tax it? As one of the Bank's attorneys, Daniel Webster first repeated the arguments used originally by Hamilton to prove that the establishment of such an institution came within the "necessary and proper" clause. Then, to dispose of the tax issue, Webster added an ingenious argument of his own. The power to tax, he said, involved a "power to destroy," and if the states could tax the Bank at all, they could tax it to death. But the Bank with its branches was an agency of the federal government: no state could take an action tending to destroy the United States itself. Marshall adopted Webster's words in deciding for the Bank.

The case of *Gibbons* v. *Ogden* (1824) brought up the question of the powers of Congress, as against the powers of the states, in regulating interstate commerce. The state of New York had granted Robert Fulton's and Robert Livingston's steamboat company the exclusive right to carry passengers on the Hudson River to New York City. From this monopoly Aaron Ogden obtained the business of navigation across the river between New York and New Jersey. Thomas Gibbons, with a license granted under an act of Congress, went into competition with Ogden, who brought suit against him and was sustained by the New York courts. When Gibbons appealed to the Supreme Court, the justices faced the twofold question of whether "commerce" included navigation and whether Congress alone or Congress and the states together could regulate interstate commerce. Marshall replied that "commerce" was a broad term embracing navigation as well as the buying and selling of goods. Though he did not exactly say that the states had no authority whatever regarding interstate commerce, he asserted that the power of Congress in regard thereto was "complete in itself" and might be "exercised to its utmost extent." He concluded that the state-granted monopoly was void.

For some time Virginia Republicans like Thomas Jefferson and John Taylor of Caroline (a Virginia county) had protested against the views of their fellow Virginian John Marshall. In *Construction Construed and Constitutions Vindicated* (1820) Taylor argued that Marshall and his colleagues were not merely interpreting but were actually changing the nature of the Constitution, which should properly be changed only by the amending process, requiring the approval of three-fourths of the states. In Congress some critics of the Court, mostly from the South and the West, proposed various means (none of which was adopted) of curbing what they called judicial tyranny.

Origin of the Monroe Doctrine

To most people in the United States, South and Central America had been "dark continents" before the War of 1812. Suddenly they emerged into the light, and Americans looking southward beheld a gigantic spectacle: the Spanish empire struggling in its death throes, a whole continent in revolt, new nations in the making with a future no one could foresee.

Already a profitable trade had developed between the ports of the United States and those of the Rio de la Plata in South America, of Chile, and above all of Cuba, with flour and other staples being exported in return for sugar and coins. Presumably the trade would increase much faster once the United States had established regular diplomatic and commercial relations with the countries in revolt.

Secretary Adams and President Monroe hesitated to take the risky step of recognition unless Great Britain would agree to do so at the same time. In 1818 and 1819 the United States made two bids for British cooperation, and both were rejected. Finally, in 1822, President Monroe informed Congress that five nations — La Plata (Argentina), Chile, Peru, Colombia, and Mexico — were ready for recognition, and he requested an appropriation for sending ministers to them. This was a bold stroke: the United States was going ahead alone as the first country to recognize the new governments, in defiance of the rest of the world.

In 1823 President Monroe stood forth as an even bolder champion of America against Europe. Presenting to Congress his annual message on the state of the Union, he announced a policy that afterward — though not for thirty years — was to be known as the "Monroe Doctrine." One phase of this policy had to do with the relationship of Europe to America. "The American continents," Monroe declared, ". . . are henceforth not to be considered as subjects for future colonization by any European powers." Furthermore, "we should consider any attempt on their part to extend their system to any portion of this hemisphere as dangerous to our peace and safety." And we should consider any "interposition" against the sovereignty of existing American nations as an unfriendly act. A second aspect of the President's pronouncement had to do with the relationship of the United States to Europe. "Our policy in regard to Europe," said Monroe, ". . . is not to interfere in the internal concerns of any of its powers."

Monroe and Adams were concerned about threats to American interests. They feared that France might attempt to retake the lost Spanish empire and threaten America's westward expansion. They feared British designs upon Cuba. And they feared that Russia, which owned Alaska, would attempt to control California, where American fur traders and whalers operated.

In issuing his challenge to Europe, Monroe had in mind the domestic situation as well as the international scene. At home the people were bogged down in a business depression, divided by sectional politics, and apathetic toward the rather lackluster administration of Monroe. In the rumors of European aggression against this hemisphere lay an opportunity for him to arouse and unite the people with an appeal to national pride.

Selected Readings

On the Confederation period and the movement for a stronger government, see the following: Merrill Jensen, *The New Nation: A History of the United States During the Confederation, 1781–1789*° (1950); G. S. Wood, *The Creation of the American Republic, 1776–1787* (1969); E. S. Morgan, *The Birth of the Republic, 1763–89*° (1956); and J. T. Main, *Political Parties Before the Constitution* (1972).

A general account of the Federalist regime is given in J. C. Miller, *The Federalist Era, 1789–1801*° (1960). The beginnings of the political parties are described in Joseph Charles, *The Origins of the American Party System*° (1956). Dealing with political rights and their repression is J. M. Smith, *Freedom's Fetters: The Alien and Sedition Laws and American Civil Liberties* (1956). Diplomacy is the subject of Alexander De Conde, *The Quasi-War: Politics and Diplomacy of the Undeclared War with France, 1797–1801* (1966), and Bradford Perkins, *The First Rapprochement: England and the United States, 1795–1805* (1955). On slavery during the Revolutionary period, see David Brion Davis, *The Problem of Slavery in the Age of Revolution, 1770–1823* (1975).

On the Jefferson administration, see Morton Borden, *Parties and Politics in the Early Republic, 1789–1815*° (1967); M. D. Peterson, *The Jeffersonian Image in the American Mind*° (1960); Adrienne Koch, *Jefferson and Madison: The Great Collaboration* (1950); and Dumas Malone, *Jefferson and His Time* (3 vols., 1948–1962).

The following deal with the second war with England: Bradford Perkins, *Prologue to War: England and the United States, 1805–1812* (1961), and Reginald Horsman, *The Causes of the War of 1812*° (1962). On the Monroe Doctrine, see Dexter Perkins, *The Monroe Doctrine, 1823–1826* (1927).

° Titles available in paperback.

Part Three
1823–1848

Sectionalism Contends with Nationalism as the Country Expands

Between the War of 1812 and the Civil War, Americans acquired a strong material basis for national unity. Capitalists, engineers, and laborers built canals and eventually railroads to link coastal cities with the interior, the East with the West, the North with the South. Telegraph lines connected all parts of the country. Merchants widened the scope of their activities until business came to be conducted on a scale more nearly nationwide than ever before. With the continued growth of industry, some workers began to show signs of self-consciousness as members of a distinct class, with common interests transcending those of their separate localities. The people as a whole, benefiting from the new developments in transportation, communication, and manufacturing, were able to raise their living standards while steadily increasing in numbers.

Despite the growth of a national marketplace, sectionalism — the rivalry of one part of the country against another — intensified. Even in colonial times there were three great areas (New England, the middle colonies, and the South) that developed characteristics different enough to set them apart as distinct sections. As the country grew after independence, the composition of the sections changed, and sectional feelings were intensified. By the 1840s three sections that could be distinguished were the Northeast, the Northwest, and the South. These were in the process of being reduced to two, the North and the South.

In each section a particular economic activity predominated, laying the basis for enhanced sec-

tionalism. In the Northeast, industry and overseas commerce prevailed; in the Northwest, most of the people were small farmers; in the South, where also the small farmers were the most numerous group, they yielded to the large planters, who exercised a controlling influence. In this section slavery persisted and, indeed, was expanding. Slavery provided the most striking difference between the South and the Northeast, where slavery had disappeared, and between the South and the Northwest, where the Northwest Ordinance had prohibited it from the beginning.

The rise of industry raised questions about the future of democracy itself. So it seemed to Alexis de Tocqueville, a twenty-six-year-old French nobleman who visited the United States in 1831–1832 and wrote a two-volume study of *Democracy in America* (1835–1840). Tocqueville feared that, with the continued growth of factories, there might eventually arise a large group of dependent workers and a small group of new aristocrats, an industrial plutocracy. For "at the very moment at which the science of manufactures lowers the class of workmen, it raises the class of masters." With this prospect of widening class differences, some Americans wondered about the wisdom of extending political rights to larger and larger numbers. President Andrew Jackson and his followers, however, generally encouraged the common man's participation in politics.

To most Americans, progress was a profound faith. However, many came to the conclusion that obstacles hindered the perfecting of society and humankind. There resulted a tumultuous and many-sided movement for social reform. From the reformers' point of view, one social evil came to stand out above all others. That was the plight of the Americans of African descent, most of whom were slaves and the rest of whom were less than wholly free. Eventually the reform drive concentrated its main force on a single goal, the elimination of slavery. The reform spirit — a "freedom's ferment" — had never stirred the South so much as it had the North, and with the development of an antislavery crusade white Southerners rallied to the defense of their "peculiar institution." Thus the nation began increasingly to divide on moral as well as economic and political grounds.

In the time of President James K. Polk the egalitarian spirit of Jacksonian Democracy broadened into a nationalistic demand for military conquest. Expansion was "Manifest Destiny," a phrase coined by a Democratic party journalist who, in 1845, prophesied "the fulfillment of our manifest destiny to overspread the continent allotted by Providence for the free development of our yearly multiplying millions." In other words, the United States had a divine mission to take the whole of North America, by force if necessary, and thus make room for its own rapidly growing people while carrying the blessings of democracy to less favored peoples who happened to occupy attractive lands nearby. Not all Americans agreed with that, nor did the expansionists themselves try to obtain the whole of the North American continent. Yet by 1848 the United States had expanded to the Pacific Coast, attaining essentially the size and shape that it still has (so far as the forty-eight contiguous states are concerned).

Expansionism rose from nationalism and would strengthen it after the Civil War. But the immediate result was to endanger national unity, for expansion provoked and aggravated sectional conflict.

Chapter 8

Toward a National Economy

Industrialization Emerges

Industrialization, or the growth of manufacturing activity relative to other forms of economic activity (particularly farming), was based on the introduction of new modes of industrial organization and technology.

In part, the new organization and technology came from England, where industrialization was beginning at the time the American Revolution occurred. The essence of industrialization was simply this: more rapidly and extensively than ever before, power-driven machines were taking the place of hand-operated tools. To tend the machines, workers were brought together in factories or mills located at the sources of power. New factory towns arose, with a new class of dependent laborers and another of mill owners or industrial capitalists. The new factory system was adapted most readily to the manufacture of cotton thread and cloth.

To protect England's superior position as a manufacturing nation, the British government tried to prevent the export of textile machinery and the emigration of skilled mechanics. Nevertheless, to take advantage of higher wages, a number of mechanics and millwrights made their way to the United States, the most important of them being Samuel Slater. In 1790, with the aid of American mechanics, Slater built a spinning mill for the Quaker merchant Moses Brown at Pawtucket, Rhode Island. Though a few inferior spinning mills already were in operation, Slater's work is generally considered as the beginning of the factory system in America.

In textiles and in some other manufactured goods the young republic did not measure up to England. Americans generally produced the coarser kinds of yarn and cloth, and though they supplied their own needs in common metalware, they still imported the finer grades of cutlery and other metal products. Yet in certain respects American industry was neither imitative nor inferior, and some American inventors and engineers were equal to the greatest in the world. They were especially advanced in techniques of mass production that saved labor and thus helped American manufacturers compete with the English, who could employ workers more cheaply.

Technology and industrial ingenuity prepared the way for future American industrial supremacy. The machine tools used in the factories of the Northeast, such as the turret lathe, the grinding machine, and the universal milling machine, were better than those in European factories. The principle of interchangeable parts, applied earlier in gun factories by Eli Whitney and Simeon North, was being introduced into other lines of manufacturing. Coal was replacing wood as an industrial fuel, particularly in the smelting of iron. Coal was also being used in increasing amounts to generate power in the steam engines that were replacing the water power that had driven most of the factory machinery in the Northeast. The production of coal, most of it mined in the Pittsburgh area of western Pennsylvania, leaped from 50,000 tons in 1820 to 14,000,000 tons in 1860.

The great technical advances in American industry owed much to American inventors. The

patent records reveal the growth of Yankee ingenuity. In 1830 the number of inventions patented
was 544; in 1850 the figure rose to 993; and in
1860 it stood at 4,778. In 1839 Charles Goodyear,
a New England hardware merchant, discovered a
method of vulcanizing rubber; his process had
been put to 500 uses by 1860, and the rubber industry was firmly established. In 1846 Elias Howe
of Massachusetts constructed a sewing machine,
upon which improvements were soon made by
Isaac Singer. The Howe-Singer machine was soon
employed in the manufacture of ready-to-wear
clothing. A little later, during the Civil War, it
would supply the Northern troops with uniforms.

In an earlier period, the dominant economic
figures in the Northeast had been the merchant
capitalists — the people who engaged in foreign
or domestic trade, who invested their surplus capital in banks, and who sometimes financed small-
scale domestic manufactures. By 1840 merchant
capitalism was in a state of decline, though the
merchant by no means disappeared. In such cities
as New York, Philadelphia, and Boston, there
were important and influential mercantile groups
that operated shipping lines to Southern ports —
carrying away cotton, rice, and sugar — or dispatched fleets of trading vessels to the ports of
Europe and the Orient. Many of these vessels
were the famous clippers, the most beautiful and
the fastest-sailing ships afloat. In their heyday
in the late 1840s and early 1850s, the clippers
were capable of averaging 300 miles a day, which
compared favorably with the best time then
being made by steamships. The value of American exports, almost entirely agricultural in
nature, increased from $124,000,000 in 1840 to
$334,000,000 in 1860.

Many business concerns were owned by one
person, by a family, or by partners. But, particularly in the textile industry, the corporation
spread rapidly as a form of organization. In their
overseas ventures, the merchants had been accustomed to diversifying their risks by buying shares
in a number of vessels and voyages. They employed the same device when they moved their
capital from trade to manufacturing, purchasing
shares in several textile companies.

Regardless of the forms of business organization, the industrial capitalists became the ruling
class, the aristocrats of the Northeast. As they

had sought and secured economic dominance,
they reached for and grasped political influence.
In politics, local or national, they liked to be
represented by highly literate lawyers who could
articulate their prejudices and philosophy. Their
ideal of a representative was Daniel Webster of
Massachusetts, whom the business people of the
section, at considerable financial cost to themselves, supported for years in the United States
Senate.

Transportation: Oceans and Roads

Before the full potential of the Industrial Revolution could be realized in the United States,
transportation had to be improved. What was
needed was a system of roads and waterways that
would connect all parts of the country and create
a market extensive enough to justify production
on a reasonably large scale. In the late eighteenth
and early nineteenth centuries, goods still moved
far more cheaply by water than by land. For the
Atlantic seaports, ocean commerce with other
continents was more easily carried on than overland trade with American settlements west of the
Appalachian range.

When, in 1785, the *Empress of China* returned
to New York from Canton, the ship brought back
a cargo of silk and tea, which yielded a fabulous
profit. Within five years Yankee ships were trading regularly with the Far East. Generally these
ships carried various manufactured goods around
Cape Horn to California, which the Spanish had
begun to settle during the 1760s and 1770s. There
New England merchants acquired hides and furs,
and with these proceeded on across the Pacific, to
barter them in China.

Not only in China but also in Europe and the
Near East enterprising Yankees from Salem and
other ports sought out every possible opportunity
for commerce. These Yankees were aided by two
acts of the new Congress (1789) giving preference
in tariff rates and port duties to home-owned
ships. American shipping was greatly stimulated
(despite the loss of ships and cargoes seized by the
belligerents) by the outbreak of European war in
the 1790s. Neutral Yankee vessels took over most
of the carrying trade between Europe and the European colonies in the Western Hemisphere. That

trade stimulated a period of vigorous urban growth that continued until the War of 1812. As early as 1793, the young republic had come to possess a merchant marine and a foreign trade larger than those of any other country except England.

Transportation and trade within the United States labored under handicaps, but improvements were steadily being made. In river transportation a new era began with the development of the steamboat. Oliver Evans' high-pressure engine, lighter and more efficient than James Watt's, made steam more feasible for powering boats as well as mill machinery and eventually the locomotive. The perfecting of the steamboat was chiefly the work of the inventor Robert Fulton and the promoter Robert R. Livingston. Their *Clermont*, equipped with paddle wheels and an English-built engine, voyaged up the Hudson in the summer of 1807, demonstrating the practicability of steam navigation even though taking 30 hours to go 150 miles.

Meanwhile, during the expansive 1790s, the turnpike era had begun. In 1792 a corporation constructed a toll road the sixty miles from Philadelphia to Lancaster, with a hard-packed surface of crushed rock. This venture proved so successful that similar turnpikes (so named from the kind of tollgate frequently used) were laid out from other cities to neighboring towns. Since the turnpikes were built and operated for private profit, construction costs had to be low enough and the prospective traffic heavy enough to assure an early and ample return. Therefore these roads, radiating from Eastern cities, ran for comparatively short distances and through rather thickly settled, highly productive, agricultural areas.

At the same time, private companies began to build a rudimentary road system, linking the Eastern seaboard states with the Ohio River Valley. Although these interregional roads were often little more than widened trails, they permitted large herds of cattle and hogs to pass eastward from the frontier, and by 1800 so much whiskey from Kentucky and Tennessee traveled these roads that it replaced rum as the national beverage. The profits from road construction, however, were too low to induce private parties to improve this simple system, and interest in public revenues increased. When Ohio was admitted as a state in 1803, the federal government agreed that part of the proceeds from the sale of public lands there should be used for building roads. In 1807 Jefferson's secretary of the treasury, Albert Gallatin, proposed that a national road, financed partly by Ohio land sales, be built from the Potomac to the Ohio. Construction began in 1811 but moved slowly until the War of 1812 demonstrated inadequacies in the nation's road system. After the war, building of the National Road accelerated, and by 1818 this highway, with a crushed-stone surface and massive stone bridges, was completed to Wheeling, Virginia (now West Virginia), on the Ohio River.

The Canal Age

Despite the road improvements of the turnpike era (1790–1830) Americans, as in colonial times, depended wherever possible on water routes for travel and transportation. The larger rivers, especially the Mississippi and the Ohio, became increasingly useful as steamboats grew in number and improved in design.

New waterways were needed, particularly to link Eastern cities with Northwestern farmers who had to rely upon poor East-West roads or the Mississippi for long-distance commerce. However, sectional jealousies and constitutional scruples stood in the way of action by the federal government, and necessary expenditures were too great for private enterprise. If extensive canals were to be dug, the job would be up to the various states.

New York was the first to act. It had the natural advantage of a comparatively level route between the Hudson River and Lake Erie, through the only break in the entire Appalachian chain. Yet the engineering tasks were imposing. The distance was more than 350 miles, and there were ridges to cross and a wilderness of woods and swamps to penetrate. The Erie Canal, begun in 1817 and completed in 1825, was by far the greatest construction job that Americans ever had undertaken. It quickly proved a financial success as well. The prosperity of the Erie encouraged the state to enlarge its canal system by building several branches.

The range of the New York canal system was

still further extended when the states of Ohio and Indiana, inspired by the success of the Erie Canal, provided water connections between Lake Erie and the Ohio River. These canals made it possible to ship or to travel by inland waterways all the way from New York to New Orleans, though several changes between canal, lake, and river craft would be necessary. By way of the Great Lakes it was possible to go by water from New York to Chicago. After the opening of the Erie Canal, shipping on the Great Lakes by sail and steam rapidly increased.

Before the canal age had reached its height, however, the era of the railroad was already beginning.

Railroads and the Telegraph

By 1804 both English and American inventors had experimented with steam engines for propelling land vehicles as well as boats. In 1820 John Stevens ran a locomotive and cars around a circular track on his New Jersey estate. Finally, in 1825, the Stockton and Darlington Railroad in England began to operate with steam power over a short length of track and to carry general traffic.

This news quickly aroused the interest of American business people, especially in those seaboard cities that sought better communications with the West. First to organize a railroad company was a group of New Yorkers, who in 1826 obtained a charter for the Mohawk and Hudson and five years later began running trains the sixteen miles between Schenectady and Albany. First to begin actual operations was the Baltimore and Ohio. The only living signer of the Declaration of Independence, Charles Carroll of Carrollton, dug a spadeful of earth in the ceremonies to start the work on July 4, 1828, and a thirteen-mile stretch opened for business in 1830. In that same year the Charleston and Hamburg ran trains over a segment of its track in South Carolina; when this line was completed, in 1833, it was the longest in the world (136 miles). By 1836 a total of more than 1,000 miles of track had been laid in eleven states.

From the outset railroads and canals were bitter competitors. For a time the Chesapeake and Ohio Canal Company blocked the advance of the Baltimore and Ohio Railroad through the narrow gorge of the upper Potomac, and the state of New York prohibited railroads from hauling freight in competition with the Erie Canal and its branches. These restrictions and the slow pace of railroad building meant that canals carried twice as much tonnage as railroads even as late as 1852. But railroads had the advantages of speed and year-round operation (canals closed down for the winter freeze) and could be located almost anywhere, regardless of terrain and the availability of water. These assets, combined with a slight price advantage, produced a victory for railroads during the 1850s. By the end of the decade, they took most of the nation's passenger traffic and carried more freight than the canals.

A new feature in railroad development — and one that would profoundly affect the nature of sectional alignments — was the trend toward the consolidation of short lines into trunk lines. By 1853 four roads had surmounted the Appalachian barrier to connect the Northeast with the Northwest. Chicago became the rail center of the country, served by 15 lines and over 100 trains daily. The appearance of the great trunk lines tended to divert traffic from the water routes — the Erie Canal and the Mississippi River. By lessening the dependence of the West upon the Mississippi, the railroads helped to weaken the connection between the Northwest and the South. By binding more closely the East and West, they prepared the way for a coalition of those sections.

The railroads obtained significant assistance from the federal government in the shape of public land grants. In 1850 Senator Stephen A. Douglas and other railroad-minded politicians persuaded Congress to grant lands to the state of Illinois to aid the Illinois Central, then building toward the Gulf of Mexico; Illinois was to transfer the land to the Central as it carried its construction forward. Other states and their railroad promoters demanded the same privileges, and by 1860 Congress had allotted over 30,000,000 acres to eleven states.

Accompanying the expansion of the railroad was the spread of the electromagnetic telegraph system. Together, they dramatically increased the speed with which information flowed. The telegraph became operational in 1844 when Samuel F. B. Morse transmitted from Washington to Bal-

Sources of Economic Growth

By the end of the nineteenth century, the annual per capita income (the fundamental measure of economic growth) in the United States was several times as large as it had been at the beginning of the century. Historians have generally agreed that industrialization was the central source but have disagreed as to the importance of other factors and as to the timing of economic growth.

In *The Rise of American Civilization* (1927), Charles and Mary Beard emphasized the influence of the Civil War and the accompanying government policies on industrialization. The Beards realized that by 1860 industry already rivaled agriculture in importance, but they thought that industrialization received a great boost from the Republican economic program. This interpretation was scarcely questioned until 1960, when Thomas C. Cochran, in his essay "Did the Civil War Retard Industrialization?" showed that the production of certain industrial commodities had increased at a lower rate during the Civil War decade than during either the preceding or the following decade.

By 1960 economic historians had begun to focus upon the prewar period because of newly developed data that clearly indicated that the most important acceleration in growth and industrialization occurred before the Civil War. The most influential of these historians, W. W. Rostow, in *The Stages of Economic Growth* (1960), found that the industrial "take-off" of the United States occurred during the 1840s. This, according to Rostow, was the time when the economy managed to reach a certain critical level of industrialization. The take-off resulted most importantly, Rostow believed, from the construction of railroads.

Many economic historians agreed with Rostow's concept of take-off but disagreed as to its precise timing and its sources. For example, Douglass C. North, in *The Economic Growth of the United States, 1790–1860* (1966), emphasized the 1830s and the agricultural sector, explaining the take-off in terms of the great increase in the exports of cotton. These exports, North argued, stimulated growth by generating income that Northern merchants who handled cotton exports could invest in manufacturing, and by promoting expansion of the agricultural sector that stimulated gains in agricultural productivity and growth in the size of the market for manufactured goods. Robert W. Fogel, on the other hand, in *Railroads and Economic Growth: Essays in Econometric History* (1964), stressed the contributions of canals and canal building and picked the 1820s as the locus of take-off. Others had their own candidates for crucial periods and leading sectors or industries.

None of the various interpretations has survived intact, although transportation innovations — in the form of turnpikes, canals, and railroads — and industrialization are commonly seen as central to the American growth process. Perhaps most important, the accumulated scholarship has eroded the concept of take-off. Economic historians now tend to see economic growth as a slow, incremental increase in per capita income, a result of the complex interaction of many elements in all sectors of the economy, agriculture as well as manufacturing, over a long period of time, beginning as early as the last half of the eighteenth century.

timore the message "What hath God wrought!" The Morse telegraph seemed, because of the relatively low cost of constructing wire systems, the ideal answer to the problems of long-distance communication. By 1860 more than 50,000 miles of wire connected most parts of the country, and a year later the Pacific telegraph, with 3,595 miles of wire, was open between New York and San Francisco. Nearly all of the independent lines had been absorbed into one organization, the Western Union Telegraph Company.

The development of the telegraph, together with the invention in 1846 of the rotary press (eliminating the need to move flat beds of type), allowed much speedier collection and distribution of news than ever before. In 1846 the Associated Press was organized for the purpose of cooperative news gathering by wire; no longer did publishers have to depend on exchanges of newspapers for out-of-town reports. Also with the advent of the telegraph and the railroad, the center of news transmission shifted from Washington to New York. Newspapers became more national in their coverage and began to record the most recent news, the happenings of the day. One result of this increased communication within the country was a feeding of the fires of sectional discord; the rapid reporting of detailed information regarding differences between the sections prompted people to anger more quickly and more often than otherwise would have been the case. But viewed in a longer perspective, the revolution in news was a unifying factor in American life. It provided the information network necessary for a genuinely national economy.

The Northeast: Farms and Labor

The story of agriculture in the Northeast after 1840 is largely one of dramatic transformation. The reason for the transformation is simple: the farmers of this section could not produce goods in competition with the new and richer soil of the Northwest. Eastern farmers turned to a system of production that aimed at a rude self-sufficiency or to the cultivation of products that would not suffer from Western competition.

Many went West and took up new farms or moved to mill towns and became laborers. As a result, the rural population in many parts of the Northeast continued to decline.

The centers of production shifted westward for wheat, corn, grapes, cattle, sheep, and hogs. In 1840 the leading wheat-growing states were New York, Pennsylvania, Ohio, and Virginia; in 1860 they were Illinois, Indiana, Wisconsin, Ohio, and Michigan. In the case of corn, Illinois, Ohio, and Missouri supplanted New York, Pennsylvania, and Virginia. In 1840 the most important cattle-raising areas in the country were New York, Pennsylvania, and New England, but by the 1850s the leading cattle states were Illinois, Indiana, Ohio, and Iowa in the West and Texas in the South.

In some lines of agriculture, the Northeast held its own or even surpassed the Northwest. As the Eastern urban centers increased in population, many farmers turned profitably to the task of supplying foods to the city masses, engaging in truck gardening (vegetables) or fruit raising. New York led all other states in apple production. Also stimulated by the rise of cities was dairy farming. The profits to be derived from supplying milk, butter, and cheese to local markets attracted many farmers in central New York, southeastern Pennsylvania, and various parts of New England. Approximately half of the dairy products of the country were produced in the East; the other half came from the West, with Ohio being the dairy center of that section. Partly because of the expansion of the dairy industry, the Northeast led other sections in the production of hay. New York was the leading hay state in the nation, and large crops were grown in Pennsylvania and New England. The Northeast also exceeded other areas in producing potatoes.

Most of the workers in Northeastern factories during the decade of the 1840s came from the native population of the section — from the farming classes that were being pinched off the land by Western competition. Almost half of the laborers were women and children, and in some industries, notably textiles, the percentage was much higher. The rural people who flocked to the mill towns in the hope of finding a better life earned more income than they could have in the countryside but often found their living and working conditions worse than those back on the farms. Most mill towns were cheerless, ugly places in which to live, and most factories were unsanitary, unhealthful places in which to work. The average workday was no longer than it had been on the farm, twelve to fourteen hours, but the work, especially in the mills, was more routine and exhausting. In response to the needs of industry a considerable class of wage earners finally began to form. Its members came mostly from the marginal farms of the East (those farms unable to compete with the fertile fields of the West) and, somewhat later, from the British Isles and Europe.

In the textile mills, two different methods of labor recruitment were used. One of these, which prevailed in the middle states and parts of New England, brought whole families to the mill. Father, mother, and children, even those no more than four or five years old, worked together in tending the looms. The second, the Waltham or Lowell system, which was common in Massachusetts, enlisted young women in their late teens and early twenties. These unmarried girls went from farms to factories to work for only a few years and then returned with their savings. They did not form a permanent working class.

Much worse off were the construction gangs that performed the heavy, unskilled work on turnpikes, railroads, and canals. A large and growing number of these men were Irish immigrants. They received low pay and, since their work was seasonal and uncertain, did not make enough in a year to maintain a family at what was generally considered a decent living standard; many of them lived in the most unhealthful of shanties. After about 1840, Irish men and women began to be employed in textile mills. As these newcomers replaced the native farm girls, working conditions deteriorated somewhat. Piece rates were paid instead of a daily wage; these and other devices were used to speed up production and to employ the labor force more efficiently.

Neither ditchdiggers nor mill hands, however, were the first to organize and act collectively to improve the conditions of their work. Skilled artisans formed the earliest labor unions and arranged the first strikes (shortly before 1800). From the 1790s on, the printers and cordwainers took

the lead. The cordwainers — makers of high-quality boots and shoes, each person fashioning the entire product — suffered from the competition of manufacturers who put out work to be performed in separate tasks. These artisans sensed a loss of security and status with the development of mass-production methods, and so did members of other skilled trades, such as carpenters, joiners, masons, plasterers, hatters, and shipbuilders. In cities like Philadelphia, Baltimore, Boston, and New York, the skilled workers of each craft formed societies for mutual aid. During the 1820s and 1830s the craft societies began to combine on a city-wide basis and set up central organizations known as trade unions. Since, with the widening of the market, workers of one city competed with those at a distance, the next step was to federate the trade unions or to establish craft unions of national scope. In 1834 delegates from six cities founded the National Trades' Union, and in 1836 the printers and the cordwainers set up their own national craft unions.

This labor movement soon collapsed. Labor leaders struggled against the handicap of hostile laws and hostile courts. By the common law, as interpreted by judges in the industrial states, a combination among workers was viewed as, in itself, an illegal conspiracy. But adverse court decisions did not halt, though they handicapped, the rising unions. The death blow came from the Panic of 1837 and the ensuing depression, but the most serious flaw in this first labor movement was its reliance on workers whose skills were obsolete.

During the 1840s the factory labor supply of the Northeast was augmented by immigrants from Europe. The immigrant flood helped to delay the development of the labor organizations that had experienced a vigorous growth in the 1830s but had been hard hit by the depression after 1837. Generally the newcomers were willing to work for less than the wages demanded by native workers. Labor never recovered, before 1860, the ground it had lost in the lean depression years. By the 1850s several national craft unions had been formed by such groups as machinists, hat workers, printers, molders, stonecutters, and a few others. But these were organizations of skilled workers, representing only a tiny minority of labor and manifesting almost no class awareness. The mass of laborers remained unorganized.

The Northwest

There was some industry in the Northwest, more than in the South, and in the two decades before the Civil War the section experienced a steady industrial growth. Along the southern shore of Lake Erie was a flourishing industrial and commercial area of which Cleveland was the center. Another manufacturing locality was in the Ohio River Valley, with the meat-packing city of Cincinnati as its nucleus. Farther west, the rising city of Chicago, destined to be the great metropolis of the section, was emerging as the national center of the agricultural machinery and meat-packing industries. The most important industrial products of the West were farm machines, flour, meats, distilled whiskey, and leather and wooden goods.

But the West predominantly was a land of family farms and small farmers. The average size of Western farms was 200 acres, and the great majority of the farmers owned their own land.

In concentrating on corn, wheat, cattle, sheep, and hogs, the Western farmer was motivated by sound economic reasons. As the Northeast became more industrial and urban, it enlarged the domestic market for farm goods. At the same time England and certain European nations, undergoing the same process, started to import larger amounts of food. This steadily increasing worldwide demand for farm products resulted in steadily rising farm prices. For the farmers, the 1840s and early 1850s were years of prosperity.

The expansion of agricultural markets had profound effects on sectional alignments in the United States. Of the Northwest's total output, by far the greatest part was disposed of in the Northeast; only the surplus remaining after domestic needs were satisfied was exported abroad. The new well-being of Western farmers, then, was in part sustained by Eastern purchasing power. Eastern industry, in turn, found an augmenting market for its products in the prospering West. Between the two sections a fundamental economic relationship that was profitable to both was being forged.

To meet the increasing demands for its products, the Northwest had to enlarge its productive capacities. The presence of large blocks of still unoccupied land made it possible to enlarge the area under cultivation during the 1840s. By 1850 the growing Western population had settled the prairie regions east of the Mississippi and was pushing beyond the river. Of greatest importance were the improvements that Americans continued to introduce in farm machines and tools. During the 1840s more efficient grain drills, harrows, mowers, and hay rakes were placed in wide use. The cast-iron plow, devised earlier, continued to be popular because its parts could be replaced when broken. An even better implement appeared in 1847, when John Deere established at Moline, Illinois, a factory to manufacture plows with steel moldboards, which were more durable than those made of iron and were also self-scouring.

Two new machines heralded a coming revolution in grain production. The most important was the automatic reaper, invented by Cyrus H. McCormick of Virginia. The reaper, taking the place of sickle, cradle, and hand labor, enabled a crew of six or seven men to harvest in a day as much wheat (or any other small grain) as fifteen men could harvest using the older methods. McCormick, who had patented his device in 1834, established in 1847 a factory at Chicago, in the heart of the grain belt. By 1850 he was turning out 3,000 reapers a year; by 1860 more than 100,000 were in use on Western farms.

The Northwest was the most democratic of the three sections in the sense that the farmers, the majority, were the dominant economic class and generally had their way in politics. Theirs was a capitalistic, property-conscious, middle-class kind of democracy. Abraham Lincoln, an Illinois politician, voiced the economic opinions of many of the people of his section. "I take it that it is best for all to leave each man free to acquire property as fast as he can," said Lincoln. "Some will get wealthy. I don't believe in a law to prevent a man from getting rich; it would do more harm than good. . . . When one starts poor, as most do in the race of life, free society is such that he knows he can better his condition: he knows that there is no fixed condition of labor for his whole life."

The democratic conservatism of the West was apparent in the economic program it advocated in national politics: internal improvements, cheap or preferably free lands, and territorial expansion.

King Cotton's Country

The Southern agricultural system was organized around the great staples: tobacco, rice, sugar, and above all cotton. These were the section's money crops, but they did not constitute by any means its only forms of agricultural effort. What might be termed general or diversified farming was carried on in many areas, notably in the Shenandoah Valley of Virginia and the Bluegrass Region of central Kentucky. Most planters aimed to produce on the plantation the foodstuffs needed by the family and the slaves. On some large plantations, more acres were planted in corn than in cotton, and in 1850 half the corn crop of the country was raised in the South. The section produced 87 percent of the nation's hemp supply (in Kentucky and Missouri) and 80 percent of its peas and beans. Other important products of Southern husbandry were apples, peaches, peanuts, sweet potatoes, hogs, and mules.

But the staples dominated the economic life of the section and absorbed the attention of the majority of the people. Climatic and geographic conditions dictated the areas where each was produced. Tobacco, which needed only a fairly short growing season (six months), was grown in tidewater Maryland west of the Chesapeake, in the foothills of Virginia and adjacent North Carolina, in northern and western Kentucky, in northwestern Tennessee, and in the Missouri River Valley of Missouri. Rice demanded a growing season of nine months and irrigation, and hence was restricted to the coastal region of South Carolina and Georgia. Sugar, with a similar period necessary for maturation, was concentrated in southern Louisiana and a small area in eastern Texas (around Galveston). Cotton, which required

a growing season of seven to nine months and could be produced in a variety of soil formations, occupied the largest zone of production. The cotton kingdom stretched from North Carolina to Texas.

The production of cotton had been expanding since the invention of the cotton gin in 1793. The earlier expansion of the textile industry in England had created a tremendous demand for cotton, but the only cotton that could be grown in the Southern interior required excessive labor to separate the seeds fron the cotton. With the gin, one slave could clean cotton as fast as several could by hand. Soon the gin enabled cotton production to spread into the upland South and meet the needs of textile producers. By 1830 Southern production had reached 1,000,000 bales and increased to 4,000,000 bales in 1860. In that year Southern cotton brought $191,000,000 in European markets and constituted almost two-thirds of the total export trade of the United States. (By way of contrast, the annual value of the rice crop was $2,000,000.) No wonder Southerners said smugly, "Cotton is king."

As cotton culture expanded, the centers of production moved westward into the fresher lands of Alabama, Mississippi, Arkansas, Louisiana, and Texas. The extension of the cotton kingdom into this area bore certain resemblances to the rush of gold seekers into a new frontier. The prospect of tremendous profits drew settlers by the thousands. Some who came were wealthy planters from the older states who transferred their assets and slaves to a cotton plantation. Most were small slaveholders or slaveless farmers who intended to become planters.

On the whole, the planters made profits that compared very favorably with those earned elsewhere in the economy. Indeed, at least in the short run, the preoccupation with the production of staples in such high demand was the most effective way for Southern planters to maximize their profits. (However, there can be little doubt that the concentration on cotton production and the heavy reliance on slave labor retarded Southern development in the long run.) As a consequence of the high profits earned from cotton production, the largest planters were among the nation's wealthiest men.

Three Southern families in four owned no slaves. These farmers, and those who owned only a few slaves, lived lives of rude plenty, devoting more attention to subsistence farming than did the planters. Most of them owned their land. During the 1850s the number of nonslaveholding landowners increased much faster than the number of slaveholding landowners.

The comparatively few wealthy planters represented the social ideal of the South. Enriched by vast annual incomes, dwelling in palatial homes, surrounded by broad acres and many black servants, they were the class to which all others paid a certain deference. Enabled by their wealth to practice the leisured arts, they cultivated gracious living, good manners, learning, and politics. Their social pattern determined to a considerable degree the tone of all Southern society.

The Southern planters constituted the closest approach to an aristocracy to be found in the United States. They enjoyed in their section a higher social position, a greater political power, a more unquestioned leadership than did the factory owners of the Northeast.

Class distinctions were more sharply drawn in the South than in other sections. Some Southerners spoke scornfully of democracy. Yet, particularly in the newer states, an ambitious person might move from one class to another. Farmers nursed the hope of becoming small slaveholders, and small planters aimed to become large ones. In fact, the great majority of the cotton lords of the Mississippi Valley states had come from the ranks of the obscure and the ordinary. Planters who wished to exercise political influence, whether or not they believed in majority rule, had to affect democratic manners and mouth principles that would please the multitudes.

In Southern society the business classes — the manufacturers and merchants — were of considerable importance, though comparatively few in numbers. Flour milling and textile and iron manufacturing were the main Southern industries, with the principal mill areas being located in Virginia, the Carolinas, and Georgia. The Tredegar Iron Works in Richmond compared favorably with the best iron mills in the Northeast. The value of Southern textile goods increased from $1,500,000 in 1840 to $4,500,000 in 1860. Despite some promising beginnings, however, Southern industry before 1860 remained largely in a formative stage.

More important than the budding manufacturers were the merchants, particularly the brokers or factors who marketed the planters' crops. These individuals, in such towns as New Orleans, Charleston, Mobile, and Savannah, acted as selling agents for the planters, and sometimes also as purchasing agents. Frequently the broker became a banker to the planter, furnishing money or goods on credit. In such cases the planter might be in debt to his factor for a long period, during which time he would have to consign his entire crop to the broker. The merchant-broker, dominating as he did the credit facilities of the rural South, was in a position to exert great economic pressure on the planter.

Closely linked economically with the planters were the professional classes — lawyers, editors, doctors, and others. Because their well-being largely depended on planter prosperity, the professional groups usually agreed with and voiced the ideals of the dominant class.

In the Southern mountains — the Appalachian ranges east of the Mississippi and the Ozarks west of the river — lived the Southern highlanders, the white groups set most apart from the mainstream of Southern life. These mountaineers practiced a crude form of subsistence agriculture, with practically no slaves. They had a proud sense of seclusion, and they held to old ways and old ideals, which included the ideal of loyalty to the nation as a whole. The mountain region was the only part of the South that defied the trend toward sectional conformity.

Occupying the lowest position in Southern white society was that tragic and degraded class known as poor whites, who in 1850 totaled perhaps half a million. The poor whites were distinct from the ordinary farmers and from the highlanders. The "crackers," "sand hillers," or "white trash" occupied the infertile lands of the pine barrens, the red hills, and the swamps. Here they lived in miserable cabins surrounded by almost unbelievable squalor. Their degradation resulted partly from dietary deficiencies and disease. Afflicted by pellagra, hookworm, and malaria, the poor whites resorted to eating clay, a practice which in itself indicated a serious shortcoming in their diet.

The "Peculiar Institution"

Slavery was an institution established by law and regulated in detail by law. The slave codes of the Southern states forbade slaves to hold property, to leave their masters' premises without permission, to be out after dark, to congregate with other slaves except at church, to carry firearms, to strike whites even in self-defense. The codes prohibited teaching slaves to read or write and denied the right of slaves to testify in court against whites. They contained no provisions to legalize slave marriages or divorces. Any person showing a strain of African ancestry was presumed to be a slave unless he or she could prove otherwise. If an owner killed a slave while punishing the individual, the act was not considered a crime.

The routine of plantation life was governed by a system of rules created by custom and the planters. Small planters directly supervised the work on their places. Medium or large planters hired overseers and perhaps assistant overseers to represent them. The "head drivers," trusted and responsible slaves, acted under the overseers as foremen. Under each one might be several subdrivers. Two methods or systems of assigning slave labor were employed. One was the task system, most widely used in rice culture. Here a slave was allotted a particular task in the morning, say to hoe one acre; when the job was complete the slave was free for the rest of the day. The other was the gang system, employed on the cotton, sugar, and tobacco plantations. Here the slaves were simply divided into groups, each of which was directed by a driver, and were worked for as many hours as the overseer considered a reasonable workday.

Slaves were provided with at least enough necessities to enable them to live and work. They were furnished with an adequate if rough diet, consisting mainly of corn meal, salt pork, and molasses. Many were allowed to raise gardens for their own use and were issued fresh meats on special occasions. They received issues of cheap clothes and shoes. They lived in rude cabins, called the slave quarters. Slaves worked hard, beginning with light tasks as children; and their workday was longest at harvest time. They sometimes had time off to hunt and fish, and they attended the church services and some of the social festivities of their white families.

The closing of the transatlantic slave trade in 1808 had put slaves in short supply, and the master consequently had an economic interest in taking reasonably good care of his slaves. The master was likely to use hired labor, when available, for the most unhealthful or dangerous tasks. A traveler in Louisiana noted, for example, that Irishmen were employed to clear malarial swamps and to handle cotton bales at the bottom of chutes extending from the river bluff down to a boat landing. If an Irishman died of disease or was killed in an accident, the master could hire another for a dollar a day or less. But he would be out perhaps $1,000 or more if he lost a prime field hand. Still, a cruel master might forget his pocketbook in the heat of momentary anger. And slaves were often left to the discipline of an overseer, who had no pecuniary stake in their well-being; he was paid in proportion to the amount of work he could get out of them.

Slavery in the cities differed significantly from slavery in the country. On the more or less isolated plantation the slaves were kept apart from free blacks and lower-class whites. The master, his family, and his overseers maintained a fairly direct and effective control. A deep and unbridgeable chasm yawned between slavery and freedom. In the city, however, the master often could not supervise his slaves closely and at the same time use them profitably. Even if they slept at night in carefully watched backyard barracks, they went about by day on errands of various kinds. Others were hired out, and after hours they fended for themselves, with neither the owner nor the employer looking after them. Thus the urban slaves gained numerous opportunities to mingle with free blacks and with whites. A line between slavery and freedom remained, but it became less and less distinct.

Indeed, slavery was basically incompatible with city life, and as Southern cities grew, the number of slaves in them dropped, relatively if not absolutely. Fearing conspiracies and insurrections, urban slaveowners sold off much of their male property to the countryside, where slaveowners could, in fact, control slaves more easily. The cities were left with an excess of black women while continuing to have an excess of white men (a circumstance that helped to account for the birth of many mulattoes). While slavery in the cities declined, segregation of blacks both free and slave increased. Segregation was a means of social control intended to make up for the loosening of the discipline of slavery itself.

The transfer of slaves from one part of the South to another (when the slaves were not carried by their migrating owners) was accomplished through the medium of professional slave traders. In long-distance traffic the slaves were moved on trains or on river or ocean steamers. Or they were moved on foot, trudging in coffles of hundreds along the dusty highways. Eventually they arrived at some central market such as Natchez, New Orleans, Mobile, or Galveston, where purchasers collected to bid for them. At the auction the bidders checked the slaves like livestock, watching them as they were made to walk or trot, inspecting their teeth, feeling their arms and legs, looking for signs of infirmity or age. It paid to be careful, for traders were known to deceive buyers by blacking gray hair, oiling withered skin, and concealing physical defects in other ways. A sound, young field hand would fetch a price that, during the 1840s and 1850s, varied from $500 to $1,700, depending mainly on fluctuations in the price of cotton. The average figure was about $800. A good-looking "fancy girl," desirable as a concubine, might bring several times that much.

The domestic slave trade dehumanized all who were involved in it. It separated children from parents, and parents from one another. Even in the case of a kindly master who had kept families together, they might be broken up in the division of the estate after the master's death. Planters condoned the trade and eased their consciences by holding the traders in contempt and assigning them a low social position.

The Population

The dynamic industrial economy and the highly expansive agricultural sector shaped the nature of the population. The most distinctive feature of the population was its dynamic growth and, as in the colonial period, the primary source of growth was natural increase — the excess of births over deaths. Responding to rising incomes, increasing industrial employment, and abundant land, Americans continued to multiply almost as fast as in the colonial period. The population still doubled every twenty-five years or so, even though the nation's birth rate began to decline by 1810. The total figure, lower than 4,000,000 in 1790, rose to about 17,000,000 in 1840, and then, fueled by accelerating immigration, to more than 31,000,000 in 1860. The United States was growing much more rapidly in population than the British Isles or Europe: by 1860 it had gone ahead of the United Kingdom and had nearly overtaken Germany and France.

With its more fertile, abundant land, the West (including both Northwest and Southwest) continued to grow much more rapidly than the rest of the country. By 1830 more than a fourth of the American people lived to the west of the Appalachians; by 1850, nearly a half. Some of the seaboard states suffered serious losses of manpower and womanpower, not to mention the personal property that departing migrants took away. Year after year the Carolinas gave up nearly as much in human resources as they gained by natural increase; their populations remained almost stationary. The same was true of Vermont and New Hampshire. Many a village in these two states was completely depopulated, its houses and barns left to rot, as its people scattered over the country in search of an easier life than the granite hills afforded.

Not all the migrating villagers and farmers sought the unsettled frontier; some moved instead to the centers of economic opportunity: increasingly crowded cities. Urban places (considered as communities of 2,500 or more) grew faster than the nation as a whole, and in the 1820s their growth rate was accelerated. While the vast majority of Americans continued to reside in the open country or in small towns, the number of city dwellers increased remarkably. In 1790 one person in twenty lived in a community of 2,500 or more; in 1840, one in ten.

The rise of New York City was phenomenal. By 1810 it had surpassed Philadelphia, which earlier had replaced Boston as the largest city in America. New York steadily increased its lead in both population and trade. Its growth was based on the possession of a superior natural harbor and on several historical developments after the War of 1812. After the war the British chose New York as the chief place to "dump" their manufactured goods and thus helped make it an import center. State laws, which were liberal with regard to auction sales, encouraged inland merchants to do their buying in New York. The first packet line, with regularly scheduled monthly sailings between England and the United States, made New York its American terminus (1816) and hence a more important center of overseas commerce than ever. The Erie Canal (completed in 1825) gave the city unrivaled access to the interior. And New York's sheer size and concentration of population gave it advantages as a commercial center.

Immigration accounted for little of the population growth before the 1840s. Then the floodgates opened. From 1840 to 1850 over 1,500,000 Europeans moved to America; in the last years of the decade the average number arriving yearly was almost 300,000. Of the 23,000,000 people in the United States in 1850, 2,210,000 were foreign-born; of these almost 1,000,000 were Irish and over 500,000 were German. Special reasons explained the prevalence of immigrants from Ireland and Germany: widespread unemployment produced by the dislocations of the Industrial Revolution; famines resulting from the failure of the potato and other crops; dislike of English rule by the Irish; and the collapse of the liberal revolutions of 1848 in Germany. The great majority of the Irish settled in the Eastern cities, where they swelled the ranks of unskilled labor. But they never outnumbered the native-born in the labor population of Eastern cities. Most of the Germans, having a little more money than the Irish, who had practically none, moved on to the Northwest, where they tended to become farmers or went into business in the Western towns.

The number of immigrants who came in the fifties exceeded even that of the previous decade, reaching an estimated aggregate of over 2,500,000. As before, the overwhelming majority of the newcomers hailed from Ireland and Germany. Other nationalities represented in the immigrant tide were the English, the French, Italians, Scandinavians, Poles, and Hollanders. Most of the foreigners collected in the urban centers of the Northern states.

Few immigrants settled in the South. Only 500,000 lived in the slave states in 1860, and a third of these were concentrated in Missouri; of the Southern cities, only New Orleans contained a large number of foreign-born residents. Immigrants avoided the South partly because of the climate, partly because most of them were opposed to slavery or feared the competition of slave labor, and also because the bulk of them landed at Northern ports and from these points gravitated easily to areas in the North that attracted them.

Chapter 9

Freedom's Ferment

Democracy and Civilization

Having won political independence, many Americans promoted cultural independence. The Connecticut schoolmaster and lawyer Noah Webster, for example, contended that the American schoolboy should be educated as a patriot. "As soon as he opens his lips," Webster wrote, "he should rehearse the history of his own country; he should lisp the praise of liberty, and of those illustrious heroes and statesmen who have wrought a revolution in her favor."

To foster a distinctive culture and unify the nation, Webster insisted upon a simplified and Americanized spelling — "honor" instead of "honour," for example. His *American Spelling Book* (1783), commonly known as the "blue-backed speller," eventually sold over 100,000,000 copies. Webster also wrote grammars and other schoolbooks. His school dictionary (1806) was republished in many editions and eventually was much enlarged to form *An American Dictionary of the English Language* (1828). By means of his speller and his dictionary he succeeded in establishing a national standard of words and usages for the United States.

In their first constitutions, several of the states endorsed the principle of public education, but none actually required the establishment of free schools. A Massachusetts law of 1789 reaffirmed the colonial laws providing for the support of schools by the various towns. But the enforcement of the law was lax in many places. Even in Boston only seven public schools existed in 1790, and most of these were poorly housed; more than twice as many private schools were in operation.

At the outbreak of the Revolution there had been a total of nine colleges in all the colonies; in 1800 there were twenty-two in the various states, and the number continued steadily to increase thereafter. Whereas all but two of the colonial colleges were sectarian in origin and spirit, a majority of those founded during the first three decades of independence were nondenominational. Especially significant in foreshadowing the future pattern of higher education was the fact that five were state institutions: the universities of Georgia (1785), North Carolina (1789), Vermont (1791), Ohio (1804), and South Carolina (1805).

During the first decades of independence, the most widely read American writings — and some of the greatest ones (such as *The Federalist*) — were polemical and political, not esthetic. In pamphlets and newspapers, Americans followed the arguments about British colonial policy, the aims of the Revolution, the question of a new Constitution, and the party contests of the young republic. The literate American became a "news-paper-reading animal," as an English visitor observed. This preoccupation with the news of the day drew attention away from literature of a more artistic and permanent kind. Consequently, colonial attitudes persisted in America as far as literature was concerned. Seldom was an American author appreciated at home until he or she had been praised by critics abroad, and sometimes not even then. Despite the rise of book publishing in several American cities, especially in New York, the great majority of books published and sold were written, as before, by English authors. The romantic novels of Charles Dickens and Sir Walter Scott were as much the rage in the United States as in the British Isles.

In 1837 Ralph Waldo Emerson, in his Phi Beta Kappa address at Harvard, declared American literary independence. He called for a literature of democracy and called upon American writers to celebrate the individual. He urged them to abandon European themes and to attend to the everyday lives and potential of Americans. What followed was a golden age of American literature. James Fenimore Cooper emphasized the nobility, innocence, and strength of frontier Americans. Henry David Thoreau proclaimed that individuals could achieve fulfillment without relying upon the trappings of civilized society. In his poetry, Walt Whitman embraced the potential of American democracy, celebrating the humanity and strength of all its members. Less optimistic were Nathaniel Hawthorne and Herman Melville, who dwelt on the vanities, corruption, and excesses of untrammeled individualism. And, a group of women novelists treated social issues with a concern for the situation of women. Like Hawthorne and Melville, they complained about excessive individualism but advocated their own solution: affirmation of a special role for women as moral reformers. About a dozen women novelists, including Catharine Maria Sedgwick and Harriet Beecher Stowe, gained great popularity, reaching mass audiences with more success than any of the leading men authors.

Spirit of Social Reform

"In no country in the world has the principle of association been more successfully used, or more unsparingly applied to a multitude of different objects, than in America," Tocqueville observed. "Societies are formed to resist enemies which are exclusively of a moral nature, and to diminish the vice of intemperance: in the United States associations are established to promote public order, commerce, industry, morality, and religion; for there is no end which the human will, seconded by the collective exertions of individuals, despairs of attaining."

This reform spirit derived from a variety of sources, religious and rational, domestic and foreign. The Christian doctrine of human worth, the Revolutionary philosophy of the equality of

man — these were part of the general background. More immediately, the rise of industrialism in the British Isles and Western Europe as well as the United States produced social dislocations and suffering but at the same time gave promise of a more abundant life for all. No doubt, with some people, a determination to improve human welfare was stimulated by the contrast between what actually was and what apparently might be. The humanitarian stirrings of the time were to be found in many lands at once, and most conspicuously in those countries that were being most rapidly industrialized.

Contributing to reformism were the religious movements of the day. On one extreme of these movements was the growing interest in deism, the rational religion of Enlightenment philosophers, especially those in France. The deists believed in God but considered Him a rather remote being who had created the universe, not an intimate presence who was concerned with human individuals and their sins. Franklin, Jefferson, and others among the founders had held deistic views. Such views, at first confined to the well educated, spread, and by 1800 books and articles attacking religious "superstitions" found eager readers all over the country.

The popularity of such views fed the development in New England of Universalist and Unitarian doctrines. Increasingly, Congregationalists rejected not only the idea of predestination but also the idea of the Trinity, and split from established churches to found their own congregations. The Unitarian emphasis on universal salvation — the availability of salvation to all — and on the bonds that unite all humans energized the reform spirit both directly and indirectly through the transcendental movement initiated by Ralph Waldo Emerson. Emerson evolved the doctrine of the Oversoul, or spiritual essence from which all things derived, including the soul of human beings. Since all humanity shared in this essential Being, this all-in-all, there existed a very real kinship among all. And since the Oversoul was good, there could be no such thing, in the last analysis, as evil. This philosophy, for all its obscurities and inconsistencies, had practical consequences for its believers. It made them optimistic. It taught them that they were potentially divine and could increase their divinity by identifying themselves more and more fully with the Oversoul, with

Being, with Truth. It led them to believe in the perfectibility of humankind.

Outside New England, the far more emotional movements of religious revivalism also became a powerful force in reform. Beginning at the turn of the century and extending through the 1850s, during what became known as the Second Awakening, waves of evangelical Protestantism swept across much of the nation. Presbyterians, Methodists, and Baptists gained many converts, in part through the camp meeting, an outdoor revival that lasted several days. Crowds of sinners as well as salvation seekers attended these open-air get-togethers, and the atmosphere sometimes was far from churchlike. But many evangelical leaders came to frown on the camp meeting, deploring in particular the worst outbreaks of frenzy, when men and women had fits, rolled in the dust, and lay twitching with the "holy jerks." And, in fact, the success of evangelical Protestantism was based on much more than camp meetings. Americans of diverse class and section found deeply appealing the evangelical vision that Christianity and political democracy were joined in a common enterprise of elevation and purification. And invocation of this vision became an important part of the call to reform.

Particularly influential on behalf of reform were the preachings of Charles G. Finney, who was first a Presbyterian and later a Congregationalist. From 1825 through the early 1830s, Finney began a series of revivals along the route of the newly constructed Erie Canal. Emphasizing the possibilities of individual salvation through good works as well as faith and believing that revivals were necessary to preserve the spirit of American democracy, Finney maintained that "the church must take the right ground on the subject of Temperance, and Moral Reform, and all the subjects of practical morality which come up for decision from time to time."

The reform spirit cannot be viewed as an outgrowth of the labor movement, except in certain cases, notably the drive for free public schools. Most reform leaders disbelieved in unions, opposed strikes, and were indifferent to the plight of the unemployed. William Lloyd Garrison, the abolitionist, denounced labor agitators for trying "to inflame the minds of our working classes against the more opulent, and to persuade men that they

are contemned and oppressed by a wealthy aristocracy." A few of the "more opulent," such as the merchants Arthur and Lewis Tappan of New York and Amos and Abbott Lawrence of Boston, contributed vast sums to finance various reforms. Reform, however, was essentially a middle-class movement, receiving its greatest support from the reasonably well-to-do farmers, shopkeepers, and professional people of the Northeast and the Northwest.

Advancing Education

As of 1830 no state could yet boast a general system of free public education in the modern sense — with full tax support, compulsory attendance, and enforced maintenance of schools — though Massachusetts, as in earlier times, came fairly close to it. A very high proportion of American children had the benefit of the three R's, but most of them still got their learning from church schools, other private schools, private tutors, or members of their own families.

Then, during the 1830s, a widespread demand for state-supported primary education arose. This demand came from reformers who feared the consequences of allowing every man to vote, including in many cases even the newly arrived immigrant, without making public provision for his literacy at least. The demand came also from workers who hoped that book learning would enable their children to rise in the world. Opposition was forthcoming, however, from taxpayers (especially childless ones) who objected to paying for the education of other people's families, and from Lutherans, Roman Catholics, and other religious groups, who already supported their own church schools and did not wish to be taxed for public education besides.

Educational reformers made considerable headway against such opposition in several of the states. The greatest of these leaders was Horace Mann, the first secretary of the Massachusetts Board of Education, which was established in 1837. He reorganized the state's school system, lengthened the school year (to six months), doubled teachers' salaries, enriched the curriculum, improved teacher training and teaching methods, and promoted the employment of young women,

arguing that they were well educated and required only modest salaries.

By the 1850s the principle of tax-supported
elementary schools was accepted in all the states,
and all of them were making at least a start toward putting the principle into practice. Still,
there were vast differences in the quantity and
quality of public schools from place to place, the
poorest performances and the lowest literacy
rates being found in the newly settled areas of the
West and in the more sparsely populated parts of
the South. In the country as a whole, only a small
proportion of children of school age were actually
going to school — one white child out of every
seven in the South and one out of every six elsewhere (1860). American society as a whole did not
significantly increase the share of its resources devoted to education until the 1880s.

Most teachers were poorly paid and poorly
prepared, and many of them were scarcely able to
read, write, and cipher. In rural district schools,
containing husky youths along with tender tots,
what the schoolmaster needed was a strong arm
rather than a well-stocked mind. Under the circumstances the majority of teaching positions
continued to be filled by men, even in the elementary schools. Seldom did these men look upon
teaching as a career; often they were aspiring
lawyers or preachers who worked their way
through college by doubling as schoolmasters in
vacation periods. Nevertheless, teaching was beginning to be looked upon as a profession, and an
increasing number of young women were going
into it. With Mann taking the lead, Massachusetts, in 1839, established the first American
state-supported teacher-training, or "normal,"
school at Lexington. In 1845 he organized a state
association of teachers.

Since so many teachers were poorly prepared,
both they and their pupils had to rely heavily
upon textbooks. Noah Webster's spellers and
grammars continued to be widely used. Supplementing them and rivaling them in popularity
were the six graded *Eclectic Readers* (1835–1857)
prepared by William Holmes McGuffey, who was
an Ohio professor and college president and then
for many years a professor at the University of
Virginia. The McGuffey readers were filled with
moral lessons, patriotic declamations, sentimental
verse, and fascinating facts. Eventually adopted

in thirty-seven states, the McGuffey books gave
thousands of schoolchildren a shared background
of popular culture and helped to mold the literary
tastes of the reading public.

Private colleges multiplied, about eighty being
founded between 1830 and 1850. Almost all of
these were denominational colleges, with close
church connections, and their chief though not
their only purpose was to prepare a learned
clergy. Their enrollments were small, in many
cases fewer than 100 in the 1850s (even Harvard
and Yale had only 400 or 500 students apiece,
though the College of William and Mary had
nearly 1,000). Generally, endowments were
scanty, facilities poor, salaries low, and professors
unscholarly, though self-sacrificing and sincere.

None of these institutions admitted women
until, in 1837, Oberlin accepted four women as
regular students and thus became the first coedu-
cational college. Some outsiders feared that coed-
ucation was a rash experiment approximating free
love, but the Oberlin authorities were confident
that "the mutual influence of the sexes upon each
other is decidedly happy in the cultivation of
both mind & manners." Only a few other institutions copied Oberlin's example before the Civil
War. Interest in higher education for women
generally led to the creation of women's colleges.
The first to have a curriculum equivalent to those
of men's colleges was Mount Holyoke, founded by
Mary Lyon in 1837.

The idea of state support for higher education
had to contend against the prevailing concept of
private, denominational control. Besides the older
states with public universities, the newer states of
Indiana, Michigan, Kentucky, Missouri, Mississippi, Iowa, Wisconsin, Minnesota, and Louisiana
committed themselves to the support of higher
learning before the Civil War. None of these state
institutions, whether old or new, was a true university in the European sense of an institution devoted to high-level, graduate training.

The standard curriculum, whether in the private college or the state university, still emphasized the old-fashioned liberal arts. A young man
who desired training for a professional career
(other than the ministry) had few institutions to
choose from. He could study engineering at the
United States Military Academy, Rensselaer Poly-
technic Institute (1824), or Yale or Harvard,

which set up engineering schools in 1846 and 1847. He could study law or medicine at one of several institutions, but no American medical school compared with the best ones abroad. In most cases, as in earlier times, he apprenticed himself to a practicing physician, learned engineering on the job (the Erie Canal was a most productive "school" for engineers), or "read law" in the office of some successful lawyer.

Remedying Society's Ills

While many reformers hoped to make possible a better life by creating opportunities through education or by eliminating specific social evils, some of the more advanced thinkers aspired to start afresh and remake society by founding ideal communities based on cooperative values. America seemed to be spacious enough to allow models of a perfect society to be established that could be isolated from the influence of competitive life-styles and ideologies. Presumably success would lead to imitation, until communities free of crime, poverty, and other evils would cover the land. Among the dozens of experimental communities were New Harmony, founded in Indiana by the philanthropic Scottish mill owner Robert Owen; Brook Farm, an association of intellectuals, near Boston; and the Oneida Community in upstate New York, where the followers of John Humphrey Noyes abandoned private property and monogamous marriage in the belief that both institutions made people slaves to sinful possessiveness and therefore prevented the attainment of spiritual perfection.

From the 1820s on, the states one by one abolished imprisonment for debt, and some of them greatly improved their handling of the criminal and the insane. In the 1830s several states ended public hangings and began to hold executions within the privacy of prison walls, and later a few states did away with capital punishment entirely. The Boston schoolmistress Dorothea Dix, shocked by her chance visit to the Cambridge jail (1841), devoted her life to securing the establishment of insane asylums in Massachusetts and other states.

In looking for causes of insanity, pauperism, and crime, many reformers concluded that these evils could be traced largely to strong drink. An organized temperance movement had begun with the formation of local societies in New England, and in 1826 the American Society for the Promotion of Temperance appeared as a coordinating agency for the various groups. As the temperance forces grew and spread over the country, the crusaders diverged, some advocating total abstinence and others seeing no harm in wine or beer; some favoring prohibition laws and others relying on the individual conscience. Massachusetts and other states experimented with legislation for local option, allowing communities to regulate or prohibit liquor sales, and Maine passed a statewide prohibition law in 1851.

The Movement for Women's Rights

The Industrial Revolution shaped the movement for women's rights in a complicated fashion. On the surface it seemed to limit economic opportunities for women. It sharpened the lines of demarcation between the home and the marketplace and accentuated the division of labor within the home. Women worked less in the production of goods (within a household workshop, for example) and devoted themselves more to supporting the employed members of the family. Beneath the surface, however, the change in the roles of women within the family created a basis for greater independence and power. Drawing on the enhanced esteem attached to their family roles and reinforcing each other through intensified community and kinship ties with other women, new middle-class women fostered a common identity in "womanhood" and used it to enlarge their influence over decisions in all areas of family life, including the bearing of children and their husbands' choice of work. For most middle-class women, greater influence over family life was enough. But some seized upon the logic implicit in the emphasis on the moral role of women to increase their involvement outside their homes.

Many young women from middle-class families in New York and New England entered the public arena through the spiritual revivals of the 1820s and 1830s. Energizing women by emphasizing individual free will and providing a central role for women in proselytizing, the revivals involved women more deeply in community life, enhanced their self-esteem, and make them receptive to participation in other reform movements, such as educational reform.

Education attracted even more women committed to reforming American life. During the 1840s and 1850s thousands of young, middle-class women took up teaching. Their intellectual leader was Catharine Beecher, who founded academies for young women in Hartford and Cincinnati during the 1820s and 1830s. She wrote that women should have a special commitment to education because they had a more general obligation to foster moral development. Since "to enlighten the understanding and to gain the affections is (*sic*) a teacher's business," and since "the mind is to be guided chiefly by means of the affections," she asked: "Is not *woman* best fitted to accomplish these important objects?"

Some women reformers, led by Catharine Beecher, also called for an elevation of family life. They wrote books on "domestic economy," urging Christians to infuse their homes with love and altruism. In the form of manuals and magazines, such as *Godey's Lady Book*, women were instructed on how to make their homes at once more efficient and more moral. Catharine Beecher's *Treatise on Domestic Economy* (1841) was reprinted almost every year during the 1840s and the 1850s, becoming the standard text on housekeeping and child rearing. She hoped that women would further increase their power in the domestic arena.

Some women, however, began to find Catharine Beecher too conservative. They rejected the implicit bargain she had made for enlarging the realm of women: they could not agree to her acceptance of a restricted role in society in return for greater control over domestic life and a central role in education. Shaping the ideas of the radical wing of the women's movement were two women, Angelina and Sarah Grimké, who were daughters of a South Carolina planter and active advocates of the abolition of slavery. In 1838 Angelina debated Catharine Beecher, declaring that "it is a woman's right to have a voice in all the laws and regulations by which she is governed, whether in Church or State." Consequently, she said, "the present arrangements of society, on these points are a *violation of human rights, a rank usurpation of power,* a violent seizure and confiscation of what is sacredly and inalienably

hers." By 1840 the Grimkés were asserting that the traditional allocation of roles within the family instituted the "domestic slavery" of women to men.

Not all women reformers shared these views; followers of both the Grimké sisters and Catharine Beecher worked together in reform movements, especially abolitionism. And, all women reformers gained confidence outside the home, refined their ideas, and learned much about the organizational requirements for success. During the 1840s women reformers developed a pragmatic course of action to advance women's rights, one that remained within the existing social and political structure and did not threaten the existing division of labor within the family. They adopted the objective of strengthening women's legal position.

In 1848 women reformers took a critical step, the calling of a rights convention that met in Seneca Falls, in upstate New York. Led by abolitionists Elizabeth Cady Stanton and Lucretia Mott, who had met at the World's Anti-Slavery Convention in 1840, the convention outlined, for the first time, a coherent and elaborate philosophy and program to achieve equality. The women adopted resolutions patterned directly on the Declaration of Independence. Among their declared principles were "that all men and women are created equal; that they are endowed by the Creator with certain inalienable rights; that among these are life, liberty and the pursuit of happiness." They asserted, however, that "the history of mankind is a history of repeated injuries and usurpations on the part of man toward woman, having in direct object the establishment of an absolute tyranny over her."

Subsequently, during the 1850s, national women's rights conventions became an annual occurrence and were accompanied by numerous local and regional meetings. They emphasized establishing the right of married women to control their own property and earnings, guaranteeing guardianship of their children in the event of divorce, ensuring the right to sue or bear witness, revising concepts of female inferiority found in established religious theology, and winning the suffrage for women.

The campaign for the suffrage made no headway before the Civil War, although it became increasingly important to the ideology and organization of the women's movement. Those who argued for the suffrage began to question the ideal of separate spheres by suggesting that the interests of men and women were not necessarily compatible. The national convention of women that met in 1851 resolved that "the Right of Suffrage for Women is, in our opinion, the corner-stone of this enterprise, since we do not seek to protect woman, but rather to place her in a position to protect herself."

The accomplishment of the 1850s that proved most significant for women was that they learned how to organize. The meetings and publicity widened the participation of women in feminist issues, and the feminist leadership grew, with Susan B. Anthony its most important addition.

While the women leaders of the 1830s and 1840s had been gifted lecturers, Susan B. Anthony's foremost talents were organizational. She was a member of a Massachusetts Quaker family that had moved to a farm near Rochester, New York. She had participated in a women's antislavery society, lectured widely on antislavery and religion, resigned a teaching position with bitterness over discrimination, and joined the temperance movement as a paid fundraiser. In 1851, when she was thirty-one years old, she joined the movement for women's rights and forged an enduring friendship with Elizabeth Cady Stanton. In promoting the cause of feminist reforms during the 1850s, Susan B. Anthony created a network of political "captains" in each of New York's sixty counties, thereby developing the ability to collect thousands of signatures on petitions. She lobbied the legislature relentlessly. In 1860 her efforts culminated in New York's legislating the right of women to collect their own wages, to bring suit in court, and to enjoy, if widowed, full control over their own property.

The organizational and legislative successes of the women's rights movement during the 1850s provided the basis for the more aggressive movement that followed the Civil War.

The Nativist Movement

Reform enthusiasm had its darker side; the presence of huge numbers of aliens occasioned the first important organized nativist movement in American history. While some natives recognized the contribution that the newcomers were making to the cultural and material development of their adopted land, many others disliked their ways and feared their influence. These critics contended that many of the immigrants were mentally and physically defective, that they created slums, and that they corrupted politics by selling their votes. Laborers complained that the aliens, willing to work for low wages, were stealing their jobs. Protestants, impressed by the aptitude that the Catholic Irish demonstrated for politics, believed, or affected to believe, that the Church of Rome was attaining an undue power in American government. Evangelical revivalism seemed to accentuate the differences between Protestants and Catholics. Many Americans of older stock were honestly concerned that the immigrants would not assimilate into national life or would inject new and radical philosophies into national thought.

In 1834 an anti-Catholic mob set fire to a convent in Charlestown, Massachusetts, and the next year Samuel F. B. Morse (who is better remembered as a portrait painter and as the inventor of the telegraph) published his *Foreign Conspiracy*, which served thereafter as a textbook for nativists crusading against what they imagined was a popish plot to gain control of the United States. Still, the federal government did nothing to check immigration, and shipowners, employers, and some of the states took measures to encourage it.

Out of the tensions and prejudices emerged a number of secret societies to combat the "alien menace." Originating in the East and later spreading to the West and South, these groups combined in 1850 to form the Supreme Order of the Star-Spangled Banner. Included in the official program of the order were opposition to Catholics or aliens holding public office and support of stricter naturalization laws and literacy tests for voting. When members were asked to define their platform, they replied, because of the secrecy rule, "I know nothing," and hence were dubbed "Know-Nothings."

Soon the leaders, deciding to seek their objectives by political methods, formed the so-called American party. In the East the new organization scored an immediate and astonishing success in the elections of 1854, casting a large vote in Pennsylvania and New York and winning control of the state government in Massachusetts. Elsewhere the progress of the Know-Nothings was more modest and tempered by local conditions. Western members of the party, because of the presence of many German voters in the area, found it expedient to proclaim that they were not opposed to naturalized Protestants. In the South, where Catholics were few, the leaders disavowed any religious bias, and Catholics participated in the movement. The party's spectacular growth would soon be interrupted by the rise of the larger issue of slavery.

North of Slavery

In the 1850s there were more than 4,000,000 black Americans, of whom about 95 percent were confined to the South. That left nearly a quarter of a million of them living in the North. These people were concentrated mainly in the cities, about 22,000 in Philadelphia and about 12,000 in New York. Many were fugitives from slavery.

Blacks faced severe handicaps in the North. They had little or no political influence: They could vote only in New England (not including Connecticut), and in New York only if they owned a certain amount of property, which was not required of white voters. In most places they were excluded from the public schools that whites attended. They faced the constant danger of being attacked by white mobs or kidnapped by slave dealers and sold, or resold, into slavery. Usually they had no choice but to take a low-paying job as a domestic servant or unskilled laborer.

In the early 1800s a Massachusetts free black, Paul Cuffe, tried to begin a back-to-Africa movement so as to give his people a new life in their ancestral homeland. Cuffe had spent $4,000 on the project, without success, when he died in 1817. That same year a group of prominent white Virginians organized the American Colonization Society to "colonize" freed slaves in Africa. Some Northern blacks feared this was a scheme to get rid of them, and James Forten, a prosperous black businessman, called a mass meeting of Philadelphia blacks to object to it. The American Colonization Society received private contributions and appropriations from Congress and the Virginia

and Maryland legislatures to carry on the work. Though shipping out of the country fewer blacks in a decade than were being born in it each month, the society succeeded in founding and governing on the west coast of Africa the colony of Liberia, which it converted into an independent black republic in 1846.

Meanwhile, in Massachusetts, a new note of black militancy had been struck. David Walker, born free in North Carolina, made his living by selling secondhand clothes in Boston. There, in 1829, he published a pamphlet entitled *Walker's Appeal . . . to the Colored Citizens*. In it he ridiculed the "Christian" pretensions of the slaveholders and urged slaves to cut their masters' throats. "Kill, or be killed!"

A number of other black critics of slavery, most of them less bitterly outspoken than Walker, appeared in the North. The greatest of all — and one of the most electrifying orators of his time, black or white — was Frederick Douglass. Born a slave in Maryland, Douglass ran off to Massachusetts in 1838, made a name for himself as an antislavery leader, and lectured for two years in England, where he was lionized. (More than a dozen other black abolitionists also visited the British Isles and made a strong impression there.) After returning to the United States in 1847, Douglass purchased his freedom from his Maryland owner and founded an antislavery newspaper, the *North Star*, in Rochester, New York.

As early as 1830, black abolitionists had held their first national convention. It was largely their example that inspired white reformers to launch an aggressive antislavery movement.

The White Abolitionists

During the 1820s the most active white crusader against slavery was the New Jersey Quaker Benjamin Lundy, who published the leading antislavery newspaper of the time, the *Genius of Universal Emancipation*, in Baltimore. Lundy used moderate language and advocated a mild and gradual program.

In 1831 his helper, the young Massachusetts-born printer William Lloyd Garrison, sounded a much more strident note when he presented the first issue of his own weekly, *The Liberator*, in

Boston. From the outset Garrison condemned the thought of gradual, compensated emancipation and demanded immediate abolition, without reimbursement for slaveholders. He denounced the American Colonization Society as no emancipationist agency but the reverse, a group whose real aim was to strengthen slavery by ridding the country of blacks already free. He got support from free blacks, who bought most of the subscriptions to *The Liberator.* Despite his strong language, he was no advocate of slave rebellions, and he criticized *Walker's Appeal* as a "most injudicious publication."

Under the leadership of Garrison the New England Antislavery Society was founded in 1832 and the American Antislavery Society the following year. But he shocked many friends of freedom, including Frederick Douglass, by the extremes to which he went. He opposed the government, characterizing the Constitution as "a covenant with death and an agreement with hell," and he opposed the churches on the grounds that they were bulwarks of slavery. In 1840 he split the American Antislavery Society by insisting upon the right of women to participate fully in its activities, even to speak before audiences that included men as well as women.

By that time there were in existence nearly 2,000 local societies with a total of almost 200,000 members. These societies remained alive, active, and growing after the disruption of the national organization.

Another outstanding leader, busy in New York and the Northwest, was Theodore Weld. Converted to reform by Charles G. Finney's preaching, Weld worked within the churches, especially the Presbyterian and Congregational. He married Angelina Grimké and, with the aid of his wife, he compiled an overwhelming factual indictment of the institution in the book *American Slavery As It Is: Testimony of a Thousand Witnesses* (1839).

The Campaign for Liberation

Most of the active members of organized societies were "abolitionists" in the sense that they favored immediate abolition. But this did not mean precisely what it seemed to mean. The abolitionists aimed at what they called "immediate abolition gradually accomplished." That is, they hoped to bring about a sudden and not a gradual end to slavery, but they did not expect to achieve this for some time. At first, they counted on "moral suasion": they were going to appeal to the conscience of slaveholders and convince them that slaveholding was a sin.

Later they turned more and more to political action, seeking to induce the Northern states and the federal government to aid the cause where possible. They helped runaway slaves find refuge in the North or in Canada, though in doing so they did not set up any such highly organized system as the term "Underground Railroad" implies. After the Supreme Court (in *Prigg* v. *Pennsylvania*, 1842) held that the states need not aid in enforcing the federal fugitive-slave law of 1793, abolitionists secured the passage of "personal liberty laws" in several of the Northern states. These laws forbade state officials to assist in the capture and return of runaways. Above all, the antislavery societies petitioned Congress to abolish slavery in places where the federal government had jurisdiction — in the territories and the District of Columbia — and to prohibit the interstate slave trade. Only a very few of the abolitionists supposed that Congress constitutionally could interfere with a "domestic" institution like slavery within the Southern states themselves.

While the abolitionists engaged in pressure politics, they never formed a political party with an abolition platform. In 1840 the Liberty party was launched, with the Kentucky antislavery leader James G. Birney as its presidential candidate, but this party and its successors did not campaign for outright abolition: they stood for "free soil," that is, for keeping slavery out of the territories. Some free-soilers were friends of the slave; others feared blacks, cared nothing about slavery, and desired to make the West a country for whites only. Garrison said free-soil-ism was really "white-man-ism."

The real friends of blacks were quite aware that, to be consistent, they would have to help the free as well as the enslaved, since so-called freedom was "but an empty name — but the debasing mockery of true freedom." Garrison assured his "free colored brethren" that the attainment of equal rights for them was "a leading object." He and other abolitionists did try to open new opportunities for them. They had little success in appealing to employers to hire additional blacks and give them training as apprentices. But the reformers made other rather modest gains. They established schools for blacks (by 1837 there were 100 young white women teaching black children in Ohio) and even colleges (Wilberforce in Ohio, Avery in Pennsylvania). They opened Oberlin College to black students. They brought about the desegregration of all Massachusetts public schools in 1855, six years after Charles Sumner had argued in a Boston lawsuit (as opponents of segregation elsewhere were to do a century later) that, no matter how good the facilities provided for black pupils, "the separate school is not equivalent." The reformers also secured the repeal of Massachusetts and Ohio laws requiring separate cars for blacks on the railroads.

The abolitionists might have accomplished more reforms in the North had it not been for the widespread antiblack if not proslavery feeling there. Prejudice was reinforced by the desire of many Northern business people to keep on good terms with Southern customers or suppliers, and by the fear on the part of wage-earning Northern whites that blacks, if freed and given equal opportunities, would be dangerous competitors for jobs. The antislavery movement provoked much hostility in the North, especially during the early years. When Prudence Crandall undertook to admit black girls to her private school in Connecticut, local citizens had her arrested and threw filth into her well, forcing her to close the school. A mob burned the Philadelphia abolitionists' "temple of liberty" and started a bloody race riot (1834). Another mob seized Garrison on the streets of Boston and threatened to hang him, and a member of still another group shot and killed the antislavery editor Elijah Lovejoy in Alton, Illinois (1837). Throughout the North antislavery lecturers, risking their health if not their lives, time and again were attacked with rotten eggs or stones.

In the South the reaction was far stronger, and if no abolitionists were killed there, it was only because (from the 1830s on) very few of them dared even venture into that part of the country.

The Slave's Response

For the vast majority of slaves, there was no way out of bondage. A few were allowed to earn money with which they managed to buy their own and their families' freedom. Some had the good luck to be set free by their master's will after his death — like the more than 400 slaves belonging to John Randolph of Roanoke (1833). From the 1830s on, however, state laws made it more and more difficult, and in some cases practically impossible, for an owner to manumit slaves. The laws, when permitting manumission, often required the removal of the freed slaves from the state. The masters objected to the very presence of free blacks, who set a disturbing example for the slaves and provided cover for escaping slaves.

By 1860 there nevertheless were about 250,000 free blacks in the slaveholding states, more than half of them in Virginia and Maryland. A few, as in the North, attained wealth and prominence. A few themselves owned slaves, usually relatives whom they had bought in order to assure their ultimate emancipation. Most lived in abject poverty, even worse than in the North. Law or custom closed many occupations to them, forbade them to assemble without white supervision, and placed numerous other restraints upon them. They were only quasi-free, and yet they had all the burdens of freedom, including the obligation of paying taxes.

Great as were the hardships of freedom, blacks preferred them to the hardships of slavery. Occasionally slaves sought freedom through flight. They might succeed in hiding out for a time, but the chance of escaping to the North or to Canada was exceedingly slim except for those who lived fairly close to the free-state border and who got help from free blacks and friendly whites on the so-called Underground Railroad. For fugitives from the deep South, the hazards of distance and geographical ignorance, of white patrols and bloodhounds, were hard if not impossible to overcome, especially since every black at large was presumed to be a runaway slave unless carrying documentary proof to the contrary.

Discontented slaves could express their feelings through individual acts of resistance. They might be deliberately careless with their master's property, losing or breaking tools, setting fire to houses or barns. They might make themselves useless by cutting off fingers or even commiting suicide. Or, despite the terrible consequences, they might turn upon the master and kill him.

The idea of combining with other blacks, rising up, and overthrowing the masters occurred to slaves and free blacks from time to time. In 1800 Gabriel Prosser gathered 1,000 rebellious slaves outside Richmond, but two blacks gave the plot away, and the Virginia militia was called out in time to head it off. Prosser and thirty-five others were executed. In 1822 the Charleston free black Denmark Vesey and his followers — rumored to total 9,000 — made preparations for revolt, but again the word leaked out and retribution followed. In 1831 Nat Turner, a slave preacher, led a band of slaves who armed themselves with guns and axes and, on a summer night, went from house to house in Southampton County, Virginia. They slaughtered sixty white men, women, and children before being overpowered by state and federal troops. More than 100 slaves were put to death in the aftermath. Nat Turner's was the only actual slave insurrection in the nineteenth-century South, but slave conspiracies and threats of renewed violence continued throughout the section as long as slavery lasted.

For most slaves, however, the central instrument for coping with an increasingly rigid system of slavery was neither simple accommodation nor outright rebellion. It was, instead, the development of a unique culture that gave slaves a sense of personal worth. The institution responsible for elaborating and transmitting this culture was the slave family, the origins of which are obscure but which had emerged to become remarkably resilient by the time of the Civil War despite the lack of legal protection for marriage and parenthood. Many slaves had marriages that lasted throughout their adult lives. Slave trading often broke up marriages and families, but even then, strong family life normally continued. Slaves separated from their families often made successful efforts to continue relations with them; the result was an elaborate set of kinship networks that, for generations, connected slaves on numerous plantations. Within these kin groups, children were assigned familial surnames, and incest taboos against first-cousin marriages were observed faithfully. Herbert Gutman concludes that "communication networks were built upon these enlarged kin networks and undercut the dependence of slaves upon those who owned them." If distances were too great for such arrangements, slaves, retaining a powerful belief in the value of familial obligations, commonly started new families in their new location. Reinforcing the cultural impact of family life was the slaves' interpretation of Christianity, which Eugene Genovese describes as strengthening "slaves' love for each other and their pride in being black people."

The Proslavery Reaction

By the 1830s slavery was being threatened from three directions — from the slaves themselves, from Northern abolitionists, and from Southern slaveless farmers. There were still antislavery societies in the South, and as late as 1827 there had been a larger number than in the North. They were most numerous in the border slave states, where a few antislavery activists, notably Cassius M. Clay of Kentucky, kept up their campaign through the 1850s. Between 1829 and 1832 a Virginia constitutional convention and then the state legislature, responding to demands from nonslaveholders in the western part of the state, seriously considered ending slavery through compensated emancipation but were discouraged by the tremendous expense it would have required.

Meanwhile the news of the Turner insurrection terrified whites in Virginia and all over the South. They had always been uneasy, always mindful of the horrors of the successful slave uprising in Santo Domingo (in the 1790s). Now they were reminded of their insecurity, and they were especially horrified because there had been long-trusted house servants among Turner's followers who, axe in hand, had suddenly confronted their masters' sleeping families. Who among the blacks could the whites really depend upon? Many of the master class now blamed Garrison and the abolitionists for the slaves' defection. Planters were determined to make slavery secure against all dangers.

While the Southern states strengthened their slave codes, controlling the movement of slaves and prohibiting their being taught to read, Southern leaders proceeded to elaborate an intellectual defense of slavery. According to the proslavery argument it was good for slaves because they were inferior creatures who needed the master's guidance and who were better off — better fed, clothed, and housed, and more secure — than the Northern factory workers. It was good for South-

The Slave's Response to Slavery

For many years, Ulrich B. Phillips' *American Negro Slavery* (1918) was accepted as the standard authority on the subject. Phillips assumed that the typical plantation slave was lazy, childlike, irresponsible, contented, and submissive — all because of race. Further, Phillips believed that the American slave kept little if any African cultural inheritance.

Eventually strong dissenters appeared. In *The Myth of the Negro Past* (1941) the anthropologist Melville J. Herskovits emphasized the number of "Africanisms" that survived through slavery times. In *American Negro Slave Revolts* (1943) the historian Albert Aptheker claimed to have discovered "approximately two hundred and fifty revolts and conspiracies in the history of American Negro slavery" and concluded that "discontent and rebelliousness" were "characteristic of American Negro Slaves." In *The Peculiar Institution* (1956) Kenneth M. Stampp viewed the black slaves as "ordinary human beings" who reacted to slavery in a variety of ways, much as white people would have done in the same circumstances.

In 1959 Stanley M. Elkins provoked controversy with his *Slavery: A Problem in American Institutional and Intellectual Life*. Elkins agreed with Phillips that the typical slave had a "Sambo" personality but accounted for it in terms of the psychological shock of enslavement and the enforced "adjustment to absolute power" in the hands of the master. In the process the slaves lost the tribal or cultural identity that might have helped them to maintain their personal independence.

Several historians have taken issue with Elkins by pointing to aspects of slave culture that provided slaves with a sense of independence. John Blassingame, in *The Slave Community* (1973), found that American-born slaves were able to retain their ancestors' culture, largely through the slave family, which enabled members to "cooperate with other blacks" and maintain self-esteem. Eugene D. Genovese, in *Roll, Jordan, Roll: The World the Slaves Made* (1974), emphasized the development of the slaves' religion as "the organizing center of their resistance within accommodation." Genovese concluded that it "gave the individual slave the wherewithal to hold himself intact and to love his brothers and sisters in the quarters, even as it blocked the emergence of political consciousness."

On the basis of an elaborate quantitative study, Robert W. Fogel and Stanley L. Engerman concluded, in *Time on the Cross: The Economics of American Negro Slavery* (1974), that planters themselves, out of self-interest, encouraged stable family relationships and provided slaves with a standard of living comparable with that of free people. Moreover, they found the slaves to have been neither lazy nor rebellious types but extremely productive workers. But their findings encountered immediate criticism, led by historian Herbert G. Gutman and a group of economists in *Reckoning with Slavery* (1976). While agreeing that slaves developed a supportive culture and displayed real achievement, they stressed the low standard of living of the slaves, the obstacles faced in maintaining a stable family life, and the violence used by planters to maintain order.

ern society because it was the only way two races so different as the black and the white could live together in peace. It was good for the nation as a whole because the entire Southern economy depended on it, and the prosperity of the nation depended on the prosperity of the South. It was good in itself because the Bible sanctioned it — did not the Hebrews of the Old Testament own bondsmen, and did not the New Testament apostle Paul advise, "Servants, obey your masters"? These and other arguments convinced most Southerners, even those (the great majority) who owned no slaves and had no direct interest in the peculiar institution.

While spreading proslavery propaganda, Southern leaders tried to silence the advocates of freedom. In 1835 a mob destroyed sacks containing abolition literature in the Charleston post office, and thereafter Southern postmasters generally refused to deliver antislavery mail. Southern state legislatures passed resolutions demanding that Northern states suppress the "incendiary" agitation of the abolitionists. In Congress, Southern representatives with the co-operation of Northerners secured the adoption of the "gag rule" (1836), according to which anti-slavery petitions were automatically laid on the table without being read

As a champion of freedom of speech and petition, John Quincy Adams led a struggle against the gag rule, finally (1844) securing its repeal. Throughout the North many people who were not abolitionists began to feel that civil liberties were endangered in the entire country, not just the South. These people were inclined to sympathize with the abolitionist as a martyr for freedom in the broadest sense. They came to suspect that there really existed, as the abolitionist claimed, a kind of "Slave Power Conspiracy" to destroy the liberties of the country as a whole. Thus the majority of Northerners, though not usually for love of blacks, eventually came to sympathize in varying degrees with the antislavery cause, while an even larger and more determined majority of Southerners rallied to the defense of the peculiar institution, thereby laying the foundation for a "solid South."

Chapter 10

Jacksonian Democracy

More and More Voters

When Ohio and other new states in the West joined the Union, they adopted constitutions that gave the vote to all adult white males and allowed all voters the right to hold public office. Thus the new states set an example for the older ones. After 1815 the Eastern states began to revise their constitutions by calling conventions that served as grand committees of the people to draw up new documents and submit them for public approval. Eventually all the states (some of them not till after the Civil War) changed their constitutions in the direction of increased democracy.

In most of the states there was at first no popular vote for President. As late as 1800, the legislature chose presidential electors in ten of the states, and the people in only six. The trend was toward popular election, however, and after 1828 the legislature made the choice in only one state, South Carolina. There the people had no chance to vote in presidential elections until after the Civil War.

The number of voters increased far more rapidly than did the population as a whole. In the presidential election of 1824 fewer than 27 in 100 adult white males voted (though previously, in some of the states, more than 50 had done so). In the election of 1828 the proportion rose to about 55 in 100 — more than twice the figure for 1824 — and in the elections of 1832 and 1836 the proportion remained approximately the same as in 1828. Then, in 1840, people flocked to the polls as never before, 78 in 100 white men casting their ballots. The multiplication of voters was due only in part to the widening of the electorate. It was due in greater measure to a heightening of interest in politics and a strengthening of party organization. Citizens were aroused, and those who in former times had seldom bothered with elections now came out to vote.

Political parties became more important as both the electorate and the elections grew in number and complexity. Parties were necessary for bringing together voters of diverse interests and providing common goals so that the will of the people could express itself in a united and meaningful way. Parties were also necessary to give central direction to governments made up of independently elected officials. Hence, as the states became more democratic, political organizations within them became more tightly knit. Political machines and party bosses appeared in states like New York and Pennsylvania which had large and heterogeneous electorates with a variety of conflicting interests. By 1840 mass political parties, carefully organized throughout every precinct and mobilizing voters in great numbers, had clearly emerged.

"Corrupt Bargain"

From 1796 to 1816, presidential candidates had been nominated by caucuses of the members of each of the two parties in Congress. In 1820, when the Federalists declined to oppose his candidacy, Monroe ran as the Republican nominee without the necessity of a caucus nomination. If the caucus system were revived and followed in

1824, this would mean that the nominee of the Republicans in Congress would run unopposed, as Monroe had done. Several men aspired to the Presidency, however, and they and their followers were unwilling to let a small group of congressmen and senators determine which one was to win the prize.

In 1824 "King Caucus" was overthrown. Fewer than a third of the Republicans in Congress bothered to attend the gathering that went through the motions of nominating a candidate (William H. Crawford), and he found the caucus nomination as much a handicap as a help in the campaign. The rest of the candidates — John Quincy Adams, Andrew Jackson, and Henry Clay — received nominations from state legislatures and endorsements from irregular mass meetings throughout the country.

In those states where the people chose the presidential electors, Jackson led all the rest at the polls. In the electoral college also he came out ahead, with 99 votes to Adams' 84, Crawford's 41, and Clay's 37. He lacked the necessary majority, however. So, in accordance with the Twelfth Amendment, the final decision was left to the House of Representatives, which was to choose among the three candidates with the highest electoral vote.

If Clay, in 1825, could not be President, he could at least be President maker, and perhaps he could lay the ground for his own election later on. As speaker, he was in a strategic position for influencing the decision of the House of Representatives. In deciding among the three leading candidates, the House was to vote by states, the delegation from each state casting one vote. Clay, as the winner of the recent election in Kentucky, Ohio, and Missouri, could swing the congressional delegations of those three states at least. Finally Clay gave his support to Adams, and the House elected him.

The Jacksonians were angry enough at this, but they became far angrier when the new President made known his appointments. Clay was to be the secretary of state! The State Department being the well-established route to the Presidency, Adams thus appeared to be naming Clay as his own successor. The two must have agreed to make each other President — Adams now, Clay next — or so the Jacksonians exclaimed, and

they pretended to be horrified by this "corrupt bargain." Very likely there had been some sort of understanding, and though there was nothing improper in it, it proved to be politically unwise for both Adams and Clay.

Soon after Adams' inauguration as President, Jackson resigned from the Senate to accept a renomination for the Presidency from the Tennessee legislature and to begin a three-year campaign for election in 1828.

The Second President Adams

John Quincy Adams, the son of John Adams, had made a brilliant record in diplomacy, serving as the American minister in one foreign capital after another and then as one of the most successful of all secretaries of state. As President (1825–1829), however, he endured four ineffectual years. His frustration in the White House shows that the Presidency demands more than exceptional ability and high-mindedness, for John Quincy Adams possessed both. The Presidency also requires political skill and political luck, and these he did not have.

In his inaugural address and in his first message to Congress he boldly stated a broad conception of the powers and duties of the federal government. He recommended "laws promoting the improvement of agriculture, commerce, and manufactures, the cultivation of the mechanic and of the elegant arts, the advancement of literature, and the progress of the sciences, ornamental and profound." The most he could get was a few million dollars for improving rivers and harbors and for extending the National Road westward from Wheeling.

Adams was worsted also in a contest with the state of Georgia. That state attempted to remove the remaining Creek and Cherokee Indians so as to gain additional soil for cotton planters. The Creeks, however, had a treaty with the United States (1791) that guaranteed them the possession of the land they occupied. A new treaty (1825) ceded the land to the state, but Adams refused to enforce this treaty, believing that it had been obtained by fraud. The Georgia governor defied the President of the United States and went ahead with plans for Indian removal. At last the Creeks agreed to still another treaty (1827) in which they yielded their claims. Adams' stand had been honorable but unpopular. Southerners condemned him for encroaching upon state rights, and Westerners as well as Southerners disapproved of his interfering with efforts to get rid of the Indians.

Southerners again denounced the administration and its supporters on account of the tariff of 1828. The bill of 1828 contained high duties not only on woolens but also on a number of other items, such as flax, hemp, iron, lead, molasses, and raw wool. Thus it displeased New England manufacturers, for it would raise the cost of their raw materials as well as the price of their manufactured goods. A story arose that the bill had taken its shape from a Jacksonian plot to embarrass New Englanders and discredit Adams. Supposedly it was intended to put Adams in a dilemma that would lose him friends whether he signed or vetoed it. While some politicians did see the measure as an electioneering device, others intended it seriously as a means of benefiting the farmers and manufacturers of the middle states and the West.

When the bill was considered item by item, Southerners voted against reductions in the hope that some of its outrageous duties would so antagonize New Englanders that they would help defeat it. But when it came to a final test, the bill got enough New England votes to pass. Adams signed it. The Southerners, whose tactics had backfired, cursed it as the "tariff of abominations."

The Common Man's President

By 1828, the Republican party having split completely, there were again two parties in the campaign — the Adamsites, who called themselves National Republicans, and the Jacksonians, who took the name of Democratic Republicans. Adams himself once had been a Federalist, and most of the old Federalists joined his party, though some became followers of Jackson.

Issues figured little in the campaign of 1828, though much was said about the "corrupt bargain" and something was said about the "tariff of abominations." Regarding the tariff, Adams was on record, having signed the abominations bill, but nobody knew exactly where Jackson stood.

More was made of personalities than of policies, and there was far worse mudslinging than ever before. Though the majority voted for Jackson, a large minority (44 percent) favored Adams, who received all but one of the electoral votes from New England.

Though the new President was no democratic philosopher like Jefferson, he nevertheless held certain democratic convictions, notably that government should offer "equal protection and equal benefits" to all the people. His enemies denied that he ever really championed the people's cause, but they could not deny that he became a living symbol of democracy or that, far more than any of his predecessors, he gave a sense of participation in government to the common man.

As President, Jackson promptly set about to "reform" the personnel procedures of the federal government. For a generation, ever since the downfall of the Federalists in 1800, there had been no complete party turnover in Washington. Officeholders accordingly stayed on year after year and election after election, many of them growing gray and some of them growing corrupt in office. "Office is considered as a species of property," Jackson told Congress, "and government rather as a means of promoting individual interests than as an instrument created solely for the service of the people." He believed that official duties could be made "so plain and simple that men of intelligence may readily qualify themselves for their performance." According to him, offices belonged to the people, not to the entrenched officeholders. Or, as one of his henchmen, William L. Marcy of New York, more cynically put it, "To the victors belong the spoils."

A corollary to the spoils system was the doctrine of rotation in office. Since ordinary people were fit or could easily be fitted for government service, and since loyal members of the victorious party deserved government jobs, a particular position should not be held too long by any one person but should be passed around, or rotated, among several deserving applicants.

The Nullification Theory

President Jackson had taken office with no clearly announced program to carry out. His followers — who soon began to call themselves simply Democrats — had interests so diverse that a statement of definite aims would have alienated many of the party at the outset. This is not to say that Jackson himself was lacking in convictions. Far from it. Besides believing in government by and for the common man, he stood for strong presidential leadership and, while respecting what he considered the legitimate rights of the states, he was devoted to the national Union. He did not hesitate to assert his principles when South Carolina tried to put into effect the nullification (or interposition) theory of John C. Calhoun.

Vice President in John Quincy Adams' administration, Calhoun in 1828 was running as the vice-presidential candidate on the Jackson ticket. And he could look forward to the Presidency itself after a term or two for Jackson — if all went well.

But the tariff question placed Calhoun in a dilemma. Carolina cotton planters were disturbed because their plantations were less profitable than it seemed they should have been. The Carolinians reasoned correctly that protective duties raised the prices of the things they had to buy, whether they bought them at home or from abroad, and lowered the price of the cotton they sold, most of which was exported.

Quietly Calhoun worked out a theory to justify state action in resisting the tariff law. He intended for this action, if and when it became necessary, to be strictly legal and constitutional, not revolutionary. So he had to find a basis for his plan in the Constitution itself. He believed he was following the lines laid down by Madison and Jefferson in their Virginia and Kentucky resolutions of 1798–1799. Indeed, his reasoning was quite similar to theirs, but he carried it farther than they had done, and he provided a definite procedure for state action, which they had not. If Congress enacted a law of doubtful constitutionality — say, a protective tariff — a state could "interpose" to frustrate the law. That is, the people of the state could hold a convention, and if (through their elected delegates) they decided that Congress had gone too far, they could declare the federal law null and void within their state. In that state the law would remain inoperative until three-fourths of the whole number of states should ratify an amendment to the Constitution specifically assigning Congress the power in question. And if the other states should ever get around to doing this, the nullifying state would then submit — or it could secede. The legislature of South Carolina published Calhoun's first statement of his theory, anonymously, in a document entitled *The South Carolina Exposition and Protest* (1828).

Removing the Indians

As an old Indian fighter, Jackson was no lover of Indians, and he desired to continue and expedite the program, which Jefferson had begun, of moving all the tribes to territory west of the Mississippi. The land between the Missouri and the Rockies, according to such explorers as Lewis and Clark, was supposed to be a vast desert, unfit for white habitation. Why not leave that land for the Indians? By the Indian Removal Act of 1830 Congress proposed to exchange tribal lands within the states for new homes in the West, and by the Indian Intercourse Act of 1834 Congress marked off an Indian country and provided for a string of forts to keep the Indians inside it and the whites outside. Meanwhile the President saw that treaties, nearly a hundred in all, were negotiated with the various tribes and that reluctant tribes were moved west, with the prodding of the army.

In the process of Indian removal there was much tragedy and violence. When (in 1832) Chief Black Hawk with a thousand of his hungry Sac and Fox followers — men, women, and children — recrossed the Mississippi into Illinois to grow corn, the frontier settlers feared an invasion. Militiamen and regular troops soon drove the unfortunate Indians into Wisconsin and then slaughtered most of them as they tried to escape down the Wisconsin River. In Florida a war began when Chief Osceola led an uprising of his tribe (including runaway slaves), and the fighting lasted off and on for several years. Jackson sent troops to Florida, but the Seminoles and fugitive slaves were masters of guerrilla warfare in the jungly Everglades. Even after Osceola had been treacherously captured under a flag of truce and had died in prison, the rebels continued to resist.

Unlike the Sacs and Foxes or the Seminoles, the Cherokees in Georgia had a written language of their own (invented by Sequoyah in 1821) and followed a settled way of life as farmers. Yet the state of Georgia, after getting rid of the Creeks, was eager to remove the Cherokees also and open their millions of acres of land good for cotton to white occupation. In 1827 these Indians adopted a constitution and declared their independence as the Cherokee Nation. Promptly the Georgia legislature extended its laws over them and directed the seizure of their territory. Hiring a prominent lawyer, the Cherokees appealed to the Supreme Court. In the case of *Cherokee Nation* v. *Georgia* (1831), Chief Justice Marshall gave the majority opinion that the Indians were "domestic dependent nations" and had a right to the land they occupied until they voluntarily ceded it to the United States. In another case, *Worcester* v. *Georgia* (1832), Marshall and the Court held that the Cherokee Nation was a definite political community with territory over which the laws of Georgia had no force and into which Georgians could not enter without permission.

President Jackson did not sympathize with the Cherokees as President Adams had done with the Creeks. Jackson's attitude is well expressed in the comment attributed to him: "John Marshall has made his decision; now let him enforce it." The decision was never enforced.

In 1835 a few of the Cherokees were induced to sign a treaty giving up the nation's Georgia land in return for $5,000,000 and a reservation in Indian Territory (Oklahoma). The great majority of the 17,000 Cherokees were unwilling to leave their homes, so Jackson sent an army of 7,000 men under General Winfield Scott to drive them westward at bayonet point. About a thousand fled across the state line to North Carolina, where eventually the federal government provided a reservation for them. Most of the rest made the long forced trek west, beginning in midwinter 1838. Several thousand perished before reaching their undesired destination. The survivors were never to forget the hard march to Indian Territory. They called it "The Trail Where They Cried," the trail of tears.

South Carolina Interposes

After waiting four years for Congress to undo the "tariff of abominations," the South Carolina followers of Calhoun lost all patience when Congress denied them any real relief in the tariff of 1832. Calhoun had come out openly for nullification, elaborated the doctrine further, and induced the extremists to adopt it as their remedy. The legislature now called for the election of delegates to a state convention. The convention adopted an ordinance of nullification that declared null and void the tariffs of 1828 and 1832 and forbade the collection of duties within the state. The legislature then passed laws to enforce the ordinance and make preparations for military defense. Needing a strong man to present the South Carolina case ably in Washington, the nullifiers arranged for Calhoun to resign as Vice President and become senator.

Unofficially President Jackson threatened to hang Calhoun. Officially he proclaimed that nullification was treason and its adherents traitors. He also took steps to strengthen the federal forts in South Carolina, ordering General Winfield Scott and a warship and several revenue cutters to Charleston. When Congress met, the President asked for specific authority with which to handle the crisis. His followers introduced a "force bill" authorizing him to use the army and navy to see that acts of Congress were obeyed.

At the moment Calhoun was in a predicament. South Carolina, standing alone, itself divided, could not hope to prevail if a showdown with the federal government should come. If the nullifiers meekly yielded, however, they would lose face and their leader would be politically ruined. Calhoun was saved by the timely intervention of the Great Pacificator, Henry Clay. Newly elected to the Senate, Clay in consultation with Calhoun devised a compromise scheme by which the tariff would be lowered year after year, reaching in 1842 approximately the same level as in 1816. Finally Clay's compromise and the force bill were passed on the same day (March 1, 1833).

Though Calhoun and his followers, having brought about tariff reduction, claimed a victory for nullification, the system had not worked out in the way its sponsors had intended. Calhoun had learned a lesson: no state could assert and maintain its rights by independent action. Thereafter, while continuing to talk of state rights and nullification, he devoted himself to building up a sense of Southern solidarity so that, when another trial should come, the whole section might be prepared to act as a unit in resisting federal authority.

The Bank War

The Bank of the United States, with its headquarters in Philadelphia and its branches in twenty-nine other cities, had become important to the national economy: it provided credit, its bank notes circulated throughout the country as a dependable medium of exchange, and it restrained the less well-managed banks chartered by the various states.

Nicholas Biddle, president of the Bank from 1823 on, had done much to put the company on a sound and prosperous basis. A banker, not a politician, he had no desire to mix in politics. But he finally concluded it was necessary to do so in self-defense when, with the encouragement of Jackson, popular opposition to the Bank rose to a threatening pitch.

Opposition came from two very different groups. The first, consisting largely of state bankers and their friends, objected to the Bank of the United States because it competed with state banks and restrained the state banks from issuing notes as freely as some of them would have liked, through its policy of collecting such notes and presenting them for payment in cash. These critics of the Bank desired more paper money (that is, bank notes circulating as money), not less, and could be categorized as "soft money" people. The second set of critics, the "hard money" people, had the opposite complaint. Believing in coin as the only safe currency, these people condemned all banks of issue — all banks issuing bank notes — whether chartered by the states, as all but one of them were, or by the federal government, as the Bank alone was.

To preserve the institution, Biddle began to grant banking favors to influential people in the hope of winning them to his side. At first he sought to cultivate Jackson's friends. Then he turned more and more to Jackson's opponents. He extended loans on easy terms to several prominent newspaper editors, to a number of important state politicians, and to more than fifty congressmen and senators. In particular, he relied upon Senators Clay and Daniel Webster, the latter of whom was connected with the Bank in various ways — as legal counsel, director of the Boston branch, frequent and heavy borrower, and Biddle's personal friend.

Clay, Webster, and other advisers persuaded Biddle to apply to Congress for a recharter bill in 1832, four years ahead of the expiration date. After investigating the Bank and its business, Congress passed the recharter bill. At once Jackson vetoed it, sending it back to Congress with a stirring message in which he denounced the Bank as unconstitutional, undemocratic, and un-American. The veto stood, for the Bank's friends in Congress failed to obtain the two-thirds majority necessary for overriding it. And so the Bank question emerged as the paramount issue of the coming election, just as Clay had fondly hoped it would. In 1832 Clay ran as the unanimous choice of the National Republicans, who had held a nominating convention in Baltimore late in the previous year.

Jackson took his decisive reelection as a sign that the people endorsed his views on the Bank of the United States. As soon as the nullification crisis had been disposed of, he determined to strike a blow at this banking "monster," this dangerous money power, as he saw it. He could not put an end to the Bank before the expiration of its charter, but at least he could lessen its power by seeing to the removal of the government's deposits. The government opened accounts with a number of state banks, depositing its incoming receipts with them. Jackson's enemies called them his "pet banks."

Biddle soon struck back. He felt that the loss of government deposits, amounting to several millions, made it necessary for him to call in loans and raise interest rates, since the government deposits had served as the basis for much of the Bank's credit. He realized that, by making borrowing more difficult, he was bound to hurt business and cause unemployment, but he consoled himself with the belief that a short depression would help to bring about a recharter of the Bank.

The banker finally carried his contraction of credit too far to suit his own friends among the anti-Jackson business people of the Northeast. To appease the business community he at last reversed himself and began to grant credit in abundance and on reasonable terms. The "Bank War" was over, and Jackson had won it. But, with the passing of the Bank of the United States (in 1836), the country lost a valuable financial institution.

Whigs Against Democrats

During the bank war the opponents of Jackson not only formally censured him in the Senate but also denounced him throughout the country for his allegedly high-handed and arbitrary actions. His opponents often referred to him as a tyrant, "King Andrew I," and they began to call themselves "Whigs," after the party which in England stood traditionally for limiting the power of the King.

The Whig party, organized in time for the congressional elections of 1834 and the presidential election of 1836, was an aggregation of dissimilar groups. It included the National Republicans who had opposed Jackson in 1828 (some of these were old Federalists, others former Jeffersonian Republicans), and it also included many people who had supported Jackson in 1828 but had turned against him afterward. Some of the Whigs, as in Virginia, were really state-rights Democrats who had broken with the President when he threatened to use force against a sister state, South Carolina. On the whole the new party was strongest among the merchants and manufacturers of the Northeast, the wealthier planters of the South, and the farmers most eager for internal improvements in the West. But the party as a rule did not appeal very strongly to the mass of voters. Throughout its existence of twenty years or so the party was able to win only two presidential elections (1840 and 1848), both of them with military heroes as its candidates.

Jackson and his party, in the course of his two presidential terms, developed a fairly definite and coherent political philosophy. The Jacksonians believed in laissez faire. That is, they believed that the government should let economic activities pretty much alone. They proposed the elimination of governmental favors to private enterprise and the destruction of government-granted monopolies and other corporate privileges. Then in theory the people through free and fair competition would be able to take care of themselves, prospering in accordance with their own labor and skill. The worst of poverty and of social in-

equality would thus be done away with when the government ceased to help the rich and hinder the poor. While the Democrats did not advocate social revolution, the more radical of them (known as "Loco Focos") maintained that revolutionary violence might unfortunately appear unless economic inequalities were removed.

Senator Daniel Webster from Massachusetts, the leading Whig philosopher, stoutly denied the contentions of the more radical Democrats. If there was any revolutionary discontent among the American people, he charged, it was due to the policies of the Jackson administration and the clamor of Democratic agitators. He maintained that the people had common interests rather than conflicting ones, at least so long as the government pursued the correct policies. He believed that a wise and active federal government, by stimulating and regulating economic activity through a national banking system, a protective tariff, and expenditures for internal improvements, could assure the economic well-being of all the people and thereby harmonize the interests of every section and class.

As the presidential election of 1836 approached, the Democrats had the advantages of patronage, Jackson's prestige, and a superior party organization. Jackson, not desiring a third term for himself, was able to choose the President to succeed him. The Democratic convention readily nominated his favorite, Martin Van Buren, who had resigned the governorship of New York to become Jackson's secretary of state.

The Whigs in 1836 could boast no such unity and discipline. Indeed, they could not even agree upon a single candidate. Their strategy, masterminded by Biddle, was to run several candidates, each of them supposedly strong in part of the country. Webster was the man for New England, and Hugh Lawson White of Tennessee was to seek the votes of the South. The former Indian fighter and hero of the War of 1812 from Ohio, William Henry Harrison, was counted upon in the middle states and the West. The three Whigs proved to be no match for the one Democrat.

Parties and Ethnicity

The division between Jacksonians and Whigs over economic issues was reinforced by cultural conflicts. Many Jacksonians who challenged the Whig economic program for lining the pockets of the wealthy were also distinctly anti-Yankee. America's wealthy were, in fact, largely of English stock, associated with the socially prestigious Protestant denominations, and, in the North, disproportionately Whig in political affiliation. In Illinois, for example, the settlers of Scotch-Irish descent who moved into the southern counties from the upper South not only supported Jackson's economic program but also resented the growing political power and cultural influence of the New England immigrants who increasingly populated the state's northern counties and occupied the best land and commercial sites. For their part, many Whigs of New England stock viewed Andrew Jackson and his supporters in the same stereotyped way they tended to view the Scotch-Irish and, later, the Irish: as shiftless and mildly barbaric. In contrast, the Democrats, in the 1830s and 1840s, welcomed non-English immigrants, including the Irish, into their ranks. Meanwhile, Whigs tried to deny the ballot to immigrants and to impose temperance and adherence to Sabbath laws. Leading Northern clergy, who advertised their Whig associations, increasingly indulged in hysterical anti-Catholic propaganda. In the 1850s the most fervent opponents of Catholic immigration among the Whigs would unite with anti-Catholics among the Scotch-Irish Democrats to support the Know-Nothing movement. Thus, cultural issues — issues based on loyalties that went beyond economic self-interest — intensified political competition, even in the 1820s and 1830s, and contributed to heightened party identification by voters and to the upsurge of mass participation in politics.

Buren's time. Consequently Van Buren recommended no significant antidepression measure, except for the borrowing of $10,000,000 to meet expenses during the emergency. However, Van Buren did favor the development of an economic program that would please the dominant farmer-labor segment of his party. Accordingly, he urged Congress to reduce the price of public lands and to pass a general preemption bill giving settlers the right to buy 160 acres at a set minimum price before land in any particular area was opened for public sale. These programs failed in Congress, but Van Buren was able to satisfy his urban followers through his presidential order that established a ten-hour work day on all federal projects.

The most important measure in the President's program, and the most controversial, was his proposal for a new fiscal system. With the Bank of the United States destroyed and with Jackson's expedient of "pet banks" discredited, some kind of new system was urgently needed. Van Buren's fiscal ideas demonstrate both his mental ingenuity and his sincere devotion to Democratic principles. The plan he suggested, known as the "Independent Treasury" or "Subtreasury" system, was simplicity itself. Government funds would be placed in an independent treasury at Washington and in subtreasuries in specified cities throughout the country. Whenever the government had to pay out money, its own agents would handle the funds. No bank or banks would have the government's money or name to use as a basis for loans. The government and the banks would be "divorced." Not until 1840, the last year of Van Buren's Presidency, did the administration succeed in driving the measure through both houses of Congress.

Van Buren and Hard Times

President Van Buren had been in office less than three months when the Panic of 1837 broke. The ensuing depression, while mild by twentieth-century standards, was the worst the American people ever had experienced and lasted for about five years.

The modern concept that government can successfully fight depressions, and has an obligation to do so, simply did not exist in President Van

The Log Cabin Campaign

As the campaign year of 1840 approached, the Whigs scented victory. The depression still gripped the country, and the Democrats, the party in power, could be blamed for it. The veteran Whig leader Henry Clay expected the nomination, but the party bosses decided otherwise. Clay had too definite a record; he had been defeated too many times; he had too many enemies. Passing him over, the Whig convention nominated William Henry Harrison of Ohio, and for Vice President, John Tyler of Virginia. The Democrats renominated Van Buren.

The campaign of 1840 set a new pattern in American politics. It introduced the circus-carnival atmosphere that would mark presidential elections for years in the future and that would awe or amuse European beholders — vast meetings, shouting parades, party badges and other insignia, and campaign songs.

Throughout the campaign the eager Whigs were on the offensive. They depicted themselves as the party of the people and the party that could save the nation from depression. They said Van Buren was an aristocrat who used cologne, drank champagne, and engaged in other undemocratic and un-American practices. A Democratic newspaper unwisely sneered that Harrison was a simple soul who would be glad to retire to a log cabin if provided with a pension and plenty of hard cider. In a country where many people lived or had lived in log cabins, this was almost handing the election to the Whigs, and they took the cue. Yes, their candidate was a simple man of the people, they proclaimed, and he loved log cabins and cider (actually he was a man of substance and lived in a large and well-appointed house).

Thereafter the log cabin was an established symbol at every Whig meeting, and hard cider an established beverage. Hundreds of Whig orators bragged that they had been born in log cabins or apologized for having been brought into the world in more sumptuous edifices. Thousands of Whig auditors listened to these effusions and happily chanted the songs that turned every Whig gathering into a frenzy of enthusiasm: "Tippecanoe and Tyler too" (referring to Harrison's fight against Tecumseh) and "Van, Van is a used-up man." Against such techniques and the lingering effects of the depression the Democrats could not avail.

Chapter II

Manifest Destiny

Frustration of the Whigs

The Whigs found themselves divided and frustrated despite their overwhelming victory in the "log cabin" campaign of 1840, which had brought into office their appealing ticket of "Tippecanoe and Tyler too."

"Old Tippecanoe," William Henry Harrison, was never to have a chance to demonstrate what sort of President he would have made. Though he seemed to be in good health, he was sixty-eight years old in 1841, and the strain of the campaign and the inauguration and the pressing demands of his office-seeking supporters were apparently too much for him. He contracted a cold which turned into pneumonia, and he died on April 4, 1841, exactly one month after he had been inaugurated — the first President to die in office. In his brief presidential tenure he had looked for advice to the accepted leaders of the party, particularly to Clay and Webster. Webster became secretary of state, and four of Clay's friends went into the cabinet. Clay and Webster had expected to guide the old soldier through the political jungle.

Vice President John Tyler, though some contended he was merely the second officer acting as the first, immediately assumed the title as well as the powers of the Presidency. For the time being, he kept Harrison's cabinet. A member of an aristocratic Virginia family, Tyler had left the Democratic party in protest against Jackson's overly equalitarian program and imperious methods. Clay apparently had the impression that the new President would support a national bank and other Whig projects, but Tyler soon broke with Clay.

A part of Clay's program was enacted without causing serious division in the party. With near unanimity the Whigs passed a measure, which Tyler signed, abolishing the Independent Treasury system. They also agreed on a bill, the Tariff of 1842, which raised the rates to approximately the same level as in 1832. Tyler accepted this bill, too, but with no great show of enthusiasm.

Part of the Whig legislative program made a bid for the approval of Western settlers and farmers. The frontier was continuing its steady expansion. Arkansas became a state in 1836, Michigan in 1837, and Florida in 1845. The greatest rush of settlers was into the future states of Wisconsin, Iowa, and Minnesota. To attract Western voters the Whig leadership put through the Preemption Act of 1841, which made it possible for a "squatter" on public land to claim 160 acres before they were offered for sale and to pay for them later at $1.25 an acre. This "log cabin bill" was hailed by the Whigs as a relief measure for sufferers from the depression and as a proof of their party's devotion to the welfare of the common man.

The Whig leadership was committed to restoring a financial system similar to the Bank of the United States. But Tyler desired a kind of "state-rights national bank," one that would confine its operations to the District of Columbia and establish branches in the states only with their consent. He twice vetoed bills for setting up what the Whigs tried to disguise as a "Fiscal Corporation."

Lacking a sufficient majority to override the veto, the Whigs fumed with rage at the President, who added to their anger by vetoing a number of internal improvement bills. In an unprecedented action, a conference of congressional Whigs read Tyler out of the party. All the cabinet members resigned except Webster, who had some diplomatic business with Great Britain that he wished to settle. To fill their places, the President appointed five men of his own stripe — former Democrats.

A portentous new political alignment was taking shape. Tyler and a small band of conservative Southern Whigs who followed him were getting ready to rejoin the Democrats. When the office of secretary of state became vacant in 1844, Tyler appointed John C. Calhoun — who had left the Democratic party in the 1830s and had since rejoined it. Into the common man's party of Jackson and Van Buren came a group of men who had aristocratic ideas about government, who thought that government had an obligation to protect and even expand the institution of slavery, and who believed in state rights with a single-minded, almost fanatical devotion.

Webster's Diplomacy

Starting in the late 1830s a series of incidents brought Great Britain and the United States once again close to war. In 1837 rebellion broke out in the eastern provinces of Canada, and many Americans applauded the rebels and furnished them with material aid. The rebels chartered a small American steamship, the *Caroline*, to carry supplies across the Niagara River from New York. One night while the ship was moored at a wharf on the American side, the Canadian authorities sent over a force that took possession of the *Caroline* and burned it; in the melee one American was killed. Excitement flared on both sides of the border.

In an attempt to stamp out the African slave trade, Great Britain was asking for the right to search American merchant ships suspected of carrying black cargoes. Since the American government, sensitive on the matter of search, had always refused the British request, slavers of other nations frequently sought to avoid capture by hoisting the American flag. Complicating the issue was the domestic slave trade, in which slaves were carried by sea from one American port to another. Sometimes the ships in this trade were blown off their course to the British West Indies, where the authorities, acting under English law, freed the slaves. In 1841 an American brig, the *Creole*, sailed from Virginia for New Orleans with over 100 slaves aboard. En route the slaves mutinied, took possession of the ship, and took it to the Bahamas. Here British officials declared the bondsmen free. Although Webster protested, England refused to return the slaves. Many Americans, especially Southerners, were infuriated.

At this critical juncture a new government came to power in Great Britain, one that was more disposed to conciliate the United States and to settle the outstanding differences between the two countries. The new ministry sent to America an emissary, Lord Ashburton. He liked Americans, and Webster admired the English. To avoid war, both were willing to compromise. The result of their deliberations was the Webster-Ashburton Treaty of August 9, 1842.

By the terms of this arrangement, the United States and Great Britain agreed on a Canadian-American boundary from the Atlantic Ocean to the Rocky Mountains. It was also agreed that both Great Britain and the United States would maintain naval squadrons off the African coast, the American ships being charged with chasing slavers using the American flag.

Webster used secret funds to inspire newspaper propaganda favorable to his arrangements with Ashburton, and the treaty proved quite popular. War talk was forgotten for the time being, as Anglo-American relations suddenly looked better than they had for many years.

Election of Polk

In 1844 Henry Clay expected to be the Whig candidate, and Van Buren the Democratic nominee. Both wanted to avoid taking a stand on the annexation of Texas, because a stand, no matter on which side, was certain to lose some votes.

Consequently, they issued separate statements, so similar in tone as to indicate previous consultation between the authors. They both favored annexation, but only with the consent of Mexico. Since this consent was most unlikely to be forthcoming, the statements had little or no meaning.

Clay's action did not harm his candidacy. The Whig convention nominated him unanimously, although the platform discreetly omitted any reference to Texas. But Van Buren had destroyed his chances with the Democrats, particularly with those from the South, who were enraged by his equivocal stand on annexation. The Democratic convention threw him aside and nominated James K. Polk, a champion of expansion. The platform caught the prevailing mood in its key resolution: "that the re-occupation of Oregon and the re-annexation of Texas at the earliest practicable period are great American measures." The words "*re*-occupation" and "*re*-annexation" were intended to imply that, in taking Oregon and Texas, the United States would only be confirming its claim to territories that had already belonged to it. By combining Oregon and Texas, the Democrats hoped to appeal to both Northern and Southern expansionists.

Too late Clay realized that he had muffed the expansion issue. In mid-campaign he announced that under certain circumstances he might be for the acquisition of Texas. His tardy straddling probably cost him more votes than it gained. Polk carried the election by 170 electoral votes to 105, though his popular majority was less than 40,000. The Liberty party, running James G. Birney a second time, polled 62,000 votes (as compared with 7,000 in 1840), most of which were cast by Whigs who turned against Clay.

"Who is James K. Polk?" the Whigs had sarcastically asked during the campaign. Actually, he was not so obscure as all that. Born in North Carolina, he had moved, when in his mid-twenties, to Tennessee, thus following the pattern of the man who became his political mentor, Andrew Jackson. Elected to the national House of Representatives, he held his seat for fourteen consecutive years, serving for four of them as speaker. He was thin, worn, even grim-looking, and his public manners comported with his appearance. But he had a good mind, he worked hard at his job, and above all he had an iron, implacable will. Probably no other President entered office with so clearly defined a program and accomplished so much of it as did Polk.

Partitioning of Oregon

The ownership of Oregon had long been in dispute, but its boundaries were clearly defined — on the north the latitude line of 54° 40′, on the east the crest of the Rocky Mountains, on the south the forty-second parallel, and on the west the Pacific Ocean. Included in its half-million square miles were the present states of Oregon, Washington, and Idaho, parts of Montana and Wyoming, and half of British Columbia.

At various times in the past the Oregon country had been claimed by Spain, Russia, France, England, and the United States. By the 1820s only the last two nations remained in contention. The American and British claims were equally valid — or invalid. Both countries could assert title on the basis of the activities of their explorers, maritime traders, and fur traders. The English had one solid advantage: they were in actual possession of a part of the area. In 1821 the powerful British fur trading organization, the Hudson's Bay Company, established a post at Fort Vancouver, north of the Columbia River.

Several times the English government proposed the Columbia as a suitable line of division. The United States, also showing a desire to compromise, countered by suggesting the forty-ninth parallel. This difference in official views prevented an early settlement of the Oregon question. Unable to agree on a demarcation line, the diplomats of the two powers agreed that the citizens of each should have equal access to Oregon for ten years. This arrangement, called joint occupation, was renewed in 1827 for an indefinite period, with either nation empowered to end it on a year's notice.

Beginning in 1841, thousands of American pioneers set out for Oregon. Amazed observers remarked upon the "Oregon fever." Two thousand miles in length, the Oregon Trail penetrated Indian country and crossed mountains and semi-desert regions. To the emigrants, traveling in caravans of covered wagons and accompanied by

ring it to London. Abruptly Polk took a more militant attitude. Saying America should look John Bull "straight in the eye" and hinting at war, he asserted claim to all of Oregon. Though there was loose talk of war on both sides of the Atlantic, neither nation really wished to resort to force. The British government now offered to divide Oregon at the forty-ninth parallel — that is, to accept Polk's original proposal. In the 1846 treaty the United States secured the larger and better part of the Oregon country and certainly all that it could have reasonably expected to get.

Annexation of Texas

Southwest of the United States stretched the northern provinces of Mexico — Texas, New Mexico, and Upper California — once parts of Spain's colonial empire in North America but, since 1822, states in the independent republic of Mexico. Under Spanish rule the provinces had been subject to only the lightest supervision from the government of the vice-royalty in Mexico, and only a few thousand whites had settled in them. The same conditions prevailed under the republic, which lacked the power, the population, and the economic incentive to govern and settle such distant areas. At one time the United States had advanced a claim to Texas as a part of the Louisiana Purchase but had renounced the claim in 1819. Twice thereafter, however, in the presidencies of John Quincy Adams and Jackson, the United States had offered to buy Texas, only to meet with indignant Mexican refusals.

In the early 1820s the Mexican government encouraged American immigration by offering land grants to men like Stephen Austin who promised to colonize the land, swear loyalty to Mexico, and abandon Protestantism. Thousands of Americans, attracted by reports of the rich soil in Texas, took advantage of Mexico's welcome. The great majority, by the very fact of geography, came from the Southern states, sometimes bringing with them slaves, although slavery was forbidden in Mexico after 1829. By 1835 approximately 35,000 Americans were living in Texas, which was ten times the number of native Mexicans there.

Almost from the beginning there was friction

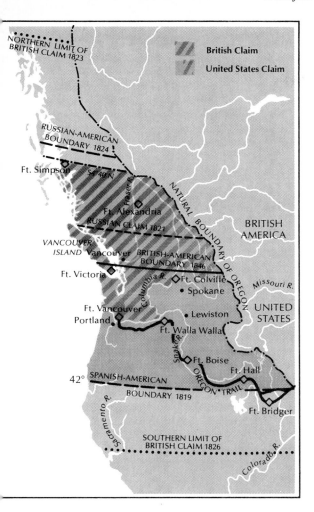

American Expansion in Oregon

huge herds of cattle, it presented enormous problems in transportation. The average period required for the journey was from May to November. Some never lived to complete it. But the great majority got through. By 1845, 5,000 Americans were living south of the Columbia — and demanding that their government take possession of Oregon.

When Polk assumed office, he was willing to compromise — to effect a division on the line of the forty-ninth parallel. The British minister in Washington rejected Polk's offer without refer-

between the settlers and both the Mexicans and the Mexican government. The Americans failed to appreciate the gentility of Spanish culture and blamed the illiteracy of the Mexican peasants on racial inferiority; they were convinced that their life-style was in every way superior to that of the original Mexicans and believed that it was their mission to bring progress to a backward society. By the 1830s the numerically and financially dominant settlers had relegated the native Mexicans to inferior status.

Finally the Mexican government, realizing that its power over Texas was being challenged by the settlers and recognizing the plight of the native Mexicans, moved to exert control. A new law reduced the powers of the various states of the republic, a measure that the Texans took to be aimed specifically at them; another law threatened to prohibit slavery after 1842; and when protesting in Mexico City, Stephen Austin found himself thrown in jail. In 1836 the Texans proclaimed their independence.

The Mexican dictator Santa Anna advanced into Texas with a large army. Even with the aid of volunteers, money, and supplies from private groups in the United States, the Texans were having difficulty in organizing a resistance. Their garrison at the Alamo mission in San Antonio was exterminated; another at Goliad suffered substantially the same fate when the Mexicans murdered most of the force after it surrendered. But General Sam Houston, emerging as the national hero of Texas, kept a small army together, and at the battle of San Jacinto (April 21, 1836, near present-day Houston) he defeated the Mexican Army, killing more than 600 Mexican soldiers in retaliation, and taking Santa Anna prisoner. Although the Mexican government refused to recognize the captured dictator's vague promises to withdraw Mexican authority from Texas and limited fighting continued into the early 1840s, Texas had won its independence.

The new republic desired to join the United States and through its president, Sam Houston, asked for recognition, to be followed by annexation. Though President Jackson favored annexation, he proceeded cautiously.

Abolitionism was beginning to make its influence felt in politics. Many Northerners expressed a conviction that it would be immoral to extend the dominion of slavery. Others were opposed to incorporating a region that would add to Southern votes in Congress and in the electoral college. Jackson feared that annexation might cause an ugly sectional controversy and bring on a war with Mexico. He did not, therefore, propose annexation and did not even extend recognition to Texas until just before he left office in 1837. His successor, Van Buren, also refrained, for similar reasons, from pressing the issue.

President Tyler, eager to increase Southern power and worried about Texas becoming a British protectorate, persuaded Texas to apply again, and Secretary of State Calhoun submitted an annexation treaty to the Senate in April 1844. Unfortunately for Texas, Calhoun presented annexation as if its only purpose were to extend and protect slavery. The treaty was soundly defeated.

President Tyler, who remained in office until March 1845, viewed the election returns of 1844 as a mandate to carry annexation through. He proposed to Congress that Texas be annexed by a joint resolution of both houses, a device that would get around the necessity of obtaining a two-thirds majority in the Senate for a treaty. In February 1845, Congress voted to admit Texas to the Union. It became a state in December 1845.

Promptly, the Mexican government broke off diplomatic relations with the United States. To make matters worse, a dispute over Texas' boundary with Mexico now developed. The Texans claimed that the Rio Grande constituted the western and southern border, an assertion that would place much of what is now New Mexico in Texas. Mexico, while not formally conceding the loss of Texas, replied that the border had always been the Nueces River and pointed out that Texans had not settled between the Nueces and the Rio Grande. Polk recognized the Texan claim, and in the summer of 1845 he sent a small army under General Zachary Taylor to the Nueces line and massed a naval force in the Gulf to protect Texas, he said, against the Mexicans.

Lands Beyond Texas

New Mexico, another of Mexico's frontier provinces, supported a scanty population on a semi-primitive economy. Its small metropolis and trade center, Santa Fe, was 300 miles from the most northern settlements in Mexico. Under Spanish

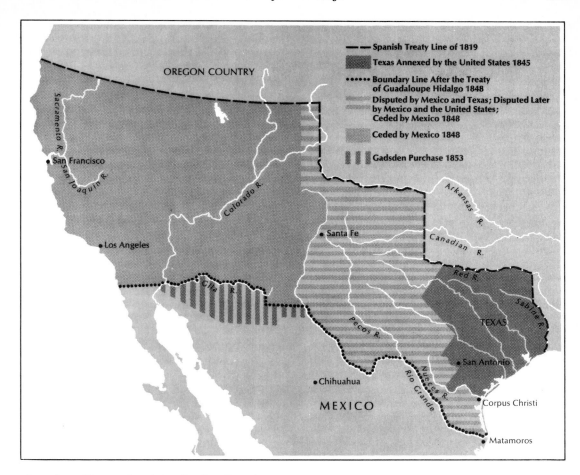

Spanish Treaty Line of 1819

Texas Annexed by the United States 1845

Boundary Line After the Treaty of Guadaloupe Hidalgo 1848

Disputed by Mexico and Texas; Disputed Later by Mexico and the United States; Ceded by Mexico 1848

Ceded by Mexico 1848

Gadsden Purchase 1853

American Expansion into the Southwest

rule the New Mexicans had to export their few products over 1,000 miles to Mexico City and Vera Cruz and from these economic centers import their meager supply of finished goods. Mexico, after achieving independence from Spain, let it be known that traders from the United States would be welcome in New Mexico.

An American wagoned a load of merchandise to Santa Fe in 1821 and sold it at a high profit. Out of his success arose the famous and colorful "Santa Fe trade." Every year traders with a stock of manufactured goods gathered at Independence, Missouri, and traveled in an organized caravan over the Sante Fe Trail, more than 800 miles long. The merchants brought back gold, silver, furs, and mules. The Sante Fe trade opened

up another route to the West and pointed another direction for expansion.

Even more distant from Mexico City and even freer from Mexican supervision was the third of the northern provinces, California. In this vast, rich region lived perhaps 100,000 Indians and 3,000 Mexicans, descendants of Spanish colonists, who engaged in agricultural pursuits, chiefly ranching, lived lives of primitive plenty, and carried on a skimpy trade with the outside world.

The first Americans to enter California were maritime traders and captains of ships engaged in whaling or in harvesting sea otters for their furs. Following them came merchants, who established stores, imported merchandise, and conducted a profitable trade in furs, hides, and tallow with the

Mexicans and Indians. Thomas O. Larkin, who set up business in Monterey in 1832, soon attained the status of a leading citizen. Although Larkin maintained close and friendly relations with the Mexican authorities, he secretly longed for the day when California would become an American possession. In 1844–1845 he accepted an appointment as United States consul, with instructions to arouse sentiment among the Californians for annexation.

As reports spread of the rich soil and mild climate, immigrants began to enter California from the east by land. These were pioneering farmers, of the type who were penetrating Texas and Oregon in search of greener pastures. By 1845 there were 700 Americans in California, most of them concentrated in the valley of the Sacramento River and thus removed from the centers of Mexican power on the coast.

President Polk feared that Great Britain wanted to acquire or dominate California as well as Texas — a suspicion that was given credence by the activities of British diplomatic agents in the province. His dreams of expansion went beyond the Democratic platform. He was determined to acquire for his country New Mexico and California and possibly other parts of northern Mexico.

At the same time that he sent Taylor to the Nueces, Polk also sent secret instructions to the commander of the Pacific naval squadron to seize the California ports if he heard that Mexico had declared war. A little later Consul Larkin was informed that, if people wanted to revolt and join the United States, they would be received as brethren. Still later an exploring expedition led by Captain John C. Frémont, of the army's corps of topographical engineers, entered California. The Mexican authorities, alarmed by the size of the party and its military aspects, ordered Frémont to leave. He complied but moved only over the Oregon border.

"American Blood"

After preparing measures that looked like war, Polk resolved on a last effort to achieve his objectives by diplomacy. He dispatched to Mexico a special minister, John Slidell, a Louisiana politi-

cian, with instructions to settle with American money all the questions in dispute between the two nations. If Mexico would acknowledge the Rio Grande boundary for Texas, the United States would assume the damage claims, amounting to several millions, which Americans held against Mexico. If Mexico would cede New Mexico, the United States would pay $5,000,000. And for California, the United States would pay up to $25,000,000. Slidell soon notified his government that his mission had failed. Immediately after receiving Slidell's information, on January 13, 1846, Polk ordered Taylor's army to move across the Nueces to the Rio Grande.

If Polk was hoping for trouble, he was disappointed for months. Finally, in May, he decided to ask Congress to declare war on the grounds that Mexico had refused to honor its financial obligations and had insulted the United States by rejecting the Slidell mission. While Polk was working on a war message, the news arrived from Taylor that Mexican troops had crossed the Rio Grande and attacked a unit of American soldiers. Polk now revised his message. He declared: "Mexico has passed the boundary of the United States . . . and shed American blood upon the American soil" — "war exists by the act of Mexico herself." Congress accepted Polk's interpretation of events and on May 13, 1846, declared war by votes of 40 to 2 in the Senate and 174 to 14 in the House.

Although Congress had accepted war with near-unanimity, there was more opposition than appeared on the surface. Opposition increased and intensified as the war continued and costs and casualties came home to the people. The Whigs in Congress supported the military appropriation bills, but they became ever bolder and more bitter in denouncing "Mr. Polk's war" as aggressive in origin and objectives.

War with Mexico

In the opening phases of the war President Polk assumed the planning of grand strategy, a practice that he continued almost to the end of the war. His basic idea was to seize key areas on the Mexican frontier and then force the Mexicans to make peace on American terms. Accordingly, he

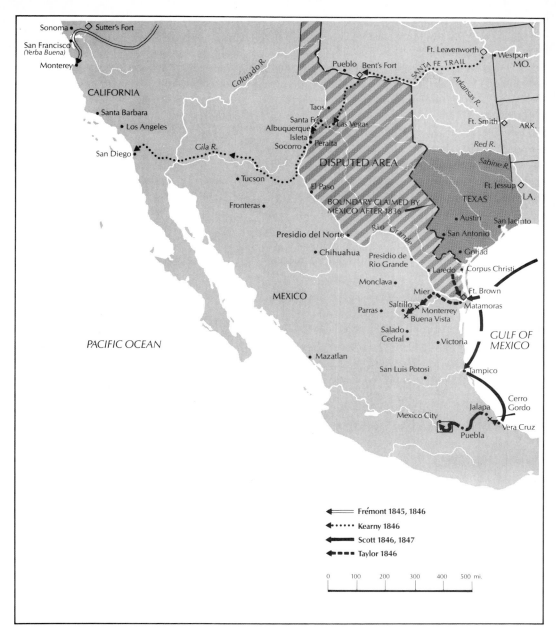

The Mexican War

ordered Taylor to cross the Rio Grande and occupy northeastern Mexico, taking as his first objective the city of Monterrey. Taylor, "Old Rough
and Ready," attacked Monterrey in September
1846 and took it, but at the price of agreeing to
let the garrison evacuate without pursuit.

Two other offensives planned by Polk were
aimed at New Mexico and California. In the summer of 1846 a small army under Colonel Stephen
W. Kearny made the long march to Santa Fe and
occupied the town with no opposition. Then he
proceeded with a few hundred troopers to California to take charge of operations there. In California a combined revolt and war was being
staged by the settlers, Frémont's exploring party,
and the American Navy. With some difficulty,
Kearny brought the disparate American elements
under his command, and by the autumn of 1846
completed the conquest of California.

In addition to northeastern Mexico, the United
States now had possession of the two provinces
for which it had gone to war. In a sense, the objectives of the war had been achieved. The only
trouble was that Mexico would not agree to a
peace and cede the desired territory. At this point
Polk turned to General Winfield Scott, the commanding general of the army and its finest soldier,
for help. Together Polk and Scott devised a plan
to force the Mexicans to accept peace. From Vera
Cruz, on the Gulf coast, Scott would move west
along the National Highway to Mexico City.

While Scott was assembling his army off the
coast, General Santa Anna, again in power as
Mexican dictator, decided to take advantage of
the division of American forces by marching
northward and crushing Taylor and then returning to deal with Scott. With an army much larger
than Taylor's, Santa Anna attacked the Americans
at Buena Vista (February 1847). Santa Anna could
not break the American line and had to return to
defend Mexico City.

In the meantime Scott had taken Vera Cruz by
siege and was moving inland, in one of the most
brilliant campaigns in American military annals.
With an army that never numbered more than
14,000, he advanced 260 miles into enemy territory, conserved the lives of his soldiers by using
flanking movements instead of frontal assaults,
and finally achieved his objective without losing a
battle. At Cerro Gordo, in the mountains, he inflicted a smashing reverse on the Mexicans. He
met no further resistance until he was within a
few miles of Mexico City. After capturing the fortress of Chapultepec in a hard fight, the Americans occupied the enemy capital.

Polk, in his growing anxiety to get the war finished, had sent with the invading army a presidential agent who was authorized to negotiate an
agreement. On February 2, 1848, the agent concluded the Treaty of Guadalupe Hidalgo. Mexico
agreed to cede California and New Mexico and to
acknowledge the Rio Grande boundary of Texas.
In return, the United States contracted to assume
the claims of its citizens against Mexico and to
pay $15 million to Mexico.

Settlers in the Far West

When the war ended, a portion of the territory
acquired from Mexico was already settled by
Americans who, ironically, had left their country
because they were unhappy there. These people
were adherents of a religious sect formally known
as the "Church of Jesus Christ of Latter Day
Saints" and more commonly known as Mormons.
The Mormon faith, one of the numerous new religions that flowered in America in the 1820s and
1830s, had originated in western New York. The
Mormons believed in a tightly knit and disciplined community life directed by the church
elders. Seeking a more congenial environment,
under the leadership of their prophet, Joseph
Smith, they moved to Ohio, then to Missouri, and
finally to Nauvoo, Illinois. Everywhere they met
with resentment, largely caused by their economic and community organization. At Nauvoo
they particularly outraged the opinions of their
neighbors by introducing polygamy. Their troubles came to a climax when a mob lynched Smith.

Smith's successor, Brigham Young, now decided that if the Mormons were to escape further
persecution they would have to move outside the
United States. In 1846 almost the entire Mormon
community left Nauvoo. Their destination,
picked out by Young, was the Great Salt Lake
basin in Utah, so arid that no other people would
have the courage to live there. By 1850 over
11,000 people were settled in and around the
Mormon metropolis of Salt Lake City. With the

aid of irrigation they made the desert bloom. They established thriving industries, and they built up a profitable trade with emigrants on the way to California.

In January 1848 gold was discovered in the Sacramento Valley in California. As word of the strike spread, inhabitants of California and the whole Far West, fired by hopes of becoming immediate millionaires, stampeded to the area to stake out claims. By the end of summer the news had reached the Eastern states and Europe. Then the gold rush really started. From the United States and all the world, thousands of "Forty-Niners" poured into California. Those who left from the older states could choose between three routes of travel: overland by covered wagon, inexpensive but involving a long journey over the Great Plains and across the Rockies; by ship around Cape Horn, quicker but more expensive; or the dangerous, difficult shortcut across the Isthmus of Panama. By all three routes, disdaining hunger, thirst, disease, and even death, the seekers after gold came — more than 80,000 of them in 1849. By the end of that year, California had a population of approximately 100,000, more than enough to entitle it to statehood.

Wartime and Postwar Politics

In domestic politics President Polk was as aggressive — and successful — as he was in foreign policy. At his insistence Congress reestablished the Independent Treasury system, thus pleasing all sections of the Democratic party and redeeming one of its platform promises. Again at his demand, Congress fulfilled another platform pledge by lowering the tariff. The Tariff of 1846 reduced the average rates enough to delight the South, but it could not have been passed without the votes of Northwestern Democrats.

Naturally, the Westerners expected something in return, and specifically they expected Southern support for internal improvements. Two internal improvements bills passed Congress, but Polk, who sincerely believed that the national government had no legal power to finance such projects, vetoed both of them. The Westerners were disappointed and angered.

Before Polk left office, a much more dangerous issue emerged. In August 1846, while the war was in progress, he had asked Congress to provide him with $2,000,000 that he could use to purchase peace with Mexico. When the appropriation was introduced in the House, David Wilmot of Pennsylvania, an antislavery Democrat from a high-tariff state, moved an amendment that slavery should be prohibited in any territory secured from Mexico. The so-called Wilmot Proviso passed the House but failed in the Senate. It would be called up again and be debated and voted on for years.

Diametrically opposed to the Wilmot Proviso was the formula of the Southern extremists. They contended that the states jointly owned the territories and that the citizens of each state possessed equal rights in them, including the right to move to them with their property, particularly slave property. According to this view, Congress, which was the only agent for the joint owners, had no power to prohibit the movement of slavery into the public domain or to regulate it in any way except by extending protection. Neither could a territorial legislature, which was a creature of Congress, take any action to ban slavery.

Two compromise plans were presented. One, which numbered President Polk among its advocates, proposed to run the Missouri Compromise line of 36° 30′ through the new territories to the Pacific coast, banning slavery north of the line and permitting it south. The other, first prominently espoused by Lewis Cass, Democratic senator from Michigan, was originally called "squatter sovereignty." Later, when taken up by Stephen A. Douglas, an Illinois senator of the same party, it was given the more dignified title of "popular sovereignty." According to this formula, the question of slavery in each territory should be left to the people there, acting through the medium of their territorial legislature.

Congress and the country debated the various formulas, but at the end of Polk's administration no decision had been reached. No territorial government had been provided for California or New Mexico (New Mexico included most of present New Mexico and Arizona, all of Utah and Nevada, and parts of Colorado and Wyoming). Even the organization of Oregon, so far north that obviously slavery would never enter it, was held up by the controversy. Southern members of Congress, hoping to gain some advantage in the regions farther south, blocked a territorial bill for Oregon until August 1848, when a free-soil government was finally authorized.

The debate was partially stilled by the presidential campaign of 1848. Both the Democrats and the Whigs tried to avoid definite and provocative references to the slavery question. The Democrats nominated as their candidate Lewis Cass of Michigan, an elderly, honest, dull wheel horse of the party. Although their platform was purposely vague, it was capable of being interpreted as an endorsement of squatter sovereignty. The Whigs adopted no platform and presented as their candidate a military hero with no political record — General Zachary Taylor of Louisiana.

Ardent abolitionists and even moderates who merely opposed the expansion of slavery found it difficult to swallow either Cass or Taylor. The situation was ripe for the appearance of a third party. The potential sources for such a group were the existing Liberty party and the antislavery members of the old organizations. Late in the campaign, third-party promoters held a national convention, adopted a platform endorsing the Wilmot Proviso, free homesteads, and a higher tariff, and nominated former President Van Buren for the Presidency. Thus was launched the Free-Soil party.

Taylor and the Whigs won a narrow victory. Though Van Buren failed to carry a single state, he polled an impressive 291,000 votes, and the Free-Soilers elected ten members to Congress. It is probable that Van Buren pulled enough Democratic votes away from Cass, particularly in New York, to throw the election to Taylor.

Selected Readings

General accounts of economic development are W. E. Brownlee, *Dynamics of Ascent: A History of the American Economy* (1974), and D. C. North, *The Economic Growth of the United States, 1790–1860°* (1961). On transportation and communication, see G. R. Taylor, *The Transportation Revolution, 1815–1860* (1951). Immigration and nativism are discussed in Oscar Handlin, *Boston's Immigrants°* (1941), and P. Taylor, *The Distant Magnet°* (1971).

On Jacksonian politics and democratic trends, see the following: Alexis de Tocqueville, *Democracy in America°* (2 vols., 1945); R. P. McCormick, *The Second American Party System: Party Formation in the Jacksonian Era* (1966); and A. M. Schlesinger, Jr., *The Age of Jackson°* (1945). See also Edward Pessen, *Jacksonian America* (1970). Indian policy is treated in F. P Prucha, *American Indian Policy in the Formative Years* (1962), and R. N. Satz, *American Indian Policy in the Jacksonian Era* (1975); nullification in W. W. Freehling, *Prelude to Civil War: The Nullification Controversy in South Carolina, 1810–1836* (1966), and R. N. Current, *John C. Calhoun°* (1963); and the "bank war" in Bray Hammond, *Banks and Politics in America from the Revolution to the Civil War* (1957), and Peter Temin, *The Jacksonian Economy°* (1969). Whig politics are seen in R. N. Current, *Daniel Webster and the Rise of National Conservatism°* (1955).

On cultural trends and the reform spirit, see A. F. Tyler, *Freedom's Ferment: Phases of American Social History to 1860°* (1940), and R. G. Walters, *American Reformers, 1815–1860* (1978). On women and the rise of feminism, see Nancy Cott, *The Bonds of Womanhood: "Women's Sphere" in New England, 1780–1835°* (1977), and Nancy Woloch, *Women and the American Experience°*

(1984). The following deal with abolitionist activity: L. F. Litwack, *North of Slavery: The Negro in the Free States, 1790–1860* (1961); Benjamin Quarles, *Black Abolitionists* (1969); Louis Filler, *The Crusade Against Slavery, 1830–1860* ° (1960); and G. H. Barnes, *The Antislavery Impulse, 1830–1844* ° (1933). Slavery is the subject of K. M. Stampp, *The Peculiar Institution: Slavery in the Ante-Bellum South* ° (1956); S. M. Elkins, *Slavery: A Problem in American Institutional and Intellectual Life* ° (1959); E. D. Genovese, *The Political Economy of Slavery* ° (1965) and *Roll, Jordan, Roll* ° (1974); Herbert G. Gutman, *The Black Family in Slavery and Freedom, 1750–1925* (1976); and Paul A. David *et al., Reckoning with Slavery* ° (1976). On expansion, see O. A. Singletary, *The Mexican War* ° (1960), and Frederick Merk, *Slavery and the Annexation of Texas* (1972).

° Titles available in paperback.

North and South Separate, Fight, and Rejoin, While the Slaves Gain Partial Freedom

George Washington on leaving the Presidency had cautioned his fellow citizens that it might "disturb our Union" if political parties should ever be organized on a geographical basis — Eastern against Western or Northern against Southern — "whence designing men may endeavour to excite a belief that there is a real difference of local interests and views." He explained: "One of the expedients of party to acquire influence, within particular districts, is to misrepresent the opinions and aims of other districts."

From the beginning the parties had been national, not sectional. From the 1830s on, Whigs from North and South cooperated against Democrats from North and South. Partisan loyalties cut across geographical lines and served as bonds of national union. Then, during the 1850s, the Whig party disintegrated. In the North it was replaced by a new party, the Republican, which had no members in the South. For a while the Democratic party continued to have a nationwide membership, but the party was weakened by sectional strains, and in 1860 it split into Northern and Southern wings. The time was at hand against which George Washington had warned.

No doubt some of the politicians of each section had misrepresented the "opinions and aims" of the other. Still, the sectionalization of parties was due not merely to the influence of "designing men" but also to a "real difference of local interests and views." The breaking of the bonds of union and of the Union itself could hardly have occurred without real and substantial causes —

the rise of opposition to slavery on moral grounds, the rapid industrialization of the North, and the westward movement of population. The political disputes that led to national disruption centered on the question of future slavery in the West, not present slavery in the South, but that was largely due to the nature of the American Constitution. Opponents of slavery could hardly contend that the Constitution gave the federal government power to abolish it in the states where it already existed. These people did maintain — though defenders of slavery denied — that the federal government could, and should, prevent its spread to new territories.

After the new Northern party had won a presidential election, the Southern states seceded, and war came. From the seceders' point of view, it was a war for Southern independence. Afterward (but not at the time) Southerners were to call it "the War between the States," thus implying that secession and resistance to federal authority had been legitimate, constitutional exercises of state rights. Yet the Southerners both during and after the fighting were proud to call themselves "rebels," and from the Northern view they were certainly engaging in rebellion as well as war. The official name that the Union government gave the conflict was "the War of the Rebellion."

This was the first great military experience of the American people. Compared to it the earlier wars — the one with Mexico, the War of 1812, even the Revolutionary struggle itself — were minor and episodic. It has been called the first modern war. It involved masses of men and new kinds of technology: railroads and railroad artillery, the telegraph, armored ships, balloons, the Gatling gun (precursor of the machine gun), repeating rifles, trenches, wire entanglements, water and land mines (including what were then called "infernal machines" and would now be known as "booby traps"), torpedo boats, even submarines. It compelled both sides to concentrate a high proportion of their resources on the pursuit of total victory. More than most wars, this one settled some things and settled them permanently. It brought about the destruction of slavery and the preservation of the Union. But it did not settle the question of the precise relationship of the states to the Union or of blacks to whites.

When Americans of a later generation looked back on the 1860s and 1870s, it seemed to many of them that there had been a sharp break between the Civil War and the ensuing period of Reconstruction. The war itself, for all its suffering and sacrifice, was remembered on the whole as an ennobling experience, one of high purpose and gallantry on both sides. The postwar years, by contrast, appeared to have been a time of low, unscrupulous politics, a time when vengeful men among the victors disgraced the country while unnecessarily delaying a real, heartfelt reunion of the North and the South.

That view contains elements of historical reality, but it misses an essential truth about the trou-

bled postwar period. The struggle over Reconstruction was, in part, a continuation of the Civil War. It was a struggle, as the war had been, that involved (among other things) the question of both state rights and human rights. The victory for Union and emancipation had not been completely won on the battlefield. In the postwar years an effort was made to confirm the supremacy of the national government over the Southern states and to assure the benefits of freedom to the millions of emancipated slaves. This effort, provoking resistance as it did, had the effect of keeping the country psychologically divided.

The struggle over Reconstruction ended in the Compromise of 1877. This arrangement, a combination of "reunion and reaction," brought the sections together at the expense of the black people. The federal government gave up the attempt to enforce the rights of blacks and left the Southern states in the hands of the conservative whites. Yet two great charters of human liberty still stood as documents of the Reconstruction era — the Fourteenth and Fifteenth amendments to the federal Constitution — which had been intended to assure citizenship and the suffrage to the former slaves. For the time being these documents were disregarded, but a day was to come, several decades later, when they would provide the legal basis for a renewed drive to bring true freedom and equality to all Americans.

Chapter 12

The Road to Disunion

Taylor and the Territories

Zachary Taylor was the first man to be elected President with no previous political training or experience. He was also the first professional soldier to sit in the White House. Although he came from the South and was a slaveholder, Taylor was a Southerner only in a technical sense. From his long years in the army he had acquired a national outlook and an attachment to the concept of nationalism.

He had to face immediately the problem of providing civil government for the area annexed from Mexico, which was being administered by military officials who were responsible to the President. The old soldier had a penchant for simple solutions, and a ready answer came to him — statehood for these territories. Statehood would not only provide civil government but prevent a controversy over slavery in the territories, because it was universally conceded that a territory on becoming a state could do whatever it wanted about slavery. Therefore, after assuming office in March 1849, he encouraged California and also New Mexico to frame constitutions and apply for statehood.

California needed no prodding; by October the Californians had prepared and ratified a constitution in which slavery was prohibited. Without waiting for congressional approval of their work, as required by law, they elected a state government and representatives to Congress. New Mexico, with a smaller population and less pressing governmental problems, moved more slowly, but prepared to call a constitutional convention. When Congress assembled in December 1849,

Taylor proudly described his efforts, and recommended that California be admitted as a free state and that New Mexico, when it was ready, be permitted to come in with complete freedom to decide the status of slavery.

Immediately it became apparent that Congress was not going to accept the President's program. For one reason, the legislative branch felt a natural jealousy of the power of the executive, a feeling that had been increasing since Jackson's time; many legislators believed Taylor should have consulted Congress before acting.

Simultaneously a number of side issues emerged to worsen the situation. One of them arose out of the demand of the antislavery forces that slavery be abolished in the District of Columbia, a demand that was angrily resisted by Southerners. Another concerned the "personal liberty" laws enacted by many Northern states, laws that forbade their courts and police officers to assist in the return of fugitive slaves. In retaliation, some Southerners were calling for a stringent *national* fugitive-slave law.

A third issue related to the boundary between Texas and New Mexico. Texas claimed the portion of New Mexico east of the Rio Grande, although the national government had assigned this region to New Mexico. Texans resented this action and also the government's refusal to assume the Texas war debt. Southern extremists supported the pretensions of Texas, while their fellows in the North upheld New Mexico.

Finally, there was the fear felt by the South at the prospect of two new free states being added

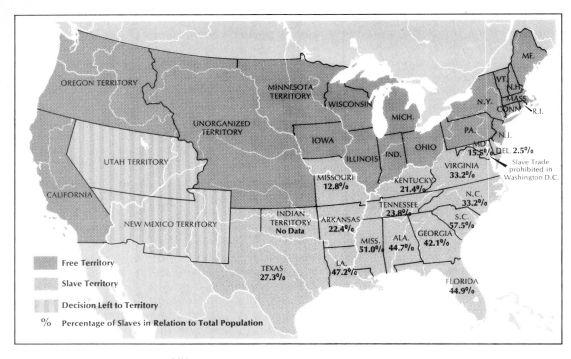

Slave and Free Territory 1850

to the Northern majority. In the structure of
the national government the South retained an
equal voice only in the Senate. The number of
free and slave states was equal in 1849; there
were fifteen of each. But now the admission of
California would upset the balance and deprive
the South of its last constitutional protection —
and New Mexico, Oregon, and Utah were yet
to come.

Responsible Southern leaders declared that if
California was to be admitted, and if slavery was
to be prohibited in the territories, the time had
come for the South to secede from the Union. At
the suggestion of Mississippi, a call went out for a
Southern-rights convention to meet in June 1850
at Nashville, Tennessee, to consider whether the
South should resort to secession. In the North excitement ran equally high. Every Northern state
legislature but one adopted resolutions demanding that slavery be barred from the territories;
public meetings all through the free states called
for the Wilmot Proviso and the abolition of slavery in the District of Columbia.

The Compromise of 1850

As the crisis worsened, moderate men in Congress naturally turned their thoughts to the framing of a compromise that would satisfy both sections and restore tranquility, and for a leader they
turned to Henry Clay, the venerable Kentuckian.
Clay believed that no compromise would have
any significant or lasting effects unless it settled
all the issues in dispute between the sections. Accordingly, he took a number of separate measures
which had been proposed by various members of
both parties and combined them into one set of
resolutions that, on January 29, 1850, he presented to the Senate. His proposals were as follows: (1) that California be admitted as a free
state; (2) that, in the rest of the Mexican cession,
territorial governments be formed without restrictions as to slavery; (3) that Texas yield in its
boundary dispute with New Mexico and be compensated by the federal government's taking over
its public debt; (4) that the slave trade, but not
slavery itself, be abolished in the District of Co-

lumbia; and (5) that a new and more effective fugitive-slave law be passed.

These resolutions started a debate that raged for months in Congress and throughout the country. Clay himself opened the oratorical tournament with a defense of his measures and a plea to North and South to be mutually conciliatory and forbearing.

Early in March, John C. Calhoun, who had less than a month to live, presented the views of the Southern extremists. Too ill and weak to speak, he sat grimly in his seat while a colleague read his speech. Almost ignoring Clay's proposals, he devoted his argument to what to him was the larger and the only subject — the minority South — and he asked more for his section than could be given: The North must admit that the South possessed equal rights in the territories, must agree to observe the laws concerning fugitive slaves, must cease attacking slavery, and must accept an amendment to the Constitution guaranteeing a balance of power between the sections.

After Calhoun came the third of the elder statesmen, Daniel Webster. His "Seventh of March address" was probably the greatest forensic effort of his long oratorical career. Although he still nourished White House ambitions, he now sought to calm angry passions and to rally Northern moderates to the support of compromise, even at the risk of alienating the strong antislavery sentiment of his native New England.

Other speakers now entered the debate. Some recommended popular sovereignty; others advocated extending the Missouri Compromise line. Of particular import were the views of the Northern extremists, voiced by the New York Whig William H. Seward. There was a higher law than the Constitution, Seward proclaimed, the law of God, which required opposition to slavery.

After most of the speeches had been made, Clay's resolutions were referred to a special committee, headed by Clay, which was to frame them into acceptable laws and report back to the Senate. When the bills were introduced, popular sentiment in all sections was slowly swinging in favor of some kind of compromise. The country was entering upon a period of prosperity, and conservative economic interests everywhere wanted to terminate the sectional dispute and concentrate the attention of the nation upon internal expansion. Even in the South excitement seemed to be abating. The Nashville convention met in June and, after adopting some tame resolutions, adjourned to await final action by Congress.

For a time, however, it seemed that Congress was not going to act. One reason was the opposition of Taylor. The President persisted in his stand that the admission of California, and possibly New Mexico, must come first and alone; after that, it might be possible to discuss other measures. In the meantime, if the South wanted to try anything like secession, "Old Zack" was ready to use force against his native section and to lead the armed forces in person.

On July 9, President Taylor suddenly died, the victim of a violent stomach disorder following an attack of heat prostration. He was succeeded by the Vice President, Millard Fillmore of New York. The new chief executive was a practical politician who understood the importance of compromise in statecraft. At once he ranged himself on the side of the advocates of adjustment, using his powers of persuasion and patronage to swing Northern Whigs into line. At about the same time, Clay, exhausted by his labors, temporarily left Congress, and Stephen A. Douglas took over the leadership of the compromise forces. Discarding the Kentuckian's all-or-nothing strategy, Douglas broke up the various measures reported by Clay's committee and presented them one by one. By mid-September the series of measures had been enacted by both houses of Congress and signed by the President.

It was one thing to pass the Compromise through Congress and another to persuade the country to accept it. In the North the task of winning popular acceptance was easier than in the South. The only provision that really gagged Northern opinion was the Fugitive Slave Act. By this measure blacks accused of being runaways were denied trial by jury and the right to testify in their own behalf. Their status was to be decided by a federal judge or by a special commissioner appointed by the federal circuit courts. They could be remanded to slavery on the bare evidence of an affidavit presented by the individual who claimed to be the owner.

The advocates of the Compromise in the South had to fight hard to carry the day. The adjourned session of the Nashville convention met in November 1850 (with only about a third of the original delegates present) and condemned the Compromise. Eventually, the South brought itself to accept the Compromise, but only after much agonizing, and then only conditionally. Several states declared that if in the future Southern rights were denied, the section would have to consider secession.

Renewed Agitation

At their national convention in 1852 the Democrats adopted a platform pledging their devotion to the Compromise of 1850 and their opposition to all attempts to renew the agitation of the slavery question. Not so unanimous when it came to choosing a candidate, they wrangled through forty-nine ballots, with no one of the leading contenders — General Lewis Cass of Michigan, Douglas, or James Buchanan of Pennsylvania — being able to secure a two-thirds majority. Finally, the prize went to one of the more obscure aspirants, Franklin Pierce of New Hampshire. The Whigs likewise endorsed the Compromise but in much milder terms and over the opposition of many antislavery, or "Conscience," Whigs. Instead of nominating a man connected with the Compromise, they named General Winfield Scott, whose views were unknown and whose support by Northern delegates made him suspect to Southerners. Only the Free Soilers, with John P. Hale of New Hampshire as their candidate, repudiated the Compromise.

Probably because they had taken the strongest stand in its favor, the Democrats won at the polls. Pierce carried twenty-seven states and Scott four, and the Democrats got 254 electoral votes to the Whigs' 42 — the largest majority that any candidate had attained since Monroe's victory in 1820. The Free Soilers received only about half the number of votes they had polled in 1848.

When Franklin Pierce was inaugurated in 1853, he was, at the age of forty-nine, the youngest man up to that time to become President. Amiable and charming, he had been selected as the Democratic nominee largely for reasons of party harmony. In his short political career he had held few opinions and made few enemies. He was to make many enemies as President.

The Compromise did not dissolve the abolitionist organizations nor stop their crusade to convince the Northern masses that slavery was a sin. In the 1850s the abolitionists intensified their efforts and found a growing audience.

The most powerful, the most telling document in the abolitionist propaganda attack was a novel, *Uncle Tom's Cabin*, written by Harriet Beecher Stowe and published in 1852. Mrs. Stowe belonged to a famous New England ministerial family (her father and her seven brothers were preachers), and she had married a minister. For several years she had lived in Cincinnati and from there had made several forays into Kentucky to view slavery and plantation life. Her novel, written after she and her husband had left Cincinnati for Maine, was an indictment of slavery although not of the slaveholders; her purpose was to show that the slave system had a brutalizing effect on all who were connected with it.

The book had a terrific impact on the Northern mind. Other abolitionists had attacked slavery in the abstract or as an evil institution, but Mrs. Stowe assailed it in terms of human personalities. In such a form, her message appealed to emotions and sympathies as nothing had done before, and it inspired other similar novels. The book sold over 300,000 copies in its first year. Dramatized, it reached other thousands who attended the play.

Northern hostility to the new Fugitive Slave Act was intensified when Southerners appeared in the Northern states to pursue fugitives or to claim as slaves blacks who had been living for years in Northern communities. Mobs attempted to impede enforcement of the law. In 1851 a crowd in Boston took from a federal marshal a runaway named Shadrach and sent him on his way to Canada. Later there were similar rescues or rescue attempts in other places throughout the North.

These displays of violence alarmed the South, and so did the new personal-liberty laws passed by several Northern legislatures. The frank purpose of the statutes was to nullify the Fugitive Slave Act. They interposed state power between the accused fugitive and the federal authority. In Wisconsin and Massachusetts, state courts were instructed to issue writs of habeas corpus (requiring an appearance before a judge) against any person detaining a fugitive and to grant the fugitive a judicial hearing in which the burden of proof was placed on the pursuer. The supreme court of Wisconsin, in the case of *Ableman* v. *Booth* (1857), declared the national law void. When the Supreme Court of the nation decided against the state, the Wisconsin court ignored the decision. Thus legal and judicial barriers were being thrown in the way of the one provision of the Compromise that the South considered a victory, and Southerners were deeply angered.

Latin American Ambitions

The Pierce administration attempted to maintain a national base of support for the Democratic party in part by promoting foreign expansion, as had the Polk administration. Whigs would support efforts to open new trade; the Fillmore administration had sent Commodore Matthew C. Perry to open Japan to American merchants. And Americans across party lines believed the United States should support the liberal and nationalist revolutions that had appeared in Europe in 1848. The old Whig Daniel Webster, who returned to the office of secretary of state in 1850 until his death in 1852, had supported Hungary in its efforts to gain independence from Austria. The Democrats who felt most strongly about this organized the "Young America" movement and advocated American expansion into areas of Latin America controlled by European monarchies.

In practice, the Pierce administration favored ambitions in Latin America above all others. Southern Democrats blocked initiatives to annex Canada and acquire Hawaii and they forced Pierce to focus on Cuba. Earlier Polk had tried to purchase Cuba from Spain; then, from 1849 to 1851, Southern expansionists, trying to stir up revolution in Cuba in order to add it as a slave state, had funded three expeditions to Cuba by a Cuban exile, General Narciso López. Pierce privately supported another expedition to Cuba, which would be led by John A. Quitman, a former governor of Mississippi. He instructed Pierre Soulé, American minister to Spain, to attempt "to detach that island from the Spanish dominion." After failing to purchase Cuba, Soulé, collaborating with James Buchanan, the minister to Great Britain, sent Pierce what became known as the

"Ostend Manifesto." In it Soulé declared that the United States would be justified "by every law, human and Divine" in "wresting" Cuba from Spain "if we possess the power." By November 1854, when the document arrived in Washington, Pierce realized that Northern politicians, including many Democrats, would prevent the United States from undertaking a war to add a new slave state. Pierce also knew that supporting a Cuban revolution would lose him support among Northern Democrats, and he persuaded Quitman to abandon his expedition. In 1855, the Manifesto, when leaked to the public, produced a wave of outrage in the North.

Another Southern adventurer, William Walker, kept the ambition of slavery in Latin America before the American public. In 1854, with fifty-eight followers, he landed in Nicaragua, and by 1855 he had succeeded in making himself dictator of that country. He had the support of an American company that was trying to secure a route across Central America to the goldfields of California, but he had a grander scheme: creating and heading a new nation embracing Central America and Cuba. Most of his followers had a simpler mission: to bring Nicaragua into the Union. In 1856 Walker announced the reestablishment of slavery in Nicaragua, received recognition for his government from the Pierce administration, and won an endorsement from the Democratic party in its platform. However, Walker, having alienated the neighboring countries, was driven out of power in 1857 and died before a Honduran firing squad in 1860.

The Kansas-Nebraska Act

By the 1850s the line of frontier settlement had reached the great bend of the Missouri. Beyond the western boundaries of Minnesota, Iowa, and Missouri stretched the vast expanse of plains earlier called the Great American Desert and designated as an Indian reserve. Now it was known that large sections of this region were suited to farming, and in the Northwest people were saying that the national government should open the area to settlement and provide it with a railroad.

The idea of a transcontinental railroad had been discussed in and out of Congress for years and found wide approval in principle. Disagreement arose when people talked about the eastern terminus of the road and its specific route. Several cities pressed their claims, but the leading contenders were Chicago, St. Louis, Memphis, and New Orleans. The transcontinental railroad, like nearly everything else in the fifties, became entangled in sectionalism. People talked about a "southern road" or a "northern road."

One argument against a southern route had been removed through the foresight of Secretary of War Jefferson Davis. Surveys had indicated that a road from a southern terminus would probably have to pass through an area south of the Gila River, in Mexican territory. At Davis' suggestion, Pierce appointed James Gadsden, a Southern railroad builder, to negotiate with Mexico for the sale of this region. Gadsden persuaded the Mexican government to dispose of a strip of land that today comprises a part of Arizona and New Mexico, the so-called Gadsden Purchase (1853), which cost the United States $10,000,000.

The leading advocate of a northern route was Senator Stephen A. Douglas, and his interest influenced him to introduce in Congress a fateful legislative act, one that accomplished the final destruction of the truce of 1850. As a senator from Illinois and a resident of Chicago and, above all, as the acknowledged leader of the Northwestern Democrats, Douglas naturally wanted the transcontinental railroad for his own city and section. He realized too the potency of the principal argument urged against the northern route: that west of the Mississippi it would run largely through unsettled Indian country. Hence in January 1854 he introduced a bill to organize a huge new territory, to be known as Nebraska, west of Iowa and Missouri.

Douglas seemed to realize that his bill would encounter the opposition of the South, partly because it would prepare the way for a new free state, the proposed territory being in the Louisiana Purchase area north of the 36° 30′ line of the Missouri Compromise and hence closed to slavery. In an effort to make the measure acceptable to Southerners, Douglas inserted a provision that the status of slavery in the territory would be determined by the territorial legislature, that is, by popular sovereignty. The concession was not enough to satisfy extreme Southern Democrats, particularly those from Missouri who feared that

their state would be surrounded by free territory. They demanded more, and Douglas had to give more to get their support. He agreed to a clause specifically repealing the territorial section of the Missouri Compromise and to a provision creating two territories, Nebraska and Kansas, instead of one. Presumably the latter, because of its more southern location, would become a slave state. In its final form the measure was known as the Kansas-Nebraska Act.

Douglas induced President Pierce to endorse his bill, and so it became an official Democratic measure. But even with the backing of the administration, it encountered stiff opposition and did not become a law until May 1854. Nearly all the Southern members of Congress, whether Whigs or Democrats, supported the bill, and nearly all the Northern Whigs opposed it. The Northern Democrats split, with half of their votes in the House going for the act and half against it.

Probably no other piece of legislation in congressional history produced as many immediate, sweeping, and ominous changes as the Kansas-Nebraska Act. It destroyed the Whig party in the South except in the border states. At the same time, as many Southern Whigs became Democrats, it increased Southern influence in the Democratic party. It destroyed the popular basis of Whiggery in the North, with the result that by 1856 the national Whig party had disappeared and a conservative influence in American politics had been removed. It divided the Northern Democrats and drove many of them from the party. Most important of all, it called into being a new party that was frankly sectional in composition and creed.

People in both the major parties who opposed Douglas' bill took to calling themselves Anti-Nebraska Democrats and Anti-Nebraska Whigs. In their anger at the South they were in a mood to defend their opinions by forming a new party. And in 1854 this took form — the Republican party. Originating in a series of spontaneous popular meetings throughout the Northwest, the Republican movement soon spread to the East. In the elections of 1854 the Republicans, often acting in concert with the Know-Nothings, elected a majority to the House and won control of a number of Northern state governments. For the moment the new party was a one-idea organization: its only platform was opposition to the expansion of slavery into the territories. Composed mainly of former Whigs and Free Soilers but including also a substantial number of former Democrats, it represented in large part the democratic idealism of the North. But it contained, in addition, Northern power groups who felt that the South — the champion of a low tariff, the enemy of homesteads and internal improvements — was blocking their legitimate economic aspirations.

Republican Ideology

Republicans framed an ideology that had great appeal to free-soilers, abolitionists, and conservative Northern Whigs. The Republicans justified free-soil with ideas drawn from both Whig ideology and the ideas of the evangelical reform movements.

Republican ideology emphasized the class nature of the South. The planters seemed dangerous to both slaves and free society because they occupied positions of incredible power. There seemed to be no restraint on their passion and will. They could gratify every whim, inflict whatever injustice they wished. They even denied their slaves the uplifting influence of family and evangelical religion. By contrast, Republicans described the North as class-free. Abraham Lincoln, a Whig who became a Republican after the passage of the Kansas-Nebraska Act, described Northern society with the flat assertion that "there is no permanent class of hired laborers among us." He explained that "if any continue through life in the condition of the hired laborers, it is not the fault of the system, but because of either a dependent nature which prefers it, or improvidence, folly, or singular misfortune." Republican moralists saw only diligent, independent, and moral artisans, trades people, and farmers: a disciplined citizenry pursuing individualism within a context of Christian restraint. Citizens of a free society, Republicans said, met the responsibilities of family, church, and community. By claiming to protect this virtuous free society, Republicans at once defended the Northern status quo and identified themselves as the inheritors of the evangelical reform movements.

This Republican ideology had strong appeal for members of the Know-Nothing movement, many of whom were artisans, small manufacturers, and trades people. Many Know-Nothings saw the Republicans as sharing their concern for eliminating from America obstacles that blocked climbing the economic ladder in accord with the Protestant work ethic. While Know-Nothings wished to exclude immigrants from American life, many Western Republicans wished, through free-soil, to exclude blacks from their communities. Republicans and many Know-Nothings identified their common enemies as blacks, immigrants, and Democrats.

"Bleeding Kansas"

The pulsing popular excitement aroused in the North by the Kansas-Nebraska Act was sustained by events occurring during the next two years in Kansas. Almost immediately settlers moved into this territory. Many of them came to Kansas simply to make homes. But there were some who came for the specific purpose of engaging in a struggle over ideologies. They were dedicated people who were determined to make Kansas free — or slave. Those who came from the North were encouraged by press and pulpit and the powerful organs of abolitionist propaganda; often they received financial help from antislavery organizations. Those who came from the South were stimulated by similar influences of a Southern nature; often they received financial contributions from the communities they had left.

In the spring of 1855 elections were held for a territorial legislature. Thousands of Missourians, some traveling in armed bands, moved into Kansas and voted. Although there were probably only some 1,500 legal votes in the territory, over 6,000 votes were counted. With such conditions prevailing, the proslavery forces elected a majority to the legislature, which proceeded immediately to enact a series of laws legalizing slavery. The outraged free-staters, convinced that they could not get a fair deal from the Pierce administration, resolved on extralegal action. Without asking permission from Congress or the territorial governor, they elected delegates to a constitutional convention that met at Topeka and adopted a constitution excluding slavery. They then chose a governor and legislature, and petitioned Congress for statehood. Pierce stigmatized their movement as unlawful and declared that the government would support the proslavery territorial legislature.

A few months later a proslavery federal marshal assembled a huge posse, consisting mostly of Missourians, to arrest the free-state leaders in Lawrence. The posse not only made the arrests but sacked the town. Retribution came immediately. Among the more extreme antislavery proponents was a fierce, fanatical old man named John Brown who considered himself an instrument of God's will to destroy slavery. Estimating that five antislavery men had been murdered, he decided that it was his sacred duty to take revenge. He gathered six followers and in one night murdered five proslavery settlers (the "Pottawatomie massacre"). The result was to touch off civil war in Kansas — irregular, guerrilla war conducted by armed bands, some of them more interested in land claims or loot than in ideologies. People all over the country talked about "Bleeding Kansas."

In May 1856 Charles Sumner of Massachusetts arose in the Senate to discuss affairs in the strife-torn territory. He entitled his speech "The Crime against Kansas." Sincere, doctrinaire, Sumner embodied the extreme element of the political antislavery movement. In his address he fiercely denounced the Pierce administration, the South, and slavery; and he singled out for particular attention as a champion of slavery Senator Andrew P. Butler of South Carolina.

Particularly enraged by the attack was Butler's nephew, Preston Brooks, a member of the House from South Carolina. He resolved to punish Sumner by a method approved by the Southern code — by publicly and physically chastising the senator. Approaching Sumner at his desk when the Senate was not in session, he proceeded to beat his kinsman's traducer with a cane until Sumner fell to the floor in bloody unconsciousness. The injured senator stayed out of the Senate four years, and during his absence his state refused to elect a successor. Brooks, censured by the House, resigned and stood for reelection. He was returned by an almost unanimous vote.

The violence in Congress, like that in Kansas, was a symbol. It showed that Americans were becoming so agitated by their differences that they could not settle them by the normal political processes of debate and the ballot.

Buchanan and Sectional Politics

The presidential campaign of 1856 got under way with the country convulsed by the Brooks assault and the continuing violence in Kansas. The Democrats adopted a platform that endorsed the Kansas-Nebraska Act and defended popular sovereignty. The leaders wanted a candidate who had not made many enemies and who was not closely associated with the explosive question of "Bleeding Kansas." So the nomination went to James Buchanan of Pennsylvania, a reliable party stalwart who had been minister to England and hence had been safely out of the country during the recent troubles.

The Republicans, engaging in their first presidential contest, faced the campaign with confidence. They denounced the Kansas-Nebraska Act and the expansion of slavery but also approved a program of internal improvements, thus beginning to combine the idealism of antislavery with the economic aspirations of the North. Just as eager as the Democrats to present a safe candidate, the Republicans nominated John C. Frémont, who had made a national reputation as an explorer of the Far West, and who had no political record to embarrass the new party.

The American, or Know-Nothing, party was beginning to break apart on the inevitable rock of sectionalism. At its convention, many Northern delegates withdrew because the platform was not sufficiently firm in opposing the expansion of slavery. The remaining delegates nominated ex-President Millard Fillmore. His candidacy was endorsed by the sad remnant of another party, the few remaining Whigs who could not bring themselves to support either Buchanan or Frémont.

The results of the election seemed to indicate that the prevailing mood of the country was conservative. Buchanan carried all the slave states except Maryland (whose eight votes went to Fillmore) and five Northern states (Illinois, Indiana, New Jersey, Pennsylvania, and California). Frémont won the other eleven Northern states, and he received a large minority vote in the five states carried by Buchanan. In fact, his popular vote was only 400,000 less than Buchanan's.

James Buchanan had been in politics and in public office almost continuously since he was twenty-three years old. At the time of his inauguration he was nearly sixty-six. Undoubtedly his age and general physical infirmity had something to do with the indecision he often displayed. He seemed to be obsessed by one idea — to meet every crisis by giving the South what it wanted.

In the year Buchanan took office, a financial panic struck the American economy, but the following depression, instead of drawing the nation closer together in a sense of common misfortune, sharpened sectional differences. The South was not hit as hard as the North. The result was to confirm the opinion of Southern leaders that their economic system was superior to that of the free states; and, smarting under previous Northern criticisms of Southern society, they loudly boasted to the North of their superiority.

In the North the impact of the depression had the effect of strengthening the sectional Republican party. Distressed economic groups — manufacturers and farmers — came to believe that the depression had been caused by unsound policies forced upon the government by Southern-controlled Democratic administrations. They thought that prosperity could be restored by a program embracing such items as a high tariff (the tariff was lowered again in 1857), a homestead act, and internal improvements — all measures to which the South was opposed. Northern resentment at what seemed to be Southern restraint of the nation's economic future was one important reason why the Democrats lost their majority in the House in the election of 1858.

The Dred Scott Case

Two days after Buchanan was inaugurated, the Supreme Court of the United States projected itself into the sectional controversy with its decision in the case of *Dred Scott* v. *Sanford*.

Dred Scott was a Missouri slave, once the property of an army surgeon, who on his military pilgrimages had carried him to Illinois, a free state, and to Minnesota Territory, where slavery was forbidden by the Missouri Compromise. Eventually both the owner and the slave returned to Missouri, where the surgeon died. Scott was persuaded by some abolitionists to bring suit in the Missouri courts for his freedom on the ground that residence in a free territory made him a free

man. The state supreme court decided against him, but meanwhile the officer's widow had married an abolitionist. Her brother, J. F. A. Sanford, a New Yorker, became executor of her estate. Since Sanford was a citizen of another state, Scott's lawyers were able to get his case into the federal courts with the claim that the suit lay between citizens of different states. Regardless of the final decision, Scott would be freed, as his abolitionist owners would not keep him a slave. The case was intended to secure a federal decision on the status of slavery in the territories.

Of the nine justices, seven were Democrats (five of them from the South), one was a Whig, and one was a Republican. Chief Justice Taney, in the majority opinion, announced two important principles. First, the chief justice declared that Scott was not a citizen of Missouri and hence could not bring a suit in the federal courts. Second, Scott's residence in territory north of the Missouri Compromise line had not made him free. Slaves were property, said Taney, and the Fifth Amendment prohibited Congress from taking property without "due process of law." Consequently, Congress possessed no authority to pass a law depriving persons of their slave property in the territories. The Missouri Compromise, therefore, had always been null and void.

Few judicial opinions have stirred as much popular excitement as this one. Southerners were elated: the highest tribunal in the land had invested with legal sanction the extreme Southern argument. Republicans denounced the decision as a partisan opinion by a partisan body. As for settling the status of slavery in the territories, that section of the opinion was an *obiter dictum* and had no legal justification. Boldly the Republicans announced that when they secured control of the national government they would reverse the decision — by altering the personnel of the Court.

Kansas Again

President Buchanan, who had known in advance the nature of the Dred Scott decision (having been tipped off by two of the justices), had said in his inaugural address that he hoped the forthcoming opinion would end the agitation over slavery in the territories. With equal blindness, he decided that the best solution for the Kansas troubles was to force the admission of that territory as a slave state.

The existing proslavery territorial legislature called an election for delegates to a constitutional convention. The free-state people refused to participate. As a result, the proslavery forces won control of the convention, which met in 1857 at Lecompton and framed a constitution establishing slavery. When an election for a new territorial legislature was called, the antislavery groups turned out to vote and won a majority. Promptly the legislature moved to submit the Lecompton constitution to the voters. The document was rejected by more than 10,000 votes. The picture in Kansas was now clear enough. The majority of the people did not want to see slavery established. Unfortunately Buchanan could not see, or did not want to see, the true picture. He urged Congress to admit Kansas under the Lecompton constitution, and he tried to force the party to back his proposal. Douglas and other Western Democrats refused to accept this perversion of popular sovereignty. Openly breaking with the administration, Douglas denounced the Lecompton proposition. And although Buchanan's plan passed the Senate, Western Democrats helped to block it in the House. Partly to avert further division in the party, a compromise measure, the English bill, was offered (1858) and passed. It provided that the Lecompton constitution should be submitted to the people of Kansas for a third time. If the document was approved, Kansas was to be admitted and given a federal land grant; if it was disapproved, statehood would be postponed until the population reached 93,600, the legal minimum for a representative in Congress. Again, and for the last time, the Kansas voters decisively rejected the Lecompton constitution. Not until the closing months of Buchanan's administration, in 1861, when a number of Southern states had withdrawn from the Union, would Kansas enter the Union — as a free state.

Lincoln Against Douglas

The congressional elections of 1858 were unusually hard fought. The contest that excited the widest public attention was the senatorial election in Illinois. There Stephen A. Douglas, the most prominent Northern Democrat, was a candidate for reelection, and he was fighting for his political life. He faced a Republican opponent who was an exceptionally able campaigner, Abraham Lincoln.

Lincoln had been the leading Whig in Illinois. After the passage of the Kansas-Nebraska Act he had, after some hesitation, joined the new party, and he was now the leading Republican in his state. But because he was not as well known as Douglas, Lincoln challenged the senator to a series of seven joint debates. Douglas accepted, and the two candidates argued their cases before huge crowds in every congressional district in the state. The Lincoln-Douglas debates, as the oratorical jousts came to be known, were widely reported by the nation's press, and before their termination the Republican who had dared to challenge the "Little Giant" was a man of national prominence.

Douglas devoted his principal efforts to defending popular sovereignty and attacking the Republicans. Popular sovereignty was a democratic way of settling the slavery issue in the territories, he said. Although his formula would keep slavery out of the territories, he did not seem to think it was important to call the institution wrong.

Lincoln, for his part, wanted not only to bar slavery from the territories but also to call it wrong. If slavery was prevented from expanding into the territories, he claimed, it would eventually die a natural death.

In the debate at Freeport, Lincoln asked Douglas a question that made this meeting historically the most significant of all the debates. His query was: Can the people of a territory exclude slavery from its limits prior to the formation of a state constitution? Or in other words, is popular sovereignty still a legal formula despite the Dred Scott decision? The question was a trap, for no matter how Douglas answered it, he would lose something. If he disavowed popular sovereignty, he would undoubtedly be defeated for reelection and his political career would be ended. But if he reaffirmed his formula, Southern Democrats would be offended, the party split deepened, and his chances of securing the Democratic nomination in 1860 damaged if not destroyed.

Boldly Douglas met the issue. The people of a territory, he said, could, by lawful means, shut out slavery prior to the formation of a state constitution. Slavery could not exist a day without the support of "local police regulations," that is, without territorial laws supporting slave ownership. The mere failure of a legislature to enact such laws would have the practical effect of keeping slaveholders out. Thus a territory could still exclude slavery. Douglas' reply became known as the Freeport Doctrine or, in the South, as the Freeport Heresy. It satisfied his followers sufficiently to win him a return to the Senate, but throughout the North it aroused little enthusiasm.

The elections went strongly against the Democrats, who lost ground in almost every Northern state. The administration retained control of the Senate but lost its majority in the House, where the Republicans gained a plurality. The rise of Republican strength was another frightening manifestation to the South.

John Brown's Raid

But more frightening was an event occurring in 1859. John Brown, the grim fanatic of the Pottawatomie killings, now made a spectacular appearance on the national scene. Still convinced that he was God's instrument to destroy slavery, he decided to transfer his activities from Kansas to the South itself. With encouragement and financial aid from certain Eastern abolitionists, he devised a wild scheme to liberate the slaves. His plan was to seize a mountain fortress in Virginia from which he could make raids to free slaves; he would organize his freed slaves, whom he intended to arm, into a Negro state within the South, and eventually he would force the South to concede emancipation. Because he needed guns, Brown fixed on Harpers Ferry, where a United States arsenal was located, as his base of operations. In October, at the head of eighteen followers, he descended on the town and captured the arsenal. Almost immediately he was attacked by citizens and local militia companies, who were shortly reinforced by a detachment of United States Marines sent to the scene by the national government. With ten of his followers killed, Brown had to surrender. He was promptly tried in a Virginia court for treason against the state, found guilty, and sentenced to death by hanging. Six of his followers met a similar fate.

Probably no single event had as much influence as the Brown raid in convincing Southerners that the welfare of their section was unsafe in the Union. Despite all the eulogies of slavery they penned, one great fear always secretly gnawed at their hearts: the possibility of a general slave insurrection. But now it seemed that such an uprising might be encouraged by people in the North, specifically by Republicans.

Chapter 13

The Nation Divided

The Great Decision of 1860

The election of 1860, judged by its consequences, was the most momentous in our history.

As the Democrats gathered in convention at Charleston, South Carolina, in April, most of the Southern delegates came with the determination to adopt a platform providing for federal protection of slavery in the territories. The Western Democrats were angered at the rule-or-ruin attitude of the Southerners but hoped to negotiate a face-saving statement on slavery that would hold the party together. They vaguely endorsed popular sovereignty and proposed that all questions involving slavery in the territories be left up to the Supreme Court. When the convention adopted the Western platform, the delegations from eight lower South states withdrew from the hall. The remaining delegates then proceeded to the selection of a candidate. Stephen A. Douglas led on every ballot, but he could not muster the two-thirds majority (of the original number of delegates) required by party rules. Finally the managers adjourned the convention to meet again in Baltimore in June. At Baltimore most of the Southerners reappeared, only to walk out again. The rest of the Southerners had assembled at Richmond. The rump convention at Baltimore nominated Douglas. The Southern bolters at Baltimore and the men in Richmond nominated John C. Breckinridge of Kentucky. There were now two Democratic candidates in the field, and, although Douglas had supporters in the South and Breckinridge in the North, one was the nominee of the Northern Democrats and the other of the Southern Democrats.

The Republicans held their convention in Chicago in May. The party managers were determined that the party, in both its platform and its candidate, should appear to the voters as representing conservatism, stability, and moderation. No longer was the Republican party a one-idea organization composed of crusaders against slavery. It now embraced, or hoped to embrace, every major interest group in the North that believed that the South, the champion of slavery, was blocking legitimate economic aspirations.

The platform endorsed such measures as a high tariff, internal improvements, a homestead bill, and a Pacific railroad to be built with federal financial assistance. On the slavery issue, the Republicans affirmed the right of each state to control its own institutions. But they also denied the authority of Congress or of a territorial legislature to legalize slavery in the territories.

The leading contender for the nomination was William H. Seward, whose very prominence and long record hurt his availability. Passing him and other aspirants over, the convention nominated on the third ballot Abraham Lincoln — who was prominent enough to be respectable but obscure enough to have few foes, and who was radical enough to please the antislavery faction in the party but conservative enough to satisfy the ex-Whigs.

Still a fourth party entered the lists — the Constitutional Union party. Although posing as a new organization, it was really the last surviving remnant of the oldest conservative tradition in the country; its leaders were elder statesmen, and most of its members were former Whigs. Meeting in Baltimore in May, this party nominated John Bell of Tennessee and Edward Everett of Massachusetts. Its platform declared for the Constitution, the Union, and enforcement of the laws.

In the November election Lincoln won a majority of the electoral votes and the Presidency, though only about two-fifths of the popular votes. The Republicans had elected a President, but they had failed to secure a majority in Congress; and of course they did not have the Supreme Court.

The Secession of the South

During the campaign various Southern leaders had threatened that if the Republicans won the election the South would secede from the Union. Southern threats of secession had been voiced at intervals since 1850, without any action following, and Northerners had come to believe they were intended as bluffs. This time, however, the threats were serious.

For most whites in the lower South, the appropriate response to Lincoln's election seemed to be immediate secession. Since the shock of John Brown's raid, waves of hysteria over slave rebellion had swept through the region. The panic intensified during the presidential campaign. Fires of unknown origin and peculiar deaths of whites inspired reports of arson and poisoning. Southerners became convinced that Lincoln would challenge slavery not only in the territories but in the South itself. They knew that Lincoln thought that slavery was morally wrong; they believed that he would appoint abolitionists or free blacks to federal jobs in the South, and reopen the flow of abolitionist literature to Southern blacks. By the time of Lincoln's election in November, whites in the lower South were united in a fear of cataclysm — a fear that they believed no decent Christian or loyal American should have to endure. The relief could be found immediately: in secession from the Union.

The South believed that secession was a legal process. Sovereign states could leave the Union they had entered. But the process had to be a solemn one — the voters of a state elected a convention that had the power to take the state out of the Union.

South Carolina, long the hotbed of Southern separatism, led off the secession parade, its convention taking the state out of the Union on December 20, 1860, by a unanimous vote. It was followed quickly by six other states — Mississippi, Florida, Alabama, Georgia, Louisiana, and Texas. And in February 1861 representatives of the seceded states met at Montgomery, Alabama, and formed a new, Southern nation — the Confederate States of America.

Northern opinion was puzzled by secession, and the indecision was reflected in the thinking of President Buchanan. In his message to Congress of December 1860 he denied the right of a state to secede; but he added that he did not think the federal government possessed the power to coerce a state back into the Union. He intended to avoid a collision of arms and to maintain the symbolic authority of the national government until his successor could take office.

As the various states seceded, they took possession of federal property within their boundaries, but they lacked the strength to seize certain offshore forts, notably Fort Sumter in the harbor of Charleston, South Carolina, and Fort Pickens in the harbor of Pensacola, Florida. South Carolina, aggressively "independent," sent commissioners to Washington to ask for the surrender of Sumter, garrisoned by a small force under Major Robert Anderson. Buchanan, fearful though he was of provoking a clash, refused to yield the fort.

Buchanan also recommended to Congress that it frame compromise measures to hold the Union together. The Senate and the House appointed committees to study plans of adjustment. Outside Congress, representatives from twenty-one states met in a peace convention at Washington to try to shape a compromise. None of the compromise efforts succeeded. The one that came closest to adoption was offered by the Senate committee, the Crittenden Compromise. But it foundered on the issue that destroyed the others. The contending parties could agree on several questions, such as a constitutional amendment guaranteeing the permanence of slavery — but on the question of slavery in the territories they split apart.

And so nothing had been resolved when Abraham Lincoln was inaugurated President on March 4, 1861. In his inaugural address he laid down the following basic principles: the Union was older than the Constitution, no state could of its own volition leave the Union, the ordinances of secession were illegal, the acts of violence to support secession were insurrectionary or revolutionary. He declared that he meant to execute the laws in all the states and to "hold, occupy, and possess" the federal property in the seceded states (Forts Sumter and Pickens).

Lincoln soon found an opportunity to apply his policy in the case of Fort Sumter. Major Anderson was running short of supplies; unless he received fresh provisions the fort would have to be evacuated. After much deliberation Lincoln decided to dispatch to the fort a naval relief expedition. His move placed the Confederates in a dilemma. If they permitted the expedition to land, they would be bowing tamely to federal authority. But the only alternative was to reduce the fort before the ships arrived — in short, to invoke war. The government in Montgomery ordered General P. G. T. Beauregard, in charge of Confederate forces at Charleston, to demand Anderson's surrender and, if the demand was refused, to reduce the fort. Beauregard made the demand and Anderson rejected it. The Confederates then bombarded the fort for two days, April 12–13, 1861. On April 14 Anderson surrendered.

War had come. Lincoln moved to increase the army and called on the states to furnish troops to restore the Union. Now four more slave states seceded and joined the Confederacy: Virginia (April 17); Arkansas (May 6); Tennessee (May 7); and North Carolina (May 20). The mountain counties in northwestern Virginia refused to accept the decision of their state, established their own "loyal" government, and in 1863 secured admission to the Union as the new state of West Virginia. The four remaining slave states, Maryland, Delaware, Kentucky, and Missouri, cast their lot with the Union. Lincoln kept a keen watch on their actions, and in two, Maryland and Missouri, helped to ensure their decision by employing military force.

War Potential, North and South

The North had a larger labor reservoir from which to draw its armed forces. In the North, or the United States, were twenty-three states with a population of approximately 22,000,000. In the South, or the Confederate States, were eleven states with a population of some 9,000,000. Of these, approximately 3,500,000 were slaves, leaving a white population of something under 6,000,000.

The Northern economy was vastly superior to that of the South, especially in industrial production. Eighty percent of the factories of the country were concentrated in the North. The transportation system of the North was superior to that of the South. The North had more and better inland water transport (steamboats, barges), more surfaced roads, and more wagons and animals. The North had approximately 20,000 miles of railroads, while the South, containing at least as large a land area, had only 10,000 miles. The trackage figures, however, do not tell the whole story of Southern inferiority. There were important gaps between key points in the South, which meant that supplies had to be detoured long distances or carried between railheads by wagons. As the war wore on, the Confederate railroad system steadily deteriorated, and by the last year and a half of the struggle it had almost collapsed.

The material factors give the impression that the South had absolutely no chance to win the war. Actually, these odds were not so great as they appear at first glance. The South, for the most part, fought on the defensive in its own country and commanded interior lines. The Northern invaders had to maintain long lines of communication, to supply themselves in areas where transportation was defective, and to garrison occupied regions. Furthermore, the North had to do more than capture the enemy capital or defeat enemy armies. It had to convince the Southern civilian population that the war was hopeless by seizing and holding most of the Confederacy. The South was fighting for something very concrete, very easy for its people to understand. It simply wanted to be independent, to be let alone; it had no aggressive designs on the North. If the South could have convinced the North that it could not be conquered or that the result would not be worth the sacrifices, it might, even after 1863, have won its independence.

The North's Economic Program

For Northern industry and agriculture the wartime years were a period of significant legislative gains. The Republicans represented Northern industry and agriculture, and, now that the war had removed Southern opposition, they proceeded to put into effect the kind of program their supporters expected.

The Homestead Act (1862) and the Morrill Land Grant Act (1862) were measures the West had long sought. The first provided that any citizen, or any alien who had declared the intention to become a citizen, could register claim to a quarter section of public land (160 acres), and, after giving proof of having lived on it for five years, receive title on payment of a small fee. The Morrill Law provided federal aid for the promotion of agricultural education and, in turn, agricultural productivity. By its terms each state was to receive 30,000 acres of public land for each of its congressional representatives, the proceeds from the donation to be used for education in agriculture, engineering, and military science.

Industry scored its first gain a few days before President Buchanan left office. Congress passed the Morrill Tariff Act, which provided a moderate increase in duties, bringing the rates up to approximately what they had been before 1846. Later measures enacted in 1862 and 1864 were frankly protective. By the end of the war the average of duties was 47 percent, the highest in the nation's history, and more than double the prewar rate.

Other legislative victories for business were achieved in connection with railroads and immigration. Two laws (1862, 1864) created two federal corporations: the Union Pacific Railroad Company, which was to build westward from Omaha, and the Central Pacific, which was to build eastward from California. The government would aid the companies by donating public lands and advancing government loans. Immigration from Europe fell off in the first years of the war, and the decrease, coupled with the military demands for personnel, threatened to cause a labor shortage. President Lincoln and business leaders asked Congress for governmental encouragement of immigration. In 1864 Congress passed a contract labor law authorizing employers to import laborers and collect the costs of transportation from future wages.

Perhaps the most important measure affecting the business-financial community was the National Bank Act, enacted in 1863 and amended in 1864. The act created the National Banking System, which lasted without serious modification until 1913. Its architects thought of it as a law that would provide a badly needed national banknote currency; at the outbreak of the war 1,500 banks chartered by twenty-nine states were empowered to issue notes. Furthermore, the new system would enable the government to market its bonds more cheaply, and thus aid the financing of the war.

The act spelled out a process by which a "banking association" (an existing state bank or a newly formed corporation) could secure a federal charter of incorporation and become a National Bank. Each association was required to possess a minimum amount of capital and to invest one-third of its capital in government securities, thereby supporting the war effort. Upon depositing the securities with the national treasury, it would receive, and could issue as bank notes, United States Treasury notes up to 90 percent of the current value of the bonds. Various clauses in the law provided for federal supervision and inspection of the banks. When many of the state banks, disliking the regulatory features, held aloof from the new system, Congress (in 1865) placed a tax on all state bank notes. This action forced state notes out of existence, induced many state banks to seek federal charters, and made the nation's currency more uniform. By the end of the war the system numbered 11,582 National Banks that were circulating notes amounting to over $200,000,000.

The North financed the war from three principal sources: taxation, loans, and paper money issues. From taxes, including the tariff, the government received approximately $667,000,000; loans, including U.S. Treasury notes, accounted for $2,600,000,000; and $45,000,000 of paper currency ("greenbacks") was issued.

Not until 1862, when mounting war expenses forced the country to face realities, did Congress pass an adequate war tax bill. Then it enacted the Internal Revenue Act, which placed sales taxes on practically all goods and introduced (in 1861) the nation's first income tax, a duty of 3 percent on incomes above $800. Later (in 1862 and 1865) the rates were increased to 5 percent on incomes between $600 and $5,000, and to 10 percent on incomes above the latter figure.

The greenbacks, because they bore no interest, were not supported by a specie reserve, and depended for redemption on the good faith of the government, fluctuated in value. In 1864 a greenback dollar, in relation to a gold dollar, was worth only 39 cents, and even at the close of the war its value had advanced to but 67 cents.

Mobilizing the Union Armies

Congress, the only agency authorized by the Constitution to raise armies, was not in session when hostilities started. Lincoln met the crisis with bold decision. He called for 42,000 volunteers for national service for three years and authorized an increase of 23,000 in the regular army. When Congress met in July 1861, it legalized the President's acts and, at his recommendation, provided for enlisting 500,000 volunteers to serve for three years. All in all, the government of the North, despite some minor bungling, adopted a sound military policy from the beginning. It acted to raise a large force (numbers were on the side of the North), and it avoided the mistake of short-term enlistments.

At first the volunteering system brought in enough men to fill the armies. But soon the initial enthusiasm waned, and men came forward to enlist in diminishing numbers. Even the generous cash bounties held out to prospective volunteers by the federal government and by the states were insufficient lures. Finally, in March 1863, Congress enacted the first national draft law in American history. (The South had employed conscription almost a year earlier.) Few exemptions were permitted: only high national and state officials, preachers, and men who were the sole support of a dependent family. But a drafted man could escape service by hiring a substitute to go in his place or by paying the government a fee of $300. Eventually this cash commutation was repealed.

The purpose of the draft law was to spur enlistments by threatening to invoke conscription. Each state was divided into enrollment districts, and at announced intervals was assigned a quota of men to be raised. If a state, by bounties or other means, could fill the quota, it escaped the draft completely. Although the draft directly inducted only 46,000 men, it stimulated enlistments enormously. The federal armies increased steadily in size, reaching a maximum number in 1865. The number of enlistments was 2,900,000, but this figure includes many who enlisted several times or served short terms. A reasonably accurate estimate is that 1,500,000 served for three years (as contrasted with 900,000 in the Confederate forces).

The casualty rate was tremendous. This was due to two factors, one military and the other medical. The weapons employed in the war — rifles and artillery with a faster rate of fire and a longer range than those used in previous wars — gave armies a vastly increased firepower. In many battles the proportion of men killed and wounded ranged from 20 to 32 percent.

To cope with the carnage, the Lincoln administration expanded and professionalized the army's medical services. Along with congressional reorganization of the Union Army Medical Bureau and the appointment in 1862 of an innovative surgeon general, William A. Hammond, the federal government increased the numbers of surgeons, built more general hospitals, and organized a trained ambulance corps. It also integrated the services of the United States Sanitary Commission into the war effort. Organized by civilians, the Sanitary Commission, through 7,000 local auxiliaries, gathered supplies; distributed clothing, food, and medicine to the army; raised the sanitary standards of camp life; and provided its own system of recruiting nurses and doctors for the battlefield.

The results of all this organized effort were not readily visible. Disease — mainly dysentery, typhoid, and malaria — killed twice as many Union soldiers (about 250,000) as did combat. Surgeons took more lives by spreading infection than they saved by treating wounds and amputating limbs. However, the incidence of mortality from disease and wounds was substantially less than in other major nineteenth-century wars, partly because of the attention given to sanitation and the quality of food.

Most of the thousands of nurses and workers for the Sanitary Commission were women. Inspired by the example Florence Nightingale had set in the Crimean War and organized by Dorothea Dix, who was the only woman to receive a major federal appointment, the nurses overcame resistance to women treating the bodies of men who

The Causes of the Civil War

On the causation of the Civil War, historians' views have changed with changing times, illustrating that history reflects the period *in* which it is written as well as the period *about* which it is written. In the 1890s the Civil War seemed to have been concerned with the destruction of slavery. Such was the theme of the leading authority of the time, James Ford Rhodes, in his *History of the United States from the Compromise of 1850* . . . (7 vols., 1893–1900).

This view prevailed until the 1920s, when Charles and Mary Beard challenged it in *The Rise of American Civilization* (2 vols., 1927). The Beards believed that the basic causes of the Civil War were economic. According to them, the war arose out of a clash between Northern industrialists and Southern planters, each group seeking to control the federal government in its own interest, and both groups using arguments about slavery and state rights only as smoke screens. The Beards had doubts about the results of the "Second American Revolution," as they called the war, for it brought on the evils associated with the rise of big business.

In the 1930s the Beardian interpretation began to be superseded by the views of the "revisionists." The recent war to "end war" and "make the world safe for democracy" (World War I) had obviously done neither, and American participation in it seemed now like a great mistake. The Civil War, too, had been unfortunate and useless according to the revisionists, such as Avery Craven and James G. Randall, who blamed it on the fanaticism of abolitionists and Southern firebrands and the political ineptitude of a "blundering generation" of leaders.

After World War II, which appeared to have saved democracy from the threat of Hitlerism, historians took a new look at the Civil War and concluded, once again, that it had been necessary and worthwhile. Arthur Schlesinger, Jr., explained that violence was sometimes indispensable for clearing away obstacles to social progress and that slavery had been such an obstacle. As the civil rights movement gained momentum in the 1950s and 1960s, historians gave more and more attention to slavery and race relations as central issues in the sectional conflict of the 1850s and 1860s. Eugene Genovese, for one, saw the war as growing out of the Southern planters' efforts to protect and expand the slave system.

More recently, in an era of declining faith in liberalism, historians have called into question the motives of the Northern opponents of slavery, as did Charles Beard. Eric Foner, in *Free Soil, Free Labor, Free Men* (1970), argued that most Northerners, including Abraham Lincoln, opposed slavery because they feared it might spread to the North and threaten free laborers. And Michael Holt, in *The Political Crisis of the 1850s* (1978), emphasized the extent to which Republican politicians, as well as Democratic politicians in the South, manipulated the slavery issue for their own advancement.

were not close relatives and opened up a new occupation to women. Nurse Clara Barton said, "At
the war's end, woman was at least fifty years in
advance of the normal position which continued
peace would have assigned her." Barton exaggerated, perhaps, but the organized war effort did
provide middle-class women with a great range of
new civic involvement; unprecedented experience in large, complex bureaucracies, such as the
Sanitary Commission, which included both men
and women; and new jobs as clerks in government
offices. Moreover, with the men away, women
dramatically increased their responsibilities in
schools, in their own households, and on their
farms. Women in both public and private life
emerged from the war with greatly increased
confidence in their abilities.

Northern Politics, to 1862

When Lincoln first came to Washington, he
was almost universally considered a small-time
prairie politician, unfit for his job. He strengthened this impression by his unpretentious air. Actually, he was well aware of his great abilities and
of his superiority over other Northern leaders. His
supreme confidence in himself was demonstrated
by his choice of a cabinet. Representing every
faction of the Republican party and every segment of Northern opinion, it was an extraordinary
assemblage of advisers and a difficult set of prima
donnas to manage. Three of the secretaries, William H. Seward (State), Salmon P. Chase (Treasury), and Edwin M. Stanton (War), were able men
who thought they could dominate Lincoln — but
in the end were dominated by him.

Lincoln's confidence in his inner strength was
revealed by his bold exercise of the war powers of
his office. In order to accomplish his purposes, he
was ready to violate parts of the Constitution, explaining that he would not lose the whole by
being afraid to disregard a part. In this spirit he
called for troops to repress the rebellion (an act
equivalent to a declaration of war), illegally increased the size of the regular army, and proclaimed a naval blockade of the South.

Opposition to the war came from two sources:
from Southern sympathizers in the Union slave
states and from the peace wing of the Democratic
party. War Democrats were willing to support
the war and even to accept offices from the administration. Peace Democrats or, as their enemies called them, "Copperheads," feared that
agriculture and the West were being subordi-
nated to industry and the East and that state
rights were going down before nationalism. Simply stated, their war policy was as follows: to call
a truce in the fighting, invite the South to attend a
national convention, and amend the Constitution
to preserve state rights. On the whole, the Peace
Democrats were unionists, in that they did not
favor a division of the country. But some of them
were willing to countenance Southern independence.

To deal with opponents of the war, Lincoln resorted to military arrests. He suspended the right
of habeas corpus, so that an alleged offender
could be arrested and held without trial or, if
tried, had to appear before a military court. At
first Lincoln denied the civil process only in specified areas, but in 1862 he proclaimed that all
persons who discouraged enlistments or engaged
in disloyal practices would come under martial
law. In all, over 13,000 persons were arrested and
imprisoned for varying periods. The most prominent Copperhead in the country, Clement L. Vallandigham of Ohio, was seized by military authorities, although not at Lincoln's instigation, and
later exiled to the Confederacy. (After the war, in
1866, the Supreme Court held, in *Ex parte Milligan*, that military trials in areas where the civil
courts were capable of functioning were illegal.)

There were factions too in the dominant Republican party — the Radicals and the Conservatives. On most questions, including economic
matters, they were in fundamental agreement,
but they differed on the disposition to be made of
slavery. The Radicals wanted to seize the opportunity of the war to strike slavery down — abolish
it suddenly and violently. The Conservatives, who
were also antislavery, wanted to accomplish the
same result in a different way — easily and gradually. Lincoln, who tended to be a Conservative,
made several notable although unsuccessful attempts to persuade the loyal slave states to agree
to a program of compensated gradual emancipation. He feared, at first, that the introduction of

abolition as a war aim would divide Northern opinion and alienate the border slave states.

Emancipation

As the war intensified, the Republicans broadened their war aims beyond restoration of the Union to include the destruction of slavery. The abolitionists contributed to the shift in official war aims. Shrewdly, they adopted arguments of "military necessity." They emphasized the military importance of slaves to the Confederate war effort. Frederick Douglass wrote that "the very stomach of this rebellion is the negro in the form of a slave. Arrest that hoe in the hands of the negro, and you smite the rebellion in the very seat of its life."

All Republicans were ready for some kind of emancipation. They divided into three groups over the timing and method. The conservatives, the smallest of the three groups, looked forward to slavery's ultimate death but believed that the federal government should only block the extension of slavery into the territories. Emancipation should be left to state governments. More numerous were the radicals, who wanted the federal government to abolish slavery immediately, everywhere. Most numerous were the moderates. They wanted emancipation to proceed more rapidly than did the conservatives but feared the disruptive consequences of immediate abolition. One of the consequences might be the loss of Union support in the border states of the upper South.

As battlefield casualties mounted, so did popular support for making the slaveowners pay for rebellion with the loss of their slaves, so did moral enthusiasm for freeing the slaves, and so did the power of the Republicans who were radical emancipationists. The leaders of the radical Republicans included the chairs of key congressional committees, such as Charles Sumner, chair of the Senate Committee on Foreign Affairs, and Thaddeus Stevens, chair of the House Ways and Means Committee, who could, and did, pressure the moderates, including the leader of the moderates, Abraham Lincoln.

Together, Lincoln and congressional Republicans moved rapidly toward abolition of slavery.

Their measures were moderate, shaped by the practical objectives of winning the war. Thus, when Congress took its first step in April 1862, abolishing slavery in the District of Columbia, it promised compensation to the former owners in order to maintain their loyalty to the Union. Its second step, abolishing slavery in the national territories (June 1862), affected few slaves; it was the enactment of the Wilmot Proviso and the fulfillment of the free-soil platform.

Lincoln waited for a favorable turn on the battlefield before he extended emancipation significantly. After Antietam he decided that his opportunity had arrived. On September 23, 1862, he issued a preliminary Emancipation Proclamation. He declared that on January 1, 1863, by virtue of his war powers as commander in chief, the slaves in all states that were still in rebellion were to be free. He gave the rebellious states 100 days to return to the Union and yet keep slavery intact. None did.

Lincoln played astute politics. He left slavery intact in the border states because he wanted to *hold* their loyalty. He left slavery untouched in areas occupied by Union armies (western Virginia, the state of Tennessee, and southern Louisiana, including New Orleans) because he wanted to *win* their loyalty. The Emancipation Proclamation had no instant, practical effect on the life of a single slave. But, as the Union armies advanced, it did provide for the freeing of hundreds of thousands of slaves and it did clearly change the meaning of the war.

Equally important in the process of emancipation was the induction of many former slaves into the armed forces: some 186,000 served as soldiers, sailors, and laborers, thereby making a substantial contribution to the cause of freedom. Furthermore, the impulse to abolition, which the Proclamation symbolized, increased in intensity throughout the country. The final and inevitable action was taken early in 1865, when Congress approved the Thirteenth Amendment (ratified by the required number of states several months after the war closed), which freed all slaves everywhere and abolished slavery as an institution.

Early in the war, and particularly after the election of 1862, in which the Republicans suffered heavy losses, the party leaders proceeded to form a broad coalition of all groups who supported the war, trying particularly to attract the War Democrats. The new organization, which was composed of a Republican core with a fringe of War Democrats, was known as the Union party. It encountered its major political test in the presidential election of 1864, which was the first national election held in the midst of a great war.

When the Union convention met in June, it nominated Lincoln, with the chilly assent of the Radicals, and, for Vice President, Andrew Johnson of Tennessee, a War Democrat who had refused to follow his state into secession. In August the Democratic convention nominated George B. McClellan, a former Union general whose opposition to emancipation made him an object of hatred to all good Radicals. The peace faction got a plank into the platform denouncing the war as a failure and calling for a truce to be followed by an invitation to the South to enter a national convention. Although McClellan repudiated the plank, the Democrats stood before the country as the peace party. At the same time several Northern military victories, particularly the capture of Atlanta, Georgia, early in September, rejuvenated Northern morale and gave promise of Republican success in November.

The outcome of the election was a smashing electoral triumph for Lincoln, who got 212 votes to McClellan's 21 and carried every state except Kentucky, New Jersey, and Delaware. Lincoln's popular majority, however, was uncomfortably small.

The Confederate Government

Although the first seven Southern states to secede had left the Union as individual sovereignties, they had no intention of maintaining separate political existences. It was understood from the first that they would come together in a common confederation to which, they hoped, the states of the upper South would eventually adhere. Accordingly, representatives of the seceded states assembled at Montgomery, Alabama, early in February 1861 to create a Southern nation. Montgomery, "the cradle of the Confederacy," was the capital of the new nation until after Vir-

ginia seceded. Then the government moved to Richmond, partly out of deference to Virginia, partly because Richmond was one of the few Southern cities large enough to house the government.

There was significance in the name of the Southern government: it was a confederation of sovereign states, not a federation of united ones. State sovereignty was expressly recognized in the constitution. Interestingly enough, proposals to insert the right of a state to secede failed of adoption; the right was implied but never mentioned. In structure, the Confederate government was an almost exact duplicate of the model that Southerners had just discarded.

As President the Montgomery convention elected Jefferson Davis of Mississippi, and as Vice President, Alexander H. Stephens of Georgia. Davis had been a firm but not extreme advocate of Southern rights in the former Union; he was a moderate but not an extreme secessionist. Stephens had been the chief among those who had contended that secession was unnecessary.

Although Davis was intelligent and honest, he showed grave defects as a war leader. In particular, he spent too much time on routine items, on what one observer called "little trash." Having been an officer in the Mexican War and U.S. secretary of war (1853–1857), Davis took particular interest in the details of military policy. Second, Davis failed to grasp the all-important fact that the Confederacy was not an established, recognized nation but a revolution. He proceeded on the basis that the Confederacy was a legal and permanent organization that could fight a war in the normal fashion of older countries. Whereas the situation demanded that the South act with ruthless efficiency, Davis assumed that it should observe every constitutional punctilio. Lincoln, without clear constitutional sanction, suspended habeas corpus; Davis asked his Congress to let him suspend it and received only partial permission.

Southern Money and the Draft

The people seeking to devise measures for financing the Confederacy's war effort, Treasury Secretary Christopher G. Memminger and the congressional leaders, had to reckon with a number of hard facts. Southern banking houses were fewer and, except in New Orleans, smaller than those of the North. Because excess capital in the South was usually invested in slaves and land, the sum of liquid assets on deposit in banks or in individual hands was relatively small. The only specie possessed by the government was that seized in United States mints located in the South.

The Confederate Congress, like its counterpart in the North, was reluctant to enact rigorous wartime taxes. In 1861 the legislators provided for a direct tax on property to be levied through the medium of the states. If a state preferred, it could meet its quota by paying as a state. Most of the states, instead of taxing their people, assumed the tax, which they paid by issuing bonds or their own notes. This first tax measure produced a disappointing return of only $18,000,000. Moving more boldly in 1863, the Confederate Congress passed a bill that included license levies and an income tax. A unique feature was "the tax in kind." All farmers and planters had to contribute one-tenth of their produce to the government. Although Congress later raised the rates in the internal revenue measure and enacted other taxes, the revenue realized from taxation was relatively small. The Confederacy raised only about 1 percent of its total income in taxes.

The bond record of the Confederacy was little better than its tax program. Congress authorized a $100,000,000 loan to be paid in specie, paper money, or produce. The expectation was that the bulk of the proceeds would be in the form of products — "the loan in kind." The loan was subscribed, partly in paper currency and mostly in produce or pledges of produce. But many of the pledges were not redeemed, and often the promised products were destroyed by the enemy. The Confederacy also attempted to borrow money in Europe by pledging cotton stored in the South for future delivery, but it secured little from this source.

Since ready revenue was needed and since cash was scarce, the government resorted in 1861 to the issuance of paper money and treasury notes. Once it started, it could not stop. By 1864 the staggering total of $1 billion had been issued. In addition, states and cities issued their own notes. The inevitable result was to depreciate the value

of the money. Prices skyrocketed to astronomical heights. Some sample figures for 1863–1864 are as follows: flour, $300 a barrel; broadcloth, $125 a yard; chickens, $35 a pair; beef, $5 a pound; men's shoes, $125 a pair. Many people, particularly those who lived in towns or who had fixed incomes, could not pay these prices. They did without and lost some of their will to victory.

Like the United States, the Confederate States first raised armies by calling for volunteers. By the latter part of 1861 volunteering had dropped off badly. As the year 1862 opened, the Confederacy was threatened by a manpower crisis.

The government met the situation boldly. At Davis' recommendation, Congress in April enacted the First Conscription Act, which declared that all able-bodied white males between the ages of eighteen and thirty-five were liable to military service for three years. A man who was drafted could escape his summons if he furnished a substitute to go in his place. The prices for substitutes eventually went up to as high as $10,000 in Confederate currency. The purpose of this provision was to exempt men in charge of agricultural and industrial production, but to people who could not afford substitutes it seemed like a special privilege for the rich. It was repealed in 1863 after arousing bitter class discontent.

The first draft act and later measures provided for other exemptions, mostly on an occupational basis. The laws erred in excusing men who were not doing any vital services and in permitting too many group exemptions. The provision most bitterly criticized was that exempting one white man on each plantation with twenty or more slaves. It caused ordinary men to say; "It's a rich man's war but a poor man's fight."

In September 1862 Congress adopted a second conscription measure, which raised the upper age limit to forty-five. At the end of the year, an estimated 500,000 soldiers were in the Confederate armies. Thereafter conscription provided fewer and fewer men, and the armed forces steadily decreased in size.

As 1864 opened, the situation was critical. In a desperate move, Congress lowered the age limits for drafted men to seventeen and raised them to fifty, reaching out, it was said, toward the cradle and the grave. Few men were obtained. War weariness and the certainty of defeat were making their influence felt. In 1864–1865 there were 100,000 desertions. On the army rolls 200,000 names were carried, but at the end probably only 100,000 were in service. In a frantic final attempt to raise men, Congress in 1865 authorized the drafting of 300,000 slaves. The war ended before this incongruous experiment could be tried out.

Confederate Politics

Only in the mountain areas of the South did organized opposition to the war exist. The mass of the people were united in support of the war. But they became bitterly divided on how it should be conducted.

The great dividing force was, ironically enough, the principle of state rights. State rights had become a cult with Southerners, to the point that they reacted against any sort of central control, even to controls necessary to win the war. If there was an organized faction of opposition to the government, it was that group of quixotic people who counted Vice President Stephens as their leader and who are usually known as the state-rights party. They had one simple, basic idea. They believed first in state sovereignty and then in the Confederacy. They wanted the Confederacy to win its independence, but they would not agree to sacrificing one iota of state sovereignty to achieve that goal. If victory had to be gained at the expense of state rights, they preferred defeat.

The state-righters fought every attempt of the government to impose centralized controls. They concentrated their fire against two powers that the central government sought to exercise: the suspension of habeas corpus, and conscription.

Recalcitrant governors, such as Joseph Brown of Georgia and Zebulon M. Vance of North Carolina, contending that the central government had no right to draft troops, tried in every way to obstruct the enforcement of conscription. Their chief weapon was certifying state militia troops as exempt. In the spring of 1862 an estimated 100,000 men throughout the South were held in state service. In Georgia in 1864 more men between eighteen and forty-five were at home than had gone into the army since 1861. Unwittingly, the state-righters helped to bring about the Confederacy's defeat.

Chapter 14

The Civil War

The Commanders in Chief

It was the responsibility of the President as commander in chief of the army and navy — of Abraham Lincoln for the Union and Jefferson Davis for the Confederacy — to see to the making and carrying out of an overall strategy for winning the war. Lincoln, a civilian all his life, had had no military education and no military experience except for a brief militia interlude. Yet he became a great war President, and a great commander in chief, superior to Davis, who was a trained soldier. By the power of his mind, Lincoln made himself a fine strategist, often showing keener insight than his generals. He recognized that numbers and matériel were on his side, and immediately he moved to mobilize the maximum strength of Northern resources. He urged his generals to keep up a constant pressure on the whole defensive line of the Confederacy until a weak spot was found and a breakthrough could be made. At an early date he realized that his armies ought to seek the destruction of the Confederate armies rather than the occupation of Southern territory.

During the first three years of the war, Lincoln performed many of the functions that in a modern command system would be done by the chief of the general staff or the joint chiefs of staff. He formulated policy, devised strategic plans, and even directed tactical movements. Some of his decisions were wise, some wrong, but the general effect of his so-called interfering with the military machine was fortunate for the North.

In the command system arrived at in 1864, Ulysses S. Grant, who had emerged as the North's greatest general, was named general in chief. Charged with directing the movements of all Union armies, Grant, because he disliked the political atmosphere of Washington, established his headquarters with the Army of the Potomac but did not technically become commander of that army. As director of the armies, Grant proved to be the man for whom Lincoln had been searching. He possessed in superb degree the ability to think of the war in overall terms and to devise strategy for the war as a whole. Because Lincoln trusted Grant, he gave the general a relatively free hand.

Southern command arrangements consisted mainly of President Davis. The Confederacy failed to achieve a modern command system. Early in 1862 Davis assigned General Robert E. Lee to duty at Richmond, where, "under the direction of the President," he was "charged" with the conduct of the Confederate armies. Despite the fine words, this meant only that Lee, who had a brilliant military mind, was to act as Davis' adviser, furnishing counsel when called on.

The Role of Sea Power

The Union had the advantage of overwhelmingly preponderant sea power, and President Lincoln made the most of it. It served two main functions. One was to enforce the blockade of the Southern coast that he proclaimed at the start of the war (April 19, 1861). The other was to assist the Union armies in combined land-and-water operations.

In the Western theater of war, the vast region between the Appalachian Mountains and the Mississippi River, the larger rivers were navigable by vessels of considerable size. The Union Navy helped the armies to conquer this area by transporting supplies and troops for them and joining them in attacking Confederate strong points. In defending themselves against the Union gunboats on the rivers, the Confederates had to depend mainly on land fortifications because of their lack of naval power. These fixed defenses proved no match for the mobile land-and-water forces of the Union.

At first, the blockade was too large a task for the Union Navy. Even after the navy had grown to its maximum size, it was unable to seal off completely the long shoreline of the Confederacy. Small blockade runners continued to carry goods into and out of some of the Southern ports. Gradually the Federal forces tightened the blockade by occupying stretches of the coast and seizing one port after another. Fewer and fewer blockade runners got through, and the blockade increasingly hurt the South.

In bold and ingenious attempts to break the blockade, the Confederates employed some new weapons, among them an ironclad warship. They constructed this by plating with iron a former United States frigate, the *Merrimack*, which the Yankees had scuttled in Norfolk harbor when Virginia seceded. On March 8, 1862, the *Merrimack* steamed out from Norfolk to attack the blockading squadron of wooden ships in Hampton Roads. The *Merrimack* destroyed two of the ships and scattered the rest. But the federal government had several ironclads of its own. One of these, the *Monitor*, arrived at Hampton Roads on the night of March 8. When the *Merrimack* emerged on the following day to hunt for more victims, the *Monitor* met and engaged it in the first battle between ironclad ships. Neither vessel was able to penetrate the other's armor, but the *Monitor* put an end to the depredations of the *Merrimack*.

To weaken the blockade, the Confederates had meanwhile decided to build or buy fast ships to prey on the Northern merchant marine on the high seas. The hope was that the Union would detach ships from the blockade to pursue the commerce raiders. The Confederates also hoped

to get, from abroad, a specially built "ram" with which to smash the wooden blockading ships.

Europe and the Disunited States

In the relationship of Europe to the Civil War, the key nations were Great Britain and France. These two had acted together against Russia in the Crimean War and were united by an entente, one of the understandings of which was that questions concerning the United States fell within the sphere of British influence. Napoleon III, therefore, would not act in American affairs without the concurrence of Britain.

In the minds of Southern leaders, cotton was their best diplomatic weapon. The analysis was as follows: the textile industry was basic to the economies of England and France, which depended on the South for the bulk of their cotton supply; deprived of Southern cotton, these countries would face economic collapse. Therefore they would have to intervene on the side of the Confederacy.

But this diplomacy based on King Cotton never worked as its champions envisioned. In 1861 English manufacturers had a surplus of cotton on hand. Thereafter the supply became increasingly short, and many mills were forced to close. Both England and France, however, managed to avoid a complete shutdown of their textile industries by importing supplies from new sources, notably Egypt and India.

No European nation extended diplomatic recognition to the Confederacy. Though several times England and France considered offering mediation, they never moved to intervene in the war. Neither could afford to do so unless the Confederacy seemed on the point of winning and the South never attained a prospect of certain victory.

Immediately after the outbreak of hostilities, Great Britain issued a proclamation of neutrality, thus attributing to the Confederacy the status of a belligerent. France and other nations followed suit. Although the Northern government, which officially insisted that the war was not a war but a domestic insurrection, furiously resented England's action, the British government had proceeded in conformity with accepted rules of neutrality and in accordance with the realities of the situation. The United States was fighting a *war*, a fact that Lincoln himself had recognized in his proclamation establishing a blockade. Thereafter three crises or near-crises between England and the United States developed.

The first crisis, and the most dangerous one — the so-called *Trent* affair — occurred late in 1861. The Confederate commissioners to England and France, James M. Mason and John Slidell, had slipped through the then ineffective blockade to Havana, Cuba, where they boarded an English steamer, the *Trent*, for England. Hovering in Cuban waters was an American frigate, the *San Jacinto*, commanded by Captain Charles Wilkes, an impetuous officer who knew that the Southern diplomats were on the *Trent*. Acting without authorization from his government, Wilkes stopped the British vessel, arrested the commissioners, and bore them off in triumph to Boston. The British government drafted a demand for the release of the prisoners, reparation, and an apology. Lincoln and Seward, well aware that war with England would be suicidal, spun out the negotiations until American opinion had cooled off, then returned the commissioners with an indirect apology.

The second issue — the case of the Confederate commerce destroyers — generated a long-lasting diplomatic problem. Lacking the resources to construct the vessels, the Confederacy contracted to have them built and equipped in British shipyards. Six cruisers, of which the most famous were the *Alabama*, the *Florida*, and the *Shenandoah*, were sold to the Confederacy. The British government knew what was going on but winked at the practice. The United States protested that it was in violation of the laws of neutrality.

The third incident — the affair of the Laird rams — could have developed into a crisis, but did not because the British government suddenly decided to mend its ways. In 1863 the Confederacy placed an order with the Laird shipyards for two powerful ironclads with pointed prows for ramming and sinking Union vessels and thus breaking the blockade. The British government acted to detain the rams and to prevent the Confederacy from obtaining any other ships.

If Napoleon III had had his way, France and England would have intervened at an early date. Unable to persuade Britain to act, he had to content himself with expressing sympathy for the Southern cause and permitting the Confederates to order commerce destroyers from French shipyards. The Emperor's primary motive for desiring an independent South was his ambition to establish French colonial power in the Western hemisphere: a divided America could not block his plans. He seized the opportunity of the war to set up a French-dominated empire in Mexico.

Napoleon's Mexican venture was a clear violation of the Monroe Doctrine. The United States viewed it in such a light, but, during the war, for fear of provoking France into recognizing the Confederacy, it could do no more than register a protest.

The Opening Battles   1861

The one big battle of 1861 was fought in Virginia in the area between the two capitals. Just south of Washington was a federal army of over 30,000 under the command of General Irvin McDowell. Opposing it was a Confederate Army of over 20,000 under P. G. T. Beauregard based at Manassas in northern Virginia about thirty miles southwest of Washington; and there were other Confederate troops in the Shenandoah Valley, commanded by Joseph E. Johnston.

In mid-July McDowell marched his inexperienced troops toward Manassas, his movement well advertised to the Confederates by Northern newspapers and Southern spies. Beauregard retired behind Bull Run, a small stream north of Manassas, and called on the government to order Johnston to join him. Most of Johnston's army reached Beauregard the day before the battle, making the Northern and Southern armies approximately equal in size, each numbering something over 30,000.

The Battle of Bull Run, or Manassas (July 21), might be summarized by saying that Beauregard never got his offensive into motion and that McDowell's attack almost succeeded. The Confederates stopped a last strong Union assault. Beauregard then ordered a counterattack. As the Confederates slashed forward, a sudden wave of

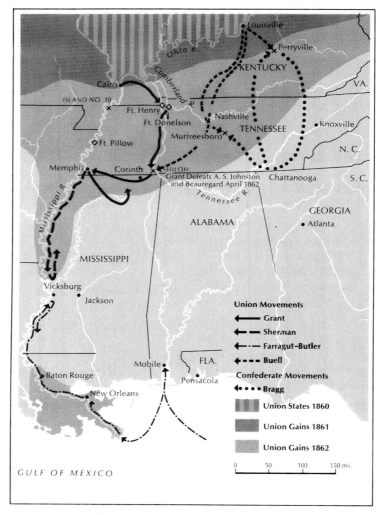

Union Movements

←—— Grant

←–– –– Sherman

←–·–·– Farragut–Butler

←···· Buell

Confederate Movements

◄···· Bragg

▨ Union States 1860

▨ Union Gains 1861

▨ Union Gains 1862

0   50   100   150 mi.

The War in the West 1861–1862

panic struck through the Union troops, wearied after hours of hot, hard fighting and demoralized by the abrupt change of events. They gave way and crossed Bull Run in a rout. Unable to get them in hand north of the stream, McDowell had to order a retreat to Washington.

The Confederates, as disorganized by victory as the federal troops were by defeat and lacking supplies and transport, were in no condition to undertake a forward movement. Lincoln replaced McDowell with General McClellan, the victor of earlier fighting in western Virginia, and took measures to increase the army. Both sides girded themselves for real war.

The Western Theater   1862

The first decisive operations in 1862 were in the Western theater. Here federal troops were trying to secure control of the Mississippi line by moving on the river itself or parallel to it. Most of their offensives were combined land-and-naval operations. To achieve their objective, they advanced on the Mississippi from the north and south, moving down from Kentucky and up from the Gulf of Mexico toward New Orleans.

In April a Union squadron of ironclads and wooden vessels forced the civil authorities to surrender the city. For the rest of the war federal troops held New Orleans and the southern part of Louisiana. They closed off the mouth of the great river to Confederate trade, grasped the South's largest city and greatest banking center, and secured a base for future operations.

A fatal weakness marked the Confederate line in Kentucky. The center, through which flowed the Tennessee and Cumberland rivers, was thrown back (southward) from the flanks and was defended by two forts, Henry on the Tennessee and Donelson on the Cumberland. The forts had been built when Kentucky was trying to maintain a position of neutrality and were located just over the Tennessee line. If federal troops, with the aid of naval power, could pierce the center, they would be between the two Confederate flanks and in position to destroy either.

This was exactly what they did in February. Grant proceeded to attack Fort Henry, whose defenders, awed by the ironclad river boats accompanying the Union Army, surrendered with almost no resistance (February 6). Grant then marched to Donelson while his naval auxiliary moved to the Cumberland River. At Donelson the Confederate troops put up a scrap, but eventually the garrison of 20,000 had to capitulate (February 16). Grant had inflicted a near-disaster on the Confederacy. As a result of his movement, the Confederate Army was forced out of Kentucky and had to yield half of Tennessee.

Grant, with about 40,000 troops, now advanced up the Tennessee (southward). The immediate objective was to destroy Confederate railroad communications in the Corinth, Mississippi, area. Grant debarked his army at Pittsburg Landing about thirty miles from Corinth. The battle that ensued (April 6–7) is usually known as Shiloh. The Confederate troops caught Grant by surprise and by the end of the first day's fighting drove him back to the river, but here the attack was halted. The next day Grant, reinforced by 25,000 fresh troops, went over to the offensive, and regained his original lines. Shiloh turned out to be an extremely narrow Union victory. Federal troops eventually seized Corinth and the railroads of which it was the hub. By early June they had occupied the river line down as far as Memphis.

The Confederate forces held approximately the eastern half of Tennessee. They hoped to recover the rest of the state and, if possible, carry the war back to Kentucky. When Confederate General Braxton Bragg moved from Tennessee into Kentucky, Union General Don Carlos Buell followed him. The two armies met in the indecisive Battle of Perryville (October 8), and Bragg returned to Tennessee.

The Virginia Front   1862

In the Eastern theater in 1862 Union operations were directed by young George B. McClellan, commander of the Army of the Potomac and the most controversial general of the war. McClellan was a superb trainer of men but lacked the fighting instinct, necessary in a great captain, to commit his soldiers to decisive battle.

During the winter of 1861–1862 McClellan had remained inactive, training his army of 150,000 men near Washington. He finally settled on a plan of operations for the spring campaign. Instead of striking for Richmond by moving southward from Washington, he would have the navy transport his army to Fort Monroe on the Virginia coast in the region between the York and James rivers known as the Peninsula. Late in March McClellan started putting his troops on transports to begin his Peninsula campaign.

The Confederate high command (Davis and Lee) had misgivings about General Joseph E. Johnston's strategy of drawing McClellan closer to Richmond before fighting and they were worried by the possibility that reinforcements might join McClellan. To prevent this, the commander of the Confederate forces in the Shenandoah Valley, Thomas J. ("Stonewall") Jackson, was directed to move northward, giving the impression that he meant to cross the Potomac. Partly to defend the approaches to Washington and partly to trap Jackson, Lincoln rushed forces to the Valley. Jackson slipped back to safety before the various Union forces could converge on him.

While these events were unfolding in the Valley, Johnston at last attacked McClellan at Fair Oaks or Seven Pines (May 31–June 1). The attack failed to budge McClellan, and Johnston was so seriously wounded that he had to relinquish the command. To replace him Davis named the man who would lead the Army of Northern Virginia for the rest of the war, Robert E. Lee.

Lee, a brilliant field commander, realized that the Confederacy could not win its independence merely by repelling offensives. He decided to call Jackson from the Valley, bringing his total numbers up to 85,000 (as compared to McClellan's 100,000), mass his forces, and attack. The operation that followed, which involved several engagements, is known as the Battle of the Seven Days (June 25–July 1). It did not proceed as Lee expected. He drove back McClellan, who headed southward. Lee followed, trying desperately to destroy federal forces, but McClellan extricated his army, even inflicting a bloody repulse on Lee at Malvern Hill. He reached Harrison's Landing on the James, where with naval support, he was safe from any attack Lee could launch.

At Harrison's Landing federal troops were only twenty-five miles from Richmond and had a secure line of water communications. But Lincoln, instead of replacing McClellan with a more aggressive commander, decided to evacuate the army to northern Virginia, where it would be combined with a smaller force under John Pope — to begin a new operation on the Washington-to-Richmond "overland" route.

As the Army of the Potomac left the Peninsula by water, Lee, understanding what was happening, moved his army northward with the purpose of striking Pope before he was joined by McClellan. Pope, who was rash where McClellan was timid, attacked the Confederate forces in the Second Battle of Manassas or Bull Run (August 29–30). Lee easily halted the assault, and in a powerful counterstroke swept Pope from the field. The beaten federal troops retired to the Washington defenses, where Lincoln relieved Pope and placed all the troops around the city under McClellan's command.

Lee gave federal troops no respite. Early in September he went over to the offensive, invading western Maryland. With some misgivings, Lincoln let McClellan go to meet Lee. Lee had

time to pull most of his army together behind Antietam Creek near the town of Sharpsburg. Here, on September 17, McClellan, with 87,000 men, threw a series of powerful attacks at Lee's 50,000. McClellan might have won with one more assault. But his caution asserted itself, and he called off the battle. Lee retired to Virginia, and after an interval of reorganization McClellan followed. Lincoln, disgusted by McClellan's failure to exploit his victory, removed him from command in November.

As McClellan's successor Lincoln appointed Ambrose E. Burnside, a modest mediocrity. He planned to drive at Richmond by crossing the Rappahannock at Fredericksburg, the strongest defensive point on that river. On December 13 he flung his army at Lee's defenses in a hopeless, bloody attack. At the end of a day of bitter failure and after suffering 12,000 casualties, he withdrew to the north side of the Rappahannock. Soon he was relieved at his own request.

Year of Decision   1863

As 1863 opened, the Union Army in the East was commanded by Burnside's successor, Joseph Hooker — "Fighting Joe," as the newspapers called him. His army, which numbered 120,000, fell back to a defensive position at Chancellorsville in the desolate area of scrub trees and brush known in Virginia as the Wilderness. Here Lee came up to attack him.

The Battle of Chancellorsville (May 1–5) was one of Lee's most brilliant exploits. With an army of only 60,000 (part of his force had been detached for other service), he took great but justified risks. He divided his army and sent Jackson to hit the Union right, which was exposed, while he struck from in front. Again Lee had won, but he had lost his ablest lieutenant. Jackson, wounded in the fighting, died soon afterward.

While the Union Army was failing in the East, a different story unfolded in the West. U. S. Grant was driving at Vicksburg, the most strongly fortified Confederate point on the Mississippi River. After failing to storm the strong works, he settled down to a siege, which endured for six weeks, Vicksburg capitulating on July 4.

At last federal forces had achieved one of their

principal strategic aims; they had gained control of the Mississippi line. The Confederacy was split into two parts, and the trans-Mississippi area was isolated from the main section. A great turning point in the war had been reached.

When the siege of Vicksburg began, the Confederate high command in Richmond was dismayed at the prospect of losing the great river fortress. Various plans to relieve the city were discussed, the principal one being a proposal to send part of Lee's army to Tennessee, possibly with Lee himself in command, to launch an offensive. But Lee put forward a counterscheme: he would invade Pennsylvania. If he could win a victory on Northern soil, he said, great results would follow. The North might abandon the war, England and France might intervene, and the pressure on Vicksburg and other fronts would be broken. The government assented, and in June Lee started his movement, swinging his army west toward the Valley and then north through Maryland into Pennsylvania.

As Lee advanced, Hooker moved back to confront him, marching parallel to the line of Lee's route. But Hooker, unnerved by his experience at Chancellorsville, soon found an excuse to ask to be relieved. To replace him Lincoln appointed an army corps commander, George G. Meade, a solid if unimaginative soldier. Meade followed Lee and approached what might be called the strategic rear of the Confederate Army in southern Pennsylvania. Lee, who had not expected the Union Army to move so rapidly, was astounded when he learned of its nearness. With his army marching in three columns, he was in a dangerous position; hurriedly he had to concentrate his forces. Meade, realizing that Lee in enemy country had to attack or retreat, selected a strong defensive site at the little town of Gettysburg, a road hub in the region, and Lee, seeking contact with federal forces, moved toward the same spot. Here on July 1–3 was fought the most celebrated battle of the war.

Lee finally withdrew his shattered forces to Virginia. Meade made but a feeble pursuit. Although he had thrown away an opportunity to end the war, Gettysburg was another turning point. The total Confederate losses in the campaign were close to 25,000. Never again would Lee feel strong enough to fight offensively.

A third turning point against the Confederacy was reached in Tennessee. In the autumn Union General William S. Rosecrans moved toward Chattanooga. Bragg evacuated the town. Rosecrans rashly plunged over the Georgia line in pursuit, where Bragg, reinforced by troops from Lee's army, was lying in wait. Rosecrans barely got his scattered forces in hand before Bragg delivered his crushing assault at Chickamauga (September 19–20). The beaten Union Army fell back into the Chattanooga defenses.

Bragg eventually occupied the heights south of Chattanooga. Mounting batteries on these points, he commanded the roads leading into the city and virtually shut off its supplies. Grant was named departmental commander of the West. Immediately he came with part of his own army to the relief of the beleaguered city. At the Battle of Chattanooga (November 23–25) the Union Army hurled Bragg from his lines on Missionary Ridge and Lookout Mountain and back into northern Georgia. They then proceeded to occupy most of east Tennessee.

From the Chattanooga base federal troops were in position to split the Confederacy again — what was left of it. Chattanooga deserves to be ranked with Vicksburg and Gettysburg as a decisive Union victory. After 1863 the Confederacy had no chance on any front to win its independence by a military decision. Now it could hope to triumph only by exhausting the Northern will to fight.

The Ending   1864–1865

Grant's plans for 1864 called for two great offensives. The Army of the Potomac, commanded by Meade but accompanied and directed by Grant, was to seek to bring Lee to decisive battle in northern Virginia. From near Chattanooga the Western army, commanded by William T. Sherman, was to advance into northern Georgia, destroy the Confederate Army, now commanded by Joseph E. Johnston, and wreck the economic resources of Atlanta.

From its position in northern Virginia the Army of the Potomac, 115,000 strong, crossed the Rappahannock and Rapidan rivers, and plunged into the Wilderness area. Grant's plan was to en-

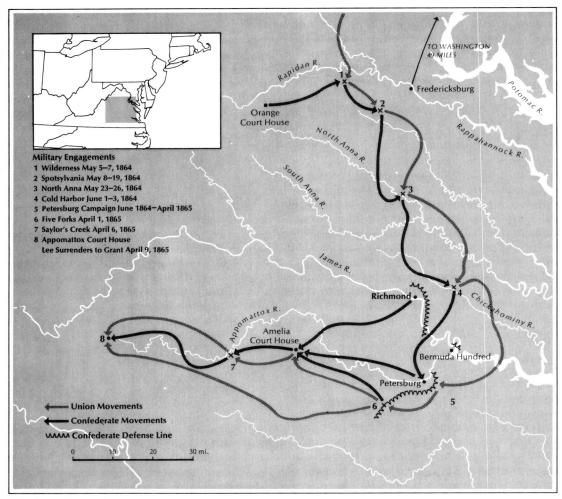

Virginia Campaigns

velop Lee's right and force him to a showdown battle. Lee, whose army numbered about 75,000 at the beginning of the campaign, was determined to avoid a showdown unless he saw a chance to deal a decisive blow. In the battles of the Wilderness (May 5–7), Spotsylvania Court House (May 8–19), and Cold Harbor (June 1–3), Grant pressed stubbornly on toward Richmond, at tremendous human cost. In a month of fighting he lost a total of 55,000 men — killed, wounded, and captured — and Lee lost 31,000.

Now Grant had to alter his strategy. If he re-

mained where he was, Lee would retire into the Richmond defenses to stand a siege, something Grant wanted to avoid. Masking his movements from his adversary, Grant moved southward across the James heading for Petersburg, directly south of Richmond. Petersburg was the hub of all the railroads feeding into the capital; if Grant could secure it, he could force Lee to come into the open to fight for his communications. He almost succeeded, but finally had to resort to a siege. He dug in, and so did Lee. The trench lines of the two armies stretched for miles above and

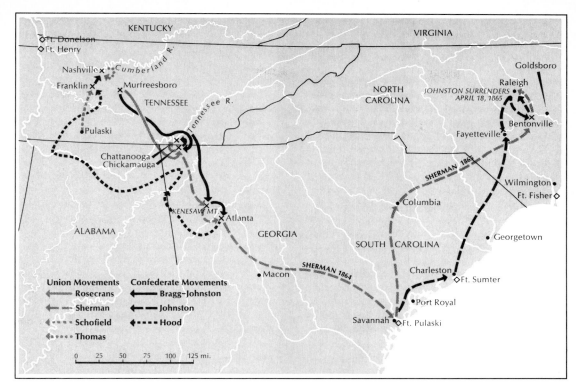

Sherman's March Through the Confederacy 1864–1865

below Petersburg. Always Grant strove to extend his left around Lee's right so as to get on the railroads that were the lifeline of the Southern army. It would be nine months before he reached his objective.

Meanwhile Sherman, with an army of over 90,000, moved toward Atlanta against Johnston's army, which numbered 60,000 at the beginning. Johnston's plan was to delay Sherman, to fight for time, and not to commit his forces unless the conditions were exceptionally favorable. As Sherman was approaching Atlanta, President Davis replaced Johnston with John B. Hood. Combative by nature, Hood threw two successive attacks at Sherman, both of which failed. The Union Army occupied Atlanta on September 2.

Sherman had not destroyed the enemy army. Eager to strike deeper into Georgia, he sent 30,000 of his army to Tennessee under George H. Thomas and prepared to move for Savannah on the coast. At the same time Hood decided to in-

vade Tennessee, hoping to force Sherman to follow him. Despite disastrous losses at Franklin, Tennessee (November 30), Hood moved on northward and took up a position outside Nashville. In the Battle of Nashville (December 15–16) Thomas drove Hood from the field. As the Confederate forces retreated toward Mississippi, they were harried by the most merciless cavalry pursuit of the war. Only a few units reached Mississippi intact. The Confederate Army of Tennessee had, in effect, ceased to exist.

In the meantime Sherman was marching almost unopposed across Georgia, inaugurating a new kind of warfare. He was the prophet of modern total war — war against the civilian population of the enemy, war intended to break the enemy people's will to resist. His army marched on a sixty-mile front, destroying property and supplies that might be used by the Confederate forces and committing many individual depredations as well. By December 20 Sherman was at Savannah.

Sherman then turned into South Carolina, still facing slight opposition and still ripping up enemy property. When he advanced into North Carolina, the Confederate government got together an army of 30,000 under Johnston to oppose him, but this small force could do little more than delay his march.

In April 1865 Grant finally passed a part of his army around Lee's right to the vital railroads. The Confederates evacuated Petersburg and Richmond, and Lee moved westward with his army, now shrunk to about 25,000. His one forlorn hope was to reach a rail line to North Carolina and unite with Johnston. But the pursuing Union Army barred his escape route. At last he realized that further fighting was hopeless, and on April 9 he met Grant at Appomattox and surrendered the Army of Northern Virginia. In North Carolina Joe Johnston reached the same conclusion, and on April 18 he surrendered to Sherman near Durham. Jefferson Davis, defiant to the last and unable to recognize defeat, fled southward, and was captured in Georgia. The war was soon over.

The War's Aftermath

In the North, the postwar years were prosperous, but Northerners who visited the South were appalled when they gazed upon the desolation left in the wake of the war — gutted towns, wrecked plantations, neglected fields, collapsed bridges, and ruined railroads. Confederate bonds and currency were now worthless. Nearly 260,000 Confederate soldiers had been killed and other thousands went home wounded or sick.

If conditions were bad for Southern whites, they were generally worse for the 4,000,000 Southern blacks who were emerging from bondage. As the war ended, freedom appeared to be on the way, but its arrival was uncertain. The Thirteenth Amendment, which would make slavery unconstitutional, had yet to be ratified by the requisite number of states. (It had passed Congress on February 1, 1865, and was to be proclaimed in effect on December 18, 1865.) On many plantations the blacks were still being detained and forced to work. Most planters agreed with a former Confederate leader who was saying (in June 1865) that slavery had been "the best system of labor that could be devised for the Negro race" and that the wise thing to do now would be to "provide a substitute for it."

To get away from their old masters, thousands of blacks continued to leave the plantations. Old and young, many of them feeble and ill, they trudged to the nearest town or city or roamed the countryside, camping at night on the bare ground. Few had any possessions except the rags on their backs. Somehow they managed to stay alive.

What blacks wanted was, first of all, to be assured of their freedom — to feel it, to exercise it, and to know it was not going to be taken from them. Next, they needed immediate relief from the threat of starvation. Then, looking ahead, they desired land, farms of their own, a bit of economic independence. A few of the freed slaves had already settled on abandoned plantations, notably on the Sea Islands along the South Carolina coast and on land in Mississippi that had belonged to the Davis family. Blacks also longed for schooling for their children if not for themselves. In some places, above all in New Orleans, there were well-educated and highly cultured communities of blacks who had been free for generations. But education was a rare and precious thing to the newly liberated blacks, most of whom were as illiterate as the slave codes had intended them to be. Finally, a number of blacks were beginning to demand political rights. "The only salvation for us besides the power of the Government is in the *possession of the ballot*," a convention of black people of Virginia resolved in the summer of 1865. "All we ask is an *equal chance*."

Presidential Reconstruction: Lincoln

When the North defeated the Confederate armies, many questions remained to be answered. Would the North readmit the South to the Union? Would the North punish Southern whites? How would the federal government implement the eradication of slavery called for by the Thirteenth Amendment? Would the South continue to resist?

At first an expeditious reconciliation seemed possible. Ex-Confederate soldiers were inclined to accept defeat, to abstain from further resistance. Most ex-slaves hoped to live in peace with whites. They desperately hoped and pleaded to acquire the land they tilled, but they did not plot violent retribution against their former masters. Northerners had accomplished their original war aims — the defeat of Southern resistance and the crushing of the Slave Power — and had even made slavery unconstitutional. While some Northerners insisted on punishment to pay for the 360,000 Union deaths, the typical Union soldier took a compassionate view of the conflict, believing that 260,000 Confederate deaths and surrender had been payment enough.

Lincoln initiated the process of Reconstruction while the war was still being fought. Whenever federal troops occupied large portions of the South, he employed a policy of moderation and reconciliation, in order to restore a harmonious Union as quickly as possible and to subvert the Southern war effort.

In December 1863 Lincoln offered a general amnesty to all Confederates except, for the time being, the high officials of the Confederacy. His simple plan called for Confederates to take an oath (1) pledging their *future* loyalty to the Union, and (2) accepting the wartime acts and proclamations concerning slavery. When 10 percent of the number of people who had voted in 1860, in each state, had taken the loyalty oath, new state governments could form in the areas of secession. Lincoln aimed his plan at Southern Whigs, many of whom he knew well. He hoped that they would step forward, declare their allegiance to the Union, and take charge of Southern governments. Lincoln's constitutional assumption was simple: states could not legally secede and were therefore still in the Union.

Lincoln's plan encountered opposition in Congress from members of his own party. A group of Radical Republicans, most of whom had abolitionist backgrounds, opposed it most strenuously. Led by Senator Charles Sumner and Representative Thaddeus Stevens, these Radical Republicans wanted the federal government, in Stevens' words, to "revolutionize Southern institutions, habits, and manners." Stevens declared that "the foundations of their institutions . . . must be broken up and relaid, or all our blood and treasure will have been spent in vain."

The Radicals were united by the belief that ex-slaves must vote. Without it the ex-slaves could not enjoy genuine independence from their ex-masters. All the Radicals believed that the federal government must establish a program that would guarantee that ex-slaves could vote. They disagreed, however, as to whether the suffrage alone would produce a revolution in the South. Charles Sumner, for example, believed that black suffrage alone would do it while Thaddeus Stevens believed that the redistribution of land to the ex-slaves was necessary as well.

More moderate Republicans formed the majority of the party and did not agree with the Radicals that the federal government should promote black voting. They did, however, along with the Radicals, oppose Lincoln on three other Reconstruction objectives. Both the Radicals and the Moderates, unlike Lincoln, wished (1) to punish the South, (2) to guarantee the abolition of slavery, and (3) to establish the Republican party in the South. Combining their forces, the Radicals and the Moderates controlled Congress and refused to accept the new governments that Lincoln established in occupied Louisiana, Arkansas, and Tennessee.

In July 1864, to advance its own objectives for Reconstruction, the Republican Congress passed the Wade-Davis bill. Based on the old Whig theory of congressional government, the bill asserted that Congress, not the President, was primarily responsible for Reconstruction. Toward the South, Congress took the constitutional position, promoted by Thaddeus Stevens, that the seceded states had actually left the Union and now were no more than conquered territory. For readmission as states, the bill insisted that the conquered provinces meet a series of stiff requirements. A majority of a state's adult white males had to swear an oath of allegiance; each state had to write a new constitution; only those who had taken an iron-clad oath that they had never carried arms against the United States or voluntarily aided the Confederacy could participate in writing the constitution; and the new constitution had to abolish slavery, disfranchise Confederate civil and military leaders, and repudiate war debts.

The Wade-Davis bill, however, was essentially a Moderate plan because it did not establish national control over race relations or guarantee the participation of ex-slaves in the new state governments. In these respects the bill was no different from Lincoln's plan. Grounds for a compromise between Lincoln and Congress clearly existed, and Lincoln astutely kept his options open. After giving the Wade-Davis bill a pocket veto (holding the bill, unsigned, until Congress adjourned), Lincoln began informal discussions directed toward a compromise.

John Wilkes Booth, however, intervened. On Good Friday, April 14, 1865, he and a band of ex-Confederates assassinated Lincoln and made abortive attempts on the lives of Vice President Andrew Johnson and Secretary of State William H. Seward. The assassination came before Lincoln had reached a compromise over Reconstruction.

Presidential Reconstruction: Johnson

When Vice President Johnson succeeded to the Presidency, compromise between the President and a Republican Congress became more difficult. An old Jacksonian Democrat from Jackson's home state, Johnson had risen from poverty to property ownership (including a farm and slaves) and to a political career that led from the Tennessee legislature to the U.S. Senate and, because of his support for the Union, to the Vice Presidency.

Johnson opposed the Republican policy of using the national government to foster economic development, believing that the policy would foster dangerous monopolies. He hated what he called the "bloated, corrupt aristocracy" of the Northeast. Johnson also despised blacks. He would accept their legal freedom but he wanted to maintain white supremacy — through the systematic denial of any rights to blacks. Because he opposed both the economic and the racial plans of the Republicans, Johnson did not want to see the Republican party prevail in either the North or the South. Johnson's interest in Reconstruction extended no further than punishing the elite of ex-slaveholders — a class that he resented.

Despite their differences, President Johnson and the Republican Congress could have avoided a deadlock. In the North, Democrats and conservative Republicans were not far apart in their racial policies. Most Republicans in Congress favored the moderate approach to Reconstruction outlined by the Wade-Davis bill. In the South, the ex-Confederates, accepting their defeat in total war, were prepared to submit even to a Reconstruction that was somewhat punitive.

Johnson, however, proved to be politically inept. His difficulties in consulting and cooperating with Congress produced an erratic policy. It first encouraged and then punished ex-Confederates. This alternating policy intensified Southern resistance to federal power and, in turn, stimulated Republican retaliation. Consequently, the kind of compromise peace that seemed very close at hand in 1865 was long in coming.

Johnson risked confrontation with Congress when he announced his own lenient plan, one of restoration, and proceeded to execute it during the summer of 1865. Congress was not in session and could not be consulted, but Johnson thought Reconstruction should be exclusively an executive function. Moreover, he thought it should do little more than restore the Union.

Johnson insisted on only three conditions: that the states revoke ordinances of secession, abolish slavery, and repudiate the debts they had acquired during the rebellion. He assumed that virtually all whites would participate in the process of framing new state governments. Johnson's plan offered amnesty and a return of all property except for slaves to almost all Southerners if they took an oath of future allegiance to the Union. He excluded several categories of Southerners from his amnesty: high-ranking Confederate officers and civil officials and, revealing his distaste for planter aristocrats, persons with taxable property of more than $20,000. These excluded individuals were invited to petition him personally for pardons. His intention was to humble them and then grant most of them pardons.

By December all of the former Confederate states were ready to rejoin the Union under Johnson's plan. They had functioning civil governments and had met Johnson's requirements for re-entry. Each state of the former Confederacy, however, had laws designed to ensure that blacks remain permanently on the land as agricultural laborers and that they work there under terms highly favorable to landowners. Passage of these laws, known as the Black Codes, was a blatant effort to give whites as much control over blacks as they had had under slavery.

Chapter 15

Radical Reconstruction

Congress Takes Over

Most Republicans supported Johnson's program at first, despite his failure to consult with Congress. They believed that they could work with Johnson to amend his program so that it would achieve the objectives of the Wade-Davis bill, and they hoped that Southern governments would respond positively to Johnson's conciliation and offer the vote to at least some blacks. Johnson did, in fact, unofficially advise Southern states to undertake some enfranchisement of blacks.

Johnson, however, made the mistake of advertising his reason for supporting limited black suffrage. In an August 1865 telegram that became public, Johnson told the provisional governor of Mississippi that if he gave the vote to literate blacks, "the radicals, who are wild upon negro franchise, will be completely foiled." This embarrassed Moderate Republicans and, to compound Johnson's problem, provisional governments in the South paid no attention to his advice on black suffrage. Moderate Republicans began to doubt Johnson's leadership on the suffrage issue.

During the autumn of 1865, Moderate Republicans became more sympathetic with the situation of blacks and more concerned with the way Johnson's plan was working in the South, as reports reached the North of frequent attacks on ex-slaves and Union supporters, and of ex-Confederates taking control of Southern governments. Under their new constitutions, the Southern voters sent to Congress nine prominent individuals who had served in the Confederate Congress,

seven officials from Confederate state governments, four generals and four colonels from the Confederate Army, and Alexander Stephens, the Vice President of the Confederacy. Radical Republicans such as Charles Sumner and Thaddeus Stevens began to attack Johnson for his failure to reconstruct the South.

Meanwhile, Johnson increasingly viewed himself as the savior of the Democratic party. Democrats in both the North and the South praised Johnson as the leader they needed to restore their party on a national basis. Northern Democrats, whose antiblack passions were stronger than those of Northern Republicans, cheered Johnson's racial policy. As Johnson soaked up Democratic applause, and as he heard the criticism of Radical Republicans, he concluded that he should move even further toward the position of ex-Confederates.

Moderate Republicans shifted from mild doubt about Johnson's leadership over Reconstruction to conviction that his plans were inadequate. In September they resolved to exclude the new Southern representatives until Johnson and Congress had agreed on a Reconstruction program. By December, when Congress convened, the Moderate Republicans had become convinced that they had to do more to protect the rights of the ex-slaves and establish the Republican party in the South. Nonetheless, the Moderate Republicans still wished to work with Johnson. They believed that the Northern public would not support an aggressive defense of blacks. And, Moderates wished to avoid assaulting Johnson for fear of increasing public support for him and for the Democratic party.

The Moderate Republicans controlled Congress when it convened in December 1865. They rejected the new Southern representatives and then formed a joint House-Senate committee of fifteen to develop a plan of Reconstruction. They still hoped to cooperate with President Johnson. He seemed to support the right of Congress to evaluate the qualifications of its members and seemed to favor some increased protection for the rights of the ex-slaves.

When the joint committee conducted hearings on conditions in the former Confederacy, it heard alarming reports from army officers, federal officials, and white and black Southerners that the level of violence was rising and that Southern legislatures were enacting Black Codes. Moderate Republicans drafted two bills in response to the complaints they had heard. The first extended the life of the Bureau of Refugees, Freedmen, and Abandoned Lands. Known as the Freedmen's Bureau, this was an agency created in March 1865 to feed and clothe refugees of both races, to rent confiscated land to "loyal refugees and freedmen," to draft and enforce labor contracts between ex-slaves and planters, and to cooperate with voluntary associations, such as the Freedmen's aid societies, which sent missionaries and teachers south to establish schools for ex-slaves. The new bill sought to empower the Bureau to establish courts that would function as military tribunals, protecting the rights of ex-slaves until the time states in rebellion were restored to the Union. The bill also sought to extend the occupation by ex-slaves of confiscated land in the Sea Islands of South Carolina and Georgia. The second bill was a civil rights bill that defined the citizenship rights of the ex-slaves and gave *federal* courts appellate jurisdiction in cases involving these rights.

Republicans were almost unanimous in passing the Freedmen's Bureau bill, and they expected Johnson to sign it into law. In February 1866 Johnson vetoed the bill. He argued that the bill was unconstitutional because the Constitution did not authorize a "system for the support of indigent persons" and because "there was no Senator or Representatives in Congress from the eleven States which are to be mainly affected by its pro-

visions." The veto enraged Moderates. They could not accept Johnson's implication that *any* Reconstruction legislation they passed without Southern representation was *necessarily* unconstitutional. Moderates tried to override the veto but failed, just barely, to collect the two-thirds majority they needed.

Democrats applauded Johnson's firmness, and, in a celebration, a group of them went to the White House to serenade him. The President emerged to deliver a speech that suggested to many that he was under the influence of alcohol. Johnson went so far as to accuse the Radical Republicans of being traitors who were plotting to assassinate him.

Johnson's veto and public disgrace pushed the Moderates in Congress closer to a complete break. Nonetheless, they still expected cooperation over the civil rights bill. In March 1866 Republicans passed it, declaring that blacks had the right to enjoy "full and equal benefit of all laws and proceedings for the security of person and property as it is enjoyed by white citizens." Republicans intended that the bill would wipe out the Black Codes and thus ensure the eradication of slavery. They did not mean for the bill to guarantee that blacks could exercise the vote. It was, therefore, a distinctly Moderate bill, one that Republicans expected Johnson to sign. Johnson, however, vetoed the civil rights bill. He called it unconstitutional and, with the votes of Democratic wards in the large cities in mind, argued that it discriminated against whites by providing citizenship for newly freed slaves while immigrants had to wait five years for the privilege.

Johnson's veto persuaded almost all Moderate Republicans that they must take charge of Reconstruction and adopt a completely independent plan. In April they overrode Johnson's veto to pass the Civil Rights Act of 1866. In July, after amending the Freedmen's Bureau bill by replacing the provision extending the occupation of confiscated land on the Sea Islands with one offering ex-slaves an opportunity to buy that land, they passed the bill over another Johnson veto. At the same time, the Joint Committee on Reconstruction drafted and submitted to Congress its proposal for the Fourteenth Amendment to the Constitution. The amendment would guarantee blacks citizenship — status that the Dred Scott decision had said the Constitution did not provide them — and encourage their suffrage. Thus, the resistance of ex-Confederates and President Johnson had moved Moderates toward the Radical position. Radicals, however, complained that the amendment did not *guarantee* the vote to blacks and that the amendment would have little effect on Northern states that refused to give blacks the vote.

Johnson attacked the Fourteenth Amendment, despite its moderation, and blamed it on the Radicals. Disregarding precedent, he campaigned personally in the 1866 congressional elections to attack the Radicals. In August and September he made a whistle-stop tour from Washington to Chicago to St. Louis and back, charging that Congress had acted illegally by approving the Fourteenth Amendment without the representation of all the Southern states. He declared that Southerners were loyal while the real traitors were the Radical Republicans in Congress who stalled restoration of the Union. "Why not hang Thad Stevens and Wendell Phillips?" he asked a crowd.

Under Johnson's assault, Moderates began to take a more radical tone. They reminded Northern voters of vicious race riots over suffrage that had occurred in Memphis and New Orleans during the late spring and early summer. In the latter city, a mob attacked the delegates to a black suffrage convention and killed forty people, including thirty-seven blacks. Republicans escalated their attacks on the Democrats. In what became known as "waving the bloody shirt," Republicans blamed the Democrats for the Civil War. Governor Oliver Morton of Indiana described the Democratic party as "a common sewer and loathsome receptacle, into which is emptied every element of treason North and South, every element of inhumanity and barbarism which has dishonored the age."

The outcome of the 1866 elections was a humiliating defeat for the President. The Republicans won a three-to-one majority in Congress. They gained control of every Northern state and the states of West Virginia, Missouri, and Tennessee.

Moderates moved even further toward the Radicals. They interpreted the elections as calling clearly for the reconstruction rather than the restoration of the South. And they were shocked to watch the state governments that Johnson had organized refusing to ratify the Fourteenth Amendment. Finally, Moderates accepted the Radical proposition that the federal government must guarantee black suffrage in the defeated Confederacy.

In the months following the elections of 1866, Moderates and Radicals together hammered out a more demanding plan of Reconstruction. By March, Congress had passed, over Johnson's persistent vetoes, the Reconstruction acts of 1867. These acts divided the South into five military districts and placed each district under a military commander, who was responsible for registering voters. The acts ordered the commanders to register all adult black males but allowed them considerable discretion in registering former Confederates. After voter registration the commander would call on voters to elect a constitutional convention that would write a state constitution with guarantees for black suffrage. Congress would readmit the state to the Union if the state's voters would ratify the new constitution, if the new constitution proved acceptable to Congress, if the new state legislature would approve the Fourteenth Amendment, and if enough states had ratified the Fourteenth Amendment to make it part of the Constitution.

Republicans also took action to ensure that President Johnson did not thwart Reconstruction by using his executive authority. Congress passed the Tenure of Office Act; it required congressional consent for the removal of any official, such as cabinet members, whose initial appointment had needed congressional approval. Congress also required the President to issue orders to the army through the general of the army, Ulysses S. Grant. In the wake of the 1866 elections, Grant supported more radical Reconstruction policies, and Congress wanted to make certain that Johnson worked through him in implementing the Reconstruction acts. In effect, Congress attempted to reconstruct the Presidency.

Radicals and Moderates had joined together in enacting the new Radical program. However, some Radicals did not believe that even the new measures went far enough in guaranteeing equality for blacks. They would have preferred land redistribution to ex-slaves, federal support for black schools, and continued disfranchisement of ex-Confederates. Nonetheless, the Radicals hoped that the policies would work and that, if they did not, the Northern public would move in an even more radical direction. They were willing to accept the new Reconstruction policies as the best that they could get in 1867.

The President Impeached

In August 1867, after Congress had adjourned and was therefore unable to review dismissals, Johnson made his move to challenge Congress. He fired Secretary of War Edwin M. Stanton, who was the only member of Johnson's cabinet to support congressional Reconstruction. To replace him Johnson appointed Ulysses S. Grant on a temporary basis. He next replaced four Republican generals who commanded Southern districts. One of those replaced, the commander of the Louisiana–Texas district, was Philip H. Sheridan, who had been one of Grant's favorite cavalry generals.

Johnson had underestimated Grant. Grant wrote a letter of protest over this thwarting of Congress and deliberately leaked it to the press. In January 1868, after learning that Congress had overruled Stanton's suspension, Grant countered Johnson again by moving out of the office of the secretary of war and allowing Stanton to return. Johnson, protesting that Grant had assured him that he would retain the office, engaged Grant in a public exchange of sharp letters. The popular Grant emerged openly as an enemy of Johnson, which eroded Johnson's support even further.

Johnson, still wishing to challenge congressional power, decided to test unequivocally the constitutionality of the Tenure of Office Act. In February 1868, without having sought congressional approval, he dismissed Stanton again. Stanton barricaded the door of his office, refusing to admit Johnson's appointee.

Republicans in Congress responded with an impeachment effort. Radicals led it; they had sought impeachment for a year, but only now did they have the support of Moderates in their party. Many Moderates now saw impeachment as the only way to deal with a President whose ineptitude made it impossible to carry out any Reconstruction of the South. On February 24, 1868, the

House impeached the President with support from the Moderate wing of the Republican party. Dominated by Radicals, the committee that was appointed to bring charges of "high crimes and misdemeanors" against Johnson concentrated on alleged violations of the Tenure of Office Act.

The Senate, however, acting as a court, failed to convict Johnson of the charges. After deliberating for eleven weeks, on May 26 thirty-five Senators voted for impeachment, but this fell one vote short of the two-thirds required for conviction. Seven Republicans had broken ranks, voting with twelve Democrats in support of Johnson. These Moderate Republicans reached their decision only partly because they believed that Johnson was innocent. Primarily, they worried about the precedent of Congress deposing a President with whom it disagreed over an issue of policy. They feared weakening the Presidency. They believed that the Civil War had demonstrated the need for a strong federal government administered by a powerful executive. They doubted whether the nation could preserve internal unity, advance the Republican economic program, and defend itself against foreign enemies without a strong Presidency.

Radical Republicans failed to convict Johnson, but they defeated him on Reconstruction. Chastened, Johnson subsided for the remainder of his term, letting Reconstruction proceed under congressional direction.

In 1869 the Republicans added the last major piece of Reconstruction legislation, the Fifteenth Amendment, which forbade states to deny its citizens the right to vote on the grounds of race, color, or previous condition of servitude. Once again, some Radicals would have preferred more. They had wanted to close off the loopholes of property or literacy qualifications that state governments might use to disfranchise blacks. Moderates, however, had prevailed; they feared that Northern and Western states would want to protect their ability to deny immigrants the vote and would therefore oppose a more rigorous proposal. Still, the Fifteenth Amendment was much tougher in protecting black suffrage than the Fourteenth. Passing the amendment in February 1869, Congress required the unreconstructed states of Virginia, Mississippi, Texas, and Georgia to ratify the amendment before readmission.

The Reconstructed States

Between 1868 and 1871, all Southern states met the stipulations of Congress and rejoined the Union. Reconstructed governments remained in power for periods ranging from a few months, in the case of Virginia, to the extreme of nine years in the cases of South Carolina, Louisiana, and Florida. In each government the Republican party was in control and blacks played an important role, although in no state did blacks dominate Reconstruction. In Alabama, Florida, South Carolina, Mississippi, and Louisiana, where blacks constituted a majority of all registered voters, they contributed heavily to Republican victories. Blacks held positions of importance in all Reconstruction governments, although they were more poorly represented among officeholders than among the population at large in every government except for South Carolina's.

Black political leaders came largely from an elite that had been freed before the Civil War. Some of these leaders were the sons of planters who had provided them with educations. Blanche K. Bruce, one of the two black senators from Mississippi, had received tutoring on the plantation of his white father. Another, P. B. S. Pinchback, a Louisiana lieutenant governor, went to school in Cincinnati, sent there at age nine by his planter father. They, and the other black artisans, shopkeepers, teachers, and ministers who held office in the Reconstruction South, emphasized the suffrage and the need for public improvements of all kinds, especially schools and roads.

On the whole, whites dominated the reconstructed state governments, holding the vast majority of state offices. These whites were a diverse group. Among them were nonslaveholding whites, labeled "scalawags" by their Democratic opponents. Some were wealthy individuals, often former Whigs who wanted Southern industrial development. Still others were settlers from the North, whom the Democrats called "carpetbaggers." The carpetbaggers held more than half the Republican governorships and almost half of the congressional positions.

The Southern supporters of Reconstruction did not fit the stereotypes that the Democrats advertised. Carpetbaggers often sought personal profit, but they usually made long-run commitments to Southern society. Most had been Union Army officers who had fallen in love with the South. Many brought far more than carpetbags in which to carry off the wealth of the South; they brought capital and skills to invest in the South's future. Many were college graduates and professionals — lawyers, engineers, and teachers. The scalawags were poorer but often owned their own farms. They wished to see a South free of a slave-owning aristocracy and usually had fought against, or at least refused to support, the Confederacy. Blacks were the poorest of the elements in the Republican coalition, but three quarters of the blacks who held office in the postwar South were literate.

In wielding power, Southern Republicans established a record of real accomplishment. It is true that, just as in Northern legislatures, Republicans were sometimes corrupt and inefficient. But the Southerners accomplished much more. They widened the franchise, for both blacks and whites, and made many offices, especially in the judicial system, elective. They built modern public schools serving both black and white children. Both blacks and poor whites, thirsting for the knowledge denied them under slavery, flocked to the new schools. In 1867 a young black student in Augusta, Georgia, explained simply that "I'm going to school now to try to learn some thing which I hope will enable me to be of some use to my race." By 1877 over half a million black children were enrolled in public schools. The Republicans engaged in major public works programs, including the replacement of railroads destroyed during the war, and they subsidized manufacturing investment. They did all of this without any federal financing. Their mission was to promote an alternative to cotton agriculture; they sought economic growth based on manufacturing, capital intensity, and a skilled people.

A Soldier in the White House

At the end of the war both parties had angled to make General Grant their candidate, and he could have had the nomination of either party. But Grant concluded that the Radical Reconstruction policy expressed the real wishes of the

The Nature of Reconstruction

Historical writing on Reconstruction like that on the Civil War, reflects the patterns of thought that have prevailed at different times. The first professional historian of Reconstruction, William A. Dunning, who taught at Columbia University from the 1880s to the 1920s, carried on his work during a period when scholars generally held that certain racial and ethnic groups were inherently superior to others. Dunning assumed that blacks were inferior and hence unfit to receive the vote. In his *Reconstruction, Political and Economic* (1907), he argued that the Republicans imposed their Radical program upon the South mainly to keep their party in power. Under the Radical plan, the Southern states suffered the agonies of "bayonet rule" and "Negro rule," when with army support the blacks and their unscrupulous white accomplices plundered the people in an unbelievable orgy of corruption, ruinous taxation, and astronomical increases in the public debt.

The first historian seriously to challenge the Dunning interpretation was the black scholar William E. B. Du Bois. In *Black Reconstruction* (1935), Du Bois pointed out that the misdeeds of the Reconstruction state governments had been exaggerated and their achievements overlooked. These governments were expensive, he explained, because they undertook to provide public education and other public services on a scale never before attempted in the South. Du Bois described Reconstruction politics in the Southern states as an effort on the part of the masses, black and white, to create a true democratic society. Writing under the influence of Marxism, he assumed a class consciousness for which few other historians could find much evidence.

By the 1940s the attitudes toward race, on the part of scholars at least, had drastically changed. Since that time a new generation of historians has arisen — among them C. Vann Woodward, John Hope Franklin, Kenneth M. Stampp, Eric McKitrick, and John and La Wanda Cox — who argue that the Radical Republicans were motivated less by partisan or economic interests than by a determination to guarantee basic rights to the former slaves and thus to secure the war aims of reunion and freedom. There was little if anything in the South that could properly be called "Nego rule," and the black, carpetbagger, and scalawag politicians were at least as honest and capable as others of their time. The mistake in Reconstruction was not the attempt to confer civil and political rights upon blacks, but the failure to provide an adequate economic and educational basis and sufficient governmental protection from the assurance of those rights.

Where historians now tend to disagree is on why Reconstruction fell short of guaranteeing racial justice. Some scholars claim that conservative obstacles to change were so great that the Radicals, despite their good intentions, simply could not overcome them. Others claim that the Radicals lacked sufficient commitment to the principle of radical justice; they concluded too quickly that they could not win. Others, however, reemphasize the achievements of Reconstruction, particularly the Fourteenth and Fifteenth amendments, which strengthened federal responsibility for protecting the rights of citizenship.

people. He was receptive when the Radical leaders approached him with offers of the Republican nomination.

The Republicans endorsed Radical Reconstruction and black suffrage for the South but declared that in the North the question of black voting should be determined by each state. (Thus during the campaign the Republicans opposed the suffrage amendment, the Fifteenth, which they were to pass soon after the election.)

Unwisely the Democrats decided to meet the Republican challenge. Their platform also emphasized Reconstruction, denouncing in extravagant terms the Radical program and demanding restoration of "home rule" in the South. Thus the Democrats chose to fight the campaign on an issue that was related to the war and its emotions — an issue that enabled their opponents to associate them with rebellion. They did, however, attempt to inject a new question of an economic nature into the contest. In 1868 approximately $356,000,000 of the Civil War greenbacks were in circulation, and Middle Western Democrats wanted to keep the paper currency and use it when legally possible to pay off the national debt. Behind this so-called Ohio idea was the larger question of retaining the greenbacks as a permanent part of the money supply. This proposal appealed to the debtor farmers of the West and also to many hard-pressed business people of the East. The Westerners succeeded in writing the Ohio idea into the platform, but the party nominated Horatio Seymour of New York, a gold or "sound money" proponent, who repudiated the currency plank.

After a bitter campaign revolving around Reconstruction and Seymour's war record as governor of New York (he had been a Peace Democrat), Grant carried twenty-six states and Seymour only eight. But Grant got only 3,012,000 popular votes to Seymour's 2,703,000, a scant majority of 310,000, and this majority was due to black votes in the reconstructed states of the South.

Ulysses S. Grant was the second professional soldier to be elected to the Presidency (Zachary Taylor having been the first), and the last to be chosen until Dwight D. Eisenhower was selected in 1952. Grant had little knowledge of political issues or political ways, and he was naive in choosing people to help him, often appointing

rascals or mediocrities. His greatest defect was that he did not understand his function as President. He regarded the Presidency as a ceremonial and administrative office and failed to provide real leadership in trying times.

Successes in Foreign Affairs

In foreign affairs the Grant administration achieved its most brilliant successes, as the Johnson administration also had done. These were the accomplishments of two outstanding secretaries of state: William H. Seward (1861–1869) and Hamilton Fish (1869–1877).

An ardent expansionist and advocate of a vigorous foreign policy, Seward acted with as much daring as the demands of Reconstruction politics and the Republican hatred of President Johnson would permit. By exercising firm but patient pressure, he persuaded Napoleon III of France to abandon his Mexican empire, which was established during the war when the United States was in no position to protest. Napoleon withdrew his troops in 1867, his puppet Emperor Maximilian was executed by the Mexicans, and the validity of the Monroe Doctrine was strikingly reaffirmed.

When Russia let it be known that it would like to sell Alaska to the United States, the two nations long having been on friendly terms, Seward readily agreed to pay the asking price of $7,200,000. Only by strenuous efforts was he able to induce the Senate to ratify the treaty and the House to appropriate the money (1867–1868). Critics jeered that the secretary had bought a useless frozen wasteland — "Seward's Icebox" and "Walrussia" were some of the terms employed to describe it — but Alaska, a center for the fishing industry in the North Pacific and rich in natural resources, was a distinct bargain. Seward was not content with expansion in continental North America. In 1867 he engineered the annexation of the tiny Midway Islands west of Hawaii.

The United States had a burning grievance against Great Britain that had originated during the Civil War. At that time the British government, according to the American interpretation, had violated the laws of neutrality by permitting Confederate cruisers, the *Alabama* and others, to be built and armed in English shipyards and let loose to prey on Northern commerce. American demands that England pay for the damages committed by these vessels became known as the "Alabama claims." Although the British government realized its diplomatic error in condoning construction of the cruisers (in a future war American-built *Alabamas* might operate against Britain), it at first hesitated to submit the issue to arbitration.

Seward tried earnestly to settle the Alabama claims before leaving office. Secretary Fish continued to work for a solution, and finally in 1871 the two countries agreed to the Treaty of Washington, one of the great landmarks in international pacification, providing for arbitration of the cruiser issue and other pending controversies. The Alabama claims were to be laid before a five-member tribunal appointed by the governments of the United States, England, Italy, Switzerland, and Brazil. In the covenant Britain expressed regret for building the *Alabama* and agreed to a set of rules governing neutral obligations that virtually gave the British case away. In effect, this meant that the tribunal would have only to fix the sum to be paid by Britain. Convening at Geneva in Switzerland, the arbitrators awarded the United States $15,500,000.

The Evils of "Grantism"

Through both his foreign and his domestic policies, President Grant antagonized and alienated a number of prominent Republicans, among them the famous Radical, Charles Sumner.

Sumner and other Republican leaders joined with civil service reformers to criticize Grant for his use of the spoils system, his reliance on ruthless machine politicians. Republican critics of the President also denounced him for his support of Radical Reconstruction. He continued to station federal troops in the South, and on numerous occasions he sent them to the support of black and carpetbag governments that were on the point of collapsing. To growing numbers in the North, this seemed like dangerous militarism, and they were more and more disgusted by the stories of governmental corruption and extravagance that came up from the South. Some Republicans were begin-

ning to suspect that there was corruption not only in the Southern state governments but also in the federal government itself. Still others criticized Grant because he had declined to speak out in favor of a reduction of the tariff. The high wartime duties, used as a means of paying off the war debt, remained substantially unchanged.

In 1872, hoping to prevent Grant's reelection, his opponents bolted the party. Referring to themselves as Liberal Republicans, they proceeded to set up their own organization for running presidential and vice-presidential candidates. For the Presidency they named Horace Greeley, veteran editor and publisher of the New York *Tribune*. The Democratic convention, seeing in his candidacy the only chance to unseat the Republicans, endorsed him with no great enthusiasm. Despite his recent attacks on Radical Reconstruction, many Southerners, remembering Greeley's own Radical past, prepared to stay at home on election day. Greeley carried only two Southern and four border states.

During the campaign the first of a series of political scandals had come to light. Although the wrongdoing had occurred before Grant took office, it involved his party and the onus for it fell on his administration. This scandal originated with the Crédit Mobilier construction company that helped build the Union Pacific Railroad. In reality, the Crédit Mobilier was controlled by a few Union Pacific stockholders who awarded huge and fraudulent contracts to the construction company, thus milking the Union Pacific, a company of which they owned a minor share, of money that in part came from government subsidies. To avert a congressional inquiry into the deal, the directors sold at a discount (in effect gave) Crédit Mobilier stock to key members of Congress. A congressional investigation revealed that some high-placed Republicans had accepted stock, including Schuyler Colfax, now Grant's Vice President.

One dreary episode followed another during Grant's second term. Benjamin H. Bristow, secretary of the treasury, discovered that some of his officials and a group of distillers operating as a "Whiskey Ring" were cheating the government out of taxes by means of false reports. Among the prominent Republicans involved was the President's private secretary, Orville E. Babcock. Grant defended Babcock, appointed him to another office, and eased Bristow out of the cabinet.

The Greenback Question

Meanwhile the Grant administration along with the country as a whole had suffered another blow when the Panic of 1873 struck. It was touched off by the failure of a leading investment banking firm, Jay Cooke and Company, the "financier of the Civil War," which had done well in the handling of government war bonds but had sunk excessive amounts in postwar railroad building. Depressions had come before with almost rhythmic regularity — in 1819, 1837, and 1857 — but this was the worst one yet. It lasted four years, during which unemployment rose to 3,000,000, and agricultural prices fell so far that thousands of farmers, unable to meet mortgage payments, went more deeply into debt or lost their farms.

Debtors hoped the government would follow an inflationary, easy-money policy, which would have made it easier for them to pay their debts and would have helped to stimulate recovery from the depression. But President Grant and most Republicans preferred what they called a "sound" currency, which was to the advantage of the banks, moneylenders, and other creditors.

As a relief measure after the Panic of 1873, the Treasury increased the amount of greenbacks in circulation. For the same reason Congress, in the following year, voted to raise the total again. Grant, responding to pressures from the financial interests, vetoed the measure. In 1875 the Republican Congress enacted the Resumption Act, providing that after January 1, 1879, the government would exchange gold dollars for greenbacks and directing the government to acquire a gold reserve for redemption purposes. The law had its intended result: with the specie value of greenbacks assured, they were equal in worth to gold. The fundamental impact of the law was to produce deflation and thus protect the interests of the creditor classes, but at the same time, the

debtor groups could take some comfort in the retention of the greenbacks.

Southern Republicans Lose

Ex-slaveowners opposed the entire Republican program in the South and sought to regain control of Southern state governments. They based their appeals to Southern whites on calls for racial solidarity. Consequently, mass hostility to the Republicans and their programs focused not on the economic issues but on black suffrage and, more generally, black social independence. In the seven states in which whites formed a majority of the population (all except for Louisiana, Mississippi, and South Carolina), planters sought to return ex-Confederates to the rolls of registered voters and unite them under the Democratic banner. In every state planters resorted, when necessary, to techniques of intimidation and terror. In effect, the "redeemers," as they began to call themselves, resumed the Civil War — as a kind of guerrilla war.

Ex-Confederates organized secret societies to frighten blacks and Republican whites from political action. These societies coerced whites into joining the Democratic party and prevented blacks from supporting the Republican party. The most widespread of these secret groups was the Ku Klux Klan, first organized in Tennessee in 1865. It quickly spread throughout the South. As Reconstruction advanced, terrorist resistance became more open and more elaborate. Paramilitary groups, carrying names like Rifle clubs and Red Shirts, operated openly. They became most visible in Mississippi, where their procedures became known as the Mississippi Plan. The first step in the Mississippi Plan was to force all whites into the Democratic party. Organizers used every means possible to compel the state's white Republicans to change sides. The second step was the relentless intimidation of black voters. In Mississippi's 1875 elections, in which the Republican party went down to defeat, local Democratic clubs paraded as full militia companies, listed black leaders in "dead-books," broke up Republican meetings, and provoked rioting that killed hundreds of blacks.

To contain the terror, Southern Republicans needed the intervention of federal forces, but they received little help. In 1870–1871 Congress did pass the Force acts, which authorized the President to use military force and martial law in suppressing felonies and conspiracies where the Ku Klux Klan was active. Under the acts, federal agents penetrated the Klan and gathered evidence that provided the basis for thousands of arrests. And federal grand juries indicted over 3,000 Klansmen. The Justice Department, however, lacked the resources necessary to prosecute effectively, especially when trials were held before all-white juries. Only about 600 major offenders received convictions and, of these, only a handful served major prison sentences. The ex-Confederates who used terror suffered only a temporary setback.

To defeat the resistance of the paramilitary forces, the federal government would almost have had to resume the Civil War. The Grant administration and Moderate Republicans in Congress, however, were unwilling to enlarge what was already a costly, bloody guerrilla war.

Democrats began a national comeback after Grant's reelection victory in 1872. In the 1874 elections, Democrats gained seats in both houses of Congress and won control of the House of Representatives for the first time since 1856. The Democrats based their gains on the appeal of their alternative economic program, especially low tariffs and an inflationary currency, and on Northern weariness with the spilling of blood and treasure to support Reconstruction. With each election, Republican "waving the bloody shirt" had less effect.

To Republicans, softening Reconstruction seemed to offer an opportunity to recoup part of their 1874 losses. With a milder approach to Reconstruction, they hoped to recapture wavering Republicans and even find new supporters among Northern Democrats. And most Republicans, including some Radicals, concluded that they had done all that they needed to do on behalf of ex-slaves and that the ex-slaves could enjoy their freedom without additional federal assistance. Republicans moved toward a consensus that the federal government had accomplished its Civil War objectives and should put an end to Reconstruction.

Southern terrorists gradually overwhelmed the Republican governments, which lacked federal reinforcements. During 1870 Democrats, supported by a vigorous Klan, recovered power in Virginia, Georgia, and North Carolina. Democrats overthrew Republicans in Texas in 1873, in Alabama and Arkansas in 1874, and in Mississippi in 1875. By 1877 Republican governments and token federal forces remained in only three states: Louisiana, South Carolina, and Florida.

The Compromise of 1877

In 1876 the Republican managers, seeking to reunite the party, secured the nomination of Rutherford B. Hayes, governor of Ohio and a symbol of honest government. The Democrats nominated Samuel J. Tilden, governor of New York and also a symbol of honest government. Between the two candidates there was little difference. Both were conservative on economic issues, and both were on record as favoring the withdrawal of troops from the South.

The November election revealed an apparent electoral and popular majority for Tilden. But disputed returns had come in from three Southern states, Louisiana, South Carolina, and Florida, whose total electoral vote was nineteen. In addition, there was a technical dispute in Oregon about one elector. Tilden had for certain 184 electoral votes, one short of a majority. The twenty votes in controversy would determine who would be President.

With surprise and consternation, the public now learned that no measure or method existed to determine the validity of disputed returns. The Constitution stated: "The President of the Senate shall, in the presence of the Senate and House of Representatives, open all the certificates and the votes shall then be counted." The question was how and by whom? The Senate was Republican and so, of course, was its president, and the House was Democratic. The country was threatened with crisis — and possibly with chaos.

Not until the last days of January 1877 did Congress act to break the deadlock. Then it created a special Electoral Commission to pass on all the disputed votes. It was to be composed of five senators, five representatives, and five justices of the

Supreme Court. Because of the party lineup, the congressional delegation would consist of five Republicans and five Democrats. The creating law named four of the judicial commissioners, two Republicans and two Democrats. The four were to select their fifth colleague, and it was understood that they would choose David Davis, an independent Republican, thus ensuring that the deciding vote would be wielded by a relatively unbiased judge. But at this stage Davis was elected to the Senate from Illinois and refused to serve. His place on the Electoral Commission fell to a Republican. Sitting throughout February, the commission by a partisan vote of eight to seven decided every disputed vote for Hayes. Congress accepted the final verdict of the agency on March 2, only two days before the inauguration of the new President.

But the findings of the Electoral Commission were not final until approved by Congress, and the Democrats could have prevented action by filibustering. The success of a filibuster, however, depended on concert between Northern and Southern Democrats, and this the Republicans disrupted by offering the Southerners sufficient inducement to accept the commission's finds. They promised to the Southerners control of the federal patronage in their states, generous internal improvements, federal aid for a Southern transcontinental railroad, and withdrawal of federal troops from the South. The Southerners accepted the package, and the crisis was over.

The withdrawal of the troops, which President Hayes effected soon after his inauguration, was a symbol that the national government was giving up its attempt to control Southern politics and to determine the place of blacks in Southern society.

Selected Readings

The controversy between the sections that finally erupted in civil war is treated in a number of general studies. Among the best of these is Allan Nevins, *Ordeal of the Union* (2 vols., 1947). On the 1850s, see David Potter, *The Impending Crisis, 1848–1861* (1976); and Michael F Holt, *The Political Crisis of the 1850s* (1978). On the ideas motivating Republicans there is Eric Foner's *Free Soil, Free Labor, Free Men: The Ideology of the Republican Party before the Civil War*° (1970). On Lincoln's role, see B. F. Thomas, *Abraham Lincoln*° (1952), and J. G. Randall, *Mr. Lincoln* (1957), distilled by R. N. Current from Randall's four-volume *Lincoln the President* (1945–1955 with vol. 4 completed by R. N. Current). The critical events of 1860–1861 are related in R. N. Current, *Lincoln and the First Shot*° (1963).

The literature on the Civil War is so vast as to defy summary. Excellent bibliographies appear in the convenient survey by James M. McPherson, *Ordeal by Fire: The Civil War and Reconstruction* (1981). There is the massive survey of Allan Nevins, *The War for the Union* (4 vols., 1959–1972). Informative for the Southern side is C. P. Roland, *The Confederacy*° (1960).

On special aspects of the North at war, see T. H. Williams, *Lincoln and the Radicals*° (1941), and H. L. Trefousse, *The Radical Republicans* (1969), which offer somewhat contrasting views; and J. M. McPherson, *The Struggle for Equality* (1964), on the abolitionists in the war.

On Civil War campaigns, begin with T. H. Williams, *Lincoln and His Generals*° (1952).

The older but now questioned view of Reconstruction appears in W. A. Dunning, *Reconstruction, Political and Economic*° (1907). It was first challenged by W. E. B. Du Bois in *Black Reconstruction*° (1935). Later and more telling challenges came in E. L. McKitrick, *Andrew Johnson and Reconstruction* (1966), and J. H. Franklin, *Reconstruction* (1965). The best overall account is K. M. Stampp's *Era of Reconstruction* (1965). On blacks during Reconstruction, see Joel Williamson, *After Slavery* (1966); Willie Lee Rose, *Rehearsal for Reconstruction* (1964); and Leon Litwack, *Been in the Storm So Long* (1979). On the New South, see C. V. Woodward, *Origins of the New South, 1877–1913* (1951), and *The Strange Career of Jim Crow* (1953).

---

*Titles available in paperback.

Part Five
1865-1917

Modern America Emerges

"With a stride that astonished statisticians, the conquering hosts of business enterprise swept over the continent; twenty-five years after the death of Lincoln, America had become, in the quantity and value of her products, the first manufacturing nation of the world," the historians Charles and Mary Beard have written. "What England had accomplished in a hundred years, the United States had achieved in half the time."

The rate of industrial growth increased so rapidly in the postwar decades that these came to constitute a new age of industrialization. It was also an age of urbanization, in which cities assumed a greater and greater importance. The tremendous increase in the output of goods — and the multiplication of conveniences that city life afforded — made possible a higher and higher average level of living and increasing real income for most Americans. But the people did not share equally in the benefits of the industrial system. There were gross inequalities, and these provoked severe criticism of the system and sometimes violent attempts to bring about a redistribution of income.

Opportunities for individual success seemed to be shrinking with the near disappearance of good free land in the West. The census report for 1890 noted that the unsettled areas of the West had been "so broken into by isolated bodies of settlement" that a continuous frontier line could no longer be drawn. Three years later a young historian from the University of Wisconsin, Frederick

Jackson Turner, startled the American Historical Association with a memorable paper, "The Significance of the Frontier in American History." The roots of the national character, Turner asserted, lay not so much in the East or in Europe as in the West. As he saw it, "The existence of an area of free land, its continuous recession, and the advance of settlement westward explain American development." This experience, by stimulating individualism, nationalism, and democracy, had made Americans the distinctive people that they were. "Now," Turner concluded ominously, "four centuries from the discovery of America, at the end of a hundred years of life under the Constitution, the frontier has gone, and with its going has closed the first period of American history."

Political leaders were slow to respond to the challenges of the time — to the serious problems arising out of the development of big business, the organization of labor and the resulting industrial conflict, the decline of agricultural prices and the worsening position of the farmer, and the economic instability that brought collapse in 1873 and again in 1893.

By the early 1890s a tide of protest was swelling and dashing against politics as usual. It was headed by discontented farmers, but it included other dissatisfied groups whose numbers were increased by the onset of the depression. It encountered the forces of conservatism and partially recoiled before them but recovered to reach a roaring climax in the election of 1896. Thereafter the protest movement receded, as the economic system demonstrated its capacity to enlarge the general well-being, and the political system showed its ability to absorb dissenters into the traditional two parties.

Opening the two-party system to new groups and concerns in the first decades of the twentieth century was a new political impulse that came to be known as "progressivism." Those who thought of themselves as "progressives" saw with great concern the nation's rapid technological development and growing involvement in international affairs. They wanted to make sure that the United States, as an industrial giant and a world power, held on to the democratic ideals that it had inherited from the past.

There were many wrongs to be righted, and the progressives differed among themselves in both their aims and their methods. To some, the main evil was monopoly; to others, corruption in city government; to still others, the unequal status of women. And so it went. Various groups combined and cooperated, or they divided and worked against one another, on certain issues. For example, some favored and others opposed imperialism. Thus progressivism may be considered as an aggregate of causes rather than a single movement. Still, most progressives had in common the following convictions: (1) "the people" ought to have much more influence in government and the "special interests" much less, and (2) government ought to be much stronger, more active, and more efficient in serving the public welfare.

In certain respects progressivism was a continuation of Populism. Progressives advocated some (though not all) of the reforms that the Populists had proposed, and some of the former Populists joined the progressive movement. But progressivism and Populism differed in important respects. The People's party members had been mostly distressed farmers of the Southern and the Great Plains and Rocky Mountain states. The progressive ranks included men and women from all parts of the country, but especially from the Northeast and the Midwest, and prominent among the progressives were persons of the urban middle class. The progressives had a broader concept of both "the people" and the public welfare than the Populists had had.

Prominent figures of both major parties brought progressivism into national politics. Among the leading Republicans were Robert M. La Follette and Theodore Roosevelt; among the Democrats, William Jennings Bryan and Woodrow Wilson. From 1901 to 1916 politics and government largely reflected the opinions and ambitions of these men — especially Roosevelt and Wilson — and their respective followings.

Meanwhile the United States took a new direction in foreign affairs when it began to acquire possessions overseas. From the very beginning, of course, the republic had been expansionist. As the American people moved relentlessly westward across the continent, their government from time to time acquired new lands for them to occupy. Almost all these acquisitions — the fruits of what might be called the old Manifest Destiny — were contiguous with existing territories of the United States. But the expansionism of the 1890s, the new Manifest Destiny, was in some respects different. It meant acquiring island possessions, some of which were already thickly populated, were unsuitable for settlement by migrants from the United States, and were expected to be held indefinitely as colonies, not as states or even territories. The new expansion was motivated largely (though not entirely) by considerations of trade. Thus it represented a kind of commercial imperialism.

After 1900 Americans clung to the old idea of keeping out of Europe's quarrels, but the nation drifted toward the twentieth-century maelstrom of world conflict. The industrial developments in Europe and America had brought, along with increased material abundance, a heightened competition for markets, sources of raw materials, places for investment, and sheer national prestige. As the foremost of all industrial nations, the United States could scarcely remain unaffected by world events for long. Its emergence from the Spanish-American War with Pacific and Caribbean colonies intensified the risks of involvement. So did certain phases of the progressive spirit itself, which stimulated increased activity in foreign affairs. Some progressives aspired not only to revitalize democracy here but to extend it abroad.

World War I brought the greatest challenge in 100 years to the time-honored policy of neutrality and diplomatic independence. For three years, from 1914 to 1917, the United States remained at peace, and then it joined in the hostilities. Its entrance hardly meant that the traditional policy had failed, for strict neutrality had not been tried. The American people had closer ties of kinship and commerce with one set of European belligerents than with the other.

According to this country's constitutional system, one man has the ultimate responsibility for war or peace — the President. In 1917 President Woodrow Wilson made the decision for war. He saw it as a war to end war, to bring about an international organization for keeping the future peace, and thus to "make the world safe for democracy." Wilson thereby took progressivism abroad; America's decision to enter World War I was a decision to wage progressivism by the sword.

Chapter 16

Economic Life, 1865–1917

Industrialization

Between the Civil War and World War I, the American economy experienced a sensational expansion. This was most apparent in industry — in these years America became the first manufacturing nation of the world. Its rise to eminence rested on firm bases: the inventive and organizational skills of its people; the willingness of its people to forgo current consumption and save at high rates; its possession of unparalleled national resources; and its ever-growing, mobile population, which constituted a vast interior market and source of labor. These elements provided the means for not only increasing industrial production but also increasing efficiency. Thus, although American manufacturers produced 76 percent more goods in 1914 than in 1899, they did so with only 36 percent more workers and 13 percent more establishments.

Among the important inventions and innovations of the period were the telephone, the typewriter, the adding machine, the cash register, and the use of electricity as a source of light and power. Drawing on these innovations and others, and utilizing increasing amounts of capital, manufacturing firms adopted mass-production techniques, used large-scale factories, reached national markets, developed techniques of national advertising, and adopted sophisticated management practices. By World War I, the modern manufacturing enterprise as we know it today had emerged to lead the process of industrialization.

Railroads

American industrial expansion relied heavily on the nation's railroad system. Not only did that network create the basis for a genuinely national economy, but it also provided significant increases in the volume, rate, and regularity of the flow of goods through the production and marketing systems. The resulting flows established the basis for the adoption of mass-production and distribution techniques and, in turn, for the marked gains in productivity and per capita income that characterize the period. The railroads had been the first giant American industry, and after the Civil War they continued to expand. Their trackage figure quadrupled between 1860 and 1900, when the United States had the most extensive transportation system in the world.

Railroad development included the building of the great "transcontinental" lines. During the Civil War, Congress had acted to make the dream of a road from the Mississippi Valley to the Pacific coast a reality. It had chartered two railroad corporations, the Union Pacific and the Central Pacific. The Union Pacific was to build westward from Omaha, Nebraska, and the Central Pacific eastward from Sacramento, California, until they met.

To provide the financial aid deemed necessary to initiate the roads, Congress donated a right of way across the public domain and offered the companies special benefits. By the terms of the war legislation, the Union Pacific and the Central

Pacific stood to receive approximately 20,000,000 acres of land and $60,000,000 in loans.

The companies started work in 1865. Appalling obstacles faced the builders — mountains, deserts, hostile Indians. In addition, supplies and labor had to be brought in from distant points. The Central Pacific imported several thousand Chinese laborers, while the Union Pacific hired thousands of Irish immigrants. Nevertheless, the job was pushed on, and in the spring of 1869 the nation was linked by rail from the Atlantic to the Pacific. The event set off a national celebration. At the end of the century five transcontinental systems were in operation. All but one were built with some form of assistance from the national government or from state governments.

As the network of rails covered the country, it became evident that the railroad industry was being overbuilt and overextended; many railroad corporations, including some of the largest ones, were afflicted with impossible debt burdens. In some areas of the country certain railroads enjoyed monopolies, but wherever competition existed, it was savage and sustained. The inevitable effects of overexpansion and cutthroat competition were apparent in the depression of the seventies, when 450 roads went into bankruptcy. Twenty years later, in the hard times of the nineties, 318 companies controlling 67,000 miles fell into the hands of receivers.

The Rise of Big Business

After the economic crises of 1873 and 1893, railroad capitalists moved to curb competition by creating larger systems and to enhance stability by introducing more efficient management. Reorganizing the railroads required huge sums of cash and credit, which could be supplied only by the big New York investment banking houses. The bankers, led by J. P. Morgan, were eager to finance consolidation in order to stop the railroads, with their wild financing and frenzied speculating, from ruining the investment business. But the bankers, as the price for their aid, insisted on being given a voice in the management of the roads, a condition that the railroad promoters had to accept. By the end of the century a few

railroad systems controlled over half the mileage in the country, and these systems were wholly or partially controlled by two banking houses: J. P. Morgan and Co. and the Rockefeller-controlled National City Bank.

Until 1900, the railroad empires were the nation's biggest businesses. But they were gradually eclipsed by giant manufacturing corporations. Prior to the late nineteenth century, manufacturing activity tended to be small-scale, rooted in discrete locations, family-owned, organized as a single proprietorship or a partnership, and often based on the work of a household unit. But during the 1870s the increasing scale of manufacturing activity, promoted by the access to larger markets that the railroad provided, led manufacturers to incorporate their enterprises for the first time. The limited liability to investors that the corporate form provided allowed manufacturers to more easily mobilize capital.

The corporation, however, was not the ultimate form of organization. Even larger were forms combining a number of corporations — pools, trusts, and holding companies. A pool was an informal organization of several corporations in the same business. A trust came into being when the stockholders of a number of corporations transferred their stock to a directing board of trustees. A holding company was born when the directing company actually bought the stock of competing corporations.

Behind the movement toward concentration were powerful economic forces. The expanded number of business units intensified competition and the scramble for profits. More potent was the steady decline in prices between 1865 and 1897, forcing business executives to consider every device that might cut costs. Equally powerful was the economy's increasing instability, which led business leaders to search for ways of making their world more predictable. Organization into larger units would eliminate competition, lower costs, and increase profits.

Thus American industry moved with unconscious purpose toward concentration. Fewer and fewer companies produced more and more of the nation's goods. By 1900 less than 2 percent of the manufacturing establishments were turning out almost 50 percent of all the manufactured goods in the country.

Leaders of Big Business

Reflecting the division of public opinion, contemporary writings about late-nineteenth-century business leaders usually were either flattering or denunciatory. In the "muckraking" years of the early twentieth century, denunciation came to predominate. Thus Ida M. Tarbell, *The History of the Standard Oil Company* (1904), presented John D. Rockefeller as a predatory character who drove smaller oil entrepreneurs out of business by unscrupulous means. Gustavus Myers, *The History of the Great American Fortunes* (1907), undertook to show that other business leaders had also amassed their wealth by crushing competitors and corrupting politicians, not by practicing the old-fashioned American virtues of honesty, thrift, and hard work.

The treatment of these business leaders became more favorable during the prosperous 1920s. In *The Rise of American Civilization* (1927) Charles and Mary Beard described them as "captains of industry" who contributed to industrial development through their remarkable powers of organization. During the depression of the 1930s, however, the pioneers of big business again fell into disrepute. Matthew Josephson gave them a name that most historians accepted in his popular book *The Robber Barons* (1934). Josephson compared them to feudal lords who got rich by preying on legitimate commerce.

Allan Nevins challenged the Josephson view in *John D. Rockefeller: The Heroic Age of American Enterprise*, which was originally published in 1940 and republished with revisions and elaborations in 1953. Nevins depicted Rockefeller as an industrial statesman who brought order and efficiency to the oil business. The Nevins interpretation reflected the changed attitude that came with World War II and the cold war, when it seemed to many Americans that the industrial greatness of the United States made possible a successful effort to save the world from totalitarianism.

Meanwhile, from the 1920s on, historians at the Harvard Business School and elsewhere were writing business history without moral judgments. These "entrepreneurial historians," among them Thomas C. Cochran, Alfred D. Chandler, Jr., and Kenneth W. Porter, were primarily interested in accurately describing and explaining, with heavy emphasis on economic forces, the development of business institutions and practices. The most elaborate expression of their approach is found in Chandler's *The Visible Hand, the Managerial Revolution in American Business* (1977).

Bigness in Specific Industries

The timing of the movement toward business consolidation varied a great deal by industry, depending on the difficulty of the technological change required for manufacturers to adopt mass-production techniques. Such techniques were adopted first by industries processing liquids or semiliquids, such as crude oil. Thus, the petroleum industry was among the first to adopt a modern corporate structure.

Petroleum production was centered in Pennsylvania, Ohio, and West Virginia, the region where oil had first been discovered. Relatively little capital was required to drill for oil or to refine it, and a host of small companies, particularly refineries, competed savagely for business. But soon there appeared to bring order to the industry the greatest consolidator of the time. John D. Rockefeller was a comparatively young Cleveland businessman who decided that his future lay with oil. He and various associates built the Standard Oil Company of Ohio to a position of dominance. They bought up competing companies or forced them out of existence with price wars and formed the Standard Oil trust in 1882. More importantly, they also set up an integrated system of production, controlling both the refining and marketing of oil. And, along with adopting integrated mass production, Standard Oil developed a modern bureaucracy, which consisted of a staff of salaried managers who coordinated the complicated flow of resources through production and marketing.

Similar organizational changes came next to food-processing industries. Like the petroleum industry, they underwent integration and consolidation as they grew larger. By the turn of the century, the meat-packing industry, centered in Chicago, supplied its products to a national market. So did the flour-milling industry in Minneapolis. Changes in the metal-using and metal-working industries, however, came more slowly because of the necessity for more significant technological changes to allow mass production. In the steel industry the master innovator and consolidator was Andrew Carnegie, a Scottish immigrant who had worked his way up as a boy in the railroad industry and then moved into steel. Gradually he built up his company to dominance in the industry, buying out or forcing out competitors and integrating the processing of steel from mine to market. In 1901 the Carnegie Steel Company and other concerns were combined in a gigantic holding company, United States Steel.

The Automobile

A new transportation revolution was beginning. Since the introduction of railroads, people had been intrigued with the idea of installing some kind of engine in carriages or cars that would run on roads. In the 1870s designers in France, Germany, and Austria began to develop the internal-combustion engine using the expanding power of burning gas to drive pistons, and the gasoline engine soon supplanted all other types.

In 1893 the Duryea brothers (Charles E. and J. Frank) built and operated the first gasoline-driven motor vehicle in the United States. Three years later Ford produced the first of the famous cars that would bear his name, a two-cylinder, four-horsepower affair. In 1901 Ransom Olds built 1,500 curved-dash Oldsmobiles, thus becoming the first mass producer of automobiles.

In 1900 the several automobile companies turned out over 4,000 cars, a trifling production compared to what would shortly come. A number of factors held back production. For one thing, the country's roads were not adequate for automobile transportation. Only 150,000 miles, 7 percent of the total mileage, were improved with gravel, oil, shell, or other forms of surfacing. The greatest deterring force was the expense involved in the manufacturing process, which resulted in cars priced too high for the mass market. The first builders had to order their parts from many sources, including sewing-machine and bicycle companies, and then begin the job of assembling, but soon they turned to assembly-line techniques and mass-production methods.

There had been only four automobiles on the American highways in 1895; by 1917 there were nearly 5,000,000, and the automobile was beginning to remake American life. Automobiles then had become commonplace among upper-middle-class families, just as telephones were almost essential in middle-class homes.

Crucial to the mass consumption of automobiles was the innovation of Henry Ford. In 1914 Ford became the first of the automobile manufacturers to replace stationary assembly with a moving assembly line. This revolutionary technique cut the time for assembling a chassis from twelve and a half hours to one and a half. While Ford raised the wages and lowered the hours of his workers, he cut the base price of his Model-T car from $950 to $290. Other industrialists, following his example, soon electrified their factories and adopted the moving assembly line.

Distribution of Wealth

Whatever pride Americans might have felt over the success of the economy was mingled with serious misgivings. For millions of Americans the economic system meant personal poverty and misery. There was a dramatic disparity between the incomes of the wealthy few and the poor multitudes. One percent of the American families owned nearly seven-eighths of the physical assets; 99 percent of the families owned only one-eighth. While a fifth of the families were comfortable or even rich, four-fifths lived on modest or marginal incomes. A careful estimate in 1904 indicated that about one-eighth of the people, or a total of ten million, lived in poverty.

Ranking particularly low in the wage scale were women. One woman in five worked, and often for wages as low as $6 or $8 per week. It was almost impossible for a woman to exist upon these wages unless they were supplemented by the earnings of a husband or father. Advocates of a minimum wage law to protect women created a sensation in Chicago by bringing several women to a hearing to testify that low pay and poverty had driven them to prostitution. Nevertheless, the Illinois legislature failed to enact the desired law.

Child labor was becoming an increasingly serious problem by the early 1900s. At least 1,700,000 children under sixteen were employed in factories and fields. Ten percent of the girls between ten and fifteen, and 20 percent of the boys, were gainfully employed. At least thirty-eight states had laws to protect children, but these typically applied only to children employed in factories and set a minimum age of twelve years and a maximum workday of ten hours. Sixty percent of the child workers were employed in agriculture, which could mean a twelve-hour day picking or hoeing the fields. In the cotton mills of the South, children working at the looms all night were kept awake by having cold water thrown in their faces. In canneries, little girls cut fruits or vegetables sixteen hours a day. Some children worked at dangerous machines without safety devices.

The widening gap between the richest and the poorest troubled many Americans, but their concern was often mitigated by their own economic success. During this period, and especially after 1900, the growing importance of technical knowledge meant that incomes were determined to an increasing extent by skills and educational level rather than by mere ownership of property. Consequently, for the first time in American history, the distribution of income became less concentrated. The lowest-income groups did not benefit from this distribution, but middle-class families did. Not only did they enjoy increasing income levels, but, as a class, they received a growing share of the nation's income.

Labor Organizes

As business became big, consolidated, and national, labor attempted to create its own organizations that would match the power of capital. The economic revolution changed workers from artisans who owned their own tools to factory laborers who operated machines owned by an employer more powerful than any individual worker. To counter corporate power, labor formed unions that sought to bargain collectively with employers. During the Civil War twenty craft unions were formed, nearly every one of which represented skilled workers. The first attempt to federate separate unions into a single national organization came in 1866, when, under the leadership of William H. Sylvis, the National Labor Union was founded. Claiming a membership of 640,000, it was a polyglot association that included, in addition to a number of unions, a variety of reform groups having little direct relationship with labor.

The trade unions experienced stormy times during the hard years of the 1870s, and after the panic of 1873 the National Labor Union disintegrated and disappeared. Their bargaining power weakened by depression conditions, unions faced antagonistic employers eager to destroy them, and a hostile public that rejected labor's claim to job security. Several of the disputes with capital were unusually bitter and were marked by violence, some of it labor's fault and some not, but for all of which labor received the blame. A near-hysteria gripped the country during the railroad strikes of 1877. The trouble started when the principal Eastern railroads announced a 10 percent slash in wages. Immediately railroad workers, whether organized or not, went out on strike. Rail service was disrupted from Baltimore to St. Louis, equipment was destroyed, and rioting mobs roamed the streets of Pittsburgh and other cities.

The strikes were America's first big labor conflict and a flaming illustration of a new reality in the American economic system: with business becoming nationalized, disputes between labor and capital could no longer be localized but would affect the entire nation. State militia were employed against the strikers, and finally, and significantly, federal troops were called on to suppress the disorders. The power of the various railroad unions was seriously sapped by the failure of the strikes, and the prestige of unions in other industries was weakened by similar setbacks.

Meanwhile, another national labor organization appeared on the scene, the Noble Order of the Knights of Labor, founded in 1869 under the leadership of Uriah S. Stephens. Instead of attempting to federate unions, as the National Labor Union had done, the Knights organized their association on the basis of the individual. Membership was open to all who "toiled," and the definition of toilership was extremely liberal: the only excluded groups were lawyers, bankers, liquor dealers, and professional gamblers. The amorphous masses of members, including many unskilled workers, were arranged in local "assemblies" that might consist of the workers in a particular trade or a local union or simply all the members of the Knights in a city or district. Presiding laxly over the entire order was an agency known as the General Assembly. Much of the program of the Knights was as vague as the organization. Although they championed an eight-hour day and the abolition of child labor, the leaders were more interested in long-range reform of the economy than in the immediate objectives of wages and hours, which appealed to the trade unions. Under the leadership of Terence V. Powderly, the order entered upon a spectacular period of expansion that culminated in 1886 with the total membership reaching 700,000.

Rise of the AFL

A rival organization appeared in 1881, when representatives of a number of craft unions formed the Federation of Organized Trade and Labor Unions of the United States and Canada.

Five years later this body took the name it has borne ever since, the American Federation of Labor (AFL). Under the direction of its president and guiding spirit, Samuel Gompers, the AFL soon became the most important labor group in the country. As its name implies, it was a federation or association of national trade unions, each of which enjoyed essential autonomy within the larger organization. Rejecting completely the idea of individual membership and the corollary of one big union for everybody, the AFL built on the principle of the organization of skilled workers into craft unions.

The program of the AFL differed as markedly from that of the Knights as did its organizational arrangements. Gompers and his associates accepted the basic concepts of capitalism; their purpose was to secure for labor a greater share of capitalism's material rewards. Repudiating all notions of fundamental alteration of the existing system or long-range reform measures or a separate labor party, the AFL concentrated on labor's pressing objectives: wages, hours, and working conditions.

As one of its first objectives, the AFL called for a national eight-hour day, to be attained by May 1, 1886, and to be obtained, if necessary, by a general strike. On the target day, strikes and demonstrations for a shorter workday took place all over the country. Although the national officers of the Knights had refused to cooperate in the movement, some local units joined in the demonstrations. So did a few unions that were dominated by anarchists — European radicals who wanted to destroy "class government" by terroristic methods. The most sensational demonstrations occurred in Chicago, which was a labor stronghold and an anarchist center.

At the time, a strike was in progress at the McCormick Harvester Company; and when the police harassed the strikers, labor and anarchist leaders called a protest meeting at the Haymarket Square. During the meeting, the police appeared and commanded those present to disperse. Someone — his identity was never determined — threw a bomb that resulted in the death of seven policemen and injury to sixty-seven others. The police, who on the previous day had killed four strikers, fired into the crowd and killed four more people. News of the Haymarket affair struck cold fear into Chicago and the business community of the nation. Blinded by hysteria, conservative, property-conscious, middle-class Americans demanded a victim or victims — to demonstrate to labor that it must cease its course of violence. Chicago officials finally rounded up eight anarchists and charged them with the murder of the policemen on the grounds that they had incited the individual who hurled the bomb. In one of the most injudicious trials in the record of American juridical history, all were found guilty. One was sentenced to prison and seven to death. Of the seven, one cheated his sentence by committing suicide, four were executed, and two had their penalty commuted to life imprisonment.

Although some of the Haymarket tragedy was unloaded on the AFL, most fell on the Knights, who had had almost nothing to do with the May demonstrations. In the public mind the Knights were dominated by anarchists and socialists. The Knights never managed to free themselves from the stigma of radicalism as the AFL did, and 1886 marked the eclipse of the Knights by the AFL. By 1890 the membership of the Knights had shrunk to 100,000, and within a few years the order was a thing of the past.

Major Strikes

Some of the most violent strikes in American labor history occurred in the nineties. Among the largest strikes were those at the Homestead plant of the Carnegie Steel Company in Pennsylvania and at the Pullman Palace Car Company in the Chicago area.

The Amalgamated Association of Iron and Steel Workers, which was affiliated with the American Federation of Labor, was the most powerful trade union in the country. It had never been able, however, to organize all the plants of the Carnegie Steel Company, the largest corporation in the industry; of the three major steel mills in the Carnegie system, the union was a force only in one, the Homestead plant. In 1892, when the strike occurred, Carnegie was in Scotland, visiting a castle that he maintained as a gesture of ancestral pride, and the direction of the company was in the hands of Henry Clay Frick, manager of Homestead and chairman of the Carnegie firm.

Carnegie was nevertheless responsible for the company's course. Despite his earlier fine words about labor, he had decided with Frick before leaving to operate Homestead on a nonunion basis, even if this meant precipitating a clash with the union.

The trouble began when the management announced wage cuts. Frick abruptly shut down the plant and asked the Pinkerton Detective Agency to furnish 300 guards to enable the company to resume operations on its own terms. (The Pinkerton Agency was really a strikebreaking concern).

The hated Pinkertons, whose mere presence was enough to incite the workers to violence, approached the plant on barges in an adjacent river. Warned of their coming, the stikers met them at the docks with guns and dynamite, and a pitched battle ensued on July 6, 1892. After several hours of fighting, which brought death to three guards and ten strikers and severe injuries to many participants on both sides, the Pinkertons surrendered and were escorted roughly out of town. The company and local law officials then asked for militia protection from the Pennsylvania governor, who responded by sending the entire National Guard contingent, some 8,000 troops, to Homestead. Public opinion, at first sympathetic to the strikers, turned abruptly against them when an anarchist made an unsuccessful attempt to assassinate Frick. Slowly workers drifted back to their jobs.

A dispute of greater magnitude and equal bitterness, although involving less loss of life, was the Pullman strike in 1894, a depression year that saw over 700,000 workers throughout the country out on strike. Near Chicago were the works of the Pullman Palace Car Company. This corporation leased sleeping and parlor cars to most of the nation's railroads; it also manufactured and repaired its own cars and also freight and passenger cars. Over 5,000 workers were employed in the various shops and factories of the company. At the instigation of George M. Pullman, inventor of the car that bore his name and president of the firm, the company had built the 600-acre town of Pullman, containing dwellings that were rented to the employees, churches, schools, parks and playgrounds, a bank, and a library — all owned and operated by the company. Pullman liked to exhibit his town as a model solution of the industrial problem and to refer to the workers as his "children"; his attitude was completely feudalistic and patronizing.

Nearly all of the workers were members of a union, a very militant one, the American Railway Union; this association had recently been organized by Eugene V. Debs, a sincere and idealistic labor leader formerly active in the Railroad Brotherhoods. Becoming disgusted with the brotherhoods' lack of interest in the lot of the unskilled workers, he had formed his own union, which soon attained a membership of 150,000, mainly in the Middle West.

The strike at Pullman began when the company during the winter of 1893–1894 slashed wages by an average of 25 percent and refused to reduce rentals in the model town. The strikers appealed to the Railway Union for support, and that organization voted to refuse to handle Pullman cars and equipment.

The General Managers' Association, representing twenty-four Chicago railroads, prepared to fight the boycott. Switchmen who refused to handle Pullman cars were summarily discharged. Whenever this happened, the union instructed its members to quit work. Within a few days thousands of railroad workers in twenty-seven states and territories were on strike, and transportation from Chicago to the Pacific coast was paralyzed.

Ordinarily, state governors responded readily to appeals from strike-threatened business, but the governor of Illinois was different. John P. Altgeld had pardoned the Haymarket anarchists remaining in prison.

Bypassing Altgeld, the railroad operators sought the national government to send regular army troops to Illinois. At the same time federal postal officials and marshals were bombarding Washington with information that the strike was preventing the movement of mail on the trains. President Grover Cleveland was inclined to gratify the companies and so was his attorney general, Richard Olney, a former railroad lawyer and a bitter foe of labor. Cleveland and Olney decided that the government could employ the army to keep the mails moving, and in July 1894 the President, over Altgeld's strident protest, ordered 2,000 troops to the Chicago area.

At Olney's suggestion, government lawyers obtained from a federal court an order restraining Debs and other union officials from interfering with the interstate transportation of the mails. This "blanket injunction" was so broad in scope that it practically forbade Debs and his associates to continue the strike. They ignored the injunction and were arrested, tried for contempt of court (without a jury trial), and sentenced to six months in prison. With federal troops protecting the hiring of new workers and with the union leaders in a federal jail, the strike quickly collapsed.

It left a bitter heritage. Labor was convinced that the government was not a neutral arbiter representing the common interest but a supporter of one side alone. Debs emerged from prison a martyr, a convert to socialism, and a dedicated enemy of capital.

Unionization Slows

With the return to prosperity during McKinley's administration, a "honeymoon" period between capital and labor ensued. Surrounded by opportunities for expansion and faced with developing increasing needs for labor, many big business concerns preferred to negotiate with labor rather than risk a strike. Taking advantage of the changing disposition of business, some labor leaders, such as Samuel Gompers, preached that labor could cooperate with capital. One result of the new mood was that union membership jumped from less than half a million in 1897 to over two million in 1904.

The "honeymoon" did not last, however. Not all laborers were ready to accept the assumption of such leaders as Gompers that differences with capitalists could easily be adjusted around a conference table. The socialist minority within the American Federation of Labor succeeded in capturing unions of machinists and miners. Militant Western miners in 1905 founded the Industrial Workers of the World, which tried to organize the great masses of unskilled workers, mostly immigrants, whom the AFL ignored. The IWW aimed ultimately to form "one big union" including all workers, hold one big strike, and thus paralyze and then take over the government. Its members, popularly known as "Wobblies," were accused of responsibility for acts of violence. Employers and state and local authorities certainly did not hesitate to use violence against the Wobblies. Two episodes, neither the work of the IWW, especially outraged orderly progressives. These were the murder of a former governor of Idaho and the dynamiting of the plant of the *Los Angeles Times,* which was militantly antiunion.

Such episodes prompted many middle-class Americans to listen to the antiunion slogans of the National Association of Manufacturers and kindred organizations. The NAM, which proclaimed itself against union recognition in 1903, was predominantly made up of people who ran small plants and were dependent upon low labor costs to survive in highly competitive markets. It called the open shop the "American plan," and the independent worker (strikebreaker) the "American hero."

The manufacturers had the backing of federal judges. The most spectacular court blow against collective bargaining grew out of the Danbury Hatters' strike of 1902. The courts held that the union's efforts to obtain a nationwide boycott of Loewe hats was a violation of federal antitrust law and assessed triple damages of $240,000 against the union. Union officials began a concerted and vigorous campaign to exempt labor organizations from antitrust legislation and to outlaw antilabor injunctions.

Thus, by World War I, an overwhelming majority of employers still looked upon labor as a force to be disregarded when possible and to be crushed when practicable, and the American public, in overwhelming numbers, considered unions as alien and dangerous elements in the national economy. In that hostile environment the progress of unionization, even when managed by a cautious Gompers, was slow. Between 1904 and 1914, union membership grew by little more than half a million.

The Last West

During the late nineteenth century, at the same time the Industrial Revolution was accelerating, a dramatic transformation of the American scene was occurring west of the Mississippi River. There, in the vast area stretching from the middle valley to the far western highlands, a propulsive movement of population settled the last frontier in America. The last frontier was made up of three distinct natural, or physiographic, areas: the Great Plains, the Rocky Mountains, and the Basin and Plateau region between the Rockies on the east and the Sierra Nevada–Cascade range on the west. By the turn of the century practically every part of the region had been organized into states or territories.

The lure of minerals drew the first settlers to the last West. They began to come on the eve of the Civil War, came even during the war, and entered in larger numbers after its close. The mining frontier had a brief but brilliant existence, beginning around 1860, flourishing until 1880, and then abruptly declining. The settlement of the region followed a pattern. News of a gold or silver strike in some part of it — Colorado, Nevada, South Dakota — would bring a stampede of prospectors. These people, using pan and placer mining, exploited and quickly exhausted the shallower deposits of ore and then moved on to other places. Next corporations moved in to engage in lode or quartz mining of the deeper deposits. But even these resources eventually thinned or ran out, and though commercial mining might continue on a restricted basis, the population of a typical mining area declined. It would not rise until agriculture was developed to give the region a more stable economy.

Soon after the mineral empire burst into being, another great economic province took shape, the cattle kingdom of the Great Plains. Like the mining frontier, it had a brief and brilliant existence, from about 1865 to 1885. The rise of the cattle kingdom was directly related to the developing industrial society of urban America — the concentration of population in cities created a new market for meat and other foods. Two factors enabled the cattle industry to spread from Texas over the West. First, the open range, the unclaimed grasslands of the public domain, provided a vast area where cattle raisers could graze their herds free of charge. Second, the ever-expanding railroads gave the cattle raisers access to the Eastern markets. To various towns on these roads, Sedalia, Abilene, and others, ranchers drove their herds, sometimes numbering in the thousands, in the famous "long drives."

The profits to be made in the cattle industry

were tremendous and inevitably tempted more investors into it. The ranges became overstocked, and prices fell drastically. As abruptly as it had risen, the cattle kingdom fell. Cattle raisers turned to more modest operations, acquiring title to lands, fencing in their tracts, and becoming settled ranchers.

Some farmers had drifted into the last frontier during its first stages of settlement. More came in the late seventies, and a rush of them in the eighties. They gradually converted the area to an agricultural economy.

The Western Indians

The expansion of the mining and cattle frontiers was costly, however, since it met the determined opposition of the Plains Indians. The highest price was paid by the Indians themselves, but this was an irrelevant consideration to most Americans, who generally regarded the Indians as inferior beings with no legitimate stake in America. Excluded from American society, the Indians often used force to defend themselves but were not able to resist the power that industrial technology and organization provided for their opponents. On the rolling, semiarid, treeless plains, these Indians followed a nomadic life. Riding their small but powerful horses, which were descendants of Spanish stock, the tribes roamed the spacious expanses of the grasslands. The magnet that drew the wanderers and guided their routes was the buffalo, or bison. This huge grazing animal provided the economic basis for the Plains Indians' way of life. Its flesh was their principal source of food, and the skin supplied materials for clothing, shoes, tepees, blankets, robes, and utensils. To the Indians, the buffalo was, as someone had said, "a galloping department store." They trailed the herds, estimated to number at least 15,000,000 head in 1865, all over the plains.

The Plains Indians were almost uniformly martial, proud, and aggressive. Mounted on their horses, they were a formidable foe, whether armed with bow, spear, or rifle. No previous Indians possessed such mobility, and students of war have ranked them among the best light cavalry in military history.

It was the traditional policy of the federal government to regard the tribes as independent nations (but also as wards of the Great White Father in Washington) and to negotiate agreements with them in the shape of treaties that were solemnly ratified by the Senate. This concept of Indian sovereignty was responsible for the attempt of the government before 1860 to erect a permanent frontier between whites and Indians, to reserve the region west of the bend of the Missouri as permanent Indian country. But by the 1860s the related principles of tribal independence and a perpetual line of division were breaking down before harsh realities. Administration of Indian matters was divided between the Bureau of Indian Affairs, located in the Department of the Interior, and the army. The bureau was vested with general powers to supervise the disposition of Indian lands, disburse annuities, and, through its agents in Western posts, distribute needed supplies. From top to bottom, the personnel was shot through with the spoils system. Although some agents were conscientious and able, more were dishonest and incompetent.

The army came into the picture only when trouble developed — when bands of Indians attacked homes or stagecoach lines or when a tribe went on the warpath. In short, its principal function was to punish, not to police. In its "wars" with the Indians, the army frequently experienced rugged going. The mobile plains tribes were fully a match for cavalry armed with carbines. But soon the superior technology of the whites shifted the balance. The Colt repeating revolver gave the army increased fire power, the railroads facilitated quick troop concentrations, and the telegraph reported almost immediately the movements of hostile bands. Even so, the business of suppressing Indians was expensive to the government. Three wars in the 1860s cost $100,-000,000, and one official estimated that the cost per Indian killed was $1,000.

The subjection of the fierce Plains Indians was accomplished by economic as well as orthodox warfare — by the slaughter of the buffalo herds that supported their way of life. After the Civil War the demand for buffalo hides became a national phenomenon. It was partly based on economics — a commercial demand for the hides developing in the East; and it was partly a fad — suddenly everyone east of the Missouri seemed to require a buffalo robe from the romantic West. Gangs of professional hunters swarmed over the plains to shoot the huge animals, divided by the Union Pacific Railroad into Southern and Northern herds. Some hunters killed merely for the sport of the chase, though the lumbering victims did not present much of a challenge. The Southern herd was virtually exterminated by 1875, and within a few years the smaller Northern herd met the same fate. Fewer than 1,000 of the magnificent beasts survived. The army and the Indian agents condoned and even encouraged the killing. With the buffalo went the Indians' source of food and supplies and their will and ability to resist the white advance.

There were almost incessant Indian wars from the 1860s to the 1880s as the army slowly forced the tribes onto smaller reservations. Those who resisted included Sitting Bull, who tried to protect the Sioux holy grounds in the Black Hills from the exploitation of goldminers. In 1876, when three army columns were sent to disperse the Sioux, the Indians succeeded in surprising and killing the entire Seventh Cavalry under George A. Custer at the battle of Little Bighorn. Custer rode into something that no white man would have believed possible at the time. On this occasion, the chiefs had concentrated between 2,500 and 4,000 warriors, the largest Indian army ever assembled at one time in the United States.

The Indians, however, did not have the political organization or the commissary to keep their troops united. Soon they drifted off in bands to elude pursuit or search for food, and the army ran them down singly and returned them to their Dakota reservation. The power of the Sioux was now broken. The proud leaders, Crazy Horse and Sitting Bull, accepted defeat and the monotony of agency existence, and both were later killed by reservation police after being tricked or taunted into a last pathetic show of resistance. In similar fashion, the army subdued other great Indian leaders such as Chief Red Cloud of the Sioux, Chief Joseph of the Nez Percé, and Geronimo of the Apaches.

In 1887 Congress had finally moved to destroy the tribal structure that was the cornerstone of Indian culture. Although the motivation was partially a humanitarian impulse to help the Indians,

the action was frankly designed to force them to become landowners and farmers, to abandon their collective society and culture, to become, in short, whites. The Dawes Severalty Act provided for the gradual abrogation of tribal ownership of land and the allotment of tracts to individual owners: 160 acres to the head of a family, 80 acres to a single adult or orphan, 40 acres to each dependent child. Adult owners were accorded the status of citizenship, but, unlike other citizens, they could not give away or sell their property for twenty-five years. The act failed because the Indians lacked the economic resources required for a shift from a collective society to individualism. Congress attempted to facilitate the transition with the Burke Act of 1906. Citizenship was deferred until after the completion of the twenty-five-year period contemplated in the Dawes Act, but Indians who proved their adaptability could secure both citizenship and land ownership in a shorter period. Full rights of citizenship were technically conferred on all Indians in 1924.

The Farmers' Grievances

One of the great agricultural changes of the nineteenth century reached its culmination in the years after 1865 — the change from subsistence, or self-sufficient, farming to commercial farming. In commercial farming, the producers specialized in a cash crop, sold it in an outside market, and in the same market bought the household supplies they had previously made. This kind of farming, when it was successful, raised the farmers' living standards, and, for most farmers, it was successful. But it also made them more dependent on other factors and groups in the economy. They had become business people, but unlike many large manufacturers, they could not regulate production or control prices.

Impelling economic forces had dictated the shift to commercial farming — an expanding national and world demand for farm products. In answer to this demand, the farmers of America increased their output, putting huge new areas of land under cultivation, especially in the West; utilizing labor-saving machines — the reaper, thresher, and others; and going into debt to finance purchases of land and machinery. But while farmers were going more deeply into debt, they faced declining prices — a result of the failure of the money supply to keep up with the pace of production between the Civil War and the late 1890s. Like all debtor capitalists, including most small business people during the period, the farmers found their debts increasing as prices declined; they encountered severe difficulty in paying off those debts during the depressions of the 1870s and 1890s. The farmers were too numerous and their interests too diverse to unite in restricting production to raise prices.

The farmers were painfully aware that something was wrong and first turned their attention and anger to the brokers with whom they dealt. Farmers contended that the banks charged too-high interest rates, sometimes as much as 10 to 25 percent, and were reluctant to lend to farmers. Also, they accused speculators and bankers of conspiring to fix prices to benefit themselves. Farmers also believed that there was a conspiracy to fix the prices of supplies.

The most burning grievance was against the railroads. The farmers believed that the roads charged high and discriminatory rates to small producers while favoring large shippers. They were also convinced that the railroads controlled the elevator-warehouse facilities in buying centers and levied arbitary storage rates. The anger of the farmers at the railroads shook their traditional individualism and prepared them to turn for the first time to organized political action.

Chapter 17

Society and Culture in the Industrial Era, 1865-1917

Population

Between 1860 and 1900, the population of the United States more than doubled, increasing from about 31,000,000 in 1860 to almost 76,000,000 in 1900. By 1920 the population had reached more than 106,000,000. The birth rate, however, declined sharply. Increasingly, families, especially those in the burgeoning middle classes, consciously restricted family size. The birth rate was still high by European standards, but the increase in population was led by the rising tide of foreign immigration. Some 14,000,000 aliens arrived between 1860 and 1900, and then the pace accelerated: nearly that many more arrived before World War I. In 1907 alone nearly 1,300,000 immigrants arrived — the peak year of immigration in American history — and that total was nearly matched in five other years between 1900 and 1914. Most of the immigrants settled in the industrial cities, causing the urban population to increase more than ninefold, three times as rapidly as the total population. By 1920 immigrants and their children comprised about half of the nation's total urban population, almost two-thirds of the population residing in large cities (those with over 100,000 people), and an even larger share of the large cities of the New England, Middle Atlantic, and Great Lakes states.

The Newer Immigrants

Up to 1880 the great majority of the immigrants had originated in the countries of western and northern Europe: England, Ireland, Germany, and the Scandinavian countries. Although there had always been friction between these people and "native" Americans, most of the newcomers were in culture and outlook essentially similar to those among whom they settled, and they were eventually assimilated. But in the eighties the immigrant stream began to flow from another source — southern and eastern Europe. Among the new ethnic stocks were Austrians, Hungarians, Bohemians, Poles, Serbs, Italians, Russians, and Jews from Poland and Russia. After 1900 the flow of the "old immigrants" from northern and western Europe continued, but the flow from southern and eastern Europe, comprising about 72 percent of the total between 1900 and 1910, became a flood. They came for the reasons that had always brought immigrants to the United States: the desire to escape unfavorable economic and political conditions at home; knowledge of the opportunities in America gained from friends and relatives who had already crossed the Atlantic; and the demand for cheap labor by industry.

The later immigrants flocked to the industrial cities of the East and became unskilled laborers. They did not have the capital to begin farming operations in the West; they had to have immediate employment, and this was offered them by the meat packers, railroads, coal producers, and steel manufacturers, hungry for cheap labor; and in a strange land the immigrants felt the need for association with their fellows that only city life could give.

The new immigrants, like the old ones, came with high hopes to what they expected to be a land of opportunity. Needy families, both native and foreign-born, could look to private charitable societies for assistance, but generally these were run by middle-class humanitarians who insisted on middle-class standards of morality. Such societies operated on the belief that poverty was more commonly due to laziness and vice than to misfortune. After careful investigation they confined their help to the "deserving poor." In 1879, a year after its founding in London, the Salvation Army began its work in American cities, but at first it concentrated on religious revivals rather than on the relief of the homeless and hungry. Social workers established settlement houses in the foreign neighborhoods to entice the aliens from the saloons and streets and bring them under religious influences. The most famous of the houses were the Henry Street Settlement in New York, founded by Lillian D. Wald, and Hull House in Chicago, directed by Jane Addams. By 1900 fifty such centers were operating in American cities.

For most of the urban poor, especially the foreign-born and their families, the main welfare agency was the political machine, headed by a boss, who himself was typically of foreign birth or parentage, most commonly Irish. To maintain his power, the boss needed votes, and in exchange for these he offered favors of various kinds. He provided the poor with occasional relief, such as a basket of groceries or a bag of coal. He stepped in to save from jail those arrested for petty crimes. When he could, he found work for the unemployed. Most important, he rewarded his followers with political jobs, with opportunities to rise in the party organization.

With the mounting of the alien tide, demands for immigration restrictions rose in the land. In 1882 Congress closed Chinese immigration, passed a general immigration law denying entry to certain undesirables (such as convicts and paupers), and placed a tax of 50 cents on every person admitted. Later legislation of the nineties enlarged the proscriptive list and increased the tax. The laws kept out only a small number of aliens, however, and were far from fulfilling the purposes of the extreme exclusionists. The exclusionists worked for a literacy test, a device intended to exclude immigrants from eastern and southern Europe. Congress passed a literacy law in 1897, but President Cleveland vetoed it.

The American Federation of Labor (whose president, Samuel Gompers, was himself an im-migrant) became increasingly active in fighting to cut off this flood of cheap, unskilled foreign labor, which was said to keep wages down and hamper unionization. Many Americans were susceptible to the popular dogma of Anglo-Saxon superiority and joined in the anti-immigration movement. They feared the high birth rate among immigrants as compared with the low birth rate among natives in the higher-income groups. They feared the spread of disease from urban ghettos. They blamed the squalor of the slums and the power of the political bosses largely upon the immigrants and felt that through restriction could come improvement. As a result of their agitation, the United States government negotiated in 1907 a "gentlemen's agreement" with Japan that stopped the immigration of Japanese laborers to the Pacific coast. A series of restrictive laws blocked entry for various groups, ranging from ex-convicts to alcoholics, thought to be undesirable. In 1917, over the veto of President Wilson, Congress passed a law setting up a literacy test as a means of reducing the number of immigrants.

The Urban Scene

The fast-growing American cities were places of violent contrast — of poverty and wealth, of palatial homes and dingy slums. They were also places faced by many perplexing problems, most of them the result of a suddenly expanded population.

An urgent urban problem was disease. In the dark and dirty slums, where families were huddled in single rooms with inadequate toilet and sanitary facilities, thousands died annually of epidemics. From the slums, disease spread into other sections. At the time of the Civil War, most cities took no precautions to guard the purity of their water supply and no satisfactory measures to dispose of their sewage and garbage. A common practice was to empty sewage into nearby rivers, sometimes into the stream from which the city secured its water; in other cases the sewage was dumped into open ditches within the city limits. Garbage was customarily placed on the streets, where it might remain indefinitely.

Out of the urban environment arose the first

American public health movement. First cities and then states created boards of health empowered to correct slum conditions, enforce sanitation measures, and improve sewage and garbage disposal. The water closet (flush toilet) was perfected in the 1870s. Covered sewers were installed in many cities, and in others sewage was dumped at sea. Garbage was collected on regular schedules and was burned in furnaces or fed to hogs, an unfortunate practice that spread disease. Many cities built reservoirs and pressed water-purification programs. As a result, spectacular reductions in death rates occurred in many overcrowded districts. At the turn of the century the life of the urban dweller was still dangerous from the medical standpoint, but it was immeasurably safer than it had been.

Improvements in urban services were engineered politically by the city bosses. While the bosses personally profited from the bribes extracted for the granting of public contracts, those contracts provided urban centers with needed streets, sewers, public buildings, reservoirs, parks, and playgrounds. Boss rule was made possible by the weakness of existing city government. Within the government, no single official held decisive power. Power was divided among a number of officeholders — the mayor, the aldermen, and others — and was limited by the state legislature, which had ultimate authority over municipal affairs. Centralizing power in their own hands, the bosses together with their machines formed a sort of "invisible government" that made up for the inadequacy of the regular government. From time to time middle-class reformers sought to overthrow a boss. But they succeeded only when they had support from powerful, dissident elements within the machine who believed that the boss had abused power and taken exorbitant graft. Such an instance was the overthrow of New York City's William M. Tweed, and the "Tweed Ring" in 1871. The system of boss rule continued to flourish in New York and other large cities because the conditions that produced it remained essentially unchanged.

Women: Outside the Home

Because of their race or sex, some Americans had distinctive experiences in this expansive society. Among them, of course, were women.

The huge demand for labor that sustained immigration also contributed to the employment of large numbers of women. This demand bid up the wages of women, and these wages made employment attractive. From 3,750,000 in 1870, the number of women employed at full-time jobs increased to about 8,000,000 in 1910, accounting for over 20 percent of the labor force, as contrasted with less than 15 percent in 1870. Many women continued to work as farm laborers, largely in the South, and as industrial laborers, particularly in the growing garment industry. But, most important, women became increasingly employed in the "service" sector — not so much in domestic service, which had been important but was declining in significance, as in clerking, sales, stenography, bookkeeping, teaching, nursing, and social work (including the settlement house movement of Jane Addams). In 1890 women comprised two-thirds of the nation's high-school graduates, and they took up service jobs in large numbers. The jobs provided working conditions that were pleasant by the standards of the day and that required a certain degree of skill, in contrast to available jobs in the manufacturing sector, where hostile employers and male workers denied women access to skilled positions.

Some women embarked upon careers in the professions, and many of these women made marked contributions to their fields. In medicine, for example, Alice Hamilton, trained in Europe and at the Johns Hopkins Medical School, went to Northwestern University in 1897 and became a pioneer in the study of diseases resulting from occupational hazards. Medicine in particular proved attractive to women interested in professional careers. By 1900, about 10 percent of all the students in conventional medical schools were women, numbering more than 5,000. By 1910, their numbers grew to nearly 10,000.

Women and Family Life

The movement of women away from traditional roles within the household and toward market employment was advanced by a set of important changes in the household. The decline of the birth rate eased the burden, both physical and economic, of child rearing. And it was during this period that the country witnessed the beginnings of a technological revolution in the household. As early as the 1870s, well before the electrification of the home that began during the 1910s, an array of consumer durable goods (including washing machines, wringers, and sewing machines) proliferated to lighten household tasks. In addition, consumer goods (especially clothing) and services (laundry and meal preparation, for example) were increasingly available outside the home at lower prices, thereby reducing the pressure on housewives' time and easing the need for the employment of servants. Finally, household manufacturing and the family farm became less important as sources of employment for women.

As a consequence of these changes, the rate at which women took up jobs outside the home increased significantly. While only about 15 percent of women (over the age of fourteen) worked after the Civil War, nearly 25 percent worked by 1910. But the new working women were typically young, unmarried women. The older women who worked tended to be either lower-class married women, often black, who desperately needed to supplement family incomes or to provide the only possible support for a family, or upper-class women who had renounced marriage in order to take up an independent professional life. It remained the normal expectation for women to be married and for married women to stay in their homes. Thus, even as late as 1920, only about 9 percent of married women had marketplace employment. It appears that the potential for increased employment provided by the social changes of the period was enjoyed largely by older daughters who were relieved of responsibilities from household chores. For the average housewife and mother, little had changed except that she had more time at her disposal.

The reasons why the life of married women remained fundamentally unchanged are various. One factor is that the enormous growth of urban populations made it difficult for public expenditures on education, health services, and recreation to grow rapidly enough to meet the needs of middle-class families and families aspiring to middle-class status. Such families decided to devote more of their resources — in the form of mothers' time — to the education of their children. Also, married women faced discrimination in the form of restricted job opportunities. Employers, union leaders, and husbands tended to agree that married women belonged in the home,

caring for their families. Finally, the period was one of unusually intense enthusiasm for family life. Perhaps the confusion and insecurity that attended massive immigration and rapid urbanization fostered what was a powerful, pervasive preoccupation among the upper and middle classes with the virtues of the family as an institution that could promote social order. They saw the family and, within the family, traditionally defined motherhood as offering the only effective means of protecting threatened values. Consequently, prominent cultural and political leaders — Theodore Roosevelt, most visibly — spoke out forcefully on behalf of keeping women within their traditional domestic roles. Mothers were expected to devote their increasing free time to a more intense preoccupation with childrearing.

Despite the increasing esteem granted to motherhood, some women who sought independent, professional careers chose to forgo marriage and family altogether. Such women, ususally of upper-class or genteel middle-class families, were common among the graduates of prestigious women's colleges. Characterized as "new women," they were apt to agree with the criticism of modern marriage rendered by Charlotte Perkins Gilman, who wrote a brilliant series of books, including *Women and Economics* (1899), on the place of women. Describing the home, she wrote: "Among the splendid activities of our age it lingers on, inert and blind, like a clam at a horse race."

Black Americans

Until the mobilization for World War I, over 90 percent of all blacks lived in the South under circumstances that had changed but little after Reconstruction. Those who came to power in the South after 1877 were not in the old agrarian, planter tradition. Known as Bourbons or Redeemers, they preached the industrialization of the South through the importation of Northern capital, a policy of low taxes to attract business, and the provision of cheap labor, both white and black. Controlling state governments through the medium of the Democratic party, which as a result of Reconstruction was virtually the only party in the section, they practiced a program marked by economy in government and few social services. They did not attempt to abolish black suffrage but instead sometimes used the black vote to maintain their power. Blacks continued to vote after the return of white rule, but in reduced numbers.

Not until the 1890s did the Southern states pass laws to disfranchise blacks. Poor white farmers demanded disfranchisement because they were convinced that rich whites were able to manipulate black votes to defeat programs of economic justice. Wealthy whites lent their support, fearing an alliance of poor whites and blacks.

In devising laws to disfranchise blacks the Southern states had to take care to evade the intent of the Fifteenth Amendment, to exclude blacks without seeming to do so because of color. Two devices were widely employed before 1900. One was the poll tax or some form of property qualification. The other was the literacy and understanding test, which required a voter to demonstrate an ability to read and to interpret the Constitution. Many states passed so-called grandfather laws, which permitted white men who could not meet the literacy and property qualifications to be admitted to the suffrage if their ancestors had voted before 1867 or some date before Reconstruction began.

The Supreme Court proved compliant in ruling on the various Southern laws. Earlier, in the Civil Rights Cases of 1883, it had held that while the Fourteenth Amendment prohibited states from imposing segregation because of color, it did not enjoin such private institutions as railroads or hotels. Then in *Plessy* v. *Ferguson* (1896), a case involving separate seating arrangements on railroads, it affirmed that a state could enforce segregation if the separate arrangements were equal. The separate but equal principle was shortly applied to education.

The Court was equally cooperative in accepting the disfranchising laws. Although it voided the grandfather laws, it validated the literacy tests and manifested a general willingness to let the Southern states define suffrage standards — provided the evasions of the Fifteenth Amendment were not too glaring. At the turn of the century, the South seemed to have won a complete victory over the outside influences that had sought to disturb its way of life.

After 1900 the plight of black Americans appeared to worsen. Between 1895 and 1907 every state of the former Confederacy except Tennessee took formal steps, by law or constitutional amendment, to exclude all blacks from the suffrage. Meanwhile blacks suffered more and more at the hands of lynching mobs in the South and rioters in both the South and the North. In 1908, while the city's leaders were planning a 1909 celebration of the centennial of Abraham Lincoln's birth, a bloody race riot broke out in Springfield, Illinois, Lincoln's hometown. This event led directly to the rise of the first effective nationwide organization for black rights.

The emerging leader in the cause was William E. Burghardt Du Bois, a black historian and sociologist with a Harvard Ph.D. Du Bois openly challenged Booker T. Washington as the spokesperson for their race. Washington taught blacks that they must be patient and submissive until they had proved their worth, and thus he "tended to make the whites, North and South, shift the burden of the Negro problem to the Negro's shoulders and stand aside as critical and rather pessimistic spectators," Du Bois charged, "when in fact the burden belongs to the nation, and the hands of none of us are clear if we bend not our energies to righting these great wrongs."

At first, Du Bois and a group of like-minded reformers, black and white, met from time to time in a fellowship known as the Niagara Movement. Then, on Lincoln's birthday in 1909, they organized the National Association for the Advancement of Colored People. White men were named to most of the offices of the NAACP, but Du Bois as its director of publicity and research remained the guiding sprit. From 1909 on, the NAACP worked slowly but steadily for equal rights, mainly through legal strategy, through filing and winning one lawsuit after another in the federal courts.

The NAACP was so preoccupied with civil rights that it found little time to devote to economic opportunities, though blacks continued to suffer from discrimination in employment and pay. So blacks and sympathetic whites formed interracial organizations to improve economic and social conditions for blacks, especially in New York City. Three of these organizations combined in 1911 to form the National League on Urban

Conditions among Negroes, which came to be known as the National Urban League. The league, with branches in many of the large cities, undertook to meet black newcomers, to find lodgings and jobs for them, and to provide training in social work.

Toward Universal Schooling

Mary Antin, a Russian girl who came as an immigrant to the United States, had heard that in America everything is free. Best of all: "Education was free. That subject my father had written about repeatedly, as comprising his chief hope for us children, the essence of American opportunity, the treasure that no thief could touch, not even misfortune or poverty." Education in America after the Civil War was indeed free or in the process of becoming so — free, public, and almost universal. Education was becoming the central means for transmitting democratic virtue, for providing a skilled labor force, and for acculturating immigrants.

In 1860 there were only 100 public high schools in the country, but by 1900 the number had reached 6,000. Between 1860 and 1900 the share of the nation's resources devoted to education had doubled. Still much remained to be accomplished. In 1900 the average elementary school term was only 143 days, of which a child was likely to attend half the time. Both the term and the attendance figures had risen by 1900, but even then most children went to school only an average of slightly more than six years. However, by 1917 effective compulsory education laws were in force and had begun to reduce the number of child workers.

Powerfully stimulating the expansion of higher learning were huge new financial resources made available by the national government. The national government, by the Morrill Land Grant Act of the Civil War period, donated land to states for the establishment of colleges to teach, among other subjects, agriculture and mechanical arts. After 1865, particularly in the West and the South, states began to exploit the possibilities of the act to strengthen existing institutions or to found new ones. In all, sixty-nine "land grant" institutions came into existence, among them the universities of Wisconsin, California, Minnesota, and Illinois.

Two groups in American society — women and blacks — did not receive the full benefits of higher education, although both made some gains in access to education during this period. Before the Civil War, girls had been generally admitted on an equal basis to elementary and secondary schools, but the doors of most colleges were closed to them. A few private colleges for women had been founded, and a very few schools (three, to be exact) admitted women to study with men. After the war a number of additional women's colleges came into existence, generally as the result of donations from philanthropists: Vassar, Wellesley, Smith, Bryn Mawr, and Goucher. Some of the largest private universities established on their campuses separate colleges for women. Also, a number of independent medical colleges for women provided increasing opportunities for women until those schools were absorbed by large universities, which admitted fewer women to medical study. But the greatest educational opportunities for women opened in the Middle West, where the state universities began to admit women along with men.

Blacks reaped the fewest advantages from the educational renaissance. In the South, and also in most parts of the North, they attended segregated elementary and secondary schools that were nearly always poorer than the white schools. Blacks desiring a higher education were almost universally barred from white institutions and had to attend one of the colleges established for their race by Northern philanthropy: Howard University, in Washington; Fisk University, in Nashville; Straight University, in New Orleans; or Shaw University, in Raleigh. Some black leaders were disturbed by the tendency of their people to seek a "classical" education that did not fit them for the economic position they occupied in the South. For the transitional period after emancipation, these leaders believed that an industrial education, stressing vocational training and the dignity of labor, was preferable. The result of their thinking was the establishment, with aid from private sources, of the Hampton Normal and Industrial Institute in Virginia and the Tuskegee Institute in Alabama, the latter presided over by Booker T. Washington.

New Uses of Leisure

Many Americans, especially those of the urban middle and professional classes, found that they had more leisure at their command, and they had incomes sufficient to gratify their demands for pleasure. Even the workers had more free time, and they too sought satisfactory forms of recreation. The late nineteenth century marked the expansion and specialization of urban entertainment industries. The circus, vaudeville, burlesque, popular theater, and the legitimate stage evolved as distinct forms. Saloons, beer gardens, houses of prostitution, dance halls, and billiard parlors flourished. Rapid-transit companies, in conjunction with suburban amusement parks, provided new opportunities for weekend outings. Americans in the larger cities could enjoy stage plays and vaudeville skits that were booked out of New York City by a national syndicate. But most Americans found their entertainment in the newly developed motion picture. The first film telling a continuous story was a melodrama, *The Great Train Robbery*, produced in 1903. In 1915 the lengthy, impressive feature film arrived with *The Birth of a Nation*. It was as significant in marking the coming of age of a new art form as it was deplorable in its glorification of the Ku Klux Klan. Its popularity revealed that racial prejudice abounded in all sections of the country. By 1914 motion pictures had become a multimillion-dollar industry and were moving into large and impressive theaters.

Most dramatic was the rise of organized spectator sports, such as horse racing, prize fighting, and baseball; by 1900 sports had become a business. The most popular of all the organized sports was baseball. As early as 1744, the word "baseball" had appeared in England, where it was applied to a primitive ball and stick game. But it was in the United States that baseball acquired its modern form. The first baseball club appeared in 1831, and by the end of the Civil War interest in the game had spawned over 200 teams, some of which toured the country playing rivals. They belonged to the "National Association of Base Ball Players," which had proclaimed a set of standard rules. The players were amateurs or semi-professionals, but as the game waxed in popularity, it offered opportunities for profit. The first

professional team, the Cincinnati Red Stockings, appeared in 1869. Other cities soon fielded professional teams, and in 1876 the present National League was organized by William A. Hulbert and Albert G. Spaulding. Soon a rival league appeared, the American Association. Competition between the two was intense, and in 1882 they played a postseason contest, the first "world's championship series." The American Association eventually collapsed, but in 1900 the current American League was organized.

The Publishing Business

Newspapers and magazines provided the reading matter for most Americans. During the period 1870–1910 the circulation of daily newspapers had a nearly ninefold increase (from less than 3,000,000 to more than 24,000,000), which was over three times as great as the increase in population.

Meanwhile, journalism changed in various ways. Newspapers became predominantly news organs, while editorial opinion and the editorial page declined in importance. Newspapers became corporations, impersonal business organizations similar to those emerging in industry, their worth often reckoned in millions of dollars. At the same time, they tended to become standardized. The press services furnished the same news to all their subscribing papers, and syndicates came into existence to provide their customers with identical features, columns, editorials, and pictures. By the turn of the century there were several newspaper chains, harbingers of a development that would become stronger in the future. Thus the newspapers conformed to and reinforced the trend toward uniformity that characterized American society as a whole.

Book publishing became a business and in line with the trend in industry, a big business. The corporation replaced the individual publisher, and publishing became more impersonal and increasingly commercial. By 1900 most of the big publishing houses were centered in New York City, the recognized publishing capital of the country and also the largest literary market. The passage by Congress in 1891 of an International Copyright Law prevented American publishers from pirating foreign books without payment (and also prevented foreign pirating of American books). The result was that publishers had to rely more on American authors and pay them better.

Reflections in Literature

In a novel, *The Gilded Age* (1873), Mark Twain and Charles Dudley Warner satirized the men and manners of industrial society and thus provided a name that is sometimes applied to the last decades of the nineteenth century. The novel deals with greedy men and their get-rich-quick schemes. It suggests that American life, though showy on the surface, was essentially acquisitive and corrupt. Its authors thus reflected the economic and social changes of the time. Different writers responded to these changes in a variety of ways. Some faced up to the realities of the industrializing and urbanizing trend; others sought a vicarious escape for themselves and for their readers.

Mark Twain (born Samuel Clemens) began his career on a newspaper, and he long considered himself to be a journalist. The public long insisted on regarding him as merely a humorist, but he was probably the greatest American novelist in the era between 1865 and 1900. His first important success, *The Innocents Abroad* (1869), a tale of American tourists in Europe, was a loud and scornful laugh at Old World decay and hypocrisy — and also at American worship of European institutions. His literary fame, however, rests primarily on *The Adventures of Tom Sawyer* (1876) and *The Adventures of Huckleberry Finn* (1885), sensitive and sympathetic accounts of life in rural mid-America.

Some writers viewed with misgiving the culture of their own times and deplored its materialism and economic inequalities. Gradually there developed a literature of protest, expressed chiefly in the medium of the problem novel. The dissenters attacked their targets from many and varied angles. A few, like Henry Adams in *Democracy* (1880) and John Hay in *The Breadwinners* (1884), spoke for the old aristocracy, the former ruling class; in criticizing the crassness of the new rich, they merely expressed the resentment of their group of being dethroned. No novelist of

stature voiced the aspirations of labor, although Stephen Crane in *Maggie: A Girl of the Streets* (1893) described slum conditions and urban poverty with somber realism. For rural America and its small towns, Hamlin Garland and Edgar W. Howe grimly performed a similar descriptive job. Garland, smashing the traditional idyllic picture of pastoral culture, exposed in *Main-Travelled Roads* (1891) the ugliness, isolation, and drudgery of farm life, and Howe in *The Story of a Country Town* (1883) starkly painted the narrow, provincial nature of the American village.

A few literary critics of the American scene retreated from its vigor and materialism and found refuge in Europe. Preeminent among them was Henry James, who studied and described his country from England. In such novels as *The American* (1876), *An International Episode* (1878), and *Daisy Miller* (1879), he detailed the psychological impact of Europe's ancient culture upon visiting Americans. In his coldly realistic volumes, the Americans are usually frustrated or defeated by Europe, but nearly always they appear more noble than the civilization they cannot understand. During his later years, James confessed he wished he had remained in America.

After the turn of the century, novelists turned from realism to naturalism — an emphasis on the sordid or grotesque side of reality. Drawing for inspiration upon the French writer Émile Zola and European literary movements, American realities were presented harshly, in the spirit of rural and urban revolt. Theodore Dreiser's blunt, powerful *Sister Carrie* (1900) dealt so frankly with sex that it was suppressed by its publisher; it was not until 1911 when the public attitude had changed that his next novel appeared. Then in *The Financier* (1912) and *The Titan* (1914) he portrayed a ruthless Chicagoan who destroyed his business competitors. Frank Norris also wrote of unscrupulous businessmen: California railroad barons in *The Octopus* (1901) and Chicago grain speculators in *The Pit* (1903).

Business Philosophy and Its Critics

The economic revolution produced a new ruling class among business managers. They were a class with little tradition of culture and little concept of social responsibility beyond that dictated by the marketplace. In their view, they had won their wealth by work and merit, and they would do with it as they pleased. Their philosophy was epitomized by a much quoted statement of one of them: "Can't I do what I want with my own?"

To a few business executives, the formula of Social Darwinism seemed to explain both their own success and the nature of the society in which they operated. Social Darwinism was Charles Darwin's doctrine of evolution applied to social organization. (This doctrine was that all living things had evolved from earlier forms and that the various species had resulted from a process of natural selection.) As expounded by the Englishman Herbert Spencer, it taught that struggle was a normal human activity, especially in economic life. The weak went down, the strong endured and became stronger, and society was benefited because the unfit were eliminated and the fit survived.

According to Social Darwinism, all attempts by labor to raise its wages by forming unions and all endeavors by government to regulate economic activities would fail, because economic life was controlled by a natural law, the law of competition, which could not be superseded by human restraints. This aspect of Darwinism coincided with another "higher law" that seemed to justify business practices and business dominance: the economic law of supply and demand as defined by Adam Smith and the classical economists. According to the economists, the economic system was like a great machine functioning by natural and automatic rules. The most basic of these rules was the law of supply and demand, which determined all economic values — prices, wages, rents, interest rates — at a level that was just to all concerned. Business leaders justified themselves by this economic theory even though the combinations they were creating threatened to undermine the foundations of the free competitive market. However, for those business people requiring ideological reassurance, most compelling was a popular "gospel of success," which held that the acquisition of a material fortune was a sure measure of divine blessing.

The beliefs of business leaders were not shared by all Americans. Many books — a whole literature of protest — questioned or denounced various aspects of the economic system. Henry George's angrily eloquent *Progress and Poverty,* published in 1879, was an immediate success; reprinted in successive editions, its world-wide sales reached millions. George addressed himself to the question of why poverty existed amidst the wealth created by modern industry. "This association of poverty with progress is the great enigma of our times," he wrote. He blamed poverty on monopoly, and he proposed a remedy, a "single tax" on unimproved land. An increase in the value of such land resulted from the growth of society around it. Thus when land increased in value, George argued, the private owner had not earned the increment, and the community should receive the increase. Such a tax supposedly would destroy monopolies, distribute wealth more equally, and eliminate poverty. Single-tax societies sprang up in many cities, and in 1886 George, backed by labor and the Socialist party, narrowly missed being elected mayor of New York.

Rivaling George in popularity was Edward Bellamy, whose *Looking Backward,* published in 1888, became a best seller within a few years and eventually topped the million mark. Bellamy's book was a novel, a romance of a socialist Utopia. It described the experiences of a young Bostonian who in 1887 went into a hypnotic sleep from which he awakened in the year 2000. He found a new social order, based on collective ownership of property, where want, politics, and vice were unknown, and where people were incredibly happy. Shortly, over 160 "Nationalist Clubs" sprang up to propagate Bellamy's ideas, and the author devoted the remainder of his life to championing Utopian socialism.

Also calling for a larger role for government in controlling the economy was Henry Demarest Lloyd's *Wealth Against Commonwealth,* published in 1894. A tremendous, if not always accurate, attack on the Standard Oil trust, it contended that competition in industry had disappeared. Therefore industry would have to submit to strict government ownership.

The call for the assistance of the government in controlling the economy received support from the growing popularity of a new philosophy that was peculiarly American and peculiarly suited to America's changing material civilization. The name of the philosophy was pragmatism, and its principal formulators were Charles Peirce and William James in the period before 1900, and John Dewey later.

Pragmatism is difficult to define, partly because its advocates differed as to its meaning, but mainly because it avoided absolutes and dealt with relative standards. According to the pragmatists, who accepted the idea of organic evolution, the validity of human institutions and actions should be determined by their consequences. If the ends of an institution or the techniques of a group did not satisfy social needs, then a change was in order. In blunt terms, the pragmatists applied one standard: Does it work? Looking at the economy, many Americans often came to the conclusion that it did not work and urged government-arranged changes — as a natural part of the evolutionary process. Pragmatists employed the test of consequences to truth, as well. There were no final truths or answers, they contended, but a series of truths for each generation and each society. Truth, like institutions, had to be validated by consequences. Said James: "The ultimate test for us of what a truth means is the conduct it dictates or inspires."

Chapter 18

Politics, 1865–1917

The Politics of Complacency

Economic discontent made little impression on the political leaders of the years between 1877 and 1890, a transitional period in politics. The politicians were not unaware of the new economic problems that were emerging, but they were complacent about the need for reform. They were primarily concerned, when they became disturbed, with improving the processes of government.

The politics of the era was exemplified in the administration of Republican Rutherford B. Hayes, who became President after the disputed returns of 1876–1877 were settled. Hayes was an intelligent and high-minded man, but his administration was only partially successful. Hayes took up the problem of governmental reform. Long an advocate of civil service reform, he instructed cabinet heads and other officials to award appointments on the basis of merit. Some of them complied, but others ignored or evaded his wishes. The spoils system was so embedded in the government that not even a President could uproot it. Hayes had even less luck with Congress. Despite his repeated appeals, the legislators refused to appropriate money to renew the civil service commission created under Grant.

On economic questions that emerged during his administration Hayes evinced a conservative attitude. In Congress a coalition of Western Democrats and Republicans from the farming states introduced a free silver measure that would commit the government to buying and coining all the silver offered to it. Their objective was to expand the nation's money supply and thereby halt the downward movement of prices. They were forced, however, to accept a compromise, the Bland-Allison Act, which provided that the government each month would purchase a specified amount of silver and coin it into dollars at the ratio of sixteen-to-one (the silver dollar having sixteen times as much silver as the gold dollar had gold). The specter of price inflation horrified Hayes, who vetoed the bill. Congress, however, repassed it. The silver forces had won a partial victory.

For the presidential election of 1880 the Republicans nominated a veteran member of the House of Representatives from Ohio, James A. Garfield. The Democrats, lacking a strong leader, finally settled on Winfield Scott Hancock, who had been a secondary general in the Civil War. The November election, coming after a bitter personal campaign, showed that Garfield had won a decisive electoral but narrow popular victory.

Garfield, four months after his inauguration, was shot by a deranged office seeker. For over two months he lingered in pain before dying.

The Vice President, Chester A. Arthur of New York, took over the Presidency and pushed zealously for civil service. The public, shocked by Garfield's assassination, was more favorably disposed toward civil service reform, and in 1883 Congress passed the Pendleton Act. By its terms a limited number of federal jobs were to be "classified": applicants for them were to be chosen on the basis of competitive written examinations. At first only about 14,000 of some 100,000 offices were placed on the classified list. But the act provided that future Presidents might by executive order enlarge the list. Every President thereafter extended the list, primarily to "blanket" his appointees into office.

Return of the Democrats

The election of 1884, with its absence of national issues and its emphasis on the personal qualities of the candidates, epitomized the politics of the era of complacency. The Republicans nominated their most popular man, James G. Blaine of Maine, known to his admirers as "the plumed knight." He was also their most vulnerable candidate because of an alleged involvement in a railroad scandal. His selection split the party. The reform element, now known as the Mugwumps, announced that they were prepared to support an honest Democrat. Rising to the bait, the Democrats nominated Grover Cleveland, the reform governor of New York. The platforms of the two parties were almost identical on the tariff, trusts, and other issues.

With no real issues between the parties, the campaign developed into a mudslinging contest as to the personal fitness of the candidates. The Democrats exposed Blaine's none too savory past record. The Republicans unearthed a story that Cleveland as a young man had been accused of fathering an illegitimate child. Cleveland did not specifically deny the charge, and so sex became an issue in the contest. In the November election Cleveland won a narrow electoral victory and a bare popular plurality.

Uninterested in economic issues, Cleveland was absorbed with plans to improve the efficiency and honesty of government. He enlarged the civil service list, although not as much as the reformers wished. He vetoed a number of "pork barrel" appropriations and Civil War pension bills. He sponsored two major bills in Congress. The Electoral Court Act, passed with the election of 1876 in mind, stipulated that Congress was to accept the returns certified by the government of each state. The Presidential Succession Act, designed to ensure a safer succession to the chief office, provided that after the Vice President the heads of cabinet departments were to succeed in the order of the establishment of their agencies.

Despite Cleveland's preoccupation with political reform, economic issues obtruded into his administration. The Interstate Commerce Act was passed in 1887, and he signed it. This prohibited various discriminatory practices by railroads and provided that rates in interstate commerce should be "reasonable and just." The act was to be administered by the Interstate Commerce Commission, which had the power to hear complaints from shippers and, if it thought a complaint was justified, to order a carrier to lower its charges. If the road refused, the ICC had to take its case to the courts and prove the fairness of its order, a cumbersome procedure that militated against effective regulation. The law failed immediately to force rates down, but it was still a landmark measure, the first major American regulatory act.

Also, Cleveland decided that the high tariff rates were responsible for the Treasury surpluses that tempted Congress to reckless appropriation bills. Therefore in December 1887 he asked Congress to lower the rates — but not to such a point that the interests of industry would be endangered.

The Democrats, who controlled the House, responded to the President's leadership by passing the Mills bill, which provided for moderate tariff reductions. But the Republicans, who controlled the Senate, rejected the Mills bill and offered as an alternative a protective measure. Action was thus deadlocked, and the tariff became an issue in the election of 1888.

The Democrats nominated Cleveland and pledged support to his tariff policy. The Republicans, meeting the challenge, endorsed protection and nominated Benjamin Harrison of Indiana. The election was the first one since the Civil War that was fought out on a definite issue. Curiously, the November results revealed that the voters had not registered a definite decision. Harrison had a small electoral majority, but Cleveland led slightly in the popular vote. Harrison would take office as a new wave of protest rolled over the country.

Ethnic Politics

As before the Civil War, political affiliations continued to be shaped by issues associated with race, religion, national origin, and, more generally, ethnicity as well as economic issues. Indeed, the massiveness of immigration, particularly during the 1880s, increased the salience of these issues and intensified political rivalries based upon ethnicity. During the 1880s many Republicans became enthusiastic supporters of efforts to suppress alcohol, restrict parochial schools (both Lutheran and Catholic), and close off immigration. In response, immigrants increasingly tended to identify with the Democratic party, which united them with white Protestant Southerners in defense of threatened cultures. Even German Lutherans, who had usually been sympathetic to Republican policies, often voted in the ranks of the Democrats. And as Catholic immigration increased in volume, the Democratic party overcame the weakening effect of secession to become a close competitor of the Republican party. Cleveland's victories in the popular voting in both 1884 and 1888 clearly indicated that the Democrats had regained national strength. In addition, the Democrats won significant victories at the state and local level, especially in the Midwest, where they took advantage of the "backlash" against the anti-immigrant posture of the Republicans. In Wisconsin, for example, the Republicans secured a law (1889) requiring the use of English in parochial schools, many of which taught exclusively in German. As a result, the Republicans alienated many of their Lutheran followers and lost the next state election. The Republicans, however, learned from their defeats and began to deemphasize cultural issues and to emphasize their support of the protective tariff and the gold standard. This strategy of stressing economic issues, aided by the economic troubles of the 1890s and a dramatic split in the Democratic party, proved to be the basis of Republican dominance of national politics from the 1896 election until the Great Depression and the election of 1932.

Rise of the Populists

As prices continued to decline during the 1880s, embittered and frustrated farmers turned to militant forms of organization. A multitude of farm societies sprang into existence, but by the end of the decade they had united into major organizations: the National Farmers' Alliance, centered in the prairie states west of the Mississippi and usually known as the Northern Alliance, and the Farmers' Alliance and Industrial Union, largely restricted to the South and known as the Southern Alliance. Loosely associated with the Southern order was a black branch, the Colored Farmers' Alliance. Although the latter group functioned separately, Southern Alliance leaders preached that the farmers of both races faced the same problems and had to work together.

Almost immediately the leaders in both sections turned to politics as a means of saving the farmer. They decided that farm problems would have to be solved by national legislation and that this legislation could not be secured from the Democrats or the Republicans. Therefore farmers had to form their own party. Alliance candidates first ran in state and congressional elections in 1890, appearing under diverse party labels in the West and usually as Alliance Democrats in the South.

The farm forces surprised conservatives and probably themselves with their success in 1890. They won control of the legislatures in eight Southern and four Western states and elected six governors, three United States senators, and some fifty representatives to the House. The sweep of the vote encouraged the Alliance leaders, who now laid plans to form a national third party. In July 1892 delegates from the farm states gathered at Omaha, Nebraska, to proclaim the new party and its principles. The party already had by common consent a name, the People's or Populist party. The delegates almost ignored such traditional issues as civil service or the tariff. "We believe that the power of government . . . should be expanded," they announced, "to the end that oppression, injustice and poverty shall eventually cease in the land."

The Populist platform demanded national government ownership and operation of the railroad, telephone, and telegraph systems; a flexible national currency issued by the government and not by the banks; the free and unlimited coinage of silver; government-operated postal savings banks; a graduated income tax; and the subtreasury plan. Under this plan farmers could deposit nonperishable produce in government warehouses and borrow in United States Treasury notes up to 80 percent of the current value of their commodities, thus enabling them to withhold crops from sale until the price was right. Bidding for the support of labor, the platform also demanded shorter hours for workers and restrictions on immigration, and denounced the employment of private detective agencies as strikebreakers in labor disputes. Other planks called for new political techniques to place government more directly under democratic control: the Australian, or secret, ballot; the popular election of United States senators (instead of election by the state legislatures); the initiative, a device whereby state legislation could be introduced or enacted by the voters; and the referendum, a method whereby the voters could veto actions of state legislatures.

The new party was launched, but its appearance of strength was somewhat illusory. Its popular vote was restricted to the South and the prairie West, the one-crop regions where agricultural distress was most acute, and the Rocky Mountain states, where its advocacy of free silver appealed to the mining interests. The Populists aroused little response in the older states of the Middle West, now converted to diversified farming and a new prosperity. The Populists also failed to attract the forces of urban protest. The Knights of Labor endorsed the new party, but the Knights were a dying organization. The rising but still small American Federation of Labor was interested primarily in wages and hours and felt no communion of interests with the farmers. The mass of laborers, whether organized or not, noted the Populist emphasis on free silver and concluded that expansion of the currency would raise prices and hence their cost of living.

The Populists came increasingly to stress the free silver issue. In large part, the strategy was forced on them. Currency expansion was a simple matter to explain to the voters, much easier than extolling the benefits of government ownership of key industries. Moreover, it was already a popular issue with debtor farmers, who were correct in believing that price inflation would lighten their burdens and that free silver would produce inflation. The Populists badly needed money to finance their campaigns, and the only source of help was the silver-mine owners, who insisted on an elevation of the money question. Lastly, many Populist leaders were professional politicians and had a natural desire to win office, and free silver seemed to offer the best promise of achieving that objective. This concentration on an immediate reform could, however, lead to another result. One of the major parties might seek to absorb the Populists by taking over free silver for itself.

Harrison and Then Cleveland Again

Benjamin Harrison, the victor in the election of 1888, assumed the Presidency the following year in the nation's centennial inauguration. Just forty-eight years before, his grandfather, William Henry Harrison, had entered the same office and died almost immediately. Benjamin Harrison served out his term, but he left behind a slight record of accomplishment. Not a strong leader, he left the framing of a legislative program to the party leaders in Congress. They were content to push for bills for more generous internal improvements and pensions.

Public opinion, however, forced Congress to consider legislation affecting broad areas of the economy. The public was most stirred by the issue of the trusts, demanding that they be curbed. In response, Congress passed the Sherman Antitrust Act in 1890. Based on the power of Congress to regulate interstate commerce, the measure declared that any "combination" in restraint of trade between the states was illegal. The language was general but could mean that any company big enough to influence the price of a commodity in interstate trade was illegal. But for over a decade after its passage, the government made little effort to enforce the Sherman Act. It brought few suits in the courts against trusts and lost nearly every one it brought.

Having blunted the movement against big business, the Republicans next had to turn back a new demand for currency inflation by the silver forces in the party. These groups wanted free silver, but once again they had to accept a compromise, the Sherman Silver Purchase Act. This measure directed the Treasury to buy 4,500,000 ounces of silver each month and to pay for the bullion in Treasury notes.

In the presidential election of 1892 Harrison was again the Republican nominee and Cleveland the Democratic one. Once more the platforms of the two parties were almost identical except for the tariff, which the Republicans' McKinley Tariff Act had raised in 1890, and which the Democrats attacked. Only the Populists, offering their first presidential candidate, James B. Weaver, emphasized economic reform. The result of the election indicated that the people desired some kind of change. Cleveland was elected, and the Democrats won a majority of both houses of Congress. Weaver polled twenty-two electoral votes and over 1,000,000 popular votes, and the Populists elected at least a dozen candidates to Congress.

As Cleveland began his second term in 1893, a severe depression struck the country. Brought on by an overexpansion of productive facilities and exacerbated by a sharp contraction of the money supply, it lasted until almost the end of the decade. Thousands of business concerns and banks failed, farm prices tumbled, and 1,000,000 workers, 20 percent of the laboring force, were thrown out of jobs.

The behavior of the unemployed workers indicated that new forces of protest were loose in the country. Workers demanded that the national government should provide jobs for them. The most specific proposal for a federal relief program was advanced by Jacob S. Coxey, an Ohio Populist, who tried to dramatize his plan by organizing a march of the unemployed on Washington. Only 500 of "Coxey's army" were able to make their way to Washington, and these were barred from the Capitol and herded into camps on the pretext that their presence endangered public health.

Cleveland, however, continued to be concerned solely with the effect of the panic on the government's monetary system. Its onset, coupled with the threat to the gold standard posed by the Populists, caused holders of greenbacks and silver certificates to present their notes to the Treasury and demand redemption in gold, and soon the reserve sank below the level necessary to maintain the gold standard. Cleveland had always disliked the Sherman Silver Purchase Act, and now he could point out that it was a major factor draining gold from the Treasury.

In one of his rare moods of leadership, the President summoned Congress into special session and demanded the repeal of the Sherman Silver Pur-

chase Act. He worked his way but only by swinging the patronage lash hard on recalcitrant Democrats and enlisting the support of Eastern Republicans. Western and Southern Democrats fought repeal to the last and in defeat were incredibly bitter.

Repeal slowed but did not stop the drain on the Treasury, however, as persons with Treasury notes continued to present them for redemption. Cleveland, in desperation, went for help to the most powerful source of power he knew — the big New York bankers. A syndicate headed by J. P. Morgan agreed to take up a $65,000,000 bond issue and to use the influence of the financial community to check the flow of gold to Europe. As a result, confidence in the ability of the government to maintain the gold standard was renewed, the stampede to redeem notes ended, and the depression eased. But to agrarian Democrats and to Populists it seemed that Cleveland had sold out to Wall Street, perhaps for personal profit. Actually, no corruption was involved, although the bankers turned a large profit. In the absence of a central banking system (like the Federal Reserve System) only the international bankers had power sufficient to resolve the monetary crisis.

The fight over the money issue revealed a dangerous division within Democratic ranks, and this split was deepened by the party's course on the tariff. After the silver question was disposed of, Cleveland called on his party to redeem its campaign pledge to lower the existing tariff rates. A bill was introduced in the House providing for moderate downward revision while retaining adequate protection for domestic producers. To get the support of Populists and Populist-minded Democrats, the bill contained an income tax of 2 percent on incomes over $4,000. When the bill reached the Senate, over 600 amendments were added to it. Most of them were made by Eastern Democrats and had the effect of raising the duties. Strong pressure from the Democratic leadership induced the House to accept the Senate version, which became law as the Wilson-Gorman Tariff. Cleveland stigmatized it as a violation of the party's platform but allowed it to become law without his signature.

The measure reduced the general scale of duties only 10 percent and was denounced by Western and Southern Democrats and Populists as a sham. Even the one crust thrown to the agrarians, the income tax, was shortly snatched away by the Supreme Court. In a case testing the right of the government to levy an income tax (*Pollock* v. *The Farmer's Loan and Trust Co.*), the Court declared in a five–four decision that a tax on incomes was a "direct" tax and hence had to be apportioned among states according to population. Since an income tax, by its very nature, would be effective only if applied on a basis of individual wealth, the Court had made it impossible to levy such a tax. The 1895 decision was bitterly condemned in agrarian circles as another concession to big business. The lines were being drawn for the election of 1896.

The Choice of 1896

As the election approached, the Republicans were confident of victory. The recent Democratic years had been ones of depression and dissension, and some Republicans boasted that the party could elect any candidate it nominated. But one leader was determined that the party should put up a safe candidate. This was Senator Marcus A. Hanna of Ohio, a wealthy industrialist who was emerging as the boss of the party. Hanna had picked out his candidate — former Ohio Congressman William McKinley, author of the tariff of 1890, and now governor of his state. On every occasion Hanna presented his candidate as "Bill McKinley, the advance agent of prosperity."

By the time the convention met, Hanna had lined up enough delegates to nominate McKinley on the first ballot. The platform endorsed the protective tariff, ignored completely such issues as the income tax and railroad and trust abuses, and opposed the free coinage of silver except by international agreement with the leading commercial nations. As these countries were unlikely to abandon the gold standard, the Republicans were in reality supporting gold.

The Democrats met amid scenes of drama seldom equaled in American political history. The Southern and Western delegates, a majority, came to the convention determined to seize control of the party from the Easterners. To counter the rise of Populist strength in their sections, they intended to write free silver and other planks of the third party into the platform and to nominate a silver candidate.

The resolution committee presented to the convention two reports. The majority platform demanded tariff reduction, endorsed the principle of the income tax, denounced the issue of currency notes by the national banks, condemned the use of injunctions in industrial disputes, pledged a "stricter control" of trusts and railroads, and — this was the issue that headlined the platform — called for free silver. The minority resolution opposed the free coinage of silver except by international agreement, a stand identical to that of the Republicans.

Various speakers then debated the two platforms before the convention. Last to appear was a young Nebraskan, only thirty-six years of age: William Jennings Bryan. His political experience was limited to two terms in the House of Representatives, but he was widely known in the plains country as a magnetic orator, and he had been mentioned as a possible nominee of the party. He delivered one of the great speeches in American political history.

He devoted most of his remarks to a plea for free silver. But he also called for the Democratic party to steer a new course — to represent the "struggling masses" and to support national legislation to better the life of the masses. He ended with a peroration that brought the delegates and the spectators to their feet in thunderous applause: "You shall not press down upon the brow of labor this crown of thorns; you shall not crucify mankind upon a cross of gold." The majority platform was quickly adopted, and on the following day Bryan was nominated on the fifth ballot. The agrarians had found a cause and a leader.

The action of the Democratic convention placed the Populists in a quandary. They had expected both of the major parties to adopt conservative platforms and nominate conservative candidates. But now the Democrats had taken over part of the Populist program, such as free silver and the income tax, while ignoring such demands for fundamental change as government ownership of key industries. Some Populists argued that the party should retain its identity and fight for broad reform. Others contended that endorsement of Bryan offered the party a chance to get some of its ideas adopted. The Populists at their convention finally voted to support Bryan, and the party thereby lost its identity.

The campaign of 1896 had drama, excitement, and a clean-cut issue. The Republicans, amply financed by business and banking and directed by "Mark" Hanna, presented McKinley as the champion of stability, prosperity, and order. They also stigmatized Bryan as a dangerous radical, as, in the words of one campaign document, "an apostle of atheism, repudiation, and anarchy."

Bryan, breaking with precedent, embarked on a stumping tour of the country, traveling 18,000 miles and addressing an estimated 5,000,000 people. His reception frightened the Republicans, who in the closing days of the campaign resorted to the weapon of economic pressure. Employers told their workers not to report for work in case of a Democratic victory, for all industry would be taken over by the government. There were banks that let it be known that farmers supporting the Democrats would have their mortgages foreclosed or at least not renewed. But the crucial source of Republican votes was the honest worry of urban workers over tariff reductions and monetary expansion.

The election results recorded a decisive victory for the Republicans in both the electoral and the popular vote. Bryan carried the Confederate South plus Missouri, swept the plains and mountain states with the exception of North Dakota, but lost California and Oregon on the Pacific coast. In short, he won only the mining regions and the areas where staple farming was predominant and agricultural prices were lowest. The appeal of the Democrats and Populists had been too narrowly agrarian to win a national election.

And so the "battle of the standards" ended in a victory for gold. Economic developments after 1898 seemed to prove that the supporters of gold had been right. Prosperity returned to America. Business entered another cycle of booming expansion. Farm prices shot up because of crop failures in Europe. Actually, the adherents of silver had a point. The world supply of money had not kept pace with the expansion of the world economy. It so happened that the supply was greatly increased after the Republicans came into power. A new technique for extracting gold from low-content ores, the cyanide process, made it possible to work mines previously considered mar-

ginal, and huge new gold deposits were discovered in Alaska, South Africa, and Australia. Within a few years the currency supply was expanded far beyond the level proposed by Bryan and that expansion halted the prolonged price decline of the late nineteenth century. In the glow of prosperity Americans did not pause to analyze economic subtleties; instead, they turned their eyes to the expanding economy.

Origins of Progressivism

It was against this social and economic background that a new political movement developed — the progressive movement. Progressives were concerned at the social ills they saw in America and were disturbed by the growing economic and political power of big business.

Progressive leaders were chiefly from the urban middle class, to a remarkable extent college-educated, self-employed professional or small business people, of native-born Protestant background. For the most part they were about forty years old, financially secure civic leaders who had earlier been McKinley Republicans.

Following these leaders was a middle class, like them still clinging to the traditional agrarian values but caught up in the social whirlpool of the new industrial age. The older segment of the middle class, the independent professional and business people, somewhat more than doubled between 1870 and 1910. This meant it grew as rapidly as the population as a whole. But there was another group, a new middle class of white-collar workers — the clerks, sales people, and technicians who worked for corporations or service enterprises. It increased almost eight times, from 756,000 to 5,609,000 people, thus reaching a number almost double the size of the older middle class. These two groups, the white-collar class and the older middle class, along with many of the more successful farmers and some of the laborers, were ready to accept the new progressive creed.

Middle-class people were frightened by urban political bosses, not only because of their corrupt ties with the industrial moguls but also because of their hold over the laboring masses (often largely immigrants) of the cities. Moreover, these mid-

The Nature of Progressivism

The first historians of the progressive movement had lived through it and enthusiastically hailed its achievements. Sometimes in their writings they fell a little short of some progressive memoirists who remembered the movement as the coming of the millennium.

One of the first and best interpretations, sympathetic but balanced, was that of Charles and Mary Beard, who in a notable chapter of *The Rise of American Civilization* (1927) linked Populism and progressivism as a single heroic surge toward social democracy. In the *Quest for Social Justice* (1931), Harold U. Faulkner embellished this theme. "To many thoughtful men in the opening years of the twentieth century it seemed that America in making her fortune was in peril of losing her soul," wrote Faulkner. "Crude and chaotic as was this civilization in many respects, its essential soundness became manifest in the next decade and a half as the rising social consciousness of the people directed the national energy into fresh and nobler channels." This optimistic and rather agrarian-based view of progressivism as a triumph of the Jeffersonian tradition dominated academic thinking into the 1940s.

Skeptical scholarly appraisals of progressivism began to appear after World War II. George Mowry and Richard Hofstadter emphasized the middle-class urban background of the progressive leaders. In *The Age of Reform* (1955), Hofstadter suggested that these leaders were drawn to progressivism as a means of regaining the political status and power that had been draining away from their class, and that rising prices created a consumer consciousness that "gave mass appeal and political force to many Progressive issues and provided the Progressive leaders with a broad avenue of access to the public."

A succeeding group of historians believed, on the contrary, that progressivism meant no more than a successful maneuver on the part of business people to obtain government regulation that would further their own economic interests. The most vigorous of these historians, Gabriel Kolko, in *The Triumph of Conservatism* (1963), wrote: "Progressivism was initially a movement for the political rationalization of business and industrial conditions, a movement that operated on the assumption that the general welfare of the community could be best served by satisfying the concrete needs of business." Richard H. Wiebe, in *The Search for Order, 1887–1920* (1971), agreed that progressivism was a quest for a more stable society. But he argued that support for that quest was spread throughout middle- and upper-class America.

In the face of the criticisms of progressivism, some historians have continued to insist that it was a movement for social democracy. In 1962 J. Joseph Huthmacher argued that members of the working class, including immigrants, were instrumental in enacting labor reforms. And David P. Thelen, in *The New Citizenship* (1972), claimed that Wisconsin progressivism at least involved a clash between the "public interest" and "corporate privilege."

dle-class people had some fear of the new rising labor unions. Populist farmers had also been suspicious of the moguls and the masses. One of the Populist papers had said the purpose of the party was to serve as a "bulwark against the anarchy of the upper and lower scums of society."

Progressives were not a cohesive group. Reflecting the political situation in their cities or states, some were Republicans and some were Democrats. Often they had divergent goals. To one progressive, regulation of trusts might be the great end; to another, clean municipal government; to a third, equal rights for women; to a fourth, restriction of immigration. Sometimes progressives would coalesce to attain common objectives; occasionally they would even oppose each other. Thus some progressives favored imperialism while others fought it bitterly. Out of all these varying drives there emerged two great streams of progressivism — the movement for social justice and the demand for political reform, which dominated progressivism until World War I.

Social Justice

The social justice movement was already well advanced by the turn of the century. It had its roots in European, especially English, reform movements. Almost every prominent English reformer visited the United States, and conversely almost every American progressive leader fell under the influence of the British. Young Jane Addams had worked at the newly established Toynbee Hall in the Limehouse section of London; in 1889 she returned to the United States to establish Hull House, a slum relief center, in Chicago. Settlement houses, slum clearance programs, and a great variety of other English reforms quickly developed counterparts in the United States.

The Salvation Army, which had recently come to the United States from England, by 1900 boasted a corps of 3,000 officers and 20,000 privates. It offered aid as well as religion to the dregs of the cities. So did ministers, priests, and rabbis, who by the nineties were working in the slums; these religious leaders were united in their determination to improve the existence of the miser-

able people around them in addition to saving their souls. "One could hear human virtue cracking and crushing all around," Walter Rauschenbusch wrote of Hell's Kitchen in New York City. Thus many an American Protestant minister arrived at the "social gospel." Catholics like Father John Augustine Ryan joined in the fight for social justice under the authority they found in Pope Leo XIII's encyclical *Rerum Novarum.* It declared that "a small number of very rich men have been able to lay upon the masses of the poor a yoke little better than slavery itself. . . . No practical solution of this question will ever be found without the assistance of religion and the church."

Close behind the ministry in advocacy of social justice were middle-class and upper-class women. In the 1890s many of them had taken more schooling and read more widely than their husbands or brothers, joining literary circles and women's clubs. By the early 1900s these clubs were beginning to display a remarkable growth; the General Federation of Women's Clubs, from a membership of 50,000 in 1898, grew to over 1,-000,000 by 1914. In the new era, the members of the clubs were quick to take up the fight for the ballot and legal equality for themselves, and for a wide array of reforms on behalf of children and working women.

Another small but mighty social justice group consisted of those who carefully gathered data and statistics on the need for reform. They were often social welfare workers or crusaders working for federal or state agencies. In many a state before 1900 there were bureaus of labor that could and did, as in the case of Illinois, compile great quantities of data on deplorable working and living conditions. But research alone could not gather a great force of public opinion behind the progressive movement. That was the task of a group of men and women called by a critic the "muckrakers."

Reform in the Cities

The muckrakers were the many journalists who dramatized the need for reform by writing exposés of the unsavory in business and government. The muckraking writers found a huge national audience in the new popular magazines, selling for 10 cents or 15 cents, which were then building mass circulation. *McClure's*, already a magazine of broad appeal, began publishing Ida Tarbell's series on Standard Oil. The publisher, S. S. McClure, sent a new editor, Lincoln Steffens, out to see the country firsthand; this experience led Steffens to begin a series on municipal corruption. *The Shame of the Cities* was the title Lincoln Steffens gave to his notable series of exposés that appeared in *McClure's*, and shame was what civic-minded progressives felt. They tried to wrest control of their city governments away from the machines, reorganize the governments scientifically, and use them as instruments of economic and social reform.

Municipal reform began in response to a tragedy in Galveston, Texas, where the old, ineffective government broke down in the wake of a tidal wave. The citizens replaced it with a commission of five, whose members by 1908 were jointly enacting ordinances and were singly running the main city departments. In 1907 Des Moines adopted the commission plan with modifications to make it more democratic, and other cities followed. Another variation was the city manager plan, which placed a trained expert, similar to the manager of a business, in charge of the city, and made that person responsible to the commission or the mayor and council. Staunton, Virginia, hired a city manager in 1908; the new device attracted national attention when Dayton, Ohio, adopted it in 1913 to speed rehabilitation from a serious flood. By the end of the progressive era some 400 cities were operating under commissions, and another 45 under city managers.

Progressives fought also to destroy economic privilege on the municipal level. They favored municipal ownership of streetcar and other franchises; if the franchises were privately owned, progressives battled to force the often high rates down. The most notable of the reform mayors was Tom Johnson of Cleveland, who had invented the streetcar fare box. He was a "traction magnate" (a street-railway entrepreneur) converted to the ideas of Henry George. As mayor, Johnson fought to raise the ridiculously low assessments upon railroad and utility property, introduce city planning, and above all, lower streetcar fares to 3 cents. After his defeat and death, his brilliant

aide, Newton D. Baker, was elected mayor and helped maintain Cleveland's position as the best-governed American city.

Many of the urban gains of progressivism were permanent, but in some cities, as soon as progressives relaxed, the old forces recaptured city hall. In other municipalities, state control over city government made reform almost impossible. Cities derived all of their powers from the state, and many a state legislature granted new charters only reluctantly or controlled a large city within the state through special legislation.

Statewide Reforms

Sometimes progressives tried to obtain state laws allowing cities to write their own charters. More often, urban progressive leaders moved into state politics, running for governorships and trying to control legislatures. They wanted to help their cities, but also to establish progressivism on a larger scene.

At the state level, progressives enacted a wide array of legislation to increase the power of crusading governors, give the people more direct control over the government, and decrease the functions of legislators. The most important measures, the initiative and the referendum, were first enacted in Oregon in 1902 as a result of the quiet but persistent advocacy of the secretary of several voters' organizations, William S. U'Ren. The initiative enabled voters to short-circuit the legislature and vote upon measures at general elections; the referendum forced the return of laws from the legislature to the electorate. By 1918 twenty states had adopted these schemes.

Progressives also believed that elective government would be more honest if placed more directly under popular control. Hence they supported the direct primary, a device whereby the voters of a party instead of a machine-dominated convention would nominate the party's candidates. By 1915 every state had adopted some form of the direct primary.

The most controversial of the progressive reforms was the recall, which made possible the removal of officials at a special election to be called after sufficient numbers of the electorate had signed petitions. Many states enacted recall laws, but because of the difficulty of obtaining the required number of signatures the device was little used.

Aided by the new devices and supported by public opinion, progressive leaders won control of a number of states. Robert M. LaFollette in Wisconsin pushed through firm regulation of railroads, compensation for workers injured in industrial accidents, and graduated taxation of incomes. Charles Evans Hughes in New York obtained a commission to regulate public utilities. When Woodrow Wilson, fresh from the presidency of Princeton University, became governor of New Jersey in 1911, he obtained from the legislature a substantial array of measures to transform the state into one of the progressive leaders.

Nevertheless, much social justice legislation came only late and after great struggle. New York failed to enact factory-safety legislation until it was shocked into action by the Triangle Shirtwaist Factory fire in New York City in 1911, in which 148 people, mostly young women, were helplessly trapped and killed in a few minutes. But eventually in some urban states, New York and others, the city machines joined the progressives in supporting factory legislation. The bosses found that such measures won them votes among their working-class constituents.

Throughout the era, progressive legislators ran the risk that the Supreme Court would invalidate their handiwork. The Court made one great, although temporary, shift toward progressivism. This came in 1908 when Louis D. Brandeis argued in support of an Oregon law to limit women workers to a ten-hour day. He presented a brief in which he devoted only 2 of 104 pages to the legal precedents and the remainder to proofs that Oregon's police power was necessary to protect the health and general welfare of the mothers, and thus of all humankind. The Supreme Court accepted this argument and thus moved toward a "sociological jurisprudence" that adjusted "principles and doctrines to [the] human conditions they are to govern rather than to assumed first principles."

As a final measure in their program to place government more directly under popular control, progressives sought to eliminate the election of United States senators by state legislatures and to substitute popular election. They charged that too many legislatures were influenced by corporations and elected officeholders chosen by the corporations.

By 1902 the House of Representatives had already five times passed resolutions for a constitutional amendment for direct election of senators; each time the Senate blocked the amendment. Impatient progressives in various states provided in effect for direct election by means of preferential votes for senators; the legislatures were obligated to choose the candidate whom the voters preferred. By 1912 twenty-nine states had adopted these devices. Finally the Senate in 1912 passed the Seventeenth Amendment, for the direct election of senators, and by 1913 the requisite number of states had ratified it. The new amendment did not startlingly modify the nature of the Senate, since most progressive states had already elected senators of a new mettle.

Women's Causes

Women took an active part in many of the progressive reforms, such as those for the protection of female employees. Women were especially important in the furthering of two causes that long antedated the progressive period but received new impetus from the reform spirit of the time. These two were temperance and woman suffrage.

Since 1874 the Woman's Christian Temperance Union, whose greatest leader was Frances E. Willard, had worked through schools and churches to arouse public opinion against strong drink. The Anti-Saloon League, containing both men and women, joined the crusade in 1893. For many years the cause gained publicity from the one-woman campaign of Carry Nation, who took out after the saloons in her home state of Kansas with a hatchet.

Since 1880 Kansas had had an antiliquor law, but it was poorly enforced. The temperance crusaders undertook to get antiliquor legislation in other states and also to obtain a national prohibition amendment. By 1917 more than half of the states had banned liquor sales, and several others had permitted counties or municipalities to do so (through "local option"). In 1917 Congress approved an amendment prohibiting the manufacture, sale, or transportation of intoxicating beverages throughout the country. This, the Eighteenth Amendment, went into effect in 1920.

Of all the rights that women sought, the right to vote became the most important. Often frustrated in their campaigns, particularly those on behalf of working women, feminist leaders of the late nineteenth and early twentieth centuries gradually came to believe that the right to vote was necessary to secure other rights. A great many women contributed to the suffrage movement, but the two who had the most to do with its ultimate success were Susan B. Anthony and Carrie Chapman Catt.

In 1866 Anthony along with Elizabeth Cady Stanton had led in founding the American Equal Rights Association to promote universal suffrage. In 1868 they were shocked to find women excluded from the protections of the Fifteenth Amendment and persuaded a congressman to introduce a constitutional amendment enfranchising women. When most abolitionists failed to support it, Anthony and Stanton denounced the Fifteenth Amendment and broke with the abolitionists by forming a new association, the National Woman Suffrage Association, which developed a comprehensive feminist position. Women now began to develop political strategies independently of other reform movements.

In 1878 the suffragists introduced another amendment in Congress, and they reintroduced it in every session after that for more than forty years. While urging the federal government to act, they also carried their campaign to the state legislatures. But before the 1890s gains were minimal, limited to the granting of suffrage to women for certain school elections in nineteen states. After taking over the leadership of the movement in the 1890s, Carrie Chapman Catt decided to concentrate on state action, so as to produce enough "suffrage states" to compel the federal government to go along. When Wyoming entered the Union in 1890, it was the only state with equal suffrage, having adopted it as a territory in 1869. During the 1890s the neighboring states of Colorado, Utah, and Idaho followed the example of Wyoming. By 1914 a total of eleven states, all but one of them west of the Mississippi River, allowed women the same voting privileges as men. In 1916 the women voters of Montana helped to elect the first woman to serve as a member of Congress, Jeannette Rankin.

Progress with state action was so slow that, in the meantime, Catt and most of the feminists had returned to the earlier emphasis on federal action. They disagreed, however, on the methods they should use. One leader, Alice Paul, favored imitating the "nuisance tactics" of radical English suffragists who smashed windows, destroyed mailboxes, and disrupted public meetings to get attention for the cause. American suffragists did march in parades and picket the White House, but Catt and the majority of the leaders in the United States preferred the more conventional methods of persuasion and political pressure.

Resistance was strong. Antifeminists formed the Association Opposed to Woman Suffrage and chose a woman to head it. They had the support of the "liquor interests," who feared that women with the vote would hasten the day of national prohibition. The opponents also had the support of "preparedness" advocates, who argued that woman suffrage would weaken the nation in the face of possible war.

Congresswoman Rankin did, indeed, oppose the declaration of war in 1917 (and she was to be the only member of Congress to vote against it in 1941). But Catt, though herself a pacifist, believed that the cooperation of women in the war effort would help them to gain the vote. She was right. Women, suffragists among them, contributed to victory in World War I by working on farms and in factories, assisting in the sale of war bonds, and joining in other patriotic activities on the home front. In 1919, more than half a century after the introduction of the first woman suffrage proposal, Congress finally endorsed the Nineteenth Amendment, which made it unconstitutional to deny or abridge the right to vote "on account of sex." This was ratified in time for the election of 1920.

T. R. and the Trusts

Progressivism appeared first in cities, then shifted to state government, and finally and inevitably developed into a national movement. In the years between 1900 and 1917 most Americans accepted in one form or another the faith of progressivism. It was important to the movement that in its early years the man who was President was sympathetic to its ideals. Theodore Roosevelt, probably the most popular American of the era, was, in part, a progressive.

Roosevelt, elected Vice President in 1900, became President in the following year when McKinley died at the hands of an assassin. The new chief executive was young — only forty-two years of age — dynamic, and sensitive to the growing desire for reform. But he felt that he had to proceed cautiously. Conservative Republicans controlled the party machinery in Congress and throughout the country, and they would look coldly on a too ambitious accidental President. Hence Roosevelt devoted his first major effort to gaining control of the party organization. But at the same time he let it be known that he was on the side of the progressives.

In his first annual message to Congress, December 3, 1901, he set forth his basic policy toward trusts: "There is a widespread conviction in the minds of the American people that . . . trusts are in certain of their features and tendencies hurtful to the general welfare. This . . . is based upon sincere conviction that combination and concentration should be, not prohibited, but supervised and within reasonable limits controlled; and in my judgment this conviction is right."

Specifically, Roosevelt asked for legislation to give the government the right to inspect and examine the workings of great corporations, and subsequently to supervise them in a mild fashion, rather similar to the regulation of banks. What he desired first was the power to investigate trusts and publicize their activities; on the basis of these data, Congress could later frame legislation to regulate or tax the trusts. Consequently he requested the establishment of a Department of Commerce and Labor, containing a Bureau of Corporations to carry on investigations. Congress set up such a department in 1903.

The establishment of a great railroad monopoly in the Northwest, after a bitter and spectacular stock market battle in 1901, gave Roosevelt an opportunity to begin prosecution under the Sherman Antitrust Act. And so he did, even though his avowed purpose had been to regulate, not destroy, and to stamp underfoot only "malefactors of great wealth," while sparing large corporations

that were benign. The new Northern Securities Company had emerged out of the struggle for control of the Northern Pacific between E. H. Harriman of the Union Pacific on the one side and James J. Hill of the Great Northern and J. P. Morgan on the other. In the eyes of progressives, these men were malefactors.

When the Supreme Court in 1904 dissolved the Northern Securities combine, it in no material way injured Harriman, Hill, or Morgan. But it did convince progressives that Roosevelt, however cautious his avowed policies might be, was a heroic "trust buster."

Trust busting was popular and proceeded apace. Roosevelt's attorneys obtained twenty-five indictments altogether and instituted suits against the beef, oil, and tobacco combinations. In these, the government was ultimately successful, but the Supreme Court instituted a "rule of reason," declaring in effect that the Sherman Act prohibited only unreasonable restraints upon trade. The end result of the trust-busting policy was disappointing. Instead of forming trusts, business consolidators increasingly engaged in simple merger. As one critic said, trust busting was like trying to unscramble eggs. But Roosevelt's campaign probably slowed the pace of business concentration.

Government and Labor

Roosevelt foresaw an active role for government as *neutral* regulators of relations between capital and labor. Presidential intervention in labor disputes was nothing new — there had been, for example, the Pullman strike — but the government had usually acted as a strikebreaker for the captains of industry. Now Roosevelt was ready to make the government an impartial arbiter instead. He found an opportunity to demonstrate his views when in 1902 a strike broke out in the anthracite coal mining industry, which was controlled by eight railroads under the domination of the Morgan banking house. The United Mine Workers, led by John Mitchell, demanded an eight-hour day, a 20 percent wage increase, and recognition of the union. Mitchell so effectively presented the miners' claims, and George F. Baer, spokesperson for the operators, was so truculent, that public sympathy was aligned with the strikers. Roosevelt toyed with schemes to send federal troops to take over the mines. In the end he persuaded Morgan to force arbitration upon the operators. The miners after their long strike failed to gain union recognition but did obtain a 10 percent wage increase.

Roosevelt, despite some setbacks, was satisfied with his administration — but wanted another in his own right. He could not be denied the Republican nomination, although some conservatives were disturbed by his progressive gestures. The Democrats, as though playing for the conservative vote, nominated a virtual unknown, Cleveland's former law partner, Alton B. Parker. After a dull campaign Roosevelt swept to a resounding electoral and popular victory in November.

Regulation and Conservation

Roosevelt interpreted the election as a mandate to continue his program of moderate progressive reform. His course alienated some of the business people who had contributed money to his campaign. Henry Clay Frick, the steel magnate, complained: "We bought the ——— and he didn't stay bought." He equally offended the advanced progressives of the Middle West with his undisguised disdain for "the La Follette type of fool radicalism."

Some progressives urged Roosevelt to move for tariff reduction, but he showed little interest in this issue. He was primarily interested in obtaining more effective railroad rate reductions by strengthening the Interstate Commerce Act of 1887. By a series of intricate maneuvers, Roosevelt managed to force a new regulatory law through Congress. At one point he seemed to join Senator La Follette in demands for really drastic regulation of railroads. La Follette wished to give the ICC power to evaluate railroad property as a base for determining rates. He felt betrayed when Roosevelt abandoned him, but Roosevelt had been intent only upon obtaining a moderate law. Although the Hepburn Act of June 1906 was in La Follette's eyes only half a loaf, it was at least the beginning of effective national railroad regulation. It empowered the ICC to put into effect reasonable rates, subject to later court review; extended its jurisdiction to cover express, sleeping car, and pipeline companies; separated railroad management from other enterprises such as mining; prescribed uniform bookkeeping; and forbade passes and rebates.

Although Roosevelt continued to press suits against trusts, he, as well as other progressives, turned increasingly to regulation as the remedy for the problems of an industrial society. The President worked with progressives in Congress to secure the enactment of the Meat Inspection Act and the Pure Food and Drug Act. Passed largely because of public anger at the unsanitary practices of the meat packers, the laws provided for federal inspection of certain products destined for interstate commerce. They were not as immediately effective as their sponsors hoped, but their mere passage was significant — two additional industries had been brought under federal regulation.

In line with the regulatory pattern was Roosevelt's policy on conservation of natural resources. The President had long believed that the United States should develop great national forests like those of European countries, and now he became convinced that the government should act to conserve other resources for the public good. By executive order he withdrew practically all remaining forests in the public domain from exploitation by private interests, and then all the remaining coal lands. He also prepared the way for a new government policy on electric power by reserving water power sites that expanding private utility companies wanted to obtain.

At the end of his second administration Roosevelt could look back at a record of varied achievement. The trust-busting policy had had disappointing results. But the regulatory measures of the administration had been more successful — they marked the direction in which progressivism would go.

Taft and the Progressives

On the night of his election in 1904 Roosevelt had announced that he would not seek another term. He kept his word, but as the election of 1908 approached he was determined that the Republicans should nominate a candidate of his choosing, one who would carry on the Roosevelt policy of moderate progressivism. His choice fell on his secretary of war, William Howard Taft of Ohio, who had a long and solid record of service in state and national government. The Republican convention obediently nominated Taft, while the Democrats named William Jennings Bryan, now running for a third time. Both candidates advanced progressive ideals during the campaign, but between the two, most business people preferred Taft. So did the voters in November, but although Taft's electoral majority was substantial, his popular lead over Bryan was only half the size of Roosevelt's plurality in 1904. The vote portended that many progressives were not sure Taft was one of them.

Taft was a progressive but he lacked Roosevelt's political skills. The result was that during his administration a division between progressives and conservatives split the party. Such a division had threatened under Roosevelt, but T. R. had been able to face it down. Taft, who did not subscribe to the principle of strong presidential leadership, sat back while the split widened. To progressives it seemed that he was betraying their cause — and Roosevelt.

The first of these seeming betrayals occurred when Taft called Congress into special session to redeem the Republican platform pledge to revise the tariff downward. The revision that progressives had in mind would have accomplished only a moderate reduction, but even this was not acceptable to conservative Republicans and high-tariff Democrats. They added over 800 amendments to the tariff bill that had been introduced, and the Payne-Aldrich Act that finally emerged was on the whole a protective measure. Taft gave the progressives no help in their fight to lower the rates, and then infuriated them by signing the bill, which he declared to be the "best" tariff the Republicans had ever passed.

The most important betrayal came in the Ballinger-Pinchot controversy. Richard Ballinger had been appointed by Taft to be secretary of the interior. As the head of this office, he had charge of government lands containing natural resources; he was known to favor a policy of permitting private interests to exploit these lands. Gifford Pinchot was in charge of the Forestry Service in the Department of Agriculture, a Roosevelt appointee and zealous conservationist. Pinchot precipi-

tated the controversy by charging that Ballinger was conniving to turn over valuable coal lands in Alaska to a private syndicate in return for a financial consideration. Taft stood by his secretary and discharged Pinchot for insubordination. Although the President correctly judged that Ballinger was personally honorable, he had placed himself in the position of supporting an anticonservationist. Progressives cried that Taft was scuttling the Roosevelt conservation program.

In their mounting anger at Taft the progressives overlooked that he had followed a partly progressive course. In his one administration the government brought twice as many antitrust suits as Roosevelt had in two administrations. And Taft supported the Mann-Elkins Act of 1910, which extended the authority of the ICC over railroads and brought two additional industries, the telephone and the telegraph, under national regulation.

A Rift in Republican Ranks

Roosevelt, after seeing Taft inaugurated, had departed for Africa to hunt big game and then traveled through Europe. Arriving home in 1910, he was met by indignant progressives who told him they were ready to oppose Taft's renomination at the Republican convention. Some of them were supporters of Senator La Follette, but most of them hoped that Roosevelt himself could be persuaded to run. At first he said that he wished only to unify the party. Being T. R., he could not stay out of a fight. "My hat is in the ring," he announced finally. He also announced his platform, which he called the New Nationalism. Abandoning trust busting, it proposed that the government should regulate the economy in the public interest. Boldly Roosevelt declared that the advocate of property rights "must now give way to the advocate of human welfare, who rightly maintains that every man holds his property subject to the general right of the community to regulate its use to whatever degree the public welfare may require it."

Roosevelt's enormous popularity led many progressives to flock immediately to his standard. In the states that chose delegates to the convention in primary elections he defeated Taft. But in most states the delegates were selected by the state organizations, which were often under the influence of the administration and picked representatives pledged to Taft. When the convention convened in Chicago, the Taft forces were in firm control and demonstrated their strength by denying seats to a number of delegates supporting Roosevelt. T. R., breaking with tradition, had come in person to Chicago to direct his followers. But when his delegates were denied admission, he angrily announced that he was bolting the party. He left the city, and left the convention to Taft, who was nominated.

Before leaving, Roosevelt had discussed with associates the desirability of forming a new party. Quickly the Progressive party came into being, and it convened in Chicago shortly after the Republican convention adjourned. In an almost religious atmosphere the delegates nominated Roosevelt and adopted a platform embodying the ideals of the New Nationalism. T. R., in agreeing to run, declared he was fit as a bull moose, thus giving the new party a symbol.

Woodrow Wilson Wins

Between the Progressive bolt of the Republican convention and the nomination of Roosevelt, the Democrats met in Baltimore, exultant with the heady knowledge that, though they were a political minority, they almost certainly were nominating the next President. The two leading contenders for the nomination were Governor Woodrow Wilson of New Jersey and Speaker Champ Clark of Missouri. Wilson's reform record in New Jersey made him the favorite of progressive Democrats, while Clark had the support of conservatives and most of the bosses. Clark led on the early ballots, but the forces of Wilson and other aspirants stood firm, preventing the Missourian from attaining the necessary two-thirds majority. Finally, on the forty-sixth ballot, the convention turned to Wilson. His aspiration had always been to become a political leader, but when he had found the road rough as a beginning lawyer in Atlanta, he had taken a Ph.D. degree at Johns Hopkins, had become a professor of political economy, and then served as president of Princeton University.

Both as president of Princeton and as governor of New Jersey, Wilson demonstrated the courageous strength and alarming weaknesses that would characterize his Presidency. He had the vision to inspire multitudes but was dogmatic and distant with individuals. He could lecture the opposition in high moral terms, but his sense that he and he alone was absolutely right prevented him from stooping to necessary political negotiations.

The Democratic platform had emphasized trust busting as the solution to the problems of an industrial society. This older strategy of progressivism appealed to Wilson, who had his own program, which he called the New Freedom. He believed that the federal government should create an economic climate in which competition could flourish. Roosevelt's New Nationalism, Wilson charged, would mean the federal licensing of the juggernauts of big business to crush the American people. In contrast, Wilson proclaimed his New Freedom as the fight for emancipation of the small business person, the "man on the make." He proclaimed: "If America is not to have free enterprise, then she can have freedom of no sort whatever."

In November, because of the three-cornered contest, Wilson won an overwhelming electoral victory. Roosevelt trailed far behind and Taft was a poor third. But the combined popular vote of Roosevelt and Taft exceeded that of Wilson, who garnered less than 42 percent of the total. Still the result revealed that the country was in a progressive mood. All three candidates were in varying degrees progressive, and in 1913, the year that Wilson took office, two amendments to the Constitution backed by progressives were ratified: the Sixteenth, authorizing Congress to levy an income tax, and the Seventeenth, providing for the direct election of United States senators.

Enacting the New Freedom

In his inaugural address Wilson called for action on three broad fronts: tariff revision, banking and currency reform, and antitrust legislation. He immediately demonstrated that he was going to be a President who would try to influence what Congress did. Summoning the legislators into special session, he appeared before them in person to read his message, thus breaking a precedent in effect since Jefferson's time. He demanded as a first priority a reduction of the tariff.

Responding to the President's leadership, the Democratic majority pushed through the Underwood-Simmons Tariff. The reductions still retained protection for domestic manufacturers, but they represented the first substantial lowering of duties since before the Civil War. One section of the measure provided for a graduated income tax. This first modern income tax imposed upon individuals and corporations a tax of 1 percent on all income of $4,000, and an additional surtax of 1 percent on income over $20,000, ranging up to a maximum of 6 percent on income over $500,000. It was the beginning of a change in the American tax structure; the United States was beginning to place upon those of large income a proportionately greater share of the cost of the government.

Rather than lose momentum, President Wilson held Congress in session through the sweltering summer, to begin work on banking reform. In 1911 he had declared: "The great monopoly in this country is the money monopoly. So long as that exists, our old variety and freedom and individual energy of development are out of the question." Early in 1913 a House investigating committee headed by a Democrat, Arsene Pujo, published a frightening set of statistics to back Wilson's accusation. Thus the Morgan-Rockefeller empire held "in all, 341 directorships in 112 corporations having aggregate resources or capitalization of $22,245,000,000." This was in 1913, when the entire national wealth was estimated at less than ten times this figure.

To President Wilson evidence like this indicated a need to break the money trust. At the same time, one of the serious ills of the American banking system was its decentralization and independence, except through the loose tie of urban clearing houses. This meant that in time of financial crisis and deflation, banks lacked adequate reserves to meet all their obligations. In a crisis, banks would call in their loans, thereby worsening the contraction. Reform was obviously necessary, but Wilson and most progressives rejected the idea of a single central bank or too great a degree of government control over the banking system. Instead they favored a decentralized system under loose federal regulation. Their concepts were embodied in the Federal Reserve Act of 1913.

This measure created central banks for each of twelve regions. Each bank was to serve and be owned by the banks of its district. The decentralization was designed in part to increase the availability of credit in the West and South. The Federal Reserve bank would rediscount the notes held by member banks, thereby lending money to member banks, and issue a new type of paper currency: Federal Reserve notes. The act required national banks to become members, and encouraged other banks to do so. Although the American Bankers' Association had criticized the legislation, nearly half the nation's banking resources were represented in the system within its first year of operation, and four-fifths by the late 1920s. The Federal Reserve system provided the federal government with the means to create currency or bank reserves in periods of crisis. It did not destroy the so-called money trust, but it did mark a significant start toward government management of the money supply in the United States.

Wilson gave his strong support to a bill prohibiting unfair trade practices and establishing a Federal Trade Commission to prohibit unfair methods of competition such as price discrimination or exclusive dealing contracts. The FTC would police business through cease-and-desist orders, engaging in prevention as well as punishment. Thus Wilson intended to restrict practices that might lead to monopoly.

The result was the Clayton Antitrust Act. Conservatives, however, put qualifying clauses around the sections outlawing interlocking directorates or stockholdings and exclusive selling contracts, so that the clauses, as a progressive Republican senator complained, did not have enough teeth to masticate milk toast. As a concession to labor, the act stated that labor was not a commodity and declared that unions were not conspiracies in restraint of trade. President Gompers of the AFL chose to hail the Clayton Act as "Labor's Magna Carta" and insisted that organized labor was now exempted from antitrust prosecution.

The passage of his program seemed to satisfy Wilson that enough reform had been accomplished. But as the election year 1916 opened, progressive Democrats in Congress were not satisfied. They noted that the Progressive party was disintegrating and concluded that unless the Democrats, who were normally a minority, presented a vigorous progressive program, they would be swamped by the reunited Republicans. Wilson accepted the challenge and went beyond the New Freedom, allying himself with the progressives, farmers, and laborers to advocate a series of laws that in some respects enacted the Progressive party program of 1912. In May 1916 he accepted a farm-loan bank system in the Federal Farm Loan Act. At the urging of progressives, he applied pressure on the Democratic leaders in the Senate to obtain a "workmen's compensation" system for federal employees, and the first federal child labor law. The child labor law, the Keating-Owen Act of 1916, prohibited the shipment in interstate commerce of products manufactured by underage children. It marked not only a significant reversal on the part of Wilson but also a new assumption of federal control over manufacturing through the commerce clause. The Federal Highway Act of 1916 appropriated $75,000,000 to be spent for road building over a period of five years. Without attracting much attention, this act undermined state rights by granting subsidies on a dollar-matching basis for states to undertake highway programs. Another effect, in combination with the highly progressive income tax rates established by the Revenue Act of 1916, was to take money out of the wealthier Northeastern areas and redistribute it in the South and West.

Altogether, the first Wilson administration had gone far beyond the limited reform program of the New Freedom. It demonstrated that progressives, whether or not they wanted to, were moving away from the negative policy of trust busting to the positive solution of regulation. Wilson was justified in his boast that the Democrats had come close to carrying out the platform of the Progressive party as well as their own.

Chapter 19

Emergence of a World Power, 1865-1917

The New Manifest Destiny

In the years following the Civil War the American people, occupied with domestic problems, were little interested in foreign affairs. By the 1890s the American people were ready to resume the course of expansion that in the forties had been characterized as Manifest Destiny.

Various forces shaped the new national mood. The rapid settlement of the last frontier shifted popular attention from the continental limits to lands beyond. The bitter class strife of the nineties alarmed many leaders, who thought that a more aggressive foreign policy might divert the popular mind from domestic dissensions. The swelling value of foreign trade directed American interests to foreign markets — and to the possible necessity of securing foreign colonies. Finally, America was influenced by the imperialism of the powers of Europe, which had partitioned most of Africa between them and were turning eager eyes on Asia. America "must not fall out of the line of march," one leader cried.

Hawaii and the Pacific

The first area into which the United States directed its imperialist impulse after the Civil War was the vast Pacific Ocean region.

The islands of Hawaii in the mid-Pacific had been an important stopover station for American ships in the China trade since the early 1800s. The first American settlers to reach Hawaii were New England missionaries, who advertised the economic possibilities of the islands in the reli-

gious press. Soon other Americans arrived to become sugar planters and to found a profitable new industry. Eventually, officers of the growing navy looked longingly on the magnificent natural base of Pearl Harbor on the island of Oahu.

The McKinley Tariff of 1890 dealt the planters a bad blow; by removing the duty on foreign raw sugar and giving domestic producers a bounty, it deprived Hawaii of its privileged position in the American sugar market. Annexation seemed the only alternative to economic strangulation. At the same time there ascended to the throne a new ruler, Queen Liliuokalani, who was determined to eliminate American influence in the government.

The American residents decided to act at once. They started a revolution (1893) and called on the United States for protection. At a critical moment the American minister, John L. Stevens, an ardent annexationist, ordered 160 marines from a warship in Honolulu harbor to go ashore to aid the rebels. The queen yielded her authority, and a delegation representing the triumphant provisional government set out for Washington to negotiate a treaty of annexation. They found President Harrison highly receptive, but before the resulting treaty could be acted on by the Senate he was succeeded by Cleveland.

Cleveland had old-fashioned reservations about taking other people's property. Suspicious of what had happened in Hawaii, he withdrew the treaty and sent a special representative to the islands to investigate. When this agent reported that the American element and Stevens had engineered the revolution, Cleveland endeavored to restore the queen to her throne. But the Americans were in control of the kingdom and refused to budge. Reluctantly the President had to accord recognition to their government as representing the "republic" of Hawaii. Cleveland, however, had only delayed the inevitable. In 1898, with the Republicans again in power, Hawaii was annexed by joint resolution of both houses of Congress.

Controversy over Cuba

Not all the territory falling to the rising imperialist republic was obtained by annexation agreements with native rulers. A substantial area was wrenched from Spain by war in 1898.

The immediate background of the Spanish-American War lay in the Caribbean island of Cuba, which with nearby Puerto Rico comprised nearly all that was left of Spain's once extensive Latin American empire. The Cubans had long resented Spanish rule and several times had tried unsuccessfully to throw it off. In 1895 they rose again in revolt.

This revolution immediately took on aspects of ferocity that shocked Americans. Determined to repress the insurrection, the Spanish resorted to extreme methods of coercion. General Valeriano Weyler — or "Butcher" Weyler, as he soon came to be known in the American press — in an effort to stamp out the Cuban guerrilla forces, ordered the entire civilian population in certain areas confined to hastily prepared concentration camps, where they died by the thousands, victims of disease and malnutrition.

The Cuban revolt came when Joseph Pulitzer with his New York *World* and William Randolph Hearst with his New York *Journal* were revolutionizing American journalism. This new "yellow press" specialized in lurid and sensational news; when such news did not exist, editors were not above creating it. Both Hearst and Pulitzer sent batteries of reporters and illustrators to Cuba with orders to provide accounts of Spanish atrocities. "You furnish the pictures," Hearst supposedly told a too scrupulous artist, "and I'll furnish the war."

The mounting storm of indignation against

Spain left President Cleveland unmoved. Convinced that both sides in Cuba were guilty of atrocities and that the United States had no interests justifying involvement in the struggle, he issued a proclamation of neutrality.

When McKinley took over the Presidency in 1897, he protested to Spain against its "uncivilized and inhuman" conduct. The Spanish government, alarmed that McKinley's course might forebode American intervention in Cuba, recalled Weyler, modified the concentration policy, and took steps to grant the island qualified autonomy. At the end of 1897, with the insurrection losing ground, it seemed that war might be averted.

If there had been any chance of a peaceful settlement, it was extinguished in February 1898 by the news that the battleship *Maine* had been blown up in Havana harbor with a loss of over 260 lives. This vessel had been ordered to Cuban waters in January to protect American lives and property against possible attacks by Spanish loyalists. Many Americans jumped to the conclusion that the Spanish had sunk the ship — "an act of dirty treachery," Theodore Roosevelt announced. (The source of the explosion has never been established, however.) As war hysteria swept the country, Congress unanimously appropriated $50,000,000 for military preparations. "Remember the *Maine*" became a national chant for revenge.

After the *Maine* episode there was little chance that the government could keep the people from war. In March 1898 McKinley asked Spain to agree to an armistice, with negotiations for a permanent peace to follow, and an immediate ending of the concentration system. After a slight delay, Spain essentially accepted the American demands on April 9. Two days later McKinley asked Congress for authority to use military force to end the hostilities in Cuba — in short, for a declaration of war. After reviewing the reasons that impelled him to recommend war ("in the name of humanity, in the name of civilization, in behalf of endangered American interests") he mentioned only casually, at the end of the message, that Spain had capitulated to his requests. By huge majorities Congress passed a joint resolution declaring Cuba free and authorizing the President to employ force to expel the Spanish from the island.

The "Splendid Little War"

To many Americans, the Spanish-American War was, in the words of John Hay, McKinley's secretary of state and Roosevelt's close friend, "a splendid little war." It was the last small, short, individualistic war before the huge, protracted, impersonal struggles of the twentieth century. Declared in April, it was over by August. Newspaper readers easily and eagerly followed the campaigns and the heroic exploits of American soldiers and sailors. Only 460 Americans were killed in battle or died of wounds, but some 5,200 perished of disease: malaria, dysentery, typhoid, and other ills.

Blithely and confidently the United States embarked on a war it was not prepared to fight. The regular army, numbering only 28,000 troops and officers scattered around the country at various posts, was a tough little force, skilled at quelling Indian outbreaks, but with no experience in anything resembling large-scale war. Hastily Congress directed the President to increase the army to 62,000 and to call for 125,000 volunteers. It was expected that the National Guard, the state militia, would furnish the bulk of the volunteers.

The Spanish Army numbered almost 130,000 troops, of whom 80,000 were already in Cuba at the beginning of the war. Despite its imposing size, it was not an efficient army; its commanders seemed to be paralyzed by a conviction of certain defeat. The American Navy, fifth largest in the world, was far superior to the Spanish in ships, gunnery, and personnel.

No agency in the American military system was charged with strategic planning, and on the eve of the war only the navy had worked out an objective. The commander of the Asiatic Squadron, Commodore George Dewey, had received instructions that when war came, he was to attack the Spanish fleet in the Philippines. Immediately after war was declared, Dewey left the China coast and headed for Manila, where a venerable Spanish fleet was stationed. He destroyed the enemy with no damage to his ships. But the Spanish still held Manila City, and Dewey could not dislodge them. While he waited, the government assembled an expeditionary force to relieve him. The Americans, aided by native insurgents, were soon able to take Manila. The American leaders who gave Dewey his orders may have meant only to strike a blow at Spanish power. But whatever the case, the war was now becoming a struggle for colonies.

While the navy was monopolizing the first phases of the war, the War Department was trying to mobilize and train an army. The entire mobilization process was conducted with remarkable inefficiency. There were appalling shortages of arms, ammunition, food, clothing, and medical supplies.

The army's commanding general, Nelson A. Miles, a veteran of the Civil War, had planned to train the troops until autumn, then to occupy Puerto Rico and in conjunction with the Cuban rebels attack Havana. But with a Spanish naval force at Santiago, plans were hastily changed. It was decided to send General William R. Shafter with his force of 17,000 regulars to take Santiago.

Once landed, Shafter moved his army toward Santiago, planning to surround and capture it. On the way he fought and defeated the Spaniards at two battles, El Caney and San Juan Hill. Shafter was now before Santiago, but his army was so weakened by sickness that he feared he might have to abandon his position. When he besought the navy to unite with him in a joint attack on the city, he received the answer that mines in the harbor made it too dangerous.

At this point disaster seemingly confronted the Americans, but unknown to them the Spanish government had decided that Santiago was lost. On July 3 the Spanish fleet broke from the harbor to attempt an escape; the waiting American squadron destroyed the entire fleet. Shafter then pressed the Spanish Army commander to surrender, and that official, after bargaining Shafter into generous terms, including free transportation back to Spain for his troops, turned over Santiago on July 16. While the Santiago campaign was in its last stages, an American army landed in Puerto Rico and occupied it against virtually no opposition.

Through the medium of the French ambassador in Washington Spain asked for peace, and on August 12 an armistice ended the war.

Decision for Imperialism

In agreeing to a preliminary peace, the United States had laid down terms on which a permanent settlement must be based: Spain was to relinquish Cuba, cede Puerto Rico to the United States, cede also to the victor an island in the Ladrones, midway between Hawaii and the Philippines (this turned out to be Guam), and permit the Americans to hold Manila pending the final disposition of the Philippines.

In October 1898 commissioners from the United States and Spain met at Paris, France, to determine a permanent peace. With little protest Spain agreed to recognize Cuba's independence, to assume the Cuban debt, and to cede Puerto Rico and Guam to the victor. Then the American commissioners, acting under instructions from McKinley, startled the conference by demanding the cession of all the Philippines. Stubbornly the Spanish resisted the American demand, although they realized they could retain the islands only by resuming the war. They yielded to the inevitable when the United States offered payment of $20,-000,000. The Treaty of Paris was signed on December 10, 1898, and was sent to the United States for ratification by the Senate.

When the treaty was submitted to the Senate, it encountered immediate and fierce criticism and occasioned in that body and throughout the country one of those "great debates" that frequently precede a departure in American foreign policy. The chief point at issue was the acquisition of the Philippines, denounced by many, including prominent Republicans, as a repudiation of America's high moral position in the war and a shameful occupation of a land that wanted to be free. Favoring ratification were the imperialists, the big navy lobby, Protestant clergy who saw in a colonial empire enlarged fields for missionary enterprise, and most Republicans. Business, which had opposed the war, swung over to support the treaty, converted by the notion that possession of the Philippines would enable American interests to dominate the Oriental trade. Among the forces opposing the treaty were old-fashioned Americans who objected to their country's annexing other people's land against their will, traditionalists who feared that a colonial empire would necessitate large armaments and foreign alliances, a majority of the intellectuals, economic interests like the sugar growers who foresaw colonial competition, and most Democrats.

After weeks of bitter wrangling, the treaty was ratified February 6, 1899, but only because it re-

ceived an unexpected assist from William Jennings Bryan, who expected to be his party's candidate in the election of 1900. He persuaded a number of Democratic senators to vote for ratification. It has been charged that he was looking for a campaign issue, and in his defense it has been said that he thought the question of the Philippines should be decided by a national referendum: if the Democrats won in 1900 they would free the islands.

Bryan was the Democratic standard bearer in 1900, running against McKinley again. The principal issue was imperialism, and Bryan went down to a crushing defeat. The Republicans claimed, with some justification, that the result constituted a mandate for imperialism.

The Colonial Empire

The new colonial empire was extensive enough to warm the heart of the most ardent imperialist. Stretching from the Caribbean to the far reaches of the Pacific, it embraced Puerto Rico, Alaska, Hawaii, a part of Samoa, Guam, the Philippines, and a chain of minor Pacific islands.

Immediately, the nation faced the problem of how to govern its dependencies. Three of the dependencies, Hawaii, Alaska, and Puerto Rico, were given territorial status as quickly as Congress considered them ready for it. For Hawaii, with its large American population and close economic ties with the United States, a basis for government was provided by an act of 1900. This measure granted American citizenship to all persons who were citizens of the Hawaiian republic, authorized an elective two-house legislature, and vested executive authority in a governor appointed from Washington. By the terms of an act of 1884 Alaska was governed by appointed civil officials. The discovery of gold in 1896 caused the first substantial influx of Americans, and in 1912 Alaska received territorial status and a legislature, and its inhabitants were given the rights of citizenship. Because Puerto Rico's population readily accepted American rule, military occupation of the island was ended in 1900, and civil government was established by the Foraker Act. The governor and upper house of the legislature were to be appointed from Washington, while only the lower house was to be elected. The act did not declare the Puerto Ricans to be American citizens, this privilege being deferred until 1917.

American military forces remained in Cuba until 1902. The occupation was protracted to enable American administrators to prepare the island for the independence promised in the peace treaty of 1898. The vigorous occupiers built roads, schools, and hospitals, reorganized the legal, financial, and administrative systems, and introduced far-reaching sanitary reforms.

Then a convention assembled to draft a constitution for independent Cuba. To the disappointment of the American government, the document contained no provisions concerning relations with the nation responsible for Cuba's freedom. The United States was quite willing to relinquish Cuba, but, with its expanding interests in the Caribbean, it expected to exercise some kind of control over the island republic. The nature of this control was spelled out by Congress in 1901 in the Platt Amendment, a rider to an army appropriation bill, which Cuba was pressured into incorporating in its constitution. The Platt Amendment stated that Cuba should never impair its independence by treaty with a foreign power (this was equivalent to giving the United States a veto over Cuba's diplomatic policy), that the United States had the right to intervene in Cuba to preserve its independence and life and property, and that Cuba must sell or lease to the United States property for naval stations. The amendment left Cuba only nominally independent. It was in fact, if not in name, an American appendage.

Alone among the possessions in the imperial system, the Philippines offered resistance to American rule. The Filipinos, rebellious against Spain before 1898, had hailed Dewey and the expeditionary force sent to Manila as their deliverers from tyranny, but they soon realized that American altruism for a free Cuba did not include them. When the hard fact sank in that the Americans had come to stay, the Filipinos resolved to expel the new invaders. In 1899 they resorted to war (by the American definition, rebellion) and, ably led by Emilio Aguinaldo, they fought the army of occupation from island to island until 1901. In the end the Americans repressed the up-

rising but only after employing methods unpleasantly reminiscent of Weyler's tenure in Cuba, including the use of concentration camps. Civil government began taking over from the military in 1901, and the Filipinos, with great adaptability, began the process of adjusting to American culture. Thus they started on the long road that would lead, in 1946, to the independence that they so ardently desired.

The Open Door

The acquisition of the Philippines made the United States an Asian power, necessarily interested in anything that happened in the area and particularly in its largest nation, China. At the same time other nations were casting covetous eyes on China. By the turn of the century the great European imperialistic powers — England, France, Germany and Russia — and one Asian power, Japan, were beginning to partition China into "spheres of influence." The process, if continued, threatened to destroy American trade with China.

The situation posed a delicate problem for those directing American foreign policy. Knowing that public opinion would not support any use of force, they had to find a way to protect American interests in China without risking war. McKinley's secretary of state, John Hay, attempted an audacious solution. In September 1899 he addressed identical notes to England, Germany, and Russia, and later to France, Japan, and Italy, asking them to approve a formula that became known as the "Open Door." It embodied three principles: (1) each nation with a sphere of influence was to respect the rights and privileges of other nations in its sphere; (2) Chinese officials were to continue to collect tariff duties in all spheres (the existing tariff favored the United States); and (3) each nation with a sphere was not to discriminate against other nations in levying port dues and railroad rates.

The nations addressed replied that they accepted the idea of the Open Door but could make no commitment to support it. Although the American public applauded his diplomacy, Hay had won little more than a theoretical victory. The United States could not prevent any nation that wanted to violate the Open Door from doing so — unless it was willing to resort to war.

T. R. and World Politics

In addition to upholding the pledge of the Monroe Doctrine, the American government felt an urge to support the economic activities of its citizens abroad, and it believed it had to maintain control of its colonies, including the distant Philippines. Not all Americans understood that the recent commitments might necessitate a change in the time-honored policy of diplomatic isolation. One American who did understand the necessity was Theodore Roosevelt, who played an even more active role in foreign affairs than in domestic policy.

Roosevelt's concept of the role of the United States in world politics emphasized sea power. Now that the United States had colonies, it needed to build a navy powerful enough to keep the sea lanes open to them. It also needed to build an Isthmian canal so that naval units could sail quickly from one ocean to another. In addition it needed to protect the Caribbean approaches to the canal from encroachment. All this predicated a strong naval policy at a time when the key to strength in the world was a powerful fleet. This meant a navy second only to that of Great Britain.

At the same time Kaiser Wilhelm's Germany was launching upon a gigantic naval race with Great Britain. The German fleet laws of 1898 and 1900 committed Germany too to a navy second only to England's and set forth plans for one that could even challenge England. As Britain in 1905 picked up the gauntlet by beginning construction on the first dreadnought (a giant battleship), both Germany and the United States embarked upon an intensive naval race, amidst increasing alarms of war.

Under the strong urging of President Roosevelt, who was himself the most effective of naval lobbyists, Congress between 1902 and 1905 voted for ten battleships and four armored cruisers. These were far stronger than the relatively light vessels of the nineties; they were no longer being built primarily to defend the American coastline. By 1906 the American Navy was second only to the British but in the next few years was surpassed by the German.

The Asian Balance

In the Far East Roosevelt thought that it was vital to the Open Door policy to block Russian expansion in Manchuria. Therefore he encouraged Japan to oppose the Russian drive. When the Japanese made a surprise attack upon the Russian fleet at Port Arthur, Manchuria, in 1904, he warned the French and Germans against aiding Russia. Nonetheless, he did not wish to see the Japanese totally victorious, since this might "possibly mean a struggle between them and us in the future."

The Japanese, however, even after winning a series of spectacular victories, faced such serious financial difficulties that they asked Roosevelt to mediate. He agreed and called a peace conference at Portsmouth, New Hampshire, in the summer of 1905. But Roosevelt lost Japan's good will by opposing its demand for an enormous indemnity, even though he approved the territorial gains.

Japanese-American relations, thus suddenly made worse, were improved somewhat by a secret Japanese-American agreement effected at the time of the Portsmouth conference. President Roosevelt had dispatched Secretary of War Taft from Manila to Tokyo to reach a Far Eastern understanding with the Japanese. In the resulting Taft-Katsura executive agreement of July 1905, the Japanese acknowledged American sovereignty in the Philippines, and the United States recognized the suzerainty of Japan over Korea.

Shortly another issue fanned anger between the United States and Japan. In 1906 the San Francisco school board ordered the segregation of Oriental schoolchildren. This step was taken in response to the feelings of Californians against the 500 to 1,000 Japanese immigrants coming in each year, feelings that were intensified by lurid "Yellow Peril" articles in the Hearst and other newspapers. Resentment in Japan flared and patriots in each country fanned the flames still higher.

Roosevelt worked skillfully to douse the flames. He persuaded San Francisco to desegregate its schools, and in return in 1907 he negotiated a "gentlemen's agreement" with Japan to keep out agricultural laborers. Then, lest the Japanese government think he had acted through fear, he launched a spectacular naval demonstration. He sent sixteen battleships of the new navy, "the Great White Fleet," on an unprecedented 45,-000-mile voyage around the world. It gave the navy invaluable experience in sailing in formation while demonstrating the danger of dependence on foreign-owned coaling stations. Most important, the Japanese invited this formidable armada to visit Yokohama and gave it a clamorous welcome. Thus Roosevelt felt that through brandishing the big stick he had helped the cause of peace.

For the moment, the United States had demonstrated sufficient naval strength to restore an unsteady balance in Asian waters. In 1908, before the fleet had returned home, Japan and the United States negotiated the comprehensive Root-Takahira Agreement. Both countries agreed to support the Open Door in China. The United States tacitly seemed to give Japan a free hand in Manchuria (where rivalry with Russia continued) in return for an explicit guarantee of the status quo in the Pacific.

The Panama Canal

Roosevelt's preoccupation with the American strategy of defense in the Caribbean led him to start work on a canal in Panama. There were two possible routes. The shortest one would be across the Isthmus of Panama, but the rights there were owned by a French company, the successor of an earlier company that had tried and failed to dig a canal. The French company wanted $109,000,000 for its franchise, which would make a Panama canal more expensive than a Nicaraguan one. Consequently a commission, Congress, and President Roosevelt all favored the Nicaraguan route. But the French company had expert agents in Philippe Bunau-Varilla, its chief engineer, and William Nelson Cromwell, an attorney who had contributed heavily to the Republican campaign fund in 1900. Hastily they cut the price of their rights to $40,000,000; unless sold to the United States and sold quickly, the rights would be worthless, for they would expire in 1904. This price cut — and able lobbying — caused Con-

gress and the President to change their minds.

Impatient to begin digging the canal, Roosevelt put pressure upon Colombia, which owned Panama, to conclude a treaty authorizing the United States to dig a canal. In 1903 Secretary of State Hay signed one with the Colombian chargé d'affaires Tomás Herrán, which was most unfavorable to Colombia. It authorized the United States to construct a canal in return for a payment of only $10,000,000 and an annual rental of $250,000. The Colombian Senate rejected the treaty.

Roosevelt was furious. Fuming that the Colombians were "inefficient bandits," he considered seizing Panama through twisting a technicality in an 1846 treaty with Colombia (then New Granada) guaranteeing the neutrality and free transit of the Isthmus. Roosevelt's intended seizure became unnecessary, because Bunau-Varilla helped organize a Panamanian revolution. At its outset, the United States landed troops from the U.S.S. *Nashville,* and, invoking the 1846 treaty obligation to maintain order, prevented Colombian troops from putting down the revolution. Three days later the United States recognized the new republic of Panama and, soon after that, negotiated a treaty paying Panama the sum Colombia had rejected, in return for the grant of a zone ten miles wide. The minister from Panama who arranged the treaty was Bunau-Varilla.

Work on the canal proceeded smoothly and efficiently. The elimination of tropical diseases in the area, the digging of the tremendous cuts, and the installation of huge locks at a total cost of $375,000,000 filled Americans with patriotic enthusiasm. The achievements demonstrated that the United States, like other imperial nations, could undertake enormous projects in the tropics. The canal opened in 1914.

The "Roosevelt Corollary"

Meanwhile, in 1902 and 1903, Roosevelt had to deal with an apparent German grab at Venezuela. That country had not honored its debt to a group of German, English, and Italian bankers, and Germany responded by blockading and bombarding Venezuela's principal port. Roosevelt, fearing that the German intervention might lead to establishment of a naval base, warned the German ambassador that the United States would use force if Germany tried to acquire territory anywhere in the area.

The Germans, wishing to avoid an incident, quickly agreed to arbitration. The episode seemed, nevertheless, to confirm American fears that the Germans were scheming to get a foothold in the Caribbean. There was, in particular, a persistent fear that the Germans might try to acquire the Danish West Indies. In 1902 the Senate ratified a treaty for their purchase, but the Danish parliament rejected it. Finally in 1917 the United States acquired the poverty-stricken islets, which were then renamed the Virgin Islands, for an exorbitant $25,000,000.

The Venezuela incident led to a new Caribbean policy usually called the "Roosevelt corollary" to the Monroe Doctrine. Roosevelt declared that if the Latin American nations could not meet their obligations to outside creditors, the United States reluctantly would police them and collect debt payments from them in order to forestall European intervention. In effect, Uncle Sam would act as a bill collector for European bankers. Roosevelt declared to the Congress in 1904 that the United States might be forced "however reluctantly, in flagrant cases of . . . wrongdoing or impotence, to the exercise of an international police power."

As a part of an American strategy of defense, Roosevelt's Caribbean policy was doubtless successful. As a means of securing the support and cooperation of nations to the south, it left much to be desired. Roosevelt's tactics inspired fear rather than friendship.

Taft and Dollar Diplomacy

President Taft was neither so vigorous nor so able as Roosevelt in exercising leadership in foreign affairs. He and his secretary of state, Philander C. Knox, made no real effort to maintain a balance of power in Europe or Asia. Rather, they promoted expansion of American business and banking activities to enhance American political power overseas. This policy became known as "dollar diplomacy."

In the Caribbean, dollar diplomacy resulted in a series of interventions, going far beyond Roose-

velt's limited ones, to establish firm military and political control over several unstable republics to the south. Advocates of this program argued that American investors must be invited in to replace European investors, who otherwise might in time bring about European intervention. A perhaps inevitable step had been taken beyond the Roosevelt corollary.

With the active support of the government, American bankers acquired holdings in Honduras, Haiti, and other countries. The government even sent marines to Nicaragua to protect revolutionaries, sponsored by an American mining company, who were fighting to overthrow a hostile dictator. Secretary Knox negotiated a treaty with the new friendly government giving the United States financial control, but the United States Senate failed to approve it. However, American bankers accepted Knox's invitation to move in. By 1912 the new pro-American government was so unpopular that revolution broke out. Taft sent marines to crush the uprising, and some of them remained as late as 1925.

Wilsonian Intervention

President Wilson brought to the determination of foreign policy a flair for idealistic pronouncements. He was never unsure of his moral position but was often uncertain how to reach it. He disapproved of the crasser aspects of dollar diplomacy, but at the same time he felt an urge to use American force to uplift the nations to the south. He also convinced himself that an American-sponsored stability in the Caribbean was vital to national defense.

The Wilson administration not only regularized through treaty the continuing occupation of Nicaragua but also initiated new interventions in Santo Domingo and Haiti. In spite of American customs control, revolution after revolution had swept through and impoverished Santo Domingo. The United States took over all Dominican finances and the police force, but the Dominicans would not agree to a treaty establishing a virtual protectorate. In 1916 Wilson established a military government. During the eight years that it continued, the United States forcibly maintained order, trained a native constabulary, and promoted education, sanitation, and public works.

On the other end of the island of Hispaniola, the black republic of Haiti was even more revolution-wracked. Wilson again sent in the marines, established another military government, and began the task of improving living conditions in Haiti. The marines demonstrated their efficiency in 1918 when they supervised an election to ratify a new American-sponsored constitution.

Making Mexico Behave

American business interests had invested about $1 billion in Mexico during the regime of a friendly dictator, Porfirio Díaz. They owned over half the oil, two-thirds of the railroads, and three-fourths of the mines and smelters. Popular though Díaz was in the United States, he came to be hated in Mexico because, while he encouraged foreigners to amass huge profits, he suppressed civil liberties and kept the masses in peonage. In 1910 the aged Díaz was overthrown by a democratic reform leader, who in turn was murdered and succeeded by the reactionary Victoriano Huerta just before Wilson took office. Wilson turned a deaf ear to American investors who saw in Huerta's presidency an opportunity to return to the "good old days." Rather, he refused to recognize "the government of butchers."

Wilson hoped that, by refusing recognition to Huerta's government, he could bring about its collapse and the development of constitutionalism in Mexico. He offered to mediate between Huerta and the opposing Constitutionalists of Venustiano Carranza, but both sides refused.

Wilson was in a dilemma: he might have to choose between recognizing Huerta, stronger than ever, or intervening with armed force, which could mean war against all the Mexican factions. An unforeseen incident gave Wilson a way out. The commander of one of the American naval vessels hovering off the coast of Mexico gave some of his men permission to go ashore at Tampico. One of Huerta's officers promptly arrested them; a superior officer quickly released them and apologized. But the American admiral demanded in addition a twenty-one-gun salute to the United States flag. At this Huerta balked. Wilson, decid-

ing to back the admiral, sent all available warships to Mexican waters, and asked Congress for authority to take drastic action. But before Congress could act, Wilson ordered the navy to seize Vera Cruz. It did so, but not in the bloodless way that Wilson had anticipated. Both sides sustained substantial casualties.

At this difficult point, Argentina, Brazil, and Chile offered to mediate. With relief, Wilson accepted, and sent his delegates to confer with Huerta's at Niagara Falls, Canada. As the negotiations went on and on, the Carranzists advanced on Mexico City, finally bringing the result Wilson wished, the abdication of Huerta.

Under Carranza's presidency, the Mexican muddle became worse. By 1914 civil war was again devastating Mexico, as a former general of Carranza's, Francisco ("Pancho") Villa, tried to overthrow him. In 1915 the United States gave de facto recognition to Carranza's government.

This antagonized Villa, who was still roaming northern Mexico. He tried to bring about a war between the United States and Mexico by shooting sixteen Americans he seized from a train. When that failed he raided Columbus, New Mexico, just across the border, killing nineteen more Americans. Wilson retaliated by ordering a punitive expedition under Brigadier General John J. Pershing to hunt down Villa. Wilson tried not to offend Carranza, but as Villa drew the American forces 300 miles into Mexico, two skirmishes occurred with Mexican troops that almost led to a war. In 1916 Carranza suggested the appointment of a Joint High Commission to consider the problem. After long debate the commission broke up without establishing a basis for the withdrawal of American troops. By then the United States was so close to war with Germany that it nevertheless withdrew the troops and in 1917 gave de jure recognition to Carranza's government.

War in Europe

In Europe, most of the nations, big and small, had become aligned in two potentially hostile diplomatic blocs. On one side was the Entente, led by England, France, and Russia; on the other was the Central Alliance, represented by Germany and Austria-Hungary. Economic and power rivalries between the two blocs exploded into war in the summer of 1914 following the assassination of an Austrian archduke by a young man of Serbian ancestry. The conflict eventually involved so many nations that it became known as the World War.

Bewildered Americans congratulated themselves that at least the explosion could not extend to their shores; the New World was still secure. A minority of Americans, mainly those of German descent, sympathized with the Central Powers. But the great majority, bound by cultural or sentimental ties to England and France, sympathized with the Entente nations, now known as the Allies. They were pro-Allies without being at all sure what the war was about. None of them in August 1914 envisaged American entrance into the war.

Neutral Trade and Neutral Rights

At the outbreak of the war Wilson issued a proclamation of neutrality in which he asked the American people to be impartial even in their thinking. But it soon became evident that there were problems involved in being a neutral. As a maritime nation, the United States was in a position to take over the carrying trade of the nations at war. These nations, however, were not disposed to permit neutral trade with the enemy. Great Britain particularly, the greatest naval power in the world, was determined to wage economic warfare against Germany. The British established a naval blockade of Germany and stopped and searched American ships for "contraband" goods that might aid the enemy. Wilson protested these acts but not too vigorously because of American sympathy for Britain and its allies.

On the whole, the British blockade proved to be no economic handicap for the United States, since by early 1915 heavy war orders were arriving from Britain and France. While trade with the Central Powers almost came to an end, that with the Allies jumped between 1914 and 1916 from $824,000,000 to $3,214,000,000 — a staggering figure for that time. In March 1915 the

government relaxed its regulations so as to allow the Allies to float huge loans in the United States for financing their purchases. In effect the United States, embarking upon the greatest boom in its history, was becoming the great banker and arsenal for the Allies.

This the Germans could not permit. During the first weeks of the war they imposed no blockades but concentrated upon trying to win a decision in France. The German armies drove deep but were halted short of Paris in the Battle of the Marne in September 1914. Although on the Russian front great armies continued to move back and forth for several years, in the west the war turned into the grinding attrition of trench combat along lines extending from the North Sea to Switzerland. As a relative stalemate developed along the western front, Germany turned toward the relatively new weapon of the submarine as a possible means of breaking the British blockade. Submarines had the advantage of surprise but were so vulnerable to attack by an armed ship that they could scarcely follow the accepted rules of international law. These rules called for visit and search of enemy merchant ships and allowed sinking only if provision were made for the safety of passengers and crew. The sinking of merchant vessels without warning seemed to Americans to add a new and frightful dimension to warfare.

Beginning in 1915, this was what Germany set out to do. It announced that it would sink enemy vessels in a broad zone around the British Isles. This policy, the Germans explained, was in retaliation for the British food blockade, which they claimed would starve women and children in Germany. President Wilson declared on February 10 that he would hold Germany to "strict accountability" for unlawful acts.

A serious crisis developed when a submarine fired a torpedo without warning into the Cunard liner *Lusitania*. The ship went down in eighteen minutes, drowning 1,198 people, among them 128 Americans.

Shortly before, the Germans had launched against the Allied lines at Ypres a new weapon of frightfulness, poison gas. On May 13 American newspapers carried lengthy excerpts from an official British report on almost unprintable alleged German atrocities in Belgium. This report contained fabrications, yet few Americans questioned its authenticity, for by this time most people were ready to believe almost anything against Germany. Even in their revulsion, however, they were not ready to fight.

Wilson came close to the point of coercion over the *Lusitania* incident, in an exchange of notes with Germany. In his first note he virtually demanded that Germany end its submarine blockade. When the Germans sent an argumentative reply, he drafted a still stronger second note. Apparently Wilson was ready to risk war rather than surrender to Germany what he considered to be American maritime rights, even though he had said: "There is such a thing as a man being too proud to fight."

New trouble developed in the early months of 1916 when the Allies began arming merchant vessels and ordering them to attack submarines. Germany gave notice that it would sink them without warning. Wilson reiterated his doctrine of "strict accountability," and when the channel steamer *Sussex* was torpedoed, he threatened to break off diplomatic relations if Germany did not abandon its unrestricted submarine campaign. He made the threat at a time when Germany still lacked sufficient submarines to maintain a tight blockade and did not wish to bring the United States into the war. Consequently the German Foreign Office pledged that submarine commanders would observe rules of visit and search. The President had won a diplomatic victory, and relations with Germany became less tense during the eight months that followed.

The Preparedness Program

With the outbreak of war, the leaders of the military establishment and civilian advocates of a larger military machine began to advocate a preparedness program. Leading the agitation were "big navy" advocates, who declared that despite its expansion in the T. R. era the navy was not strong enough to take on a first-rate foe.

The army was much less ready than the navy to fight a major war. The establishment of the General Staff and other administrative reforms had come into effect in the Roosevelt administration,

but the older officers were still antagonistic toward such changes. The quartermaster corps in 1913 was thinking about using trucks but as yet not seriously testing them. The air force, consisting of seventeen planes, was part of the signal corps; its 1913 appropriation was $125,000. The army numbered less than 80,000; a large part of this force was required to maintain the posts within the United States. The National Guard was somewhat larger, but was scarcely professional.

President Wilson opposed new armaments, and so did public opinion, until the crisis over submarine sinkings frightened the nation into preparedness. In November 1915 the President proposed a long-range program that by 1925 would give the United States a navy second to none and would reorganize the army and provide a reserve force of 400,000 soldiers. This proposal touched off a hot debate in Congress and throughout the country. Progressives in the House fought the program vigorously. Throughout the country, the pleas of peace organizations strongly appealed to farmers and workers. Wilson took the issue to the country in a series of speeches, but the House would not budge.

Wilson ultimately got part of what he wanted. Congress passed legislation providing for substantial increases in the army, the navy, and merchant shipping. The Merchant Marine Act of 1916 established the United States Shipping Board, which was empowered to own and operate vessels and regulate shipping.

Conservatives wished to finance the defense expenditures through bonds, but the administration proposed new, heavier taxes. Progressives denounced the tax proposals as falling too heavily upon the masses and in Congress fought through a tax measure frankly aimed at making the wealthy, whom they blamed for preparedness demands, pay the bill. The Revenue Act of 1916 levied heavy income and inheritance taxes upon the rich for the first time in American history.

In 1916 Democrats and Republicans fought the presidential campaign over the issue of foreign policy before a seriously divided people.

The Democrats renominated Wilson and adopted as their slogan "He kept us out of war." They went into the campaign in a strong position.

Many of the ex-Bull Moosers, Republican farmers in the Midwest, and workers who had once voted for a full dinner pail now favored the Democrats. They did so because of Wilson's progressive domestic policy but still more because of their hope that the President could continue to keep the country out of the war.

As for the Republicans, they persuaded Charles Evans Hughes, who had an impeccable progressive record, to resign from the Supreme Court and accept the nomination. Primarily because of the whooping of Roosevelt and others on the sidelines, the Republicans gradually began to look like the war party, and Hughes was made to seem like a war candidate.

The people's wish to keep out of war was disclosed in the election returns. Wilson received 3,-000,000 more popular votes than he had in 1912, although his electoral majority was narrow. The Democrats also retained a thin majority in Congress.

Leading the People to War

So far as elections can be regarded as national plebiscites, Wilson had received a narrow mandate to continue along the path of progressivism and peace. Undoubtedly he intended to follow such a course.

Even before the war began, he had tried to bring an end to the armaments race. Since the outbreak of the war he had repeatedly sought means to bring the warring nations into a peace conference. But both sides had invested too heavily in the conflict and were still too hopeful of realizing gain upon their investment to talk of a negotiated peace.

Immediately after the election, Wilson renewed negotiations looking toward a settlement. The Germans, successful on the eastern front, for a while appeared to be receptive. But the top German generals did not want any conference because they believed they could win a decisive victory. Early in 1917 Wilson spread his plan before the Senate, calling for a lasting peace that the American people would help maintain through a league of nations. It would be a peace with freedom of the seas, disarmament, national self-determination for subject peoples, and equality among nations. "Peace among equals" — a lasting peace — could come only through "peace without victory."

But the military leaders of Germany had decided upon one final cast of the iron dice. They had resolved to return to unrestricted submarine warfare even though it would bring the United States into the war. They hoped that they could crush France on land and starve Britain from the sea before America could make its weight felt. Consequently Germany announced that, beginning the following, day, submarines would sink all ships, enemy or neutral, in a broad zone around the British Isles.

President Wilson now faced a dilemma of his own making. Earlier he had issued what amounted to an ultimatum to Germany — the demand that American citizens and vessels had the right to travel on the high seas in time of war — and he had threatened Germany with war if it should disregard the demand. He now had to take the step made inevitable by his policy. He broke off diplomatic relations with Germany, knowing this was probably a prelude to hostilities.

Events now carried Wilson and the country rapidly toward war. The British turned over to the American government an intercepted note from the German foreign secretary, Arthur Zimmerman, proposing that in the event of war, Mexico should attack the United States and receive in return its lost provinces north of the border. Americans were infuriated. At about the same time, the Russian Revolution eliminated one of the moral problems in Wilson's mind by replacing a despotism among the Allies with a constitutional monarchy. (This government lasted only until November 1917 when Lenin and the Communists came into power.) It seemed increasingly clear to Wilson — despite the horrors and losses of war and the way in which it would bring brutality even at home and damage progressive reforms — that American participation would be worthwhile. He had faith that at the conference table the United States could bring about a just and lasting peace.

In 1917 news came that submarines had torpedoed three American ships. Thereupon the cabinet unanimously advised the President to ask Congress for a declaration of war.

On the evening of April 2, 1917, President Wilson delivered his war message to Congress. After enumerating the German transgressions of American neutral rights, he declared: "It is a fearful thing to lead this great peaceful people into war, into the most terrible . . . of all wars. . . . But the right is more precious than peace, and we shall fight for the things which we have always carried nearest our hearts — for democracy, . . . for the rights and liberties of small nations, for a universal dominion of right by such a concert of free peoples as shall bring peace and safety to all nations and make the world itself at last free."

Four days later, Congress passed the war declaration and the President signed it. The American people had yet to learn what this would entail and to realize the broad aims for which they were struggling.

Selected Readings

The Industrial Revolution in America has received detailed attention from historians. A survey is found in W. E. Brownlee, *Dynamics of Ascent: A History of the American Economy* (1979). An account of big business is Alfred D. Chandler, Jr., *The Visible Hand: The Managerial Revolution in American Business*° (1977).

There are several textbook treatments of the West, including R. A. Billington, *Westward Expansion* (1960). A classic regional study is W. P. Webb, *The Great Plains* (1931). On Indians, see Dee A. Brown, *Bury My Heart at Wounded Knee: An Indian History of the American West*° (1971).

On the women's movement see Eleanor Flexner, *Century of Struggle: The Woman's Rights Movement*° (1959); Aileen Kraditor, *The Ideas of the Woman Suffrage Movement, 1880–1920*° (1965); and Ellen C. Dubois, *Feminism and Suffrage: The Emergence of an Independent Women's Movement in America, 1848–1869*° (1978).

Politics in the years following the Civil War is treated in a variety of works. The movement for civil service receives attention in Ari Hogenboom, *Outlawing the Spoils* (1961). On the money issue see Irwin Unger, *The Greenback Era* (1964), and W. T. K. Nugent, *Money and American Society* (1968).

Politics in the age of protest is analyzed in H. U. Faulkner, *Politics, Reform and Expansion*° (1959), and Richard Hofstadter, *The Age of Reform*° (1955). See also H. W. Morgan, *William McKinley and His America* (1963). A classic on the farm uprising is J. D. Hicks, *The Populist Revolt*° (1931). For the progressive period convenient surveys are G. E. Mowry, *The Era of Theodore Roosevelt, 1900–1912*° (1958); R. H. Wiebe, *The Search for Order, 1877–1920*° (1967); and O. L. Graham, Jr., *The Great Campaigns: Reform and War in America, 1900–1928*° (1971). A critical view of progressivism is registered in Gabriel Kolko, *The Triumph of Conservatism*° (1963). On the aspirations of blacks see August Meier, *Negro Thought in America, 1880–1915* (1968). On Wilson's first years in the presidency, go to A. S. Link, *The Road to the White House*° (1947), and *Woodrow Wilson and the Progressive Era, 1900–1917*° (1954); and J. M. Blum, *Woodrow Wilson and the Politics of Morality*° (1956).

On foreign policy and the imperialist urge, there are a number of good works, including E. R. May, *Imperial Democracy** (1961), and Walter LaFeber, *The New Empire** (1963). A vivid account of the war with Spain is Frank Freidel, *The Splendid Little War* (1958). On foreign policy and American entrance into the World War see G. F. Kennan, *American Diplomacy, 1900–1950** (1951); A. S. Link, *Woodrow Wilson: Revolution, War, and Peace** (1979), and *Wilson: The Struggle for Neutrality* (1968); Ernest May, *The World War and American Isolation* (1959).

---

* Titles available in paperback

Part Six
1917–1941

From Total War Through Depression

In a real sense America did not enter the twentieth century until 1917. Among the hallmarks of the twentieth century have been total war, economic calamity, and a vast expansion of centralized government. In contrast, the nineteenth century was far more an era of peace, economic stability, and diffused, weak governmental authority. The intervention of 1917 launched America into the mainstream of the twentieth century.

When Americans accepted the idealistic statement of war aims set down by Woodrow Wilson, they proceeded to build an enormous war machine commensurate with their moral obligation to the war effort. The creation and operation of more than 5,000 government war agencies involved an unprecedented amount of planning and regimentation in American life. Although most of these agencies were abandoned after the war, they showed that the federal government could meet a national emergency through a coordinated, centrally directed effort. This lesson would be remembered in the 1930s.

One government power tested by the mobilization effort was that of manipulating public opinion through propaganda. To win the full support of Americans for the war the Wilson administration persuaded newspaper and magazine editors to engage in voluntary self-censorship; disseminated tons of literature; and enlisted the services of 150,000 writers, lecturers, actors, and artists. Much of the message was idealistic, directly reflecting Wilson's own aims, but much appealed to fear and hate as well. A consequence of the propaganda and the insecurity of a public disturbed by war and social change was a campaign for 100 percent Americanism that sought to suppress dissent and deviant social behavior. The making of the peace at Versailles only enhanced American insecurity as it tragically brought into question Woodrow Wilson's assumption that world peace and stability would logically result from American participation in the war. An embittered public viewed with even more enthusiasm the national crusade for conformity that included not only the Red Scare of 1919 but enactment of prohibition and later the drastic restriction of immigration.

To find relief from Wilsonian idealism the American public turned to Warren G. Harding and elected him President in 1920. He said that "America's present need is not heroics, but healing; not nostrums, but normalcy" and thereby captured the electorate and provided a catch phrase for the period following World War I.

The 1920s were a time of remarkable prosperity and economic stability. The people generally assumed — and experts in business, economics, and government told them — that this was veritably a new era in human history. The country had reached a "permanent plateau" of prosperity and need never worry again about the possibility of a serious slump. But prosperity, like "normalcy," proved to be only temporary. Eventually the country fell into much the worst economic depression it had ever known.

During 1917 and 1918 the government of the United States, in order to win a war, had undertaken to control nearly all aspects of the economy. But never before the 1930s had the government intervened in so many ways to overcome a depression. Between 1933 and 1938, under the leadership of President Franklin D. Roosevelt, the government launched a bewildering variety of programs and set up a jumble of "alphabetical agencies" — AAA, NRA, TVA, and so on — to administer them. Some of these were intended to provide immediate relief for people facing a loss of income or property. Others were expected to stimulate economic activity and bring about recovery from the depression. Still others were designed to reform the economic system in order to reduce poverty and insecurity and avoid future depressions. Some of the programs served two or all three of these aims. All together, the series of measures constituted the New Deal.

The New Deal failed to bring about complete recovery; not until after 1941 did war, the greatest of public works, take up the slack in the employment of human and other resources. But the New Deal did produce a very rapid rate of recovery from the exceptionally depressed conditions of 1933. And the relief measures enabled both the people and the economic system to survive the depression; the reform measures made significant and enduring changes in the system itself. The role of government in economic life was vastly increased; the nation had become a welfare state. Henceforth the principle was to be generally accepted — though not always completely realized — that it was the government's duty to "provide for the general welfare" by controlling business and agriculture, maintaining full employment, and assuring at least a basic level of economic security to all members of society.

Having fought a war to end war and make the world safe for democracy, Americans of the 1920s were generally optimistic about the prospects whenever they gave thought to international affairs. Optimism faded after the depression struck. During the 1930s Japan under fanatical militarists, Germany under Hitler and the Nazis, and Italy under Mussolini and the Fascists each launched programs of domestic tyranny and foreign conquest. Opposed to these aggressive nations were Great Britain, France, and the Soviet Union, which disagreed on many things but had a common interest in maintaining the status quo.

The American government faced a choice between two broad lines of policy. On the one hand, the United States might back Great Britain, France, and the Soviet Union in the hope that all somehow could and would provide for their "collective security," prevent aggression, and maintain peace — though in this there was the real risk of hastening a general war. On the other hand, the United States might follow a policy of so-called isolation. That is, this country might strengthen its position in the Western Hemisphere and concentrate on keeping out of war instead of preventing it.

Most of the American people favored the second of these alternatives. They were preoccupied with the depression and were determined to set their own country to rights, regardless of what might go on in the rest of the world. They were disillusioned about their earlier effort to bring peace through war, and they were in no mood to go on a second crusade.

Ever regardful of public opinion, President Franklin D. Roosevelt hesitated to come out openly and clearly in favor of collective security even after the long-expected war had broken out in Europe in 1939. He continued to talk the language of isolationism, representing his policy as one of keeping out of war, while he committed the country to greater and greater support of Great Britain and its allies. The issues became more and more confused as the debate between "interventionists" and "isolationists" grew hotter. On December 7, 1941, the debate was stilled.

Chapter 20

The War to End War and Its Aftermath, 1917–1920

Mobilizing Labor and Resources

World War I was a total war. The nations that fought it had to mobilize their entire resources, human and material, to wage the struggle. As the United States had entered the conflict largely unprepared, it had to mobilize its resources hurriedly. It performed the task, sometimes clumsily but in the end with impressive results.

Both the President and the Congress realized that the mass armies required in this war could not be raised using only volunteers. Soon after war was declared, Congress enacted the Selective Service Act, which required that all males between the ages of eighteen and forty-five register for military service. Nearly 3,000,000 were inducted under the act. With the existing regular army and National Guard, the United States eventually had an army of 3,500,000 men, of whom 2,000,000 were sent overseas. (Blacks were drafted along with whites and for the second time, the Civil War being the first, blacks served in large numbers in an American conflict — but in segregated units.)

It was also necessary to mobilize the country's vast economic resources. Indeed, it was thought at first by the Allies that America's greatest contribution to the war effort would be in furnishing supplies. To accomplish the task, the War Industries Board was established by executive order. When it seemed unable to do the job, Wilson asked Congress to delegate to him almost unlimited power over the economy. Congress responded with the Overman Act, which authorized the board to fix priorities on raw materials, standardize products, and set prices. With Bernard Baruch, a shrewd Wall Street broker, as

its chair, the board used its great powers to achieve what was called "the miracle of production."

In addition to arms and munitions, it was expected that the United States would provide food for its allies as well as itself. "Food will win the war" became a popular slogan. To increase production, Congress authorized the creation of the Food Administration. Administered by Herbert Hoover, an able mining engineer, this agency persuaded consumers to conserve food by observing meatless and wheatless days. But it did not rely on voluntary appeals to convince farmers to increase production — it set prices and set them high. As an example of the results of its work, wheat acreage jumped from 45,000,000 acres to 75,000,000 acres.

Increased industrial and agricultural production would be useless unless the supplies could be delivered to Europe. The chaotic railroad system was unable to deliver raw materials to factories or munitions and personnel to embarkation ports. Consequently the lines were put under the control of a single agency, the Railroad Administration, and operated as a unit. The Shipping Board was authorized to increase the merchant marine by building new vessels or buying or leasing existing ones. It too accomplished a miracle of production, and the ships crossed the Atlantic in what was called a "bridge of ships": great convoys guarded by the navy.

To prevent industrial disputes from impeding production, the War Labor Board was established. Made up of representatives from organized labor and business, it discouraged strikes and sought to mediate disputes. At the same time it recognized that labor had the right to bargain collectively and deserved a fair wage. As a result, wages rose faster than prices, and the unions almost doubled their membership.

The great American war effort was extremely costly, and the task of financing it fell to Secretary of the Treasury William G. McAdoo. He sought to raise as much of the money as possible through taxes, but opposition to the war limited his success. Only a third of the total cost, $32 billion, was raised through taxes. The War Revenue Act imposed a variety of excise taxes, raised income tax rates to a new high, and imposed heavy corporation and excess profits duties. The remainder was secured through loans. Banks provided some of the loans, but the government also asked ordinary men and women to lend money by buying Liberty Bonds. All of the loans were facilitated by the decision of the Federal Reserve system to allow the money supply and credit to expand dramatically during the war.

Altogether nearly 5,000 special agencies operated during the war. They brought the American economy and people under a regulation not previously known.

Mobilizing Opinion

In this total war the government acted to mobilize minds as well as military personnel and materials. Congress created a special agency to rally opinion behind the war, the Committee on Public Information, headed by progressive journalist George Creel. It published tons of propaganda designed to demonstrate that America and its allies were fighting a war for democracy and justice; much of the propaganda was written by volunteers: authors, professors, and others.

Much of the Committee's material was idealistic in nature. On the other hand, some of the publications preached hatred of the enemy, especially Germany, and inevitably the result was to arouse in this country hatred of German-Americans, pacifists, or any individuals who opposed the war or even criticized its conduct. Eventually a mood of hysteria gripped the country. German books were removed from some libraries, and the teaching of the German language was dropped

from some schools. In some cities and states patriots enforced their own repression on dissenters by tarring and feathering or hanging.

The government gave official approval to a policy of repression with the Espionage Act and the Sedition Act. The Espionage Act prescribed severe penalties of fine and imprisonment for anyone who interfered with the draft or encouraged obstruction of the war effort. The Sedition Act, even more sweeping, imposed the same penalties for anyone who spoke, wrote, or printed any "disloyal language." Over 1,500 persons were arrested under these laws, and some of them were sentenced to prison terms for as long as twenty years. President Wilson had feared that in the stress of war the American people might lose their sense of tolerance, and events seemed to be proving that he had been right.

The AEF in France

The war was truly global in extent. It was fought in Europe, Asia, Africa, and on the oceans. Shortly after the United States entered the war, it seemed that Germany and its allies were on the point of achieving victory. In the fall of 1917 Germany in effect knocked Russia out of the war. The government of the tsar fell and was briefly replaced by a constitutional democracy. This government was in turn replaced by a Communist regime that concluded peace with Germany. At the same time the Germans and Austrians inflicted a near-fatal blow to the Italians. Relieved of pressure on its eastern border, Germany was able to give almost its full attention to the war on the western front in France.

Across France the contending armies, German on the one side and French and British on the other, faced each other in complex lines of trenches. The Germans had struck into France in 1914, but after an initial successful advance they had been stopped. In this war new weapons gave the defense an advantage — improved small arms, quick-firing artillery, and above all the machine gun. Attacking armies made only limited advances and suffered appalling casualties. The war had settled down to one of position rather than maneuver.

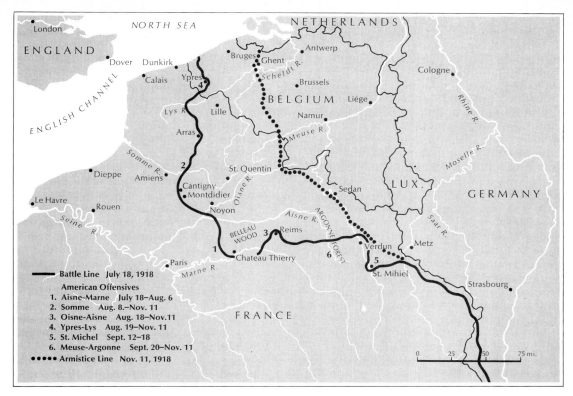

Battle Line   July 18, 1918
American Offensives
1. Aisne-Marne   July 18–Aug. 6
2. Somme   Aug. 8.–Nov. 11
3. Oisne-Aisne   Aug. 18–Nov.11
4. Ypres-Lys   Aug. 19–Nov. 11
5. St. Michel   Sept. 12–18
6. Meuse-Argonne   Sept. 20–Nov. 11
Armistice Line   Nov. 11, 1918

U.S. Participation in Allied Offensives 1918

Although the Allies desperately needed soldiers, they at first regarded with doubts the arriving American Expeditionary Force under General John J. Pershing. The American troops had had only a brief training, and the British and French generals did not feel that this green army could be relied on. They therefore proposed that the Americans be mixed in with their more experienced units. Pershing, however, insisted that his force should operate as a separate army and was backed up by President Wilson. The Allied Supreme War Council had to agree, but the Americans were stationed on a relatively quiet sector of the front.

In the spring of 1918 the Germans launched a great offensive that they hoped would end the war. All along the line they surged forward and at first scored impressive gains. The shaken Allies for the first time appointed a commander in chief,

French Marshal Ferdinand Foch, and threw in everything they had to resist the Germans. In the crisis Pershing permitted some of his troops to be brigaded with Allied units. Fighting mixed or separately, the Americans surprised the French and British by their efficiency, performing with particular brilliance at Château-Thierry, only fifty miles from Paris. By July the German offensive was contained. At this time reinforcements had brought the AEF up to over 1,000,000 men.

Almost immediately the Allies went over to the offensive. The Americans, forming the southern wing of the attack, first erased a German salient that jutted into the Allied line at St. Mihiel. Then by Foch's command they were turned northward in the great Meuse-Argonne offensive that lasted for forty-seven days and carried the AEF toward the German border. In other sectors the Allied thrusts were equally successful, and the Germans knew they would have to sue for peace. Envoys from the German government aked Foch for an armistice and received terms so stiff that a resumption of hostilities would be impossible. Nevertheless the Germans signed the armistice on November 11, 1918. The German imperial government fell and was replaced by a democratic regime, and the resistance of Germany's allies collapsed. The war was in effect over.

The United States had played an important part in achieving the victory. The success of the Allied offensive rested on the addition of American forces (and also on the introduction of a new weapon by the British, the armored tank). But in comparison to its allies the United States had suffered light losses. The total American dead and missing were something over 100,000. The French lost 1,385,000 men and the English 900,-000. A frightful war had ended.

Preparing for Peace

President Wilson intended that he and his country should play a large role in determining the nature of the peace. In various public pronouncements Wilson set forth the outline of what he thought the peace should be like — a peace of idealism, a "peace without victory." In January 1918 he laid down as a basis for a settlement his Fourteen Points. The most important ones proposed "open covenants of peace openly arrived at," freedom of navigation on the seas, removal of tariff barriers, reduction of armaments, adjustment of colonial claims with consideration being given to the wishes of the colonial peoples, and a League of Nations to preserve peace. In the meantime he had learned that the Allied powers had made secret treaties among themselves to divide up the colonies of the enemy and to take other spoils. But he convinced himself that he could persuade the heads of these governments to adopt a more lofty and disinterested attitude at the peace conference that was to convene at the palace of Versailles near Paris early in 1919.

Wilson announced that he would go to Paris as the head of the American delegation. His decision was unprecedented — that a President should leave the country — and was widely criticized. But the conference was what would be later called a summit meeting, and Wilson had reason to go. The heads of the other principal Allied governments planned to be at Paris — Premier Georges Clemenceau of France, Premier Vittorio Orlando of Italy, and Prime Minister David Lloyd George of England. They, with Wilson, would comprise what came to be known as the Big Four.

Wilson did, however, commit two serious tactical errors. On the eve of the congressional elections of 1918, he asked the voters to return a Democratic majority as a vindication of his foreign policy. The people responded by electing a Republican majority to both houses. Thus in a sense Wilson went to Paris repudiated at home. His second mistake was in not taking on the American delegation a ranking Republican, especially a Republican senator, since Republican votes would be required in the Senate to muster the required two-thirds majority to ratify the treaty coming out of the conference. To many people it seemed that Wilson's peacemaking had become too partisan.

Wilson at Versailles

During the negotiations for an armistice, the Germans had asked for an agreement based on the Fourteen Points. The Allies had seemed to agree but had made certain reservations, one being that Germany had to pay financial reparations for damages to Allied civilian populations. Despite the reservations, and his knowledge of the secret treaties, Wilson arrived in Paris confident that the peace would be based on the Fourteen Points.

At Paris all the nations that had declared war on Germany were represented whether or not they had contributed much to the war effort. It was soon discovered that such a large assemblage could not conveniently arrive at agreements. Therefore the Big Four took to meeting secretly and then transmitting their decisions to the other delegates. One of the Fourteen Points, open covenants openly arrived at, had gone by the board already.

At the outset Wilson had to struggle to prevent a division of spoils under the secret treaties. He tried to block the Japanese from obtaining permanently the German treaty rights in the Shantung

Peninsula of China and the former German islands north of the equator in the Pacific, which could be Japanese strongholds. He had to give way, however, to the insistence of the British that they honor the treaty promises with which they had lured the Japanese into the war. Wilson with more success persuaded the Allies to hold former German colonies and Turkish territories on a basis of trusteeship responsible to the League of Nations. This was the new and unprecedented "mandate" system.

Simultaneously, Wilson worked on the drafting of the League Covenant. He insisted that it form the first part of the treaty and be inseparable from it, and he labored long and hard fabricating it in meticulous detail. In the League Covenant he saw the one possible way of overriding the vengeful selfishness that seemed dominant among the victorious nations. Whatever imperfections and inequities there were in the treaty he thought could be rectified through the League. In the League he envisaged a potentially powerful (but not armed) international organization through which the nations of the world could share responsibility in maintaining the security of all against any aggressor.

Opposition to the League

At the end of February 1919, as Congress prepared to adjourn, Wilson came home to sign bills. He brought with him the League Covenant, determined that he would force the Senate to accept it without compromise. He was convinced that public sentiment was overwhelmingly behind him.

But strong resistance was taking shape. Senator Henry Cabot Lodge of Massachusetts produced a round robin signed by thirty-nine senators, a number sufficient to block the treaty, announcing they would not accept the Covenant in its existing form. Wilson, about to reembark for Paris, retorted angrily. But back at the conference he did obtain some of the reservations for the United States upon which the Senate would obviously insist. These provided that a nation need not accept a mandate against its will, that a member could withdraw with two years' notice, that the League would not regulate immigration and other inter-

nal matters, and that it would not infringe upon the Monroe Doctrine.

The Versailles Treaty

While Wilson was obtaining revision of the Covenant, the conference was also grappling with the critical problem of Germany and the remaking of the European map. Together with Lloyd George, Wilson resisted the French proposal to break up western Germany into buffer states. He did sanction the return to France of Alsace-Lorraine and the establishment of a strong Poland and Czechoslovakia on Germany's borders, all in keeping with the national self-determination clauses of the Fourteen Points. He also supported German demilitarization, long-term Allied occupation of the west bank of the Rhine, and an Anglo-French-American mutual defense pact (which was never ratified).

Wilson's most important departure from the Fourteen Points was his acceptance of British and French demands for heavy reparations from the Germans. At the conference, he permitted these demands to cover even pensions for veterans; the astronomical sum was to be set later by a reparations commission. Meanwhile, the other powers insisted that Germany must accept sole responsibility for starting the war. The "war guilt" clause and reparations stuck in the craw of Germans. Even in the United States, the harsh peace meted out against Germany disillusioned many liberals and alienated them from Wilson. They regarded the treaty as a "hell's brew" that would ultimately lead to another war.

Defeat in the Senate

Wilson returned to the United States confident that the Senate, despite the difficulties Lodge was stirring up, would ratify the treaty. On July 10, 1919, when he presented it to the Senate, he asked rhetorically: "Dare we reject it and break the heart of the world?"

Through a combination of coercion and compromise he might have brought about ratification. But he was suffering from hardening of the arteries and while in Paris had been so ill that he may have been close to a stroke. His physical condition robbed him of his political suppleness; instead of using patience and tact, he was more likely to shower his opponents with self-righteous anger.

Wilson's opponents in the Senate had varied motives. The fourteen "irreconcilables" were men of conscience, of Middle Western or Far Western progressive tradition, like Republicans Borah of Idaho, Johnson of California, and La Follette of Wisconsin, and Democrat James Reed of Missouri. They acted from a deep conviction that their nation could best be served by staying out of the League. Other opponents were more concerned with constructing a winning issue for the Republicans in the 1920 election. Senator Lodge, applying all his brilliant intellect to his loathing of Wilson, was ready, as chairman of the Senate Foreign Relations Committee, to use every possible tactic to obstruct, delay, and defeat the treaty. Public sentiment seemed to favor ratification, and Lodge needed time to marshal forces against it. Consequently, he spent the first two weeks after it reached the committee reading aloud every word on its nearly 300 pages. Next, he held six weeks' of public hearings, airing the complaints of every disgruntled minority.

The strongest objection of opponents was to Article X of the League Covenant, the collective security section designed to prevent aggression. It provided that the League Council, in the unlikely event it should agree, could impose economic sanctions on an aggressor nation; or the council could recommend to member nations that they take military action against the aggressor. To many senators it seemed that this provision would involve the United States in countless wars. Wilson was told that he would have to accept a modification of this article and other reservations if he wished to obtain ratification. He replied: "Never! Never! . . . I'll appeal to the country!"

So Wilson, at the end of his physical resources, against the stern warnings of his physician, undertook a cross-country speaking tour, writing his speeches as he went along, delivering them night after night. In twenty-two days he traveled over 8,000 miles, giving thirty-six speeches averaging an hour in length. As the tour proceeded, he gained larger and more enthusiastic audiences and grew more eloquent in his moral fervor. Had it been possible to sway the United States Senate

through public opinion, the tour might have been a success. But Wilson became more and more frail. Finally, after speaking at Pueblo, Colorado, September 25, he suffered such severe headaches that he had to cancel the tour and return to Washington.

Then he suffered an acute stroke that partially paralyzed his left side. For two weeks he was close to death, and for six weeks more so seriously ill that he could attend only to what little business his devoted wife and doctor thought would not unduly upset or fatigue him. The country was in effect without a President.

At this critical period the Senate Foreign Relations Committee finally reported the treaty, recommending forty-five amendments and three reservations. Lodge managed to marshal the Republican senators so well that in November he obtained adoption of fourteen reservations. By this time Wilson had recovered sufficiently to give stern directions to the Democratic minority: they must vote only for the treaty without any reservations whatsoever. Although none of the Lodge reservations would have devitalized the League, Wilson preferred no ratification of the treaty to ratification with reservations. While he was by no means his old self, he was able to exert power enough to maintain discipline over the loyal Democrats. When the vote came, November 19, 1919, forty-two Democrats joined with the thirteen Republican irreconcilables to vote down the treaty with reservations. Next, the Senate voted on ratification of the treaty without reservations. There were thirty-eight senators, all but one of them Democrats, who voted for it; fifty-five voted against it.

On the day of the final vote, March 19, 1920, when the Senate considered the treaty with fifteen reservations, it came within seven votes of receiving the requisite two-thirds. By this time, President Wilson looked to the campaign of 1920 as the opportunity for a "solemn referendum" on the League issue.

Demobilization

Wilson and his wartime planners had been highly successful in converting a peacetime society to one that could conduct a total war. But they made a shambles of the reconversion to peace. They allowed virtually all of the wartime agencies to shut down almost immediately after the conclusion of hostilities. Moreover, they paid little attention to the continued stimulation of the money supply by the Federal Reserve (to ease the financing of the Treasury Department's 1919 borrowing by holding down interest rates and making certain funds were available), which produced overexpansion of the economy and soaring prices during 1919 and much of 1920. While prices had increased 12 percent during 1918, they rose 29 percent during 1919. By May 1920 (when a very sharp depression ensued, lasting until July 1921), prices were almost three times as high as they had been only six years earlier. The sharply rising cost of living particularly hurt white-collar workers and other middle-class people. They became bitter against not only the Wilson administration but organized labor as well.

Union workers tried to preserve their wartime economic gains by striking for higher wages to compensate for the rise in living costs. A great wave of strikes spread across the country, involving in 1919 some 4,000,000 workers. Many were successful, but they alienated much of the public, which accepted the industrialists' protests that higher wages were responsible for higher prices and that the strike leaders were radicals. The outbreak of a steel strike in September 1919 brought antilabor feeling to a boil. The grievances of the workers were serious. They were working an average of nearly sixty-nine hours a week for bare subsistence wages. United States Steel was able to swing public sentiment away from the strikers by claiming that the leaders were Communists; William Z. Foster, the main organizer, was to emerge in 1924 as the presidential candidate of the Communists. The company also tried to stir up trouble between Italian and Serb strikers, and brought in black strikebreakers. By January 1920 the workers were starved out. Steel remained unorganized for another decade and a half.

Public opinion turned even more firmly against organized labor when a police strike broke out in Boston. The police officers were working long hours on prewar salaries under unpleasant conditions. They struck when the police commissioner dismissed the leaders of a union they were organizing. Citizens were horrified when rowdies took over the streets of Boston; troops quickly restored order. When President Gompers of the AFL appealed to Governor Coolidge to permit the reemployment of the police officers who had gone on strike, Coolidge wired: "There is no right to strike against the public safety, anywhere, anytime." No strikers were ever rehired, and this one telegram made Coolidge a formidable contender for the Republican presidential nomination in 1920.

"Red" Scare and Reaction

In Washington, Attorney General A. Mitchell Palmer was becoming a leading contender for the Democratic nomination through his war on both labor and radicals. By obtaining federal court injunctions, he smashed the strike of John L. Lewis' United Mine Workers in November 1919. He attracted even more attention with his crusade against Communists. Throughout the country the violent suppression of pro-German persons during the war had been continued in the persecution of the IWW, the Socialist party members, and all other left wingers. A series of bombing outrages in 1919–1920 intensified the public revulsion against radicals and encouraged Palmer's repressive tactics. On January 1, 1920, he conducted a great Communist roundup, jailing some 6,000 suspects. Communists who were United States citizens were turned over to the states for prosecution under laws that made seeking the overthrow of the state a crime. The aliens came under the jurisdiction of the Labor Department, which deported Communists.

In Massachusetts a payroll robbery and murder in April 1920 led to the trial and conviction of two anarchists, Nicola Sacco and Bartolomeo Vanzetti. Numerous believers in civil liberties insisted that the two men were being prosecuted more on the basis of their radicalism than on criminal evidence, but in August 1927 Sacco and Vanzetti were executed. Their case was the cause célèbre of the 1920s.

Intolerance led to the persecution of not only radicals and labor organizers but also aliens, Catholics, Jews, and blacks.

No people suffered more severely than did blacks. For hundreds of thousands of them, the war had offered an opportunity to break out of the narrow caste structure of the South. Some 400,000 served in the army, half of them in Europe, which drew no color line. Several hundred thousand more moved into the industrial North, where there was less discrimination against them than in the South. Even in the North, however, they suffered from wretched housing, low pay, and the animosity of unskilled white workers who feared their competition. Many blacks in the North and South alike began to follow the militant leadership of the National Association for the Advancement of Colored People, which demanded larger economic opportunities and greater civil rights for blacks.

In both North and South, blacks faced explosive resentment against them. To intimidate blacks into their old subservience, Southerners resorted to the terrorism of the Ku Klux Klan, which grew by 1919 to a membership of 100,000, and to lynchings, which increased from thirty-four in 1917 to more than seventy in 1919. Terrible race riots broke out, beginning in July 1919, in twenty-six towns and cities. Hundreds of persons were killed or wounded, and millions of dollars worth of property was destroyed.

These terrors led as many as 500,000 blacks to follow a leader of magnetic appeal, Marcus Garvey, founder of the Universal Negro Improvement Association. In return for their contributions he promised to take them home to an African empire. Garvey, appealing particularly to poorer blacks, helped arouse their racial pride. Du Bois and the NAACP attacked Garvey's scheme as "bombastic and impracticable." Garvey badly handled the funds poor blacks invested with him, and in 1923 he was convicted of using the mails to defraud and sentenced to federal prison. Black nationalism nevertheless persisted.

Progressivism Turns Sour

The strains of demobilization, which followed so rapidly the disruptions of war and disillusionment with Wilson's idealistic war aims, produced a movement on behalf of "100 percent Americanism" — a crusade to control or destroy all that seemed alien to American society. As a consequence, progressives who had been interested in using the powers of the government to enhance efficiency, rather than to promote social justice, came to the fore and found widespread support,

not only for an anti-Communist campaign, but for prohibition and for immigration restriction.

In December 1917 Congress had adopted and sent to the nation the Eighteenth Amendment, authorizing federal prohibition of the manufacture, sale, and transportation of alcoholic beverages. The amendment was approved in January 1919, and in October 1919, over President Wilson's veto, Congress passed the drastic Volstead Act to implement the amendment. It prohibited all liquors containing more than 0.5 percent of alcohol, rather than permitting the sale of weak beer, which might have appeased millions of city-dwelling opponents of prohibition. To jubilant members of the Anti-Saloon League and the Women's Christian Temperance Union, this meant the enforcement of morality; to opponents it meant an unjustifiable infringement on their personal liberties.

During 1920–1921, as a new flood of immigration from Europe developed, labor leaders, such as Samuel Gompers, and progressives who had been hostile to immigration found that they now had great support; they quickly induced Congress to pass an emergency immigration act. That act established a quota system cutting the number of immigrants from 800,000 in the year ending June 1921 to about 300,000 in the next twelve months. Opponents of immigration were still not satisfied, so in 1924 Congress enacted the National Origins Act. This measure completely banned the people of East Asia, thus abrogating the Gentlemen's Agreement with Japan and incensing the Japanese people. It set a quota of 2 percent for Europeans, on the basis of the 1890 census, thus cutting the total inflow to 164,000 a year, heavily weighted in favor of those from northeastern Europe. The great flood of diverse peoples from Europe had been cut to a few drops.

The approval of the woman suffrage amendment (the Nineteenth) was related to the enactment of prohibition and immigration restriction. The cause of woman suffrage had won many new adherents during World War I as women expanded their participation in American society and as women's organizations became increasingly militant in seeking the vote. But the critical link to success appeared when supporters of prohibition and immigration restriction decided that women would be valuable allies in protecting and expanding their programs. Ironically, women achieved full participation in the American democracy only when the nation was in a mood for the restriction of rights. Congress ratified the suffrage amendment in June 1919, and the last state ratified it in August 1920 — just in time for women to vote in the presidential election.

Harding's Election

Domestic tensions made it impossible for the election of 1920 to serve as the "solemn referendum" on the League of Nations that President Wilson had hoped for. Rather, the "Red" scare and the rising cost of living almost guaranteed in advance a Republican victory, making it unnecessary for Republican politicians to choose a strong, popular candidate such as Herbert Hoover. Rather, when the nominating convention was deadlocked on the two leading contenders, General Leonard Wood and Governor Frank O. Lowden of Illinois, the Republicans turned to the amiable, pliable Senator Warren G. Harding of Ohio. As his running mate, the delegates chose the hero of the Boston police strike, Calvin Coolidge. These thoroughly conservative candidates ran on a thoroughly conservative platform.

The Democrats assembled at San Francisco rather confused because President Wilson, who could have designated a candidate, seemed to be waiting with pathetic coyness to be renominated for a third term. After thirty-eight ballots, the urban bosses stepped in and secured the nomination of an antiprohibition candidate who might salvage their city tickets for them — the former progressive governor of Ohio, James M. Cox. As a gesture toward the Wilsonians, Assistant Secretary of the Navy Franklin D. Roosevelt was nominated for Vice President. Cox and Roosevelt campaigned arduously to try to make the election the referendum on the League that Wilson wished it to be but faced the hostility of foreign-born city voters and great indifference elsewhere.

Harding, following the advice of his managers, made few speeches and took few positions on the issues except to promise a return to what he earlier had called "normalcy." The landslide exceeded even the expectations of the Republicans. Harding received 16,143,407 popular votes, 61 percent of the total, and carried every state outside of the South, which remained largely loyal to the Democratic party. He won even Tennessee. Cox received only 9,147,000 popular votes. Debs, running on the Socialist ticket while in the Atlanta penitentiary, received 920,000 votes. The sweep brought in large Republican majorities in Congress.

Chapter 21

From Normalcy to Depression, 1920–1933

The Tragedy of Harding

The Presidency of Warren G. Harding symbolized the mixture of solid achievement and tragic human failure that characterized the 1920s. Harding was an attractive, well-meaning President who sincerely wished to surround himself with the best qualified people. And in part he succeeded. He placed Herbert Hoover, the friend of small enterprise and expert on efficiency, in charge of the Commerce Department. Andrew W. Mellon represented big business as secretary of the treasury. When Harding was persuaded that his friend Albert B. Fall was not of a caliber to be secretary of state, he appointed the distinguished Charles Evans Hughes. But Harding placed Fall, a notorious anticonservationist, in charge of the Interior Department, and made some equally disastrous appointments to other offices. Despite good intentions, Harding's lack of executive ability and his poor choice of political friends proved his undoing.

The poker-playing and drinking companions whom Harding had placed in positions of trust betrayed him and the American people. The most spectacular fraud involved Secretary of the Interior Fall, who leased rich naval oil reserves at Teapot Dome, Wyoming, and Elk Hills, California, to Harry F. Sinclair and Edward L. Doheny. Fall, who had been in financial straits, suddenly became affluent; he had received over $400,000 in loans and a herd of cattle for his ranch. In 1929 Fall was convicted of bribery, fined $100,000, and sentenced to a year in a federal penitentiary.

In the summer of 1923 Harding journeyed to Alaska. Tired and depressed, he died of a heart attack in San Francisco on his return. In the months that followed, as exposure after exposure crowded the headlines, his reputation collapsed.

Keeping Cool with Coolidge

It was the singular good fortune of Vice President Calvin Coolidge to become President of the United States at the only time since the 1890s when his largely negative custodial approach to the Presidency could bring him popularity rather than disaster. He came to be chief executive through a curious mixture of luck, political regularity, and Yankee shrewdness. Unlike Harding, he had a clear-cut conservative philosophy; he always cooperated wholeheartedly with the big interests because he believed in them, and fought unwaveringly for what he believed.

To the older circle in Washington, Coolidge's personality was not especially appealing; Alice Roosevelt Longworth remarked that he had been weaned on a dill pickle. To the American public, however, there was an infinite appeal and security in his folksy virtues, so lavishly detailed and praised in the nation's press. Coolidge reinforced this appeal with little homilies drawn from his Vermont boyhood — exhortations (in which he fervently believed) to thrift, hard work, and respect for business.

The Coolidge administration seemed so patently incorruptible that the exposures of Harding scandals appeared if anything to backfire against the exposing Democrats. Ultimately Coolidge forced Attorney General Harry Daugherty to resign and helped clean up the scandals. There was

248

no possibility that they would be repeated; and as the election of 1924 approached, they seemed to be doing no appreciable harm to the Republican party. The nation appeared ready to heed the party's campaign slogan: "Keep cool with Coolidge."

In 1924 the Democratic party was badly split between its rural and urban wings. Democrats outside the big cities were in favor of prohibition and fearful of Catholicism; their candidate was William Gibbs McAdoo, who had been Wilson's secretary of the treasury. Big-city Democrats, holding quite reverse views, ardently supported the competent governor of New York, Alfred E. Smith, the son of Irish immigrants, a Catholic, and a "wet." The two contenders deadlocked at the Democratic convention until, on the 103rd ballot, when the nomination had become meaningless, they gave way to a compromise candidate, John W. Davis, a wealthy and able corporation lawyer.

While the Democratic convention dragged on, insurgent Republicans and allied representatives of organized labor held a third convention to organize a Progressive party and nominated Robert M. La Follette. Here, apparently, was a real contrast to the Republican and Democratic tickets, and it served as a made-to-order target for the Republicans. They urged the electorate to choose Coolidge as the only alternative to the "red radicalism" of La Follette. Before election day, labor became lukewarm toward La Follette, and Republican farmers, as crop prices rose, decided to stay within the party.

In its last thrust the old Middle Western insurgency carried only Wisconsin and secured but 16.5 percent of the popular vote throughout the country. Coolidge polled 54 percent, and Davis only 28.8 percent. In his inaugural, March 4, 1925, President Coolidge, declaring that the nation had achieved "a state of contentment seldom before seen," pledged himself to the maintenance of things as they were.

Business Is Business

Big business had a special friend in the government during the 1920s. Andrew Mellon, the Pittsburgh aluminum baron who served as secretary of the treasury from Harding's inauguration into the

Hoover administration, was widely hailed as the greatest secretary of the treasury since Hamilton. His prime mission seemed to be to promote tax cuts. Cartoonists routinely pictured Mellon slicing a tax melon. So far as he could, as a matter of principle, he divided these among wealthy individuals and large corporations to encourage them to become more productive.

Smaller business people also had a strong champion in the government, Secretary of Commerce Hoover. In his own spectacular rise as an international mining engineer, Hoover epitomized the self-made business tycoon. He made Commerce the most spectacular of the departments, as he sought to aid small business in becoming as efficient and profitable as big business.

The most significant of Hoover's aids to small business was the sponsorship of voluntary trade associations similar to the committees of the War Industries Board. By 1921 some 2,000 were in operation. These associations, free from government regulation, could establish codes of ethics, standardize production, establish efficiency, and make substantial savings. They could also, contrary to Hoover's wishes, arrive indirectly at higher standard prices that would bring them better profits. Their real value to highly competitive smaller businesses was to eliminate competition through setting up standard schedules of quality (and prices).

Voluntarism was at the heart of all Hoover's projects. As the new field of commercial radio broadcasting began to develop, Hoover fostered voluntary self-regulation for it. Only when the efforts to keep stations off each other's wavelengths completely broke down did he move toward compulsory government regulation through the Federal Radio Commission, established in 1927. In the same way, the Department of Commerce finally took over regulation of commercial aeronautics through the Air Commerce Act in 1926.

Beginning in the mid-1920s a new wave of mergers swept through American business, carrying 8,000 mining and manufacturing companies into mergers with other companies. The firms that made the most fervent efforts to promote mergers were those that experienced the most rapid growth of production during the 1920s, the manufacturers of automobiles, chemicals, and household appliances. Their strategies were to acquire greater control over prices, to diversify into new products, and to find the capital necessary to make their plants and equipment more productive.

Consumers and Workers

The growing productivity of business was a major source of the real prosperity American consumers and workers enjoyed during the 1920s. Per capita income increased almost 20 percent during the 1920s, and although the evidence is incomplete, it appears that income became distributed more evenly as the end of immigration created a shortage of unskilled labor and a consequent increase in the relative wages of unskilled workers. The decade witnessed a dramatic rise in the consumption of automobiles, furniture, and electrical appliances. Between 1921 and 1929 an unusual degree of price stability and an exceptionally low level of unemployment accompanied the high levels of income. The average annual rate of price increase was less than 1 percent, and unemployment dropped to an annual average of only 3.7 percent. That record was a significant improvement over that of the two preceding decades and has not been matched since.

The wage gains of the 1920s were achieved largely without the benefit of unions. Indeed, the living conditions of many factory workers improved sufficiently to make easier the drive of most employers against unions. The paternalistic policies of welfare capitalism, combined with a continued crusade against the closed shop (the hiring of only union labor) led to a decline in union membership during the 1920s. Many companies greatly improved working conditions by installing safety devices and cafeterias, promoting athletic teams, and providing pension plans. Company unions through which workers could voice their grievances were effective safety valves. Through such devices, companies helped fend off unionism from the new mass-production industries such as automobile manufacturing. Union membership declined from over 5,000,000 in 1920 to 4,300,000 in 1929.

The prosperity was, however, not uniform. Certain industries were depressed during the 1920s, and their problems would become even more severe during the 1930s. For example, the New England textile industry suffered from the movement of firms to the cheaper labor markets of the South. Railroads encountered stiff competition in freight and passenger service from publicly subsidized highways (including a trunk system initiated by the Federal Aid Road Act of 1916). Mining had experienced overexpansion as a result of wartime demands and was particularly depressed. In coal mining, an industry suffering competition from petroleum and natural gas, wages fell more than 10 percent between 1923 and 1929. The lumber industry was also paying the price of overexpansion, particularly in the Great Lakes states. What is most remarkable is that even in the face of these problems the economy as a whole enjoyed unmatched prosperity during the 1920s.

Thunder from the Farm Belt

The industry that suffered the greatest adversity during the 1920s was agriculture. The income of farmers drastically declined during the 1920s. In 1920 they lost their price supports at the same time that the bloated wartime European market contracted. Within agriculture, the shifting eating habits brought a doubling of truck farming and an increase by a third in dairying and citrus growing, together with profits for many of these farmers. At the same time, those who had moved on to marginal or submarginal land during the war suffered so acutely that in the five years after 1919, 13,000,000 acres were abandoned. These farmers were often heavily burdened with debts acquired at high wartime prices and unable to compete with new, expensive machinery, which especially helped contribute to the glut of wheat. These were the years when tractors almost completely replaced horses, releasing 35,000,000 acres of land for additional crops. Only big operators could enjoy good incomes from producing staples. The agricultural population dropped 3,000,000 between 1921 and 1928.

Those who remained on their farms began to agitate militantly for relief. The radical Non-Partisan League, first organized in North Dakota in 1915, evolved into the Farmer-Labor party in the 1920s, but could not win the support of farmers earning $1,000 to $4,000 a year. This middle 40 percent of the farmers rather sought through the Farm Bureau Federation to obtain federal price supports. In 1921 Midwestern congressional leaders from both parties organized a farm bloc to support these demands.

One price-raising scheme came to dominate the farmers' thinking. Behind the tariff barrier, the American protected price for crops should be raised to a "fair exchange value" based on the price of the crop during ten prewar years, compared with the general average of all prices during the same period. This price concept was called "parity." The government should obtain parity prices for farmers by buying up the surplus at the high American price and selling it abroad for whatever it would bring. To make up for the loss, an equalization fee or tax should be imposed upon the participating farmers.

Between 1924 and 1928 Senator Charles L. McNary of Oregon and Representative Gilbert Haugen of Iowa promoted this scheme in Congress. In 1924 the McNary-Haugen bill covered only grain and was defeated in the House, but in 1926 the addition of cotton, tobacco, and rice brought Southern support. In 1927 Congress passed it, but President Coolidge coldly vetoed it as being preferential legislation contrary to the principles of laissez faire and, quite correctly, as legislation that would increase surpluses without improving the farmers' income. But farmers remained unconvinced. A year later, the McNary-Haugen bill was again passed and vetoed.

The United States and the World

The problem of developing Republican alternatives to the Wilsonian foreign policy fell largely on the shoulders of Secretary of State Charles Evans Hughes. Hughes' policies involved first of all ending the war with Germany by an act of Congress, which was signed July 2, 1921, then the negotiation of separate peace treaties to obtain for the United States the benefits of the Paris treaties without the responsibilities. He persuaded President Harding in 1923 to recommend that the United States join with reservations the World Court, an almost powerless body. When

Harding's recommendation (and that of each succeeding President through Franklin D. Roosevelt) came before the Senate, irreconcilable isolationists defeated it.

Secretary Hughes' most notable substitute for American entrance into the League was the Washington Arms Conference of 1921–1922, intended to fend off a three-way naval construction race among the United States, Great Britain, and Japan. In the negotiations, Japan agreed to limit its capital ships to a total of approximately 300,000 tons compared with 500,000 tons each for the United States and Great Britain. Thus the Five Power Pact of February 6, 1922, provided a ratio of 5:5:3 for the United States, Great Britain, and Japan, and 1.75:1.75 for France and Italy. Two other treaties aimed at guaranteeing the status quo in the Far East. The Nine Power Pact pledged a continuation of the "Open Door" in China. Afterward Japan restored to China full sovereign rights in the Shantung Peninsula and promised to withdraw Japanese troops from Siberia. The Four Power Pact, among the United States, Great Britain, France, and Japan, was a mutual guarantee of insular rights in the Pacific. Upon its ratification, Japan relinquished its alliance with Great Britain. For nearly a decade these Washington treaties lowered the tension between the United States and Japan.

In European affairs the big issues were reparations and war debts. The League Reparations Commission, in the absence of Americans, set astronomically high sums for Germany to pay. Reparations payments depended to a considerable degree upon American private loans to Germany; war-debt payments from the Allies to the United States depended almost entirely upon reparations. The American public insisted that the Allies should repay the $10 billion the United States had loaned during the war. The United States pressured the former Allies to negotiate long-term schedules of debt payments. American private loans to Germany were largely what kept the system going in the 1920s.

The Jazz Age

For those who shared in the prosperity, it was a wonderful era. The national wealth of the

United States was almost as great as that of all of Europe. The average middle-class American family owned an automobile. There were 23,000,000 cars in use by 1929, and on Sundays it seemed as though they were all out on the new concrete highways. At home, people listened to the radio. The first commercial station, KDKA, broadcast the news of Harding's election in November 1920; by 1924 the National Broadcasting Company had organized a nationwide network of stations. Household appliances were supplanting the housemaid and the hired girl.

New ways of life, alarming to the older generation, swept America. Women seemed to have lost their modesty as they bobbed their hair, applied lipstick, donned short skirts and silk stockings, and unblushingly began using words previously reserved for males. Younger people talked frankly and openly about sex. Some of them further flouted the older moral standards by drinking bootleg beer or cocktails, listening to jazz, and dancing the Charleston. Many critics thought that Gertrude Stein had correctly labeled this the "lost generation"; they would not have believed that these young rebels in time would mature into censorious middle age.

Motion pictures flamboyantly heralded the new moral code and helped fabricate false stereotypes of the period. An estimated 50,000,000 people a week went to movie theaters to see the "it" girl, Clara Bow; the glamorous Rudolph Valentino; the comedian Charlie Chaplin; gangster pictures; westerns; and great spectacles such as *The Ten Commandments.* At this time nine-tenths of the world's motion pictures were made in the United States; they brought to other countries curiously distorted notions of American culture.

The prosperity of the twenties spilled over into the educational system. The per capita expenditure per pupil jumped from $24 in 1910 to $90 in 1930. Free elementary education had become established throughout the nation; illiteracy dropped from 7.7 percent to 4.3 percent. Enrollment in high schools increased 400 percent, and universities grew nearly as rapidly.

American writers made themselves heard, and often impressively. Seldom has such a remarkable galaxy appeared. Sherwood Anderson, giving up his paint factory, wrote tart Freudian sketches of small-town America in *Winesburg, Ohio* (1919).

Sinclair Lewis more spectacularly exploited the same vein in his satiric *Main Street* (1920). His onslaught against business Philistinism, in a long series of novels, at times verged close to caricature, but in time brought him a Nobel Prize. The novelist who best embodied the jazz age in both his personal life and his writing was F. Scott Fitzgerald, catapulted to success with *This Side of Paradise* (1920). Other young novelists appeared who helped set patterns for later decades. Above all, there were Ernest Hemingway and William Faulkner. The reaction against war was most vigorously stated in Hemingway's novel of disillusion, *A Farewell to Arms* (1929), which also helped set a new literary style. Faulkner, analyzing the South with morbid intensity in such novels as *The Sound and the Fury* (1929) and *Sanctuary* (1931), developed an abstruse stream-of-consciousness technique that profoundly influenced other writers.

In literature, there was a seeking for values that would be something more than the advertising executives' paeans to mass-production cultures. This seeking was the reason so many of the younger writers were rejecting the popular values of the United States for those of Europe, which did not seem to them to be caught in the new commercial maelstrom.

In music the twenties were notable for the rise of jazz. It had originated among black musicians in the South, particularly in New Orleans, who drew upon their African heritage in composing and playing tunes with improvised harmonies and a syncopated beat. Among the outstanding black creators of jazz were the guitar-playing singer Huddie Ledbetter ("Leadbelly") and the band conductor William C. Handy, the "father of the blues," whose compositions include *St. Louis Blues* (1914). The new music first became widely known when jazz players moved with the general black migration northward during and after World War I. The great trumpet player Louis ("Satchmo") Armstrong, for example, went from New Orleans to Chicago in 1922 to join a band that helped spread jazz through phonograph recordings. Meanwhile, white musicians had begun to take up the new form, modifying it and making it popular with ever-larger numbers of people. Prominent among them were the composer George Gershwin, who incorporated jazz elements into his *Rhapsody in Blue,* and the conductor Paul Whiteman, whose band presented a pioneering jazz concert in New York City in 1922.

Hoover Follows Coolidge

To many Americans, a simple and effective way of perpetuating the Coolidge prosperity after 1928 seemed to be to put the "Great Engineer," Herbert Hoover, in the White House. Hoover himself seemed to think that a continuation of the administrative policies of his predecessor would bring a continued boom. "Given a chance to go forward with the policies of the last eight years," he promised, "we shall soon with the help of God be in sight of the day when poverty will be vanished from this nation."

A scramble for the Republican nomination had begun when President Coolidge announced: "I do not choose to run in 1928." Hoover was easily nominated on the first ballot. The platform emphasized prosperity and straddled the troublesome issues of farm relief and prohibition.

Among Democrats, the experienced politicians were still almost as badly divided as in 1924, but they saw no reason to turn their convention into another brawl when their candidate had no chance of winning against Republican prosperity. Even those who were ardently dry and Protestant wanted party unity so badly that they raised no barrier against the governor of New York, Alfred E. Smith, who was a "wet" and a Catholic. For the first time, a major party had dared to confront Protestant prejudice by nominating a Catholic for President.

Smith was nominated on the first ballot to run on a platform not much more positive than that of the Republicans. It did, however, include a plank offering the farmers McNary-Haugenism. More important, Smith promised, despite a compromise plan on prohibition, that he would favor relaxing the Volstead enforcement act. This forced prohibition into the forefront of the campaign. There was little except that and religion to campaign about.

Both Hoover and Smith were self-made men and proud of it. Hoover's path, from an Iowa farm through Stanford University, had been marked by

a phenomenally successful rise as a business and government executive. Smith's path led from the East Side of New York through the Fulton Fish Market and the Tammany hierarchy to the governorship of New York. There he had demonstrated a consummate political and administrative skill. He had reorganized the state government; fought to build schools, parks, and parkways; and struggled for public development of the great power sites. Both candidates were mild progressives, dedicated to perpetuating the intimate ties between business and government.

This contest between two people of high character degenerated into one of the lowest mudslinging campaigns in American history. Hoover himself stressed prosperity, which was popularly translated into the notion of a chicken in every pot and two cars in every garage. This left the political storms to sweep around Smith, who evoked more enthusiastic loyalty and venomous hatred than any candidate since Bryan. Millions of the urban masses, mostly of immigrant and Catholic background, saw in Smith their spokesperson, their great hero. In the Protestant South belief in prohibition was still almost an act of faith, and the Ku Klux Klan was boisterous in its anti-Catholicism. Fiery crosses greeted Smith near Oklahoma City, where he courageously denounced the Klan. Smith had no effective defense against the religious and prohibition issues; they overrode rural Americans' disgust with Hoover's coldness toward their demands.

The Hoover landslide far exceeded expectations, with a popular vote of 21,391,000 to 15,016,000 for Smith.

Repeal of Prohibition

To some observers, the 1928 election seemed to be a great national referendum in favor of prohibition, yet prohibition was not to last much longer than prosperity. Though Hoover had referred to it as a "noble experiment," enforcement was breaking down so badly that Congress stiffened the penalties for violating the Volstead Act and authorized the new President to appoint a National Law Enforcement Commission. This commission, headed by a former attorney general, George Wickersham, ultimately reported in 1931 that prohibition was not only not being enforced but was virtually unenforceable.

Rampant gangsterism and the open flouting of the law by millions of otherwise respectable citizens convinced many thoughtful Americans that prohibition was not worth its price in lawlessness. With the coming of the depression, some well-to-do people redoubled their efforts in the hope that repeal would increase liquor taxes, thereby reducing income taxes, and promote prosperity by stimulating the liquor, beer, and wine industries. In the campaign of 1932 prohibition, compared with the depression, evaporated as a serious issue, and the Democrats bluntly advocated repeal. In February 1933 Congress submitted to the states the Twenty-first Amendment, which repealed prohibition; by December it had been ratified, and the experiment was at an end.

The Wall Street Crash

Almost every action of the Hoover administration revolved around the depression, which began in the summer of 1929. The initial downturn occurred because manufacturers had grossly overestimated the ability of the consuming public to buy their products, particularly automobiles and appliances. The result was accumulating inventories, cutbacks in production, the laying off of workers, and reduced incomes and buying power. At first, this downturn was a normal business contraction; the economy had tolerated many such episodes in the past without developing long periods of severe unemployment and extraordinarily low incomes. What helped make the post-1929 contraction unusually severe was the collapse of the stock market in October and November. From the latter part of 1927 on, the New York Stock Exchange had been in a grotesquely inflated condition. Full of flaws, the stock market had become for many speculators a great national gambling casino. By 1929 disaster became inevitable and the recession that began in the summer produced the pinprick of doubt that burst the bubble on October 21. Within three weeks, stocks had lost over 40 percent of their former value.

To Americans of all walks of life the stock market had become the symbol of national economic stength and the embodiment of a faith in big busi-

ness. When the crash came, the public became deeply pessimistic about the future not only of the stock market but also of the economy. Thus, the impact of the crash was to sharpen and prolong the crisis of confidence, which grew worse as the depression dragged on. Expectations of extended depression inhibited the consumption and investment necessary to stimulate the economy.

Hoover Faces the Depression

President Hoover was far more energetic and imaginative than any previous American President in trying to develop a program to combat the depression. He determined that the government should intervene positively but in a very limited way, seeking the voluntary cooperation of business and labor.

First, to restore confidence, Hoover declared: "The fundamental business of this country, that is, production and distribution of commodities, is on a sound and prosperous basis." Next, he held a number of highly publicized meetings of business, farm, and labor leaders in an effort to rally the country to adopt a voluntary program. Business participants pledged themselves not to cut payrolls or production; labor leaders, not to ask for better wages or hours. In addition, Hoover used the government to fight deflation. He announced a significant tax cut and arranged for the Federal Reserve to provide liberal credit for business. He asked Congress for an increase of $423,000,000 in public works — a huge sum for the period — and called upon mayors and governors to engage in the "energetic yet prudent pursuit" of them. In the spring of 1931 conditions seemed to be improving. The depression up to this point had not been much more serious than that of 1920–1921; perhaps, Hoover and others thought, it was nearly over.

Instead, the nation was dragged down into far worse conditions as the repercussions of European panic hit these shores. Since the flow of long-term American loans to central Europe had slackened several years previously, Germany and Austria had depended upon short-term credit. French bankers cut this off in March 1931, and by May the largest bank in Austria had collapsed. Germany, appealing to the United States in June, obtained from President Hoover the proposal of a one-year moratorium on reparations and war debt payments, but France destroyed much of the good effect by delaying in accepting the plan. By September England and most other nations of the world went off the gold standard. The crisis in western Europe hit the United States severely in the spring of 1931 as European gold was withdrawn from American banks in anticipation of American abandonment of the gold standard.

In October 1931, because of the conviction that maintenance of the gold standard was essential to recovery from the depression, the Federal Reserve responded to the outward flow of gold by taking a series of actions designed to protect the dollar and to encourage a return of gold to American shores. By contracting the nation's money supply and raising short-term interest rates the Federal Reserve succeeded in keeping the United States on the gold standard, but the monetary contraction was so severe (over 30 percent of the nation's money supply had disappeared by February 1932) that immediate economic recovery became impossible. Americans became further convinced that prices would continue to fall and even more insistent on increasing their holdings of cash, which were gaining in value. To make things worse, the monetary contraction made it difficult for banks to meet their obligations, and fearful depositors withdrew their savings. Consequently, instead of improving in 1931, the economy sank lower and lower. Security and commodity prices continued to fall; bankruptcies and bank failures multiplied; unemployment soared. By December 1931 when Congress met, conditions were so frightening that President Hoover abandoned his reliance upon voluntary measures and proposed direct governmental action of an unprecedented sort to combat the depression.

In January 1932 Congress created a giant loan agency, the Reconstruction Finance Corporation, which during 1932 loaned $1.5 billion, mostly to banks, railroads, and other businesses. Hoover, trying to parry criticism that he had set up a bread line for big business, asserted that his purpose was to stop deflation and thus increase employment, mainly by helping relatively small companies.

Hoover believed that while people must not go cold and hungry, feeding them was a voluntary and local responsibility. "If we start appropriations of this character," he had declared, "we have not only impaired something infinitely valuable in the life of the American people but have struck at the roots of self-government." It was hard to impress the niceties of distinctions like this upon desperate people. Hoover, who for so many years had been one of the most popular of American heroes, became the scapegoat for the depression.

The People in Hard Times

The chain reaction of unemployment slowly spread from 1930 into 1933. At first those in marginal or poorer jobs were hit hardest, as those who had been in better jobs moved downward. In time millions who had never been unemployed for any length of time were jobless and unable to find work of any sort. They had been brought up in the sturdy tradition of self-reliance and had accepted the doctrine of rugged individualism — that opportunities were limitless if only one had the ambition and energy to take advantage of them. Now these people were humiliated and baffled at not being able to provide for themselves and their families.

Care of the unemployed had always been a responsibility primarily of private charity, and for several years the President and governors exhorted citizens to contribute to the Red Cross or to emergency funds. But the task soon became far too great for private charity to handle. By 1931 the Red Cross could provide only 75 cents a week to feed each hungry family in southern Illinois.

Although several European nations had maintained unemployment insurance programs for decades, not a single state in the United States enacted such a law until January 1932 when Wisconsin passed one. Even as the distress grew, many magazines and newspapers proclaimed that any permanent system of direct unemployment relief like the British dole would bankrupt the government and undermine the moral fiber of the recipients. Not until September 1931 did the New York legislature at the insistence of Governor Franklin D. Roosevelt establish the first relief organization of any state, the Temporary Emergency Relief Administration, which became the model for other states and the prototype of the later federal relief agency.

To some of the unemployed who had recently moved to cities, the solution seemed to be to return to the farm; the migration away from farms was now reversed. But farm prices fell so low that once again, on parts of the plains, farmers burned corn to keep warm. A rancher sold seven lambs in the Denver livestock market and, after paying commissions and fees, received a check for 75 cents. In a railroad diner, two lamb chops cost the same amount. Prices of manufactured goods were relatively so high that it took ten bushels of wheat to buy a cheap pair of shoes.

Some bewildered farmers around Sioux City, Iowa, in 1932 embargoed milk bound for the city, because they were receiving 2 cents a quart and it retailed for 8 cents. Many more Iowa farmers participated in Milo Reno's militant Farmers' Holiday Association to block all farm products from the market until prices went higher.

Through the summer of 1932, some 12,000 to 14,000 unemployed veterans congregated in Washington to demonstrate for the immediate payments of their bonus for wartime service, not due until 1945. For weeks they lived in squalor in abandoned tenements and in shanties on the mud flats of the Anacostia River. After Congress failed to pass a bonus bill, about half of them, discouraged, went home. The continued presence of the rest alarmed Hoover and many Washingtonians. After a riot, the President called upon the army to oust the veterans. Under the personal command of General Douglas MacArthur, and his officers Dwight Eisenhower and George Patton, the army did so with tanks, gas masks, and fixed bayonets. "That was a bad looking mob," MacArthur declared. "It was animated by the essence of revolution."

As the depression deepened, there were surprisingly few signs of social disorder or outbursts of violence within the United States. Communists agitated, won a few converts among intellectual leaders, and made almost no impact upon the masses. The farmers' strike and the bonus march did not really threaten revolution. Even in this period of extreme despair, Americans were willing to depend upon the ballot box.

The Election of 1932

Republicans meeting in Chicago renominated Hoover in a spirit far from jubilant; they had little illusion about the outcome of the election. The Democrats, assembling later in an excited, expectant mood, saw almost certain victory after twelve years out of power. Almost anyone they nominated was sure to be elected.

Well over a majority of the delegates came pledged to vote for Governor Roosevelt of New York. Roosevelt astutely had been working for the nomination for years. To a considerable degree he bridged the gulf between the urban and rural Democrats. He was ready to emphasize economic issues and ignore the earlier divisions over prohibition and religion.

Breaking precedent, Roosevelt flew immediately to Chicago to deliver his acceptance address before the convention. He endorsed the Democratic platform, which except for a promise of prohibition repeal was not much bolder than that of the Republicans. He declared: "I pledge you, I pledge myself, to a new deal for the American people." Thus the Roosevelt program acquired a name before the electorate had more than the haziest notion of what it might embody.

Nor did the voters learn much during the campaign, for Roosevelt astutely confined himself to warm generalities that would offend few and yet would bring him the enormous vote of protest against Hoover. Through Roosevelt's speeches ran many of the old progressive themes, together with new suggestions for economic planning. An able team, largely of university professors under the leadership of Raymond Moley, helped devise policies and draft speeches for him. Newspaper reporters dubbed this group of advisers the "Brain Trust." At the Commonwealth Club in San Francisco, Roosevelt broke furthest from the past by insisting that the government must assist business in developing a well regulated economic system. Everyone, he said, had a right to a comfortable living; the nation's industrial and agricultural mechanism could produce enough for everyone with some to spare. If need be, to achieve this end, government must police irresponsible economic power. Roosevelt felt he was doing no more than to restate the objectives of Jefferson and Wilson in terms of the complexities of the thirties when he proposed that government should act as a regulator for the common good within the existing economic system.

President Hoover, tired and grim, took to the road in October to warn the populace that without his program things might be infinitely worse. His speeches, though earnest, were dull and dreary in both style and delivery compared with Roosevelt's breezy, optimistic performances. Hoover was the last of the Presidents to scorn the aid of speechwriters.

Some voters, disappointed because they could detect little difference between Roosevelt's program and Hoover's, turned to Norman Thomas and the Socialists or to William Z. Foster and the Communists. Yet, even in this year of despair, the Socialists polled only 882,000 votes, and the Communists only 103,000. Roosevelt received 22,822,000 popular votes, or 57.4 percent, to 15,762,000, or 39.7 percent, for Hoover; he carried the electoral college 472 to 92. The Democrats carried both houses of Congress by top-heavy majorities. Roosevelt had won an overwhelming mandate — but for what?

Actually, there had been discernible differences between the two candidates' programs. Hoover had seen the depression as world-wide in origin and development; he was ready to combat it internationally through currency stabilization. Roosevelt chose to regard the depression as domestic, specifically Republican, in origin. During the campaign Hoover had forced him to equivocate on the old Democratic low-tariff position; Roosevelt was ready to move toward economic nationalism. Like Hoover, he believed in economy and a balanced budget, although these would run contrary to his advocacy of social and economic planning. Unlike Hoover, he was so far from being doctrinaire that inconsistencies in his program would bother him little.

The Interregnum

President Hoover faced an agonizing four months before Roosevelt would take office on

March 4: The Twentieth ("lame duck") Amendment to end this long carryover of a defeated President and Congress was not ratified until February 1933. As the economy plummeted once again, Hoover ascribed the drop to lack of business confidence in the incoming President. There was a brief economic upswing in the spring months of 1932, reaching a peak in July, as the Federal Reserve relaxed its policies. But then gold resumed its outward flow because investors expected Roosevelt to devalue the dollar, and the Federal Reserve resumed a tight-money policy. Hoover felt he was bringing an end to the depression and that only the threat of unsettling measures from Roosevelt was preventing continued recovery. Hence, in a series of interchanges with Roosevelt during the winter of 1932–1933, Hoover tried to bind the President-elect to his programs.

The first negotiations were over the question of European debts. Both Hoover and Roosevelt opposed cancellation, but Hoover wished to use the debts as a lever to reestablish an international gold standard. Tied in with this was the proposed International Economic and Monetary Conference, which Hoover hoped would restore financial stability. Roosevelt would make no commitments.

By February 1933 an acute banking crisis had developed. Bank resources and deposits had been declining at an alarming rate. In the previous three years, 5,000 banks had failed, and now one after another was collapsing as depositors lined up to withdraw their deposits. To prevent failures, governors began proclaiming banking holidays in their states, beginning with Michigan on February 14. By March 4 banking was at a halt or drastically restricted in all states but one.

President Hoover penned a lengthy longhand letter to Roosevelt, charging that the crisis was due to "steadily degenerating confidence" in the President-elect, and calling upon him to give prompt public assurance that there would be no tinkering with the currency, no heavy borrowing, and a balanced budget. Roosevelt had not the slightest intention of adopting Hoover's views.

Chapter 22

The New Deal

F. D. R. Takes Command

When Roosevelt was inaugurated, on March 4, 1933, most of the nation's banks were closed. At least 13,000,000 people were unemployed, some of them so close to starvation that they were scrabbling for food scraps on garbage dumps. Millions of farmers were on the brink of foreclosure; many others had fallen over the brink.

In his inaugural address, President Roosevelt spoke with vigor and confidence. "This great Nation will endure as it has endured, will revive and will prosper," he declared. "So, first of all, let me assert my firm belief that the only thing we have to fear is fear itself." Somehow these words, although they said nothing new, helped inspire the American people. From their depths of helplessness they were ready to be commanded, and in Roosevelt they saw someone ready to take strong leadership. Such leadership he promised. If Congress did not act, he announced, he would ask for "broad executive power to wage a war against the emergency, as great as the power that would be given to me if we were in fact invaded by a foreign foe."

Few Presidents have been better trained for the White House. Roosevelt had served in the New York state senate, been wartime assistant secretary of the navy, and had been twice elected governor of New York. He was skilled in both legislative and administrative techniques as well as in practical politics. As a youth he had spent much time in Europe and maintained a continuing interest in foreign affairs. Roosevelt's ideology was progressive, influenced by his wife's uncle, Theo-

dore Roosevelt, whom he adored, and his former chief, Woodrow Wilson, whom he revered.

Neither he nor his advisers were clear-cut in their thinking. What was important was that Roosevelt, while basically rooted in the older economics and the social justice tradition of the progressives, was ready to experiment. His program would be flexible, not doctrinaire; the new economic theories would grow from it, not it from the theories. When one of the brain trusters warned of perils ahead, Roosevelt declared: "There is nothing to do but meet every day's troubles as they come."

With the banking crisis at its height, he might well have taken drastic steps, but the background of Roosevelt was such that he resorted to only the mildest of expedients.

The Bank Holiday

During his first days as President, Roosevelt seemed bent above all upon restoring the confidence of business leaders. He met the banking crisis in a manner pleasing to the banking community. He issued a proclamation on March 6, 1933, closing all banks and stopping transactions or exports in gold for four days until Congress could meet in special session. On March 9, he sent in a conservative bill that would bolster the stronger banks. It authorized the Federal Reserve system to issue notes against their assets, and the Reconstruction Finance Corporation to make them loans. The bill dealt a death blow to weaker banks; inspectors would deny them licenses to re-open. It stopped the ebb of gold from the Treasury and from the country by prohibiting hoarding and exportation. Congress passed the bill within four hours of its introduction.

On March 12, in the first of his "fireside chats" over the radio, the President, speaking in a warm, intimate manner, told the American people that the crisis was over. And so indeed it was; by this simple legislation and his confident leadership, Roosevelt had averted the threat to banks and the capitalist system. Three-fourths of the banks in the Federal Reserve system reopened within the next three days; $1 billion in hoarded currency and gold flowed back into them within a month.

Thus far, the Roosevelt program had done little more than improve the confidence of business people. Roosevelt, political expert that he was, knew the psychological moment was at hand for pushing a more comprehensive program through Congress. During the next hundred-odd days a remarkable array of laws came forth. The New Deal began to take form.

Emergency Relief

The first step was to feed the millions of hungry unemployed. While Roosevelt subscribed to his predecessor's maxim that relief was primarily the task of states and communities, he proposed that the federal government provide grants rather than loans to states. Congress established the Federal Emergency Relief Administration and appropriated an initial $500,000,000 for it. Roosevelt appointed the director of the New York state relief agency, Harry Hopkins, to run the federal program. Hopkins was a dedicated social worker with a lively tongue and a keen sense of professional ethics. He ardently believed in work relief rather than direct relief, but in the spring of 1933 everyone hoped recovery was at hand so that relief would be needed only for a few months.

But recovery lagged, and some new ways had to be found to care for the unemployed through the winter of 1933–1934. Relief administrator Hopkins persuaded the President to establish a temporary work relief program, the Civil Works Administration. Between November and April it put 4,000,000 people to work at emergency projects. Sometimes it was make-work like leaf raking, to which critics applied an old Texas term, "boondoggling." Some of the projects, despite lack of funds for materials and tools, made substantial improvements. The output was of secondary importance; the work raised the morale of the unemployed and increased their buying power by $950,000,000.

Congress also created an organization that reflected Roosevelt's keen interest in preserving natural as well as human resources, the Civilian Conservation Corps. It received a grant of $300,000,000 to enroll 250,000 young men from relief families and 50,000 veterans and forest workers in reforestation and flood control. Ultimately the CCC enrolled 500,000 young men, but this was only a fraction of the unemployed young men in the nation. And, despite advocacy by Eleanor Roosevelt, the President's wife, Congress never established counterparts to the CCC camps for young women.

Mortgage relief was a pressing need of millions of farm owners and home owners. Roosevelt quickly consolidated all farm credit organizations into a new Farm Credit Administration. Congress voted such large additional funds for it that within two years it had refinanced a fifth of all farm mortgages in the United States. A comparable Home Owners' Loan Corporation, established in June 1933, in a three-year period loaned $3 billion to refinance the mortgages of over 1,000,000 distressed householders. Altogether it carried about a sixth of the nation's urban mortgage burden. A year later Congress established a Federal Housing Administration to insure mortgages for new construction and home repairs — more properly a recovery than a relief agency. All these mortgage agencies not only rescued mortgage holders but also eased the burden on banks and insurance companies, thus filling a recovery function.

The First AAA

The Agricultural Adjustment Administration (AAA), created in May 1933, marked the tri-

The Nature of the New Deal

Denouncing the New Dealers, former President Herbert Hoover once said they professed the "three Rs" of Relief, Recovery, and Reform but secretly espoused the "fourth R" of Revolution. How revolutionary was the New Deal in fact? To what extent did it break with the American past? Historians have given a wide variety of answers to these questions.

Some authors maintained that the New Deal was more evolutionary than revolutionary, that in essence it was an extension of the progressive movement. In *Rendezvous with Destiny* (1952) Eric F. Goldman saw the "first" New Deal (1933–1935) as similar to Theodore Roosevelt's New Nationalism, the "second" (1935–1938) as reminiscent of Woodrow Wilson's New Freedom, though Goldman thought "there was something more to New Deal liberalism," since it included such unprecedented measures as social security.

Dominant, however, has been the liberal, approving interpretation that the New Deal, in the words of Richard Hofstadter, was a "drastic new departure" and was "different from anything that had yet happened in the United States." In *The Age of Reform* (1955), Hofstadter argued that with the New Deal the federal government, for the first time, became a positive force for promoting the welfare of the American people. Even more enthusiastic has been Arthur M. Schlesinger, Jr., who argued in *The Age of Roosevelt* (1957–1960) that Roosevelt had reformed capitalism by significantly enhancing the power of workers, farmers, and consumers. Carl N. Degler, in *Out of Our Past* (1959), called the New Deal the "Third American Revolution."

The first important dissent from this liberal consensus came in 1963 when William Leuchtenburg, in *Franklin D. Roosevelt and the New Deal*, wrote that the New Deal, despite its idealism, was only a "halfway revolution," helping many disadvantaged groups but doing little or nothing for blacks, sharecroppers, and the urban poor. During the 1960s historians, including Barton Bernstein, Paul Conkin, and Howard Zinn, catalogued the mistakes and opportunities missed by the New Deal.

By the mid-1980s, however, the criticisms of the New Deal had gained little momentum. Most historians seemed to agree that the New Deal, despite the limits within which it worked, had accomplished more significant restructuring of society than any other reform movement since the Civil War.

umphant conclusion of the farmers' long struggle to get government aid for raising farm prices. Roosevelt was mainly interested in the relatively substantial, more commercial farmers, such as the 300,000 who even in 1922 were paying dues of $10 a year or more to the Farm Bureau Federation. They desired a program to limit crops. Poorer members of other farm organizations like the Farmers' Union and the National Farmers' Holiday Association opposed production cuts, seeking instead direct relief and, above all, inflation. Roosevelt hoped to develop a program that would fit the Farm Bureau formula and yet would not drive poorer farmers into new revolt. He let the various farm organization leaders devise their own plan. Fifty of them met in Washington early in March 1933 and drafted an omnibus bill that contained scraps and reworkings of most of the old schemes, but it moved toward the production controls that had been lacking in both McNary-

Haugenism and Hoover's schemes. Producers of seven basic commodities were to receive benefit payments if they cut acreage or production. Funds for these payments would come from a tax upon the processing of commodities — for example, a tax on the milling of wheat. The tax would be added to the price of the flour or other product, and so it would be passed on to the consumer, who would thus indirectly pay the farmer for growing less. Farm prices were to be brought up to "parity," that is, a level that would provide the same price relationship of farm products to manufactured goods as during the period 1909–1914.

Because the 1933 farm season was well under way when the AAA began operations, large-scale destruction was necessary to cut surpluses. Six million pigs and 220,000 sows about to farrow were slaughtered. Nine-tenths of their weight was inedible and processed into fertilizer, but they nevertheless provided 100,000,000 pounds of pork for needy families. Bad weather so drastically cut the wheat crop that the AAA did not have to intervene to reduce it. Cotton farmers plowed under a quarter of their crop — but it was the poorest quarter and they so intensively cultivated the rest that 30,000,000 acres produced more than 36,000,000 had done the previous year.

The NRA

Hard-pressed business executives sought measures providing for government stabilization of business. Since 1931 leaders of the United States Chamber of Commerce and others had been urging an antideflation scheme that involved price fixing through trade associations. This plan would have necessitated suspension of the antitrust laws. President Hoover, who earlier had given strong support to the trade association movement, indignantly opposed price-fixing schemes.

In the spring of 1933 business people sought from Roosevelt what Hoover had refused them. Many of them also demanded government enforcement of their agreements in order to raise prices and stabilize production. The New Deal was ready to give them what they wanted if they would accept wages-and-hours regulation and other concessions for labor. This was the genesis

of the National Industrial Recovery Act, which passed Congress in June 1933.

A new era of government alliance with business for the common good seemed to be opening. Roosevelt as he signed the act called it "the most important and far-reaching legislation ever enacted by the American Congress." On the same day, the President appointed as administrator of the National Recovery Administration (NRA) the volatile, colorful General Hugh S. Johnson, who pictured himself as a sort of benign dictator presiding over the economy.

President Roosevelt and NRA administrator Johnson called upon an excited nation to accept an interim blanket code, providing minimum wages of 30 cents or 40 cents an hour, maximum working hours of thirty-five or forty per week, and the abolition of child labor. Employers who agreed with the code were to display the NRA blue-eagle symbol; consumers who cooperated were to sign pledges that they would buy only from blue-eagle establishments. In much the spirit of 1917, the nation participated in NRA parades and rallies. As Johnson began negotiating codes with big industries, recovery seemed really imminent.

By the beginning of September 1933, specific codes for most of the big industries were in operation. In the drafting of the codes, Johnson had tried to serve as arbiter to balance the conflicting interests of business, labor, and the consumer. All three were represented at the bargaining table and received some degree of protection. Nevertheless, the real power in drawing up the regulations went to the business owners themselves, to the leaders within each industry. The codes often contained provisions that were difficult for small units in the industry to maintain. Most of them provided for limiting production and, though often in disguised form, for price fixing.

Production, after a sharp rise, skidded downward during the fall of 1933, even as prices began to creep upward. The New Deal honeymoon was over, and as General Johnson had predicted, the dead cats began to fly.

A case involving the National Recovery Administration finally reached the Supreme Court. The constitutional basis for the NRA was the power of Congress to regulate commerce among the states, but the test case involved alleged code violations by the Schechter brothers, who were operating a wholesale poultry business confined to one locality, Brooklyn. Among the charges against them were the selling of poultry in poor condition and the unfair treatment of employees. The Court (1935) unanimously held that the Schechters were not engaged in interstate commerce and that Congress had unconstitutionally delegated legislative power to the President to draft the codes.

The "sick chicken" decision outraged Roosevelt. Seeing in it a threat to the whole New Deal, he lashed out at the judges for thinking in terms of the horse-and-buggy era. Actually, the decision proved to be more a blessing than a catastrophe for the New Deal, since it ended the decrepit NRA code system with its tacit suspension of the antitrust laws. "It has been an awful headache," Roosevelt confessed privately.

TVA and Conservation

Increasingly New Dealers turned their attention to measures that would remedy conditions they felt had helped bring on the depression. Their indignation burned especially hot against the private power interests, which they felt had gulled investors and overcharged consumers. The first and most far-reaching of the New Deal reform measures was the creation of the Tennessee Valley Authority (TVA).

Through the twenties, millions of progressive Americans of both parties had shared the dream of Senator George Norris of Nebraska that the government might develop the nation's great water resources to provide cheap electric power. Millions of others accepted the educational program of the utilities companies, which spent $28,000,000 to $35,000,000 per year combating the idea of a national power program. The battle centered on the great dam that had been started at Muscle Shoals on the Tennessee River but had not been finished in time to provide nitrates during the war. Coolidge and the conservatives wished to sell it to Henry Ford for private development. Norris and his cohorts in Congress blocked them. Norris wished to make Muscle Shoals the center for developing the resources of the area and bringing abundance to millions of

people living in poverty. His bill was vetoed by Coolidge and again by Hoover but was approved by Roosevelt in May 1933.

Basically, the TVA aimed to prevent the devastating floods that all too frequently had rolled down the rivers of the area, and to provide cheap, plentiful electricity as a yardstick for the measurement of private rates. More than this, the project became a great experiment in regional planning and rehabilitation.

Under a three-person board of directors with wide powers, the TVA in the next twenty years improved five existing dams and constructed twenty new ones. It stopped floods in the largest heavy-rainfall region in the nation and, by holding back the water, provided an inland waterway system with a nine-foot channel 652 miles long, soon heavy with traffic. From water power, and increasingly from steam plants, the TVA became the greatest producer of electricity in the United States. It also manufactured low-cost phosphate fertilizers. It taught farmers how to use them, how to restore the fertility of their soil, and how to end erosion by means of contour plowing and reforestation. TVA worked no miracles, but it did bring a higher living standard to the farmers of the area. It brought new light industry and increased business. When World War II came, the new power plants provided indispensable electricity for the production of munitions, aluminum, and plutonium.

In its "yardstick" function, TVA drove down the price of power in the area from 10 cents a kilowatt hour to 3 cents. Throughout the country, because of TVA and other pressures, the average residential rate dropped from 5.52 cents in 1933 to 3.67 cents in 1942.

Other great public power and irrigation developments were under way in the West during the same year. On the Colorado River, the Hoover Dam (begun during the Hoover administration) was finished in 1936, and on the Columbia River the Bonneville Dam was constructed in 1937 and the Grand Coulee Dam in 1942. In 1937 Norris proposed the creation of six additional regional authorities like the TVA; Congress failed to act, and the debate over public versus private development of power continued.

To combat drought conditions in the West, Roosevelt in 1934 by executive order set aside

$15,000,000 to build a "shelter belt" of trees on the Great Plains, to break the wind, collect moisture, and harbor wildlife. Critics scoffed, but somehow the trees grew where no one had believed they would. A Soil Erosion Service (later Soil Conservation Service), using much Civilian Conservation Corps labor, was active, especially in the West. Homesteading on the range, which meant dry farming under almost insuperable difficulties, came to an end with the passage of the Taylor Grazing Act of 1934, which withdrew overgrazed land and set regulations for the use of public rangeland. Spoliation of Indian lands came to at least a temporary halt with the passage of the Indian Reorganization Act of 1934, intended to preserve the tribal domain, customs, and civil liberties of the Indians.

Money and Banking

Much of the early New Deal was aimed at raising prices as a means of stimulating recovery. One way was to cut production, as the AAA tried to do for agriculture and the NRA for industry. Another way was to put money into circulation through government spending, as was done in the relief programs (though recovery was not the primary aim of these). Still another way was to increase the money supply.

As a result of a variety of programs the money supply increased at the rapid rate of almost 11 percent per year between April 1933 and March 1937. Many economists now see that expansion as the critical factor in explaining the exceptionally rapid rate of economic recovery that occurred during the same period.

The New Deal's promotion of monetary expansion began as a program of banking reform. In June 1933, following the bank holiday and the Emergency Banking Act, Roosevelt signed the Glass-Steagall Act aimed at curbing speculation by banks. This bill also established the Federal Deposit Insurance Corporation, which for the first time insured depositors against bank collapse, making them more willing to put their funds in the custody of banks. With increased deposits banks were able to expand their loan activities. To prevent the kind of errors by the Federal Reserve that had produced severe monetary con-

traction between 1931 and 1933, Roosevelt engineered passage of the Banking Act of 1935, which centralized control of the system in the hands of the Federal Reserve Board and moved the board's locus of power from New York to Washington in the hope that it would be more responsive to the desires of politicians. Chastened by the strength of their opponents, between 1933 and 1937 the Federal Reserve abstained from any actions that might restrict monetary expansion.

The restraint of the Federal Reserve system permitted Roosevelt to stimulate rapid monetary growth. In May 1933 Congress authorized the President to reduce the gold content of the dollar by as much as 50 percent. From November 1933 through January 1934 Roosevelt kept the announced price of gold, in terms of dollars, higher than the price abroad. The subsequent Gold Reserve Act of 1934 made his devaluation official by fixing a buying and selling price for gold of $35 an ounce rather than the $21 an ounce adhered to formerly. (Also, this act modified the gold standard by permitting the selling of gold only for foreign payments.) The new gold price provided a bonanza for foreigners holding gold and for world gold production because the pegged price was substantially higher than the world price. Consequently both gold production and the importation of gold into the United States soared, the stock in Fort Knox more than tripling between early 1934 and the end of 1940. Correspondingly, currency paid out for gold imports underwent a large increase. This provided a massive growth in the nation's money supply, which stimulated loan activity, encouraged the upward movement of prices, broke the deflationary psychology that had prevailed until 1933, and helped unleash the forces of production. If Roosevelt and Congress had allowed the Federal Reserve to be independent in the 1930s and if the system had adhered to its earlier policies, it would have taken action to cut off the large influx of gold and thus forcefully inhibited economic expansion.

Expression and Escape

Both the depression and the government's efforts to combat it left a mark on the cultural life of the time. The federal government became a patron and promoter of culture on a scale it had never attempted before. The Federal Art Project enrolled 5,000 artists, and many of them turned their attention, sometimes satirically, to the American scene. This was the heyday of Grant Wood, with his patterned Iowa landscapes and austere rural portraits, and of Thomas Hart Benton, who with dramatic sympathy portrayed sharecroppers and blacks. In sculpture, responding to the new government aid and the resurgent nationalism, Gutzon Borglum finished the enormous heads of Washington, Jefferson, Lincoln, and Theodore Roosevelt that were carved on a rocky mountainside in the Black Hills. The Federal Music Project employed 15,000 persons. They brought concerts to 100,000,000 people and gave free music lessons to over 500,000 pupils, most of whom could have afforded neither concerts nor lessons. After depression and competition from motion pictures had thrown most actors and old vaudeville performers out of work, the Federal Theatre Project found employment for 12,500 of them. It brought performances to millions who had never previously seen a stage production. Some of these were highly successful as entertainment, some were of an advanced experimental nature, and some were so far to the left that they kindled the wrath of Congress, which killed the project in 1939.

Reading was one of the most inexpensive pursuits of the depression years, and although libraries suffered from slashed funds, book circulation increased considerably. Popular tastes ranged from John Steinbeck's novel about the Oklahomans' trek to California, *The Grapes of Wrath* (1939), to the romantic escape of Margaret Mitchell's *Gone with the Wind* (1936). Depression likewise cut the cost of radios and enlarged the size of audiences. In 1929, 12,000,000 families owned radios; by 1940, 28,000,000 families, comprising 86 percent of the population, owned them. This in part explains why Roosevelt, the master of the radio "fireside chat," campaigned so successfully with at least 70 percent of the metropolitan newspaper circulation opposing him. A radio serial, *Amos and Andy,* was so popular that Huey Long took the name of one of its characters, the Kingfish, as his sobriquet. Motion picture audiences dropped one-third early in the depression, then by 1939 boomed to a yearly box-office average of $25 per family. Like radio seri-

als, motion pictures dispensed mostly escapist themes; because of the vigor of the Catholic-led Legion of Decency, founded in 1934, it was a less sexy escape than in the twenties. As yet, television was still in the engineering laboratory — a curiosity exhibited at the New York World's Fair of 1939. It was not until the late 1940s that television sets could be produced inexpensively enough to be purchased widely.

Thunder from the Left

As the congressional elections of 1934 approached, conservatives campaigned against the New Deal on the grounds that it was destroying the Constitution and driving the country toward bankruptcy. All they succeeded in doing was to drive the dispossessed millions closer to the New Deal. Instead of losing ground to the Republican party — which would have been normal in a midterm election — the Democrats gained an additional ten seats in the Senate and also in the House.

Throughout the nation leaders arose who promised much to those despairing people whom the New Deal had not yet rescued. An elderly physician in California, Dr. Francis E. Townsend, attracted a following of 5,000,000 destitute old people with his plan to obtain a federal pension of $200 per month for everyone over sixty. The Townsendites claimed that since the pensions would have had to be spent within the month, "the velocity of money" would have ended the depression. The promoters of the movement raised nearly $1,000,000 in two years and commanded a formidable bloc of votes.

Among restless people in Northern cities, Father Charles Coughlin's politico-religious broadcasts attracted a wide following. Starting with a mixture of papal encyclicals and Populism, he at first supported, then went far beyond, Roosevelt. Coughlin advocated expansion of silver coinage and nationalization of banks, utilities, and natural resources. Ultimately, in 1938, he founded the antidemocratic, anti-Semitic Christian Front. In January 1935 he was able to demonstrate his power by inspiring an avalanche of letters and telegrams to senators protesting against the World Court.

From the South, Senator Huey P. Long of Louisiana succeeded in launching a far more telling assault upon the New Deal. A skillful politician, he built a powerful organization in Louisiana and a rapidly growing following that spilled out first into neighboring states, then by 1935 into the Middle West, the Pacific coast, and indeed every part of the country. Within Louisiana, he built bridges, roads, hospitals, and a modern educational system. It was an era of dictators in Europe, and it was easy to accuse the self-styled Louisiana Kingfish of ambitions to be a Fuehrer, although his techniques were the time-honored ones of the American political boss. Ambitious to become President, he lured the masses by offering them more than Roosevelt. His "Share Our Wealth" program promised through confiscatory taxes on great fortunes to provide every family with what in those depression years seemed in itself a fortune: an income of $2,500 per year and a homestead worth $5,000. The New Dealers' political tactician, Postmaster General James A. Farley, estimated in the spring of 1935 that Long could poll up to 4,000,000 votes on a third-party ticket and possibly could throw the 1936 election to the Republicans.

The Second New Deal

The "thunder from the left" was so ominous early in 1935 that many despairing New Dealers, chafing at Roosevelt's apparent inertia, predicted defeat in 1936. Roosevelt, who never liked to explain his tactics, remarked confidentially that he had no intention of engaging in public debate with the leaders of the "lunatic fringe." Rather, he quietly went about stealing their thunder with reform programs that represented a change in the emphasis of New Deal policy. "We have not weeded out the overprivileged," the President told Congress in January 1935, "and we have not effectively lifted up the underprivileged." His new programs, he claimed, were designed to do both. Together, the new initiatives became known as the Second New Deal.

Frances Perkins, the first woman cabinet member, had accepted the office of labor secretary only with Roosevelt's pledge that he would support a social security program. For several years, she and a group of New Dealers sought to win converts in the cabinet, in Congress, and throughout the country to their view that social

insurance would not only aid the unemployed but also help prevent future depressions.

The Social Security Act of 1935 provided two types of assistance for the aged. Those who were destitute could receive federal aid up to $15 per month, depending upon the matching sums the states provided. Those who were working could receive upon retirement annuities provided from taxes upon their earnings and their employer's payroll. The 1935 law specified payments, to begin in 1942, ranging from $10 to $85 per month, and excluded wide categories of workers from the program — but it was a beginning. The act also provided for unemployment insurance, aid for the blind and crippled, and assistance for dependent mothers and children — all such funds to be administered by the states in keeping with minimum federal standards. A Social Security Board supervised the entire system.

Social security could not immediately help those already unemployed in 1935; to aid them, Congress in April voted $5 billion to supplant direct relief with the Works Progress Administration. The WPA under Harry Hopkins did much to "help men keep their chins up and their hands in." It enrolled an average of 2,100,000 workers between 1935 and 1941 on a wide variety of projects. Since the WPA workers were, theoretically, the least employable segment of the working force, and since almost all WPA money went for wages rather than tools and materials, its undertakings could not compare in efficiency with private construction projects. Nevertheless, WPA built nearly 600 airports and built or rebuilt 110,000 public buildings, more than 500,000 miles of roads and streets, over 100,000 bridges, 500,000 sewers, and over 1,000,000 privies.

While Roosevelt had always maintained cordial relations with labor leaders, he was little inclined to give them firm collective bargaining guarantees in place of the weak provisions of the National Industrial Recovery Act. Congress, under the leadership of Senator Robert F. Wagner, felt differently. In May 1935 the Senate passed Wagner's bill providing strong government protection for the unions. Roosevelt, bowing to the inevitable, signed the measure. The Wagner Act, passed at a time when unions were relatively weak, outlawed a number of the "unfair practices" by which management had been bludgeoning them, and created a powerful National Labor Relations Board to police the employers.

In January 1936 the Supreme Court held that it was unconstitutional for the AAA to regulate farm production or to impose a tax for such a purpose. Congress hastily passed a law (the Soil Conservation and Domestic Allotment Act) to meet the Court's objections and yet continue the crop-reduction effort. Under the new law, Congress appropriated money to pay farmers for conserving the soil by leaving part of their land uncultivated.

To improve the condition of the poorer farmers, those on submarginal soil, the government undertook to resettle them on better land. The Resettlement Administration (1935) made short-term loans for rehabilitation and long-term loans for purchasing farms but succeeded in moving only a few thousand farm families. More farmers were benefited by the Rural Electrification Administration, which was established in 1935 to extend power lines to farms through cooperatives. Since its activities also stimulated private power companies to extend into the country, it was effective both directly and indirectly. Power lines had reached only 4 percent of the farms in 1925; they reached 25 percent by 1940.

In 1935 Roosevelt proposed democratizing the federal tax structure by placing far higher levies upon big corporations and wealthy people. He pointed out that a person receiving $6,000 per year paid twice as high a tax as one receiving $4,000, yet the tax upon a $5,000,000 income was only about five times as high as on $1,000,000. Conservative newspapers immediately attacked this proposal as a "soak the rich" tax scheme, but it passed Congress. It wiped away the last vestiges of Secretary Mellon's influence on tax policy, as it established the highest peacetime rates in history at the top: a maximum 75 percent income tax, 70 percent estate tax, and 15 percent corporate income tax.

AFL and CIO

Even before the adoption of the Wagner Act, union membership had risen from a depression low of less than 3,000,000 to 4,200,000. A group of leaders of industrial unions (which offered membership to everyone within an industry) had chafed over the conservation of the craft unions (which took in only those working at a given trade). In 1934 labor leaders such as John L. Lewis of the United Mine Workers, and Sidney Hillman of the Amalgamated Clothing Workers, and David Dubinsky of the International Ladies' Garment Workers had forced President William Green of the AFL and the craft unionists to agree to charter new industrial unions in the big unorganized industries.

In 1935 organization of these industries began. It led to violent opposition not only from the corporations but also from the AFL craft unions, which feared they would be submerged by the new giant unions. Jurisdictional fights led to a schism between the AFL leadership and the industrial unionists, who formed a Committee for Industrial Organization (within the AFL) in November 1935. Industrial warfare followed, as both the AFL and the CIO mounted great rival organizational drives.

President Roosevelt and a few industrial leaders favored industrial unionism. Gerald Swope of General Electric told Roosevelt that his company could not conceivably negotiate with a large number of craft unions but might find advantages in contracting with a single industrial union. Generally, however, in the spring of 1936 much of big business had yet to see advantages in big labor. Small manufacturers were particularly hostile. They often forced young organizers to battle it out, often by physical force, with "loyal" strong-arm squads, occasionally with the police, and sometimes with rival organizers.

Through 1936 the United Automobile Workers gained recruits despite vigorous company opposition. There was good reason, for in 1934, at about the time the organizing drive began, nearly half the auto workers were receiving less than $1,000 per year. General Motors alone, in an effort to keep down union organization, spent almost $1,000,000 on private detectives between 1934 and 1936. In the first two months of 1937, workers closed seventeen General Motors plants through the new device of the sit-down strike, the workers staying by their machinery inside the plants. General Motors soon recognized the UAW, and other automobile companies gradually did the same. Rubber and other industries were similarly organized. Newspapers saw in the sit-down strikes a menace to private property, and much of the public became thoroughly alarmed.

In 1936 the CIO voted a $500,000 fund to organize the steel industry and began its great on-slaught, winning tens of thousands of workers from company unions. United States Steel chose to capitulate rather than face a long strike just as prosperity seemed to be returning. In March 1937, to the amazement of the nation, one of the company's subsidiaries signed a contract with the Steel Workers' Organizing Committee. For the first time, "Big Steel" was unionized.

The unions' gains had little to do directly with the Wagner Act. But the passage of the act had inspired workers, giving them confidence that their cause had significant public support.

Mandate from the People

Roosevelt's vigorous reform program, enacted in its main outlines by 1936, made him a sure winner in the election of that year. Many millions felt that their personal lot had been improved by the New Deal. The violent attacks upon it from the right convinced them even more that Roosevelt was their friend. Despite the misgivings of many conservatives within the party, the Democratic convention in 1936 renominated him by acclamation.

As for the Republicans, they nominated their strongest candidate. Ignoring former President Hoover and the right wing, which was crying calamity, they chose a one-time Bull Mooser who had never strayed far from the 1912 Progressive position. This was the competent governor of Kansas, Alf M. Landon. The Republican platform promised to do most of what the New Deal was undertaking — but more competently, constitutionally, and without running a deficit.

The election demonstrated the extent to which the New Deal depended upon a coalition of farmers, union workers, and the poor. The unions were the heaviest Democratic campaign contributors, providing $1,000,000. Blacks switched en masse from the party of Lincoln to that of Roosevelt. The "lunatic fringe" coalition against Roosevelt stirred hardly a ripple.

A preelection postcard poll by the *Literary Di-gest* had indicated that Landon would win by a big margin. How could it be so wrong? The names and addresses of those polled were taken from old telephone directories. A majority of people who could afford telephones and had not been forced to move favored Landon. In the election he received 16,680,000 popular votes, compared with 27,477,000 for Roosevelt, and got the electoral votes of only Maine and Vermont.

In the campaign Roosevelt had challenged his right-wing opponents — "economic royalists," he called them — and now he had not ony received an overwhelming endorsement for himself but he carried with him many members of Congress pledged to his support. Nevertheless, those economic royalists would still have the upper hand so long as the Supreme Court continued to check New Deal laws. Roosevelt felt he had a mandate from the people to do something about the obstructionist Court.

Storm over the Court

Foes of the National Labor Relations Act and the Social Security Act were openly flouting these laws, confident that the Supreme Court would disallow them as it had already done the NRA and the first AAA. The Court, through its narrow interpretation of the federal power over commerce and taxation and its broad interpretation of freedom of contract in the Fourteenth Amendment, seemed to have created an economic no man's land within which neither the federal nor the state governments could act.

Critics of the Court had been urging passage of some sort of constitutional amendment to provide the federal government with more extensive economic powers. Roosevelt's opinion (which subsequent Supreme Court decisions were to sustain) was that the Constitution granted adequate powers. All that was wrong was the Court's antiquated interpretation, he felt, but the four or five justices firmly opposed to the New Deal enjoyed excellent health and showed no signs of resigning. Consequently Roosevelt decided to propose adding to the Supreme Court — and to lower federal courts — new justices (presumably sharing his viewpoint) to match superannuated ones. Without informing congressional leaders in advance, in

February 1937 Roosevelt sent a surprise message proposing a needed general overhauling of the federal court system and the appointment of as many as six new Supreme Court justices.

There was no real question about the constitutionality of Roosevelt's proposal, since Congress had from time to time changed the number of justices on the Supreme Court. Nevertheless, the plan aroused a great furor throughout the country. Many thoughtful people who had supported Roosevelt in 1936 heeded the warning of conservatives that through such constitutional shortcuts, dictators came into power. Within Congress, the controversy cut across party lines. Roosevelt used every device of party discipline to round up votes in Congress. He might have succeeded in obtaining at least a compromise measure, had not the Supreme Court itself eliminated the necessity for one.

Just before the President sent his court plan to Congress, the Court, in the case of *West Coast Hotel* v. *Parrish*, validated by a 5-to-4 decision a state minimum-wage law. This reversed a 5-to-4 decision of the previous year invalidating a similar law. The decision was announced on March 29, 1937. Two weeks later, the Court, again 5 to 4, upheld the Wagner Act, and in May, the Social Security Act. Since there no longer seemed to be any pressing need for judicial reform, Congress voted down Roosevelt's court plan.

Almost at once the older justices began retiring, and Roosevelt replaced them one by one with his appointees. In the next decade the Roosevelt Court rewrote large sections of constitutional law. The new justices interpreted the commerce and tax clauses so broadly and the Fourteenth Amendment so narrowly that there remained few restrictions upon economic regulation by either the federal or the state governments.

Recovery and Recession

A sharp recession developed in the fall of 1937. It came just as many economists were fearing that an inflationary boom might get out of hand. There had been a remarkable recovery. But the depression had been so deep in 1932 that there were still 7,500,000 unemployed and nearly 4,500,000 families on relief.

Both Hoover and Roosevelt had been forced to incur budgetary deficits as a result of their spending programs and the depressed tax base. By 1937 the national debt had risen to $30 billion, an amount which Roosevelt found abhorrent. He actually feared another disastrous crash — one resulting from excessive government competition with private borrowers for capital. He had the Federal Reserve tighten credit, and he tried to balance the budget by drastically reducing government spending. Between January and August 1937, he cut the WPA in half, sending 1,500,000 workers on unpaid "vacations." The new boom collapsed and sent the economy plummeting. The index of production dropped from 117 in August 1937 to 76 in May 1938; 4,000,000 additional workers were thrown out of work. It seemed almost like 1932 all over again.

In October 1937 the President called Congress into special session. Congress passed an emergency appropriation of $5 billion; the public works and work relief programs once again poured these large sums into the economy, and by June 1938 recovery was under way at the rapid pace experienced between 1933 and 1937.

The experience of the recession of 1937–1938 and the subsequent recovery convinced Roosevelt that there was some merit in new economic theories that argued that the government could help pull the nation out of a depression by liberal expenditures. This theory, known as Keynesianism, after the British economist John Maynard Keynes, would not receive wide acceptance until much later, but never again would a national administration cut expenditures or raise taxes in the face of a recession.

For farmers, Congress passed the Agricultural Adjustment Act of 1938. The "second AAA" provided a number of devices to cut back production: soil conservation payments, marketing quotas, export subsidies, and crop loans. The 1938 act also established a Surplus Marketing Administration to channel surpluses to needy persons and provide food for school lunches.

Since questions of constitutionality no longer seriously interfered after the changes in the Supreme Court, New Dealers fought the Fair Labor Standards Act through Congress in 1938. This established a minimum wage of 25 cents an hour (to be raised gradually to 40 cents by 1945) and a maximum work week of forty-four hours (to be lowered to forty) for most laborers, excepting agricultural, domestic, and maritime workers. It also forbade employment of children under sixteen in most areas except agriculture. Low though these standards were, they raised the pay of 300,000 workers and shortened the workweek for 1,300,000. In subsequent years the standards were raised repeatedly, and the scope of the law was broadened to include additional categories of workers.

Nonetheless, by the end of 1938, the New Deal was close to its limits. The court-packing episode had energized conservatives and given Southern Democrats in Congress an excuse to vote against Roosevelt's measures. The recession of 1937–1938 had further undermined public confidence in the New Deal. In the 1938 elections the Republicans gained eighty seats in the House and seven in the Senate. And the threat of a Second World War was beginning to overshadow even the most critical domestic problems. The President could lead Congress, with its Southern committee chairs, in the direction of strong defense legislation and a vigorous foreign policy only if he conciliated them by abandoning reform.

A Discriminatory Deal

If, in the 1930s, white Americans needed a New Deal, red and black Americans needed something more than that — a new game with new rules. Indians and blacks did benefit from the Roosevelt reforms, but they got less, not more, than a fair and honest reshuffling of the cards.

By this time, all Indians were citizens. They had received citizenship in the Snyder Act of 1924 as a token of gratitude for the services of Indians who had volunteered in World War I. But citizenship did them little good. Those who continued to live on reservations were still treated as "wards of the nation" with practically no control over their own affairs. They suffered from poverty, dirt, disease, ignorance, and despair. Most of those who had left the reservations were little better off.

An investigation showed that federal policy was largely responsible for the Indians' plight. The policy, as laid down in the Dawes Severalty Act of 1887, was intended to assimilate them, that is, to make them over in the image of the whites. The actual effect was merely to weaken the tribal culture and organization of the Indians and to deprive them of land. (After they received their individual allotments under the Dawes Act, the leftover land was sold.)

The tribes were promised a New Deal in the Indian Reorganization Act of 1934. This act brought an end to allotments and provided for federal loans, better schooling and medical care, and religious freedom. It also encouraged a degree of tribal self-government and a revival of native customs. Conditions improved somewhat under the new law, but the Bureau of Indian Affairs did little to encourage Indians to take advantage of it, and Congress failed to appropriate sufficient funds for its full implementation.

At the beginning of the depression most blacks still clung to the party of Abraham Lincoln and emancipation. The lone black representative in Congress, Oscar DePriest of Chicago, had been elected (in 1928) as a Republican. In the election of 1932 the majority of black voters preferred Hoover to Roosevelt. Once in office, however, Roosevelt soon gained a large following among blacks. The shift in loyalty was reflected in 1934, when Arthur W. Mitchell was elected to replace DePriest and become the first black Democrat ever to sit in Congress.

Unlike the last Democratic president, Wilson, who had allowed many blacks to be removed from federal jobs, Roosevelt saw to a considerable increase in the number of black government employees. He regularly sought advice in black affairs from leaders in various walks of life who constituted an unofficial "black cabinet." And blacks did indeed benefit from much of the New Deal legislation. Almost one-third of the federal housing units, for example, went to blacks. But, on the whole, black Americans gained less than whites.

In almost every law setting up a relief agency, Congress included a clause against discrimination on the grounds of race. Southern white politicians, however, insisted on regional wage differentials in agencies such as the WPA. These differentials meant lower pay for blacks — and also whites — in the South. Benefits under the AAA went mainly to landowners rather than to black or white tenants on Southern farms; the biracial Southern Tenant Farmers' Union struggled to protect the sharecroppers' livelihood. CCC camps in the South were segregated. Though the New Deal helped blacks as well as whites to survive the depression, it did nothing to change the longstanding caste system.

The wage-and-hour law and the Social Security Act did not apply to the great majority of blacks, since they were in agriculture or domestic service, and these occupations were exempted from coverage. The minority of blacks in industry were unskilled workers and were excluded from the craft unions. They shared, however, in the gains of industrial unionism with the rise of the CIO, which welcomed black members. Even so, as late as 1940 fewer than 4 in 100 automobile workers were black.

Northern as well as Southern blacks felt exploited by white landlords and shopkeepers. In the Harlem section of New York City, feelings flared up on a March night in 1935 as rioters broke into 200 stores, causing merchants a $2,000,000 loss. Three of the rioters were killed. After the investigation, the black sociologist E. Franklin Frazier reported that the outbreak of lawlessness had been provoked by "resentments against racial discrimination and poverty in the midst of plenty."

Chapter 23

From Isolation to Intervention

American Ambivalence

Throughout the 1930s, the American people were well aware that cataclysmic events were preparing the way for the Second World War, which broke out in 1939. While the United States was seeking nationalistic but peaceable internal policies to restore prosperity, some other nations were trying to find their way out of depression by intimidating or even conquering other weaker countries. Adolf Hitler and the Nazis who won control of Germany in 1933 became an immediate and frightening menace to peace; the military leaders who determined policy in Japan continued their efforts to dominate East Asia. The American people and their government were quite ambivalent toward the acts of aggression of these nations. On the one hand, Americans wished to help the victims; on the other, they lacked the power to limit aggression by economic sanctions and did not wish the United States to become involved in armed conflict. This ambivalence continued through the thirties, as the United States more and more became involved in the struggle against the aggressors. Ultimately, through the Japanese attack on Pearl Harbor, the country was plunged into war.

Seeking Friends and Customers

In 1933 there still seemed the possibility that United States foreign policy could confine itself to economic questions growing out of the depression, and the encouragement of world disarmament. President Hoover had hoped through

concessions on war debts to obtain currency stabilization and other international agreements to promote recovery. After equivocating for several months, Roosevelt decided to modify the gold standard and hence rejected stabilization until a time more favorable to the United States. In July 1933 he cabled Secretary of State Cordell Hull at the London Economic Conference a "bombshell message," disavowing stabilization and ending any faint possibility that the United States would seek international routes to recovery.

The hope of stimulating foreign trade led Roosevelt in November 1933 to recognize Soviet Russia. Since the revolution of November 1917 the Russian government had gone unrecognized while a number of irritating questions between the two nations continued to fester. Americans, hungry for what they unrealistically dreamed would be a substantial Russian trade, were eager for recognition. The Russians had even stronger motives for obtaining recognition, for they were afraid of being attacked by Japan. Maxim Litvinov, the Russian foreign minister, after discussions with Roosevelt at the White House, agreed that Russia would end its propaganda activities in the United States, guarantee religious freedom and protection in the courts to Americans resident in Russia, and negotiate a settlement of debts and claims.

By January 1934 Roosevelt was ready to listen seriously to Hull's homilies on the necessity of lowering tariff barriers in order to improve foreign trade. With Roosevelt's support, Congress in June 1934 passed Hull's cherished program, the

Reciprocal Trade Agreements Act. It authorized the administration to negotiate agreements, lowering tariffs by as much as 50 percent on specified goods coming in from individual nations in return for their reducing tariffs on American goods. The legislation, which Congress periodically renewed, replaced the framing of new tariff legislation, and ultimately led to much lower rates.

Reciprocal trade was a key ingredient in the Good Neighbor policy toward Latin America, which the Roosevelt administration fabricated. At the Inter-American Conference at Montevideo in 1933, Hull not only offered this economic succor, he reiterated to the people of Latin America that the United States was opposed to armed intervention in Latin America. Hull even signed a convention declaring: "No state has the right to intervene in the internal or external affairs of another."

In 1933, when revolutions exploded in Cuba, Sumner Welles, one of the chief drafters of the new Latin American policy, was sent into Cuba to offer the "good offices" of the United States. Welles helped bring pacification without calling in the marines. In 1934, when a more conservative government came into power in Cuba, the United States gave up its right of intervention under the Platt Amendment. It also withdrew the last marines from Haiti and negotiated a treaty (not ratified until 1939) relaxing the restrictions upon Panama.

The new Good Neighbor policy of nonintervention received a severe testing in 1938 when Mexico expropriated all foreign oil holdings, including property valued by its American owners at $200,000,000. The United States conceded the right of expropriation but at first contended that the price the Mexicans wished to pay was so trivial that the takeover amounted to confiscation. In 1942 after years of involved controversy, a commission evaluated the property at $24,000,000, and the State Department then told the protesting oil companies that they must accept the settlement or receive nothing. This was a reversal of dollar diplomacy — a renunciation of the right to intervene for the purpose of protecting American property in Latin America.

As for the Philippines, primarily the depression and secondarily isolationism brought them the long-sought but economically dubious blessing of independence. American producers of sugar, fats, and oils were determined to thrust their Filipino competitors outside the tariff wall; isolationists were eager to drop this dangerous Far Eastern military commitment. The Tydings-McDuffie Act of 1934 thrust upon the Philippines complete independence rather than the dominion status they sought. In 1935 the Philippines entered upon a transitional commonwealth period; on July 4, 1946, they became a fully independent republic.

The New Neutrality

Meanwhile, the United States continued to assert a strong moral position to try to bring about substantial disarmament. But Hitler was bent upon rearming, not disarming, and in October 1933 withdrew from both the Geneva arms conference and the League of Nations. A new arms race was under way.

At the London Naval Conference of 1935, the Japanese withdrew after they failed to obtain equality with the Americans and British in place of the 5:5:3 ratio, and thus the way was opened for competitive naval building. The United States soon turned to building the fleet with which it was later to fight the opening battles of a Pacific war.

With the breakdown of the naval status quo and the threatened aggressions in both Asia and Europe, most Americans felt that at all costs they must stay out of impending wars. Some dedicated Wilsonians and advocates of the League concluded that Wall Streeters and munitions makers and Wilson's legalistic insistence upon outmoded neutral rights on the high seas had trapped the nation into World War I. Senate investigators, under the progressive Republican Gerald P. Nye of North Dakota, revealed exorbitant wartime profits and tax evasions and claimed that bankers had sought war to rescue their loans to the Allies.

The Nye Committee findings and similar sensational popular writings convinced a large part of the public that entrance into World War I had been a frightful mistake. The way to avoid its repetition seemed to be to legislate against the supposed causes. As Mussolini openly prepared to conquer Ethiopia in 1935, Americans feared that a general European war might develop. They felt that the way to avoid involvement was to isolate the nation through neutrality legislation.

President Roosevelt also favored legislation, but he and Hull desired, as Hull had proposed in 1933, a law that would enable Roosevelt to embargo war supplies to the aggressor and allow their sale to the victim. But Congress passed a neutrality act providing a mandatory embargo against both aggressor and victim and empowering the President to warn American citizens that they might travel on vessels of belligerents only at their own risk. This first Neutrality Act of 1935, a temporary measure, was renewed in 1936 and again, with even stronger provisions, in 1937.

When the attack upon Ethiopia came, in October 1935, the League branded Italy an aggressor and voted sanctions against it. England and France made gestures against Italy but showed no inclination toward determined action. Hull imposed a "moral embargo" upon oil. Mussolini easily conquered his African empire, then withdrew from the League and in October 1936 joined with Hitler to form a new Rome-Berlin axis.

The fiasco seemed to strengthen the determination of the American people to stay out of war. This anti-involvement sentiment continued to be the mood of the nation when a new danger arose in July 1936, as General Francisco Franco and the Falangists (modeled after the Fascists) revolted against the Republican government in Spain. Hitler and Mussolini sided with Franco; Russia, France, and to a lesser extent Great Britain favored the Loyalists. To prevent the Spanish civil war from spreading into a general European conflict, England and France agreed to send no aid to either side. Roosevelt tried to cooperate; he persuaded Congress to apply the existing Neutrality Act to civil as well as international wars. The result was that the United States and other Western nations denied aid to Republican Spain. The Republican government came to depend increasingly upon Russia for what little aid it received. As for Franco, he received massive aid from Mussolini and Hitler and ultimately crushed the Loyalists.

Japan's "New Order"

Japan had begun to take Chinese territory in 1931, when it seized Manchuria as a buffer against the Russians and as a source of raw mate-

rials. The Hoover administration lacked the power to do anything more than declare its moral disapproval. With the Stimson Doctrine (1932), Secretary of State Henry L. Stimson declared that the United States did not recognize the territorial change because it had been brought about by force of arms. Such protests, however, did not discourage Japan, which launched a massive drive into China's five northern provinces during the summer of 1937. Photographs of the Japanese taking major Chinese cities, including Peking and Shanghai, and bombing innocent civilians stunned Americans.

Since Japan had not declared war, Roosevelt was able to refuse to declare the existence of war and, thus, to avoid invoking the Neutrality Act. The administration's purpose was to help the Chinese, who needed American arms and munitions, by allowing Americans to continue to sell them supplies. By October 1937 the administration was ready to take a firm position against Japan. The British proposed a joint arms embargo that seemed to involve no great risk. At this time and during the next four years, the consensus of the experts was that Japan was a mediocre military power. Hull persuaded Roosevelt to make a statement to counteract isolationism. The President, speaking at Chicago, went beyond his advisers and declared: "The peace-loving nations must make a concerted effort in opposition to those violations of treaties and those ignorings of humane instincts which today are creating a state of international anarchy, international instability from which there is no escape through mere isolation or neutrality." War, he asserted, was a contagion that must be quarantined by the international community.

There is evidence that Roosevelt had in mind nothing more drastic than a collective breaking off of diplomatic relations. Immediate reaction was favorable, but within a few days, the "quarantine" speech had plunged the nation into a war fright. Roosevelt backtracked for several months.

Japan had no need to fear economic or military reprisals from the United States. On December 12, 1937, young Japanese aviators bombed and sank the United States gunboat *Panay* on the Yangtze River. The aviators claimed they bombed it in error, but visibility was excellent and an American flag was painted on the deck. As at the sinking of the *Maine* in 1898, a wave of excitement swept the country, but this time it was fear that the nation might become involved in war. The United States quickly accepted the profuse Japanese apologies and offers of indemnity.

At the end of 1938, as Japan supplanted the Open Door with the New Order, that nation was making conditions almost untenable for Americans in China. But the threat of war in Europe overshadowed the Asian impasse.

War in Europe

By 1938 Hitler had rebuilt such a strong German army and air force that he was ready to embark upon a course of intimidation and conquest. In March he proclaimed union with Austria and paraded triumphantly through Vienna. This union put western Czechoslovakia into the jaws of a German vise. Hitler began tightening it with demands on behalf of the minority of 3,500,000 Germans in Czechoslovakia. In September 1938 he brought Europe to the brink of war with his demands for the cession of the Sudeten area in which the minority lived. The Czechs, who had a strong army, were ready to fight rather than submit, but the people of other Western nations, appalled at the threat of another world conflict, were eager for a settlement on almost any terms. Roosevelt joined in the pleas to Hitler for a peaceful solution. At Munich on September 29 the French and the British signed a pact with Hitler granting his demands in Czechoslovakia. "This is the last territorial claim I have to make in Europe," he declared.

Within a few weeks, the once strong Czechoslovakia was whittled down to impotence. In March 1939 Hitler took over the remaining areas as German protectorates, thus demonstrating the worthlessness of his Munich pledge. In April he began harassing Poland. The British and French, seeing clearly that appeasement had failed, gave firm pledges to Poland and other threatened nations. They made half-hearted gestures toward Russia, which had been left out of the Munich settlement, but Stalin in August signed a nonaggression pact with Hitler. This freed Hitler to attack Poland if he could not frighten that country into submission. When Poland stood firm, Germany invaded it on September 1, 1939. True to their pledges, Great Britain and France declared war on Germany on September 3. World War II had begun.

Aiding the Allies

With the outbreak of war, Roosevelt issued a neutrality proclamation pointedly different from Wilson's 1914 plea for Americans to be impartial in thought as well as action. "This nation will remain a neutral nation," Roosevelt stated, "but I cannot ask that every American remain neutral in thought as well."

Promptly, Roosevelt called Congress into special session and, despite a heated debate, was able to muster the votes for a revision of the Neutrality Act. The 1939 measure still prohibited American ships from entering the war zones, but it allowed belligerents to purchase arms on a "cash and carry" basis. Had England and France been able to defeat Hitler with this limited assistance, Roosevelt probably would have been satisfied with it. Indeed, after the quick Nazi overrunning of Poland, overoptimistic American publicists, during the "phony war" of 1939–1940, asserted that the Allies were calling Hitler's bluff and, after a long and boring blockade on sea and land, would triumph.

Optimistic illusions about Hitler's weakness turned into panic in the spring of 1940 when the Nazis invaded Denmark and Norway, then swept across Holland and Belgium deep into France. On May 16 Roosevelt asked Congress for an additional billion for defense expenditures and obtained it quickly. On the premise that the United States must build great air armadas to hold off the Nazis, he set a goal of at least 50,000 airplanes a year.

On June 10, 1940, Mussolini joined the Germans by attacking France. Roosevelt that evening asserted: "The hand that held the dagger has struck it into the back of its neighbor." And, with France tottering from the German onslaught, he proclaimed that the United States would "extend to the opponents of force the material resources of this nation." He was taking the United States from a status of neutrality to one of nonbelligerency on the side of the democracies.

Twelve days later France fell, and in all western Europe only the shattered remnants of the British Army that had been retrieved from Dunkirk opposed the Nazis. Already the new prime minister, Winston Churchill, was showering Roosevelt with requests for destroyers and arms of all kinds to help the British defend their bastion. The odds against the British were heavy, but Roosevelt made the bold and dangerous decision to "scrape the bottom of the barrel" and make it possible for the British to buy all available matériel of war. As the Germans, preparing for an invasion, began to bomb Britain from the air, Roosevelt gave fifty overage destroyers to the British in return for ninety-nine-year leases on eight bases from Newfoundland to British Guiana. It was, as Churchill later wrote, "a decidedly unneutral act."

Isolationists vs. Interventionists

Roosevelt threw the resources of the United States behind the British as completely as Congress would let him. He did so with the feeling that an Axis victory would mean disaster to the nation. Roosevelt and the American public seemed to share incompatible aims. They wished to bring about the defeat of the Axis without involving the United States in a shooting war. Some time in the next eighteen months, Roosevelt probably came to feel that American entrance was desirable; the public never did.

The whole country was pulled into a great debate on the issue of neutrality versus all-out aid to the Allies. William Allen White, the Kansas editor, headed a Committee to Defend America by Aiding the Allies, often called the White Committee. White himself favored merely aid, but a minority wanted to go further and declare war. On the anti-involvement side, a Yale student organized an America First Committee chaired by a leading Chicago business executive, General Robert E. Wood. It drew upon the oratorical talent of the aviation hero Charles Lindbergh, General Hugh Johnson, and Senators Nye and Wheeler. It won the editorial support of some large newspapers, and it appealed to a considerable segment of patriotic Americans. Inevitably it also attracted a small fringe of pro-Nazi, anti-Semitic, and American Fascist fanatics. The debate was bitter, and through the summer and fall of 1940 it was complicated by a presidential election.

Election of 1940

The Republicans met at Philadelphia in June, at the time of the collapse of France. National defense suddenly became the most important issue. Roosevelt underscored this and stole headlines from the Republican convention by appointing to his cabinet two of the most distinguished Republicans. He made the elder statesman Henry L. Stimson secretary of war, and the 1936 vice-presidential candidate and sharp critic of the New Deal, Frank Knox, secretary of the navy.

The chagrined Republicans at Philadelphia promptly read Stimson and Knox out of the party but could not ignore the defense issue. They succumbed to the grass-roots pressure, which had been built through a careful advertising campaign, and nominated a young internationalist, Wendell Willkie. This was a startling blow to the isolationist majority among the Republican politicians, but it provided them with a tousle-haired, personable candidate who could win hysterical devotion from the amateur party workers. Both the platform and the candidate pledged that the nation would be kept out of war but would aid peoples fighting for liberty.

By the time the Democrats met in mid-July, it was a foregone conclusion that they would renominate Roosevelt. He was even able to force the Democratic politicians to swallow his choice for Vice President, Secretary of Agriculture Henry A. Wallace, who was considered an advanced New Dealer.

Willkie embarked upon an appealing but slightly amateurish campaign, whistle-stopping so vigorously that he nearly lost his voice, denouncing the bad management of the New Deal rather than its basic program.

Roosevelt, a wily old campaigner, tried to give the appearance of not campaigning at all. Defense problems were so acute, he insisted, that he had to spend his time touring army bases, munitions plants, and shipyards. He followed routes that somehow took him through innumerable cities, where he cheerily greeted quantities of voters.

Foreign policy was paramount. On this, both Willkie and Roosevelt had much the same views. Willkie approved of the destroyers-bases agreement. Both made fervent antiwar statements to placate the isolationists. Willkie declared that if Roosevelt's promise to stay out of a foreign war was no better than his pledge to balance the budget, the boys were "already almost on the transports." This was an effective campaign issue that cut into Roosevelt's support. In Boston, Roosevelt (making the mental reservation that any attack upon the United States would not be a foreign war) picked up the challenge in words the isolationists were to mock incessantly: "I have said this before, but I shall say it again and again and again: Your boys are not going to be sent into any foreign wars."

A large part of the vote of those opposing aid to the Allies went to Willkie. Those favoring vigorous aid or even intervention (including many who fervently opposed New Deal domestic policies) voted for Roosevelt. They preferred Roosevelt's sure leadership to Willkie's inexperience. It was a relatively close popular vote: 27,244,000 for Roosevelt, and 22,305,000 for Willkie; but the electoral vote was lopsided: 449 to 82.

The Lend-Lease Act

In addition to politicking, during the months after the fall of France, Roosevelt had to build makeshift defense machinery. With Willkie's aid, he pushed through the Burke-Wadsworth bill, passed in September 1940, which inaugurated the first peacetime selective service in American history. This was the summer when he arranged to send destroyers to England; returned to the factories new airplanes purchased by the American government so the British could buy them instead; and somehow ran the gauntlet of several anti-British, isolationist chairs of Senate committees.

By mid-December the British had so nearly exhausted their financial resources that they had practically stopped letting new contracts, yet Churchill warned Roosevelt that their needs would increase tenfold in the future. The Neutral-

ity Act of 1939 and the Johnson Act of 1934 forbade American loans; a request for repeal would have reawakened the old ill feelings about unpaid war debts. Roosevelt, cruising in the Caribbean after the election, thought of a formula. The United States, "to eliminate the dollar sign," should lend goods rather than money, while serving as an "arsenal of democracy."

A Lend-Lease bill went into the congressional hopper at the right moment to bear a significant number: it became House Resolution No. 1776. After fierce debate, the bill went through Congress by a wide margin and in March 1941 was signed by the President. It empowered him to spend an initial $7 billion — a sum as large as all the controversial loans of World War I.

Lend-Lease committed the United States formally to the policy the President had been following since the fall of France, the policy of pouring aid into Great Britain to help that country withstand the German onslaught. Since Lend-Lease shipments had to cross the Atlantic to be of aid, the United States acquired a vital interest in keeping the Atlantic sea lanes open against the formidable wolf packs of German submarines, which in the spring of 1941 were destroying a half-million tons of shipping a month, twice as much as could be replaced. The President did not openly dare to convoy vessels to England as Secretary Stimson urged; isolationists in Congress were too powerful. Instead he fell back upon the device of "hemispheric defense." The American republics had proclaimed an Atlantic neutrality zone in 1939; Roosevelt in 1941 extended it far to the east, almost to Iceland, and ordered the Navy to patrol the area and give warning of aggressors. This meant radioing to the British the location of Nazi submarines. The United States occupied Greenland in April 1941 and began escorting convoys as far as Iceland in July.

Toward Belligerency

In secret, the United States had gone even further, for in the spring of 1941 American and British officers in Washington reached agreement on the strategy to be followed if the United States entered the war. President Roosevelt demonstrated publicly in August 1941 how close he had come to carrying the United States from nonbelligerency to cobelligerency with England when he met with Prime Minister Churchill off the coast of Newfoundland. Roosevelt refused to make military commitments but did sign with Churchill a press release on mutual war aims, the Atlantic Charter. In it they declared that their nations sought no additional territory but favored self-determination and self-government for peoples who had been deprived of it, freedom of access and trade, collaboration in economic development, and mutual security from aggressors. As Churchill later pointed out, Roosevelt, representing a nation not at war, subscribed to a document that referred to "the final destruction of the Nazi tyranny" as a war aim.

In June 1941 Hitler unleashed against Russia a surprise attack so powerful that American military leaders predicted that Russia would collapse in a few weeks or months. The Russians fell back before the deep Nazi invasion but continued to fight, and in September Roosevelt, again gambling, extended Lend-Lease to them. This made it even more imperative to patrol the seas effectively.

The German answer was to strike back with submarines. In May 1941 they sank the American ship *Robin Moor* off the coast of Brazil. In September a submarine attacked but failed to hit the destroyer *Greer*, which was radioing the submarine's position to the British. President Roosevelt, who did not know or at least did not reveal what the *Greer* was doing, issued orders to the navy to "shoot on sight." In October another destroyer was hit, and the *Reuben James* was sunk. Congress voted legislation to arm merchant ships and allow them to sail to belligerent ports. Naval war with the Nazis was under way.

The chief of naval operations, Admiral Harold R. Stark, wrote in his diary that Hitler "has every excuse in the world to declare war on us now, if he were of a mind to." But Hitler was not, and war came from the Pacific, not the Atlantic.

Pearl Harbor

The Japanese saw in the European crisis an unparalleled opportunity to extend their empire. In the summer of 1939 they forced concessions from

the British that demonstrated their intentions. The United States promptly took a most serious step and gave it the requisite six months' notice to terminate its 1911 commercial treaty. Beginning in January 1940 this country was free to cut off its shipments of oil, scrap iron, and other raw materials.

The United States was determined to restrain Japan, even at the risk of a war. More was at stake than tin, rubber, and other vital raw materials. In September 1940 Japan signed a defensive alliance with Germany and Italy (the Tripartite Pact); any further Japanese thrusts would damage the world status quo to which the State Department was committed. The administration policy toward Japan was inseparably interrelated with that toward Germany and subordinate to it.

Under the Export Control Act, by the fall of 1940 the United States had placed an embargo upon aviation gasoline and almost all raw materials with military potential, including scrap iron and steel. Already war was close. The Japanese government of Prince Konoye wished to conciliate the United States if it could do so without serious concessions. Negotiations began in the spring of 1941 and dragged on into December. At first the Japanese informally suggested rather generous proposals, but by May they were making formal ones that were unacceptable: the United States should ask Chiang Kai-shek of China to make peace on Japan's terms, should restore normal trade with Japan, and should help Japan procure natural resources in Southeast Asia.

The German attack upon Russia relieved the Japanese of one of their greatest worries, since they thought they no longer needed to fear interference from Siberia. They decided to move into southern Indochina and Thailand. The United States had broken the Japanese code and, through intercepted messages, knew this was probably a prelude to attacks upon Singapore and the Dutch East Indies. At the end of July 1941, when the Japanese occupied southern Indochina, the United States, acting firmly with the British and the Dutch, froze Japanese assets in their respective countries so that the Japanese could not convert these assets into cash. This put the Japanese into such a desperate plight that they would either have to abandon their aggressions or attack

The Background of Pearl Harbor

After the end of World War II a number of critics charged that the Roosevelt administration had deliberately brought the United States into the war by provoking the Japanese to attack Pearl Harbor. Charles A. Beard, in his *President Roosevelt and the Coming of the War, 1941* (1948), claimed that the American government refused to compromise with Japan and allow it to buy the raw materials needed for Japan's military adventure in China. Hence Japan had little choice but to strike out in the southwest Pacific and take the necessary supplies by force. From decoded Japanese radio messages, Roosevelt and his advisers must have known, by late November, that Japan was about to begin hostilities. Indeed, as War Secretary Henry L. Stimson recorded in his diary, Roosevelt at a cabinet meeting "brought up the event that we were likely to be attacked," for the Japanese were "notorious for making an attack without warning." Stimson added, significantly: "The question was how we should maneuver them into the position of firing the first shot."

In *Roosevelt from Munich to Pearl Harbor* (1950), Basil Rauch undertook to refute Beard's argument, yet Rauch conceded that the administration had had in mind a "maneuver" of sorts. "The question" he explained, "was whether the President should ask Congress for a declaration of war *prior* to a Japanese attack on the Philippines or Guam, in order to avoid giving Japan the advantage of a surprise attack, or wait until Japan attacked American territory, that is, 'maneuver' Japan into firing the first shot."

Disagreeing with both Beard and Rauch, R. N. Current contended, in *Secretary Stimson: A Study in Statecraft* (1954), that Roosevelt and his advisers intended neither to provoke an attack on Pearl Harbor nor to await one on Guam or the Philippines. Stimson and the others were expecting the Japanese to move against Dutch or British but *not* American possessions. When Stimson said "we were likely to be attacked" he meant "we" in the sense of "our side," including the British and the Dutch. If he and his colleagues had really been anticipating a blow at Pearl Harbor, they obviously would not have had to worry about how to provoke the Japanese to attack there. The real question, as Stimson saw it, was how to make the Japanese *appear* to be firing on the United States if and when they attacked Dutch or British territory in the southwest Pacific. He assumed that such a "maneuver" as this would be necessary to persuade Congress to pass a war declaration, which he believed to be in the best interests of the United States.

Subsequent historians have found no evidence that Roosevelt knew in advance of the Japanese attack. Roberta Wohlstetter, in *Pearl Harbor: Warning and Decision* (1962), concluded that the United States would have anticipated the attack if its intelligence-gathering services had not been overwhelmed by too much information. In *At Dawn We Slept* (1981), Gordon W. Prange agreed with Wohlstetter, finding the Roosevelt administration negligent for not anticipating the attack but not guilty of foreknowledge. Despite these well-documented studies, John Toland, in *Infamy: Pearl Harbor and Its Aftermath* (1982), attempted to revive Beard's argument. However, he could produce no direct evidence that Roosevelt anticipated Pearl Harbor.

British or Dutch East India possessions to get needed supplies.

Roosevelt and Hull seemed to make the foolish error of thinking Japan was bluffing when it was not. Instead of granting limited concessions that would have strengthened the Japanese moderates and postponed or avoided a war the United States was in no position to fight in 1941, the American policy makers took an adamant moralistic position that played into the hands of the Japanese extremists.

Each nation refused to budge on the question of China. On November 20, 1941, Japan offered a temporary settlement highly favorable to itself. Hull rejected it and replied by restating the basic American terms, insisting that Japan get out of China. He not only knew Japan would not accept these but understood also, through intercepted Japanese messages, that Japan had made its last offer and that after November 29 things automatically would happen. "I have washed my hands of the Japanese situation," Hull told Stimson on November 27, "and it is now in the hands of you and Knox, the Army and Navy."

The United States knew that Japan was on the move and that war was imminent. A large Japanese convoy was moving southward through the China Sea. The administration thought an attack upon American territory unlikely. The commanders in Hawaii were routinely warned. Negligence there and in Washington, not diabolical plotting as was later charged, led to the disaster ahead. Meanwhile, on November 25, a Japanese naval task force had sailed eastward from the Kuriles.

At 7:55 on Sunday morning, December 7, 1941, the first wave of Japanese airplanes hit the United States naval base at Pearl Harbor, Hawaii; a second wave came an hour later. The attacks were successful beyond Japan's greatest expectations. Within two hours the planes destroyed or severely damaged 8 battleships, 3 light cruisers, 4 miscellaneous vessels, 188 airplanes, and important shore installations. There were 3,435 casualties. The Japanese task force withdrew, having lost 29 planes, 5 midget submarines, and less than 100 men. In this first strike, the United States was rendered almost impotent in the Pacific, but the bitterly wrangling nation was suddenly unified for the global war into which it had been precipitated.

"Yesterday, December 7, 1941 — a date which will live in infamy — the United States of America was suddenly and deliberately attacked by the naval and air forces of the Empire of Japan." Thus President Roosevelt addressed Congress on the Monday after the debacle at Pearl Harbor. Within four hours, the Senate unanimously, and the House 388 to 1, voted for a war resolution against Japan. Three days later Germany and Italy declared war against the United States, and on the same day, December 11, Congress reciprocated without a dissenting vote.

Selected Readings

A short account of the 1920s is William Leuchtenburg, *The Perils of Prosperity, 1914–32** (1958); a standard survey, J. D. Hicks, *Republican Ascendancy, 1921–1933.** A critical view is A. M. Schlesinger, Jr., *The Crisis of the Old Order* (1957). On economic history, see George Soule, *Prosperity Decade* (1947); Milton Friedman and A. J. Schwartz, *The Great Contraction, 1929–1933** (1965); and J. K. Galbraith, *The Great Crash** (1955). A careful account of the Hoover administration is A. U. Romasco, *The Poverty of Abundance** (1965).

The most notable single-volume survey of the New Deal is W. E. Leuchtenburg, *Franklin D. Roosevelt and the New Deal, 1932–1940** (1963). Two volumes in A. M. Schlesinger, Jr., *Age of Roosevelt*, cover domestic developments through the 1936 election: *The Coming of the New Deal** (1959) and *The Politics of Upheaval** (1960). On the New Deal's first year, see Frank Freidel, *Franklin D. Roosevelt, Launching the New Deal* (1973). On special topics see E. W. Hawley, *The New Deal and the Problem of Monopoly* (1966); J. M. Blum,

From the Morgenthau Diaries (3 vols., 1959–1967); Frank Freidel, *F. D. R. and the South** (1965); T. H. Williams, *Huey Long* (1969); Alan Brinkley, *Voices of Protest: Huey Long, Father Coughlin, and the Great Depression** (1982); Roy Lubove, *The Struggle for Social Security, 1900–1935* (1969); J. T. Patterson, *Congressional Conservatism and the New Deal* (1967); B. D. Karl, *Executive Reorganization and Reform in the New Deal* (1963); Bernard Sternsher, ed., *The Negro in Depression and War** (1969); and O. L. Graham, Jr., *The New Deal: The Critical Issues** (1971).

---

* Titles available in paperback.

Part Seven
1941-1960

Another Foreign Crusade with Mixed Results

With the bombing of Pearl Harbor President Roosevelt turned from the New Deal to national defense and then war abroad. About a quarter of a century earlier, President Woodrow Wilson had turned from progressive reform to a foreign crusade, with disillusioning results, but Roosevelt hoped to escape the frustrations that had befallen his predecessor.

Thus, during World War II, Roosevelt did not hold the United States somewhat aloof from its allies and call it merely an "associated" power, as Wilson had done during World War I. To the contrary, under Roosevelt this country took the initiative in drafting and signing a Declaration of the United Nations (January 1, 1942). The document set forth the war aims of the Atlantic Charter, committing the country's entire military and economic resources to the prosecution of the war, and pledging unlimited cooperation with the other signatories to fight on and make no separate peace.

In peacemaking as in warmaking, Roosevelt followed a course quite different from Wilson's. Roosevelt, with his slogan of "unconditional surrender," was determined to allow no armistice short of the enemy's utter defeat. This time there was to be no general peace conference comparable to the one at Versailles, and the new peacekeeping arrangement was to be kept quite separate from the political settlements to be made. The wartime alliance itself was to be converted into a peacekeeping body — the United Nations organization.

When, at the war's conclusion, the Senate approved American membership in the United Nations, many liberal Americans rejoiced that their country now was righting the wrong it presumably had done in rejecting the League. They assumed that with the United States as a member, the League would have prevented a second world war; surely the United Nations would prevent a third. The optimism soon passed.

As a result of World War II, Germany and Japan were temporarily eliminated as military powers. A "power vacuum" was left in Europe, and another in Asia. Only two really great powers remained in the world — the United States and the Soviet Union. The influence of the Russian Communists, and later that of the Chinese Communists, began to flow into the voids left by the war. The United States undertook to resist the spread of Communist power and thus came into collision with its recent allies, the Russians and the Chinese. It now sought new alliances not only with old associates like Great Britain and France but also with former foes, Germany (or a part of that country) and Japan, which it began to help revive and rebuild as strong nations. Such, in essence, was the "cold war" that commenced within two years after the end of World War II.

At first the United States appeared to hold the upper hand, for it had a monopoly of atomic weapons. But by 1949, the Russians had exploded an A-bomb of their own. The Americans got ahead again, in 1952, with the vastly more destructive hydrogen bomb, but the Russians produced an H-bomb, too, the following year. Each of the great contestants developed the capability, quite literally, of destroying the other. A wholly new era had arrived, in which another world war could wipe out humankind itself. Nobody really knew whether the old rules of power politics had relevance any longer.

Though the peril of nuclear annihilation hung over them, the majority of the American people, in a phrase of the time, "never had it so good." They were riding a wave of prosperity much higher and longer-lasting than any previous one in the history of the country. The boom continued through the 1950s and the 1960s, with an occasional recession or minor slump but with no real depression. A generation grew up that had never experienced such a calamity and could not believe it possible. However, a large minority of the people, perhaps 30,000,000 of them, had little share in this prosperity. Especially disadvantaged were the Americans of African, Mexican, and Indian descent.

Chapter 24

The Second World War

Mobilizing for Defense

At the time of Pearl Harbor, the United States had little armament because so much had been shipped to Great Britain and because so many of the plants had only recently begun production. The tremendous demands that followed Pearl Harbor created chaos in American war production.

But out of the confusion a pattern gradually emerged. The basic step was to coordinate the various phases of the war production program under the War Production Board, established in January 1942. The WPB eventually broke most of the bottlenecks by the Controlled Materials Plan, which allocated precise quantities of raw materials to each manufacturer.

An indispensable adjunct of the war agencies was the Senate War Investigating Committee, headed by Harry S Truman, who had been previously little known. Ruling out questions of military policy, the senators ferreted out incompetence and corruption in the war-production and military-construction programs: outrageous expense in building army camps, improper inspection of airplane engines, a quixotic scheme to build an Arctic pipeline, and the like. The Truman committee not only uncovered and stopped hundreds of millions of dollars of waste but by its vigor led war administrators to be more diligent in preventing further waste. In the wartime expenditure of $400 billion there was amazingly little corruption.

By the beginning of 1944 war production reached such high levels that factories had substantially turned out what seemed to be needed to win the war. The output was double that of all Axis countries combined. However, war needs even at their peak took only about a third of American production. While manufacture of such goods as automobiles, most electrical appliances, and nondefense housing had come to a halt in 1942, production of food, clothing, and goods for repair and maintenance was continued or even slightly increased.

Demands for consumer goods and the burgeoning of buying power in a period of renewed prosperity created an almost irresistible trend toward inflation. The Office of Price Administration, created in April 1942, issued a General Maximum Price Regulation that froze prices of consumer goods and of rents in defense areas only at their March 1942 level. In October 1942 Congress passed the Anti-Inflation Act, and under its authority Roosevelt immediately froze agricultural prices, wages, salaries, and rents throughout the country.

Altogether, the price level went up less than 29 percent from 1939 to the end of the war, compared with 63 percent between 1914 and the armistice. Consumers nonetheless suffered numerous irritations and discomforts. The OPA, through unpaid local volunteers running 5,600 price and rationing boards, administered the rationing of canned goods, coffee, sugar, meat, butter and other fats, shoes, tires, gasoline, and fuel oil. The OPA could not, however, control deterioration of quality. Black marketing and overcharging grew in proportions far beyond OPA policing capacity.

One of the most important inflationary controls was the taxation that drained off surplus purchasing power. The government raised 41 percent of its war costs through taxation, compared with 33 percent during World War I (a measure of the greater popularity of World War II). The Revenue Act of 1942, which Roosevelt hailed as "the greatest tax bill in American history," levied a 94 percent tax on highest incomes. Also, for the first time, the income tax fell upon those in lower income brackets; the number of people paying income taxes increased from about 3.9 million in 1939 to over 42.6 million in 1945. To simplify payment for these new millions, Congress enacted a withholding system of payroll deductions in 1943. Despite the heavy taxation, by the end of the war consumers possessed an estimated $129 billion in liquid savings.

From 1941 to 1945 the federal government spent twice as much as the total appropriations from the creation of the government to 1941, and ten times as much as the cost of World War I — a total of $321 billion. The national debt rose from $49 billion in 1941 to $259 billion in 1945, yet the black warnings of national bankruptcy that had punctuated the New Deal years all but disappeared.

Price controls and taxation worked in World War II to an extent they never had in earlier American wars because of the unprecedented popularity of the war. The vast majority of Americans believed that the war was both just and necessary. Most compelling was the memory of Pearl Harbor, which suggested that the nation's very survival was at stake. Consequently, Americans were willing to accept a high degree of government coercion.

Mobilization of Labor

The nation, after grappling for years with the problem of millions of unemployed, found itself hard-pressed for sufficient people to swell the fighting forces, staff the war plants, till the fields, and keep the domestic economy functioning. The armed forces had first call upon men through the Selective Service, which had been in operation since the fall of 1940. Altogether draft boards registered 31,000,000 men. Including volunteers, over 15,000,000 men and women served in the armed forces during the war. Nevertheless the working force jumped from 46,500,000 to over 53,000,000 as the 7,000,000 unemployed and many previously considered unemployable, the very young and the elderly, and several million women found jobs.

This mobilization of labor entailed the greatest reshuffling of population within such a short time in the entire history of the nation; altogether 27,300,000 people moved during the war. With the return of prosperity and the impending departure of soldiers, both marriage and birth rates rose. In 1942 and 1943 about 3,000,000 children were born each year, compared with 2,000,000 a year before the war. But young wives and mothers fared badly in crowded housing near defense plants or army bases, or, after husbands had been shipped overseas, back home with parents. Draft boards deferred fathers as long as possible, but more than 1,000,000 were ultimately inducted. More than 2,500,000 wives were separated from their husbands because of the war. The divorce rate increased slowly. Because men in the armed forces could in effect not be divorced without their consent, and many estranged wives stayed married in order to continue receiving allotment checks, a heavy backlog was built for postwar divorce courts.

The great migration to war plants was stripping the agricultural South of poor whites and blacks alike, as 5,000,000 moved within the South, and another 1,600,000 left the area completely. In the North, the exodus led to explosive tension when blacks, enjoying their new freedom, were jostled in crowded streetcars against indignant whites newly migrated from the South. A serious riot in which twenty-five blacks and nine whites were killed shook Detroit in June 1943. New York narrowly averted a similar disaster. At the very time when the United States was fighting a war against the racist doctrines of Hitler, many whites became resentful over the rapid gains blacks were making. In June 1941, after the head of the Pullman porters' union, A. Philip Randolph, threatened a march on Washington, President Roosevelt established the Fair Employment Practices Committee. It worked throughout the war against discrimination in employment. By 1944, 2,000,000 blacks were at work in war industries, and many previous barriers to economic opportunities for blacks were permanently cracked.

Scientists Against the Axis

Mobilization also included the efforts of scientists to turn basic knowledge into decisive weapons of war. Between the two wars, while the United States had neglected military research and development, Germany had sprinted far ahead.

The only way in which American scientists could catch up seemed to be through teamwork. A leading scientist, Vannevar Bush, persuaded President Roosevelt to create a committee for scientific research in June 1940. A year later, under the direction of Bush, it became the Office of Scientific Research and Development, which mobilized scientists with such effectiveness that in some areas, including radar and proximity fuses, they outstripped their German opponents.

There was a danger, little publicized, that Germany might develop an atomic weapon. In the summer of 1939 a physicist, Enrico Fermi, and a mathematician, Albert Einstein, got word to President Roosevelt that German physicists had achieved atomic fission in uranium; what had long been theoretically possible had been accomplished. Next might come a bomb. The President authorized a small research project, and a race in the dark against the Nazis began.

In December 1942 physicists produced a controlled chain reaction in an atomic pile at the University of Chicago. The problem then became the enormous technical one of achieving this release of power in a bomb. Through the Manhattan District of the Army Engineer Corps, the government secretly poured nearly $2 billion into plants to produce fissionable plutonium and into another project under the supervision of J. Robert Oppenheimer, which undertook to build a bomb. Only after the war did the United States discover that the Germans were far from developing a usable atomic device. On July 16, 1945, after the end of the war in Europe, the first A-bomb was exploded, on a tower in New Mexico — produc-

ing the most blinding flash of light ever seen on earth, and then a huge billowing mushroom cloud.

Freedoms Abroad and at Home

In January 1941 Roosevelt enunciated Four Freedoms as war aims — freedom of speech and worship and freedom from want and fear. But these never caught the public imagination as Wilson's Fourteen Points had done. The public had a practical sense of the war as a necessary evil.

The war produced far less hatred and vindictiveness at home than had World War I. Americans demonstrated little animus toward fellow citizens of German background and practically none toward Italians.

In sad contrast to this moderation, the frenzy of public fury turned on the Japanese. The fighting in the Pacific developed a fierce savagery, reflected in the public anger within the United States. On the Pacific coast, hatred of Americans of Japanese background became extreme. Wild stories circulated about sabotage at Pearl Harbor — later proven 100 percent untrue. Under public pressure, Roosevelt in February 1942 authorized the army to remove all people of Japanese ancestry from the West Coast. Some 117,000 people, two-thirds of them United States citizens, were abruptly herded behind barbed wire, and later shipped to ten "relocation centers." In fact, they were facilities little different from prisons, many of them located in the desert. The Japanese-Americans suffered the financial loss of at least 40 percent of their possessions and for several years were barred from lucrative employment. Yet Japanese-Americans in Hawaii were left unmolested without incident throughout the war. There were 17,600 Japanese-Americans in the armed forces. Their units, especially in Italy, established outstanding records for bravery under fire.

The Supreme Court in 1944 validated the evacuation and, in other decisions as well, upheld military control over civilians. In time of war or national emergency, United States citizens apparently could expect no court protection of their civil rights from military or executive authority.

Wartime Politics

At times the sound and fury in Washington seemed almost to drown out the clangor of war against the Axis. Conservatives saw in the war an opportunity to eradicate hated remnants of the New Deal. Every one of the great pressure groups in the country fought to maintain or improve its relative position; advocates for large business and small, farmers and labor, jockeyed for position in Washington. Through the election of 1942, as the United States and its allies suffered unparalleled military disasters and the war administration in Washington seemed to compound confusion, the criticism rose to a crescendo. In the election the Republicans gained forty-seven seats in the House and ten in the Senate.

President Roosevelt, to obtain crucial congressional support in prosecuting the war and planning the peace, continued to accept the sacrifice of New Deal measures. At a press conference he announced (1943) that "Dr. Win-the-War" had replaced "Dr. New Deal."

Dissatisfaction with wartime regimentation and smoldering resentments still glowing from the prewar debate over intervention seemed to give the Republicans an opportunity in 1944. In their vigorous young candidate, Governor Thomas E. Dewey of New York, who ran with Governor John W. Bricker of Ohio, they seemed to have an answer to Roosevelt and the aging New Dealers.

As for President Roosevelt, it was a foregone conclusion that he would be nominated for a fourth term if he so desired. For Vice President, the Democrats passed over Henry Wallace, the hero of most advanced New Dealers and much of the CIO membership, in favor of Senator Harry S Truman of Missouri. Truman had won newspaper approval as chairman of the Senate War Investigating Committee, was a consistent New Dealer in his voting record, and was from a border state.

The election promised to be close. This was like an injection of adrenaline into Roosevelt and he waged a strenuous campaign. The President defeated Dewey by a margin of 432 electoral votes to 99, and a popular vote of 25,602,000 to 22,006,000. The Democrats lost one seat in the Senate, but gained twenty in the House. The Democratic victory seemed to mean a revival of the New Deal at home; and the campaign promises of both parties indicated that the United States would continue to take a lead in international affairs.

The American War Strategy

As commander in chief, President Roosevelt bore responsibility for the conduct of the war. Personally, and through assistants like Harry Hopkins and cabinet members, he coordinated the war planning of the Joint Chiefs with war production and personnel and with foreign policy. He depended heavily on the advice of the Joint Chiefs and, once major strategy had been determined, seldom interfered with their implementation of it.

The first of the great policy decisions had come in 1940 when the Americans decided that even if Japan entered the war, their primary goal would be to defeat Germany with its superior military force, war production, and weapons development. This decision did not mean neglecting the war against Japan. By August 1941, when the buildup, especially of airplanes, was under way in the Philippines, and later when General Douglas MacArthur received orders to fight, the strategy was shifting to a two-front war. The war against Germany was to be offensive, while that against Japan was to be defensive.

During the first chaotic months of shocking reverses, the armed forces allotted their personnel and supplies piecemeal to try to meet each new Axis threat. Top strategists emphatically warned that such dissipation of effort might lead to defeat. No one was more insistent than Dwight D. Eisenhower, who had been brought to Washington after Pearl Harbor as a Far Eastern expert, and who by the spring of 1942 was head of the Operations Planning Division under General George Marshall. In emphatic memoranda Eisenhower hammered away at the need to build up personnel and supplies in Europe for the invasion of North Africa that Roosevelt and Churchill had decided upon in a December 1941 meeting. Because of his vigor and his important role in developing an invasion plan, Eisenhower became the logical choice to send to England in June 1942 as commanding general in the European theater.

On the Defensive   1941-1942

While the United States was building and equipping its fighting forces, it had to depend upon the Russians and the British to hold back the Germans as best they could. During the discouraging first six months of American participation, the American forces had to stand perilously on the defensive in both the Atlantic and the Pacific.

Ten hours after the strike at Pearl Harbor, Japanese airplanes hit the airfields at Manila, destroying half the American bombers and two-thirds of the fighter planes. Three days later Guam fell; then, in the weeks that followed, Wake Island and Hong Kong. The great British fortress of Singapore in Malaya surrendered in February 1942, the East Indies in March, and Burma in April. In the Philippines on May 6 the exhausted Philippine and American troops ran down the last American flag in the Far East.

Only one weak outpost, Port Moresby in southern New Guinea, stood as a bulwark against the invasion of Australia. In the Battle of Coral Sea on May 6–7, 1942, the Americans turned back Japanese invasion forces threatening Port Moresby. After the Battle of Coral Sea, the navy, having intercepted Japanese messages, knew the next move and rushed every available plane and vessel into the central Pacific. Near Midway Island, June 3–6, 1942, these forces inflicted heavy damage on a Japanese invasion fleet and headed off a drive to capture the island and neutralize Hawaii. The United States had achieved its goal of containment in the Pacific.

In the Atlantic during the early months of 1942, the Nazis tried by means of submarines to confine the Americans to the Western Hemisphere. By mid-January the Germans had moved so many submarines to the Atlantic coast, where at night they torpedoed tankers silhouetted against the lights of cities, that they created a critical oil shortage. Against convoys bound for Europe they made attacks with devastating success. In the first eleven months, they sank over 8,000,000 tons of shipping — 1,200,000 more than the Allies meanwhile built. Gradually the United States countered by developing effective antisubmarine vessels, air patrols, detecting devices, and weapons.

The submarines made it difficult to send assistance to the British and Russians in the summer of 1942 when they sorely needed it. The German *Afrika Corps* raced to El Alamein, only seventy-five miles from Alexandria, Egypt, threatening the Suez Canal and the Middle East. At the same time, German armies in Russia were plunging toward the Caucasus. In May, the Russian foreign minister, Vyacheslav Molotov, visited Washington to demand an immediate second front that would divert at least forty German divisions from Russia; the alternative might be Russian collapse. Roosevelt promised to do everything possible to divert the Germans by invading France. But Churchill arrived the next month, when the Germans were threatening Egypt, and he strongly urged an invasion of North Africa instead.

The Mediterranean Offensive

At the end of October 1942 the British opened a counteroffensive at El Alamein that sent the *Afrika Corps* reeling back. On November 8 Anglo-American forces landed at Oran, Algiers, and Casablanca, Morocco, with some bungling but gratifyingly few losses.

The Germans tried to counter the invasion by attacking in Tunisia. The green American troops lost heavily but with the aid of the British held on to their bases, gained in experience, and gradually closed a vise on the German and Italian troops. On May 12, 1943, the last Axis troops in North Africa surrendered. The Mediterranean had been reopened, and the Americans had learned lessons that would be useful in the successful invasion of France.

That invasion, despite the continued clamoring of the Russians, was not to take place immediately. The planners in London had come to recognize that an enormous buildup was necessary for a successful cross-channel invasion. Fortunately for the Allies, the tide turned for the Russians also during the winter of 1942–1943, when they successfully held the Germans at Stalingrad in the Ukraine, eliminating an army of 250,000 men.

As early as mid-January 1943 Roosevelt and Churchill and their staffs, while conferring at Casablanca, looked ahead to the next move. This was to be an invasion of Sicily. American generals

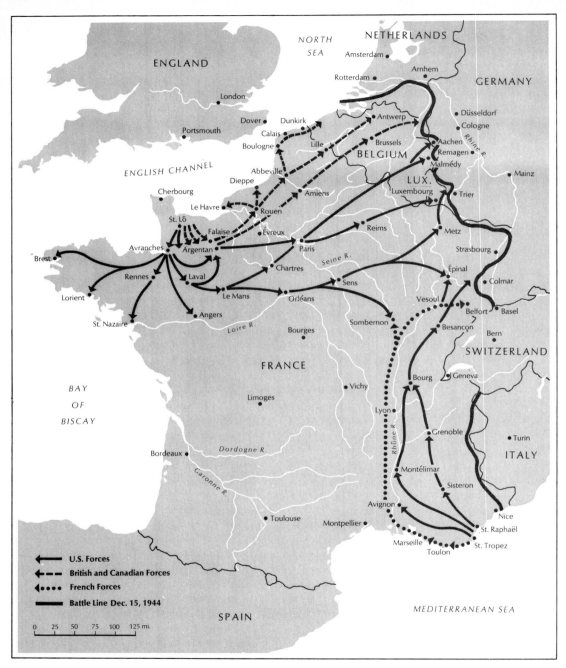

The Normandy Landings

feared that excessive casualties would result, but Churchill argued persuasively that the operation in Sicily might knock Italy out of the war and lead the Germans to tie up many divisions in defense of Italy and the Balkans.

On the night of July 9, 1943, American and British armies landed in Sicily. In thirty-eight days the Allies conquered the island and looked toward the Italian mainland. A limited but long and punishing campaign opened on the Italian peninsula on September 3, 1943, confirming the American fears. The German defenders fought so fiercely from hilly redoubts that by early 1944 they had stopped the slow and deliberately moving Allies at Monte Cassino. With relatively few divisions, the Germans were able to tie down the Allies and still concentrate upon Russia. Finally in May 1944 the Allies captured Cassino and on June 4 captured Rome, just before the cross-channel invasion of France began.

The Liberation of Europe

In the fall of 1943 Germany was already reeling under the incessant blows from the growing Allied air power. By the end of the war, the Americans were flying over 7,000 bombers and 6,000 fighters in Europe, had dropped nearly 1,500,000 tons of bombs, and had lost nearly 10,-000 bombers. British figures were similar. The bombing attacks, first upon the aviation industry, then upon transportation, did much to clear the way for the invasion in the late spring. By May 1944 the German Air Force, the *Luftwaffe*, was incapable of beating off the Allied air cover for an invasion.

D-Day (invasion day) came on the morning of June 6, 1944. The invasion came not at the narrowest part of the English channel, where the Nazis expected it, but along sixty miles of the Cotentin peninsula on the Normandy coast. While airplanes and battleships offshore incessantly bombarded the Nazi defenses, 4,000 vessels, stretching as far as the eye could see, brought in troops and supplies.

Within two weeks after the initial landings, the Allies had put ashore 1,000,000 soldiers and the equipment for them. Well into July, the Allies fought mile by mile through the Normandy hedgerows. The breakthrough came on July 25, 1944, when General Omar Bradley's First Army smashed the German lines in an enormous sweep southward, then eastward. On August 25 Free French forces rode into Paris, whose boulevards were jammed with cheering throngs. By mid-September, the Allied armies had driven the Germans from almost all of France and Belgium.

While the Allies were fighting their way through France to the Westwall (German defense line) and up the Italian peninsula, the Russian armies had been sweeping westward into central Europe and the Balkans. The Russian armies advanced more rapidly than had been expected and in late January 1945 launched an offensive of over 150 divisions toward the Oder River, deep in Germany.

The Allied armies pushed on to the Rhine, capturing Cologne on the west bank on March 6, 1945. By the end of March the last great drives were under way as the British commander "Monty" Montgomery with 1,000,000 troops pushed across the north while Bradley's army, sweeping through central Germany, completed the encirclement and trapping of 300,000 German soldiers in the Ruhr.

There were fears that the Nazis were preparing for a last stand in an Alpine redoubt centering on Berchtesgaden on the Austrian border. In fact, however, the German western front had been demolished. The only real questions were where the Americans would drive next and where they would join the Russians. The Americans could have beaten the Russians to Berlin and Prague. This would have cost American lives but would have reaped political gain in Europe. General Eisenhower decided, instead, to send American troops to capture the Alpine redoubt and then halt along the Elbe River in central Germany to meet the Russians.

On May 8, 1945, the remaining German forces surrendered unconditionally. V-E (Victory in Europe) Day arrived amidst monster celebrations in western Europe and in the United States. The rejoicing was tempered only by knowledge of the continuing war against Japan.

The Pacific Offensive

The offensive strategy against the Japanese involved amphibious warfare of a type that the marines had been developing since the early 1920s.

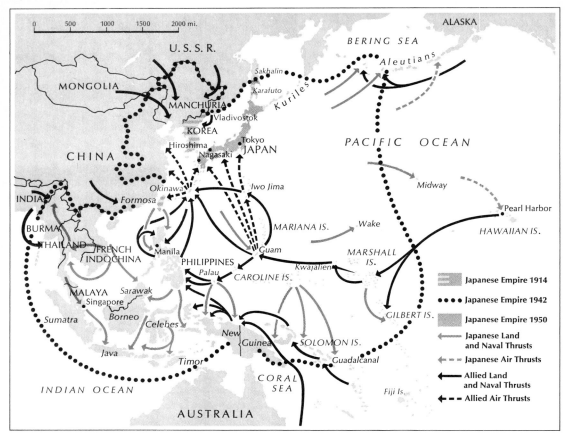

The War in the Pacific

In the Pacific these new tactics came to be so perfected that troops were able to cross and seize vigorously defended beaches when the United States could not by-pass them and immobilize advanced Japanese strong points.

The southern Solomon Islands to the east of New Guinea were being developed as a Japanese base for air raids against American communications with Australia. In August 1942 the navy and marines opened an offensive against three of these islands, Gavutu, Tulagi, and Guadalcanal. Around and on Guadalcanal a struggle of unprecedented ferocity developed as the United States and Japanese navies battled for control in a series of large-scale engagements. By the time the struggle was over, the United States and its allies had lost heav-

ily in cruisers, carriers, and destroyers but had sunk forty-seven Japanese vessels. Japan's navy had lost its offensive strength and thereafter concentrated upon defensive operations.

During the months when the great naval battles had been going against the United States, the Americans had gained control of the air and thus were able to sustain the marines, and subsequently the army, in their precarious jungle onslaught. Through 1943 the island hopping continued all around the enormous Japanese-held perimeter.

Victories in the Marshall Islands in February 1944 cracked the Japanese outer perimeter, and before the month was out the navy had plunged far within it to wreck the bastion at Truk and raid

Saipan in the Marianas. In mid-June an enormous American armada struck the heavily fortified Mariana Islands, quickly but expensively capturing Tinian, Guam, and Saipan, 1,350 miles from Tokyo. In September the Americans landed on the Western Carolines, and on October 20 General MacArthur's troops landed on Leyte Island in the Philippines. The Japanese, threatened with being fatally cut off from their new empire in Southeast Asia, threw their remaining fleets against the invaders in three major encounters — together comprising the decisive Battle of Leyte Gulf, the largest naval engagement in history — and lost almost all their remaining sea power.

Atomic Triumph over Japan

With remarkable speed but grievous losses the American forces cut still deeper into the Japanese empire during the early months of 1945. While fighting continued in the Philippines, the marines landed in February on the tiny volcanic island of Iwo Jima, only 750 miles from Tokyo. The Americans needed Iwo Jima to provide fighter cover for Japan-bound bombers and a landing place for crippled ones. The Japanese defended the island so grimly that the marines suffered over 20,000 casualties. It was the bloodiest battle in the history of the marines.

The battle for Okinawa, an island sixty-five miles long, beginning on April 1, 1945, was even bloodier. This island was 370 miles south of Japan, and its conquest clearly would be a prelude to an invasion of the main islands. On land and from the air, the Japanese fought with literally a suicidal fury. Week after week they sent Kamikaze suicide planes against the American and British ships, losing 3,500 of them but inflicting great damage. The United States and its allies suffered nearly 50,000 casualties on land and afloat before the battle came to an end in late June 1945. The Japanese lost 110,000 killed and 7,800 prisoners.

This same sort of bitter fighting seemed to await the Americans when they invaded Japan — if indeed they should ever have to invade. There were signs that the Japanese might surrender, for they had almost no ships and few airplanes with which to fight.

The atomic bomb was to be decisive in ending the war. At a meeting of Allied leaders in Potsdam, Germany, in mid-July 1945, President Truman (who had succeeded Roosevelt after his death in April) received word that the first atomic test was successful. He and Prime Minister Clement Attlee (who had succeeded Churchill) issued the Potsdam Declaration urging the Japanese to surrender or face utter devastation. The premier wished to accept the ultimatum, but the army leaders would not surrender. President Truman had set August 3 as the deadline; when it passed and the Japanese fought on, he ordered an atomic bomb to be dropped on one of four previously selected Japanese cities.

On August 6, 1945, a B-29 dropped an atomic bomb on Hiroshima, completely destroying the hitherto undamaged city, and killing 80,000 people (according to American estimates) or 200,000 (according to the Japanese). Even after the horror of Hiroshima, the Japanese army remained adamant. Russia declared war on Japan as of August 9. That same day, the air force dropped a second atomic bomb, on Nagasaki. This was the final blow. After frantic negotiations, on August 14 the Japanese government agreed to give up. On September 2, 1945, aboard the battleship *Missouri* in Tokyo Bay, the articles of surrender were signed.

World War II was at an end. Altogether, some 14,000,000 people under arms had been killed, and countless millions of civilians had died. United States casualties numbered 1,120,000; of these, about 322,000 had been killed or were missing.

The Dangerous Alliance

Only the imminent threat of Axis victory had forced an uneasy and unsatisfactory form of cooperation between Russia and its Western allies, Great Britain and the United States. As the threat began to lift in 1943, it became increasingly difficult to keep the alliance cemented together and to plan for a postwar world in which a decent peace could be maintained.

At Casablanca, Morocco, in January 1943, after previous consultation with Churchill, Roosevelt announced the doctrine of unconditional surrender by the Axis. What Roosevelt seemed to desire was to avoid the sort of negotiations that had marred the 1918 armistice, causing bickerings among the Allies at the time and German misunderstandings afterward.

With an air of optimism Roosevelt and Churchill traveled eastward in November 1943 for a long-awaited meeting with Stalin at Teheran, Iran. On the way they stopped in Cairo to confer with Chiang Kai-shek and to prepare a statement (released after the Teheran conference) drawing a map for the postwar Far East. They proposed stripping Japan of its empire in order to restore Manchuria, the Pescadores, and Formosa to China, and to create in due course a free and independent Korea.

At Teheran, Roosevelt undertook to establish a friendly, intimate relationship with Stalin of the sort he enjoyed with Churchill. Stalin reaffirmed his intention to bring Russia into the Pacific war as soon as hostilities ended in Europe and expressed his satisfaction with the Cairo communiqué on Japan. In a cordial way the three leaders discussed means, through an international organization, of keeping Germany from ever again becoming a menace. Stalin wished Russia to retain the areas it had seized in its period of collaboration with Germany, including eastern Poland as far as the so-called Curzon line proposed in 1919. Roosevelt and Churchill agreed to the Polish boundary.

The Yalta Conference

The next great conference took place at Yalta in the Crimea in February 1945. At that time American forces were having to reduce Germany mile by mile; there seemed no reason to think Japan would be different. General MacArthur insisted on the necessity for Russian aid, taking the position that otherwise the United States would have to fight a series of difficult and expensive campaigns to overcome the Japanese in Manchuria. In return for Stalin's reiterated promise to enter the Far Eastern war two or three months after German surrender, Roosevelt and Churchill promised him the Kurile Islands north of Japan and the restoration of "the former rights of Russia" lost in the Russo-Japanese War.

In its disposition of central European questions, the Yalta conference for the most part ratified previous decisions. Germany was to be divided into zones of occupation previously agreed upon. Since Berlin was to be deep in the Russian zone, the Americans and British proposed an accord providing freedom on transit into Berlin. The Russians held back, and in the general spirit of amity at Yalta, the matter was postponed. At the time, the Russian demands for heavy reparations in the form of German factories, goods, and labor seemed far more important. The British tried to scale down the Russian demand for $20 billion in such reparations, of which Russia was to obtain half. This would so strip and starve the Germans, Churchill pointed out, that the United States and Great Britain would have to feed them. Consequently he and Roosevelt agreed to the Russian figure only as a basis for discussion by a reparations commission.

One of the touchiest questions was how to define a democratic government for Poland, a matter over which Russia and the West had negotiated for months. The Russians did not wish to allow the Polish government-in-exile in London or the Polish underground to assume any substantial share of power with a government the Russians established at Lublin.

Roosevelt envisioned a complete restructuring of the Soviet-controlled government in Poland, based on free, democratic elections — which both he and Stalin knew the pro-Western forces would win. Stalin agreed only to a vague compromise whereby an unspecified number of pro-Western Poles would be granted a place in the government. Although he reluctantly consented to hold "free and unfettered elections" in Poland, he made no firm commitment to a date for them. They never took place.

For the rest of liberated or defeated Europe, the Big Three — the United States, the Soviet Union, and Great Britain — agreed to establish interim governments "broadly representative of all democratic elements" and to provide for free elections that would create "governments responsible to the will of the people."

The Yalta agreements were less a settlement of postwar issues than a general set of loose principles that side-stepped the most divisive issues. Roosevelt continued to aspire to the ideals of the Atlantic Charter and pinned his hopes upon Russian willingness to enter into an international organization for the preservation of peace.

Founding the United Nations

President Roosevelt, firmly determined to avoid Wilson's failure, included prominent Republicans in at least sketchy briefing on wartime diplomacy and let them participate more fully in postwar planning of many kinds. In March 1943 four senators, two Republican and two Democratic, introduced a resolution calling for American leadership in establishing a United Nations organization. Senator Arthur H. Vandenberg of Michigan, previously one of the most forthright isolationists, assumed Republican leadership in helping mold a "bipartisan" foreign policy. He thus gained for himself and the Republican party new power and stature.

The Big Four powers (France, the United Kingdom, the Soviet Union, and the United States), conferring in the summer and fall of 1944 at Dumbarton Oaks, drafted tentative outlines for a new international organization. These were the starting points for the drafting of a United Nations charter at a conference of fifty nations in San Francisco, opening April 25, 1945.

Basically the charter of the United Nations was a refurbishing of the old Wilsonian League covenant with the former American objections removed through giving a veto to each of the five main powers (the Big Four plus China). The Americans and British, as well as the Russians, had insisted upon the veto as a seemingly necessary protection of their sovereignty. The American delegates, led by Vandenberg, succeeded in obtaining for the small nations in the General Assembly freedom to discuss and make recommendations — in effect creating "a town meeting of the world."

The Senate quickly ratified the United Nations Charter on July 28, 1945, by a vote of 80 to 2, in remarkable contrast to the slow and painful defeat it had administered to American membership in the League of Nations.

Delayed Peacemaking

President Roosevelt lived to see neither the triumph in war nor the tragedy of peace. Already his vigor was draining away, and he could ill afford the exertions of the 1944 electoral campaign or those of the grueling trip to Yalta. Suddenly, on the afternoon of April 12, 1945, he died of a cerebral hemorrhage at his private retreat in Warm Springs, Georgia.

Roosevelt had not kept Vice President Harry S Truman well informed, and so Truman was ill prepared for the tasks that faced him when he took over as President. But he learned fast.

During the first phase of his relations with the Russians, Truman was firm but tried to give the Soviet government no cause for protest. At the Potsdam conference (July 1945) Truman could secure few satisfactory agreements on questions involving occupied and liberated countries. Despite the failure at Potsdam, Truman's secretary of state, James F. Byrnes, continued in a conciliatory fashion to seek accommodation with the Russians.

The greatest obstacle to a satisfactory settlement in Europe was Germany. The Western nations had visualized unified controls for Germany to prevent its resurgence. But the Russians had no interest in a Germany reunified in a manner acceptable to the West; Germany was to remain split indefinitely.

In occupied Germany and Japan, meanwhile, the United States pursued firm but conflicting policies compounded of harshness and idealism. During the war the American people had come to hate the enemy leaders and were insistent that they be punished for their war crimes, especially those Nazis who were responsible for the maintenance of frightful concentration camps like Buchenwald and for the gas-chamber murder of millions of Jews. This led to the trials of thousands of Nazis and war criminals, capped by that of twenty-two key Nazi leaders before an International Military Tribunal at Nuremberg in 1945–1946. Eleven were sentenced to death.

There was an equally sweeping purge of Japan, and a trial was held for twenty-five former top Japanese military and civil officials. Seven of them, including two premiers, were executed. The dangerous precedent seemed to be established, as Churchill pointed out, that "the leaders of a nation defeated in war shall be put to death by the victors."

At first the Americans seemed bent on the pastoralization as well as reform of conquered Germany. They banned all industry directly or indirectly contributing to German war potential, including even the construction of seagoing ships, drastically cut steel and chemical production, destroyed munition plants, and allowed the dismantling of some factories for shipment to the Russians. These economic policies, coming at a time when so much of German housing and industry was rubble, and when several million exiles were making their way from the East or Czechoslovakia, reduced western Germany to a living standard not much better than that of a giant relief camp. The army undertook to feed the German people between 1945 and 1948 at a subsistence level of 950–1550 calories per day.

In Japan American occupation policy suffered fewer obstacles and profited from the initial errors in Germany. During the first critical weeks General MacArthur, the supreme commander for the Allied powers, set up an overwhelmingly American occupation. The American occupation authorities in Japan acted rapidly to demilitarize and democratize the country. From the outset they recognized that Japan must be left with a healthy economy, but in practice — by limiting the nation's war potential — they reduced Japan, like Germany, to a relief state.

Postwar Readjustments and the Start of the Cold War

The Postwar Military Program

At the end of World War II, the United States speedily dismantled its army, air force, and navy. In April 1945 President Truman announced that nearly 7,000,000 people had been released from the army — "the most remarkable demobilization in the history of the world, or 'disintegration,' if you want to call it that." The gradual whittling of the armed forces continued, until by the spring of 1950 the army was down to 600,000 people, and the ceiling on defense expenditures, to $13 billion.

Lacking land armies, the United States sought to balance Soviet power with atomic bombs and an air force that could deliver them. President Truman continued the policy, initiated by Roosevelt toward the end of 1944, of maintaining secrecy about atomic research and development, despite warnings from American scientists such as Albert Einstein that no nation could maintain a monopoly of scientific information and that insistence on secrecy would intensify a nuclear arms race. Truman hoped that sole possession of atomic weapons would make the Russians more amenable to American wishes for postwar Europe.

In early 1946 Truman made one serious effort to demilitarize nuclear energy. Truman endorsed a State Department plan for giving the United Nations control over atomic raw materials and appointed Bernard Baruch to present the plan to the U.N. Atomic Energy Commission. Truman, however, allowed Baruch to amend the plan to insist on total disarmament, not just control of nuclear weapons, and to eliminate the Security Council veto in atomic energy matters. The distrustful Russians rejected the plan in the summer of 1946, demanding that the United States unilaterally destroy its atom bombs. The Soviet Union continued its own atomic research, and espionage, while the United States almost immediately resumed atmospheric testing of atomic weapons.

Meanwhile, Congress lengthily debated the domestic control of American atomic energy. Democrats wished to vest control in civilians; Senator Vandenberg and the Republicans urged giving it to the heads of the armed forces. A compromise was reached in the Atomic Energy Act of August 1946. This created a five–member civilian Atomic Energy Commission with complete control over research and development of fissionable materials; linked to it was a Military Liaison Committee.

Under the protection of an atomic umbrella, military leaders indulged in a vigorous and prolonged controversy over unification of the various armed forces. Finally in July 1947 the National Security Act provided for a secretary of defense to preside over separate Departments of the Army, Navy, and Air Force, with the Joint Chiefs of Staff serving as advisers to the secretary and to the President. To coordinate diplomacy and military planning, the 1947 act also provided for a National Security Council to consist of the President, certain cabinet members, and other advisers on foreign and military policy. This council was to be served by two other new agencies, a National Security Resources Board and a Central Intelligence Agency.

Within the reorganized Pentagon the old rivalries continued. Indeed, through the creation of a separate air force there now appeared to be three separate services where before there had been only two. The National Security Act of August 1949 forced greater unification of the services and formally established a Department of Defense.

The "Fair Deal"

On September 6, 1945, only four days after the Japanese surrender ceremonies, the President sent to Congress a twenty-one-point domestic program outlining what he later called the "Fair Deal." It requested the expansion of social security, the raising of the legal minimum wage from 40 to 65 cents an hour, a full employment bill, a permanent Fair Employment Practices Act, public housing and slum clearance, long-range planning for the protection of natural resources and building of public works (like TVA), and government promotion of scientific research. Within ten weeks, he sent additional recommendations to Congress for federal aid to education, for health insurance and prepared medical care, and for the St. Lawrence seaway project.

Congress largely ignored the President's recommendations. It focused, instead, on the problem of economic instability. Congress passed the Employment Act in February 1946. This act emphasized the commitment of the federal government to promote employment, and it established the Council of Economic Advisors to assist the President in meeting that commitment. In July 1946 Congress enacted new price-control legislation to cope with the enormous inflation that had resulted from the expiration of wartime price controls. The decontrol board Congress created studied meat prices, decided they were unreasonable, and ordered prices rolled back to the old levels. Cattle raisers held back cattle until they could force abandonment of controls; angry consumers chafed in near-empty butcher shops. Public discontent focused on the Democratic party, and politicians — already fearful of the worst in the congressional elections of 1946 — persuaded Truman to announce, on October 14, 1946, the immediate ending of meat controls. Meat came back, but like many other commodities, with new price tags so high that the old black-market price seemed to have become the new legal standard. Millions of consumers on small, inflexible salaries or pensions were hurt.

All that the Republicans needed in the fall of 1946 was the slogan, "Had Enough? Vote Republican." They captured both houses of Congress, controlling the House 246 to 188, and the Senate, 51 to 45.

President Truman, accepting the returns as a mandate to liquidate regulations, dropped almost all remaining controls on wages and prices. Retail prices moved upward 3 percent per month; the spiral of inflation was creeping upward relentlessly. Workers and others in modest circumstances began to notice that it was taking place under a Republican Congress whose leaders had asserted that laissez faire would cure the nation's ills.

Meanwhile, Congress refused to appropriate funds for public housing, even of a very moderate sort. It would not aid education or extend social security; it slashed budget allowances for reclamation and power projects in the West. It passed a tax bill that, as President Truman pointed out in vetoing it, reduced the taxes of families receiving $2,400 or less by only 3 percent, but of those receiving $100,000 or more, from 48 to 65 percent.

Congress also passed a new labor law to supplant the pro-labor Wagner Act of 1935. The Taft-Hartley Labor-Management Relations Act loosened some of the previous restrictions upon employers and added several prohibitions against the unions. It also provided for "cooling off" periods before unions could strike. President Truman stingingly vetoed it on June 20, 1947. That same day Republicans and Southern Democrats in the House overrode his veto, 331 to 83; the Senate followed three days later, 68 to 25. In practice, the Taft-Hartley Act did not cripple organized labor, partly because of the skill of labor leaders and because of President Truman's appointment to the National Labor Relations Board of members sympathetic toward labor. But the law did emphatically turn most of organized labor against the Republicans and back to the support of President Truman.

Truman Beats Dewey

When the Republicans met at Philadelphia in June 1948 to nominate a presidential candidate, they again nominated Governor Thomas E. Dewey, who favored the new role of the United States in world affairs, and whose stand on domestic issues came closer to the Fair Deal than to the Republican record in Congress. His running mate was Governor Earl Warren of California, who was even more liberal.

It seemed a winning ticket and program, especially since the Democratic party suffered from two schisms. A faction to the left followed Henry A. Wallace out of the party. Wallace ran on a "Progressive" ticket to fight for thoroughgoing reform at home and more friendly relations with Communists overseas. Around him rallied a sprinkling of Americans who felt that the Truman domestic policies were too slow and ineffective and who feared that the foreign policies would lead to a third world war.

At their convention in July 1948 the Democrats gloomily accepted the inevitable, the nomination of President Truman. Certain of defeat, the liberals salvaged what they could by fighting through a platform containing a strong civil rights plank that proposed federal legislation to prevent discrimination in employment, penalize lynching, and outlaw poll taxes. This platform was expected to help Northern and city Democrats in the local and state elections.

But it drove Southern Democrats, already angered by President Truman's espousal of a strong civil rights program, into open revolt. Waving Confederate flags, a number of them met at Birmingham, Alabama, in July 1948 to form the States Rights' Democratic Party and nominate Governor J. Strom Thurmond of South Carolina.

The revolts from both the left and the right seemed to leave President Truman in a pathetically hopeless position; all the public opinion polls showed him trailing far behind. Instead of campaigning against the cold and formal Governor Dewey, whose domestic and foreign policies were much the same as his, Truman launched his attack at the Republican Congress. Speaking extemporaneously and bluntly in a vigorous whistle-stop campaign, he won the strong support of organized labor, disgruntled farmers, and northern blacks.

On election day, to the amazement of everyone but himself, President Truman defeated Dewey, 24,106,000 to 21,969,000 in the popular vote. Thurmond's Dixiecrat ticket received 1,169,000, and Wallace 1,156,000. The Democrats also regained both houses of Congress by a margin of ninety-three seats in the House and twelve in the Senate.

Beginnings of Containment

As early as January 1946 President Truman, upset over Russian delay in withdrawing troops from Iran and Russian threats toward Turkey, wrote his secretary of state: "Unless Russia is faced with an iron fist and strong language another war is in the making."

Truman's new policy for countering Communist aggression began to unfold in the spring of 1947. Already George F. Kennan, counselor of the American embassy in Moscow, was warning the administration that it faced "a political force committed fanatically to the belief that with the U.S. there can be no permanent *modus vivendi.*" The only answer, Kennan wrote anonymously in the July 1947 issue of *Foreign Affairs*, must be "a long-term, patient but firm and vigilant containment of Russian expansive tendencies." Russian pressure on Turkey and support of Communist guerrilla forces in Greece emphasized the immediacy of the Soviet threat. The British had been aiding the Greek government but could no longer carry the burden. Unless Stalin were contained quickly, he might achieve the centuries-old Russian desire to control the straits leading from the Black Sea into the Mediterranean.

On March 12, 1947, President Truman appeared before Congress to request $400,000,000 to bolster the armed forces of Greece and Turkey, and to enunciate the doctrine that came to bear his name: "I believe that it must be the policy of the United States to support free peoples who are resisting attempted subjugation by armed minorities or by outside pressures." Senator Vandenberg again supported him, and the Republican Congress voted the Greek-Turkish Aid Act of May 1947. The initial military aid and subsequent ap-

Origins of the Cold War

According to spokespeople for the American government, the Soviet Union was entirely to blame for the cold war. Stalin violated the Yalta agreement, imposed Russian control upon eastern Europe, and schemed to spread Communism throughout the world. The United States, reacting defensively, tried to contain Soviet expansion by means of the Truman Doctrine, the Marshall Plan, and the North Atlantic Treaty Organization. At first, American historians with few exceptions agreed substantially with the official view.

As time passed, and especially after the Vietnam War disillusioned many Americans about the containment policy, an increasing number of historians undertook to "revise" the interpretation of the cold war, as earlier historians had done with previous wars. Most of the cold war revisionists belonged to the New Left. The pioneer among them was William A. Williams, who anticipated most of the revisionist themes in his *American-Russian Relations, 1781–1947* (1952) and *The Tragedy of American Diplomacy* (1959).

According to the New Left writers, the United States was mainly if not solely responsible for the cold war. At the close of World War II, the Soviet Union was exhausted and in no position to threaten the United States. But this country, with a monopoly of nuclear weapons, was in a position to threaten the Soviet Union. In the opinion of some revisionists, Franklin D. Roosevelt would have continued the wartime Soviet-American cooperation, but Harry S Truman abandoned the Roosevelt policy and adopted a hard line toward the Russians. In the opinion of other revisionists, the line would have been the same regardless of any change in the Presidency, since American foreign policy was simply a response to the needs of American capitalism, which sought American-controlled markets throughout the world.

As early as 1948 a British physicist, P. M. S. Blackett, in *Fear, War, and the Bomb,* had written that the dropping of the atomic bombs on Hiroshima and Nagasaki was "not so much the last military act of the second World War as the first major operation of the cold diplomatic war with Russia." Taking up the idea, a New Left political economist at the University of Cambridge, England, Gar Alperovitz, suggested in his *Atomic Diplomacy* (1965) that the United States dropped the bombs on an already defeated Japan in order to impress the Russians and make them more "manageable." In *The Atomic Bomb and the End of World War II* (1966), a former official in the Roosevelt and Truman administrations, Herbert Feis, argued (as Truman himself had done) that the United States used the bombs simply to assure a quick and complete victory over Japan with a minimum loss of lives.

Reviewing the work of Williams, Aperovitz, and five other revisionist authors, Robert J. Maddox in *The New Left and the Origins of the Cold War* (1973) charged them with misusing source materials and drawing conclusions at variance with their own evidence. "There is every reason to be sharply critical of recent American foreign policy," Maddox said, "but the criticisms should rest on more substantial foundations."

In *The United States and the Origins of the Cold War, 1941–1947* (1972), John L. Gaddis maintained that a variety of preconceptions had influenced the policy makers in both Washington and Moscow. He concluded that "neither side can bear sole responsibility for the onset of the Cold War."

propriations eased Russian pressure upon Turkey, and by the fall of 1949 brought an end to the long civil war against Communists in Greece.

Military aid was not enough. The Truman Doctrine logically led to a program of economic reconstruction to bolster the stability of Europe. Speaking at the Harvard University commencement in June 1947, Secretary of State George C. Marshall offered aid to all those European nations (including the Soviet Union) that would join in drafting a program for recovery.

The Soviet Union denounced the Marshall Plan as American imperialism, and intimidated the satellites and Finland and Czechoslovakia into staying away from the planning conference. Germany had no government, and Spain was not invited. Sixteen other nations of Europe joined a Committee of European Economic Cooperation, which in September 1947 presented specifications for reconstruction to create by 1951 a self-sufficient Europe. Opposition formed in Congress, but it was embarrassed from the start by possessing as unwelcome allies the American Communists, and in February 1948 it was overwhelmed by a shocked and aroused public opinion when Czech Communists seized power in Prague.

Altogether over a three-year period the United States spent $12 billion through the Marshall Plan. This helped to stimulate a remarkable recovery in Europe. By the end of 1950 industrial production was up 64 percent, economic activity was well above prewar levels, and Communist strength among voters in most areas was dwindling.

The North Atlantic Alliance

In his inaugural address, January 20, 1949, President Truman challenged the nation to aid the "more than half the people of the world" who were "living in conditions approaching misery." Point Four of his proposals for aiding them was technical assistance and the fostering of capital investment for their development. The Point Four or Technical Cooperation program began in 1950 with an appropriation of only $35,000,000, but spent $400,000,000 in the next three years.

Soviet leaders reacted vigorously against the American program. They had organized their own Warsaw Alliance of nine satellite nations in September 1947 to combat "American imperialism." Their greatest triumph was the successful coup in democratic Czechoslovakia in February 1948. Because it was as horrifying to western Europeans as it was to Americans, it helped unify them against the Communist countries. Later in the year, the pressure of Stalin and the Cominform on Marshal Tito provoked him to pull Communist Yugoslavia out of their orbit, and with American aid to embark upon an independent course between Russia and the West. The United States moved with the British and the rather reluctant French toward the creation of a self-governing, economically strong West Germany. The culmination came on June 7, 1948, when they announced plans for a new federal West German government with sovereignty over domestic matters and full membership in the European Recovery Program.

The Russians retaliated. Taking advantage of the lack of a written guarantee of land transit across the Soviet zone, they clamped a tight blockade around the western sectors of Berlin. The object was to force the Western powers to abandon either Berlin or the proposed West German republic. President Truman, unwilling to risk war by ordering in armed convoys by land, ordered the supplying of Berlin by increasing on a massive scale the airlift begun in April. Through the winter and into the spring of 1949, the airlift continued. It was a remarkable demonstration to Europeans — especially to the Germans — of what the Americans and British could achieve.

In the spring of 1949 the Russians backed down and ended the blockade. In October 1949 the German Federal Republic came into existence at Bonn in West Germany, and the Soviets established a German Democratic Republic for East Germany.

Russian intransigence led to the consolidation of the Western countries into a new grand alliance. The North Atlantic Treaty was signed April 4, 1949, by twelve nations, and subsequently also by Greece and Turkey. It declared that an armed attack against one would be considered an attack upon all and provided for the creation of joint military forces. Under it, the signatory powers established the North Atlantic Treaty Organization to construct a defense force that, while not equal to that of the Russians, would be large enough to make an attack highly costly.

The United States began to shift from economic to military aid as the Mutual Defense Act of 1949 appropriated an initial $1 billion for armaments for the signators. The governing body of NATO, the North Atlantic Council, established military headquarters near Paris early in 1951 under the supreme command of General Dwight Eisenhower.

That Russian threats were not to be taken lightly became even more clear on September 23, 1949, when President Truman issued a press statement: "We have evidence that within recent weeks an atomic explosion occurred in the USSR."

In April 1950 the National Security Council presented President Truman with a secret report, labeled NSC-68. Describing a "shrinking world of polarized power," it recommended massive increases in the military budget to check the ambitions of the Soviet Union and urged that the Truman administration mobilize public opinion behind such a policy. The administration, however, saw no way to implement the report. One aide to Secretary of State Dean Acheson remarked: "We were sweating over it, and then — with respect to NSC-68 — thank God Korea came along."

The Chinese Revolution

While the United States was struggling to contain the Soviet Union in Europe between 1947 and 1949, the Chinese Communists were destroying the armies of Chiang Kai-shek.

To prevent civil war and to effect a coalition government, the Truman administration in December 1945 had sent General George C. Marshall to China. At first he obtained a cease-fire and encouraging signs of accommodation, but irreconcilable differences kept apart the two Chinese governments — the *Kuomintang* (Nationalists) and the Communists. Finally, in January 1947, Marshall returned to Washington disgusted with both governments.

Full-scale war broke out. Although the Nationalist armies were larger and better equipped, they soon began to fall back before the better trained, more highly motivated Communist forces. As the inept Chiang Kai-shek government failed both on the fighting front and at home, where inflation and inefficiency were rampant, it was plunging toward defeat.

General Albert C. Wedemyer, who had been Chiang's chief of staff, recommended to Truman that the United States send 10,000 army officers together with massive material support. President Truman requested only limited aid for Chiang, and for this omission critics subsequently castigated him. But to do more might have interfered with the program of containment in Europe; it would have been unpopular and, in any event, would almost certainly have been too late. At the end of 1949 Chiang and the Nationalists fled to Formosa. All of China was under the new People's Republic.

Though Great Britain and some of the western European nations recognized the new government of Communist China, the United States refused to do so and blocked its entry into the United Nations.

The Japanese Ally

Beginning in 1947 the American government introduced new policies in Japan to strengthen that nation in a manner similar to the rebuilding of Germany. The American occupation in Japan brought a democratization of the government, extension of rights to women and underprivileged groups, expansion of the educational system (from a starting point as high as the goal of educational reform in China), land reform as drastic as that in China, a curbing of the power of the monopolistic *zaibatsu* industrial system, and an improvement in the status of labor. In Japan, more than anywhere else in Asia, the United States helped develop a dynamic alternative to Communism. In 1949, to stimulate Japanese recovery, the United States ended its reparations and stopped the dismantling of industrial combinations. However, the task of defending Japan continued to rest largely with the United States.

Conflict in Korea

During the hectic days at the end of the war in the Pacific, the United States had hastily pro-

The Korean War 1950–1953

posed that Americans accept the surrender of the Japanese in the lower half of Korea, up to the thirty-eighth parallel, and the Russians do the same in the northern half. At the time the arrangement was useful to the United States. Afterward, however, the Russians were willing to accept a reunited Korea only if it were Communist-dominated.

The thirty-eighth parallel became more and more an impenetrable barrier. To the north of it, the Communists developed a "people's government" with a strong aggressive army. To the south, the United Nations held elections that led to a government under the ardently nationalistic Dr. Syngman Rhee. When the United States withdrew its forces from below the thirty-eighth parallel in June 1949, South Korea was left militarily weaker than its northern twin. In January 1950 Secretary of State Dean Acheson publicly outlined a Pacific defense perimeter that did not

include Formosa or Korea. If these areas were attacked, he declared, the people invaded must rely upon themselves to resist, "and then upon the commitments of the entire civilized world under the charter of the United Nations."

The North Koreans acted swiftly, on June 24, 1950, launching a full-scale invasion that caught the South Koreans and Americans completely by surprise. Almost immediately President Truman and Congress reversed the policy of withdrawal from the Asiatic mainland. The President brought the question of the invasion before the United Nations Security Council. It could act more quickly than the General Assembly, and at that moment the Russians were boycotting it and hence had no representative present to vote a paralyzing veto. The Security Council on June 25 passed an American resolution demanding that the North Koreans withdraw behind the thirty-eighth parallel and two days later called upon members of the United Nations to "furnish such assistance to the Republic of Korea as may be necessary to repel the armed attack."

President Truman on June 27 sent United States air and sea forces to the aid of the South Koreans; on June 30 he ordered ground forces into Korea and sent the Seventh Fleet to act as a barrier between the Chinese mainland and Formosa.

The Security Council on July 7, 1950, requested those nations providing troops to place them under a unified command headed by the United States. President Truman appointed General MacArthur commander in chief. Some fifteen nations besides the United States and the Republic of Korea provided troops, but these never comprised more than 9 percent of the total fighting force. The United States sent about 48 percent; South Korea mustered 43 percent. What was officially a United Nations "police action" came to most Americans to seem a war on the part of the United States.

Until the United Nations could build strength in Korea, its forces withdrew toward the southern port of Pusan. Then in September 1950 General MacArthur launched an amphibious assault far behind the North Korean lines at Inchon, near Seoul. Within two weeks the North Korean armies, disrupted and demoralized, were fleeing as best they could to north of the thirty-eighth parallel.

Despite warnings from Communist China that it would send troops, the United States and United Nations decided to pursue the fleeing North Koreans and, in a distinct departure from containment, to liberate North Korea. But the Joint Chiefs of Staff on September 27, 1950, ordered MacArthur under no circumstances to cross the borders of China or the Soviet Union. For several weeks the advance into northern Korea went well; then Chinese troops appeared in overwhelming numbers, forcing MacArthur's troops to retreat below the thirty-eighth parallel.

In March 1951 the Eighth Army counterattacked, for a second and final time capturing Seoul and recrossing the thirty-eighth parallel. President Truman was ready again to seek a negotiated peace to restore the status quo.

General MacArthur, far from ready to accept the position of his commander in chief, repeatedly made public his eagerness to win total vic-

tory in Korea at the risk of full involvement in war with China. On March 20, 1951, he communicated his view to the Republican minority leader in the House of Representatives, Joseph W. Martin, concluding: "There is no substitute for victory."

President Truman clung to his thesis that, in the great struggle against Communism, western Europe with its concentration of heavy industry, not industrially weak Asia, was the main potential battlefield. He knew that he could not win the support of western European partners in the United Nations for a more militant policy in Asia. He would not accept the arguments of the Asia firsters that the United States should undertake unilateral action — "go it alone."

General MacArthur thus emerged as a major figure in American politics, trying to reverse the administration policies. Five days after Representative Martin released MacArthur's letter to the press, President Truman, on April 11, 1951, relieved General MacArthur of his commands. A groundswell of outrage swept the United States; MacArthur upon his return was greeted hysterically wherever he appeared; millions watched him address Congress on television.

Truman's policy of fighting a limited war of containment continued to baffle and exasperate a considerable part of the American people. It went too completely against the American tradition of total victory.

In June 1951 the Russian delegate to the United Nations hinted that settlement was possible. Armistice negotiations began on July 10, 1951, near the thirty-eighth parallel and continued for many weary months at Panmunjom. They came to revolve around the difficult questions of locating the cease-fire line, enforcing the armistice, and repatriating prisoners of war. By the spring of 1952 agreements had been reached upon all but the last question. Finally, in October 1952, the negotiations were recessed. By then, the nation was in the midst of a presidential campaign, and though there was no large-scale fighting in Korea, the interminable negotiations, endless skirmishing, and ever-growing casualties had worn out the patience of the American people.

To many of the American people the defeat of the Nationalists in the Chinese Revolution and the stalemate in Korea indicated nothing less than

Communist subversion within the Truman administration.

Trumanism and McCarthyism

As early as 1946, when the cold war was in its opening stages and spy rings were being apprehended, the public became increasingly afraid that traitors within the government were betraying it to the Russians. The federal government began extensive efforts to ferret out Communists. President Truman in November 1946 established a Temporary Commission on Employee Loyalty to recommend loyalty investigation systems and safeguards of fair hearings. This led in March 1947 to the establishment of loyalty boards to undertake a sweeping investigation of all federal employees. In August 1950 the President authorized the dismissal in sensitive departments of those deemed no more than "bad security risks." By 1951 more than 3,000,000 government employees had been cleared, over 2,000 had resigned, and 212 had been dismissed.

Against the recommendations of the Departments of Defense and Justice and of the Central Intelligence Agency, Congress passed, over the President's veto, the McCarran Internal Security Act of September 1950. This did not outlaw Communist organizations but required them to publish their records. It barred Communists from employment in defense plants and denied them passports.

Already in 1948 the attorney general had obtained indictments against eleven key Communist leaders for violation of the Smith Act of 1940, which prohibited conspiring to teach the violent overthrow of the government. They were convicted. In June 1951, in the case of *Dennis* v. *United States*, the Supreme Court in a 6-to-2 decision rejected their appeal. Chief Justice Fred Vinson held that advocating or teaching revolution in the existing state of the world, or even conspiring to do so, fell within Justice Oliver Wendell Holmes' earlier definition of what was punishable — that it constituted a "clear and present danger."

Some politicians capitalized upon the growing public hysteria over several spectacular cases. Above all there was the case of Alger Hiss, in which these politicians seemed to put on trial and condemn a whole generation of liberal intellectuals. Hiss had been a high-ranking official in the State Department. In 1948 Whittaker Chambers, a self-avowed former Communist agent, accused Hiss before the House Un-American Activities Committee. When Hiss sued him for slander, Chambers produced microfilms of classified State Department documents that Hiss allegedly had given him in 1937 and 1938.

Hiss was brought to trial for perjury (the statute of limitations prevented indictment for espionage). He called upon a number of the nation's most distinguished liberals to bear witness to his character. The first trial ended with a hung jury in July 1949; the second ended with conviction in January 1950.

Among the politicians who capitalized upon the public's fears was Representative Richard M. Nixon of California. He was already on his way to the Senate and had a national reputation for having kept the Hiss affair alive in its early stages. Most sensational in his rise was Senator Joseph McCarthy of Wisconsin. In February 1950 McCarthy charged that a large number of Communists and people loyal to the Communist party were still shaping foreign policy in the State Department. A subcommittee of the State Foreign Relations Committee took up his charges but found not a single Communist.

An excited public numbering many millions eagerly swallowed McCarthy's new claims as he went on from sensation to sensation more rapidly than his detractors could refute his unsubstantiated charges. Millions wanted to believe McCarthy when he attacked as Communists the "whole group of twisted-thinking New Dealers" who had "led America near to ruin at home and abroad." McCarthy was providing a troubled nation with a scapegoat and the Republican party with a winning issue.

A Troubled Electorate

Bipartisanship in foreign policy disappeared as the Republicans pressed their issue. They did not capture Congress in November 1950, but they gained twenty-eight seats in the House and five in the Senate. In December neo-isolationists, heart-

ened by the election results and no longer restrained by Senator Vandenberg, who was fatally
ill, opened a "great debate" in the Senate over
foreign policy. They succeeded in passing a resolution in April 1951 restraining the President
from sending troops to western Europe without
congressional authorization.

Meanwhile, President Truman made little
headway with his Fair Deal. Congress passed the
Displaced Persons Act of 1950, liberalizing the
1948 legislation that the President had denounced
as discriminatory against Catholics and Jews because its immigration quotas were unfavorable to
people from southern and eastern Europe. The
National Housing Act of 1949 provided for the
construction over the succeeding six years of
810,000 housing units for lower-income families,
together with a subsidy for forty years to bridge
the gulf between costs and the rents the tenants
could afford to pay. Congress voted increased appropriations for power development and reclamation in the West, for TVA and for the Farmers
Home Administration (which carried on the rehabilitation work of the earlier Resettlement Ad-

ministration and Farm Security Administration).
In contrast, the Fair Deal health insurance program went down to crashing defeat under the vigorous opposition of the American Medical Association, which raised a $3,000,000 fund to combat
it. Federal aid for education failed because of dissension over whether aid should go to parochial
schools.

Republicans undermined the Truman administration with charges of favor peddling and corruption, which implicated people in the White
House, though not the President himself. The
President's military aide had received as a gift a
$520 deep-freeze unit; the wife of an examiner of
loans for the Reconstruction Finance Corporation
had acquired a $9,540 mink coat. These became
the symbols of a moral malaise in Washington.

As the election of 1952 approached, there was
no indication that the majority of voters wished to
reverse either Truman's foreign policy or his domestic program. They did want to "clean up the
mess in Washington," and above all they wanted
to see an end to the drawn-out, wearying Korean
War.

Chapter 26

The Eisenhower Years

Eisenhower Elected

In Dwight D. Eisenhower, the Republican party nominated for the Presidency a successful and popular general who they felt could restore security against frightening outside threats. The conservative minority of the party had been committed to Senator Robert A. Taft. The majority sought a candidate who could pull strong support from those favoring the Democratic foreign and domestic policies. Consequently, the Republicans looked to General Eisenhower — whom some liberal Democrats had sought to draft in 1948. Senator Richard M. Nixon of California, acceptable to conservative Republicans, was nominated for the Vice Presidency. The platform was ambiguous enough to cover disagreements between the two wings of the party.

President Truman having declined to run again, the Democrats chose Governor Adlai E. Stevenson of Illinois and, as his running mate, the liberal Senator John J. Sparkman of Alabama. The platform stated the positions of the Northern Democrats: endorsement of the Truman foreign policies, civil rights, repeal of the Taft-Hartley Act, and high price supports for farmers.

Republican campaigners played upon the triple theme of "Communism, corruption, and Korea." Speaking in Detroit on October 24, 1952, Eisenhower promised to bring the war to "an early and honorable end." To help do so, he promised he would make a personal trip to Korea. The response at the polls was overwhelming, Eisenhower polling 33,936,000 votes to 27,315,000 for Stevenson. The electoral vote was 442 to 89. But the Republicans failed to gain complete control of Congress, winning a majority of eight seats in the House and only an even split in the Senate. The Republican candidate was far more popular than his party.

John Foster Dulles

A central figure in the Eisenhower administration was John Foster Dulles, who served as secretary of state from 1953 to 1959. His sturdy moralism, his skill at bureaucratic politics, and his tireless effort made him a formidable figure. Before taking office Dulles had criticized the Democratic program of "containment" as a passive one that left the initiative to the Communists. He proposed, instead, a program of "liberation" that would lead to a "rollback" of Communist expansion. As secretary of state he continued to talk of new approaches, but Eisenhower restrained him and the Eisenhower-Dulles policy was essentially a continuation of the Truman-Acheson policy. It proved difficult even to contain Communist power, without attempting a "rollback."

A Truce in Korea

Less than two months after President Eisenhower entered office, Stalin died, opening up the possibility of an end to the Korean War and perhaps some modification of the cold war. When the new Soviet premier, Georgi Malenkov, seemed conciliatory, the President called upon

the Russians to show their good faith by supporting an armistice in Korea. On July 27, 1953, a
final Korean armistice agreement was signed at
Panmunjom. It provided for a cease-fire and withdrawal of both armies two kilometers back of the
existing battle line, which ran from coast to coast,
from just below the thirty-eighth parallel in the
west to thirty miles north of it in the east.

Within three months a political conference to
seek peaceful unification of Korea was to be held,
but it never took place. Instead, the armistice
turned into an uneasy and indefinite armed truce,
marked by occasional border shootings and unre-
lenting North Korean hostility.

The Korean War (officially only a "police action") had lasted more than three years and cost
the United States alone 25,000 dead, 115,000
other casualties, and $22 billion. For Americans
who liked to think in terms of total victory, it all
seemed painfully inconclusive. The fighting had
settled no problems in the Far East except to prevent the Communist conquest of South Korea.

"Massive Retaliation"

The Eisenhower administration came into office firmly committed to a Europe-first priority.
Nevertheless, it maintained a tenuous compromise with the ardently nationalistic Asia-first
wing of the party. The hero of the Asia-firsters
was Chiang Kai-shek, and their special villain,
Communist China, which they insisted must be
curbed or destroyed at all costs. Concurring with
this group on some issues were the business leaders dominant in the Eisenhower administration,
who were determined that defense expenditures
must fit within a balanced budget.

The solution seemed to lie in a "new look" in
defense policy, equally pleasing to the secretaries
of defense, the treasury, and state. This meant
cutting the expensive army ground forces and
basic scientific research. The United States would
depend upon its thermonuclear weapons and
their delivery by the air force. Popularized, this
was the policy of "more bang for a buck."

A new foreign policy was necessary to make the
"new look" in defense operate adequately. Secretary of the Treasury George M. Humphrey, looking at it from a standpoint of cost, asserted that

the United States had "no business getting into
little wars." If the nation had to intervene, he declared, "let's intervene decisively with all we
have got or stay out." This was the economic basis
for Secretary of State Dulles' policy of "massive
retaliation." The United States would depend less
on local defense, he declared in an address on
January 12, 1954, and depend more on "the deterrent of massive retaliatory power . . . a great
capacity to retaliate instantly, by means and at
times of our own choosing."

Involvement in Vietnam

The Indochina crisis of 1954 offered the first
test of the new approach. Formerly a French colony, Indochina had been occupied by the Japanese during World War II. Against the Japanese a
Vietnamese Communist, Ho Chi Minh, in cooperation with the Americans, had led a struggle for
the liberation of Vietnam, a part of Indochina.
After the war the French undertook to recover
their former colony. Ho, issuing a declaration of
independence that echoed the American Declaration of 1776, now rallied the Vietnamese nationalists to fight the French. Ho and his followers
received supplies from the People's Republic of
China. By 1954 the Vietnamese were beseiging
and threatening to take the last French stronghold, the fortress of Dien Bien Phu.

The American government had been little concerned about events in Vietnam until the Communist victory in China and the outbreak of the
Korean conflict. Then the Truman administration, looking upon the French as foes of the
spread of Communism in Southeast Asia, began to
send substantial aid to them. Continuing to support colonialism as an alternative to Communism,
the Eisenhower administration greatly increased
economic assistance to the French. By 1954 the
American taxpayers were paying more than 70
percent of the cost of the French military effort in
Vietnam.

The administration now considered sending
planes and possibly troops to prevent Dien Bien
Phu, and with it all of Vietnam, from falling to
the forces of Ho Chi Minh. At a press conference
President Eisenhower likened the nations of
Southeast Asia to a row of dominoes. His point

was obvious: the first domino, Vietnam, must not be allowed to fall. Some of his advisers urged at least the use of carrier-based planes to bomb the Vietnamese army besieging Dien Bien Phu, but Great Britain was unwilling to cooperate in such a venture, and Senator Lyndon B. Johnson and other congressional leaders hesitated to take the United States, with few or no allies, into a conflict that might prove even more frustrating than the Korean War. So the United States declined to intervene militarily; there was no "massive retaliation," and Dien Bien Phu fell.

Later that year a settlement for Indochina was arranged at the same Geneva conference that failed to negotiate a peace for Korea. According to the Geneva agreements, Indochina was to be partitioned into three independent countries — Vietnam, Laos, and Cambodia — and Vietnam was to be divided into a Communist north and a non-Communist south, but only temporarily, until free elections could be held to unify the new nation. The United States did not sign these agreements but did promise not to use force to upset them. Later the Eisenhower administration exerted its influence against the holding of elections to bring North and South Vietnam together, and such elections were never held.

The Eisenhower administration sought new arrangements to prevent the Ho Chi Minh forces of North Vietnam from taking over the rest of Indochina. Within two months of the Geneva agreements, Secretary Dulles set up the Southeast Asia Treaty Organization (SEATO), including the United States, Great Britain, France, Australia, New Zealand, Pakistan, Thailand, and the Philippines. SEATO, unlike NATO, did not assume that an attack on one should be considered an attack on all. The SEATO members agreed only to consult one another in cases of a threat to the security of any of them or to Laos, Cambodia, or South Vietnam.

In South Vietnam the Eisenhower administration desired a ruler who could rally the people to maintain their independence. The French-sponsored puppet emperor, Bao Dai, had too many enemies, but the premier, Ngo Dinh Diem, seemed a good choice, at least to an American secret agent on the spot. In a letter to Diem, Eisenhower promised American financial aid in return for certain reforms and offered to assist "in devel-

oping and maintaining a strong, viable state, capable of resisting attempted subversion or aggression through military means." With only the unpopular Bao Dai permitted to run against him, Diem got 98 percent of the vote in a 1955 presidential election.

Between 1954 and 1959 the Eisenhower administration sent $2.3 billion to South Vietnam, besides American military advisers to help train a South Vietnamese army. But President Diem made little or no progress toward achieving the reforms that President Eisenhower had requested in return for American aid. Discontent increased among the South Vietnamese people, and growing numbers of them joined or cooperated with the Vietcong, the South Vietnamese Communist organization, which by 1959 was getting military advisers and supplies from North Vietnam. Making forays at night, murdering local leaders and terrorizing villages, Vietcong bands got control of large areas of the countryside. The authority of the Diem government was confined mostly to the cities and the main lines of communication.

Under President Eisenhower, the United States refrained from going to war to save its creature and client, the government of South Vietnam, but it had taken steps that led toward the eventual participation of the United States in the Vietnam War. Later administrations were to cite Eisenhower's Diem letter and the SEATO treaty as "commitments" that required the United States to use military force — even though Diem had failed to achieve the specified reforms and the treaty contained no very binding terms. Indeed, Secretary Dulles had told the Senate Foreign Relations Committee, when seeking its approval of SEATO, that if there should be a "revolutionary movement" in Vietnam, the SEATO members "would consult together as to what to do about it . . . but we have no undertaking to put it down; all we have is an undertaking to consult."

Meanwhile, the Eisenhower administration brought the United States close to war with the People's Republic of China over another question — the security of the Republic of China, that is, Taiwan and the nearby islands. After the negotiation of a mutual defense pact with the Chiang Kai-shek government on Taiwan, the Eisenhower administration was challenged by mainland Chinese shelling of Quemoy and Matsu, two rocky islets controlled by the Taiwan government. Here again was a challenge to Dulles' assertion of "massive retaliation." Congress hastily authorized Eisenhower to "employ the Armed Forces of the United States as he deems necessary" for the protection of Taiwan and "related positions and territories." The mainland Chinese soon stopped their shelling but resumed it again in 1958. This time the United States Seventh Fleet escorted supply ships to the islands, and Dulles talked of backing Chiang in an all-out defense. Again, the shelling stopped. Apparently forgetting about "massive retaliation," Dulles tried to persuade Chiang to renounce, at least for the moment, his fantastic hopes of recovering mainland China.

The Geneva Spirit

After the death of Stalin in 1953, some softening of Soviet policy led to demands from Europeans, Asians, and even Americans for a conference among the heads of state — a "summit conference" — to consider means of easing international tensions. But the greatest single motive for such a meeting was the knowledge that both the United States and the Soviet Union were manufacturing hydrogen bombs of staggering destructive power.

In August 1953, after the Russians had set off a hydrogen explosive, President Eisenhower warned that the physical security of the United States had "almost totally disappeared before the long-range bomber and the destructive power of a single bomb."

Against this background, the American people became enthusiastic about the meeting of the heads of the United States, Great Britain, France, and Russia at Geneva in July 1955. President Eisenhower, hopeful that he could wage "a war for peace," proposed at the meetings that the Soviet Union and the United States exchange blueprints of their armed forces and permit inspection of their military installations from the air.

The affability of the Russians at Geneva immensely relieved the American people, who were hopeful for the moment that a real change of policy had come about. This "Geneva spirit," as newspaper reporters called it, led to a general feeling on the part of most Western nations that a nuclear war between the Soviet Union and the United States would not develop. The subsequent foreign ministers' conference, however, failed dismally to agree upon German unification, disarmament, or lowering of trade barriers. The "Geneva spirit" rapidly evaporated throughout the West.

Menace in the Middle East

Soon a new Russian drive was launched toward the Middle East, where the United States had long been deeply involved because of its conflicting interests in the people of the new state of Israel and in the oil of the Arab states.

During World War II, the British, in order not to offend the Arabs, had continued restrictions upon immigration to Palestine; both political parties in the United States favored lifting these restrictions and creating a Jewish state. After the war the British brought the problem to the United Nations, which recommended partitioning Palestine between Jews and Arabs. The Jews successfully repelled military attacks by the Arabs and, on the day the British mandate ended, May 14, 1948, proclaimed a new government. President Truman recognized it within a few minutes, thus ending United Nations proposals to put Palestine under a temporary trusteeship. The new nation, Israel, fought off armies from surrounding Arab countries until the United Nations established an unstable truce in 1949. Although the United States tried to promote amity, relations between Israel and its neighbors continued close to the point of explosion, and other quarrels in the Middle East persisted.

Gradually the United States won over some of the Arab nations to the Western defense system. This country leased air bases from Saudi Arabia; and through the Baghdad Pact of February 1955 Secretary Dulles managed to bring the northern bloc of Arab states — Iraq, Iran, and Pakistan — into the defense arrangement.

Dulles' diplomacy was less successful with Egypt, which for years had quarreled with the British over the Sudan and British bases along the Suez Canal. The United States tried to mediate; in 1954 the British agreed to remove their troops from the Suez area. After Gamal Abdel Nasser came to power, the State Department tried to woo him, although he proclaimed emphatic neutralist and Arab nationalist policies and strove for leadership of the entire Arab world. Secretary Dulles tried to win him with offers of economic aid — even the sum needed to construct an enormous dam on the Nile. The Russians concluded a deal, made public in September 1955, by which they gave Nasser large quantities of armaments in exchange for cotton.

With sufficient Communist arms, Nasser might destroy Israel. He could also threaten the security system that the United States was trying to build in the Middle East. Secretary Dulles met the challenge. Instead of continuing to be conciliatory toward Egypt, in July 1956 he suddenly withdrew his promise to provide funds for a dam. A week later, Nasser retaliated by seizing the Suez Canal, purportedly to obtain money for the dam. This action gave him a stranglehold on the main oil line to Europe.

During the months of tedious negotiations with Nasser that followed, Great Britain, France, and Israel all came to feel that they were not obtaining as much support as they should from the United States. On October 29, 1956, Israeli forces struck a preventive blow at Egypt; the next day the British and French intervened to drive the Egyptian forces from the Suez Canal zone. They were militarily successful, but not before the Egyptians had thoroughly blocked the canal. The United States led the United Nations in denouncing the military intervention; the Western alliance seemed in danger of dissolving; the Soviet Union threatened to send "volunteers" to the aid of Egypt. Under these pressures, the British and French issued a cease-fire order on November 6. Another prolonged truce between Egypt and Israel began under the supervision of the United Nations.

In the Middle East positive action afterward seemed possible. The President appeared before Congress on January 5, 1957, to enunciate what came to be called the "Eisenhower Doctrine." He asked Congress to authorize military and economic aid "to secure and protect the territorial independence" of Middle Eastern nations "against overt armed aggression from any nation controlled by international communism." Congress authorized the President to use armed force as

he deemed necessary and to spend $200,000,000 on economic aid in the area.

As an instrument of pressure upon Egypt, the Eisenhower Doctrine was of little effect. Nasser reopened the Suez Canal on his own terms and with Soviet aid became increasingly involved in the governments of his neighbors. In April 1957 American policy seemed more successful when the United States rushed its Sixth Fleet to the eastern Mediterranean to bolster the government of Lebanon. Three other states — Saudi Arabia, Iraq, and Jordan — seemed to give at least tacit support to the Eisenhower Doctrine.

The Rocket Race

Communist ideology and power became especially frightening because of the failure of the United States to keep pace with the Soviet Union in the development of intercontinental ballistic missiles. In August 1957 the Soviet Union announced that it had successfully tested an intercontinental ballistic missile. In contrast, the United States had successfully tested only intermediate-range missiles that had traveled from 1,500 to 3,000 miles. The Russian claims received sobering confirmation in October when Soviet scientists, using a rocket booster engine more powerful than any yet developed in the United States, launched the first successful satellite, the "sputnik."

Nikita Khrushchev, who in a series of bold moves had just consolidated his power in the Kremlin, now issued a series of strong statements. The intent of his "sputnik diplomacy" was clearly to shake the Western alliance and impress neutral nations. The reaction within the United States, especially when the first American attempt to launch a much smaller satellite failed, was more one of angry fear than of congratulations to the Russian scientists. Three months later the United States began launching its own, smaller satellites.

Meanwhile, extensive nuclear testing by both the United States and Russia, climaxed by the Russian explosion of several "dirty" bombs, had greatly increased the fallout of radioactive isotopes. Throughout the world there was a fear of possible harmful effects. In the spring of 1958, Khrushchev announced a unilateral abstention from nuclear tests by Russia. President Eisenhower responded that the United States and its allies would suspend tests for one year beginning October 31, 1958. The suspension would continue on a year-to-year basis, provided a proper system of control could be developed and substantial progress could be made on disarmament negotiations.

In 1959 Khrushchev made much propaganda use of the failure of the United States to catch up with the Soviet Union in astronautical feats. These feats obscured the fact that the "missile gap" between the two nations was not as great as had been feared. The United States was successfully producing and testing its own, more efficient missiles and developing plans for hiding and spreading the launching sites so that it would require ten times as many Russian missiles to destroy them. The success of the navy in constructing atomic-powered submarines that could launch missiles, and in bringing the submarines up through the ice at the North Pole, was a dramatic example of American achievement. The naval development of "Project Tepee," a radio-monitoring system that could detect missile launchings anywhere in the world, was an indication of the technical advance of American defense.

A new secretary of state, Christian Herter, took over when Dulles, dying of cancer, resigned in April 1959. Although Herter was a strong secretary, President Eisenhower now assumed a larger measure of responsibility, and this led to new interchanges at the top with the Russians. In August 1959 Eisenhower announced that he would exchange visits with Khrushchev. On the whole Khrushchev received a cordial welcome during his tour of the United States, but discussions with Eisenhower brought no results. The President never made the return visit.

A second "summit" conference, to meet in Paris, was scheduled for May 1960. On May 1 an unarmed American "U-2" plane was downed inside the Soviet Union. The American government at first denied, then acknowledged and attempted to justify, that the plane had been engaged in aerial reconnaissance of a kind the United States had been carrying on, systematically but secretly, for some time. At the Paris meeting, unsatisfied by Eisenhower's belated promise to discontinue

flights over Russian territory, Khrushchev made the U-2 incident an occasion for denouncing Eisenhower and breaking up the conference.

Disgruntled Neighbors

During the cold war, the American government and people paid scant attention to Latin America. Above all, the problems from which Latin American peoples were suffering were economic. After the close of World War II, they could no longer sell raw materials from their farms and mines to the United States in such large quantities or at such favorable prices as before. The soaring costs of the American manufactured goods they imported further hurt them. At home they were undergoing an explosive population increase at the highest rate in the world, as much as 2.5 percent per year.

It seemed to Latin Americans that despite close economic ties, the United States was doing little to help them solve their problems — to provide adequate capital for large-scale development, to stabilize the prices of raw material at a profitable level, and to conquer inflation. They felt neglected as the American government poured billions into Europe and Asia while giving Latin America only a comparative pittance. Secretary Dulles was occupied elsewhere, and the Eisenhower administration, under the influence of conservative secretaries of the treasury, was cold to requests for government loans for economic development.

Despite riots and disorders, the Latin American discontent received little notice in the United States until May 1958, when Vice President Nixon was mobbed in Lima and Caracas. In the aftermath of the national shock, the State Department speeded changes in policy that were already slowly under way. When in June 1958 the president of Brazil called for an Operation Pan-America to increase economic development, the American government agreed to furnish nearly half the capital for a new billion-dollar Inter-American Bank to make development loans.

The full importance of the Communist challenge to the south became clear in 1960. Fidel Castro, whose revolutionary accession to power had been cheered by Americans at the beginning of 1959, turned his administration increasingly to the left and indulged in shrill tirades against the United States. The Eisenhower administration, acting with restraint, was slow to retaliate economically until, in the summer of 1960, Castro systematically confiscated $1 billion of American property. At this point, the United States stopped importing Cuban sugar at a subsidized price. Castro complained to the United Nations Security Council that the United States was engaging in economic aggression.

Khrushchev proclaimed that the Monroe Doctrine was dead and that if the United States were to intervene militarily, Soviet artillery could "support Cuba with rocket fire." In the fall of 1960 tension heightened as Castro tried to export his revolution to neighboring republics. President Eisenhower established a naval patrol to prevent an invasion of Guatemala or Nicaragua. At the same time, secretly, Americans were training an anti-Castro Cuban force at a camp in Guatemala. In January 1961 Castro ordered the staff of the United States embassy in Havana cut from eighty-seven to eleven. The United States then severed diplomatic relations with Cuba.

"Eisenhower Prosperity"

In the 1950s the majority of the voters seemed more interested in preserving their own economic gains than in remaking society. Viewing themselves as moderates, they gave wholehearted support to the moderate President, Dwight Eisenhower. As early as 1949 Eisenhower had indicated his own approach when, as president of Columbia University, he addressed the American Bar Association. "The path of America's future," he said then, "lies down the middle of the road between the unfettered power of concentrated wealth . . . and the unbridled power of statism or partisan interests."

Once in office, President Eisenhower established a business-oriented administration. He appointed the president of General Motors, Charles E. Wilson, to the Defense Department and other big business executives to all the rest of the cabinet posts but one. The secretary of labor was the pro-Stevenson president of the plumbers' union (who was soon to resign from the cabinet). "Eight

millionaires and a plumber," the *New Republic* disrespectfully remarked.

The new administration quickly dropped almost all the price controls that had been imposed during the Korean War, and it began to restrict credit so as to prevent inflation. By the fall of 1953, however, the threat was one of deflation, and the government reversed the scarce-money policies and eased credit. By the summer of 1955 the American economy was again booming.

Farm prices, however, remained weak because of high levels of production. The government sought to bolster the prices through $8 billion worth of purchases. The 1955 harvest was the first to be grown under a new flexible price-support system. Under the 1956 program, which was designed to cut production while creating a "soil bank" of fallow land, farmers took 12,300,000 acres out of production in return for payments of over a quarter billion dollars.

The President retained the basic general welfare programs that had been enacted during the previous twenty years. He took a firm stand against so-called socialized medicine but proposed a public health insurance program that would involve little more than limited underwriting of private insurance companies issuing health policies. Congress passed no health insurance legislation but, in 1954, extended social security to 10,000,000 more people, and unemployment compensation to an additional 4,000,000.

Decline of McCarthyism

Early in the Eisenhower administration the hunt for subversives had been intensified. Larger numbers of government employees resigned or were dismissed; the administration at one point gave their total as 2,200. But most of the serious security risks had already been ousted in the Truman administration. A study of some 400 of the Eisenhower administration cases by the Fund for the Republic indicated that in a majority of them the charges had been insupportable, and often reinstatement ultimately followed.

Senator Joseph McCarthy himself plummeted from the national limelight to relative obscurity. His downfall followed his serious blunder in obliquely attacking President Eisenhower and directly assailing Secretary of the Army Robert Stevens in January 1954. The attacks led to congressional hearings, which turned into a great national spectacle viewed by millions over television. Many people for the first time saw McCarthy in action, as for thirteen days he bullied and harried Secretary Stevens, evading issues through irrelevant countercharges and insinuations, and interrupting to object at every point. As the public watched, McCarthy seemed to change from a national hero into something of a villain, then into a low buffoon. In December 1954 the Senate voted 67 to 22 to condemn McCarthy, but his hold over the American public had already largely disintegrated.

Desegregation Begins

The Supreme Court under its new Eisenhower-appointed chief justice, Earl Warren, the former governor of California, moved toward more liberal policies on both civil liberties and civil rights. In a number of cases in the 1950s the Court protected individuals who were suspected of being subversive from undue encroachment by federal or state power. These decisions attracted relatively little attention compared with the Supreme Court rulings on desegregation.

Since the late 1930s the National Association for the Advancement of Colored People had pressed a series of cases before the Supreme Court that bit by bit broke down racial segregation in public education. Their prime target was a Supreme Court decision of 1896, *Plessy* v. *Ferguson,* which had interpreted the requirement of the Fourteenth Amendment that states give "equal protection of the laws" to mean that separate but equal facilities could be furnished to blacks. Finally, the Supreme Court reversed this doctrine in the case of *Brown* v. *Board of Education of Topeka* in May 1954. Chief Justice Earl Warren delivered the unanimous opinion of the Court: "We conclude that in the field of public education the doctrine of 'separate but equal' has no place. Separate educational facilities are inherently unequal." The Court granted that Southern states might move gradually toward desegregation.

States in the deep South and several border states resorted to every possible legal device to avoid mixed schools. Each September, mob action against integration in a few communities within the South attracted widespread attention throughout the world. By the fall of 1957, of some 3,000 biracial school districts in the South, a total of 684 had begun desegregation. Schools within these districts in large cities in the upper South or the border area, like Washington, Baltimore, Louisville, and St. Louis, opened quietly on a desegregated basis. But 2,300 districts, including all those in the deep South and Virginia, remained segregated. Some districts attempted desegregation on a very slow, "token" basis. One of these was Little Rock, Arkansas, where intervention by the governor and threats by a mob led President Eisenhower to send federal troops to maintain order.

Pressure from growing blocs of black voters in the North and from blacks rising in economic status in the South helped bring other changes. President Eisenhower completed the desegregation of the armed forces and tried to bring about greater integration in the government and the District of Columbia. "There must be no second-class citizens in this country," he wrote the black Representative Adam Clayton Powell.

Congress in August 1957, after debating sixty-three days, passed a new civil rights law — the first since Reconstruction — to give federal protection to blacks wanting to vote. In eight Southern states with an adult black population of over 3,750,000, only 850,000, or 25 percent, were registered, and still fewer went to the polls. In a 1955 election in Mississippi, only about 1 percent of the adult blacks voted. The civil rights act empowered the federal government to remove some of the obstacles that state and local officials were placing in the way of black registration and voting. Federal judges were authorized to enjoin state officials from refusing to register qualified persons. The judges could fine recalcitrant officials up to $300 and could sentence them to forty-five days in jail, without a jury trial.

A Second Term for Ike

In September 1955 President Eisenhower was at the height of his popularity. Only the anti-third-term Twenty-second Amendment, ratified in 1951 as a belated slap at Roosevelt, seemed to bar him from staying in the White House as long as he chose. Apparently his health was excellent, but while vacationing in Colorado, on the morning of September 24, he suffered a heart attack. The President began to make a promising recovery, and in 1956 he and Vice President Nixon were renominated by acclamation. Stevenson triumphed again at the Democratic convention, but in the end Eisenhower won by an even wider margin than in 1952.

It was not much of a triumph for the Republican party. The prestige of the President pulled some Republicans in Congress to narrow victories, but the Democrats continued to control both houses of Congress, as they had done since the midterm elections of 1954.

At the close of 1957 the nation skidded into the most serious recession since the war. Although recovery began in 1958, Republicans preparing for the congressional campaign of 1958 were handicapped by the economic record. The Democrats won 13 additional seats in the Senate, giving them a 62 to 34 majority. They gained an added 47 seats in the House of Representatives, providing a majority of 282 to 153 — the largest margin since Roosevelt's 1936 victory.

As prosperity returned in the spring of 1959, public opinion began to react to the incessant warnings of the President and of conservative publicists that budget balancing was the only way to avoid another ruinous round of inflation. But by the fall of 1960, the economy had again stalled into the third recession of the Eisenhower years.

In his final State of the Union message in January 1961, President Eisenhower granted that problems of recession and unemployment left little room for complacency. But he pointed out correctly that during his eight years in office the inflationary spiral had all but ceased and that the nation's output of goods and services had increased 25 percent; the income of the average American family had increased 15 percent; and the real wages of workers had increased 20 percent. "In a united determination to keep this nation strong and free and to utilize our vast resources for the advancement of all mankind," he asserted, "we have carried America to unprecedented heights."

Selected Readings

A. R. Buchanan, *The United States and World War II*° (2 vols., 1964) surveys military aspects of World War II. An excellent interpretation of strategy is S. E. Morison, *Strategy and Compromise* (1958). A momumental account of wartime diplomacy is Herbert Feis, *Churchill, Roosevelt, Stalin* (1957). An outstanding brief interpretation is Gaddis Smith, *American Diplomacy During the Second World War, 1941–1945* (1965). An important revisionist view is Gabriel Kolko, *The Politics of War: The World and United States Foreign Policy, 1943–1945* (1968). On production and domestic problems during World War II, see Eliot Janeway, *The Struggle for Survival* (1968 edition), which concentrates on policy and conflicts in Washington.

On postwar foreign policy, see Thomas G. Paterson, *On Every Front: The Making of the Cold War*° (1979), and J. L. Gaddis, *The United States and the Origins of the Cold War, 1941–1947*° (1973).

The Truman administration is discussed in E. F. Goldman, *The Crucial Decade*° (1956), and A. L. Hamby, *Beyond the New Deal: Harry S. Truman and American Liberalism* (1973). McCarthyism is dealt with in Robert Griffith, *The Politics of Fear*° (1970). On President Eisenhower and his policies, see Herbert Parmet, *Eisenhower and the American Crusades* (1972).

° Titles available in paperback.

Hope in Space, Persistent Problems on Earth

On Sunday, July 20, 1969, slowly, cautiously, a white-clad figure climbed down from his spacecraft and extended a heavy, well-insulated boot toward the surface of the moon while hundreds of millions of people throughout the world followed his movements on television or radio. As the astronaut, Neil Armstrong, placed both feet on the strange, finely powdered lunar soil, he said: "That's one small step for man, one giant leap for mankind." A human being was standing where none had ever stood before — on land beyond the earth.

The moon landing, the result of cooperative efforts by thousands of scientists and technicians, provided a spectacular illustration of what sociologists call "cultural lag," that is, the failure of social and political development to keep up with technological advances. People were acquiring the ability to visit other worlds before acquiring the capacity to put their own in order, with peace and plenty for its inhabitants. A leading example of cultural lag was the exploitation of nuclear energy with no adequate arrangement of human power to control it.

Foreign relations persisted as the central political preoccupation of Americans after 1960 as they continued to face a "hostile ideology" abroad. But there was a ray of hope. Some Americans looked toward an eventual "détente," or relaxation of tensions in world politics. Among them was President John F. Kennedy, who in his inaugural address advised: "Let us never negotiate out of fear.

But let us never fear to negotiate." Nonetheless, during the Kennedy years, as the Soviet Union and the United States faced one another over the issues of Berlin, Cuba, and nuclear testing, the spirit of negotiation was put to severe trials.

Vietnam was, without question, the major tragedy of the post-1960 era. It rang up an enormous cost in lives and resources, set generation against generation, and drastically altered national priorities. The war also delayed détente and weakened America elsewhere in the world. The 1960s began with some promise that American society, in its exceptional prosperity, would face squarely the problems of disadvantaged peoples. President Lyndon B. Johnson's "Great Society" program, in particular, suggested a significant revival of certain lines of progressive and New Deal reform. But President Johnson was himself to jeopardize his Great Society when, in 1965, he committed the country to a large-scale war in Vietnam. While starting his "war on poverty," Johnson was escalating his war in Vietnam. The enormous costs of the latter made it more and more difficult to pay for the former. And when Johnson attempted to do both, the consequence was the onset of what might prove to be the nation's most serious bout with inflation and the nation's most serious economic crisis since the depression of the 1930s.

Richard Nixon failed to "bring the American people together," as he had promised in his 1968 campaign; instead, he aroused increasing bitterness and brought division when he frustrated the hope for an early withdrawal from Vietnam. Nevertheless, he won widespread approval by finally withdrawing American troops and by redirecting basic policy in such a way as to improve the prospects for moderating the cold war and for realizing what he hailed as a "generation of peace."

As the country neared the 200th anniversary of its independence, the American people were confronted with a constitutional crisis. To carry on the Vietnam War in the face of greater and greater popular opposition to it, President Nixon had gone to unprecedented lengths in stretching his authority, silencing his critics, and hiding his illegal actions. Exposure led to impeachment and resignation. With Vice President Spiro Agnew having already resigned in disgrace, Agnew's successor, Gerald R. Ford, who had been appointed under the terms of the Twenty-fifth Amendment (ratified in 1967), became the first unelected President.

In the wake of these troubles came an economic collapse. The majority of the American people (though not the chronically poor, who made up a large minority) had been enjoying a wave of prosperity much higher and longer-lasting than any previous one in the history of the country. Beginning in the 1940s, the boom persisted through the 1950s and the 1960s, with an occasional slump but with no real depression. A generation grew up that had never experienced such a calamity and could not believe it possible. Then, in 1974, a serious recession began, the worst since the 1930s. Recovery was slow and uncertain.

The public lost much of its trust in government, partly because of the government's seeming inability to solve the economic problems, but still more because of revelations of deception, corruption, and law violation on the part of both elected and appointed officials. Of those citizens who re-

tained some faith in the electoral process, a majority looked for Presidents who seemed above the contamination. The rise to the Presidency of both Jimmy Carter and Ronald Reagan had much to do with their ability to convey a strong impression of personal honesty and decency.

Jimmy Carter retained the liberal faith in the efficacy of positive government and wished to promote human rights and weapons control and to solve the domestic problems of energy shortages, economic stagnation, and maldistribution of wealth. Unfortunately, he addressed these problems at a time when they were of staggering complexity and difficulty. Public disappointment was inevitable, especially because Carter was willing to assume heavy personal responsibility for the failures of his administration. When he left office in 1981, he was one of the least popular Presidents of the century.

Ronald Reagan and the Republicans took effective advantage of Jimmy Carter's inability to reestablish a national consensus of support for the liberalism of the Democratic party. Reagan reached the Presidency in 1980 and was reelected in 1984 by playing skillfully on disillusionment with positive government, confusion over the loss of American power in the world, and a widespread desire for more effective national leadership. Relying, ironically enough, on the power of the Presidency, the Reagan administration implemented a philosophy of negative government at home, attacking many of the institutions created by the liberal reform movements of the twentieth century. At the same time, the administration adopted foreign policies that harkened back to the cold war era. However, it remained to be seen whether Reagan would make enough progress in solving the nation's economic problems and in advancing arms control to sustain the dominance of the Republican party.

Chapter 27

The Affluent Society

The Promise of Technology and Science

Generation after generation, Americans had been preoccupied with material progress. Those of the late twentieth century saw technological achievements even more startling than those of earlier times. A future of increasing abundance seemed to be promised by the continuing development of technical innovations summed up in the term "automation."

Essential to automation as it developed after World War II were electronic controls and the development of computer systems. The first electronic computer went into operation in 1946. Its name was descriptive: ENIAC, which stood for Electronic Numerical Integrator and Calculator. At first computers were large, cumbersome, and expensive, but the discovery that complicated electronic circuits, which had been assembled by hand, could be printed on cardboard or plastic and that compact durable transistors (invented in 1948) could replace fragile vacuum tubes made possible the rapid and spectacular advance in computer technology. By the end of the sixties, computers were a hundred times faster, ten times smaller in their electronic components, and provided information in a thousandth of the time of earlier ones. They gave answers to innumerable informational problems previously so complex as to be unmanageable. They were helping industry control inventories to eliminate the periodic scarcity or glut that had contributed to irregularities in the business cycle. They could fly jet planes, guide rockets to the moon, or control almost any sort of machinery.

The public's faith in technology and science as holding the key to progress seemed confirmed by medical advances. The most visible early advance was the development of an effective polio vaccine by Dr. Jonas Salk of the University of Pittsburgh. The vaccine was first used on a large scale in 1955, and within two years the polio rate in the United States dropped 80 percent. An even more dramatic breakthrough came in the fundamental understanding of the chemistry of life. In 1953 James D. Watson of Harvard University and Francis H. C. Crick of Cambridge University worked out the chemical structure of DNA, the material in the genes that carries hereditary information. Later research revealed the mechanisms by which the genes controlled cell activity. These discoveries stimulated a biological revolution, gathering force during the 1970s and 1980s, which promised to unravel the mysteries of a number of hitherto intractable diseases and to bring from the realm of science fiction the possibility of controlling human heredity.

At the same time that humankind was dramatically advancing knowledge of its own inner space, it was venturing into outer space. However, that enterprise began not out of interest in pure science but because of the cold war.

When the Soviet Union announced in 1957 that it had launched a satellite — sputnik — into outer space, the United States reacted with shock and alarm. Strenuous efforts began to improve scientific education and research and, above all, to speed America's own efforts in space. In 1958 the

317

United States established the National Aeronautics and Space Administration (NASA) to coordinate space programs. In May 1961, a month after the Soviet Union succeeded in the first manned space flight, President Kennedy committed the United States to the goal of putting an American on the moon before the end of the decade. During the summer of 1969 two Americans became the first humans to walk on the surface of the moon.

After this symbolic victory in the space competition with the Russians, the popularity of funding for the space program waned. Nonetheless, planetary probes and laboratories orbiting the earth made significant contributions to basic scientific knowledge. And, more ominously, the air force, through the development of sophisticated electronic satellites and the space shuttle, displayed a growing interest in the strategic military uses of space.

Applications of scientific knowledge, both civilian and military, were being developed at such a rapid pace that they created a sharp pressure for additional basic research. In 1957 a Department of Defense research officer declared: "We have been chewing up the findings of basic research since World War II at a speed faster than they are being produced in the laboratories and ivory towers."

The chief agency for promotion of basic scientific research was the National Science Foundation. In 1945 Dr. Vannevar Bush, who had been wartime director of the Office of Scientific Research and Development, proposed the establishment of a peacetime government agency to promote basic research. The United States could no longer depend upon Europe, Bush warned. In 1950 Congress established the National Science Foundation but limited its annual appropriations to $15,000,000 per year and appropriated less than that until the 1956 fiscal year. In the 1959 budget, after the sputnik crisis, President Eisenhower asked for $140,000,000 for the National Science Foundation. Thereafter its budget, and its impact upon scientific research, increased significantly.

Overall federal expenditures on research and development — no more than a tenth of it for basic research — rose so spectacularly that by the end of the sixties they totaled more than the entire federal budget before Pearl Harbor. These sums were so large that many universities were dependent upon them for a considerable portion of their budgets.

The Crowding Country

A huge "census clock" in Washington continuously registers (on the basis of estimates as well as actual counts) changes in the American population. In 1967 the clock showed the total reaching and passing the 200,000,000 mark. By the mid-1970s it was indicating a steadily growing population of more than 215,000,000, with a birth every 10 seconds, a death every 16 seconds, the arrival of an immigrant every 81 seconds, and the departure of an emigrant every 15 minutes.

During the depression of the 1930s, demographic experts had predicted, on the basis of falling birth rates, that the population soon would cease to grow and might even decline. Then, during and after World War II, a "baby boom" caused pessimists to go to the opposite extreme. At the 1950s rate of growth, some warned, the population eventually would be so large that each American would have only one square foot of land to stand on. During the 1960s, however, the birth rate dropped even lower than it had during the depression. By 1970 it was down to 2.4, and by 1976 to 1.76, births per woman of childbearing age. This was less than a "zero population growth" rate. If it remained so low, after two more generations there would not be enough births to offset the number of deaths. During the early 1980s, however, the birth rate began to rise again, when members of the baby boom generation began to have babies.

Immigration accounted for approximately one-fifth of the population increase during the 1960s and 1970s. The immigration act of 1965 eliminated the national-origins quota system, which had allowed only a certain percentage of each nationality to enter the country. The new law provided that, from 1969 on, there would be a ceiling of 120,000 on immigration from the Western Hemisphere and 170,000 from the rest of the world. The law allowed parents, spouses, and children of United States citizens to enter the country without regard to the overall limitations. Thereafter, the largest numbers no longer came from Canada and the United Kingdom but from Asian countries, Cuba, and Mexico, the last of which was the source of most of the illegal immigrants as well. The Asian countries of Korea, the Philippines, and Taiwan were significant sources of immigration, but the most important sources after 1975 were the countries of Indochina. By the mid-1980s, almost 750,000 diverse Indochinese refugees — Vietnamese, Chinese-Vietnamese, Cambodians, Laotians, and Hmong-Laotians, among other groups — had reached the United States, nearly half of them settling in California.

Mobility continued to characterize Americans, as it had always done. In 1970 more than one-fourth of the natives of the United States were living in a state other than the one they had been born in. (In 1850 the proportion had been about the same.) During the 1960s, as during previous decades, the greatest interstate movement was to the Far West, especially to California, already by 1960 the most populous state and in 1970 the home of nearly 20,000,000 people. From 1920 to 1960 so many blacks had left the South that the region lost more than it gained by migration, but during the 1960s it gained 1,800,000 whites from the North while losing 1,400,000 blacks to the North. The proportion of black Americans living in the South fell from 78 percent in 1900 to 43 percent in 1975.

The flight from the farm continued, at an accelerating speed. In 1920 the people had been distributed about evenly between city and country. By 1970 the rural population had increased slightly, but the urban population had nearly tripled. The number of farms (and farmers) actually declined after 1935, from a peak of 6,800,000 in that year to less than 3,000,000 in 1970, and the figure fell to below 2,000,000 by 1980. In 1970, some 63,000,000 people were classified as rural (most of them nonfarm), about 62,000,000 as strictly urban (living in cities proper), and 75,000,000 as suburban.

Three-fourths of the people were crowded into cities and suburbs that took up only a tiny fraction of the nation's expanse. In the 1970s and 1980s, however, Americans began to move out of the largest metropolitan areas faster than they were moving in.

Rise of the Megalopolis

During the decades after World War II, metropolitan areas expanded until they met and merged with one another. From north of Boston to south of Washington a single urban region — a megalopolis — was coming into being. Other supercities were taking form along the Great Lakes from Milwaukee to Buffalo and on the Pacific coast from San Diego to Los Angeles.

Because individual metropolitan problems transcended city and sometimes state lines, special governmental authorities to deal with matters like harbor development or transit had come into existence. Together with traditional governments they led to a multiplicity of governmental agencies. Within the 212 standard metropolitan areas in the 1960s there were some 18,000 units of government, ranging from counties to school boards. There was little cooperation among them: most of these governments were ready to give little or no aid to the ailing cities. Many state, county, and suburban officials resisted the establishment of the federal Department of Housing and Urban Development, in 1965.

The problems with which metropolis and the merging megalopolis had to grapple were those long faced by city dwellers: improvement of housing, transportation, living conditions, educational and cultural opportunities, and above all the economic base for both the family and community; conversely, the elimination of pollution, blight, crime, and violence. The size of the new metropolitan areas made these problems far larger and sometimes more complex than in earlier generations.

The proper governing of these areas was a problem. It was complicated by the escape of affluent whites from city jurisdictions and tax collectors to the suburbs, and by the concentration of poor blacks in the inner cities. While the city governments needed more and more financial resources, the tax base was growing very slowly or actually shrinking.

Federal aid in one form or another had helped

make possible the vast growth of suburbia since 1945 — and then the white exodus from cities into suburbs. By 1963, 5,000,000 families owned houses built with federal housing aid; millions more lived in houses financed through the GI Bill of Rights. Federal guarantees had helped 27,000,000 homeowners borrow money for repairs. Also, the government encouraged the deposit of money in savings and loan associations, which issued millions of mortgages, by insuring the deposits and by limiting the ability of commercial banks to compete with the associations for deposits.

The federal government also promoted suburbanization by subsidizing the building of thousands of miles of expressways, beginning with the Interstate Highway Act of 1956, which provided federal funds for 90 percent of the cost of toll-free superhighways. The roadbuilding forced the leveling of countless blocks of urban buildings (including a disproportionate amount of poor people's housing). The highways reduced the costs of commuting from the suburbs but brought even more automobiles into the nation's cities.

Simultaneously with the growth of suburbs, attempts were made to rejuvenate decaying central cities through federal aid. Urban renewal projects were to transform slums into business and cultural areas and above all into attractive apartment complexes. The new buildings were expected to bring a fivefold increase in taxes, thus helping to solve urban financial problems.

A small beginning during the New Deal had involved federal clearing of slums and construction of public housing. From 1937 on, the federal government helped cities in the undertaking. Legislation in 1949 provided for a bold departure. The federal government would help cities finance the purchase of slum land, which would then be sold to private entrepreneurs at reduced costs. Federal loans or mortgage insurance gave these builders a further profit incentive.

For five years the program made little progress and thereafter seemed most effective in producing profits for the entrepreneurs. There were numerous complaints that it was the land where the poorest people (often blacks) lived that was being taken over and that these people seldom received adequate housing elsewhere at rents they could afford. Sometimes land was cleared and left idle for years while builders were sought. Sometimes the new construction was a complex of luxury apartments, as in the West End of Boston.

By the 1970s, most large American cities were in financial trouble. Their expenditures increased with rising wages and other costs, but sources of income did not keep pace. The biggest city had the biggest problems. Providing more services at higher cost than others did, New York accumulated the largest debt. In 1975 the city faced bankruptcy but managed to stave it off by state and federal loans along with municipal retrenchment. New York and the other older cities avoided fiscal crisis during the 1980s largely by postponing replacement of deteriorating sewers, water works, and roads.

Abundance and Its Costs

For the American people as a whole, the quarter century following World War II was a time of unprecedented enjoyment of material things. But abundance had its costs in the pollution of the environment and the depletion of natural resources. By the 1970s some believed that the age of plenty was about over and a new age of scarcity was at hand.

In the 1970s most Americans were still enjoying a living standard far higher than any they had previously known. Though the population had been growing, the output of goods and services had been growing much faster. Even allowing for the rise in prices and in taxes, the average person was better off than ever before. True, income continued to be very unevenly distributed, the top 5 percent of the people receiving 20 percent of the income, yet workers were getting more pay for less work than in the past. With a forty-hour instead of a forty-four hour week and with paid vacations, the average industrial employee enjoyed much more free time than his or her parent or grandparent had in 1900. Workers could afford to spend a smaller proportion of their wages for food, clothing, and shelter and a larger proportion for automobiles, appliances, medical care, and recreation.

While consumers enjoyed the bounty that industry provided, a growing number of them complained that too many of the products were useless, dangerous, falsely advertised, overpriced, defective, or lacking in durability. The complaints resulted in an accelerating movement for consumer protection. As early as the 1920s the Consumers Union had begun to test products and issue reports on them. In 1966 Ralph Nader emerged as a leading advocate of the new consumerism when he published a book, *Unsafe at Any Speed*, exposing the built-in hazards of many American cars. Nader started a number of consumer organizations to bring public pressure on both business and government.

Public services were less plentiful and of lower quality than commercial services and commodities. As population grew, the construction and maintenance of schools, hospitals, streets, sewers, public housing, and other community facilities fell behind the mounting needs. The times were characterized by private wealth and public poverty. That was the theme of John K. Galbraith's widely quoted book *The Affluent Society* (1958). "The line which divides our area of wealth from our area of poverty," Galbraith wrote, "is roughly that which divides privately produced and marketed goods and services from publicly rendered services." The contrast was symbolized by the picture he described of a prosperous middle-class family driving in an air-conditioned car, over poorly paved and trash-littered streets and billboard-cluttered highways, to lunch on "exquisitely packed food from a portable ice box" at a picnic spot beside a polluted stream.

The worsening pollution of the environment resulted from population growth and, even more, from the great increase in factory output and from the development of new industrial processes and products. The production of synthetic fibers, for example, used more energy and hence directly or indirectly yielded more pollutants than the production of cotton or wool. Synthetic detergents, plastic materials, and aluminum cans were not biodegradable as were the objects for which they were substitutes.

One of the worst offenders, with regard to air pollution, was the automobile. Motor vehicle registrations, which had amounted to only 8,000 in 1900, rose from 31,000,000 in 1945 to 109,000,000 in 1970. Many of the newer cars and trucks had more powerful, higher-compression engines than earlier models and gave poorer mileage while using high-test gasoline that contained a lead compound, an additional pollutant.

The befouling of air and water posed an immediate threat to human well-being and an ultimate threat to human existence. Environmentalists raised a demand for government action, and Congress responded with the Clean Air acts of 1963, 1965, and 1970. These encouraged states and municipalities to set up their own programs for controlling pollution from stationary sources and required car manufacturers to see that vehicle emissions were drastically cut by 1975.

The Energy Crisis

The war effort of 1941–1945 had used up tremendous quantities of raw materials, and the ensuing production boom used up still larger quantities, especially of fossil fuel. After the war, Americans turned more and more away from coal to oil and natural gas for generating electrical energy as well as for heating houses and other buildings. Manufacturers of plastics, synthetic fibers, and petrochemicals demanded increasing quantities of petroleum as a raw material. Drivers of cars, trucks, and buses added greatly to the demand.

Signs of an approaching "energy crisis" appeared in the United States as early as the mid-1960s, with the sudden failures of the electrical supply and the temporary blackouts of New York City and other areas in the Northeast. The events of 1973–1974 — the restrictions on oil exports by the Arabs and the fantastic price increases by the Arabs and other foreign producers — only made acute the seemingly chronic condition of energy shortages and price increases. Americans could take little comfort in the probability that they would not be quite so bad off as the Europeans or the Japanese. They felt the pinch during the abnormally cold winter of 1976–1977, when many schools and factories had to close for want of fuel. Then, during the next summer, they found gasoline higher in price but plentiful, and they used record quantities of it on vacation trips.

The glut was only temporary, yet it confirmed many Americans in their suspicion that no real energy problem existed. They cooperated reluctantly, if at all, with the government's efforts to induce them to conserve gasoline. Congress set a 55-mile-per-hour speed limit for all highways and imposed increasingly strict standards of fuel economy: the 1984 models of each manufacturer would have to average at least 27 miles per gallon (compared to the average consumption in 1975 of one gallon for every 15.6 miles).

Higher prices for gasoline gradually induced some conservation and promoted oil development within the United States, where there were still extensive oil resources, already discovered or yet to be discovered, in addition to vast shale deposits that could be made to yield petroleum. The Alaska pipeline, an engineering marvel completed in 1977, brought oil to the seaport of Valdez from new fields far north in the Arctic. Oil or gas could be got from the liquefaction of coal, and the country had enough coal in the ground to last for centuries. The utilization of petroleum, shale, or coal, however, endangered the environment in one way or another — through possible oil spills, destruction of the land to get at coal or shale, and pollution of the air by the burning of low-grade coal.

In the early 1900s electricity had been generated mainly by water power, but as this proved inadequate and often undependable, hydroelectric plants came to be greatly outnumbered by steam plants using oil, gas, or coal as fuel. Atomic energy seemed to promise a far superior source of electricity when the first two nuclear plants were completed in 1957. But atomic reactors were potentially far more dangerous to human well-being than were older sources of energy. Even if no serious nuclear accident should occur — no "meltdown," no explosion — there would be a persistent problem of the safe disposal of the "nuclear garbage," the radioactive waste. Protesters demonstrated against the construction of additional nuclear plants, and existing ones proved more costly to operate than had been anticipated. By 1977, power companies were deferring or canceling plans to build dozens of plants to supplement the dozens already in existence. An accident in 1979 at a nuclear power plant at Three Mile Island in Pennsylvania, which seemed to expose serious deficiencies in safety mechanisms, intensified antinuclear activity.

Distribution of Wealth

To a large extent, the amount of money that individual Americans made continued to depend on the forces of the market, that is, on competition among buyers and sellers of goods and services. To an increasing extent, however, income was being distributed or redistributed by the government, especially the federal government, through the exercise of its powers to tax, spend, and regulate. Despite the growth of governmental intervention, the overall distribution of income changed very little during the middle decades of the twentieth century. It was an extremely unequal distribution. The richest 20 percent of the people received about ten times as much as the poorest 20 percent.

Even during the best times, considerable numbers of Americans lived in poverty. Especially numerous among the poor were blacks, other minorities, families without male heads, and the elderly. From year to year the Census Bureau redefined poverty on the basis of the changing cost of living. According to the bureau's definition, 22 percent of the American people were living in poverty in 1959. The percentage had declined to 12 percent by 1975 but held at about that same level into the mid-1980s.

The persistence of poverty put a severe strain on the welfare system, which dated back to the time of the New Deal. The welfare rolls lengthened as eligibility requirements were relaxed. During the prosperous 1960s the number of persons receiving aid doubled; by 1975 it had reached a total of 25,000,000. Meanwhile annual federal expenditures on welfare had jumped from $2 billion to $18 billion and then to $45 billion. Approximately half of the welfare recipients were black. Very few were employable men. Almost all were women or children or old, blind, or otherwise disabled persons.

Nevertheless, many of the better-off Americans denounced what they viewed as extravagant handouts to the shiftless and undeserving. Certainly the system cried out for reform. Among its worst faults were the following: it denied benefits to families with able-bodied men, and so it induced husbands and fathers to desert; and it denied benefits to the poor who were employed, and so it discouraged welfare recipients from taking jobs. One President after another called for reform of the "welfare mess," but whenever a plan was proposed, it provoked bitter controversy.

Another inheritance from the New Deal, social security, also faced a crisis in the late 1970s. Old-age benefits had been raised, and the number of beneficiaries had increased to about 30,000,000. While the system was thus paying out more and more, it was receiving less than it had been, because of the persistently high unemployment and hence a loss in payroll taxes. The system approached bankruptcy as it used up its reserves. In the long run the difficulty could be expected to get worse, for the number of retired persons drawing benefits would probably continue to grow much faster than the number of the employed who contributed to the system. A reduction in benefits was unlikely, since the elderly with their growing numbers could exert more and more political power.

If retirements should be postponed, the strain on social security could be lessened somewhat. An act to raise the mandatory retirement age from sixty-five to seventy for employees of private industry passed the Congress. To save the system, however, much more than that needed to be done. An act of 1977 provided for a tripling of payroll taxes (collected from both employers and employees) in the course of the next decade. This presumably would keep the system solvent into the twenty-first century, though it would put a heavy burden on both business and labor.

Education

The prosperity of the postwar era both depended upon and supported the rapid growth of education systems. After World War II, critics of public education charged that the schools were neglecting things of the mind in favor of athletics, band contests, vocational training, and "life adjustment." When the Soviet Union launched the first artificial satellite in 1957, many Americans assumed that the Russians had proved the superiority of their education in science and technology. A demand arose for fewer "frills" and more intellectual rigor, and school-officials, teachers,

and pupils responded. So did Congress. In 1958 it passed the National Defense Education Act, which provided for the spending of nearly $1 billion over a four-year period to encourage the study of science, mathematics, and foreign languages.

Nevertheless, the schools continued to be criticized for their performance. At the end of the 1960s it appeared that 10 to 15 of every 100 pupils entering the fourth grade could not read (in ghetto schools, 35 to 50 of every 100). About 25,000,000 adults in the nation as a whole were functionally illiterate, unable to comprehend a newspaper or magazine article or to fill out an application form.

With the increasing momentum of the civil rights movement, the emphasis of school reformers had shifted from academic excellence to equality of educational opportunity. In fact, educational equality was slow to be implemented. Annual expenditures per pupil ranged from a few hundred dollars in some schools to several thousand in others, even within the same state. Schools depended mainly on local property taxes, and resources therefore varied tremendously between the poorest and the wealthiest districts. In the early 1970s, after the supreme court of California had declared the reliance on local school taxes unconstitutional in that state, suits were brought against similar financing arrangements in more than thirty other states.

During World War II colleges and universities suffered from a loss of male students to the draft. After the war the government contributed to a sudden bulge in enrollments by paying the college expenses of veterans under the GI Bill of Rights. During the 1950s and 1960s, attendance continued to swell, and at a faster rate than the college-age population, for a larger and larger proportion of young people were going on to secondary and higher education. And, at the same time, demand for professional workers grew rapidly. Consequently, graduate and professional schools were especially thriving, as the demand for university teachers and other professional workers grew. The federal government heavily subsidized many programs that were directly or indirectly related to the national defense. State universities multiplied as teachers' colleges were

converted into general colleges and these were
raised, at least in name, to university status. Large
campuses grew larger still — there were thirty-
nine with more than 20,000 students by 1969 as
compared with only two in 1941.

The first postwar generation of college students — especially the veterans, or GIs — seemed
to be mainly interested in getting a degree to get
ahead. A survey of members of the class of '49
concluded that they were "curiously old before
their time" and were concentrating on the pursuit
of economic security. Students of the 1950s also
appeared to be looking ahead to jobs, especially
corporation jobs. The prevailing campus spirit
was quiet and conformist.

Then in 1964 the campus of the University of
California at Berkeley erupted, and during
the next several years other large universities
from coast to coast experienced a succession of
student riots, with the rioters taking over and
sometimes fire-bombing university buildings and
vandalizing business properties in the neighborhood. The rioters were giving expression to a
variety of complaints — the impersonality of
the gigantic and complex "multiversity," the ir-
relevance of its curriculum to their personal
needs, and the complicity of the universities in
the Vietnam War (through war-related research
and through the training of military officers in the
ROTC).

Colleges and universities responded to demands for "relevance" and personal involvement
by relaxing requirements, adding courses in black
studies, environmental studies, and other inter-
disciplinary subjects of contemporary concern,
and giving students some voice in administration.
Some institutions, such as the City University of
New York, adopted a policy of "open admis-
sions," eliminating most entrance requirements.
By the 1970s these new programs appeared to
have wrought little basic change in the substance
of higher education. And the economic contraction of the mid-1970s, with its high unemployment rate for young people and its tightening of
university budgets, encouraged resumed enthusiasm on the part of both students and administrators for traditional programs with clear vocational objectives and some recognition of the
value of the liberal arts.

The Role of Television

Television changed the leisure habits of the
American people, made them better informed on
the news and issues of the day, and even modified
the patterns of American politics. In 1947 fewer
than 10,000 people owned television sets with
which they could view programs a few hours a
day from a handful of stations. A decade later
over 40,000,000 sets in homes, hotels, and bars
were tuned in to 467 stations.

Television even more than radio meant mass
communication to a nationwide audience. One
musical show, telecast on 245 stations one night in
March 1957, reached an estimated audience of
100,000,000 — enough people to fill a Broadway
theater every night for 165 years. Beginning with
the 1952 campaign, television remade presidential elections as candidates began to make extensive and expensive use of the new medium.

Commercial stations received and transmitted
a large share of their programs from one or another of three great networks. These sources provided not only entertainment but also news and
opinion for their affiliated stations. Bringing
world events, or chosen segments of them, visibly
into the home, the network programs had a much
greater emotional impact (as in reporting the
Vietnam War) than did newspaper accounts. A
comparatively small number of prestigious commentators, outstanding among them Walter
Cronkite of CBS, dominated the presentation of
TV news. Hence questions arose regarding the
breadth and balance of the coverage.

Vice President Spiro Agnew and others in the
Nixon administration, as well as Nixon himself,
objected strongly to what they considered hostile
treatment by the news media, especially television. Agnew demanded that commentators be
"made more responsible to the views of the nation." The director of the White House Office of
Telecommunications Policy attacked TV news reporters as "so-called professionals who confuse
sensation with sense and who dispense elitist gos-
sip in the guise of news analysis." He proposed a
law that would put the responsibility on local stations for assuring "fairness," and the administration threatened to revoke the licenses of stations
that failed to meet its standards.

An independent study (1973) by the Twentieth Century Fund concluded, however, that "presidential television" gave the President a great advantage over his critics. "Presidential television means the ability to appear simultaneously on all national radio and television networks at prime, large-audience evening hours, virtually whenever and however he wishes." Nixon exploited this advantage even more than his predecessors, taking as much TV time during his first eighteen months in office as Eisenhower, Kennedy, and Johnson together had taken during theirs. Congress, the courts, the opposition party could not keep up with the President in his ability to command free time on the air. Ronald Reagan's highly successful use of television confirmed that the medium was one of the factors that had increased the power of the executive as against that of the other branches of government. But at the same time, television exposure no doubt accelerated the demise of the Nixon administration as the relentless flow of developments on the nightly news pertaining to the Watergate scandal involving the administration contributed powerfully to the building of hostile public opinion. Similarly, coverage of the Iranian hostage crisis on the nightly news fueled opposition to the administration of Jimmy Carter. The medium of television meant that Americans had come to participate in the communal life of a giant nation with unprecedented intimacy and intensity.

Chapter 28

Seeking the "Great Society"

The "New Frontier"

"The world is very different now," said President John F. Kennedy in his inaugural address, January 20, 1961, "for man holds in his mortal hands the power to abolish all forms of human poverty and all forms of human life." To achieve the promise and avoid the peril was the twofold challenge of the time. This was what Kennedy called the "New Frontier."

Kennedy had won the Democratic nomination only after a vigorous struggle in the primaries. A forty-three-year-old senator from Massachusetts and a Roman Catholic, he was thought to be handicapped by his youth and his religion. In the primaries he had to dispose of a fellow senator, Hubert Humphrey of Minnesota, who was considered more liberal than he. Then, at the convention in Los Angeles, he had to overcome the powerful opposition of Lyndon B. Johnson of Texas, the Senate majority leader. In the 1930s Johnson had been one of the coterie of ardent New Dealers. By 1960, without entirely abandoning his earlier allegiances, he had become the most respected spokesperson of the industrialized and conservative South. When Kennedy won the presidential nomination, he offered the vice-presidential nomination to Johnson, who accepted and campaigned energetically.

The Republican nomination went almost by default to Vice President Richard M. Nixon, whom President Eisenhower favored. As Vice President, Nixon had enjoyed eight years on the front pages and had even argued with Khrushchev in Moscow. Thus he was able to offer a continuation of President Eisenhower's "peace and prosperity," and — though he was only four years older than Kennedy — mature leadership.

When Kennedy challenged Nixon to a series of television debates, Nixon's advisers thought Kennedy would be no match for their man, and they agreed to four joint appearances. In the first debate, however, everything went wrong for Nixon. Not yet recovered from an illness, he appeared tired, haggard, and heavy-jowled, in contrast to Kennedy, who seemed relaxed, self-confident, and well-informed — before an estimated 70,000,000 television viewers.

The recession of 1960–1961 also hurt the Republicans. Nevertheless, in the closing days of the campaign, a vigorous Republican campaign drive, with the aid of President Eisenhower, brought a hairline decision at the polls.

Before the election, Kennedy had hoped that on taking office he could push through Congress a legislative program as sweeping as that of Franklin D. Roosevelt during the first hundred days of the New Deal. Kennedy did not abandon his reform plans, but the closeness of the decision led him to move with caution. Unlike the Eisenhower cabinet, which had predominantly represented business, the Kennedy cabinet balanced the economic and political as well as the regional interests in the nation. The most controversial of the appointments was that of Kennedy's thirty-five-year-old brother and campaign manager, Robert F. Kennedy, as attorney general.

The Kennedy Economic Program

President Kennedy — the youngest person, except for Theodore Roosevelt, ever to occupy the White House — sent a record number of messages, twenty-five, to the first session of the Eighty-seventh Congress. Some called for long-range national undertakings: economic recovery and growth, health care for the aged, federal aid for schools, conservation and use of natural resources, highway construction, and housing and community development.

The existence of a Democratic majority in each house did not mean that Kennedy could count upon an easy enactment of his program, since many Democrats were conservative and frequently voted with the Republicans.

By dint of persuasion and compromise he managed to obtain some legislation. A new minimum-wage law provided considerably less coverage than the President had wished, but it did bring an additional 3,624,000 workers under the law. The Housing Act of 1961 fully embodied his proposals, authorizing $4.9 billion in federal grants or loans over a four-year period for the preservation of open spaces in cities, the development of local mass-transit systems, and the construction of middle-income housing.

Kennedy obtained from Congress additional expenditures for unemployment compensation, and aid to depressed areas — appropriations totaling $900,000,000. Another large addition to the federal budget was $4 billion in defense spending to meet new challenges from the Soviet Union.

Unemployment declined slowly during Kennedy's administration, partly because in his first two years in office he was determined to continue Eisenhower's resistance to inflation and, consequently, attempted to keep the budget in balance. He also used his powers energetically to prevent inflationary moves on the part of labor and industry. In the spring of 1962 he persuaded the United Steel Workers to accept a contract granting only small wage increases. When, almost immediately, United States Steel, followed by most other steel companies, unexpectedly announced large price increases, the President exploded with anger. During the three days that followed, he brought every variety of pressure he could muster, until

the steel companies returned to their old prices.

By January 1963 Kennedy had become convinced by his Council of Economic Advisers that he ought to shift budget policy to stimulate more rapid economic growth and to reduce persistent unemployment. Taking a middle course endorsed both by business leaders who wanted reductions in federal programs and by business leaders and liberals who adhered to Keynesian economics, Kennedy proposed to Congress a massive tax cut. The cut entailed a reduction of $13.5 billion in income taxes over a period of three years.

Kennedy and Civil Rights

Kennedy was becoming convinced that the government must do more than it had done for the blacks. Nearly a decade after the Supreme Court's historic decision against segregation, the equal rights movement was making little or no progress.

The National Association for the Advancement of Colored People (NAACP), which had led the cause, was still pressing lawsuits and seeking court orders, but more and more blacks were growing impatient with its methods. Blacks began to form more militant organizations. A desperate minority of perhaps 200,000 joined the Black Muslims and, in a spirit reminiscent of the Garvey black nationalism of the 1920s, proclaimed black supremacy and demanded a complete separation of the races. Others continued to struggle for integration but turned to direct action through organizations such as the Congress of Racial Equality (CORE), founded in 1941–1942, and the Southern Christian Leadership Conference. The SCLC was led by an eloquent young Baptist minister, Dr. Martin Luther King, Jr., who gained national and international fame as an advocate of passive resistance and, for his work, was to win the Nobel Peace Prize in 1964.

In the South, beginning in 1960, youthful blacks with some white sympathizers engaged in "sit-ins" to demand the right to eat in restaurants or at lunch counters or the right to use books in the main public libraries rather than in segregated branches. Blacks and whites went on "freedom rides" to desegregate interstate buses and terminals. Thousands engaged in mass demonstrations and accepted arrest; on several occasions the jails of Southern cities were filled to overflowing. Demonstrations spread to the North in mass attacks against de facto segregation in schools and housing and against the exclusion of all but a handful of blacks from various kinds of employment. In the summer of 1963, more than 200,000 demonstrators (10 to 15 percent of them white) participated in a "March on Washington," converging on the Lincoln Memorial.

In areas where federal power could be invoked, those protesting against segregation received the support of the Kennedy administration. Attorney General Robert F. Kennedy mustered federal force behind the integration of interstate transportation, and the President sent troops to the University of Mississippi to protect a black student, James Meredith, who had been enrolled by order of a federal court. Throughout the South campaigns were under way to enroll black voters under the protection of the civil rights legislation of 1957. As pressure intensified in 1963, President Kennedy threw the prestige of his administration behind the most comprehensive civil rights bill ever presented to Congress.

"Let Us Continue"

In the fall of 1963, though congressional conservatives were blocking enactment of the two major bills in the New Frontier program, the civil rights and tax-cut measures, President Kennedy felt optimistic. He was looking ahead confidently to the election of 1964 and hoped that the election would bring to Washington a more liberal Congress.

To court Southern support, Kennedy visited Florida and then Texas in November 1963. As he drove through the streets of Dallas to the cheers of an enthusiastic crowd, at least one assassin killed him and seriously wounded Governor John Connally of Texas. Police arrested Lee Harvey Oswald, a self-styled Marxist who had once tried to expatriate himself in Russia, and charged him with the murder of both the President and a police officer. Two days after the shooting, while in the Dallas city jail, Oswald himself was murdered by a Dallas night club operator, Jack Ruby, before an incredulous national television audience.

About two hours after the assassination of Kennedy, Vice President Lyndon B. Johnson was sworn in as the thirty-sixth President of the United States. When he addressed a joint session of Congress on November 27, President Johnson expressed his main theme in the words "let us continue." The most fitting memorial to Kennedy, he reminded Congress, would be the enactment of the civil rights and tax bills and, indeed, the whole agenda of the New Frontier.

The Eighty-eighth Congress responded and in its 1964 session enacted not only several vital measures of the New Frontier program but also one of President Johnson's own recommendations, an antipoverty bill designed to launch an "unconditional war on poverty." It called for the establishment of VISTA (Volunteers in Service to America), a volunteer corps of social workers, and for remedial education, vocational training, part-time employment for teen-agers and students, and federal grants to states or communities for local attacks on poverty.

Commitment to Equality

Throughout the nation the problem of civil rights was closely related to that of poverty. A large proportion of the very poor were blacks, who were unable to obtain adequately paid, secure employment. In cities like New York, blacks (together with Puerto Ricans) filled a large number of badly paid service positions and jobs not requiring skill. The average Harlem family received $2,000 a year less in income than its white neighbors. Among all blacks 13 percent (largely youths) were unemployed. Many Northern blacks were crowded into substandard housing, and their children were enrolled in poor schools integrated only in name.

A number of young Northerners went to Mississippi in the summer of 1964 to enroll several thousand young blacks in "Freedom Schools" and to conduct drives registering blacks to vote. Three of the first civil rights workers to arrive disappeared; after some weeks the FBI found their bodies buried deep beneath an earthen dam.

As the struggle intensified, President Johnson threw his weight behind the comprehensive civil rights bill that Kennedy had presented to Congress. Bipartisan leadership in the Senate finally overcame Southern opposition. In June 1964, for the first time in history, the Senate voted to end a filibuster, so that the bill could be passed. The Civil Rights Act of 1964 strengthened earlier legislation to protect the voting rights of blacks and to expedite the desegregation of schools. It also prohibited discrimination in public accommodations and facilities and in private employment. After the act went into effect, blacks ate with whites for the first time in some restaurants in the deep South, stayed in the same hotels and motels, sat in "white only" sections of motion picture theaters, and swam in previously segregated swimming pools.

Early in 1965 violence erupted in the South, especially in Selma, Alabama, where masses of blacks and a few white sympathizers demonstrated against registration procedures that kept blacks off the voting rolls. The state police brutally broke up a parade, and assassins murdered two white civil rights workers from the North. To protect the demonstrators, President Johnson called up the Alabama National Guard. He also urged upon Congress a bill to guarantee the right to vote in presidential, senatorial, and congressional elections. This bill provided for federal registration of voters in those states where there were literacy or other special tests for registering and where fewer than half the people of voting age actually went to the polls.

"One Man, One Vote"

Meanwhile, constitutional amendments and court decisions were affecting, actually or potentially, the political rights of many Americans, both black and white.

The Twenty-third Amendment (1961) gave the franchise in presidential elections to residents of the District of Columbia. Home rule for Washington, which had the highest percentage of blacks of any city in the country, continued to be withheld by Congress.

The Twenty-fourth Amendment (1964) gave symbolic, if not much practical, aid to black voters by providing that the right to vote in any primary or other federal election should not be abridged for failure to pay a poll tax. Most states in the deep South were using other methods to try to disfranchise blacks.

An issue involving the rights of representation of a large part of the American electorate came before the Supreme Court in 1962, in a case involving the apportionment of legislative districts in Tennessee. Although the state constitution called for reapportionment every ten years, none had taken place since 1901, with the result that rural dominance in the legislature was out of all proportion to population. Moore County, with a population of 3,454, sent one legislator; Shelby County (Memphis), with 627,019 residents, sent only three. By a 6-to-2 decision, the Supreme Court gave the federal district court a mandate to order reapportionment if it found a violation of the Constitution. Similar inequities existed in a surprising number of other states; in all but six states, fewer than 40 percent of the population could elect a majority of the legislature. As a result of the Tennessee decision, many states quickly made some reapportionment of their legislative districts, either as a result of court action or as a means of forestalling it.

Another important Supreme Court decision (in *Reynold* v. *Sims*, 1964) held that congressional districts within a state also must be substantially equal in population. The case before the court involved the congressional district containing the city of Atlanta, Georgia, a district that had a population of 820,000 as compared with the population of 270,000 in another Georgia district.

Johnson Thrashes Goldwater

As he took up and expanded the Kennedy program, President Johnson restated the objective as the creation of the "Great Society." "For half a century we called upon unbounded invention and untiring industry to create an order of plenty for all our people," he declared in May 1964. "The challenge of the next half century is whether we have the wisdom to use that wealth to enrich and elevate our national life — and to advance the quality of American civilization." In the presidential campaign of 1964 the moderate liberalism for which Johnson had spoken confronted extreme conservatism.

In the years following the collapse of McCarthyism, militant conservatives in the United States had organized a number of action groups. The best known was the John Birch Society, whose founder, Robert Welch, called for the impeachment of Chief Justice Earl Warren and seemed to suspect the loyalty of even President Eisenhower. Senator Barry Goldwater of Arizona, though not himself a member of the so-called radical right organizations, became the hero of most of these groups. At the Republican convention in San Francisco, the Goldwater forces were in complete command from the outset.

As Senator Goldwater carried the Republican party far to the right, President Johnson tried to dominate the center of the road. Throughout the campaign Johnson was wary of making specific, detailed promises; his best strategy seemed to be merely to gather the votes against Goldwater. And gather them he did. He received more votes, over 42,000,000, and a larger plurality than any other previous candidate.

The Johnson Program

When the Eighty-ninth Congress convened, Johnson presented to it comprehensive proposals. With unprecedented speed, almost all of this far-ranging program became law. The overwhelmingly Democratic majorities in Congress, which had accompanied the landslide victory over Goldwater, were Johnson's to command.

A new immigration law abolished the inequities of the quota system established in the 1920s. Gradually the government eliminated these quotas and began to allot visas not on a basis of national origins but giving preference on a basis of education and skills. Soon there were complaints that only an elite of professionals could enter the United States and that other nations, especially underdeveloped ones, were suffering a "brain drain" of their doctors, engineers, and highly educated specialists. In 1966 relatives of United States citizens began to receive prefer-

ence, and a quota of 17,000 was set for professionals.

Massive sustained federal aid to education at last began. President Johnson succeeded in circumventing the impasse in Congress over the question of whether parochial schools should receive a share of federal funds. He called for grants for text and library books for students in both public and parochial schools — and significantly the grants were to be made on the basis of the needs of individual students, not schools, a formula which the Supreme Court had approved when it applied to federal funds that were to provide milk or transportation to students. The Elementary and Secondary Education Act of 1965 and subsequent legislation gave aid to schools in both urban and rural areas in proportion to the number of poverty-stricken students in them. Federal funds purchased textbooks and library materials, financed special programs for adults and for the handicapped, and strengthened state educational agencies. Total federal expenditures in education and technical training rose from less than $5 billion in 1964 to more than $12 billion in 1967.

The establishment of Medicare for the 19,000,000 Americans over sixty-five through the Medicare–Social Security Act of 1965 altered the lives of old people and had great impact upon American medicine. The debate over Medicare, which had been bitter for twenty years, ended as the program went into effect. Large numbers of older people were now receiving care that they could not previously have obtained or that would have exhausted their savings. Medicare was part of the effort to eradicate the "pockets of poverty" within the prosperous nation.

The poverty program of President Johnson, continuing and expanding that of Kennedy, approached the problem in numerous ways. By 1966 the Office of Economic Opportunity, established in 1964, had put about two-fifths of its budget into a variety of community action programs. Another two-fifths went into youth programs — the Job Corps, Neighborhood Youth Corps, and College Work Study. VISTA served as a kind of Peace Corps at home.

Especially among the urban black unemployed, the job-training programs were a disappointment.

Although blacks began to penetrate the ranks of the white-collar workers, the total numbers were small. Nominally, union restrictions against them no longer existed, yet few could gain employment as skilled, highly paid construction workers. Industries that might have hired blacks were moving out of the cities, away from where they lived. The training programs could not easily provide the overall education that most of these unemployed blacks lacked. Impatient urban blacks, disappointed at the meager return that cooperation seemed to have brought them, began increasingly to turn toward other possible solutions: black power, separatism, or even violence.

Black Power

The black population had been increasing more rapidly than the white population since the 1920s and had been shifting from the rural South to the cities throughout the nation, especially in the North. In 1910 only about a quarter of the blacks lived in cities, and only a tenth outside the South; by 1966 15,000,000 blacks, 69 percent of the black population, were living in metropolitan areas; 45 percent of all blacks were living outside the South. In several of the largest cities, the proportion of blacks at least doubled between 1950 and 1968. Blacks constituted at least 30 percent of the population of seven of these cities and 66.6 percent of the population of Washington, D.C. A corresponding exodus of whites from the cities to the suburbs dramatically increased the areas of residential and school segregation in the "black ghettos."

While some urban blacks were sharing in the national prosperity, their proportional gains were decidedly less than those of the whites. Indeed, the gap between their incomes and those of whites was growing wider. The number of blacks enjoying well-paid, highly skilled employment giving them exceptional status doubled in the sixties, while the lowest-income group grew smaller. Yet 20 percent of all blacks, the 2,000,000 "hard-core disadvantaged" living in cities, were making no significant economic gains.

With increasing rapidity after 1964, the United States moved into a double crisis, compounded of rioting in the poverty-stricken "black ghettos" and escalation of the American intervention in Vietnam into a major military confrontation. White students and Northern liberals shifted their efforts from the civil rights drive to concentrate on protest against the Vietnam War. Blacks increasingly sought to take their destiny into their own hands through their own organizations, independent of aid or funds from whites.

The gradual shift from white participation and leadership to black domination of civil rights organizations was one indication of the new mood. CORE had long been the most interracial of the organizations, but by 1962 it was predominantly black; after 1965 CORE allowed only black leadership in its chapters. At their height these organizations did succeed through direct action in obtaining some votes for blacks and political participation, even in Alabama and Mississippi. In the North they helped force open new, desirable employment opportunities for well-educated blacks. But they could not change the inferior conditions under which most blacks suffered. Their failure helped stimulate feelings of separateness and militancy among black youth in the large cities.

Out of James Meredith's march southward from Memphis, Tennessee, to Jackson, Mississippi, in June 1966 there grew the concept of black power. Politically it meant separate action through which blocs of black voters would win control in Northern ghettos or the Southern black belt. Economically it meant creating black business to serve blacks. CORE and SNCC (the Student Nonviolent Coordinating Committee) became associated with the concept of black power — of black separateness. Black militants argued that blacks must attain economic and political parity with the white population before effective integration could take place.

On August 11, 1965, a black crowd gathered in Watts, a Los Angeles suburb, to protest a traffic arrest; a police officer hit a bystander with his club, and several days of violence were touched off. Before the rioting was over, thirty-four people had been killed, hundreds wounded, and some $35,000,000 in property destroyed.

In the summer of 1966 there were forty-three outbreaks, with especially serious trouble in Chicago and Cleveland. In the summer of 1967 there were eight major riots. In the worst of these, at Detroit, forty-three persons (thirty-three blacks and ten whites) were killed. On their television screens, the people of the nation saw alarming scenes of arson, plunder, and military action. President Johnson, calling for law and order, warned also that the only genuine long-range solution must be an attack upon the conditions that were causing despair and violence. He appointed a group of distinguished citizens to a commission to investigate the disorders and recommend preventive measures for the future.

The report of the Commission on Civil Disorders, which appeared in the spring of 1968, deflated numerous wild stories circulating during the riots: there had been few black snipers and no organized conspiracy instigating and directing the riots. It pointed to the complexities of the problems facing the occupants of the black ghettos, and it recommended massive spending to erase these ghettos and the inequities their occupants suffered. "Only a commitment to national action on an unprecedented scale can shape a future compatible with the historic ideals of American society," the commission concluded. "The major need is to generate new will — the will to tax ourselves to the extent necessary to meet the vital needs of the nation." But the escalation of the war in Vietnam produced an immediate response. The enormous costs of the war and the reluctance of Congress to raise taxes, and thereby increase criticism of the war, led Congress to cut rather than to increase spending for the alleviation of urban poverty.

In April 1968 the assassination of Dr. Martin Luther King, Jr., shocked the nation but scarcely altered the mood of Congress. King, whose insistence upon Gandhi-like nonviolent techniques seemed old-fashioned to black militants, was to lead a protest march on behalf of striking garbage workers in Memphis, Tennessee. While standing on a motel balcony, he was struck by a sniper's bullet and died within a few minutes. King's death touched off the most widespread rioting the nation had yet undergone in the black areas of cities from coast to coast. Looting and arson were endemic; forty persons were killed. Washington was the worst hit, as fires gutted buildings within sight of the Capitol and the White House. Simul-

taneously, the nation was preoccupied with mourning the assassinated leader, as King was given a funeral bringing together an assemblage of notables and receiving television coverage exceeded only by that for President Kennedy.

Within a week Congress responded by enacting the Civil Rights Act of 1968, which had been pending for two years. It outlawed racial discrimination in the sale and rental of four-fifths of all homes and apartments. But as poor people assembled in Washington a few weeks later in the campaign that King had been planning at the time of his death, Congress was preoccupied with frugality and was little disposed to provide economic aid for them.

The Spanish-Speaking Minority

As Afro-Americans enhanced their self-awareness during the 1960s, other racial minorities followed suit. Most numerous were people of Puerto Rican background, concentrated mainly in New York, and those of Mexican background, living mainly in California, Texas, and the Southwest.

The Mexican-Americans accounted for seven of the nine million Hispanic-Americans. They included descendants of families who had been living in Mexican territory when it was incorporated into the United States, legal immigrants and their descendants from Mexico, temporary workers ("*braceros*") brought in under special labor contracts, and illegal immigrants ("*mojados*," or "wetbacks").

The Spanish-speaking peoples had suffered from various forms of discrimination, the most visible expression of which was the "Zoot-Suit" riots in Los Angeles during June 1943. For a week mobs of white Angelenos, led by uniformed servicemen, terrorized not only the Mexican-American adolescents who sported "zoot suits," but the entire Spanish-speaking community. Beginning with that grim episode, many from the "*barrios*" began to join community organizations, but they remained localized until the 1960s. Then for the first time large numbers of Mexican-Americans were brought together in a broad, inclusive "Chicano" movement.

The hero of the Chicanos was César Chávez, an Arizona-born, California farm worker. The main focus of the movement was at first a farm workers' strike that Chávez called in 1965 and soon converted into a nonviolent crusade for social justice. He enlisted the cooperation of college students, church groups, and civil rights activists, including CORE and SNCC. To bring pressure on employers, who brought in strikebreakers, he appealed for a nationwide boycott of California table grapes. The boycott gained the support of millions throughout the country but got no assistance from the federal government, which increased its purchases of grapes to be sent to American troops in Vietnam. Chávez won a temporary victory in 1970, when the growers of half of California's table grapes signed contracts with his union.

The Pan-Indian Movement

Joining blacks and Hispanic-Americans in their quest for a decent share of the Great Society were the American Indians. They were a sizable group, numbering about 800,000 by 1970, and more than half of them lived on or near reservations. As a group they were much worse off than other Americans, even those of African descent. Annual family income for Indians was $1,000 less than for blacks, and the unemployment rate for Indians was ten times the national rate. Suicides among Indian youth were 100 times as frequent as among white youth.

The New Deal's Indian Reorganization Act had promised to revitalize aboriginal culture and tribal government, but Congress failed to provide sufficient funds. In 1953 Congress declared its intention to terminate federal relations with the tribes and leave them on their own. "Termination" led to further Indian impoverishment since it provided for no special assistance during the period of transition and abandoned any effort to preserve Indian culture. The Menominees of Wisconsin, for example, saw their reservation converted into Menominee County and experienced sharply declining real incomes.

During the 1960s more Indians than ever before joined a movement to bring tribes together and redress their common wrongs. In 1961 more than 400 members of 67 different tribes gathered in Chicago and drew up a Declaration of Indian Purpose, which stressed the "right to choose our

own way of life" and the "responsibility of preserving our precious heritage." In 1964, while Congress was considering the Economic Opportunity bill, hundreds of Indians and white sympathizers assembled in Washington to urge Congress to include Indians in the antipoverty program. A number of young, college-educated Indians began to speak of "red power," and some repudiated the name "Indian" — which, as they pointed out, whites had mistakenly given them — and insisted on being called "Native Americans." Congress did include Indians in the coverage of the Economic Opportunity Act, but beyond this neither the Kennedy nor the Johnson administration did anything to meet the Indians' needs and demands.

Frustrated Indians turned more and more to direct action, to confrontations with whites, to defiance of state and federal authority. In 1969 a group of Indians of various tribes, to dramatize the plight of their people, landed on Alcatraz Island, the site of an abandoned federal prison in San Francisco Bay, and claimed the place "by right of discovery." The anger and bitterness of many Indians found expression in the writings of Vine Deloria, Jr., a Sioux, who titled one of his books *Custer Died for Your Sins* (1969).

Women's Liberation

American women could hardly be called a minority, since 51 percent of the population was female; yet they suffered inequities comparable to those imposed upon minority groups, and women of minority groups bore a double burden of discrimination. The 1960s became for women a period of intensified activism.

True, more and more job opportunities were opening up for women, and an increasing proportion of them were working outside the home. (Fewer than 25 percent of women over sixteen had been counted as part of the labor force in 1940; more than 43 percent were so counted in 1970.) But women were paid much less than men even for comparable work, and women had fewer chances than men to make a professional or managerial career. Moreover, they composed a smaller percentage of the college population in the 1950s than in the 1920s and were granted a smaller percentage of college degrees in 1960 than in 1930. During the 1960s they were earning only one in three of all B.A.s and M.A.s and only one in ten Ph.D.s. If anything, discrimination on the basis of sex had become more pervasive than a generation earlier.

Educated women of the middle class took the lead (as they had done in earlier feminist crusades) in the dozens of "women's liberation" movements that sprang up in the 1960s. They were joined by women radicals who had been active in civil rights and antiwar groups but encountered discrimination even there. One of the most influential of the leaders was Betty Friedan, who in *The Feminine Mystique* (1963) denounced the American home as a "comfortable concentration camp" and called upon its inmates to free themselves. Friedan helped to found, in 1966, the most inclusive and effective of the new women's rights organizations, the National Organization for Women, or NOW. "There is no civil rights movement to speak for women as there has been for Negroes and other victims of discrimination," the organizers of NOW declared. The organization's 1967 "bill of rights" demanded an Equal Rights Amendment to the Constitution — "Equality of Rights under the law shall not be denied or abridged by the United States on account of sex." NOW also called for enforcement of the 1964 Civil Rights Act, which prohibited discrimination in employment on account of sex as well as race. Other NOW demands included the following: maternity leave for working women; public child-care centers to enable mothers to compete more freely for jobs; absolute equality of educational opportunities at all levels; and the "right of women to control their own reproductive lives" through contraception and abortion.

Chapter 29

The Politics of Lowered Expectations, 1968–1985

Election of 1968

The domestic turbulence of the mid-1960s, coupled with mounting criticism of American involvement in Vietnam, opened the way for a Republican electoral victory in 1968.

Lyndon Johnson, probably anticipating defeat, withdrew from the presidential race in March 1968, and the contest for the Democratic nomination turned into a bitter struggle among Senator Eugene McCarthy, Senator Robert Kennedy, and Vice President Hubert Humphrey. McCarthy and Kennedy took more liberal positions on domestic issues than Johnson or Humphrey and sharply attacked American policy in Vietnam. Humphrey entered the campaign in late April, too late to become embroiled in the primaries, but he received widespread endorsement from Democratic leaders in the many states without primaries. Meanwhile, Kennedy and McCarthy focused public attention on the primaries. Kennedy won Indiana, lost Oregon to McCarthy, and then in the last primary in California, won again. At a Los Angeles hotel, on June 5, just after he had exhorted his cheering followers to seek victory with him at the Democratic convention, he was shot and killed by an assassin.

At the Democratic convention in Chicago, McCarthy (and some Kennedy followers backing Senator George McGovern of South Dakota) were unable to prevent the nomination of Humphrey on the first ballot. The critics of Humphrey, who was heir to administration policies, were bitter. Adding to their bitterness were the rough tactics of the Chicago police who shoved and harassed delegates and spectators to the convention, and

before television cameras, clubbed and manhandled demonstrators in the streets of Chicago. An investigating committee subsequently referred to the violent police reactions to the taunts and attacks by the demonstrators as a "police riot." During the campaign, Humphrey received little support from those who had followed McCarthy and Kennedy.

The candidate who evoked the most enthusiastic responses and violent heckling wherever he spoke throughout the country was George Wallace of Alabama. Wallace had established himself as one of the leading spokesmen for the defense of segregation when, as governor of Alabama, he had attempted to block the admission of black students to the University of Alabama. In 1968 he became a third-party candidate for President, running as the American Independent party candidate. He based his campaign on a host of conservative grievances, hoping for a "backlash" to the disorder of the 1960s. He denounced the forced busing of students, condemned the proliferation of government regulations and social programs, and the permissiveness of authorities toward race riots and antiwar demonstrations. Public opinion polls showed Wallace at one point to be the favorite of one-fifth of the voters; he hoped to throw the election into the House of Representatives.

The Republicans made a parallel effort to mobilize a "silent majority" in favor of order and stability. Richard Nixon emerged as the most skillful Republican in appealing to Americans who were tired of hearing about their obligations to the poor, the sacrifices thought necessary to achieve racial justice, and the reforms proposed by more liberal leaders that seemed designed to help criminals. By offering a vision of stability, law and order, government retrenchment, and "peace with honor" in Vietnam, he easily defeated California's governor, Ronald Reagan, and New York's governor, Nelson Rockefeller, for the nomination. He chose Spiro Agnew, governor of Maryland, as his running mate.

Neither of the major candidates evoked much enthusiasm. Nixon, campaigning methodically, seemed far ahead from the outset and took a position of conciliation from strength. He declared in his acceptance address that he would heed "the voice of the great majority of Americans, the forgotten Americans, the non-shouters, the non-demonstrators, that are not racists or sick, that are not guilty of the crime that plagues the land."

In contrast to Nixon's campaign, Humphrey's seemed deficient in both planning and finance. On Vietnam, he and his opponent differed little, but on the problem of poverty he pledged federal aid for a massive "Marshall Plan for the cities" in contrast to Nixon's insistence that private capital must help the poor to help themselves. During the last weeks of the campaign, Humphrey's standing in the public opinion polls increased markedly, and the statements of both candidates became sharper. Yet, as the front runner, Nixon refused to debate Humphrey on television. Both candidates were occupying middle positions, with Nixon blaming the Johnson-Humphrey administration for the turmoil of the mid-1960s and posing as a more reasonable alternative than Wallace.

By the fairly narrow margin of some 500,000 votes, out of more than 73,000,000 cast, Nixon defeated Humphrey. The electoral vote was far more decisive, 302 for Nixon to 191 for Humphrey and 45 for Wallace. In his victory statement, Nixon returned to a theme he had frequently touched upon during the campaign and asserted that "the great objective of this Administration at the outset" would be "to bring the American people together." Nixon recognized that he had not won a decisive mandate and that the majority of the American people were more interested in the restoration of stability than in fundamental social change.

The Imperial Presidency

President Nixon took office in 1969 without having given much thought to a domestic program. However, he proclaimed the "New Federalism," which would, he said, "reverse the flow of power and resources . . . to Washington and start power and resources flowing back . . . to the people." In practice, Nixon undertook to concentrate more and more authority in the White House.

Few department heads, government officials of lesser rank, or congresspeople or senators could approach the President directly. Almost all of them had to deal with him through his top White House aide, the "keeper of the gates," H. R. Haldeman, or through the chief of his domestic policy staff, John Ehrlichman. These two old friends and veteran Nixon campaigners, now subject only to the President himself, ran the executive office with respect to domestic affairs from 1969 to 1973. The executive office was a large and rapidly swelling bureaucracy, whose numbers during that four-year period grew from 2,000 to more than 4,200.

Nixon also claimed unprecedented authority for the presidential office in relation to the legislative branch. Asserting "executive privilege" seemingly without limit, he took the position that congressional committees could not question administrative officials without the President's consent. Implying that the President, not Congress, should have the power of the purse, he ordered administrative agencies not to spend appropriated money after Congress had overridden his vetoes of appropriation bills.

Law and Order

From the beginning of his first term, President Nixon hoped to alter the direction of the Supreme Court. As Chief Justice Warren approached retirement, President Johnson had tried to replace him with Abe Fortas, whom Johnson earlier had appointed as an associate justice. Fortas, a liberal, could have been expected to keep the Court on essentially the same track it had been following under Warren. The Republicans in the Senate blocked the Fortas appointment and thus gave Nixon an opportunity to choose his own chief justice. Nixon — who insisted that it was "the job of the courts to interpret the law, not make the law" — chose a conservative strict constructionist who agreed with him. This was Warren Burger, who had served on the United States Court of Appeals for the District of Columbia and who had spoken out against what he considered the Supreme Court's protection of the rights of criminals.

Nixon soon had a chance to put another person of his choice on the Supreme Court, but this time he ran into difficulty and embarrassment. After rejecting two of Nixon's choices, the Senate finally accepted the appointment of Harry A. Blackmun, who, like Chief Justice Burger, had a reputation as a conservative jurist.

Before Nixon had been in office three years, two more Supreme Court vacancies arose, and again he ran into trouble in trying to fill them. The American Bar Association refused to endorse his first two choices, one of whom was a woman. Nixon then nominated, and the Senate approved, Lewis F. Powell, Jr., a Virginian and a former head of the American Bar Association, and William H. Rehnquist, assistant attorney general in the Nixon administration and a Goldwater Republican from Arizona. "I shall continue to appoint judges," Nixon later said, "who share my philosophy that we must strengthen the peace forces against the criminal forces in America."

In many areas the achievement of racial balance in schools would require the transporting of children from one neighborhood to another. When federal courts began to order such busing, Nixon spoke out with the many who denounced it as unthinkable if not unconstitutional. Nevertheless, the Supreme Court unanimously upheld it in a 1971 case involving Charlotte, North Carolina. The next year Nixon tried, unsuccessfully, to induce Congress to pass an antibusing law. Meanwhile, opponents of busing in Northern cities violently resisted court-ordered busing; those in Denver, Colorado, and Pontiac, Michigan, resorted to the fire-bombing of school buses. There was also resistance in the South, but on the whole desegregation proceeded faster there than in the North. Before the end of Nixon's first term — thanks to the federal courts rather than the President — the proportion of Southern blacks in all-

black schools had declined from about 80 to less than 20 percent.

Nixon Economy

In dealing with the problem of poverty, Nixon attempted to undo the Johnson poverty program by closing more than half of the Job Corps training centers. He also reduced spending on other social-welfare agencies. In his budget for 1973–1974 he proposed to abolish more than a hundred federal grant programs that were giving aid to the unemployed, the mentally ill, veterans, college students, small business owners, and other groups. He also proposed to discontinue spending for urban renewal, to end assistance for hospital construction, and to reduce expenditures on lunches for schoolchildren. In 1973 he proceeded, without congressional approval, to break up the Office of Economic Opportunity, which had been the main agency of Johnson's "war on poverty."

Many Americans had hoped that, once the United States was finally out of the Vietnam War, the government could cut its military spending and could afford to increase its domestic expenditures. Yet in his first postwar budget, the one for 1973–1974, Nixon not only demanded a reduction in domestic expenditures but also asked for an increase in military spending, from $74.8 billion to $79 billion. The extra money was to go largely for the development of new weapons and for pay raises to attract recruits to the all-volunteer armed forces.

When Nixon talked of reducing expenditures on social programs, he justified it as a necessary means of controlling inflation. He had inherited the inflation problem from his predecessor, Johnson, who had built up a tremendous inflationary pressure by increasing expenditures for both the Great Society and the Vietnam War without raising taxes. Nixon faced a dilemma, since rising prices could mean booming business, while deflationary policies might bring on widespread unemployment.

At the outset, in 1969, Nixon employed a deflationary "game plan." As a consequence a recession ensued. But anticipations of continued inflation were so strong and widespread that prices continued to rise. The country began to suffer from "stagflation," stagnation and inflation together.

If these economic conditions had persisted, they might have threatened the reelection of Nixon in 1972, just as they had contributed to the failure of Nixon's 1960 campaign. So, in 1971, he suddenly reversed his original plan of tight credit and a balanced budget. The government began to pay out so much more than it took in that the deficit for 1972 was by far the largest for any year since World War II. By Election Day, incomes were up and unemployment was down. Politically, the combination of easy credit and deficit spending proved a great success.

A Triumphant Reelection

The "real majority," according to R. M. Scammon and B. J. Wattenberg in their 1970 book of that title, was "unyoung, unblack, and unpoor." The mature, white, well-off citizens were most concerned about such things as campus protests, school integration, street crimes, and welfare costs. If these worried people could be induced to vote for Nixon, his reelection would be assured. This prospect formed the basis for the campaign strategy that Nixon's attorney general and political adviser, John Mitchell, adopted for 1972. In particular, Mitchell planned to attract to Nixon the voters who in 1968 had favored the American party candidate, George Wallace of Alabama. In addition, the Republicans hoped to win over many Northern workers, especially the Catholics of immigrant background. Thus the Nixon forces might break up the already shaky Democratic coalition — which Franklin D. Roosevelt had put together in the 1930s — and replace it with a permanent Republican majority.

To Republican strategists it was hardly encouraging when, in 1970, Congress passed a bill to lower the voting age to eighteen. Nixon signed the bill, despite the widespread assumption that most of the young would vote Democratic. The Supreme Court ruled the new law constitutional for federal but not for state or local elections. The Twenty-sixth Amendment, ratified in time for the elections of 1972, made eighteen the minimum age for voters in state and local as well as federal contests.

Nixon's chances for reelection improved when, in May 1972, in a Maryland shopping center, a would-be assassin shot George Wallace, leaving him partially paralyzed and incapable of continuing his presidential campaign. Nixon's chances improved still further when, in July, the Democratic nominating convention met in Miami.

On the first ballot the convention chose George M. McGovern, an opponent of the Vietnam War and an advocate of a $1,000 tax credit for every citizen. While still a relatively unknown senator from South Dakota, McGovern had begun openly to seek the Presidency as early as January 1971. In the primaries he outdid the early favorite, Senator Edmund Muskie of Maine, and the previous candidate, Senator Hubert Humphrey of Minnesota. At the convention, McGovern won the nomination with the help of reforms he himself had helped to bring about. The "McGovern rules" were intended to make the convention broadly representative of the party by requiring certain proportions of women, blacks, and youths among the delegates. But the rules antagonized old-line politicians and had a very divisive effect on the party, especially when the convention unseated a powerful boss, Mayor Richard J. Daley of Chicago. And from the division within the party, many voters got the impression that McGovern was the candidate of hippies, aggressive women, and militant blacks.

Nixon had the advantage of more money, most of it from large corporations, than any other presidential candidate had ever had at his disposal. Seldom appearing, Nixon was an "invisible candidate." His choice for a second time as Vice President, Spiro Agnew, carried the campaign burden for Nixon, never mentioning him by name but always referring to him as "the President." By virtue of his visits to China and the Soviet Union in 1972 and the Vietnam negotiations that Nixon was carrying on, he appeared to be a bringer of peace. Since business was booming, he could be credited with prosperity. As a foe of busing for racial balance in schools, he had the gratitude of race-conscious whites. Through his "law and order" statements and his court appointments, he had made himself the apparent champion of peace at home as well as abroad.

Nixon won by one of the most decisive margins in history. He received the largest share of the popular vote (60.8 percent) of any candidate ever, with the exception of Johnson (61.1 percent) in 1964. He received the largest proportion of the electoral vote (521 of 538) since Franklin Roosevelt (523 of 531) in 1936. McGovern carried only Massachusetts and the District of Columbia.

Watergate

As he began his second term, in January 1973, President Nixon stood at the height of his power and popularity. Soon his popularity, as measured by opinion polls, began to drop. It fell faster than that of any other President since such polls were first taken, in Franklin D. Roosevelt's time. Within a year, public confidence in Nixon was so low that serious doubts arose as to whether he should, or could, continue to lead the people. The reason for the sudden collapse of his prestige could be summed up in a word that became familiar to all newspaper readers and television viewers — "Watergate." That word designated a bewildering assortment of political scandals, easily the worst in American history.

The Watergate was a deluxe hotel-apartment-office complex in Washington. In it were located the headquarters of the Democratic National Committee. There, at about two o'clock on the morning of June 17, 1972, police arrested five men who had broken into the headquarters to tap phones and copy documents. Later two others were arrested, one of them the general counsel for Nixon's personal campaign organization, the Committee for the Re-election of the President (CREEP). Two months after the burglary, however, Nixon stated that "no one in the White House staff, no one in this Administration presently employed, was involved in this very bizarre incident." He added: "This kind of activity, as I have often indicated, has no place whatsoever in our political process."

When, after the election, the captured burglars went on trial, all but one of them pleaded guilty, and that one refused to talk. The Justice Department prosecutors failed to implicate anyone higher up than those arrested, but Federal District Judge John J. Sirica suspected that the whole truth had not been told. While sentencing the defendants to long terms in prison, Sirica intimated that if they would cooperate in getting at the truth, he would reduce the sentences. One of the defendants, James W. McCord, Jr., a former CIA agent and a "security coordinator" for CREEP, now agreed to testify before a federal grand jury and a Senate investigating committee, which was headed by Senator Sam J. Ervin of North Carolina. McCord led a long parade of witnesses who appeared, voluntarily or under subpoena, before the grand jury and the Ervin committee. The committee hearings, televised, gave the public an opportunity to draw its own conclusions about the character and conduct of those surrounding the President.

Certain undisputed facts stood out. Nixon had been much concerned about the leaking of government secrets, especially the leaking of a Defense Department study of the Vietnam War, which *The New York Times* and other journals published as "The Pentagon Papers" in 1971. So, to plug the leaks, he set up and put Ehrlichman in charge of a special group of White House employees, who called themselves "the plumbers," and who tapped the telephones of news reporters and members of the staff of Henry Kissinger, Nixon's chief adviser for national security affairs. Nixon ordered the plumbers to investigate the background of Daniel Ellsberg, the man responsible for leaking the Pentagon Papers. Using White House funds, two of the plumbers led a team of burglars who broke into the Los Angeles office of Ellsberg's psychiatrist to search for Ellsberg's psychiatric files. Nixon was eager to prosecute and convict Ellsberg. While Ellsberg was on trial before a federal court, Nixon told Ehrlichman to approach the trial judge and find out if he would be interested in a promotion to the post of FBI director. The judge dismissed the case.

Four of the burglars of the psychiatrist's office, including the two leaders, took part, with CREEP financing, in the Watergate break-in. After the arrests, CREEP members and other government officials hastily destroyed a tremendous quantity of their records. Nixon told Haldeman and Ehrlichman to meet with top CIA officials, and the CIA director concluded that the White House was trying to "use" the agency as a means of slowing down an FBI probe and covering up CREEP activities. A White House attorney suggested to one of the Watergate defendants that he, the defendant, would get a presidential pardon after a short time in prison if he would keep silent about his superiors' involvement in the affair. Nixon's personal attorney and other White House staffers covertly passed more than $400,000, most from Nixon campaign contributions, to the defendants, their families, and their lawyers.

Besides the Watergate burglary, CREEP agents had perpetrated a variety of "dirty tricks" before and during the campaign, the worst of them having been intended to destroy the reputation of Nixon's strongest potential rival, Senator Edmund Muskie, and thereby prevent his getting the Democratic nomination. "I have often thought we had too much money," one of Nixon's campaign workers said afterward in describing their willingness to undertake "dirty tricks." Part of the money came from corporations that were making unlawful contributions, part of it from persons or groups who were receiving specific government favors. Most visibly, the Justice Department compromised an antitrust suit against the International Telephone and Telegraph Company after the ITT had agreed to contribute.

A President Resigns

Many of Nixon's friends, advisers, and aides were indicted on, and some of them were convicted of, charges growing out of illegal campaign activities. The question became more and more insistent: Was Nixon himself guilty? Did he authorize any of the illegal activities or any of the attempts to cover them up? Did he have any knowledge of the misdeeds or the cover-up and fail to act on his knowledge, fail to stop what was going on and see that those responsible were punished? (Misprision — failure to inform the proper authorities of a felony — is itself a crime.) In a succession of statements Nixon altered and added to his original story, but he continued to maintain that he was innocent of any wrongdoing. "I am not a crook," he declared at one news conference.

There was a possible way of testing, at certain points, his veracity as against that of his accusers. At his direction — as one of the very few who knew about it revealed in the midst of the Senate hearings — hidden tape recorders had been recording White House conversations. But Nixon refused to give up the relevant tapes until after Judge Sirica had ruled that he must, and then Nixon's spokespeople let it be known that two of the most important tapes were nonexistent and a third had a peculiar gap in it. A team of experts concluded that part of this tape had been deliberately erased.

To a growing number of Americans it seemed that, at the very least, Nixon had shown remarkably poor judgment in choosing some of his subordinates. It turned out that he had certainly been no judge of character when he twice endorsed Spiro Agnew for the Vice Presidency. Late in 1973 Agnew, the stern advocate of law and order, resigned as Vice President and pleaded no contest to a charge of income tax evasion, the federal prosecutors agreeing in return to refrain from pressing charges of soliciting and accepting bribes. To replace Agnew, Nixon named the House Republican leader, Gerald Ford of Michigan. After a thorough investigation, Congress gave Ford its approval. He appeared to be, if not an imaginative or inspiring leader, at least an honest politician.

With Ford as the prospective successor, old demands for the resignation or impeachment of Nixon were renewed. As 1974 began, Nixon still refused to resign. The House Judiciary Committee was busily gathering evidence for the decision whether or not to impeach. After requesting a number of the presidential tapes, the committee served the President with a subpoena when he refused to give them up. Finally, at the end of April, he responded, not by delivering the tapes but by sending in and at the same time publishing 1,200 pages of selected and edited transcripts. He and other Republican spokespeople claimed that these told the whole story of his relation to the Watergate scandal and completely exonerated him. Others, especially Democrats, drew a quite different conclusion. By a partisan vote, the committee ruled that Nixon had not made an adequate response to the subpoena.

By the summer of 1974, nine men — in addition to the "Watergate seven," the burglars and their accomplices — had confessed to or been convicted of Watergate-related offenses. These nine were former members of CREEP or of the White House staff, the highest ranking of them being Ehrlichman. Several others, including Haldeman and Mitchell, had been indicted and were awaiting trial. Nixon himself had been named as an "unindicted co-conspirator" by a federal grand jury.

For use as evidence in these cases the special prosecutor for the Justice Department, Leon Jaworski, asked for tape recordings of sixty-four White House conversations. Nixon refused to give them up, claiming that "executive privilege" justified him in thus protecting the confidentiality of his office. In the case of *United States* v. *Richard M. Nixon* the Supreme Court decided unanimously against the President in July 1974.

A few days later, after several months of thorough inquiry, the House Judiciary Committee voted to recommend three articles of impeachment. These charged that Nixon had (1) obstructed justice by helping to cover up the Watergate crimes, (2) misused federal agencies so as to violate the rights of citizens, and (3) interfered with congressional powers by refusing to turn over tapes and other materials that the committee had subpoenaed.

Though Nixon continued to assert his innocence, more and more signs of his complicity were coming to light. Newly released tapes proved what he had always denied — that he had been aware of and indeed had directed the Watergate cover-up from the beginning. With impeachment and conviction finally looming as unavoidable, he did what no President had ever done before. He resigned. Immediately, on August 9, 1974, Gerald Ford was sworn in as Nixon's successor. For the first time, there was a President who had not reached the office by going through a national election.

The Ford Administration

Gerald Ford's presidency was far more modest in every way than that of his predecessor. The constitutional crisis that had vaulted Ford into the Oval Office meant that the new President had

to be cautious in advancing his prerogatives. Also, Ford was thoroughly a man of the Congress. He had been first elected to the House of Representatives in 1948, was reelected a dozen times after that, and served for nearly ten years, until he became Vice President, as House minority leader. With his respect for congressional expertise, Ford had no interest in expanding centralized executive planning. And Ford had far less taste for the trappings and show of presidential power than had Richard Nixon. Ford reduced the population of ornamental eagles that Nixon had perched in the Oval Office and removed the 307 battle streamers, commemorating engagements from Ticonderoga to Vietnam, that his predecessor had displayed behind the presidential chair.

To end speculation that he intended to be only a caretaker President and simply serve out the rest of his term, he announced that he would be a candidate for reelection in 1976. He made significant, popular gestures to the liberal wing of the Republican party and to sympathetic Democrats. He named Nelson Rockefeller, ex-governor of New York, as Vice President. By that same act he may well have eliminated from the ring his most powerful contender for the 1976 Republican nomination. And he retained Henry Kissinger as secretary of state.

All of those actions boded well for Ford's political future, but he offset their effect by his handling of the lingering Watergate affair. In September he extended a full pardon to Richard Nixon, explaining that Nixon's health was in jeopardy and that he had suffered enough. Nixon accepted the pardon, thereby admitting some element of guilt, and was, for a time, gravely ill from complications of phlebitis. But much of the American public was dissatisfied with the outcome, particularly when Ford followed the pardon with an amnesty plan for Vietnam draft evaders and deserters that was quite narrow in scope. Ford's ratings in public opinion polls nosedived as a consequence, falling to a 50 percent approval rate by late September 1974 from a favorable rating of 71 percent a week after he took office — the sharpest two-month decline in thirty-five years. And the memory of Watergate would not dissipate. In January 1975 John Ehrlichman, H. R. Haldeman, and John Mitchell were convicted of conspiracy, obstruction of justice, and giving false testimony. In February they were sentenced to a minimum of thirty months in prison, and their subsequent appeals promised to keep the cases in the public eye for some time to come.

The Great Recession

After Nixon's reelection in 1972, economic conditions deteriorated. His stimulation of the economy had produced the most rapid and extreme inflation since World War II. Then, the Arab oil embargo during the fall of 1973 triggered a recession that took hold by mid-1974. Consequently, Ford was unable to avoid the trials of a major domestic calamity — the transformation of a mild recession into the worst economic reversal since the depression of the 1930s. Beginning in the fall of 1974, the recession rapidly became acute, with the construction and automobile industries especially hard hit. By the spring of 1975 the number of unemployed in all occupations had swelled to 9.2 percent of the total work force. This meant that more than 8,400,000 Americans were unable to find jobs.

Despite the seriousness of unemployment, Ford began his approach to the recession by emphasizing the threats of inflation. Inflationary pressures were, in fact, severe. Even in mid-1975, when unemployment peaked, prices continued to rise — in part because of increases in the price of oil from the OPEC (Oil Producing and Exporting Countries) cartel. Nonetheless, the seriousness of the recession had turned Ford into a warrior against unemployment by January 1975, when he endorsed the biggest deficit — more than $50 billion for fiscal year 1976 — in peacetime history up to that time. He proposed a program of stimulation of employment through a $15 billion tax cut. Wanting even more stimulation, Congress passed and the President approved a tax cut of more than $22 billion. That action, taken in early April, contributed to the economic recovery that had begun by the summer of 1975 and continued, although more slowly, through 1976. However, the program of economic stimulation, which Congress expanded to include a deficit of nearly $60 billion, contributed to inflationary pressures. Price increases in 1975 and 1976, although less

severe than those before the 1974–1975 recession, pinched most family budgets. One result was a sharp increase in the number of wives and teenagers who sought employment to supplement eroding family incomes. The surge of new entrants into the labor force, coupled with the incompleteness of recovery from the recession, kept the rate of unemployment at nearly 6 percent, even by the end of 1978.

Election of 1976

When Ford first took office, he seemed to reassure the American people with his refreshing candor, simplicity, physical vigor, and Midwestern origins (Grand Rapids, Michigan). However, his pardon of Richard Nixon and the persistence of the frustrating conjunction of inflation and high unemployment left Ford highly vulnerable as a candidate for reelection.

Recognizing Ford's vulnerability, more than a dozen Democratic leaders entered the campaign for their party's nomination. The competition in the primaries was intense, but a former governor of Georgia, James E. Carter, Jr., or Jimmy Carter, as he insisted on being called, attracted support from a wide range of Democratic voters and emerged as the only contender to win pluralities with some consistency. By convention time almost all the other leading candidates had dropped out of the race, leaving the way clear for a smooth, party-uniting Carter nomination. Carter took liberal Senator Walter F. Mondale of Minnesota as his running mate.

Compounding the problems that a united Democratic party created for Ford, Ronald Reagan, the former governor of California, challenged Ford for the Republican nomination. As the leading spokesperson for conservative Republicans, he proved to be a formidable candidate; but Ford, with greater leverage over the party machinery and drawing on the united support of liberal Republicans, won the nomination. With a small margin of victory he was forced to take a conservative, Senator Robert J. Dole of Kansas, as his running mate, and the Republican party emerged from its August convention badly divided.

Before the primaries Jimmy Carter had been

virtually unknown outside the South. A graduate of the U.S. Naval Academy, a former career naval officer (on nuclear submarines), a moderately wealthy, small-town (Plains, Georgia) peanut farmer, Carter had limited political experience — service in the Georgia legislature and a single term as governor of Georgia. Carter campaigned as an outsider from the Washington establishment; he made much of his small-town origins; he described himself as a "populist"; he made no effort to conceal his religious faith as a "born-again" Baptist; and he ran on a platform stressing the need for greater economic stimulation and vigorous central planning to set national priorities. Ford waged his campaign largely from the White House. He put strong emphasis on his successes in foreign policy. Television advertisements stressed his sincerity, decency, and warm family life and accused Carter of extreme liberalism, inconsistency on the issues, excessive ambition, and poor judgment.

Neither candidate managed to capture the imagination of the American electorate, but Carter defeated the incumbent by a narrow electoral vote margin. However, his popular vote margin was substantially greater than Kennedy's in 1960 or Nixon's in 1968. He got his greatest support from Protestants in the South, but he also had a strong following among blue-collar workers, largely Catholic, in the Midwest and the Northeast. Without the overwhelming endorsement of black voters, he would not have won the election. But neither would he have won without the backing of organized labor and the various other groups that rallied to him. He had succeeded, at least for the moment, in putting back together the old Democratic coalition that the McGovern candidacy had torn apart in 1972.

At the inauguration, Carter became the first President who was both a native and, at the time of his election, a resident of the deep South. On the return to the White House after the ceremony at the Capitol, he suddenly got out of the presidential limousine and, with his wife and nine-year-old daughter, strolled down Pennsylvania Avenue ahead of the procession. (No President had done anything comparable since the time of Thomas Jefferson, who walked both to and from his first inauguration.) Once in the White House, Carter went to even greater lengths than Ford

had done to bring to the presidency a style of informality and simplicity as well as freshness.

Economic Dilemmas

In shaping his economic policies, Carter was torn between resisting inflation and fighting unemployment. Prices were still rising far more rapidly than they had through the 1950s and much of the 1960s. Nonetheless, unemployment continued to be a nettlesome problem. Despite rapid expansion of the economy, about 7 percent of the labor force remained out of work when Carter took office.

Some American workers lost their jobs because of foreign competition. The American steel industry, which only a few years earlier had been enjoying unusually high profits, began to suffer heavy losses and to close down mills as steel from Japan and other countries took over almost a fifth of the American market. Also losing sales to Japanese and European producers, more and more American manufacturers of textiles, shoes, and television sets went out of business or transferred their operations to cheap-labor countries. Protectionist sentiment grew in Congress, but the administration hesitated to impose tariff or other trade restrictions. These might complicate diplomatic relations, trigger a wave of protectionism abroad, and, by keeping out low-priced imports, would add to the inflationary pressure.

In initiating his economic program, Carter viewed unemployment as more serious than inflation, and he proposed a combination of increased government spending and reduced taxes. When price rises began to accelerate, however, he changed his mind. He announced that his administration would concentrate on the "pernicious problem of inflation."

The Carter administration, however, took no decisive action against inflation until late in October 1978, when the rate of inflation threatened to exceed 10 percent per year and the value of the dollar against foreign currencies, even many weak ones, had reached a post–World War II low. Carter and the chairman of the Federal Reserve Board then announced one of the most dramatic shifts in monetary policy since 1931: an increase from 8.5 percent to 9.5 percent in the rate of interest charged to banks borrowing from the Federal Reserve and a massive program of Treasury purchase (with gold and foreign currencies) of dollars held abroad. The Carter administration had taken the gamble that the increased risk of renewed recession was necessary in order to control inflation. Late in 1979 tight money pushed the economy into another recession, which lasted through the first half of 1980 and then resumed in mid-1981. Inflation, however, was slow to respond. In fact, it reached 18 percent at one time in 1980.

Energy Policy

Of all the nation's economic problems, the most urgent, as Carter saw it, was the problem of maintaining an adequate supply of energy. The Arab oil embargo of 1973–1974, with the resulting fuel shortage in the United States, had shown the risk of heavy dependence on foreign sources — a dependence that was to increase considerably during the next few years.

President Carter presented to Congress a comprehensive energy program, one designed to conserve fuel, increase domestic oil and natural gas production, bring about a shift from scarce petroleum and gas to abundant coal, and encourage the use of solar energy for heating. It included a tax on large, fuel-inefficient cars and an increase in the regulated oil and gas prices but not a deregulation of them. Carter summoned the American people to fight the "moral equivalent of war" against energy waste. When the oil companies demanded complete deregulation, he accused them of seeking the "biggest rip-off in history." The program went almost intact through the House of Representatives and passed the Senate, but not without significant modification. Signed by Carter in November 1978, the National Energy Conservation Policy Act established a tax on "gas guzzling" cars, provided a package of credits, loans, and grants for families and companies making energy-saving modifications (including the installation of solar-heating devices), and restricted the future use of oil and gas by industries and utilities (thereby promoting the use of coal). But, contrary to the President's wishes, the act provided a gradual deregulation of prices on newly discovered gas and failed to include a national policy on oil prices and imports.

In the summer of 1979 increasing instability in the Middle East produced a second major fuel shortage and a return of long lines of automobiles at the gasoline pumps. Declaring that a "national malaise" had reduced the nation to confusion, President Carter responded with a new energy program, including larger tax incentives for oil conservation and production, increased use of coal, greater research into solar and wind power, and the creation of a federal corporation to supervise the creation of a new "synthetic fuels" industry. Congress passed a scaled-down version of the President's proposals in 1980.

Women's Rights

During the 1970s the movements for women's rights continued to advance in some fields, but not in others. By 1978 more than 40,000,000 women were holding jobs or looking for them. These women constituted over 40 percent of the entire labor force. And, in 1978, for the first time, they outnumbered the women who stayed at home in traditional roles. Unfortunately for many working women, they, along with teen-agers, were heavily represented among the least trained, the lowest paid, the last hired, and the first fired. They constituted a very disproportionate number of the unemployed.

For the first time since the late nineteenth century, however, women made significant gains in higher education. During the 1970s, with the enforcement of the Civil Rights Act of 1964, which prohibited discrimination by the federal government on the basis of sex, women held an increasing share of enrollments in professional schools. Consequently, they played more important roles in medicine, law, and business management.

Women were also advancing in political life. There was a steady increase, particularly during the Carter administration, of female appointments in the executive branch. Two women held cabinet positions in that administration. And, in 1981, President Ronald Reagan appointed the first woman justice of the Supreme Court, Sandra Day O'Connor. In 1980 two women won seats in the United States Senate — the first women to serve in the Senate who were not succeeding their husbands. Numerous women served in the House of Representatives throughout the 1970s. Until 1984, however, no woman had ever competed for the Vice Presidency or the Presidency as a nominee of one of the two major parties. In that year, one of the women who had been elected to Congress, Geraldine Ferraro, representing a district in New York City, won the Democratic nomination for Vice President. By proving herself an able competitor, Ferraro paved the way for future bids by women for the nation's highest offices.

In the social sphere the movement for the right of women to abortions gathered strength during the early 1970s as advocates asserted the right of a woman to control her own body. A few states liberalized their laws so as to permit abortion under a wide range of conditions, but most of the states retained laws that made it difficult if not impossible — except for illegal and often dangerous operations. In 1973 the Supreme Court struck down those state laws that prohibited abortion during the first three months of pregnancy.

In response, "pro-life" groups insisted on the embryo's right to life. They not only opposed federal payments for abortion but also demanded a "human life" constitutional amendment that would prohibit all abortions. The groups succeeded in persuading Congress to ban all federal funding for abortions and during the early 1980s seemed to be growing as a political force.

Conservative reaction to feminism was also sufficiently strong to block ratification of the Equal Rights Amendment (ERA), which, if adopted, would presumably end all sex discrimination. Congress had overwhelmingly approved the ERA, the House (in 1971) by a vote of 354 to 24 and the Senate (in 1972) by 84 to 8. It then appeared as if the amendment would easily win ratification within the seven-year time limit that Congress set. By 1978 the amendment had indeed done so in thirty-five states, only three short of the required number. But there was little prospect that it would gain the approval of three additional states within a year. It had run against the opposition of a well-organized "Stop ERA" campaign. In response, Congress extended the ratification time limit by three years.

In 1980, however, the Republican party added to its platform a plank opposing the ERA. The Republicans, after forty years of endorsing the amendment, chose to reinforce fears that it would revolutionize relationships between the sexes. With hostility to ERA mounting, two years later, when the time allotted for ratification expired, the amendment died. It was almost sixty years since the amendment, the central demand of feminists had first been introduced in 1923. Renewal of the ERA campaign, however, remained high on the agenda of the National Organization for Women (NOW).

Election of 1980

The nation's economic woes pushed Jimmy Carter into a highly vulnerable position in his re-election effort in 1980. A challenge within the party from Senator Edward Kennedy, based largely on an appeal to those suffering from the nation's economic problems, further weakened Carter's position. He defeated Kennedy for the nomination but faced a powerful challenge from the Republican nominee, Ronald Reagan.

Ronald Reagan, the son of a shoe salesman from Tampico, Illinois, was a sports announcer on the radio, a hero in grade B movies, a leader of the Screen Actors Guild, and public relations spokesperson for the General Electric Company before entering electoral politics in 1965, at the age of fifty-four, and winning the governorship of California in 1966. During the 1930s and 1940s Reagan had supported the New Deal because he saw Franklin D. Roosevelt's cause as that of "the forgotten man at the bottom of the economic pyramid." During the 1950s and 1960s, however, he saw himself as advocate for "the forgotten American, the man in the suburbs working sixty hours a week to support his family and being taxed heavily for the benefit of someone else." To Reagan, big government had replaced big business as the enemy of individualism. Elaborating these views during two terms as governor, Reagan became the favorite presidential candidate with the conservative wing of his party and had run twice for the Presidency, in 1968 and 1976, before his nomination and victory in 1980. He always emphasized symbols rather than substance, and he chose his symbols in accord with his belief in the superiority of small-town America, a powerful faith in free enterprise and in business leaders, and a disdain for government. One of his most effective campaign lines was his promise to "get government off the people's backs."

Since the 1930s conservatives had objected to the scale of government (except for funds devoted to national defense), but by the late 1970s concerns about the rising costs of government and doubts about the effectiveness of government solutions to social problems grew powerful throughout the nation. The dissent surfaced during 1978 in a taxpayers' revolt that had its most dramatic expression in California, where voters approved Proposition 13, an amendment of the state's constitution that drastically limited property tax rates and the ability of the legislature to enact new taxes. This tax revolt — led by homeowners and business people trying to reduce their property-tax bills, conservatives attacking welfare, and people striking out at modern life — contributed significantly to the nomination of Ronald Reagan as the Republican presidential candidate in 1980.

Reagan swept to victory in the presidential election, taking full advantage of the accumulated frustrations of more than a decade of domestic and international disappointments. He won 51 percent of the ballots cast, to 41 percent for Carter, and 7 percent for John Anderson, a liberal Republican candidate who had waged an independent campaign. In addition, the Republican party won control of the Senate for the first time since the 1950s. When Reagan assumed office, he was, at age sixty-nine, the oldest man ever to do so. And, more than any of the Presidents who came into office favoring limited government, he had built his career on the proposition that the government that governs least governs best.

The Reagan Revolution

Upon assuming the Presidency in January 1981, Ronald Reagan promised a change in government more fundamental than any since the New Deal. In his inaugural address he declared that "our present troubles parallel and are proportionate to the intervention and intrusion in our lives that result from unnecessary and excessive growth of government." Central to his program was the reduction of the scale of the federal government and the adoption of what became known as "supply-side" economics: reducing taxes, particularly on wealthy individuals and corporations. It was argued that this program would stimulate investment, economic growth, and, it was hoped, government tax revenues adequate to finance the build-up in national defense that Reagan planned to undertake. Reagan's Vice President, George Bush, had described supply-side economic theory as "voodoo economics" during his challenge to Reagan in the 1980 Republican primaries. Most economists rejected the extreme claims of "Reaganomics," as this theory became known. Nonetheless, it gained wide support and became the major vehicle for Reagan to turn his rhetoric into action. It appealed to wealthy and middle-class people who resented their tax burdens; it offered an upbeat promise of curing both unemployment and inflation; and it provided symbolic satisfaction for all those angry with the federal government — perhaps especially those convinced that the federal government had become too favorable toward minorities and women.

In March 1981, as Congress debated Reagan's first budget proposals, and as he recovered from the wounds he received in an assassination attempt, his popularity ratings in public opinion polls soared. By May, with the support of conservative Democrats, Republicans passed a budget providing for sharp cuts in a wide range of social programs, including food stamps, Medicaid (federal health insurance for the poor), housing, mass transit, and student loans. The Reagan administration was even more successful in promoting tax cuts. In July Congress enacted a 25 percent rate reduction, spread over three years, on both individual and corporate taxes. Taxpayers with annual incomes of more than $50,000 would receive fully one-third of the tax benefits. This cut was at once sharper and more conservative than the Kennedy-Johnson tax cut of 1964. Critics such as Mayor Coleman Young of Detroit described Reaganomics as nothing more than the traditional "trickle down" economics of conservative Republicans. Reagan's first six months in office was often compared with Franklin D. Roosevelt's first hundred days.

Reagan's accomplishments in advancing the program of the New Right were much less substantial. Only during 1982 did Reagan declare "a crusade for national renewal," asserting his support for constitutional amendments banning abortions, preventing the forced busing of schoolchildren, and protecting prayers in school, and for laws that would establish public support for private schools. Support for this social program, however, attracted less middle-class support than did Reaganomics, and the program lost momentum after the congressional elections of 1982 returned a more Democratic Congress. Thus in March 1984 an endorsement of a constitutional amendment protecting school prayer failed to carry the Senate by eleven votes.

Democrats regained some House seats in 1982 because Reaganomics had brought severe budgetary problems. The administration made little headway in cutting "entitlement" programs such as social security, Medicare, and military retirement pensions, and it increased defense spending more than it cut domestic programs. Together with the drastic tax cutting, the growth of spending increased the size of the federal budgetary deficit. The recession beginning in 1981 proved to be the longest since the depression of the 1930s and compounded matters. National unemployment approached 11 percent by the end of 1982. The recession depressed the tax base, thus helping to push federal deficits to record-setting levels; for the first time since World War II, the debts of the federal government began to grow much more rapidly than the gross national product. Simultaneously, federal borrowing to finance these deficits soaked up domestic savings and kept interest rates high, despite the recession. High interest rates, in turn, increased the international demand for dollars and thereby depressed markets overseas for American goods.

The recession, begun by the stringent monetary policy of the Federal Reserve Board, bore most heavily on the poor, the undereducated, the unemployed, and minorities. In the industrial areas around the Great Lakes, where heavy industry prevailed, depression conditions were often as severe as they had been during the 1930s. However, the recession did have the salutary effect of dampening domestic inflation — an accomplishment that was widely popular among middle- and upper-class Americans, and one for which the Reagan administration took credit. Then, in late

1982, the Federal Reserve Board eased monetary policy, and the economy slowly emerged from the recession.

Election of 1984

By 1984 President Reagan had the luxury of campaigning for reelection in an environment of economic recovery and price stability. However, economic growth was inadequate, contrary to supply-side predictions, to solve the nagging problems of enormous budget deficits and high interest rates. These problems threatened to ruin economic recovery unless resolved by some combination of significant budget cuts and substantial tax increases. Martin Feldstein, the chairman of the President's Council of Economic Advisers, dissented from the Reagan administration's discounting of the significance of the deficit problem, and he resigned his office in May 1984.

The Democrats, however, failed to capitalize upon the vulnerability of the Reagan administration on economic issues. The Democratic party splintered among the forces of former Vice President Walter Mondale, who led a following of traditional Democrats in the South and in labor unions; Senator Gary Hart of Colorado, who attracted support from young, professional, and suburban Democrats; and Jesse Jackson, who energized the nation's black communities and attracted Democrats who regarded Mondale and Hart as too conservative. Mondale won the Democratic nomination, but millions of Americans attributed the improvement in their economic lives to administration policies and distrusted Jimmy Carter's Vice President. Voters were particularly worried about Mondale's promise to raise taxes to finance the deficit. Reagan, by contrast, throughout the campaign flatly denied that he would approve of any such tax increase.

Ronald Reagan received an overwhelming mandate in November 1984 as he swept the election everywhere except for Walter Mondale's home state of Minnesota and the District of Columbia. His 59 percent of the popular vote made him nearly as popular as Harding in 1920, Roosevelt in 1936, Johnson in 1964, and Nixon in 1972. However, it was not clear whether the mandate extended beyond an endorsement of a President who was liked for his humor, candor, and perhaps, innocence, to include all the programs of the President and his party. One columnist described Reagan's appeal as "the way he comes on as a bewildered ordinary guy, vulnerable, blundering at times, but aw shucks." The Republicans, although gaining fourteen seats in the House, failed to win control of it and lost two senators to the Democrats.

After his reelection, when he asked for a $31 billion increase for defense in the 1986 budget, Reagan had to confront the deficit problem. He did so by asking for an unprecedented $42 billion cut in virtually all social programs except for social security, justifying the cuts as part of a "new American Emancipation" to "liberate the spirit of enterprise" and leave people "free to follow their dreams." He added another symbol in his 1985 state of the union address with a call for "a Second American Revolution of hope and opportunity." Even with this projected cut, however, the administration predicted that deficits well over $100 billion would persist into the late 1980s. To reduce such deficits, Reagan allowed his secretary of the treasury to propose a "tax reform" measure to implement what Reagan called "simplification for fairness and growth." The tax reform package would close a variety of tax loopholes and indirectly raise taxes.

In June 1985, however, the President, worried about appearing to increase taxes and receiving criticism from those who would lose favored tax treatment, replaced his tax reform plan with a more moderate program. In July, mounting concern over the size of the deficit led Reagan's budget director, David Stockman, to resign and prominent Senate Republicans to criticize the President for his failure to support tax increases. As late as September, Congress and the President had not reached agreement on a budget for 1986, let alone tax reform. But the President and the Congress seemed likely to reach a budget compromise that would include some tax increases. To eliminate the budget deficits without significant tax increases, the federal government would have to halt the administration's defense build-up and slash domestic programs. The Reagan administration was unlikely to compromise on any significant aspects of defense policy, and the Congress was unlikely to make any further great departures from the domestic legacy of the New Deal.

Chapter 30

The Balance of Terror, 1961-1985

Diversified Defense

At the time Kennedy took office, the military establishment of the United States was spending half of the federal budget and nearly a tenth of the gross national product; it was directly employing 3,500,000 people. The incoming President and his new secretary of defense, Robert McNamara, were as committed as President Eisenhower had been to the theory that the strength of thermonuclear weapons on the part of both the United States and the Soviet Union was sufficiently great to constitute a "mutual deterrent" against war. They assumed, in addition, that under the umbrella of the mutual deterrence of countering nuclear forces, the Communists would seek to gain new territories by subversion or by conventional warfare. Experts pointed to areas like South Vietnam to illustrate what they meant; nuclear deterrents were of no value there. So the President wished to develop forces expert in guerrilla and jungle warfare and equipped with special arms. A million American soldiers were thus trained in "counterinsurgency." In addition, United States military missions aided other countries in establishing their own programs. During its first two years the administration also committed more of its defense expenditures to increasing its conventional forces.

Since the inception of the Truman Doctrine (1947) and the Marshall Plan (1948), the United States had depended on economic aid as well as military power to defend many areas of the world against Communism. President Kennedy continued and in some ways elaborated upon the policy of financial assistance abroad. He established the Agency for International Development (AID) to coordinate various projects and to explore means of making them more effective. He sponsored the so-called Alliance for Progress, which was not really an alliance but a set of agreements between the United States and Latin American governments for cooperative undertakings in Latin America. He also brought about the establishment of the Peace Corps, which trained and sent abroad thousands of specialists, mostly young people, to work for two years in underdeveloped areas.

Economic aid failed to work economic miracles; quite obviously economic development required far more than just the export of capital on the model of the Marshall Plan. And the amount of capital exported under programs such as the Alliance for Progress was minimal. American business leaders convinced Congress that the administration's demands for tax and land reforms, such as those included in the Alliance for Progress, were frightening investors away from the developing nations, and Latin American economic elites reinforced their advice. Consequently, foreign aid remained largely military in its substance throughout the 1960s.

Heightening Tension

The Cuban dictator Fidel Castro was drawing closer to Russia, heaping invective upon the United States, and exporting "Fidelismo" throughout Latin America. President Kennedy

349

had declared: "Communist domination in this hemisphere can never be negotiated."

Once in office, Kennedy and his advisers faced the question of whether to go ahead with a project that the Eisenhower administration had begun. Under the direction of the Central Intelligence Agency, anti-Castro Cuban emigrants were secretly being trained and equipped in Central America for a landing in Cuba. They intended to overthrow the Castro regime with the aid of discontented groups still on the island. Kennedy decided to authorize the invasion but refused to provide United States air support. On the morning of April 17, 1961, a force of about 2,000 rebels landed at the Bay of Pigs. No accompanying revolt, such as had been expected, took place in Cuba, and the invading rebels were left to the mercy of the Cuban Army and Air Force. Within two days the beachhead was wiped out. Subsequently, the Kennedy administration launched an elaborate new covert operation, code-named Mongoose by the CIA, that was designed to monitor, harass, and, if possible, remove Fidel Castro.

In the aftermath of the Bay of Pigs fiasco, Kennedy resolved to toughen his defense of West Berlin, which the Soviet Union wished to hold hostage in order to force recognition of its satellite East German government and thus undermine the claim of the West German government that it was the only legitimate representative of all the German people. Following an inconclusive June summit meeting with Premier Nikita Khrushchev in Vienna, Kennedy called for large increases in the armed forces and in civil defense projects. In a televised interview, his brother Robert said that defending Berlin was so important to the President that "he will use nuclear weapons." Khrushchev decided not to try to cut off access to West Berlin, but in August 1961 the East German government closed the border between East and West Berlin, erecting elaborate concrete block and barbed wire barriers, and put an end to the large flow of refugees from East to West Germany. The Kennedy administration decided not to challenge this face-saving device but did send a convoy of American forces to West Berlin. For a few chilling hours American and Soviet tanks faced each other across the border in Berlin before the Soviet tanks withdrew and the crisis subsided.

Throughout the crisis, fears of thermonuclear war ran high and the nation faced seriously for the first time the problem of trying to construct fallout shelters sufficient to protect the entire population. Fears were intensified during the autumn when the Soviet Union exploded approximately fifty nuclear devices, one with an estimated force of sixty-five megatons — 3,000 times more powerful than the Hiroshima bomb. The series as a whole produced double the amount of fallout of all previous atomic tests. The United States, fearing it would fall behind in the nuclear race, announced it would resume tests underground and in outer space.

Cuba: The Missile Crisis

The Berlin crisis slowly subsided during the autumn of 1961, to be succeeded a year later by a new, more frightening encounter, this time in regard to Cuba. In mid-July 1962 shiploads of Russian technicians and equipment began arriving on the island, and in August more than thirty Soviet ships unloaded 2,000 technicians and instructors, together with fighter planes, surface-to-air missiles, patrol boats with missiles, and, as it turned out, equipment for offensive missiles.

The Russian move would more than redress the missile balance that had favored the United States. According to the London *Observer* (October 28, 1962): "Seen from the Pentagon, the two most alarming features of the missile build-up [in Cuba] were proximity and speed. Radar would give 15 minutes' warning of a missile attack from Russia, but only two–three minutes from Cuba. Medium-range missile bases can be constructed in hours or days. Within a month, if the U.S. sat tight, Russia could get 200–300 missiles in position — enough, at least in theory, to knock out a large part of the U.S. retaliatory forces in a surprise 'pre-emptive' attack."

How could the United States counter the Russian move? One of the two main alternatives was to strike the bases from the air; the other was to blockade Cuba. The President and his advisers decided upon a "quarantine" — a blockade. Several days of acute tension followed as the United States instituted its naval and air blockade, uncertain what would happen if a Soviet vessel among the twenty-five bound for Cuba should refuse to stop and should be sunk.

All week long the United States negotiated with the Soviet Union, and behind the stand of each side was the threat of nuclear force. Late on the evening of October 26, President Kennedy received a long, rambling letter from Khrushchev in which he compared the United States and the Soviet Union to two men tugging on a rope, pulling a knot tighter and tighter until it could be cut only by a sword. In effect, the letter said that if Kennedy would cease tugging on his end, Khrushchev would do likewise. The letter seemed to imply that the Russians would remove the missile bases provided the Americans would promise not to invade Cuba. If Khrushchev would remove the missiles, Kennedy replied, the United States would end the blockade and not invade Cuba. The next day, October 27, Khrushchev accepted. Subsequently, Kennedy terminated operation Mongoose.

Though an armed clash had been avoided, trouble over Cuba by no means had been brought to an end. The Soviet Union did indeed remove the missiles and dismantle its bases, but Castro refused to allow on-the-spot inspection. Thousands of Russian technicians remained, and although President Kennedy pressured Khrushchev to remove them, their return to the Soviet Union was slow. Cuban refugee groups, bewildered and angered by the no-invasion pledge, engaged in private plots against Castro. In the immediate aftermath of the crisis, the national sentiment was one of profound relief, and President Kennedy's popularity rose.

Loosening of Alliances

With the onset of the cold war in 1947, world politics had become largely polarized between two power blocs: the United States and its allies, and the Soviet Union and its satellites and allies. By the early 1960s, however, strains were developing in the relations between the Soviet Union and its ally, China. This development presented new opportunities for American diplomacy.

In the summer of 1963, perhaps in part because of growing trouble with China, the Soviet Union agreed to a treaty banning atmospheric (but not

underground) tests of nuclear weapons. The treaty, the first definite step in the direction of international arms reduction since the onset of the cold war, was ratified by almost every important country except China (which was preparing to test its own nuclear bomb), France, and Cuba. A notable thaw in the cold war followed. President Kennedy announced that the United States would be willing to sell large quantities of surplus wheat to the Russians, who were suffering from a shortage.

By 1964 many Americans were thinking hopefully of the prospect for détente with the Soviet Union. But these prospects soon declined as the United States became more and more deeply involved in an anti-Communist crusade far from home in Southeast Asia.

Deeper Involvement in Vietnam

During the presidential campaign of 1964 the Republican candidate, Senator Goldwater, urged that the United States take a much more active part in the war then going on between Communist North Vietnam and non-Communist South Vietnam. But President Johnson specifically repudiated the Goldwater policy. "There are those who say you ought to go north and drop bombs, and try to wipe out the supply lines, and they think that would escalate the war," Johnson declaimed in a campaign speech. "We don't want our American boys to do the fighting for Asian boys. We don't want to get involved in a nation (China) with 700 million people and get tied down in a land war in Asia."

In fact, Johnson himself was already preparing to enlarge the American role in Vietnam, and soon he was ordering bombs dropped on the north and was sending American boys by the hundreds of thousands to fight in that faraway land. As a consequence he lost all possibility of maintaining the "consensus" he had desired and of achieving the Great Society he had proclaimed. Never before had a President been elected by such a large popular majority, and never before had a President seen his popularity dwindle away so fast and so completely.

The involvement of the United States in Vietnam had developed so slowly that when it began

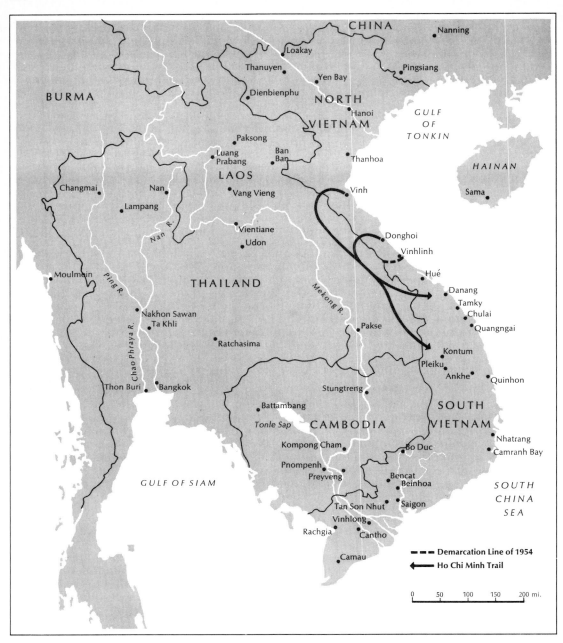

Legend:
- – – – **Demarcation Line of 1954**
- ← **Ho Chi Minh Trail**

0   50   100   150   200 mi.

Vietnam

to grow spectacularly, in 1964 and 1965, few Americans could remember how it had originated. Involvement had begun with President Truman's 1950 decision to give financial aid to the French in their war against the Vietnamese. It had been carried further by President Eisenhower when, after the defeat of the French, he gave moral and material support to the government of the southern part of divided Vietnam.

President Kennedy inherited the problem of trying to make South Vietnam a viable nation. He undertook to strengthen the resistance to Communism by sending American experts to train South Vietnamese troops in the techniques of counterinsurgency. As political and military conditions in Vietnam continued to deteriorate, President Kennedy added to the number of military advisers; by the time of his assassination in November 1963, American personnel in that country had reached a total of 15,500. Reports from American officials in Vietnam were optimistic, though internal troubles there caused newspaper reporters to cable home dark predictions. A new era of even greater instability had begun when the South Vietnamese army seized control of the government from the aristocratic nationalist Ngo Dinh Diem. In the summer of 1964 the political campaign in the United States overshadowed growing difficulties in Vietnam. The number of military advisers in Vietnam was up to 20,000, and on its way up to 25,000.

Escalating the War

In August 1964 there occurred an episode that was to give legal grounds for the reshaping of the war: American destroyers on patrol in international waters in the Gulf of Tonkin reported that they had been attacked by North Vietnamese torpedo boats. President Johnson concealed the fact that these destroyers were electronically gathering intelligence in support of a raid on two North Vietnamese islands by the South Vietnamese. Instead he ordered a reprisal aerial attack on North Vietnam, informed the nation of his action, and then asked Congress for a supporting resolution. By a vote of 88 to 2 in the Senate and 416 to 0 in the House, Congress passed a joint resolution that authorized the President "to take all necessary measures" to protect American forces and "prevent further aggression" in Southeast Asia. Senators Wayne Morse and Ernest Gruening, the only two people in Congress to vote against the resolution, opposed it as being a "predated declaration of war power." Subsequently the resolution did serve as legal authorization for the escalation of the conflict.

By the beginning of 1965 the Vietcong (the South Vietnamese Communist rebels), aided not only by supplies but also by military units coming from North Vietnam along the jungle "Ho Chi Minh trail" through Laos, were in ascendency. The American "advisers" had gradually become combatants and were already suffering serious casualties. At this point the United States began a rapid build-up of troops in Vietnam and the launching of regular bombing attacks upon supply depots, army camps, and transportation lines in North Vietnam. In 1965 United States armed forces in Vietnam grew from 23,000 to over 180,000; in 1966, the number was doubled; by the end of 1967, it was approaching an authorized 500,000. Air sorties were intensified until the tonnage of bombs dropped exceeded that dropped in Europe during World War II. Casualties mounted. By every statistic, the Vietnam War was becoming one of the most serious in United States history.

According to Johnson, the purpose of this enormous effort was to stop aggression and preserve the freedom of the South Vietnamese people. "We want nothing for ourselves," he declared in 1965, " — only that the people of South Vietnam be allowed to guide their own country in their own way." Yet the Johnson administration supported General Nguyen Van Thieu in overthrowing the previous South Vietnamese government in 1965.

While the United States increased its economic and military aid to the Thieu regime, the Soviet Union and Communist China provided larger and larger shipments of arms and other supplies to the Ho Chi Minh government of North Vietnam, and the North Vietnamese stepped up their military action and their assistance to the Vietcong. American intervention seemed to unite the rival Communist superpowers, who had a mutual interest in preventing a Communist defeat in Vietnam. There appeared to be a danger that if the

United States should press its intervention to the point of victory for Thieu, the Chinese might intervene with their own troops as they had done in Korea.

On occasions, the United States limited or halted its bombings and other offensive actions in efforts to persuade the North Vietnamese to begin negotiations. Each time North Vietnam refused, for the most part adhering to the position that the United States must unconditionally and permanently end all bombing. At times a further stipulation was attached to this condition: all American forces were to leave Vietnam.

President Johnson and his advisers refused to end the bombing unconditionally and permanently. They pointed out that during each bombing halt at the time of a holiday truce the North Vietnamese rushed soldiers and supplies southward or prepared for new attacks. American military leaders, following a policy of seeking out and destroying enemy forces, were confident at the beginning of 1968 that with enough soldiers and supplies they could eventually triumph.

Deescalation Begins

In the United States, where television brought pictures of the cruelty and destruction of the war into every living room, the war became more and more unpopular. Liberals and university students participated vigorously in demonstrations, "teach-ins," and "sit-ins." Some young men burned their draft cards. Senator J. William Fulbright of Arkansas and a group of his colleagues became bitter critics of President Johnson and Secretary of State Dean Rusk. Public opinion polls indicated that a majority of Americans still supported the Vietnam War, but it had become the transcendent issue in the nation.

The drain of enthusiasm for the Vietnam War accelerated rapidly in the early months of 1968. During a truce in the fighting to observe Tet — the Chinese New Year — the Vietcong suddenly struck in almost every city of South Vietnam. They were dislodged only after days of bitter fighting, great devastation, and heavy casualties. The single blow destroyed the homes of 500,000 South Vietnamese. The Tet offensive intensified

pressure against the war among a growing segment of the American voters.

In the fall of 1967 Senator Eugene McCarthy of Minnesota, an opponent of the war, began what seemed to be a futile protest campaign for the Presidency. He had behind him only a handful of liberals and a growing group of enthusiastic students. In the first of the primary campaigns in New Hampshire, some of the young men cut their long hair and shaved their beards before ringing doorbells for McCarthy. In the voting, McCarthy was startlingly strong against Johnson, winning almost all the delegates to the convention. The next day, Senator Robert Kennedy of New York, also a critic of the Vietnam War, announced his candidacy. There were indications that the challenge to President Johnson would be so strong that he might not be able to win renomination.

For months President Johnson had been considering a change in his course of action. On the evening of March 31, 1968, in a telecast to the nation, he suddenly announced that he was ordering a halt in the attacks upon the populous areas of North Vietnam and was inviting the North Vietnamese to join him in a "series of mutual moves toward peace": "Tonight in the hope that this action will lead to early talks, I am taking the first step to deescalate the conflict. We are reducing — substantially reducing — the present level of hostilities. And we are doing so unilaterally, and at once." At the close of his talk he made an announcement that removed any possibility that the deescalation could be looked upon as a political gesture: "I shall not seek and I will not accept the nomination of my party for another term."

The North Vietnamese government accepted President Johnson's invitation, and in May 1968 negotiations began in Paris.

Nixon-Kissinger Foreign Policy

During the presidential election of 1968, Richard Nixon had little definite to say about foreign policy. Leaving the most severe criticism of the Johnson-Humphrey administration's Vietnam policies to Democrats, Nixon made only vague references to a plan, which he refused to disclose, for bringing "peace with honor" in Vietnam.

Once Nixon took office, it became clear that he had no concrete measures in mind to extricate the United States.

Nixon, however, was far more interested in foreign than domestic affairs, and his administration emphasized foreign policy. Nixon considered himself an expert on international relations, having read and traveled widely during his years as a private citizen. And, like other Presidents, he enjoyed the freedom from legislative and political obstacles that the conduct of foreign policy, unlike domestic policy, provided. Despite his own passionate interest in diplomacy, he brought with him into government a public figure who came to overshadow the President himself in foreign policy: Henry Kissinger. He was a respected professor of international politics at Harvard when Nixon made him special assistant for national security affairs. For four years Kissinger's White House office overshadowed the Department of State. Then, after the inauguration of Nixon for a second term, the President put Kissinger at the head of the department.

Before joining the Nixon administration, Kissinger in books and articles had criticized the assumptions on which American policy was based. To him, as well as to some other observers, it seemed that the developments of the 1960s had made obsolete the containment policy of the 1950s. The signs of growing antagonism between Communist China and the Soviet Union belied the concept of a single, combined program of Communist aggression. No longer were there only two power centers, the United States and the Soviet Union; there were now at least three, with China, and potentially others if western Europe and Japan were included. For this new "multipolar" world, Kissinger proposed a flexible, many-sided, balance-of-power system to take the place of the rigid, two-sided system that had prevailed since the start of the cold war. In 1971 Nixon clearly announced the new aim of a complex equilibrium: "It will be a safer world and a better world if we have a strong healthy United States, Europe, Soviet Union, China, Japan — each balancing the other, not playing one against the other, an even balance."

When Nixon decided to open relations with the Chinese People's Republic and to improve rela-

tions with the Soviet Union, his decision was in keeping with the new diplomacy that he and Kissinger had proposed. Meanwhile Nixon continued the war in Vietnam, though Kissinger believed that American involvement had been based on "an outmoded foreign policy concept." Nixon undertook to "Vietnamize" the war — that is, to shift the burden of actual combat from Americans to the South Vietnamese — but the process was painfully slow.

Vietnamization 1969-1972

Regarding Vietnam, Nixon said in May 1969 that he hoped to achieve "a peace we can live with and a peace to be proud of." He did not specify the kind of peace he had in mind, but presumably it would be one that kept the Thieu regime in power in Saigon. Whatever the details, his kind of peace, like Lyndon B. Johnson's, remained unacceptable to the Ho Chi Minh government of Hanoi. In Paris the talks went on among the representatives of the United States, South Vietnam, North Vietnam, and the Vietcong.

As the months passed and no end to the fighting appeared in sight, "Johnson's war" began to be looked upon as "Nixon's war," and by the summer's end an opinion poll showed a clear majority of the American people believed the involvement in Vietnam was a mistake. Nixon turned opinion in favor of his Vietnam policy, however, by a television speech on November 3, 1969. He said the "silent majority" agreed with him that a "precipitate withdrawal" would be "disastrous for the future of world peace."

Making a concession to the war's critics, Nixon had announced earlier the beginning of partial troop withdrawals, the first of which would reduce by 60,000 the United States force of about 540,000 soldiers in Vietnam. These withdrawals, he explained, were steps toward the Vietnamization of the war.

Nixon also sought to lessen opposition by reforming the draft, which because of its uncertainties and inequities added to the difficulty of justifying the sacrifice of American lives in a small and distant country. To its critics, the draft seemed all the worse because of the high-handed way in which it was administered. Its director persisted in advising local draft boards to punish antiwar demonstrators by conscripting them, even after a federal court had held this to be illegal. Nixon recommended that the conscription law be changed so as to provide for a "draft lottery" that would take only nineteen-year-olds and would take them at random. Such a lottery went into effect in 1970. Going still further, Nixon urged the formation of an all-volunteer army, with improved pay and other incentives for enlistment. By 1973 Americans were no longer being drafted.

The Vietnamization plan was going so well that Nixon announced in April 1970 that he would bring home 150,000 more soldiers within a year or so. Suddenly, before the end of April, he broke the startling news that he had ordered American troops to cross into neutral Cambodia and, with their South Vietnamese allies, to seize military bases that the enemy had been using for operations in South Vietnam. He explained that "increased military aggression" by the Communists in Cambodia had begun to jeopardize the continuing success of the Vietnamization program.

Up to this point, Nixon said, it had been American policy "to scrupulously respect the neutrality" of Cambodia. What he did not tell the people was that the United States was already deliberately and systematically violating Cambodian neutrality. For more than a year he had personally authorized the secret bombing of suspected North Vietnamese bases on the Cambodian side of the border. For several years American ground forces had been carrying on clandestine operations in Cambodia and in Laos as well.

At the news of the Cambodian invasion, the languishing peace movement came to life. On campuses all over this country, during May, youthful protesters demanded that the universities close down in a "strike" against the government's war policy. A radical minority resorted to violence, smashing windows and fire-bombing buildings. The police and the national guard faced rock-throwing mobs, which they tried to disperse with tear gas and, in a few instances, with gunfire. Four students (all white) were shot and killed at Kent State University in Ohio, and two (both black) at Jackson State University in

Mississippi. A few months later a physicist died when antiwar protesters set off an explosion that wrecked several buildings at the University of Wisconsin in Madison.

American critics of "Nixon's war," like those of "Johnson's war," were appalled by the horrible sufferings it brought upon civilians, both South Vietnamese and North Vietnamese. Millions of them were deprived of life, health, shelter, or livelihood as a result of American action — napalm bombing, population transfer, village destruction, crop burning, and forest defoliation. Hundreds were shot or bayoneted by American soldiers, as in the "My Lai massacre" (March 16, 1968), for which Lieutenant William L. Calley, Jr., was convicted of premeditated murder in 1971.

Continuing troop withdrawals, Nixon announced in January 1972 that the total of American troops in Vietnam would shortly be reduced to 69,000, the lowest figure in nearly seven years. As troops were withdrawn, American casualties in the war decreased, and so did the outcry at home. Yet, while taking out ground forces, Nixon was sending in more and more air and naval forces. Eventually he authorized the dropping of a greater tonnage of bombs than Johnson had, and these bombs killed far more civilians than the 102 that Calley was charged with murdering at My Lai. Nixon ordered his greatest escalation of the war against the Vietnamese Communists after he had dramatically displayed his friendship with the Chinese and Russian Communists.

Rapprochement with China

Until 1949 the United States had sought to maintain the Open Door policy in China. Then, after the Communists under Mao Tse-tung and Chou En-lai got control of the Chinese mainland, the doors were closed on both sides. The Peking government taught hatred of Americans and excluded them from the country. The Washington government prohibited trade between the United States and the Chinese mainland, refused to recognize the Mao regime, and opposed its being represented in the United Nations. Washington continued to treat Chiang Kai-shek, after his flight to the island of Taiwan, as an ally and as the rightful head of all China.

From 1949 to 1971 no American in national politics had opposed the recognition of the Peking government more resolutely than had Richard M. Nixon. Eventually, making a complete turnabout, he reopened relations in a spectacular display of presidential diplomacy.

Recognition was long past due. China was the largest nation in the world, with about a quarter of all the world's people. It was one of the nuclear powers, having set off its first atomic bomb in 1964 and its first hydrogen bomb in 1967. By making friends with the Peking leaders, Nixon could hope to get their cooperation in ending the Vietnam War. He could also hope to use China as a counterbalance to the Soviet Union and thus as a means of inducing in the Russians a conciliatory mood and hastening a détente. The Chinese leaders, for their part, were eager to have the United States as a potentiality in their own balance-of-power arrangement against the Soviet Union.

Early in 1971 Nixon hinted at a change in American policy when, in a public statement, he used the legitimate name "People's Republic of China" for what he and other American officials always had called simply "Red China" or "Communist China." In July, he made the startling announcement that he had received an invitation to visit the People's Republic (an invitation that Kissinger had arranged on a secret trip to Peking) and would make the visit within the next several months.

Nixon's China visit, when it finally came in February 1972, proved to be a theatrical success. For a whole week American television followed the President and his entourage. Never before had a summit meeting been so elaborately staged or so extensively viewed. One effect was to reduce the anti-Chinese feelings that had been instilled in the American people for a generation.

The summit meeting was also something of a diplomatic success. In Peking the leaders of the two countries agreed to scientific, cultural, journalistic, and other exchanges and to the development of trade. They did not agree to the immediate establishment of formal relations, with an exchange of ambassadors. The Communists, looking on Taiwan as part of their country, refused to accept an embassy from the United States so long

as Taiwan had one. The United States must first break off diplomatic relations with Nationalist China. If the summit conferees arrived at any understanding in regard to the Vietnam War, they made no public announcement of the fact.

On subsequent journeys to Peking, Kissinger worked out details of trade arrangements and other matters and managed, as he put it, to "accelerate the normalization of relations." A year after the Nixon visit, the two countries agreed to set up "liaison offices" in each other's capitals. Except in name, these offices practically amounted to embassies. The United States was expected soon to remove some of the 9,000 American troops on Taiwan. By 1973 it appeared that relations with China were getting back to normal, after nearly a quarter century of nonrecognition and estrangement.

Détente with Russia

Nixon had been the first American President to make a trip, while in office, to China; he was the second to travel to the Soviet Union. From both the Russian and the American points of view, the time was ripe for a move toward a new understanding. The Soviet government, under the leadership of Communist party chief Leonid Brezhnev, looked to the United States for possible future support against China, for aid in overcoming the Soviet Union's technological lag, and for wheat and other foodstuffs to make up for its serious crop shortages. Having achieved something like nuclear parity with the United States, the Russians also were interested in the economies of slowing down the arms race. Nixon and his advisers shared the desire for a limitation of nuclear armaments, wished to promote American trade, and hoped for Soviet cooperation in ending the war in Vietnam and preventing war in other parts of the world, especially in the Middle East.

The two superpowers were engaged in a "doomsday game" of competition in the development of more and more deadly weapons and delivery systems. Each of the two was testing a multiple independently targeted reentry vehicle, or MIRV, a device that could be sent into orbit and then directed back into the earth's atmosphere above the enemy's territory, where it would drop separate nuclear warheads on widely scattered targets. Each nation was also planning an antiballistic missile system, or ABM, which was intended to protect population centers or ICBM emplacements against missile attack. In the ABM system, nuclear "antimissile missiles" would be launched to intercept and explode approaching enemy missiles before these could reach their targets. The Nixon administration's ABM project aroused considerable opposition in the United States. Critics said the ABM would have little effect on ICBMs and still less on MIRVs but would endanger civilians in its vicinity and would intensify the arms race.

The two superpowers took a step toward lessening the competition between them when, in 1969, American and Russian diplomats met in Helsinki to begin discussion of a strategic arms limitation treaty, or SALT. After continuing their talks in Vienna for two and a half years, the negotiators arrived at a temporary agreement. This first-phase treaty, or SALT I, would limit each country to only two ABMs and the existing number of ICBMs. The compromise would leave the United States superior in numbers of warheads and the Soviet Union, with its warheads of greater size, superior in total megatonnage. The limitations were to last for five years. Applying only to quantity and not to quality, they would do nothing to prevent a continuing and even heightening contest for arms improvements in the meantime.

At their Moscow meeting in 1972, Nixon and Brezhnev signed SALT I and several other agreements. One of these promised a vast expansion of trade through American tariff reductions and credit extensions. A gigantic "wheat deal" led immediately to the sale of about one-fourth of the total American wheat supply at a bargain price, one well below the market price, and the American government was to make up the difference by means of subsidies to the American wheat sellers. The prospect of a reduction in arms spending, however, did not last long. After Nixon's return from Moscow, the administration asked Congress to approve the largest military budget ever except during a declared war.

In June 1973 Nixon welcomed Brezhnev to Washington. A series of new agreements were confirmed and those of the previous year were extended. The two countries pledged to abstain from nuclear war, to speed up the conclusion of

SALT II for a permanent "freeze" on offensive nuclear arms, and to cooperate in various economic, scientific, and cultural fields. Toasting his Russian guest at a dinner, Nixon said: "The question is: Shall the world's two strongest nations constantly confront one another in areas which might lead to war, or shall we work together for peace?" The question remained to be answered, despite all the talk of détente.

Exit from Indochina

Nixon's China and Soviet diplomacy gave him added strength in his conduct of the Vietnam War. Neither Communist power stopped sending military supplies to North Vietnam, but both indicated that there were limits to their aid. Apparently each was somewhat reluctant to risk damaging its new relationship with the United States.

Between Nixon's two visits, the fighting in Vietnam actually intensified, going in some respects to greater lengths than ever before. In March 1972 the North Vietnamese launched their heaviest attack since the Tet offensive of 1968. Well equipped with tanks and artillery, they crossed into South Vietnam and proceeded to overrun much of its territory. In April Nixon responded by sending B-52 bombers to strike near Hanoi and Haiphong, thus reversing Johnson's 1968 decision to deescalate the air war in the north. On May 8 — just before his scheduled trip to Peking — Nixon ordered the mining of Haiphong harbor and six other North Vietnamese ports, so as to prevent the delivery of war supplies by ship from China or the Soviet Union. Johnson had refrained from this extreme measure for fear it would provoke retaliation from one or both of those two countries. Now they confined themselves to comparatively mild protests.

In Paris, Kissinger and North Vietnamese Foreign Secretary Le Duc Tho were meeting separately and secretly and were nearing a cease-fire agreement. "Peace is at hand," Kissinger finally announced on October 26, just before the 1972 presidential election. On December 16, Kissinger declared that the agreement was 99 percent complete, but he did not explain what the missing 1 percent consisted of.

The next day, December 17, without any announcement from the White House, American planes began to bomb North Vietnamese cities in the heaviest and most destructive raids of the entire war. The targets were docks, airfields, railyards, power plants, antiaircraft defenses, and the like, but these were located in or near residential areas, and homes, shops, schools, and even hospitals were hit. On December 30 Nixon called off the bombing and announced that the North Vietnamese had consented to resume the secret peace talks.

On January 27, 1973, representatives of the four parties (the United States and South Vietnam, North Vietnam and the "Provisional Revolutionary Government" of South Vietnam, that is, the Vietcong) signed an "agreement on ending the war and restoring peace in Vietnam." There was to be an immediate cease-fire, and within sixty days prisoners of war were to be returned and foreign military forces in South Vietnam were to be withdrawn. Contradictorily, both the South Vietnamese right of self-determination and the unity of all Vietnam, North and South, were recognized. Laos and Cambodia were to be evacuated, and their independence and neutrality were to be respected.

Nixon proclaimed that at last he had won a "peace with honor." In fact, he had gained two things in the peace arrangement. One was the return of several hundred American prisoners of war. The other gain for Nixon was to keep Thieu in power in South Vietnam for the time being. But Nixon had also yielded a lot in the truce terms. These included several references to the 1954 Geneva settlement, which the United States had never signed. They reconfirmed the Geneva principle of the ultimate reunification of Vietnam. That was what the North Vietnamese and the Vietcong had been fighting for, and they were in a strong position for achieving it, since they now occupied a large part of South Vietnam's territory.

Such were the inconclusive results of more than a decade of direct American military involvement in Vietnam, and they had been accomplished at a staggering cost. In money, this exceeded $100 billion for the United States alone. In lives, it was approximately 1,200,000 Vietnamese and 55,000 Americans. Some 300,000 Americans were wounded, half of them seriously, and many of these were permanently maimed. A total of about 3,000,000 Americans served in the war, most of

them unwillingly. Perhaps as many as 70,000 evaded service by dodging the draft or deserting after enlistment. Thousands of deserters and draft dodgers remained in hiding at home or in refuge abroad, particularly in Canada and Sweden, as Nixon with the backing of a public majority vowed to grant no amnesty. The psychological cost to Americans, both veterans and nonveterans, was incalculable. Never since the Civil War had the people been so badly divided. Understandably, the announcement of peace, after the longest war in American history, provoked no such demonstrations of popular rejoicing as had followed World War I and World War II.

Congress reacted to the conclusion of hostilities by seeking to limit the President's power to make war. Earlier, in 1971, Congress had repealed the 1964 Gulf of Tonkin resolution, which Johnson and Nixon had treated as the equivalent of a declaration of war. Congress then relied on its appropriations bills to control the war. Congress had to go further in 1973 when Nixon persisted in bombing Cambodia even after the withdrawal of American troops from Vietnam. Congress set August 15, 1973, as a deadline for the cessation of all American military activity in Indochina. Several months later Congress passed, over Nixon's veto, the war powers resolution of 1973. Under it, future Presidents could order no troops into action without reporting to Congress, and they would have to halt the action immediately if Congress objected, or in ninety days if Congress failed to give its positive permission. The new law was a response to the "imperial Presidency," an augmentation of presidential power that Congresses as well as Presidents had been fostering for many years.

Trouble in the Middle East

The Middle East, the scene of continual fighting between Arabs and Israelis, presented a particularly acute dilemma for the Nixon administration, as it had done for previous administrations. Israel had many supporters, both Jewish and non-Jewish, within the United States. The Arab countries could count upon no such American constituency, but they possessed two-thirds of the world's known oil reserve.

Violence in the Middle East had been renewed in 1967, after a United Nations peace-keeping force had been withdrawn at the demand of Egypt. Expecting an attack from Egypt, which was well equipped with Russian arms, Israel struck and in the Six-Day War defeated Egypt, Jordan, and Syria and occupied parts of their territory. A 1967 United Nations resolution called upon Israel to withdraw its armed forces from the occupied territories but recognized the right of every nation in the area to "live in peace within secure and recognized boundaries." Israel refused to budge without guarantees of security. After the 1967 war Israel rearmed with American aid, and Egypt and Syria with Russian aid.

After 1972 the détente between the United States and the Soviet Union could have been expected to defuse the explosive Middle Eastern situation. In October 1973, however, war again erupted, when on the Jewish holy day of Yom Kippur the Egyptians and the Syrians suddenly attacked. Both they and the Israelis quickly lost huge quantities of tanks, aircraft, and other equipment, and both the Russians and the Americans resorted to airlifts to make up for the losses. Only after the Israelis had gotten the upper hand did the Russians show any interest in ending the war. Then Kissinger and Brezhnev worked out, and the Security Council adopted, resolutions calling for an immediate cease-fire and for the beginning of peace negotiations on the basis of the 1967 resolution — which would presumably require Israel to give up most if not all of its 1967 conquests in return for some guarantee of its continued existence.

While Egypt and Israel disputed the details of the cease-fire and threatened to resume hostilities, the Arab countries announced plans to reduce oil production and to cut off petroleum sales to the United States. The Arabs intended, by withholding oil from Israel's friends, to pressure them into supporting a Middle Eastern settlement that would force Israel to leave the Arab territories it had conquered in 1967.

Kissinger-Ford Diplomacy

In taking over the Presidency in 1974, Gerald Ford inherited Nixon's foreign problems and policies and also his chief advisers. Among the unfin-

ished business, the main items were the strengthening of détente through a second arms treaty with the Soviet Union, the achievement of a stable peace in the Middle East, and the maintenance of the status quo in Vietnam.

Early in his term the President took off on a flight to Japan, South Korea, and Siberia. In Vladivostok he and the Soviet leader Brezhnev agreed to the holding of another round of SALT talks. These were yet to get under way, however, and a Middle Eastern settlement was yet to be negotiated when, in the spring of 1975, the administration had to contend with a catastrophe in Vietnam.

The North Vietnamese had launched a swift and powerful offensive, and the South Vietnamese were fleeing toward Saigon, leaving behind most of their equipment as they went. Ford and Kissinger were determined to honor a secret pledge that Nixon had made to Thieu — a pledge to come, if need be, to his support. Ford appealed to Congress for $722,000,000 in emergency military aid. But Thieu's cause was hopeless, and Congress refused to send good money after bad. Before Saigon fell, the 5,000 Americans still in Vietnam managed to get out and to take with them more than 100,000 South Vietnamese refugees, while having to turn back many others trying to escape. The refugees went to camps in California, Arkansas, and Florida, where they remained until they could find American sponsors who would help them get a start in American life.

Solid diplomatic successes, to offset the failure of Vietnam policy, were slow in coming. Kissinger kept shuttling back and forth between Washington and Middle Eastern capitals in an effort to prevent a recurrence of the 1973 war. Finally, in September 1975, Kissinger's "shuttle diplomacy" paid off. In Geneva the Israelis and the Egyptians agreed to separate their forces and refrain from attacking one another on condition that Americans supervise the arrangement. Congress later approved, and the United States sent 200 technicians to the Sinai to serve as monitors. For the time being, a renewal of the war had been averted, but true peace was yet to be achieved in the Middle East.

Meanwhile the policy of détente met with repeated setbacks. The Russians refused to approve a new trade agreement when Congress added a proviso that they must cease to restrict the emigration of Jews and others who wanted to leave the Soviet Union. Brezhnev and Ford, along with the heads of thirty-three other governments, did get together to sign a joint declaration at the Helsinki Conference on Security and Cooperation in Europe. In this Helsinki declaration of 1975 the participating governments promised to regard one another's boundaries as fixed and inviolable, to admit foreign publications and travelers freely, and to respect basic human rights. For détente, the agreement had some symbolic significance, but its practical effect remained to be seen.

The SALT talks lagged despite the auspicious beginning that Ford and Brezhnev had seemed to make at their Vladivostok meeting. Holding up the negotiations was a disagreement over two new war-making devices, one Russian and the other American. The Russians possessed a bomber with such a long range that it could reach the United States and return. The Americans had, in an experimental form, the "cruise missile," a bomb-carrying, jet-propelled, pilotless plane that could be launched from a plane, ship, or submarine. The Russians wanted to exempt their long-range bomber from the arms limitations, and the Americans wanted to exclude their cruise missile.

Carter Tries New Directions

In its conduct of foreign affairs, the administration of Jimmy Carter started out with a quite different tone from that of its immediate predecessors. Kissinger, to further the cause of détente, had refrained from lecturing Communist or other governments on their faults, such as their repression of their own people. The Carter approach, by contrast, was moralistic. The new President began by dedicating himself to the international cause of human rights, a theme he expounded in repeated statements, including a speech he made at the United Nations. He encouraged internal resistance to the Soviet regime by writing a personal letter to a dissident in Russia and by inviting another, an émigré, to the White House. He withdrew economic or military aid from several (non-Communist) countries — among them Argentina, Uruguay, and Ethiopia — that he accused of violating human rights. Yet he continued regular subsidies to others, notably South Korea, that were at least equally re-

pressive but were of greater strategic importance to the United States. Secretary of State Cyrus Vance explained: "In each case we must balance a political concern for human rights against economic or security goals."

High on the list of goals was the completion of SALT II, the long-awaited second Strategic Arms Limitation Treaty with the Soviet Union. The Soviets, however, resented the American hints that they ought to live up to their human rights commitments, especially those in the 1975 Helsinki accords. When Vance went to Moscow, early in 1977, to reopen the arms talks, the Russians abruptly turned down his proposals.

As the months passed, administration spokespeople had less and less to say about human rights, and eventually the Russians agreed to resume the discussion of arms. The limitations question, however, had been further complicated by the development of new weapons systems in addition to the American cruise missile and the Russian long-range bomber. Now the Americans also had the neutron bomb, which with a burst of radiation could kill human beings without damaging buildings or other structures. The Russians had the SS-20, an improved intermediate-range missile with a mobile launcher — a missile that could not reach the United States from Russian territory but could, with its multiple nuclear warheads, wreak terrible destruction on West Germany and other NATO members.

In Latin American affairs, President Carter was willing to negotiate with Brigadier General Omar Torrijos Herrera of the Republic of Panama, even though Torrijos ruled his country as a military dictator. Carter, like Presidents Johnson, Nixon, and Ford before him, recognized that the Canal Zone was not a possession of the United States and favored a revision of the treaty with Panama over the status of the zone. Perhaps Carter shared Henry Kissinger's fear that otherwise it might become the focus of "a kind of nationalist, guerrilla type of operation that we have not seen before in the Western Hemisphere." On September 7, 1977, President Carter and General Torrijos signed two new treaties in Washington. The United States agreed to transfer gradually its rights in the Canal Zone to the Republic of Panama, completing the process in the year 2000. However, the United States would permanently share the right to defend the canal and use it for the transit of warships. Opposition to the treaties among conservatives was vigorous, especially since Ronald Reagan had made the Canal Zone an issue in his effort to take the presidential nomination from Ford in 1976. Reagan and other opponents of revision contended that the treaties were a giveaway comparable to handing Alaska back to Russia or California back to Mexico. Nonetheless, in April 1978 the Senate ratified the treaties by one more vote than the two-thirds majority required by the Constitution.

To break the deadlock in the Middle East, Carter convinced Egyptian President Anwar Sadat and Israeli Prime Minister Menachem Begin to join him in a retreat at Camp David, Maryland. After ten days, Sadat and Begin emerged to announce that they were ready to sign two agreements, providing a "framework" for peace. One agreement, based on the return of the Sinai to Egypt and compensation to Israel by the United States for the loss of Sinai airfields, provided a scheme for Egyptian-Israeli peace, and the other sketched possible terms for a general Arab-Israeli peace.

In March 1979 Begin and Sadat returned together to the White House to sign a formal peace treaty. Moving beyond the agreement to a broader peace in the Middle East proved difficult, however, because of the Arab nations' increasing hostility to compromise, the assassination of Anwar Sadat by dissident Egyptian fundamentalists in 1981, and the refusal of the Israeli government to make any important concessions to the Palestinians.

As prospects for a settlement in the Middle East waned, the Carter administration made its most dramatic foreign policy move — the announcement, in December 1978, of the establishment of full diplomatic relations with the People's Republic of China and the severing of diplomatic ties with Nationalist China. The announcement was the culmination of the long process of reconciliation with China that had been initiated during the Nixon administration. In March 1979 the United States and China exchanged ambassadors.

A few months later Carter traveled to Vienna to meet with Brezhnev to complete the drafting of SALT II. The treaty set limits on the number of long-range missiles, bombers, and nuclear warheads on each side. Future negotiations, the two

sides agreed, would work toward reducing existing arsenals. Almost immediately, SALT II met with fierce opposition from a group of Senate Republicans who denounced the treaty for, among other things, restricting development of the American cruise missile while leaving the Soviets free to proceed with their new back-fire bomber. Critics also denounced concessions permitting increases in certain Soviet missile systems that would, they charged, increase an already large Russian advantage in the area. Behind the opposition was a distrust of the Soviet Union that nearly a decade of détente had not destroyed. Events in the ensuing months would provide the final blows to the treaty and to the larger framework of détente.

The Year of the Hostages

The accumulated frustrations of more than a decade culminated in late 1979 and the full year that followed. The United States, it seemed, was facing evidence of accelerating decline in the world.

The hostage crisis erupted after more than thirty years of American assistance to the shah of Iran, who had served as a bulwark against Soviet expansion in the Middle East. However, the shah's vigorous, brutal, and often corrupt efforts to Westernize his fundamentalist society produced a powerful revolutionary movement, which, in January 1979, forced the shah into exile and attacked the United States. On November 4, 1979, an armed mob stormed the American embassy in Teheran, seized the diplomats and military personnel inside, held fifty-three of them hostage, and demanded the return of the shah, who had been allowed refuge in the United States.

The hostage seizure released a surprising well of anger and emotion in the United States, and President Carter, facing a difficult reelection battle, sustained the sense of crisis. Television newscasts relayed daily scenes of angry anti-American mobs chanting "death to America" and "death to Carter" outside the embassy. Meanwhile, President Carter seemed to make no headway in obtaining the release of the hostages. Then, in April 1980, a commando mission to free them failed when two aircraft crashed in an Iranian desert.

Only weeks after the hostage seizure, the nation suffered another shock when it learned that Soviet troops had invaded Afghanistan, the nation lying between the Soviet Union and Iran. Some Americans described the invasion as an effort to prevent a fundamentalist Islamic revolution in the Soviet Union; President Carter described it as a "stepping stone to their possible control over much of the world's oil supplies" and the "gravest threat to world peace since World War II."

Afghanistan became the final blow to détente. Carter imposed economic sanctions on the Russians, called for American boycott of the 1980 summer Olympic games in Moscow, and withdrew SALT II from Senate consideration. Carter also pledged to oppose, by force if necessary, any further aggression in the Persian Gulf. The seizure of the hostages and Carter's stern response to the Afghanistan invasion lifted his campaign for reelection, but Ronald Reagan's promise to restore American "strength" in the world prevailed in the wake of more than a decade of international disappointments.

Almost at the moment of Reagan's inauguration in January 1981, the Iranian government released the hostages. Jimmy Carter, in the last hours of his Presidency, had agreed to release several billion dollars in Iranian assets that he had frozen in American banks shortly after the taking of the embassy. The next few days produced an orgy of national emotion. The euphoria marked a troubled nation grasping for reassurance.

Reagan and the World

Diplomatic relations with the Soviet Union grew even more chilly after Reagan took office. Reagan spoke harshly of the Soviet regime, describing it as an "evil empire." Indeed, the organizing theme of his defense and foreign policies was hostility to the Soviet Union. He dismissed the possibility of compromise with the Soviet Union, which he said was bent on the destruction of America and of Christianity. To Reagan, the Soviet Union represented the ultimate in big government and atheistic immorality. However, he confidently predicted that the West "will transcend Communism."

Relations with the Russians deteriorated as the Reagan administration undertook a massive military build-up — the most expensive ever in peacetime — and after the government of Poland, presumably under pressure from Moscow, imposed martial law in the winter of 1981 in response to Polish workers' demands for liberalization. Led by Secretary of Defense Caspar Weinberger, the administration recommended implementation of the MX intercontinental ballistic missile system, dismissed the importance of the SALT II agreements, and postponed arms control talks. By spring 1982, however, Reagan, recognizing the growing popularity of the nuclear freeze movement, coupled a call for nuclear superiority with a proposal for Strategic Arms Reduction Talks (START). The Reagan administration and the Soviet government initiated these talks, but Reagan concentrated upon his campaign for more defense, including a proposal, advanced first in March 1983, for a "Strategic Defense Initiative." This futuristic nuclear defense program became known as the "Star Wars" because it proposed laser, particle beam, and microwave weapons located in space. Reagan wanted to initiate research on this program even though, if implemented, it would violate the 1972 ABM treaty with the Soviet Union, a treaty that renounced all but token defense systems against missiles. In May Reagan obtained $625,000,000 for the MX, the largest American missile, one that could carry as many as ten warheads. In December the United States began deploying cruise missiles in Great Britain and, in response, the Soviet Union withdrew from the START talks in Geneva. In June 1984 the Soviets offered to resume talks if they were devoted to the banning of space weapons, but the Reagan administration insisted that the agenda include limitations on all weapons.

Dominated by anti-Soviet evangelism, Reagan foreign policy concentrated on increasing American military strength around the globe, strengthening alliances with anti-Communist regimes, regardless of their social policies, and stemming the tide of revolution in Third World nations. The administration paid closest attention to Central America. In 1983 Reagan told Congress that "if we cannot defend ourselves" in Central America, "we cannot expect to prevail elsewhere." He warned that "our credibility would collapse, our alliances would crumble and the safety of our homeland would be put in jeopardy."

The Reagan administration became most militant in El Salvador, where a repressive military regime was engaged in a hideously murderous struggle with revolutionaries who were pawns, according to the Reagan administration, of Cuba and the Soviet Union. The administration provided military and economic assistance to the conservative ruling group in El Salvador with the assertion that such support was necessary to block the advance of Soviet interests in Central America. In Nicaragua the Reagan administration provided covert support to the *contras,* guerrillas, based in sanctuaries in neighboring Honduras, who were fighting to overthrow the leftist Sandinista government in Nicaragua. Meanwhile, the administration dismissed initiatives by Fidel Castro possibly aimed at reconciliation with the United States. At the same time, the Reagan government rejected suggestions from Mexico, Colombia, Venezuela, and Panama to work out a negotiated settlement in El Savador and Nicaragua.

Congress supported increasing aid to El Salvador but began to criticize the intervention in Nicaragua. In July 1983 the House voted to end covert aid to Nicaragua. Criticism mounted after a United States helicopter pilot was killed after being shot on a mission in Nicaragua and after it was discovered that the CIA had sponsored the mining of Nicaraguan ports. In April 1984 Congress condemned the mining and then in June voted to deny additional covert aid to the *contras* by the CIA.

The Reagan administration resorted to direct military intervention in October 1983, when it sent a force of nearly 2,000 marines and army rangers to the island of Grenada to depose a hard-line Marxist regime that had taken control of the small nation the week before. After suffering a high rate of casualties in several days of intense fighting, the American forces overcame the Grenadian militia and 600 Cubans, who described themselves as construction workers; and they evacuated hundreds of United States citizens, largely medical students studying in Grenada. By mid-December, following critical world reaction, all American combat troops had left, although 300 noncombat troops remained. The political cartoonist Pat Oliphant featured a giant President Reagan, dressed in the rough-rider costume of Theodore Roosevelt, planting his foot on

a tiny island and declaring: "Bully! Where am I?"

In the Middle East as well, the Reagan administration dropped the Carter administration's emphasis on the resolution of local political issues and became preoccupied with blocking Soviet ambitions in the region. In 1981 the administration incensed Israel by giving Saudi Arabia five radar early-warning aircraft (AWACs), to be used ostensibly for patrolling the Persian Gulf, and by encouraging a Saudi plan for Israeli withdrawal from all occupied territories and the creation of a Palestinian state on the West Bank. In response, Israel formally annexed the Golan Heights, a strategic Syrian position occupied by Israel, and ruined the Reagan administration's hopes of uniting Israel and the Saudis in an anti-Soviet coalition.

In fact, conflict in the Middle East soon escalated. Israel, wishing to deflect attention from its settlement of the West Bank, to destroy the bases of the PLO, and to promote the creation of a Lebanese state that would make a peace treaty, sent its forces into Lebanon in June 1982. They quickly defeated the PLO and their Syrian allies and occupied most of Beirut, Lebanon's capital, with the cooperation of Lebanese Christian forces. The Reagan administration, trying to stay on good terms with the Israelis and the moderate Arabs, sent marine units into Beirut as part of a multinational force that would expedite both an evacuation of the disarmed PLO and a phased withdrawal of Israeli forces. However, the strategic objectives of the United States in Lebanon were very obscure, the Reagan administration was reluctant to take any military initiatives with Soviet advisers attached to Syrian troops only a few miles from American forces, the administration ignored the Syrians in its negotiations, and the marines were highly vulnerable to attack from terrorists organized by the Syrians.

In October 1983 a terror squad attacked the marine garrison at the Beirut airport, killing 241 marines and other military personnel with a truck-bomb technique that had been used successfully against the American embassy in Beirut the previous April. In February 1984, after a heavy air and naval bombardment of Syrian positions, the United States withdrew its marines from Lebanon. In September 1984 terrorists again struck, detonating 400 pounds of TNT in front of the American embassy annex in Beirut and killing fourteen people, including two Americans. Reagan acknowledged that security had been inadequate, commenting that "anyone that's ever had their kitchen done over knows that it never gets done as soon as you wish it would." Despite the heavy loss of American life and the lack of clear accomplishment, the Lebanon intervention seemed not to have damaged the credibility at home of Reagan, who had carefully avoided taking the kind of personal responsibility for the marines in Beirut that President Carter had assumed for the hostages in Teheran.

In the election of 1984 the Reagan administration faced a challenge from Democrats, who viewed the Reagan foreign policy as one that ignored the complexity of world affairs and that was apt to involve the world in a nuclear holocaust. However, the Democratic nominee, Walter Mondale, because he had been Jimmy Carter's Vice President, had great difficulty in convincing the public that his foreign policy would be any more effective than that of the Carter administration. And Reagan exploited a continuing upsurge of patriotism, which Russian withdrawal from the 1984 summer Olympic games in Los Angeles only heightened. Nonetheless, in response to Democratic pressure on foreign policy issues, President Reagan took a more positive view toward arms control negotiations in his reelection campaign.

Following the election in November, the United States and the Soviet Union agreed to meet in Geneva in January to discuss the ground rules for future discussions of arms limitations. Those meetings concluded with an agreement to resume arms control negotiations in March. The Reagan administration made a major concession by allowing those negotiations to include discussion not only of strategic weapons (START) and intermediate nuclear weapons in Europe but also of how to prevent an arms race in space. Cooperating with a more flexible President Reagan, in April 1985 Congress authorized spending $1.5 billion for additional MX missiles to strengthen the hand of American negotiators at the nuclear bargaining table.

The Reagan administration, however, stiffened its position on Central America. In February 1985 the President denounced the Nicaraguan government and declared that his goal was to remove the Sandinista government "in its present form." But in April, the new Congress handed the Reagan administration a significant defeat by refusing to release $14,000,000 for support of the *contras.* In June, Congress modified its position, authorizing the expenditure of $27,000,000 but restricting it to nonmilitary aid. Congress assumed that the American people, reading the lessons of the involvement in Vietnam, wanted the Reagan administration to adopt more moderate policies toward ferment in the Third World.

Selected Readings

On the Kennedy and Johnson administrations, see A. M. Schlesinger, Jr., *A Thousand Days: John F. Kennedy in the White House*° (1965). See also T. C. Sorensen, *Kennedy*° (1965); Herbert S. Parmet, *JFK: The Presidency of John F. Kennedy*° (1983); T. H. White, *The Making of the President, 1960*° (1961); E. F. Goldman, *The Tragedy of Lyndon Johnson*° (1969); and C. M. Brauer, *John F. Kennedy and the Second Reconstruction*° (1977).

Postwar prosperity and poverty are dealt with in Michael Harrington, *The Other America: Poverty in the United States* (1962), and H. P. Miller, *Rich Man, Poor Man*° (1964). On race and ethnicity, see Richard Polenberg, *One Nation Divisible: Class, Race, and Ethnicity in the United States since 1938*° (1980). On Indians and Chicanos, consult Vine Deloria, Jr., *Custer Died for Your Sins* (1969); W. E. Washburn, *Red Man's Land/White Man's Law: A Study of the*

Past and Present Status of the American Indian (1971); Stan Steiner, *La Raza* ° (1970); and M. S. Meier and F. Rivera, *The Chicanos: A History of Mexican Americans* (1972). Woman's place is treated in W. H. Chafe, *The American Woman: Her Changing Social, Economic, and Political Roles, 1920–1970* ° (1972).

The Nixon administration and Watergate are the subjects of Garry Wills, *Nixon Agonistes* ° (1970); Carl Bernstein and Bob Woodward, *All the President's Men* ° (1974); J. W. Dean, *Blind Ambition: The White House Years* (1976); Godfrey Hodgson, *America in Our Time* ° (1976); and Jonathan Schell, *The Time of Illusion* ° (1976).

On the Vietnam War and its background, see Neil Sheehan and others, *The Pentagon Papers* ° (1971); David Halberstam, *The Best and the Brightest* ° (1972); and George C. Herring, *America's Longest War: The United States and Vietnam, 1950–1975* (1979).

On Ronald Reagan, see Robert Dallek, *Ronald Reagan, The Politics of Symbolism* (1984), and Hedrick Smith and others, *Reagan the Man, The President* (1980).

° Titles available in paperback.

The Declaration of Independence

In Congress, July 4, 1776,

THE UNANIMOUS DECLARATION OF THE THIRTEEN UNITED STATES OF AMERICA

When, in the course of human events, it becomes necessary for one people to dissolve the political bands which have connected them with another, and to assume, among the powers of the earth, the separate and equal station to which the laws of nature and of nature's God entitle them, a decent respect to the opinions of mankind requires that they should declare the causes which impel them to the separation.

We hold these truths to be self-evident, that all men are created equal; that they are endowed by their Creator with certain unalienable rights; that among these, are life, liberty, and the pursuit of happiness. That, to secure these rights, governments are instituted among men, deriving their just powers from the consent of the governed; that, whenever any form of government becomes destructive of these ends, it is the right of the people to alter or to abolish it, and to institute a new government, laying its foundation on such principles, and organizing its powers in such form, as to them shall seem most likely to effect their safety and happiness. Prudence, indeed, will dictate that governments long established, should not be changed for light and transient causes; and, accordingly, all experience hath shown, that mankind are more disposed to suffer, while evils are sufferable, than to right themselves by abolishing the forms to which they are accustomed. But, when a long train of abuses and usurpations, pursuing invariably the same object, evinces a design to reduce them under absolute despotism, it is their right, it is their duty, to throw off such government and to provide new guards for their future security. Such has been the patient sufferance of these colonies, and such is now the necessity which constrains them to alter their former systems of government. The history of the present King of Great Britain is a history of repeated injuries and usurpations, all having, in direct object, the establishment of an absolute tyranny over these States. To prove this, let facts be submitted to a candid world:—

He has refused his assent to laws the most wholesome and necessary for the public good.

He has forbidden his governors to pass laws of immediate and pressing importance, unless suspended in their operation till his assent should be obtained; and, when so suspended, he has utterly neglected to attend to them.

He has refused to pass other laws for the accommodation of large districts of people, unless those people would relinquish the right of representation in the legislature; a right inestimable to them, and formidable to tyrants only.

He has called together legislative bodies at places unusual, uncomfortable, and distant from the depository of their public records, for the sole purpose of fatiguing them into compliance with his measures.

He has dissolved representative houses repeatedly for opposing, with manly firmness, his invasions on the rights of the people.

He has refused, for a long time after such dissolutions, to cause others to be elected; whereby the legislative powers, incapable of annihilation, have returned to the people at large for their exercise; the state remaining, in the meantime, exposed to all the danger of invasion from without, and convulsions within.

He has endeavored to prevent the population of these States; for that purpose, obstructing the laws for naturalization of foreigners, refusing to pass others to encourage their migration hither, and raising the conditions of new appropriations of lands.

He has obstructed the administration of justice, by refusing his assent to laws for establishing judiciary powers.

He has made judges dependent on his will alone, for the tenure of their offices, and the amount and payment of their salaries.

He has erected a multitude of new offices, and sent hither swarms of officers to harass our people, and eat out their substance.

He has kept among us, in time of peace, standing armies, without the consent of our legislatures.

He has affected to render the military independent of, and superior to, the civil power.

He has combined, with others, to subject us to a jurisdiction foreign to our Constitution, and unacknowledged by our laws; giving his assent to their acts of pretended legislation:

For quartering large bodies of armed troops among us:

For protecting them by a mock trial, from punishment, for any murders which they should commit on the inhabitants of these States:

For cutting off our trade with all parts of the world:

For imposing taxes on us without our consent:

For depriving us, in many cases, of the benefit of trial by jury:

For transporting us beyond seas to be tried for pretended offences:

For abolishing the free system of English laws in a neighboring province, establishing therein an arbitrary government, and enlarging its boundaries, so as to render it at once an example and fit instrument for introducing the same absolute rule in these colonies:

For taking away our charters, abolishing our most valuable laws, and altering, fundamentally, the powers of our governments:

For suspending our own legislatures, and declaring themselves invested with powers to legislate for us in all cases whatsoever.

He has abdicated government here, by declaring us out of his protection, and waging war against us.

He has plundered our seas, ravaged our coasts, burnt our towns, and destroyed the lives of our people.

He is, at this time, transporting large armies of foreign mercenaries to complete the works of death, desolation, and tyranny, already begun, with circumstances of cruelty and perfidy scarcely paralleled in the most barbarous ages, and totally unworthy the head of a civilized nation.

He has constrained our fellow citizens, taken captive on the high seas, to bear arms against their country, to become the executioners of their friends, and brethren, or to fall themselves by their hands.

He has excited domestic insurrections amongst us, and has endeavored to bring on the inhabitants of our frontiers, the merciless Indian savages, whose known rule of warfare is an undistinguished destruction of all ages, sexes, and conditions.

In every stage of these oppressions, we have petitioned for redress, in the most humble terms; our repeated petitions have been answered only by repeated injury. A prince, whose character is thus marked by every act which may define a tyrant, is unfit to be the ruler of a free people.

Nor have we been wanting in attention to our British brethren. We have warned them, from time to time, of attempts made by their legislature to extend an unwarrantable jurisdiction over us. We have reminded them of the circumstances of our emigration and settlement here. We have appealed to their native justice and magnanimity, and we have conjured them, by the ties of our common kindred, to disavow these usurpations, which would inevitably interrupt our connections and correspondence. They, too, have been deaf to the voice of justice and consanguinity. We must, therefore, acquiesce in the necessity which denounces our separation, and hold them as we hold the rest of mankind, enemies in war, in peace, friends.

We, therefore, the representatives of the United States of America, in general Congress assembled, appealing to the Supreme Judge of the world for the rectitude of our intentions, do, in the name, and by the authority of the good people of these colonies, solemnly publish and declare, that these united colonies are, and of right ought to be, free and independent states: that they are absolved from all allegiance to the British Crown, and that all political connection between them and the state of Great Britain is, and ought to be, totally dissolved; and that, as free and independent states, they have full power to levy war, conclude peace, contract alliances, establish commerce, and to do all other acts and things which independent states may of right do. And, for the support of this declaration, with a firm reliance on the protection of Divine Providence, we mutually pledge to each other our lives, our fortunes, and our sacred honor.

JOHN HANCOCK

New Hampshire

Josiah Bartlett
William Whipple
Matthew Thornton

Massachusetts Bay

Samuel Adams
John Adams
Robert Treat Paine
Elbridge Gerry

Rhode Island

Stephen Hopkins
William Ellery

Connecticut

Roger Sherman
Samuel Huntington
William Williams
Oliver Wolcott

New York

William Floyd
Philip Livingston
Francis Lewis
Lewis Morris

New Jersey

Richard Stockton
John Witherspoon
Francis Hopkinson
John Hart
Abraham Clark

Pennsylvania

Robert Morris
Benjamin Rush
Benjamin Franklin
John Morton
George Clymer
James Smith
George Taylor
James Wilson
George Ross

Delaware

Caesar Rodney
George Read
Thomas M'Kean

Maryland

Samuel Chase
William Paca
Thomas Stone
Charles Carroll,
   of Carrollton

Virginia

George Wythe
Richard Henry Lee
Thomas Jefferson
Benjamin Harrison
Thomas Nelson, Jr.
Francis Lightfoot Lee
Carter Braxton

North Carolina

William Hooper
Joseph Hewes
John Penn

South Carolina

Edward Rutledge
Thomas Hayward, Jr.
Thomas Lynch, Jr.
Arthur Middleton

Georgia

Button Gwinnett
Lyman Hall
George Walton

The Constitution of the United States

WE the People of the United States, in Order to form a more perfect Union, establish Justice, insure domestic Tranquility, provide for the common defence, promote the general Welfare, and secure the Blessings of Liberty to ourselves and our Posterity, do ordain and establish this CONSTITUTION for the United States of America.

Article I

SECTION 1.

All legislative Powers herein granted shall be vested in a Congress of the United States, which shall consist of a Senate and House of Representatives.

SECTION 2.

The House of Representatives shall be composed of Members chosen every second Year by the People of the several States, and the Electors in each State shall have the Qualifications requisite for Electors of the most numerous Branch of the State Legislature.

No Person shall be a Representative who shall not have attained to the Age of twenty-five Years, and been seven Years a Citizen of the United States, and who shall not, when elected, be an In-habitant of that State in which he shall be chosen.

[Representatives and direct Taxes[2] shall be apportioned among the several States which may be included within this Union, according to their respective Numbers, which shall be determined by adding to the whole Number of free Persons, including those bound to Service for a Term of Years, and excluding Indians not taxed, three fifths of all other Persons.][3] The actual Enumeration shall be made within three Years after the first Meeting of the Congress of the United States, and within every subsequent Term of ten Years, in such Manner as they shall by Law direct. The Number of Representatives shall not exceed one for every thirty Thousand, but each State shall have at Least one Representative; and until such enumeration shall be made, the State of New Hampshire shall be entitled to chuse three, Massachusetts eight, Rhode-Island and Providence Plantations one, Connecticut five, New York six, New Jersey four, Pennsylvania eight, Delaware one, Maryland six, Virginia ten, North Carolina five, South Carolina five, and Georgia three.

When vacancies happen in the Representation from any State, the Executive Authority thereof shall issue Writs of Election to fill such Vacancies.

The House of Representatives shall chuse their Speaker and other Officers; and shall have the sole Power of Impeachment.

---

[1] This version, which follows the original Constitution in capitalization and spelling, was published by the United States Department of the Interior, Office of Education, in 1935.

[2] Altered by the Sixteenth Amendment.
[3] Negated by the Fourteenth Amendment.

SECTION 3.

The Senate of the United States shall be composed of two Senators from each State, chosen by the Legislature thereof, for six Years; and each Senator shall have one Vote.

Immediately after they shall be assembled in Consequence of the first Election, they shall be divided as equally as may be into three Classes. The Seats of the Senators of the first Class shall be vacated at the Expiration of the second Year, of the second Class at the Expiration of the fourth Year, and of the third Class at the Expiration of the sixth Year, so that one-third may be chosen every second Year; and if Vacancies happen by Resignation, or otherwise, during the Recess of the Legislature of any State, the Executive thereof may make temporary Appointments until the next Meeting of the Legislature, which shall then fill such Vacancies.

No Person shall be a Senator who shall not have attained to the Age of thirty Years, and been nine Years a Citizen of the United States, and who shall not, when elected, be an Inhabitant of that State for which he shall be chosen.

The Vice President of the United States shall be President of the Senate, but shall have no vote, unless they be equally divided.

The Senate shall chuse their other Officers, and also a President pro tempore, in the absence of the Vice President, or when he shall exercise the Office of President of the United States.

The Senate shall have the sole Power to try all Impeachments. When sitting for that purpose, they shall be on Oath or Affirmation. When the President of the United States is tried, the Chief Justice shall preside: And no person shall be convicted without the Concurrence of two thirds of the Members present.

Judgment in Cases of Impeachment shall not extend further than to removal from Office, and disqualifications to hold and enjoy any Office of honor, Trust, or Profit under the United States: but the Party convicted shall nevertheless be liable and subject to Indictment, Trial, Judgment, and Punishment, according to Law.

SECTION 4.

The Times, Places and Manner of holding Elections for Senators and Representatives, shall be prescribed in each state by the Legislature thereof; but the Congress may at any time by Law make or alter such Regulations, except as to the Places of Chusing Senators.

The Congress shall assemble at least once in every Year, and such Meeting shall be on the first Monday in December, unless they shall by Law appoint a different Day.

SECTION 5.

Each House shall be the Judge of the Elections, Returns and Qualifications of its own Members, and a Majority of each shall constitute a Quorum to do Business; but a smaller number may adjourn from day to day, and may be authorized to compel the Attendance of absent Members, in such Manner, and under such Penalties, as each House may provide.

Each House may determine the Rules of its Proceedings, punish its Members for disorderly Behaviour, and, with the Concurrence of two thirds, expel a Member.

Each House shall keep a journal of its Proceedings, and from time to time publish the same, excepting such Parts as may in their Judgment require Secrecy; and the Yeas and Nays of the Members of either House on any question shall, at the Desire of one fifth of those Present, be entered on the Journal.

Neither House, during the Session of Congress, shall, without the Consent of the other, adjourn for more than three days, nor to any other Place than that in which the two Houses shall be sitting.

SECTION 6.

The Senators and Representatives shall receive a Compensation for their Services, to be ascertained by Law, and paid out of the Treasury of the United States. They shall in all Cases, except Treason, Felony, and Breach of the Peace, be privileged from Arrest during their Attendance at the Session of their respective Houses, and in going to and returning from the same; and for any Speech or Debate in either House, they shall not be questioned in any other Place.

No Senator or Representative shall, during the Time for which he was elected, be appointed to any civil Office under the Authority of the United States, which shall have been created, or the Emoluments whereof shall have been increased, during such time; and no Person holding any Office under the United States shall be a Member of either House during his continuance in Office.

SECTION 7.

All Bills for raising Revenue shall originate in the House of Representatives; but the Senate may propose or concur with Amendments as on other bills.

Every Bill which shall have passed the House of Representatives and the Senate, shall, before it become a Law, be presented to the President of the United States; If he approve he shall sign it, but if not he shall return it, with his Objections, to that House in which it shall have originated, who shall enter the Objections at large on their Journal, and proceed to reconsider it. If after such Reconsideration two thirds of that House shall agree to pass the bill, it shall be sent, together with the objections, to the other House, by which it shall likewise be reconsidered, and if approved by two thirds of that House, it shall become a Law. But in all such Cases the Votes of both Houses shall be determined by Yeas and Nays, and the Names of the Persons voting for and against the Bill shall be entered on the Journal of each House respectively. If any Bill shall not be returned by the President within ten Days (Sundays excepted) after it shall have been presented to him, the Same shall be a Law, in like Manner as if he had signed it, unless the Congress by their Adjournment prevent its Return, in which Case it shall not be a Law.

Every Order, Resolution, or Vote to which the Concurrence of the Senate and House of Representatives may be necessary (except on a question of Adjournment) shall be presented to the President of the United States; and before the Same shall take Effect, shall be approved by him, or being disapproved by him, shall be repassed by two thirds of the Senate and House of Representatives, according to the Rules and Limitations prescribed in the Case of a Bill.

SECTION 8.

The Congress shall have Power To lay and collect Taxes, Duties, Imposts and Excises, to pay the Debts and provide for the common Defence and general Welfare of the United States; but all Duties, Imposts and Excises shall be uniform throughout the United States;

To borrow money on the credit of the United States;

To regulate Commerce with foreign Nations, and among several States, and with the Indian Tribes;

To establish an uniform Rule of Naturalization, and uniform Laws on the subject of Bankruptcies throughout the United States;

To coin Money, regulate the Value thereof, and of foreign Coin, and fix the Standard of Weights and Measures;

To provide for the Punishment of counterfeiting the Securities and current Coin of the United States;

To establish Post Offices and post Roads;

To promote the Progress of Science and useful Arts, by securing for limited Times to Authors and Inventors the exclusive Right to their respective Writings and Discoveries;

To constitute Tribunals inferior to the Supreme Court;

To define and punish Piracies and Felonies committed on the high Seas, and Offenses against the Law of Nations;

To declare War, grant Letters of Marque and Reprisal, and make Rules concerning Captures on Land and Water;

To raise and support Armies, but no Appropriation of Money to that Use shall be for a longer Term than two Years;

To provide and maintain a Navy;

To make Rules for the Government and Regulation of the land and naval forces;

To provide for calling forth the Militia to execute the Laws of the Union, suppress Insurrections and repel Invasions;

To provide for organizing, arming, and disciplining the Militia, and for governing such Part of them as may be employed in the Service of the United States, reserving to the States respectively, the Appointment of the Officers, and the Authority of training the Militia according to the discipline prescribed by Congress;

To exercise exclusive Legislation in all Cases whatsoever, over such District (not exceeding ten Miles square) as may, by Cession of particular States, and the acceptance of Congress, become the Seat of the Government of the United States, and to exercise like Authority over all Places purchased by the Consent of the Legislature of the

State in which the Same shall be, for the Erection of Forts, Magazines, Arsenals, Dock-yards, and other needful Buildings; — And

To make all Laws which shall be necessary and proper for carrying into Execution the foregoing Powers, and all over Powers vested by this Constitution in the Government of the United States, or in any Department or Officer thereof.

SECTION 9.

The Migration or Importation of such Persons as any of the States now existing shall think proper to admit, shall not be prohibited by the Congress prior to the Year one thousand eight hundred and eight, but a tax or duty may be imposed on such Importation, not exceeding ten dollars for each Person.

The privilege of the Writ of Habeas Corpus shall not be suspended, unless when in Cases of Rebellion or Invasion the public Safety may require it.

No bill of Attainder or ex post facto Law shall be passed.

No capitation, or other direct, Tax shall be laid unless in Proportion to the Census or Enumeration herein before directed to be taken.

No Tax or Duty shall be laid on Articles exported from any State.

No Preference shall be given by any Regulation of Commerce or Revenue to the Ports of one State over those of another: nor shall Vessels bound to, or from, one State, be obliged to enter, clear, or pay Duties in another.

No Money shall be drawn from the Treasury, but in Consequence of Appropriations made by Law; and a regular Statement and Account of the Receipts and Expenditures of all public Money shall be published from time to time.

No Title of Nobility shall be granted by the United States: And no Person holding any Office of Profit or Trust under them, shall, without the Consent of the Congress, accept of any present, Emolument, Office, or Title, of any kind whatever, from any King, Prince, or foreign State.

SECTION 10.

No State shall enter into any Treaty, Alliance, or Confederation; grant Letters of Marque and Reprisal; coin Money; emit Bills of Credit; make any Thing but gold and silver Coin a Tender in Pay-

ment of Debts; pass any Bill of Attainder, ex post facto Law, or Law impairing the Obligation of Contracts, or grant any Title of Nobility.

No State shall, without the Consent of the Congress, lay any Imposts or Duties on Imports or Exports, except what may be absolutely necessary for executing its inspection Laws: and the net Produce of all Duties and Imposts, laid by any State on Imports or Exports, shall be for the Use of the Treasury of the United States; and all such Laws shall be subject to the Revision and Control of the Congress.

No state shall, without the Consent of Congress, lay any duty of Tonnage, keep Troops, or Ships of War in time of Peace, enter into any Agreement or Compact with another State, or with a foreign Power, or engage in War, unless actually invaded, or in such imminent Danger as will not admit of delay.

Article II

SECTION 1.

The executive Power shall be vested in a President of the United States of America. He shall hold his Office during the Term of four years, and, together with the Vice President, chosen for the same Term, be elected, as follows:

Each State shall appoint, in such Manner as the Legislature thereof may direct, a Number of Electors, equal to the whole Number of Senators and Representatives to which the State may be entitled in the Congress: but no Senator or Representative, or Person holding an Office of Trust or Profit under the United States, shall be appointed an Elector.

[The Electors shall meet in their respective States, and vote by Ballot for two persons, of whom one at least shall not be an Inhabitant of the same State with themselves. And they shall make a List of all the Persons voted for, and of the Number of Votes for each; which List they shall sign and certify, and transmit sealed to the Seat of the Government of the United States, directed to the President of the Senate. The President of the Senate shall, in the Presence of the Senate and House of Representatives, open all the Certificates, and the Votes shall then be counted. The Person having the greatest Number of Votes shall be the President, if such Number be a Majority of the whole Number of Electors appointed; and if there be more than one who have such Majority, and have an equal Number of Votes, then the House of Representatives shall immediately chuse by Ballot one of them for President; and if no Person have a Majority, then from the five highest on the List the said House shall in the Manner chuse the President. But in chusing the President, the Votes shall be taken by States, the Representation from each State having one Vote; a quorum for this Purpose shall consist of a Member or Members from two-thirds of the States, and a Majority of all the States shall be necessary to a Choice. In every Case, after the Choice of the President, the Person having the greatest Number of Votes of the Electors shall be the Vice President. But if there should remain two or more who have equal votes, the Senate shall chuse from them by Ballot the Vice President.][4]

The Congress may determine the Time of chusing the Electors, and the Day on which they shall give their Votes; which Day shall be the same throughout the United States.

No person except a natural-born Citizen, or a Citizen of the United States, at the time of the Adoption of this Constitution, shall be eligible to the Office of President; neither shall any Person be eligible to that Office who shall not have attained to the Age of thirty-five years, and been fourteen Years a Resident within the United States.

In Case of the Removal of the President from Office, or of his Death, Resignation, or Inability to discharge the Powers and Duties of the said Office, the same shall devolve on the Vice President, and the Congress may by Law provide for the Case of Removal, Death, Resignation, or Inability, both of the President and Vice President, declaring what Officer shall then act as President, and such Officer shall act accordingly, until the disability be removed, or a President shall be elected.

The President shall, at stated Times, receive for his Services a Compensation, which shall neither be increased nor diminished during the Period for

which he shall have been elected, and he shall not receive within that Period any other Emolument from the United States, of any of them.

Before he enter on the execution of his Office, he shall take the following Oath or Affirmation: — "I do solemnly swear (or affirm) that I will faithfully execute the Office of President of the United States, and will, to the best of my Ability, preserve, protect, and defend the Constitution of the United States."

SECTION 2.

The President shall be Commander in Chief of the Army and Navy of the United States, and of the Militia of the several States, when called into the actual Service of the United States; he may require the Opinion, in writing, of the principal Officer in each of the executive Departments, upon any subject relating to the Duties of their respective Offices, and he shall have Power to Grant Reprieves and Pardons for Offenses against the United States, except in Cases of Impeachment.

He shall have Power, by and with the Advice and Consent of the Senate, to make Treaties, provided two-thirds of the Senators present concur; and he shall nominate, and by and with the Advice and Consent of the Senate, shall appoint Ambassadors, other public Ministers and Consuls, Judges of the supreme Court, and all other Officers of the United States, whose Appointments are not herein otherwise provided for, and which shall be established by Law: but the Congress may by Law vest the Appointment of such inferior Officers, as they think proper, in the President alone, in the Courts of Law, or in the Heads of Departments.

The President shall have Power to fill up all Vacancies that may happen during the Recess of the Senate, by granting Commissions which shall expire at the End of their next Session.

SECTION 3.

He shall from time to time give the Congress Information of the State of the Union, and recommend to their Consideration such Measures as he shall judge necessary and expedient; he may, on extraordinary occasions, convene both Houses, or either of them, and in the Case of Disagreement

---

[4] Revised by the Twelfth Amendment.

between them, with respect to the Time of Adjournment, he may adjourn them to such Time as he shall think proper; he shall receive Ambassadors and other public Ministers; he shall take care that the Laws be faithfully executed, and shall Commission all the Officers of the United States.

SECTION 4.

The President, Vice President, and all civil Officers of the United States, shall be removed from Office on Impeachment for, and Conviction of, Treason, Bribery, or other high Crimes and Misdemeanors.

Article III

SECTION 1.

The judicial Power of the United States, shall be vested in one supreme Court, and in such inferior Courts as the Congress may from time to time ordain and establish. The Judges, both of the supreme and inferior Courts, shall hold their Offices during good Behaviour, and shall, at stated Times, receive for their Services, a Compensation, which shall not be diminished during their Continuance in Office.

SECTION 2.

The judicial Power shall extend to all Cases, in Law and Equity, arising under this Constitution, the Laws of the United States, and Treaties made, or which shall be made, under their Authority; — to all Cases affecting ambassadors, other public ministers and consuls; — to all cases of admiralty and maritime Jurisdiction; — to Controversies to which the United States shall be a Party; — to Controversies between two or more States; — between a State and Citizens of another State;[5] — between Citizens of different States, — between Citizens of the same State claiming Lands under Grants of different States, and between a State, or the Citizens thereof, and foreign States, Citizens or Subjects.

In all Cases affecting Ambassadors, other public Ministers and Consuls, and those in which a State shall be Party, the supreme Court shall have

original Jurisdiction. In all the other Cases before mentioned, the supreme Court shall have appellate Jurisdiction, both as to Law and Fact, with such Exceptions, and under such Regulations as the Congress shall make.

The trial of all Crimes, except in Cases of Impeachment, shall be by Jury; and such Trial shall be held in the State where the said Crimes shall have been committed; but when not committed within any State, the Trial shall be at such Place or Places as the Congress may by Law have directed.

SECTION 3.

Treason against the United States, shall consist only in levying War against them, or in adhering to their Enemies, giving them Aid and Comfort. No person shall be convicted of Treason unless on the Testimony of two Witnesses to the same overt Act, or on Confession in open Court.

The Congress shall have power to declare the Punishment of Treason, but no Attainder of Treason shall work Corruption of Blood, or Forfeiture except during the Life of the Person attainted.

Article IV

SECTION 1.

Full Faith and Credit shall be given in each State to the public Acts, Records, and judicial Proceedings of every other State. And the Congress may by general Laws prescribe the Manner in which such Acts, Records and Proceedings shall be proved, and the Effect thereof.

SECTION 2.

The Citizens of each State shall be entitled to all Privileges and Immunities of Citizens in the several States.

A Person charged in any State with Treason, Felony, or other Crime, who shall flee from Justice, and be found in another State, shall on demand of the executive Authority of the State from which he fled, be delivered up, to be removed to the State having Jurisdiction of the crime.

No Person held to Service or Labour in one State, under the Laws thereof, escaping into another, shall, in Consequence of any Law or Regu-

---

[5] Qualified by the Eleventh Amendment.

lation therein, be discharged from such Service or Labour, but shall be delivered up on Claim of the Party to whom such Service or Labour may be due.

SECTION 3.

New States may be admitted by the Congress into this Union; but no new State shall be formed or erected within the Jurisdiction of any other State; nor any State be formed by the Junction of two or more States, or parts of States, without the Consent of the Legislatures of the States concerned as well as the Congress.

The Congress shall have Power to dispose of and make all needful Rules and Regulations respecting the Territory or other Property belonging to the United States; and nothing in this Constitution shall be so construed as to Prejudice any Claims of the United States, or of any particular State.

SECTION 4.

The United States shall guarantee to every State in this Union a Republican Form of Government, and shall protect each of them against Invasion; and on Application of the Legislature, or of the Executive (when the Legislature cannot be convened) against domestic Violence.

Article V

The Congress, whenever two-thirds of both Houses shall deem it necessary, shall propose Amendments to this Constitution, or, on the Application of the Legislatures of two-thirds of the several States, shall call a Convention for proposing Amendments, which, in either Case, shall be valid to all Intents and Purposes, as part of this Constitution, when ratified by the Legislatures of three-fourths of the several States, or by Conventions in three-fourths thereof, as the one or the other Mode of Ratification may be proposed by the Congress; Provided that no Amendment which may be made prior to the Year One thousand eight hundred and eight shall in any Manner affect the first and fourth Clauses in the Ninth Section of the first Article; and that no State, without its Consent, shall be deprived of its equal Suffrage in the Senate.

Article VI

All Debts contracted and Engagements entered into, before the Adoption of this Constitution, shall be as valid against the United States under this Constitution, as under the Confederation.

This Constitution, and the Laws of the United States which shall be made in Pursuance thereof; and all Treaties made, or which shall be made, under the Authority of the United States, shall be the supreme Law of the Land; and the Judges in every State shall be bound thereby, any Thing in the Constitution or Laws of any State to the Contrary notwithstatnding.

The Senators and Representatives before mentioned, and the Members of the several State Legislatures, and all executive and judicial Officers, both of the United States and of the several States, shall be bound by Oath or Affirmation to support this Constitution; but no religious Test shall ever be required as a qualification to any Office or public Trust under the United States.

Article VII

The Ratification of the Conventions of nine States shall be sufficient for the Establishment of this Constitution between the States so ratifying the same.

Done in Convention by the Unanimous Consent of the States present the Seventeenth Day of September in the Year of our Lord one thousand seven hundred and Eighty seven, and of the Independence of the United States of America the Twelfth. In Witness whereof We have hereunto subscribed our Names.[6]

George Washington

President and deputy from Virginia

Articles in Addition to, and Amendment of, the Constitution of the United States of America, Proposed by Congress, and Ratified by the Legislatures of the Several States, Pursuant to the Fifth Article of the Original Constitution[7]

---

[6] These are the full names of the signers, which in some cases are not the signatures on the document.

[7] This heading appears only in the joint resolution submitting the first ten amendments.

New Hampshire

John Langdon
Nicholas Gilman

Massachusetts

Nathaniel Gorham
Rufus King

Connecticut

William Samuel Johnson
Roger Sherman

New York

Alexander Hamilton

New Jersey

William Livingston
David Brearley
William Paterson
Jonathan Dayton

Pennsylvania

Benjamin Franklin
Thomas Mifflin
Robert Morris
George Clymer
Thomas FitzSimons
Jared Ingersoll
James Wilson
Gouverneur Morris

Delaware

George Read
Gunning Bedford,
 Jr.
John Dickinson
Richard Bassett
Jacob Broom

Maryland

James McHenry
Daniel of
 St. Thomas Jenifer
Daniel Carroll

Virginia

John Blair
James Madison, Jr.

North Carolina

William Blount
Richards Dobbs Spaight
Hugh Williamson

South Carolina

John Rutledge
Charles Cotesworth
 Pinckney
Charles Pinckney
Pierce Butler

Georgia

William Few
Abraham Baldwin

[Article I]

Congress shall make no law respecting an establishment of religion, or prohibiting the free exercise thereof; or abridging the freedom of speech, or of the press; or the right of the people peaceably to assemble, and to petition the Government for a redress of grievances.

[Article II]

A well regulated Militia, being necessary to the security of a free State, the right of the people to keep and bear Arms shall not be infringed.

[Article III]

No Soldier shall, in time of peace, be quartered in any house, without the consent of the Owner, nor in time of war, but in a manner to be prescribed by law.

[Article IV]

The right of the people to be secure in their persons, houses, papers, and effects, against unreasonable searches and seizures, shall not be violated, and no Warrants shall issue, but upon probable cause, supported by Oath or affirmation, and particularly describing the place to be searched, and the persons or things to be seized.

[Article V]

No person shall be held to answer for a capital or otherwise infamous crime, unless on a presentment or indictment of a Grand Jury, except in cases arising in the land or naval forces, or in the Militia, when in actual service in time of War or public danger; nor shall any person be subject for the same offence to be twice put in jeopardy of life or limb; nor shall be compelled in any criminal case to be a witness against himself, nor be deprived of life, liberty, or property, without due process of law; nor shall private property be taken for public use, without just compensation.

[Article VI]

In all criminal prosecutions, the accused shall enjoy the right to a speedy and public trial, by an impartial jury of the State and district wherein the crime shall have been committed, which district shall have been previously ascertained by law, and to be informed of the nature and cause of the accusation; to be confronted with the witnesses against him; to have compulsory process for obtaining witnesses in his favour, and to have the Assistance of Counsel for his defence.

[Article VII]

In suits at common law, where the value in controversy shall exceed twenty dollars, the right of trial by jury shall be preserved, and no fact tried by a jury, shall be otherwise reexamined in any Court of the United States, than according to the rules of the common law.

[Article VIII]

Excessive bail shall not be required, nor excessive fines imposed, nor cruel and unusual punishments inflicted.

[Article IX]

The enumeration in the Constitution, of certain rights, shall not be construed to deny or disparage others retained by the people.

[Article X]

The powers not delegated to the United States by the Constitution, nor prohibited by it to the States, are reserved to the States respectively, or to the people.
[Amendments I–X, in force 1791.]

[Article XI][8]

The Judicial power of the United States shall not be construed to extend to any suit in law or equity, commenced or prosecuted against one of the United States by Citizens of another State, or by Citizens or Subjects of any Foreign State.

---

[8] Adopted in 1798.

[Article XII][9]

The Electors shall meet in their respective States and vote by ballot for President and Vice-President, one of whom, at least, shall not be an inhabitant of the same State with themselves; they shall name in their ballots the person voted for as President, and in distinct ballots the person voted for as Vice-President, and they shall make distinct lists of all persons voted for as President, and of all persons voted for as Vice-President, and of the number of votes for each, which lists they shall sign and certify, and transmit sealed to the seat of the government of the United States, directed to the President of the Senate; — The President of the Senate shall, in the presence of the Senate and House of Representatives, open all the certificates and the votes shall then be counted; — The person having the greatest number of votes for President, shall be the President, if such number be a majority of the whole number of Electors appointed; and if no person have such majority, then from the persons having the highest numbers not exceeding three on the list of those voted for as President, the House of Representatives shall choose immediately, by ballot, the President. But in choosing the President, the votes shall be taken by states, the representation from each state having one vote; a quorum for this purpose shall consist of a member or members from two-thirds of the states, and a majority of all the states shall be necessary to a choice. And if the House of Representatives shall not choose a President whenever the right of choice shall devolve upon them, before the fourth day of March next following, then the Vice-President shall act as President, as in the case of the death or other constitutional disability of the President. — The person having the greatest number of votes as Vice-President, shall be the Vice-President, if such number be a majority of the whole number of Electors appointed, and if no person have a majority, then from the two highest numbers on the list, the Senate shall choose the Vice-President: a quorum for the purpose shall consist of two-thirds of the whole number of Senators, and a majority of the whole number shall be necessary to a choice. But no person constitutionally ineligible to the office of Presi-

---

[9] Adopted in 1804.

dent shall be eligible to that of Vice-President of the United States.

[Article XIII][10]

SECTION 1.
Neither slavery nor involuntary servitude, except as a punishment for crime whereof the party shall have been duly convicted, shall exist within the United States, or any place subject to their jurisdiction.

SECTION 2.
Congress shall have power to enforce this article by appropriate legislation.

[Article XIV][11]

SECTION 1.
All persons born or naturalized in the United States, and subject to the jurisdiction thereof, are citizens of the United States and of the State wherein they reside. No state shall abridge the privileges or immunities of citizens of the United States; nor shall any state deprive any person of life, liberty, or property, without due process of law, nor deny to any person within its jurisdiction the equal protection of the laws.

SECTION 2.
Representatives shall be apportioned among the several States according to their respective numbers, counting the whole number of persons in each State, excluding Indians not taxed. But when the right to vote at any election for the choice of electors for President and Vice-President of the United States, Representatives in Congress, the Executive and Judicial officers of a State, or the members of the Legislature thereof, is denied to any of the male inhabitants of such State, being twenty-one years of age, and citizens of the United States, or in any way abridged, except for participation in rebellion, or other crime, the basis of representation therein shall be reduced in the proportion which the number of such male

citizens shall bear to the whole number of male citizens twenty-one years of age in such State.

SECTION 3.
No person shall be a Senator or Representative in Congress, or elector of President and Vice-President, or hold any office, civil or military, under the United States, or under any State, who, having previously taken an oath, as a member of Congress, or as an officer of the United States, or as a member of any State legislature, or as an executive or judicial officer of any State, to support the Constitution of the United States, shall have engaged in insurrection or rebellion against the same, or given aid or comfort to the enemies thereof. But Congress may by a vote of two-thirds of each House, remove such disability.

SECTION 4.
The validity of the public debt of the United States, authorized by law, including debts incurred for payment of pensions and bounties for services in suppressing insurrection or rebellion, shall not be questioned. But neither the United States nor any State shall assume or pay any debts or obligation incurred in aid of insurrection or rebellion against the United States, or any claim for the loss or emancipation of any slave; but all such debts, obligations, and claims shall be held illegal and void.

SECTION 5.
The Congress shall have the power to enforce, by appropriate legislation, the provisions of this article.

[Article XV][12]

SECTION 1.
The right of citizens of the United States to vote shall not be denied or abridged by the United States or by any State on account of race, color, or previous condition of servitude —

SECTION 2.
The Congress shall have power to enforce this article by appropriate legislation.

---

[10] Adopted in 1865.
[11] Adopted in 1868.

[12] Adopted in 1870.

[Article XVI]¹³

The Congress shall have power to lay and collect taxes on incomes, from whatever source derived, without apportionment among the several States, and without regard to any census or enumeration.

[Article XVII]¹⁴

The Senate of the United States shall be composed of two Senators from each State, elected by the people thereof, for six years; and each Senator shall have one vote. The electors in each State shall have the qualifications requisite for electors of the most numerous branch of the State legislatures.

When vacancies happen in the representation of any State in the Senate, the executive authority of such State shall issue writs of election to fill such vacancies: *Provided,* That the legislature of any State may empower the executive thereof to make temporary appointments until the people fill the vacancies by election as the legislature may direct.

This amendment shall not be so construed as to affect the election or term of any Senator chosen before it becomes valid as part of the Constitution.

[Article XVIII]¹⁵

SECTION 1.
After one year from the ratification of this article the manufacture, sale, or transportation of intoxicating liquors within, the importation thereof into, or the exportation thereof from the United States and all territory subject to the jurisdiction thereof for beverage purposes is hereby prohibited.

SECTION 2.
The Congress and the several States shall have concurrent power to enforce this article by appropriate legislation.

SECTION 3.
This article shall be inoperative unless it shall have been ratified as an amendment to the Constitution by the legislatures of the several States, as provided in the Constitution, within seven years from the date of the submission hereof to the States by the Congress.

[Article XIX]¹⁶

The right of citizens of the United States to vote shall not be denied or abridged by the United States or by any State on account of sex.

Congress shall have power to enforce this article by appropriate legislation.

[Article XX]¹⁷

SECTION 1.
The terms of the President and Vice-President shall end at noon of the 20th day of January, and the terms of Senators and Representatives at noon on the 3d day of January, of the years in which such terms would have ended if this article had not been ratified; and the terms of their successors shall then begin.

SECTION 2.
The Congress shall assemble at least once in every year, and such meeting shall begin at noon on the 3d day of January, unless they shall by law appoint a different day.

SECTION 3.
If, at the time fixed for the beginning of the term of the President, the President elect shall have died, the Vice-President elect shall become President. If a President shall not have been chosen before the time fixed for the beginning of his term, or if the President elect shall have failed to qualify, then the Vice-President elect shall act as President until a President shall have qualified; and the Congress may by law provide for the case wherein neither a President elect nor a Vice-President elect shall have qualified, declaring who

---

¹³ Adopted in 1913.
¹⁴ Adopted in 1913.
¹⁵ Adopted in 1918.

¹⁶ Adopted in 1920.
¹⁷ Adopted in 1933.

shall then act as President, or the manner in which one who is to act shall be selected, and such person shall act accordingly until a President or Vice-President shall have qualified.

SECTION 4.
The Congress may by law provide for the case of the death of any of the persons from whom the House of Representatives may choose a President whenever the right of choice shall have devolved upon them, and for the case of the death of any of the persons from whom the Senate may choose a Vice-President whenever the right of choice shall have devolved upon them.

SECTION 5.
Sections 1 and 2 shall take effect on the 15th day of October following the ratification of this article.

SECTION 6.
This article shall be inoperative unless it shall have been ratified as an amendment to the Constitution by the legislatures of three-fourths of the several States within seven years from the date of its submission.

[Article XXI][18]

SECTION 1.
The eighteenth article of amendment to the Constitution of the United States is hereby repealed.

SECTION 2.
The transportation or importation into any State, Territory, or possession of the United States for delivery or use therein of intoxicating liquors, in violation of the laws thereof, is hereby prohibited.

SECTION 3.
This article shall be inoperative unless it shall have been ratified as an amendment to the Constitution by conventions in the several States, as provided in the Constitution, within seven years from the date of the submission hereof to the States by the Congress.

[18] Adopted in 1933.

[Article XXII][19]

No person shall be elected to the office of the President more than twice, and no person who has held the office of President, or acted as President, for more than two years of a term to which some other person was elected President shall be elected to the office of the President more than once.

But this Article shall not apply to any person holding the office of President when this Article was proposed by the Congress, and shall not prevent any person who may be holding the office of President, or acting as President, during the term within which this Article becomes operative from holding the office of President or acting as President during the remainder of such term.

This article shall be inoperative unless it shall have been ratified as an amendment to the Constitution by the legislatures of three-fourths of the several states within seven years from the date of its submission to the states by the Congress.

[Article XXIII][20]

SECTION 1.
The District constituting the seat of Government of the United States shall appoint in such manner as the Congress may direct:

A number of electors of President and Vice-President equal to the whole number of Senators and Representatives in Congress to which the District would be entitled if it were a State, but in no event more than the least populous State; they shall be in addition to those appointed by the States, but they shall be considered, for the purposes of the election of President and Vice-President, to be electors appointed by a State; and they shall meet in the District and perform such duties as provided by the twelfth article of amendment.

SECTION 2.
The Congress shall have power to enforce this article by appropriate legislation.

[19] Adopted in 1951.
[20] Adopted in 1961.

[Article XXIV][21]

SECTION 1.

The right of citizens of the United States to vote in any primary or other election for President or Vice President, for electors for President or Vice President, or for Senator or Representative in Congress, shall not be denied or abridged by the United States or any state by reason of failure to pay any poll tax or other tax.

SECTION 2.

The Congress shall have the power to enforce this article by appropriate legislation.

[Article XXV][22]

SECTION 1.

In case of the removal of the President from office or of his death or resignation, the Vice President shall become President.

SECTION 2.

Whenever there is a vacancy in the office of the Vice President, the President shall nominate a Vice President who shall take office upon confirmation by a majority vote of both Houses of Congress.

SECTION 3.

Whenever the President transmits to the President Pro Tempore of the Senate and the Speaker of the House of Representatives his written declaration that he is unable to discharge the powers and duties of his office, and until he transmits to them a written declaration to the contrary, such powers and duties shall be discharged by the Vice President as Acting President.

SECTION 4.

Whenever the Vice President and a majority of either the principal officers of the executive departments or of such other body as Congress may

by law provide, transmit to the President Pro Tempore of the Senate and the Speaker of the House of Representatives their written declaration that the President is unable to discharge the powers and duties of his office, the Vice President shall immediately assume the powers and duties of the office as Acting President.

Thereafter, when the President transmits to the President Pro Tempore of the Senate and the Speaker of the House of Representatives his written declaration that no inability exists, he shall resume the powers and duties of his office unless the Vice President and a majority of either the principal officers of the executive departments or of such other body as Congress may by law provide, transmit within four days to the President Pro Tempore of the Senate and the Speaker of the House of Representatives their written declaration that the President is unable to discharge the powers and duties of his office. Thereupon Congress shall decide the issue, assembling within forty-eight hours for that purpose if not in session. If the Congress, within twenty-one days after receipt of the latter written declaration, or, if Congress is not in session, within twenty-one days after Congress is required to assemble, determines by two-thirds vote of both Houses that the President is unable to discharge the powers and duties of his office, the Vice President shall continue to discharge the same as Acting President; otherwise, the President will resume the powers and duties of his office.

[Article XXVI][23]

SECTION 1.

The right of citizens of the United States, who are eighteen years of age or older, to vote shall not be denied or abridged by the United States or by any State on account of age.

SECTION 2.

The Congress shall have power to enforce this article by appropriate legislation.

---

[21] Adopted in 1964.
[22] Adopted in 1967.

---

[23] Adopted in 1971.

Admission of States to the Union*

1	Delaware	*Dec. 7, 1787*	26	Michigan	*Jan. 26, 1837*
2	Pennsylvania	*Dec. 12, 1787*	27	Florida	*Mar. 3, 1845*
3	New Jersey	*Dec. 18, 1787*	28	Texas	*Dec. 29, 1845*
4	Georgia	*Jan. 2, 1788*	29	Iowa	*Dec. 28, 1846*
5	Connecticut	*Jan. 9, 1788*	30	Wisconsin	*May 29, 1848*
6	Massachusetts	*Feb. 6, 1788*	31	California	*Sept. 9, 1850*
7	Maryland	*Apr. 28, 1788*	32	Minnesota	*May 11, 1858*
8	South Carolina	*May 23, 1788*	33	Oregon	*Feb. 14, 1859*
9	New Hampshire	*June 21, 1788*	34	Kansas	*Jan. 29, 1861*
10	Virginia	*June 25, 1788*	35	West Virginia	*June 19, 1863*
11	New York	*July 26, 1788*	36	Nevada	*Oct. 31, 1864*
12	North Carolina	*Nov. 21, 1789*	37	Nebraska	*Mar. 1, 1867*
13	Rhode Island	*May 29, 1790*	38	Colorado	*Aug. 1, 1876*
14	Vermont	*Mar. 4, 1791*	39	North Dakota	*Nov. 2, 1889*
15	Kentucky	*June 1, 1792*	40	South Dakota	*Nov. 2, 1889*
16	Tennessee	*June 1, 1796*	41	Montana	*Nov. 8, 1889*
17	Ohio	*Mar. 1, 1803*	42	Washington	*Nov. 11, 1889*
18	Louisiana	*Apr. 30, 1812*	43	Idaho	*July 3, 1890*
19	Indiana	*Dec. 11, 1816*	44	Wyoming	*July 10, 1890*
20	Mississippi	*Dec. 10, 1817*	45	Utah	*Jan. 4, 1896*
21	Illinois	*Dec. 3, 1818*	46	Oklahoma	*Nov. 16, 1907*
22	Alabama	*Dec. 14, 1819*	47	New Mexico	*Jan. 6, 1912*
23	Maine	*Mar. 15, 1820*	48	Arizona	*Feb. 14, 1912*
24	Missouri	*Aug. 10, 1821*	49	Alaska	*Jan. 3, 1959*
25	Arkansas	*June 15, 1836*	50	Hawaii	*Aug. 21, 1959*

* In the case of the first thirteen states, the date given is that of ratification of the Constitution.

Presidential Elections

Year	Candidates	Parties	Popular Vote	Electoral Vote
1789	**GEORGE WASHINGTON (Va.)** *			69
	John Adams			34
	Others			35
1792	**GEORGE WASHINGTON (Va.)**			132
	John Adams			77
	George Clinton			50
	Others			5
1796	**JOHN ADAMS (Mass.)**	Federalist		71
	Thomas Jefferson	Democratic-Republican		68
	Thomas Pinckney	Federalist		59
	Aaron Burr	Dem.-Rep.		30
	Others			48
1800	**THOMAS JEFFERSON (Va.)**	Dem.-Rep.		73
	Aaron Burr	Dem.-Rep.		73
	John Adams	Federalist		65
	C. C. Pinckney	Federalist		64
	John Jay	Federalist		1
1804	**THOMAS JEFFERSON (Va.)**	Dem.-Rep.		162
	C. C. Pinckney	Federalist		14
1808	**JAMES MADISON (Va.)**	Dem.-Rep.		122
	C. C. Pinckney	Federalist		47
	George Clinton	Dem.-Rep.		6
1812	**JAMES MADISON (Va.)**	Dem.-Rep.		128
	De Witt Clinton	Federalist		89
1816	**JAMES MONROE (Va.)**	Dem.-Rep.		183
	Rufus King	Federalist		34
1820	**JAMES MONROE (Va.)**	Dem.-Rep.		231
	John Quincy Adams	Dem.-Rep.		1
1824	**JOHN Q. ADAMS (Mass.)**	Dem.-Rep.	108,740	84
	Andrew Jackson	Dem.-Rep.	153,544	99
	William H. Crawford	Dem.-Rep.	46,618	41
	Henry Clay	Dem.-Rep.	47,136	37

* State of residence at time of election.

xviii

Year	Candidates	Parties	Popular Vote	Electoral Vote
1828	**ANDREW JACKSON** (Tenn.)	Democrat	647,286	178
	John Quincy Adams	National Republican	508,064	83
1832	**ANDREW JACKSON** (Tenn.)	Democrat	687,502	219
	Henry Clay	National Republican	530,189	49
	John Floyd	Independent		11
	William Wirt	Anti-Mason	33,108	7
1836	**MARTIN VAN BUREN** (N.Y.)	Democrat	765,483	170
	W. H. Harrison	Whig		73
	Hugh L. White	Whig	739,795	26
	Daniel Webster	Whig		14
	W. P. Mangum	Independent		11
1840	**WILLIAM H. HARRISON** (Ohio)	Whig	1,274,624	234
	Martin Van Buren	Democrat	1,127,781	60
	J. G. Birney	Liberty	7,069	—
1844	**JAMES K. POLK** (Tenn.)	Democrat	1,338,464	170
	Henry Clay	Whig	1,300,097	105
	J. G. Birney	Liberty	62,300	—
1848	**ZACHARY TAYLOR** (La.)	Whig	1,360,967	163
	Lewis Cass	Democrat	1,222,342	127
	Martin Van Buren	Free-Soil	291,263	—
1852	**FRANKLIN PIERCE** (N.H.)	Democrat	1,601,117	254
	Winfield Scott	Whig	1,385,453	42
	John P. Hale	Free-Soil	155,825	—
1856	**JAMES BUCHANAN** (Pa.)	Democrat	1,832,955	174
	John C. Frémont	Republican	1,339,932	114
	Millard Fillmore	American	871,731	8
1860	**ABRAHAM LINCOLN** (Ill.)	Republican	1,865,593	180
	Stephen A. Douglas	Democrat	1,382,713	12
	John C. Breckinridge	Democrat	848,356	72
	John Bell	Union	592,906	39
1864	**ABRAHAM LINCOLN** (Ill.)	Republican	2,213,655	212
	George B. McClellan	Democrat	1,805,237	21
1868	**ULYSSES S. GRANT** (Ill.)	Republican	3,012,833	214
	Horatio Seymour	Democrat	2,703,249	80
1872	**ULYSSES S. GRANT** (Ill.)	Republican	3,597,132	286
	Horace Greeley	Democrat; Liberal Republican	2,834,125	66
1876	**RUTHERFORD B. HAYES** (Ohio)	Republican	4,036,298	185
	Samuel J. Tilden	Democrat	4,300,590	184
1880	**JAMES A. GARFIELD** (Ohio)	Republican	4,454,416	214
	Winfield S. Hancock	Democrat	4,444,952	155
1884	**GROVER CLEVELAND** (N.Y.)	Democrat	4,874,986	219
	James G. Blaine	Republican	4,851,981	182
1888	**BENJAMIN HARRISON** (Ind.)	Republican	5,439,853	233
	Grover Cleveland	Democrat	5,540,309	168

Year	Candidates	Parties	Popular Vote	Electoral Vote
1892	**GROVER CLEVELAND (N.Y.)**	Democrat	5,556,918	277
	Benjamin Harrison	Republican	5,176,108	145
	James B. Weaver	People's	1,041,028	22
1896	**WILLIAM McKINLEY (Ohio)**	Republican	7,104,779	271
	William J. Bryan	Democrat-People's	6,502,925	176
1900	**WILLIAM McKINLEY (Ohio)**	Republican	7,207,923	292
	William J. Bryan	Dem.-Populist	6,358,133	155
1904	**THEODORE ROOSEVELT (N.Y.)**	Republican	7,623,486	336
	Alton B. Parker	Democrat	5,077,911	140
	Eugene V. Debs	Socialist	402,283	—
1908	**WILLIAM H. TAFT (Ohio)**	Republican	7,678,908	321
	William J. Bryan	Democrat	6,409,104	162
	Eugene V. Debs	Socialist	420,793	—
1912	**WOODROW WILSON (N.J.)**	Democrat	6,293,454	435
	Theodore Roosevelt	Progressive	4,119,538	88
	William H. Taft	Republican	3,484,980	8
	Eugene V. Debs	Socialist	900,672	—
1916	**WOODROW WILSON (N.J.)**	Democrat	9,129,606	277
	Charles E. Hughes	Republican	8,538,221	254
	A. L. Benson	Socialist	585,113	—
1920	**WARREN G. HARDING (Ohio)**	Republican	16,152,200	404
	James M. Cox	Democrat	9,147,353	127
	Eugene V. Debs	Socialist	919,799	—
1924	**CALVIN COOLIDGE (Mass.)**	Republican	15,725,016	382
	John W. Davis	Democrat	8,386,503	136
	Robert M. LaFollette	Progressive	4,822,856	13
1928	**HERBERT HOOVER (Calif.)**	Republican	21,391,381	444
	Alfred E. Smith	Democrat	15,016,443	87
	Norman Thomas	Socialist	267,835	—
1932	**FRANKLIN D. ROOSEVELT (N.Y.)**	Democrat	22,821,857	472
	Herbert Hoover	Republican	15,761,841	59
	Norman Thomas	Socialist	881,951	—
1936	**FRANKLIN D. ROOSEVELT (N.Y.)**	Democrat	27,751,597	523
	Alfred M. Landon	Republican	16,679,583	8
	William Lemke	Union and others	882,479	—
1940	**FRANKLIN D. ROOSEVELT (N.Y.)**	Democrat	27,244,160	449
	Wendell L. Willkie	Republican	22,305,198	82
1944	**FRANKLIN D. ROOSEVELT (N.Y.)**	Democrat	25,602,504	432
	Thomas E. Dewey	Republican	22,006,285	99
1948	**HARRY S TRUMAN (Mo.)**	Democrat	24,105,695	304
	Thomas E. Dewey	Republican	21,969,170	189
	J. Strom Thurmond	State-Rights Democrat	1,169,021	38
	Henry A. Wallace	Progressive	1,156,103	—
1952	**DWIGHT D. EISENHOWER (N.Y.)**	Republican	33,936,252	442
	Adlai E. Stevenson	Democrat	27,314,992	89

Year	Candidates	Parties	Popular Vote	Electoral Vote
1956	**DWIGHT D. EISENHOWER (N.Y.)**	Republican	35,575,420	457
	Adlai E. Stevenson	Democrat	26,033,066	73
	Other	—	—	1
1960	**JOHN F. KENNEDY (Mass.)**	Democrat	34,227,096	303
	Richard M. Nixon	Republican	34,108,546	219
	Other	—	—	15
1964	**LYNDON B. JOHNSON (Tex.)**	Democrat	43,126,506	486
	Barry M. Goldwater	Republican	27,176,799	52
1968	**RICHARD M. NIXON (N.Y.)**	Republican	31,770,237	301
	Hubert H. Humphrey	Democrat	31,270,533	191
	George Wallace	American Indep.	9,906,141	46
1972	**RICHARD M. NIXON (N.Y.)**	Republican	47,169,911	520
	George S. McGovern	Democrat	29,170,383	17
	Other	—	—	1
1976	**JAMES E. CARTER, JR. (Ga.)**	Democrat	40,828,657	297
	Gerald R. Ford	Republican	39,145,520	240
	Other	—	—	1
1980	**RONALD REAGAN (Calif.)**	Republican	43,901,812	489
	James E. Carter, Jr.	Democrat	35,483,820	49
	John B. Anderson	Independent	5,719,722	—
	Ed Clark	Libertarian	921,188	—
1984	**RONALD REAGAN (Calif.)**	Republican	52,609,797	525
	Walter F. Mondale	Democrat	36,450,613	13

Index

Ableman v. *Booth*, 137
Abolitionism, 103–108, 122, 136. *See also* Slavery
Abortion laws, 345
Academy and College of Philadelphia, 22
Acheson, Dean, 300
Adams, Henry, 201
Adams, John Quincy, 32, 43, 47, 55, 62–63, 73, 108, 110–111
Adams, Samuel, 31–32
Addams, Jane, 195, 212
Afghanistan, Soviet invasion of, 363
Afrika Corps, 287
Agency for International Development, 349
Agnew, Spiro, 316, 324, 336, 338, 340
Agricultural Adjustment Act (1938), 268
Agricultural Adjustment Administration, 259–261, 268
Agriculture: slash-and-burn, 4; colonial, 15–17; in Northwest and South, 90–92; subsistence, 92; commercial farming, 192–193; railroads and, 193; Populists' rise and, 206–207; 1920s decline in, 250–251; during Great Depression, 256; New Deal and, 259–261; Second New Deal and, 266; AAA and, 268
Aguinaldo, Emilio, 226
Air Commerce Act (1926), 249
Air force, 318
Alabama claims, 173–174
Alamance, Battle of (1771), 29
Alamo, 122
Alaska, 173, 225; pipeline, 322
Albany Plan, 24–25
Albermarle settlements, 9
Algonquins, 5
Alien and Sedition Acts, 63–65
Alliance for Progress, 349
Allies. *See* World War II
Almanacs, 22
Altgeld, John P., 189
Amalgamated Association of Iron and Steel Workers, 188
America First Committee, 275
American Antislavery Society, 104
American Bar Association, 337
American Colonization Society, 103
American continents, peopling of, 1
American Equal Rights Association, 215
American Expeditionary Force, 240–242
American Federation of Labor, 187–188, 195, 207, 266–267
American Magazine, 22
American party. *See* Know-Nothings
American Philosophical Society, 23
American Railway Union, 189
Anarchists, 187–188
Anderson, John, 346
Anderson, Robert, 145, 146

Anderson, Sherwood, 252
Andros, Edmund, 11–12
Anthony, Susan B., 102, 215
Antiballistic missile system, 358
Antietam, Battle of (1862), 160
Anti-Inflation Act (1942), 283
Antin, Mary, 199
Anti-Saloon League, 214
Appeasement policy, 274
Appomattox, surrender at, 164
Arms race: weapons testing and, 350; détente and, 357–358; SALT talks and, 361, 362; under Reagan, 363, 365
Armstrong, Louis, 252
Armstrong, Neil, 315
Arthur, Chester A., 204
Articles of Confederation, 37–38, 50, 51
Artisanship, colonial, 17
Ashburton, Alexander, 119
Assemblies, colonial, 24, 27
Assembly line, 185
Associated Press, 88
Association Opposed to Woman Suffrage, 215
Atlantic Charter, 277
Atomic Energy Act (1946), 295
Atomic weapons, 281–282, 285, 291, 295
Attlee, Clement, 291
Austin, Stephen, 121, 122
Austria, 274
Automation, 317
Automobile, 185, 321

Babcock, Orville E., 175
Baby boom, 318
Bacon, Nathaniel, 6
Baer, George F., 216–217
Baghdad Pact (1955), 308
Baker, Newton D., 213
Ballinger-Pinchot controversy, 218
Bancroft, George, 39
Banking Act (1935), 263
Bank of the United States, 57, 58, 72, 77, 114–115
Banks and banking: state, 72; "pet," 114; reform under Wilson, 220; 1933 crisis in, 257–259; later New Deal action on, 263. *See also* Economy
Bao Dai, 307
Barbary pirates, 66
Barron, James, 69
Barton, Clara, 150
Baruch, Bernard, 239, 295
Baseball, 200
Bay of Pigs, 350
Beauregard, P. G. T., 146, 157–158
Begin, Menachem, 362

Belgium, 274
Bell, John, 145
Benton, Thomas Hart, 264
Berkeley, William, 6, 9
Berlin crisis, 350
Bernstein, Barton, 260
Biddle, Nicholas, 114
Big Four, 242
Bill of Rights, 55–56
Birney, James G., 104, 120
Birth rate, 194, 318
Black Codes, 166
Black Hawk, Chief, 112
Blackmun, Harry A., 337
Black Muslims, 327
Blacks: after Civil War, 164; suffrage, 165, 169, 170, 198; citizenship for, 168–169; as Reconstruction politicians, 171; pre–World War I status of, 197–199; access to education, 199; post–World War I treatment of, 245–246; New Deal and, 269–270; employment from war effort, 284–285; desegregation of, 312; job-training programs and, 330–331; black power movement and, 331–332; busing and, 337. *See also* Abolitionism; Civil rights; Slavery
Blaine, James G., 205
Bland-Allison Act (1878), 204
Blassingame, John, 107
Bonaparte, Napoleon, 63, 67–68
Booth, John Wilkes, 166
Borglum, Gutzon, 264
Bosses, political, 195, 196, 210
Boston Massacre, 31–32
Boston Tea Party, 33
Bourbons, 197
Bradley, Omar, 289
Bragg, Braxton, 159, 161
Brain Trust, 256
Brandeis, Louis D., 214
Breckinridge, John C., 144
Breeder reactor, 322
Brezhnev, Leonid, 357, 358, 360–362
Bricker, John W., 286
Bristow, Benjamin H., 174–175
Brook Farm, 100
Brooks, Preston, 140
Brown, John, 140, 143
Brown, Joseph, 154
Brown v. *Board of Education of Topeka*, 312
Bruce, Blanche K., 171
Bryan, William Jennings, 180, 209–210, 218, 225
Buchanan, James, 137, 140–141, 145
Budget, 346–348
Buffalo, 191–192
Bull Run, battles of (1861, 1862), 157–158, 160
Bunau-Varilla, Philippe, 228
Bunker Hill, Battle of (1775), 40
Bureau of Indian Affairs, 191
Bureau of Refugees, Freedman, and Abandoned Lands, 168
Burger, Warren, 337
Burgoyne, John, 40–41
Burke Act (1906), 192–193

Burke-Wadsworth bill (1940), 276
Burnside, Ambrose E., 160
Burr, Aaron, 64, 65, 68–69
Bush, Vannevar, 285, 318
Business: rise of, 183–184; in specific industries, 184–185; distribution of wealth and, 186, 322–323; philosophy of, 201–203; in Caribbean, 229; voluntarism and, 249; mergers, 249–250; NRA and, 261–262. *See also* Corporations; Economy; Industry; Labor
Busing, 337
Butler, Andrew P., 140
Byrd I, William, 19
Byrnes, James F., 293

Calhoun, John C., 71, 112, 113, 119, 122, 135
California, 123–124, 127, 133
Calley, William L., 356
Calvert, George, 5–6
Cambodia, invasion of, 356
Camp meeting, Baptist, 98
Canada, 28, 70–72, 119
Canal system, 85–86
Capitalists, types of, 84
Caribbean, 228–230
Carlos, Don, 159
Carnegie, Andrew, 185, 188
Carolina, settlement of, 9
Caroline incident, 119
Carpetbaggers, 171
Carranza, Venustiano, 230
Carroll, Charles, 86
Carter, Jimmy, 316, 342–346, 361–363
Cass, Lewis, 127–128
Castro, Fidel, 310–311, 349–351, 364
Catholics, 21, 102
Cato's Letters, 33
Catt, Carrie Chapman, 215
Cattle industry, 190–191
Caucus nomination, 109–110
Central Alliance, 230–231
Central America, Reagan and, 364, 365
Central Intelligence Agency, 295, 350, 364
Central Pacific Railroad Company, 147, 182–183
Château-Thierry, Battle of, 241
Chancellorsville, Battle of (1863), 160
Charles II, 9–10, 11
Charleston, 9
Chase, Salmon P., 150
Chattanooga, Battle of (1863), 161
Chávez, César, 332–333
Cherokee Nation v. *Georgia*, 113
Cherokees, 112–113
Chesapeake-Leopard incident, 69
Chiang Kai-shek, 292, 300, 306, 356–357
Chicano movement, 332–333
Chickamauga, Battle of (1863), 161
Child labor, 186, 221
China: trade with, 84; Open Door policy and, 226–227; Japanese attack on (1937), 273; revolution in, 300; attack on Taiwan, 307–308; Soviet Union and, 351; rapprochement with, 356–357, 362

Chinese Communists, 281

Christian Front, 264

Churchill, Winston, 275–277, 287–289, 291–292

Church of England, 3, 20–21

Cities: growth of, 94–95; immigrants in, 194–195; health problems in, 195–196; boss rule in, 196; progressive reform in, 212–213; urban renewal projects and, 320

Citizenship, 168–169, 192

City manager plan, 213

Civilian Conservation Corps, 259

Civil rights: 1866 legislation, 168; 1883 cases, 198; 1957 legislation, 312; Kennedy and, 327–328; poverty and, 328–329; 1964 legislation, 329, 344; 1968 legislation, 332

Civil service, reform of, 204–205

Civil War: industrialization and, 87; as first modern war, 131–132; events leading to, 133–146, 149; relative strengths of antagonists, 146; financing of, 146–148, 152–153; draft systems, 148, 152–154; Union mobilization for, 148–150; women and, 148–150; politics during, 150–151, 154; emancipation of slaves and, 151–152; Confederate government and, 152; commanders in chief of, 155; sea power's role in, 155–156; Europe and, 156–157; opening battles, 157–158; Western theater, 158–159; Virginia front, 159–160, 162; 1863 battles, 160–161; ending of, 161–164; aftermath of, 164

Civil Works Administration, 259

Clark, Champ, 219

Clark, George Rogers, 48

Clark, William, 68

Class structure, 18–19, 92, 139

Clay, Cassius M., 106

Clay, Henry, 71, 76–77, 110, 113, 114, 116, 118–120, 134–135

Clayton Antitrust Act, 220

Clean Air acts (1963, 1965, 1970), 321

Clemens, Samuel, 201

Clermont, 85

Cleveland, Grover, 189, 205, 207–209, 222–223

Clinton, George, 65

Clinton, Henry, 42–43

Clippers, 84

Coal, 83

Coercive Acts, 33

Cold War: origins of, 281, 298; atomic research and, 295; containment policy and, 297–299, 305; NATO and, 299–300; Korean War and, 300–303, 305–306; McCarthyism and, 303, 311–312; global political polarization and, 351. *See also* Eisenhower, Dwight D.

Colleges and universities. *See* Education

Colombia, 228

Colonial empire, 225–226

Colonies: cultural diversity of, 1–2; mercantilism and, 3, 16, 17; environment of, 3–4; Indian relations and, 4–5, 9, 28–29; settlement of, 5–11; types of, 11; Glorious Revolution (1688) and, 11–12; labor shortage in, 13–14; immigration to, 14–15; population growth in, 14–15; agriculture in, 15–17; industries in, 17–18; money and commerce in, 18; class structure of, 18–19; home and family in, 19–20; religions of,

20–22; Great Awakening and, 21–22; education in, 22–23; assemblies in, 24, 27; move toward self-government of, 24–25, 27–28; British conflicts and, 25–27; French settlements and, 25; Britain's new imperialism and, 28–30; self-interest of, 29–30; seeds of revolt in, 30–33. *See also* Revolutionary War

Colored Farmers' Alliance, 206

Columbia University, 22

Commerce, 18, 47, 78

Commercial farming, 192–193

Commission on Civil Disorders report (1968), 332

Committee for Industrial Organization, 266–267, 270

Committee for the Re-election of the President, 339, 340, 341

Committee of European Economic Cooperation, 299

Committee on Public Information, 240

Committees of correspondence, 35

Committee to Defend America by Aiding the Allies, 275

Communication, 86–88, 324–325

Communism, 245–246. *See also* China; Cold War; McCarthy, Joseph; Soviet Union

Communities, experimental, 100

Compromise: of 1850, 134–136; of 1877, 132

Computer, 317

Concord, Battle of, 35–36

Confederate States of America, 145, 152, 154, 157. *See also* Civil War

Confederation government, 49, 50

Congress: Continental, 35, 36, 37–38; powers of, 37–38, 52, 77; early Indian policy of, 48; interstate commerce and, 77–78; Reconstruction and, 167–170. *See also* Government; Political parties; Politics

Congress of Racial Equality, 327, 331

Conkin, Paul, 260

Connecticut, 8

Conscription, 355–356

Conscription Act, First (1862), 153

Conservation, 217, 262–263

Constitution, 45–46, 52–55

Constitutional amendments: Bill of Rights, 55–56; Twelfth, 65; Thirteenth, 164; Fourteenth, 132, 168–169; Fifteenth, 132, 170, 215; Sixteenth, 219; Seventeenth, 214, 219; Eighteenth, 214–215, 246; Nineteenth, 215, 246–247; Twentieth, 257; Twenty-first, 254; Twenty-second, 312–313; Twenty-third, 329; Twenty-fourth, 329; Twenty-fifth, 316; Twenty-sixth, 338

Constitutional convention, 51–52

Constitutional Union party, 144–145

Constitutions, state, 37

Construction gangs, 89

Consumers, 250, 320–322

Consumers Union, 321

Containment policy, 297–299, 305

Continental army, 40

Continental Congress: First, 35; Second, 36–38

Continental System, 69

Contract theory, 32–33

Controlled Materials Plan, 283

Conventions, state, 54

Coolidge, Calvin, 248–249

Cooper, James Fennimore, 97
Copperheads, 150
Coral Sea, Battle of (1942), 287
Cordwainers, 89
Corn, 4
Cornwallis, Charles, 42–43
Corporations, 183–185. *See also* Business
Cotton, 75, 91–92
Cotton gin, 91
Coughlin, Charles, 264
Council of Economic Advisors, 296
Courts, 55. *See also* Judiciary; Supreme Court
Cox, James M., 247
Cox, John, 172
Cox, La Wanda, 172
Coxey, Jacob S., 208
Crandall, Prudence, 105
Crane, Stephen, 201
Craven, Avery, 149
Crazy Horse, 192
Crédit Mobilier, 174
Creeks, 48, 71, 110–111
Creel, George, 240
Creole mutiny, 119
Crick, Francis H. C., 317
Crittenden Compromise, 145
Cromwell, William Nelson, 228
Cuba: attempted purchase of, 137; Spanish-American War and, 223; independence of, 226; 1933 revolutions in, 272; Castro's revolution in, 310–311; missile crisis in, 350–351
Cuffe, Paul, 103
Cultural lag, 315
Culture: colonial, 1–2; education, 22–23, 96, 98–101, 199, 252, 312, 323–324, 330; post-Revolutionary, 96–97; literature, 96–97, 201, 252; slave, 106; leisure, 200; publishing, 200–201; Jazz Age, 251–253; New Deal and, 263–264; television and, 324–325
Currency. *See* Money
Currency Act (1764), 29
Curzon line, 292
Custer, George A., 192
Customs commissioners, 31
Czechoslovakia, 274, 299

Dairy farming, 88
Daley, Richard J., 338
Danbury Hatters' strike (1902), 190
Darwinism, Social, 202
Daugherty, Harry, 248
Davis, David, 177
Davis, Jefferson, 138, 152, 155
Davis, John W., 249
Dawes, William, 35
Dawes Severalty Act (1887), 192, 269
D-Day, 289
Debs, Eugene V., 189
Debt: post-Revolutionary, 48–50; Confederate, 49; Hamilton plan and, 57–58
Declaration of Independence, 36
Declaration of Indian Purpose, 333
Declaration of the United Nations, 281

Declaratory Act (1766), 31
Deere, John, 90
Defense, 327, 349. *See also* Arms race
Deficit problem, 347, 348
De Grasse, François Joseph Paul, 43
Deism, 97
Deloria, Vine, Jr., 333
Democracy, industry and, 81
Democratic party: Whigs vs., 115–117; 1852 platform, 136; foreign expansion and, 137; 1860 division of, 144; late 19th-century ascendancy, 205–206; East's split with West and South, 208–209; urban-rural split in, 249; 1968 convention of, 335. *See also* Elections, congressional; Government; Politics; *specific Presidents*
Democratic Republicans, 111
Demography. *See* Population
Denmark, 274
Dennis v. *United States*, 303
Department of Commerce and Labor, 216
Department of Housing and Urban Development, 319
Department of the Navy, 63
Depression: of 1819–1825, 75; of 1837, 116; of 1856, 141; of 1873, 175; of 1893, 208; of 1929–1933, 238, 254–257. *See also* New Deal
DePriest, Oscar, 269
Desegregation, 312
Détente, 315, 357–358, 360–363
Detroit race riots (1943), 284
Dewey, George, 224
Dewey, John, 203
Dewey, Thomas E., 286, 297
Díaz, Porfirio, 230
Dickens, Charles, 96–97
Dickinson, John, 32
Diem, Ngo Dinh, 307
Dien Bien Phu, 306
Diplomacy: dollar, 229–230; sputnik, 309: China-Soviet relations and, 351; rapprochement with China, 356–357, 362; détente with Russia, 357–358, 360–363; Kissinger-Ford, 360–361; "shuttle," 360. *See also* Foreign policy
Direct primary, 213
Displaced Persons Act (1950), 304
District of Columbia, 329
Division of powers, 54
Divorce, 20, 284
Dix, Dorothea, 100, 148
DNA, 317
Dole, Robert J., 342
Dollar diplomacy, 229–230
Domino theory, 306–307
Douglas, Stephen A., 86, 127, 135, 138, 142–144
Douglass, Frederick, 103, 151
Draft, 148, 152–154, 355–356
Dred Scott v. *Sanford*, 141
Dreiser, Theodore, 201
Dulles, John Foster, 305, 307–309
Dumbarton Oaks, 293
Duryea, Charles E., 185
Duryea, J. Frank, 185
Dutch, 5, 10, 277

East Germany, 299
East India Company, 33
Economic Opportunity Act (1964), 333
Economy: under Jeffersonian Republicans, 66–67, 72–73, 75; transportation system and, 72, 73, 84–88, 182–183, 185; sectionalist tendencies and, 81; regional differences in, 88–94; population growth and, 94–95; turn-of-the-century industrialization, 182; labor and, 186–190; distribution of wealth and, 186; of western frontier, 190–192; commercial farming and, 192–193; government intervention in, 202–203, 207, 217; 1920s prosperity, 249–250; post–Korean War, 311; under Kennedy, 327; under Nixon, 337–338; under Ford, 342; under Carter, 343–344; supply-side theory of, 346; under Reagan, 346–347. *See also* Business; Depression; Industry
Education: colonial, 22–23; public, 96, 98–100; women and, 101, 199; differential access to, 199; universal, 199; during 1920s, 252; desegregation in, 312; in post-1960s, 323–324; federal aid to, 330
Edwards, Jonathan, 21, 23
Egypt, 308–309, 360
Ehrlichman, John, 336, 339–341
Einstein, Albert, 285
Eisenhower, Dwight D., 256, 286, 300, 305, 308–313, 353. *See also* Cold War
Eisenhower Doctrine, 309
El Caney, Battle of, 224
Elections, congressional: of 1858, 142; of 1866, 169; of 1934, 264
Elections, presidential, 109–110. *See also specific Presidents*
Electoral Commission, 176–177
Electoral Court Act (1876), 205
Elementary and Secondary Education Act (1965), 330
Elk Hills, 248
Ellsberg, Daniel, 339
Ellsworth, Oliver, 52
El Salvador, 364
Emancipation Proclamation, 151–152
Emerson, Ralph Waldo, 97
Employment: of women, 196–197; of blacks, 284–285
Employment Act (1946), 296
Empress of China, 84
Energy crisis, 321–322
Energy policy, 344
Engine, gasoline, 185
England. *See* Great Britain
English bill (1858), 142
Entente, 230
Equal Rights Amendment, 345
Era of Good Feelings, 73
Erie Canal, 85
Ernst, Joseph, 39
Ervin, Sam J., 339
Espionage Act (1917), 240
Essex Junto, 68
Ethiopia, Italian attack on, 272, 273
Ethnic politics, 115–116, 205–206
Europe, liberation of, 289
Evangelicalism, 98
Evans, Oliver, 85

Everett, Edward, 145
Executive departments, creation of, 56
Executive privilege, 336, 341
Expansionism, 82
Ex parte Milligan, 150
Export Control Act (1940), 277

Factory-safety legislation, 214
Factories, 83, 88–90
Fair Deal, 296, 304
Fair Employment Practices Act (1946), 296
Fair Employment Practices Committee, 284–285
Fair Labor Standards Act (1938), 268–269
Falangists, 273
Fall, Albert B., 248
Fallen Timbers, Battle of (1794), 60
Family: colonial, 19–20; slave, 106; women and, 196–197; middle-class attitudes toward, 197
Far East trade, 84
"Farewell Address," 62
Farley, James A., 265
Farm Bureau Federation, 251
Farm Credit Administration, 259
Farmer-Labor party, 250–251
Farmers' Alliance and Industrial Union, 206
Farmhouse, 20
Farming. *See* Agriculture
Faulkner, William, 252
Federal Art Project, 264
Federal courts, 55. *See also* Supreme Court
Federal Deposit Insurance Corporation, 263
Federal Emergency Relief Administration, 259
Federal Farm Loan Act (1916), 221
Federal Highway Act (1916), 221
Federalism: influence of, 45; party of, 54–55, 59; Hamilton's financial system and, 57–59; Jeffersonian Republicans vs., 59, 64; frontier matters and, 59–60; neutrality policy and, 60–62; 1796 election and, 62; quasi-war with France and, 62–63; repressive policies from, 63–64; "new," 336
Federalist, The, 54
Federal Music Project, 264
Federal Radio Commission, 249
Federal Reserve Act (1913), 220
Federal Reserve system, 263, 343–344, 347
Federal Theatre Project, 264
Federal Trade Commission, 220
Feldstein, Martin, 347
Feminism, 344–345
Fermi, Enrico, 285
Ferraro, Geraldine, 345
Fillmore, Millard, 135, 140
Finney, Charles G., 98
Fireside chats, 259, 264
Fish, Hamilton, 173, 174
Fisheries, 17
Fiske, John, 53
Fitzgerald, F. Scott, 252
Five Power Pact (1922), 251, 272
Florida, annexation of, 73–74
Foch, Ferdinand, 241–242
Food Administration, 239

Food-processing industries, 185
Foraker Act (1900), 225
Force acts (1870–1871), 176
Ford, Gerald R., 316, 340–343, 360–361
Ford, Henry, 185
Foreign policy: of imperialism, 28–30, 180, 224–230; of neutrality, 46, 60–61; post-Revolutionary, 47; under Grant, 173–174; of isolationism, 180–181, 238, 272–273, 275; of overseas expansion, 180; of T. Roosevelt, 227–229; in Caribbean, 228–230; dollar diplomacy, 229–230; of Wilson, 229–234; under Hughes, 251; Good Neighbor, 272; of neo-isolationism, 303–304; of "massive retaliation," 306; in Middle East, 308–309, 359–360, 362; of Kennedy, 349–351; in Vietnam, 351–356, 358–360; Nixon-Kissinger, 354–355; of rapprochement, 356–357, 362; détente, 357–358, 360–363; Kissinger-Ford, 360–361; of Carter administration, 361–363; hostage crisis and, 362–363; of Reagan, 363–365
Fortas, Abe, 336
Fort Donelson, 159
Fort Duquesne, 26–27
Forten, James, 103
Fort McHenry, 71
Fort Pickens, 145
Fort Sumter, 145–146
Foster, William Z., 245, 257
Four Freedoms (1941), 285
Four Power Pact (1922), 251
Fourteen Points, 242
Fox, George, 10
France: rivalry with England, 5; New World holdings, 25; Revolutionary War and, 41–42; American neutrality and, 60–61; quasi-war with, 62–63; Civil War and, 156–157; American Expeditionary Force in, 240–242; Nazi attack on, 274; in Vietnam, 306–308; Suez Canal and, 309
Franco, Francisco, 273
Franklin, Benjamin, 22–24, 28, 31, 41, 52
Franklin, John Hope, 172
Frazier, E. Franklin, 270
Free coinage of silver issue, 204, 207–210
Freedmen's Bureau, 168
Freedom rides, 327–328
Freeport Doctrine, 142–143
Free-soilers, 104, 128, 139
Frémont, John C., 124, 140
French and Indian War, 26–27
French Calvinists, 14
French Revolution, U.S. interest in, 59
Frick, Henry Clay, 188, 217
Friedan, Betty, 334
Fugitive Slave Act (1850), 135–137
Fulbright, J. William, 354
Fulton, Robert, 77, 85
Fur trade, 17

Gadsden Purchase, 138
Gage, Thomas, 35
Gag rule, 108
Galbraith, John K., 321
Gallatin, Albert, 66–67
Gang system, 93

Gardoqui, Diego de, 47
Garfield, James A., 204
Garland, Hamlin, 201
Garrison, William Lloyd, 98, 103–104
Garvey, Marcus, 246
Gas, poison, 231
Gates, Horatio, 40, 42
General Federation of Women's Clubs, 212
General Motors, 266–267
Genêt, Edmond, 60–61
Geneva summit (1955), 308
Gentlemen's agreement (1907), 195
George III, 27, 28, 31
German Democratic Republic, 299
German Federal Republic, 299
Germany: emigration from, 95; naval competition with England, 227; in Venezuela, 228–229; blockade of, 231; division of, 293–294; Berlin crisis and, 350. *See also* World War I; World War II
Geronimo, 192
Gershwin, George, 252–253
Gettysburg, Battle of (1863), 161
Ghent, Treaty of, 72
Ghettos, 195, 331–332
Gibbons v. *Ogden*, 77–78
Gladstone, William E., 45
Glass-Steagal Act (1933), 263
Glorious Revolution, 11–12
Gold Reserve Act (1934), 263
Gold rush (1848), 127
Gold standard, 208–210, 255, 263, 271
Goldwater, Barry, 330, 351
Goliad, 122
Gompers, Samuel, 187, 189, 220
Good Neighbor policy, 272
Goodyear, Charles, 84
Gordon, Thomas, 33
Government: self-, in colonies, 24–25, 27–28; formation of, 36–38; Confederation, 49–50; Confederate, 152; regulation by, 202–203, 207, 217; city, 213; labor and, 216–217; suburbanization and, 319–320; distribution of wealth and, 322–323; aid to education, 330
Grandfather laws, 198
Grant, Ulysses S., 155, 159–164, 169–176
Great Awakening, 21–22
Great Britain: European rivals, 5, 10, 25–27, 227; new imperialism of, 28–30; post-Revolutionary commerce with, 47; American neutrality and, 61–62; slave trade and, 119; Oregon partitioning and, 120–121; Civil War and, 156–157; Alabama claims and, 173–174; naval blockade of Germany, 231; Washington Arms Conference and, 251; Israel and, 308; Suez Canal and, 308–309. *See also* Revolutionary War
"Great Society" program, 315, 329–331
Greek-Turkish Aid Act (1947), 297–299
Greeley, Horace, 174
Greenbacks, 147–148, 173, 175
Greene, Nathanael, 42
Greenville, Treaty of, 60
Greer, attack on, 277
Grenada invasion, 364
Grenville, George, 28–30

Grimké, Angelina, 101, 104
Grimké, Sarah, 101
Gruening, Ernest, 353
Guadalcanal, Battle of (1942), 290
Guadalupe Hidalgo, Treaty of, 126
Guam, 225
Gulf of Tonkin resolution, 353, 359

Habeas corpus, Lincoln's suspension of, 150
Haiti, military government of, 230
Haldeman, H. R., 336, 339, 341
Hale, John P., 136
Hamilton, Alexander, 45, 50, 54, 56–59, 61–62, 68
Hamilton, Alice, 196
Hammond, William A., 148
Hancock, Winfield Scott, 204
Handy, William C., 252
Hanna, Marcus A., 209
Harding, Warren G., 237, 247, 248
Harlem race riots (1935), 270
Harmar, Josiah, 48
Harpers Ferry, 143
Harriman, E. H., 216
Harrison, Benjamin, 205, 207, 222
Harrison, William Henry, 70–71, 115, 117, 118
Hart, Gary, 347
Hartford Convention, 72
Harvard, 22
Hat Act (1732), 18
Haugen, Gilbert, 251
Hawaii, 222–223, 225
Hawthorne, Nathaniel, 97
Hay, John, 201, 226, 228
Hayes, Rutherford B., 176–177, 204
Haymarket Square affair, 187–188
Health, public, 195–196, 311
Hearst, William Randolph, 223
Helsinki Conference on Security and Cooperation in Europe, 361
Hemingway, Ernest, 252
Hemispheric defense, 276
Henry, Patrick, 27, 30
Henry Street Settlement, 195
Hepburn Act (1906), 217
Herrán, Tomás, 228
Herter, Christian, 310
Hill, James J., 216
Hiroshima, 291
Hispanic-Americans, 332
Hiss, Alger, 303
Hitler, Adolf. *See* World War II
Ho Chi Minh, 306
Holding companies, 183
Holland, 274
Home, colonial, 19–20
Home Owners' Loan Corporation, 259
Home rule, 30
Homestead Act (1862), 147
Homestead strike, 188
Hood, John B., 163
Hooker, Joseph, 160–161
Hoover, Herbert, 239, 248, 249, 254–257, 260, 271

Hopkins, Harry, 259
Horseshoe Bend, Battle of (1814), 71
Hostage crisis (Iran), 362–363
House Judiciary Committee, 340, 341
House of Burgesses, 6
Housing Act (1961), 327
Houston, Sam, 122
Howe, Edgar W., 201
Howe, Elias, 84
Howe, William, 40–41
Hudson's Bay Company, 120
Huerta, Victoriano, 230
Hughes, Charles Evans, 214, 233, 248, 251
Huguenots, 14
Hull, Cordell, 271–272, 273, 279
Hull House, 195, 212
Human rights, 361
Humphrey, George M., 306
Humphrey, Hubert, 326, 335, 336, 338
Hutchinson, Anne, 8
Huthmacher, J. Joseph, 211
Hydrogen bomb, 281–282

Illiteracy, 323
Immigrants: rights of, 63–64; politics and, 206
Immigration: prehistoric, 1; to colonies, 14–15; mid-19th-century, 95; 1864 contract labor law and, 147; during industrial era, 194–195; quotas on, 246, 330; 1960s population and, 318–319
Immigration Act (1965), 318–319
Imperialism, 28–30, 180, 224–230
Income tax, 147, 208–209, 220, 266
Independent Treasury system, 116, 118, 127
Indian Intercourse Act (1834), 112
Indian Removal Act (1830), 112
Indian Reorganization Act (1934), 263, 269, 333
Indians: colonial relations with, 4–5, 9, 28–29; French and Indian War and, 26–27; Washington's policy toward, 60; Jeffersonian Republicans' policy toward, 70–71; Jackson's policy toward, 112–113; army and, 191–192; citizenship for, 192; New Deal and, 269–270; Pan-Indian movement and, 333
Indigo, 16–17
Individualism, literary portrayals of, 97
Indochina, 277, 306–307, 319
Industrial capitalists, 84
Industrialization: emergence of, 83–84; Civil War and, 87; reform spirit and, 97; post-Civil War, 179; isolationism and, 180–181; growth of, 182; immigration and, 194–195. *See also* Economy
Industrial Workers of the World, 189–190
Industry: colonial, 17–18; protection of, 73; democracy and, 81; Northern advances in, 146. *See also specific industries*
Inflation: World War II and, 283–284, 296; under Eisenhower, 313; of 1970s, 337–338, 342, 343–344
Initiative, 213
Inner Light doctrine, 10
Internal Revenue Act (1862), 147
International Copyright Law (1891), 200–201
Interposition theory, 111–112
Interstate Commerce Act (1887), 205, 217

Interstate Highway Act (1956), 320
Interventionists, 275
Intolerable Acts, 34
Iran hostage crisis, 362–363
Ireland, emigration from, 14, 95
Iron Act (1750), 17
Ironclad warship, 156
Iron production, 17
Iroquois, 4, 48
Isolationism, 180–181, 238, 272–273, 275, 303–304
Israel, 308, 359–360
Iowa Jima, 291

Jackson, Andrew, 71–74, 81, 110–116, 122
Jackson, Jesse, 347
Jackson, Thomas J. ("Stonewall"), 159–160
James, Henry, 201
James, William, 203
James I, 5, 14
James II, 11–12
Jamestown, 5–6
Japan: gentlemen's agreement with (1907), 195; American colonies and, 227–228; war with Russia, 227; Shantung Peninsula and, 242–243; Washington Arms Conference and, 251; withdrawal from Five Power Pact, 272; attack on China (1937), 273; "new order" of, 273–274; American occupation policy in, 294; alliance with, 300. *See also* World War II
Japanese-Americans, imprisonment of, 285
Jaworski, Leon, 341
Jay, John, 43, 47, 54, 61–62
Jay Cooke and Company, 175
Jazz age, 251–253
Jefferson, Thomas: Declaration of Independence and, 36; on state constitutions, 37; political philosophy of, 45–46, 59; as secretary of state, 56; Hamilton's financial plan and, 58; Presidency of, 62, 65–70; Kentucky and Virginia resolutions and, 64
Jews, 21
John Birch Society, 330
Johnson, Andrew, 152, 166–170
Johnson, Hugh S., 261
Johnson, Lyndon B., 307, 315, 326, 335; Presidency of, 328–331; Vietnam War and, 351, 353–354
Johnson, Samuel, 22
Johnson, Tom, 213
Johnston, Joseph E., 156–164
Joseph, Chief, 192
Judicial review, 52, 65–66
Judiciary, 65–66, 77–78. *See also* Supreme Court
Judiciary Act: of 1789, 55–56; of 1801, 64–66
Junto club, 23

Kamikaze, 291
Kansas, 139–142
Kansas-Nebraska Act (1854), 137–139
Kearny, Stephen W., 126
Keating-Owen Act (1916), 221
Kennan, George F., 297
Kennedy, Edward, 345
Kennedy, John F., 315, 326–328, 349–351, 353

Kennedy, Robert F., 326, 328, 335, 354
Kentucky resolution (1798), 64
Keynesianism, 268
Khrushchev, Nikita, 309–311, 350, 351
King, Martin Luther, Jr., 327, 332
King George's War (1744–1748), 25
King's College, 22
King William's War (1689–1697), 25
Kissinger, Henry, 341, 354–355, 357, 358, 360–361
Knights of Labor, 207
Know-Nothings, 102–103, 139, 140
Knox, Frank, 275
Knox, Henry, 56
Knox, Philander C., 229
Konoye, Prince, 277
Korea, 292, 300–303, 305–306
Ku Klux Klan, 175, 176, 246, 253
Kuomintang, 300

Labor: colonial, 13–14; factory, 88–90; recruitment methods of, 89; 1864 contract law, 147; child, 186, 221; economy and, 186–190; unionization of, 186–190; government and, 216–217; post–World War I public opinion of, 245; 1920s prosperity of, 250; Wagner Act and, 265–266; war mobilization of, 284–285; Taft-Hartley Act and, 296. *See also* Strikes
La Follette, Robert M., 180, 214, 217, 249
Laissez faire, 115
Land Law (1820), 75
Larkin, Thomas O., 124
Latin America, 137, 310–311
Law. *See specific legislation*
League of Nations, 242, 243
League Reparations Commission, 251
Lebanon, 364–365
Lecompton constitution, 142
Ledbetter, Huddie, 252
Le Duc Tho, 358
Lee, Robert E., 155, 160–164
Legion of Decency, 264
Leisler, Jacob, 12
Leisure, 200
Lemisch, Jesse, 39
Lend-Lease Act (1941), 276, 277
Lenin, Nikolai, 233
Leo XIII, Pope, 212
Lewis, Meriwether, 68
Lewis, Sinclair, 252
Lexington, Battle of, 35–36
Leyte Gulf, Battle of, 291
Liberal Republicans, 174
Liberator, The, 103–104
Liberia, 103
Liberty Bonds, 240
Liberty party, 104, 120, 128
Liliuokalani, 222
Lincoln, Abraham, 90–91, 139; debates with Douglas, 142–143; election of, 144–145; Presidency of, 145–152; suspension of habeas corpus, 150; as war leader, 155; Reconstruction program of, 164–166; assassination of, 166. *See also* Civil War

Liquor tax, 57–58
Literacy test, 198
Literature, 96–97, 201, 252
Little Bighorn, battle of, 192
Litvinov, Maxim, 271
Livingston, Robert R., 67, 77, 85
Locke, John, 32–33, 36
Loco Focos, 115
Lodge, Henry Cabot, 243–244
Log cabin bill, 118
Log cabin campaign, 116–117
Long, Huey P., 264–265
Longworth, Alice Roosevelt, 248
López, Narciso, 137
Louis XIV, 14
Louisiana Purchase, 46, 67–69
Lowell system, 89
Loyalists, 36
Luftwaffe, 289
Lumber industry, 250
Lusitania sinking, 231–232
Lyon, Mary, 99

MacArthur, Douglas, 256, 286, 292, 294, 302
Madison, James: on centralization, 50; Constitution drafting by, 52; as Federalist, 54; Hamilton and, 58; political philosophy of, 59; Kentucky and Virginia resolutions and, 64; nomination of, 65; Marbury and, 66; *Chesapeake-Leopard* incident and, 69; territorial expansion under, 71; on transportation system, 73
Magazines, 22, 200
Maine, statehood of, 76–77
Maine incident, 223
Malenkov, Georgi, 305–306
Manassas, Battles of, 157–158, 160
Manchuria, 227, 273
Mandate system, 243
Manhattan project, 285
Manifest Destiny, 82, 180, 222
Mann, Horace, 98–99
Mann-Elkins Act (1910), 218
Manufacturing, modern, 182, 183
Manumission, 105
Marbury v. *Madison,* 66
March on Washington, 328
Marcy, William L., 111
Mariana Islands, 291
Marne, Battle of the (1914), 231
Marriage, 197
Marshall, George C., 299, 300
Marshall, John, 46, 66, 69, 77–78, 113
Marshall Islands, 290
Marshall Plan, 299
Maryland, 5–7, 11
Mary II, 11–12
Mason, James M., 157
Massachusetts, 11
Massachusetts Bay, 7
"Massive retaliation" policy, 306
Mass production, 83, 184
Mayflower, 7

McAdoo, William G., 240, 249
McCarran Internal Security Act (1950), 303
McCarthy, Eugene, 335, 354
McCarthy, Joseph, 303, 311–312. *See also* Cold War
McClellan, George B., 152, 159–160
McClure, S. S., 213
McCord, James W., Jr., 339
McCormick, Cyrus H., 90
McCulloch v. *Maryland,* 77
McDonald, Forrest, 53
McDowell, Irvin, 157–158
McGillivray, Alexander, 48
McGovern, George M., 338
McGuffey, William Holmes, 99
McKinley, William, 209, 210, 222, 223
McKinley Tariff (1890), 222
McKitrick, Eric, 172
McNamara, Robert, 349
McNary-Haugen bill (1924), 251
Meade, George G., 161–164
Meat Inspection Act (1906), 217
Medicare–Social Security Act (1965), 330
Megalopolis, rise of, 319–320
Mellon, Andrew W., 248, 249
Melville, Herman, 97
Memminger, Christopher G., 152–153
Mercantilism, 3, 16, 17
Merchant capitalists, 84
Merchant Marine Act (1916), 232
Merchants, colonial, 18
Mergers, 249–250
Merrimack, 156
Mexican-Americans, 332
Mexico: territorial acquisitions from, 121–126; war with (1846–1848), 124–126; Napoleon III and, 157; Wilson and, 230; Good Neighbor policy and, 272
Middle class: rise of, 186; attitudes about family, 197; progressive movement and, 210–212
Middle East: foreign policy in, 308–309, 359–360, 362; oil embargo, 321–322, 342, 344; conflicts in, 359–360, 362, 364–365
Middle passage, 14
Midnight appointments, 64
Midway, Battle of (1941), 287
Midway Islands, 173
Miles, Nelson A., 224
Mills, colonial, 17
Mills bill, 205
Mining, 190, 250
Minorities: Orientals, 227–228, 285; Spanish-speaking, 332–333. *See also* Blacks; Indians
Minutemen, 35
MIRV, 357–358
Missile crisis, Cuban, 350–351
Mississippi Plan, 175
Mississippi Valley, 75
Missouri Compromise, 75–77
Mitchell, Arthur W., 269
Mitchell, John, 216–217, 338, 341–342
Molasses Act (1733), 18
Moley, Raymond, 256

Molotov, Vyacheslav, 287
Mondale, Walter F., 342, 347, 365
Money: colonial, 18, 38; post-Revolutionary demand
    for, 49; trust, 220; New Deal and, 263. *See also* Banks
    and banking
Monitor, 156
Monroe, James, 46, 62, 67, 73
Monroe Doctrine, 78, 173, 228–229
Monte Cassino, capture of (1944), 289
Montgomery, Bernard L., 289
Moon landing, 315, 318
Morgan, J. P., 183, 208, 216
Mormons, 126–127
Morrill Land Grant Act (1862), 147, 199
Morrill Tariff Act, 147
Morris, Robert, 49
Morse, Samuel F. B., 86–87, 102
Morse, Wayne, 353
Mortality rate, colonial, 15
Mortgage relief, 259
Motion pictures, 200, 252, 264
Mott, Lucretia, 101
Mount Holyoke College, 99
Mowry, George, 211
Muckrakers, 212–213
Mugwumps, 205
Music, 1920s, 252–253
Muskie, Edmund, 338, 340
Mussolini, Benito, 238, 272, 274
Mutual Defense Act (1949), 300
My Lai massacre, 356

Nader, Ralph, 321
Nagasaki, 291
Nantes, Edict of (1598), 14
Napoleon III, 156, 157, 173
Nash, Gary B., 39
Nashville, Battle of (1864), 163
Nasser, Gamal Abdel, 308–309
Nation, Carry, 214
National Aeronautics and Space Administration, 318
National Association for the Advancement of Colored
    People, 198–199, 246, 312, 327
National Association of Manufacturers, 190
National Bank Act (1863), 147
National Banking System, 147
National Broadcasting Company, 252
National City Bank, 183
National Defense Education Act (1958), 323
National Energy Conservation Policy Act (1978), 344
National Farmers' Alliance, 206
National Housing Act (1949), 304
National Industrial Recovery Act (1933), 261–262
National Labor Union, 186
National Organization of Women, 334
National Origins Act (1924), 246
National Republicans, 111
National Science Foundation, 318
National Security Act: of 1947, 295; of 1949, 296
National Security Resources Board, 295
National Trades' Union, 89
National Urban League, 198–199

National Woman Suffrage Association, 215
Nativist movement, 102–103
Naturalism, 201
Naturalization Act, 63, 65
Natural resources, depletion of, 320
Navigation Acts (1660), 11, 18
Navy, 227
Nazis. *See* World War II
Neutrality Act: of 1794, 60; of 1935, 273, 274
Neutrality policy: 1793 European war and, 46; Federal-
    ists and, 60–62; World War I and, 231–232; World
    War II and, 272–273
New Deal: components of, 238; as platform, 256; bank-
    ing and, 258–259, 263; agriculture and, 259–261;
    emergency relief program of, 259; nature of, 260;
    NRA and, 261–262; Tennessee Valley Authority and,
    262–263; culture and, 263–264; money and banking
    and, 263; leftist opposition to, 264–265; Second,
    265–266; unions and, 266–267; 1936 election and,
    267; Supreme Court and, 267–268; 1937 recession
    and, 268; Indians and blacks and, 269–270
New England, 7–9, 49
New England Antislavery Society, 104
New England Confederation, 9
New Federalism, 336
New Freedom program, 219–221
New Frontier, 326
New Harmony, 100
New Jersey, 10
New Jersey Plan, 51
New Left, 298
New Mexico, 122–123, 133
New Nationalism, 218
New Netherland, 10
New Orleans, 67, 71–72
New Right, 346–347
News-Letter, 22
Newspapers, 22, 200
New York City, 9–10, 94–95, 320
Niagara Movement, 198
Nicaragua, 137, 229, 364
Nicholson, Francis, 11–12
Nine Power Pact (1922), 251
Nixon, Richard M.: Hiss case and, 303; Vice-Presidency
    of, 305, 310; public reactions to, 315–316; on televi-
    sion, 324–326; Presidency of, 335–341; Vietnam War
    and, 354–359
Noble Order of the Knights of Labor, 187
Nonimportation agreement, 31
Non-Partisan League, 250
Normalcy, 248–249
Norris, Frank, 201
Norrris, George, 262
North, Frederick, 31, 33–34
North, Simeon, 83
North Africa, invasion of, 287
North Atlantic Council, 300
North Atlantic Treaty Organization, 299–300
Northern Alliance, 206
Northern Confederacy, 68
Northern politics, 150–151
Northern Securities Company, 216

North Star, 103
Northwest Ordinance (1787), 48
Norway, 274
Noyes, John Humphrey, 100
Nuclear plants, 322
Nuclear race. *See* Arms race
Nullification theory, 111–112
Nuremberg trials, 293
Nurses, 148–150
Nye, Gerald P., 272

Oberlin College, 99
O'Connor, Sandra Day, 344
Office of Economic Opportunity, 337
Office of Price Administration, 283
Office of Scientific Research and Development, 285
Ogden, Aaron, 77
Ohio idea, 173
Oil embargo, Arab, 321–322, 342, 344
Oil Producing and Exporting Countries, 342
Okinawa, Battle of, 291
Olds, Ransom, 185
Olney, Richard, 189
Oneida Community, 100
Opechancanough, 5
Open Door policy, 226–227
Operation Pan-America, 310
Oppenheimer, J. Robert, 285
Ordinance of 1785, 48
Oregon, partitioning of, 120–121
Osceola, Chief, 112
"Ostend Manifesto," 137
Oswald, Lee Harvey, 328
Otis, James, 27–28, 31
Otis, Mercy, 23
Overman Act (1917), 239
Oversoul, 97–98
Owen, Robert, 100

Pacific front, in World War II, 289–291
Paine, Thomas, 2, 36
Palestine, partitioning of, 308
Palestine Liberation Organization, 364
Palmer, A. Mitchell, 245
Panama Canal, 228, 361–362
Panay sinking, 273–274
Panic. *See* Depression
Pan-Indian movement, 333
Paris, Treaty of (1898), 225
Parity pricing, 251
Parker, Alton B., 217
Parson's cause, trial of, 27
Paterson, William, 51
Patroons, 10
Patton, George, 256
Paul, Alice, 215
Paxton Boys, 29
Payne-Aldrich Act (1909), 218
Peace Democrats, 150
Peace movement, in Vietnam War, 354, 356
Pearl Harbor, 277–279
Peirce, Charles, 202–203

Pendleton Act (1883), 204–205
Penn, William, 10–11
Pennsylvania, 10–11
People's Republic of China. *See* China
Pequots, 9
Perkins, Frances, 265
Perry, Matthew C., 137
Perryville, Battle of (1862), 159
Pershing, John J., 230, 241
Personal-liberty laws, 136–137
"Pet" banks, 114
Petersburg, seige at, 162–164
Petroleum industry, 184–185
Philadelphia, 11
Philip, King, 9
Philippines, 225, 226, 244, 272, 291
Pierce, Franklin, 136–140
Pike, Zebulon Montgomery, 68
Pilgrims, 7
Pinchback, P. B. S., 171
Pinchot, Gifford, 218
Pinckney, Thomas, 61–62
Pinkerton Detective Agency, 188
Pirates, Barbary, 66
Pitt, William, 27, 28
Plains Indians, 191–192
Planters, Southern, 92
Platt Amendment (1901), 226, 272
Plattsburg, Battle of (1814), 71
Plessy v. *Ferguson,* 196, 312
Plymouth, 7
Pocahontas, 5
Point Four program, 299
Poison gas, 231
Poland, 274, 292
Polio vaccine, 317
Political boss, 195, 196, 210
Political parties: rise of, 59; Twelfth Amendment and, 65; increased importance of, 109; ethnicity and, 115–116; sectionalization and, 131; Kansas-Nebraska Act and, 138; progressivism and, 180. *See also* Congress; Elections, congressional; Politics; *specific parties and Presidents*
Politics: of abolitionism, 103–104; ethnic, 115–116, 205–206; sectionalist, 140–141; during Civil War, 150–151, 154; Northern, 150–151; Confederate, 154; Progressivism, 180, 181, 210–221, 246–247; during World War I, 181, 286; of complacency, 204–205; Populists' rise in, 206–207; during World War II, 286
Polk, James K., 82, 119–120, 121–128
Pollock v. *The Farmer's Loan and Trust Co.,* 209
Pollution, 320, 321
Pontiac, 28
Pools, 183
Poor Richard's Almanac, 22
Pope, John, 160
Popular sovereignty, 127, 140, 142
Population: colonial, 14–15; economic growth and, 94–95; during industrial era, 194; 1960s increase in, 318–319
Populism, 180, 206–210

Porter, Kenneth W., 184
Potsdam Conference, 291, 293
Pottawatomi massacre, 140
Poverty: single-tax remedy to, 202; post-1960 levels, 322; civil rights and, 328–329; war on, 328, 330–331
Powderly, Terence V., 187
Powell, Lewis F., Jr., 337
Power, division and separation of, 54
Powhatan, 5
Presidency: television and, 324–325; imperial, 336, 359
Presidential Succession Act, 205
Price(s) and pricing: parity, 251; fixing, 261; World War II levels of, 283. *See also* Inflation
Prigg v. *Pennsylvania*, 104
Primary, direct, 213
Princeton, 22
Printers, 89
Proclamation Line (1763), 28
Progressive party, 219, 249
Progressivism: origins of, 180, 210–212; political parties and, 180; Wilson and, 180, 214, 219–221; World War I and, 181; nature of, 211; in cities, 212–213; social justice and, 212; women and, 214–215; T. Roosevelt and, 215–219; Taft and, 217–219; decline of, 246–247
Prohibition, 214–215, 246, 253–254
Project Tepee, 310
Propaganda, 237, 240
Property, suffrage and, 37, 198
Prophet, The (Tecumseh's brother), 70
Proposition 13, 346
Prosser, Gabriel, 106
Protestantism, evangelical, 98
Protestants, 14, 21
Providence, 8
Public services, 321
Publishing business, 200–201
Puerto Ricans, 332
Puerto Rico, 225–226
Pujo, Arsene, 220
Pulitzer, Joseph, 223
Pullman strike, 188–189
Pure Food and Drug Act (1906), 217
Puritans, 7–9, 21

Quakers, 10–11
Quebec, 5, 27
Quebec Act (1774), 33–34
Queen Anne's War (1701–1713), 25
Quitman, John A., 137
Quitrents, 9

Race riots: of 1909, 198; of 1920s, 246; Harlem (1935), 270; Detroit (1943), 284; of mid-1960s, 331–332; "zoot-suit," 332
Radical Reconstruction. *See* Reconstruction
Radios, 264
Railroad Administration, 239
Railroads: development of, 86–88; transcontinental, 137–138, 182–183; business-oriented legislation and, 147; industrial expansion and, 182–183; competition against, 250; strikes of 1877, 186–187; farmers' grievance against, 193; Interstate Commerce Act and,

205, 217; Northern Securities Company monopoly, 216
Randall, James G., 149
Randolph, A. Philip, 284
Randolph, Edmund, 51, 56, 61, 62
Randolph, John, 105
Randolph, Thomas, 58
Rankin, Jeannette, 215
Rauschenbusch, Walter, 212
Reading: in colonies, 22; in New Deal era, 264
Reagan, Ronald, 316, 336, 342, 344–348, 362–365
Reaganomics, 346
Reaper, 90
Recession: of 1937, 269–270; of 1957, 313; of 1960–1962, 313, 326; of 1974, 316, 342; of 1981–1982, 347
Reciprocal Trade Agreements Act (1934), 272
Reconstruction: negative depiction of, 132; under Lincoln, 164–166; under Johnson, 166–170; Congress and, 167–170; 1867 acts, 169; black politicians during, 171; nature of, 172; terrorist resistance to, 175–176
Reconstruction Finance Corporation, 255
Red Cloud, Chief, 192
Red Cross, 255
Redeemers, 197
Redemptioners, 13
"Red" scare, 245–246
Referendum, 213
Reform: spirit of, 97–99; women's rights, 100–102, 344–345; Nativist movement, 102–103; under Jackson, 111; of civil service, 204–205; in cities, 212–213. *See also* Progressivism; Slavery
Regulator movement, 29
Rehnquist, William H., 337
Relief act (1821), 75
Religion, 20–21, 97–98
Reparations payments, 251
Representation, "virtual" vs. actual, 32
Republican party: formation of, 131, 138–139; ideology of, 139; rise in power of, 143; 1860 platform of, 144; post–Civil War coalition and, 171; loss of Southern states, 175–176; rift in, under Taft, 218–219. *See also* Elections, congressional; Politics; *specific Presidents*
Republicans, Jeffersonian: federal authority and, 45–46; Federalists vs., 59, 64; social philosophy of, 59; rights of aliens and, 63–64; Jefferson Presidency, 65–70; judiciary and, 65–66, 77–78; economic policy of, 66–67, 72–73, 75; territorial expansion under, 67–68, 73–75; Burr conspiracy and, 68–69; Anglo-French war and, 69–70; Indian policy of, 70–71; War of 1812 and, 70–72; internal improvements by, 72–73; Missouri Compromise and, 75–77; Monroe Doctrine and, 78
Rerum Novarum, 212
Research, basic, 318
Resettlement Administration, 266
Resumption Act (1875), 175
Retaliation, massive, 306
Retirement age, 323
Reuben James sinking, 277
Revenue Act: of 1916, 221, 232; of 1942, 284

Revere, Paul, 35
Revivalism, women's movement and, 100–101
Revolutionary War: start of, 35–36; government formation and, 36–38; mobilizing for, 38–40; to 1777, 40–41; French and Spanish aid in, 41–42; Yorktown victory and, 42–43; peace treaty of, 43–44
Reynolds v. *Sims*, 329
Rhee, Syngman, 301
Rhode Island, 8
Rice, 91
Riots: race, 198, 246, 270, 284, 331–332; student, 324
Roads, interregional, 85
Robin Moor sinking, 277
Rochambeau, John Baptiste Donatien de Vimeur de, 43
Rockefeller, John D., 184, 185
Rockefeller, Nelson, 336, 341
Rolfe, John, 5
Roman Catholics, 21, 102
Roosevelt, Franklin D., 238, 247, 256–257, 291–292. *See also* New Deal; World War II
Roosevelt, Theodore, 180, 197, 215–219, 227–229
Roosevelt Corollary, 228–229
Root-Takahira Agreement, 228
Rosencrans, William S., 161
Rotary press, 88
Royal Society of London, 23
Rubber vulcanization, 84
Ruby, Jack, 328
Rural Electrification Administration, 266
Russia: war with Japan, 227; revolution in, 233, 240. *See also* Soviet Union
Ryan, John Augustine, 212

Sacco, Nicola, 245
Sadat, Anwar, 362
Salk, Jonas, 317
SALT, 358, 361–363
Salvation Army, 195, 212
Sanford, J. F. A., 141
San Jacinto, 157
San Jacinto, Battle of (1836), 122
San Juan Hill, Battle of, 224
Santa Anna, Antonio López de, 122, 126
Santa Fe trade, 123
Santiago campaign, 224
Santo Domingo, military government of, 229–230
Saratoga, 41
Scalawags, 171
Scammon, R. M., 338
Schechter brothers, 261–262
Schlesinger, Arthur M., Jr., 149, 260
Schuyler, Philip, 40
Science, 22–23, 285, 317–318
Scotch-Irish immigration, 14–15
Scots, emigration of, 14
Scott, Dred, 141
Scott, Walter, 97
Scott, Winfield, 113, 126, 136
Secession: Louisiana Purchase and, 69; of South, 145–146
Second Awakening, 98
Sectionalism: economy and, 81; intensification of,

81–82; slavery and, 81–82; railroad developments and, 86; telegraph and, 88; parties and, 131; politics of, 140–141. *See also* Civil War
Sedgwick, Catharine Maria, 97
Sedition Act: under Federalists, 63–65; of 1917, 240
Segregation: purpose of, 94; of Oriental schoolchildren, 227–228. *See also* Blacks; Slavery
Selective Service Act: of 1917, 239; of 1940, 284
Senate War Investigating Committee, 283
Senators, election of, 214
Separate but equal principle, 198
Separation of powers, 54
Servitude, 6, 13
Seven Days, Battle of the (1862), 160
"Seventh of March address," 135
Seward, William H., 135, 144, 150, 166, 173–174
Sex roles, 20
Seymour, Horatio, 173
Shafter, William R., 224
Shantung Peninsula, 242–243
Shays, Daniel, 49–50
Sheridan, Philip H., 170
Sherman, William T., 161–164
Sherman Antitrust Act (1890), 207, 216
Sherman Silver Purchase Act, 207, 208
Shiloh, Battle of (1862), 159
Shipping Board, 239
Shipping industry, 17, 84–85
Shuttle diplomacy, 360
Sicily, invasion of, 287–289
Silent majority, 335, 355
Silver, free coinage of, 204, 207–210
Singapore, 277
Singer, Isaac, 84
Sirica, John J., 339, 340
Sit-down strikes, 266–267
Sit-ins, 327
Sitting Bull, 192
Six-Day War, 360
Slash-and-burn agriculture, 4
Slater, Samuel, 83
Slavery: introduction of, 6; tobacco industry and, 13; situations suiting, 16; colonials' opposition to, 37; sectionalism and, 81–82; institution of, 93–94; black critics of, 103; blacks' responses to, 105–107; defense of, 106–108; westward expansion and, 127–128, 131; emancipation from, 151–152. *See also* Abolitionism; Blacks; Civil War
Slaves: colonial class structure and, 19; three-fifths formula and, 51, 52; urban, 93; in North, 103; culture of, 106; family of, 106. *See also* Blacks
Slave trade, 13–14, 94, 119
Slidell, John, 124, 157
Slums, 195, 331–332
Smith, Abigail, 23
Smith, Adam, 202
Smith, Alfred E., 249, 253
Smith, Joseph, 126
Snyder Act (1924), 269
Social Darwinism, 202
Social justice movement, 212. *See also* Progressivism
Social security, 265, 270, 323, 330

Society: class structure, 18–19, 92, 139; urban centers, 94–95, 194–196, 212–213, 320; wealth distribution, 186, 322–323; rise of megalopolis in, 319–320; post-1960s affluence of, 320–321. *See also* Blacks; Women
Society of the Cincinnati, 50
Soil Conservation and Domestic Allotment Act (1936), 266
Soil Erosion Service, 263
Solomon Islands, 290
Sons of Liberty, 30–31
Soulé, Pierre, 137
South: agriculture in, 91–92; secession of, 145–146. *See also* Civil War
South Carolina, 113–114
South Carolina Exposition and Protest, The, 112
Southeast Asia Treaty Organization, 307
Southern Alliance, 206
Southern Christian Leadership Conference, 327
Southern Tenant Farmers' Union, 270
Sovereignty: popular, 127, 140, 142; state, 152
Soviet Union: U.S. recognition of, 271; German attack on, 277; World War II territorial gains of, 291–292; rocket race with, 309–310; Suez Canal and, 309; Berlin crisis and, 350; Cuban missile crisis and, 350–351; China and, 351; détente with, 357–358, 360–363; invasion of Afghanistan, 363; Reagan's relations with, 363. *See also* Cold War
Space research, 309–310, 317–318
Spain: rivalry with England, 5; Revolutionary War and, 41–42; post-Revolution relationship with, 47; Jay's Treaty and, 61–62; Florida annexation and, 73–74; civil war in, 273
Spanish-American War, 223–225
Spanish Civil War, 273
Sparkman, John J., 305
Spencer, Herbert, 202
Spoils system, 111, 174
Sports, 200
Sputnik, 309, 317–318
Stagflation, 338
Stalin, Joseph, 292, 298
Stamp Act (1765), 29–31
Standard Oil Company, 185
Stanton, Edwin M., 150, 170
Stanton, Elizabeth Cady, 101
Stark, Harold R., 277
"Star Wars," 363
State governments, formation of, 36–37
State rights, 154
State-rights party, 154
State sovereignty, 152
States Rights' Democratic party, 297
Steamboat, 85
Steffens, Lincoln, 213
Stein, Gertrude, 252
Stephens, Alexander H., 152
Stephens, Uriah S., 187–188
Stevens, John L., 86, 222
Stevens, Robert, 312
Stevens, Thaddeus, 151, 165
Stevenson, Adlai E., 305

Stimson, Henry L., 273, 275, 278
Stimson Doctrine, 273
Stowe, Harriet Beecher, 97, 136
Strategic Arms Reduction Talks, 363, 365
Strikes: railroad, 186–187; Homestead, 188; Pullman, 188–189; Danbury Hatters', 190; United Mine workers, 216–217; post–World War I, 245; sit-down, 266–267. *See also* Labor
Student Nonviolent Coordinating Committee, 331
Stuyvesant, Peter, 10
Submarines, atomic-powered, 310
Submarine warfare, 231, 233, 277, 287
Subtreasury system, 116, 118, 127
Suburbanization, 319–320
Suez Canal, 308–309
Suffrage: property and, 37, 198; woman, 102, 215, 246–247; black, 165, 169, 170, 198
Sugar, 91
Sugar Act (1764), 29
Sumner, Charles, 105, 140, 151, 165, 174
Supply and demand, 202
Supply-side economics, 346
Supreme Court: creation of, 55–56; separate but equal principle and, 198; on income tax, 209; on NRA, 261–262; New Deal and, 267–268; war decisions of, 285; on desegregation, 312; 1962 reapportionment decision, 329; Nixon and, 336–337, 341; on abortion, 345
Supreme Order of the Star-Spangled Banner, 102–103, 139, 140
Surplus Marketing Administration, 268
Sussex sinking, 232
Swope, Gerald, 266
Sylvis, William H., 186
Synthetics, 321

Taft, Robert A., 305
Taft, William H., 217–219, 229–230
Taft-Hartley Labor-Management Relations Act (1947), 296
Taft-Katsura executive agreement (1905), 227
Taiwan, 307–308
Talleyrand, Charles Maurice de, 62–63
Tallmadge, James, Jr., 76
Taney, Roger B., 141
Tariff: of abominations, 111, 113–114; of 1842, 118; of 1846, 127; Underwood-Simmons, 220
Task system, 93
Tax(es): internal vs. external, 31, 32; post-Revolutionary, 48–50; import, 58; income, 147, 208–209, 220, 266; poll, 198; single, 202; war costs and, 284; 1963 reduction in, 327; revolt, 346; Reagan reforms, 348. *See also specific tax legislation*
Taylor, Zachary, 122, 126, 128, 133–135
Taylor Grazing Act (1934), 263
Tea Act (1773), 33
Teaching, growth as profession, 99
Teapot Dome, 248
Technical Cooperation program, 299
Technology, 317–318
Tecumseh, 70–71

Telegraph, 86–88
Television, 324–325
Temperance movement, 100, 214–215
Temporary Commission on Employee Loyalty, 303
Temporary Emergency Relief Administration, 256
Tennessee Valley Authority, 262–263
Tenure of Office Act (1867), 169, 170
Terrorism, 364–365
Tet offensive, 354
Texas, 119–122
Textile industry, 89, 250
Thailand, 277
Thames, Battle of the (1813), 71
Thieu, Nguyen Van, 353, 360
Thomas, George H., 163
Thomas, Jesse B., 77
Thomas, Norman, 257
Thoreau, Henry David, 97
Three-fifths rule, 51, 52
Thurmond, J. Strom, 297
Tilden, Samuel J., 176
Tippecanoe, Battle of, (1811), 71
Tito, Marshal, 299
Tobacco, 5, 6, 13, 18, 91
Tocqueville, Alexis de, 81
Toleration Act (1649), 21
Tories, 36
Torrijos Herrera, Omar, 361
Towns, 8, 83, 15
Townsend, Francis E., 264
Townshend, Charles, 31
Townshend Act (1767), 31–32
Trade: slave, 13–14, 94, 119; unions, 89; associations, 249, 261; foreign, 271–272. *See also* Business; Economy
Trail of tears, 113
Transcendental movement, 97–98
Transcontinental railroad, 137–138, 182–183
Transportation system, 72, 73, 84–88, 182–183, 185
Trenchard, John, 33
Trent affair, 157
Triangle Shirtwaist Factory fire, 214
Triangular route, 13–14
Tripartite Pact (1940), 277
Tripoli, war in, 66–67
Truman, Harry S.: on Senate War Investigating Committee, 283; Vice-Presidential nomination of, 286; atomic bomb and, 291, 295; at Potsdam, 293; Fair Deal and, 296, 304; containment policy of, 297–299; election of, 297; Korean War and, 300–303; McCarthyism and, 303; Vietnam involvement of, 353
Truman Doctrine, 297–299
Trunk lines, 86
Trusts, 183, 207, 215–216, 220
Tryon, William, 29
Tunisia, 287
Turkey, 297–299
Turner, Nat, 106
Turnpikes, 85
Twain, Mark, 201
Tweed, William M., 196

Tydings-McDuffie Act (1934), 272
Tyler, John, 117–119, 122

Underground Railroad, 105
Understanding and literacy test, 198
Underwood-Simmons Tariff, 220
Unemployment, 327, 342
Union Army Medical Bureau, 148
Unionization, 186–190
Union Pacific Railroad Company, 147, 174, 182–183
Union party, 152
Unions, 89–90, 250, 266–267. *See also* Labor
Unitarian doctrine, 97
United Automobile Workers, 266–267
United Mine Workers, 216–217
United Nations, 281, 293
United States Sanitary Commission, 148
United States Shipping Board, 232
United States Steel, 185, 245, 267, 327
United States v. *Richard M. Nixon,* 341
Universalist doctrine, 97
Universal Negro Improvement Association, 246
University of Pennsylvania, 22
Urban renewal projects, 320
U'Ren, William S., 213
Utrecht, Treat of (1713), 25
U-2 incident, 310

Vallandigham, Clement L., 150
Van Buren, Martin, 115, 116, 119–120, 128
Vance, Cyrus, 361
Vance, Zebulon M., 154
Vandenberg, Arthur H., 293
Vanzetti, Bartolomeo, 245
Venezuela, German intervention in, 228–229
Vergennes, Charles Gravier de, 41, 43
Versailles, 242–244
Vesey, Denmark, 106
V-E Day, 289
Vicksburg, Battle of (1863), 160–161
Vietnamization, 355–356
Vietnam War: France and, 306–308; consequences of, 315–316; protests against, 331; escalation of, 351–356; de-escalation of, 354; conclusion of, 358–360; costs of, 359
Villa, Francisco ("Pancho"), 230
Vinson, Fred, 303
Virginia, 5–7, 11, 159–160, 162
Virginia Plan, 51
Virginia resolutions (1798), 30, 64
Virgin Islands, purchase of, 229
VISTA, 328
Volstead Act (1919), 246, 253
Voluntarism, 249
Voluntary trade associations, 249
Voting, 109, 198, 338. *See also* Suffrage

Wade-Davis bill (1864), 165–166
Wages, women's, 186
Wagner, Robert F., 265
Wagner Act (1935), 265–267

Wald, Lillian D., 195
Walker, David, 103
Walker, William, 137
Wallace, George, 335, 338
Wallace, Henry A., 275, 297
Wall Street crash, 254
Waltham system, 89
Wampanoag Indians, 9
War Democrats, 150
War Industries Board, 239
War Labor Board, 239–240
Warner, Charles Dudley, 201
War of 1812, 46, 70–72
War powers resolution (1973), 359
War Production Board, 283
Warren, Earl, 297, 312, 336
War Revenue Act, 240
Warship, ironclad, 156
Washington, Booker T., 198
Washington, George, 40, 51, 55–57, 59–60, 62
Washington, Treaty of (1871), 174
Washington Arms Conference, 251
Watergate scandal, 325, 339–341
Watson, James D., 317
Wattenberg, B. J., 338
Wayne, "Mad" Anthony, 60
Wealth, distribution of, 186, 322–323
Weaver, James B., 208
Webster, Daniel, 77, 84, 114–115, 118–119, 135, 137
Webster, Noah, 96
Webster-Ashburton Treaty (1842), 119
Wedemyer, Albert C., 300
Weinberger, Caspar, 363
Welch, Robert, 330
Weld, Theodore, 104
Welfare state, 238
Welfare system, 322–323
Wesley, Charles, 21
Wesley, John, 21
West: post-Revolutionary, 48; securing, 60
West Coast Hotel v. *Parrish*, 268
Western Union Telegraph Company, 88
West Germany, establishment of, 299
West Indies trade, 18
West Virginia, 146
Weyler, Valeriano, 223
Wheat, demand for, 16
Whigs: Democrats vs., 115–117; decline of, 118–120;
  Kansas-Nebraska Act and, 138
Whiskey Rebellion (1794), 59
Whiskey Ring, 174–175
White, Hugh Lawson, 115
White, William Allen, 275
Whitefield, George, 21
Whiteman, Paul, 253
Whites, poor, 92
Whitman, Walt, 97
Whitney, Eli, 83
Wickersham, George, 253–254
Wilkes, Charles, 157
Willard, Frances E., 214

William and Mary College, 22
William of Orange, 11–12
Williams, Hannah, 23
Williams, Roger, 8–9
Willkie, Wendell, 275–276
Wilmot Proviso, 127
Wilson, Charles E., 311
Wilson, Woodrow: progressivism and, 180, 214, 219–221; declaration of war by, 181; Presidency of, 219–221; bank reforms by, 220; foreign policy of, 229–234. *See also* World War I
Wilson-Gorman Tariff, 208–209
Winthrop, John, 7–8
Wobblies, 189–190
Wolfe, James, 27
Women: demand for rights for, 100, 333–334, 344–345; education and, 101, 199; suffrage, 102, 215, 246–247; effect of Civil War on, 148–150; wage scale of, 186; employment of, 196–197; family life and, 196–197; social justice movement and, 212; progressive reforms and, 214–215
Women's Christian Temperance Union, 214
Wood, Grant, 264
Wood, Robert E., 275
Woodward, C. Vann, 172
Woolen Act (1699), 17
Worcester v. *Georgia*, 113
Workers. *See* Labor
Workmen's compensation system, 221
Works Progress Administration, 265
World War I: politics during, 181, 286; progressivism and, 181; neutrality policy and, 231–232; preparedness program and, 232–233; entry into, 233–234; propaganda and, 237, 240; mobilization for, 239–240; American Expeditionary Force in, 240–242; aftermath of, 242–247
World War II: American ambivalence toward, 271, 275; events leading to, 272–274; neutrality policy and, 272–273; material aid to Allies and, 274–276; election of 1940 and, 275–276; Pearl Harbor attack and, 277–279; inflation and, 283–284; mobilization for, 283–285; Four Freedoms and, 285; politics during, 286; U.S. strategy for, 286; in Mediterranean, 287–289; European liberation and, 289; in Pacific, 289–291; peace process, 291–294
Writing, in colonies, 22
Writs of assistance, 27

X. Y. Z. Affair, 62–63

Yale, 22
Yalta Conference, 292
Yorktown, 42–43
Young, Brigham, 126–127
Young, Coleman, 346
Youth programs, 330

Zimmerman, Arthur, 233
Zinn, Howard, 260
Zola, Émile, 201
"Zoot-suit" riots, 332

About the Authors

RICHARD N. CURRENT is University Distinguished Emeritus Professor of History at the University of North Carolina at Greensboro. He is co-author of the Bancroft Prize–winning *Lincoln the President*. His books include *Three Carpetbag Governors, The Lincoln Nobody Knows, Daniel Webster and the Rise of National Conservatism*, and *Secretary Stimson*. Professor Current has lectured on United States history in Europe, Asia, South America, Australia, and Antarctica. He has been a Fulbright Lecturer at the University of Munich and the University of Chile at Santiago, and has served as Harmsworth Professor of American History at Oxford. He is a past president of the Southern Historical Association.

T. HARRY WILLIAMS was Boyd Professor of History at Louisiana State University. He was awarded both the 1969 Pulitzer Prize and the National Book Award for his biography of *Huey Long*. His books include *Lincoln and His Generals; Lincoln and the Radicals; P. G. T. Beauregard; Americans at War; Romance and Realism in Southern Politics; Hays of the Twenty-Third; McClellan, Sherman, and Grant; The Union Sundered;* and *The Union Restored*. Professor Williams was a Harmsworth Professor of American History at Oxford and president of both the Southern Historical Association and the Organization of American Historians.

FRANK FREIDEL is Bullitt Professor of History at the University of Washington and Charles Warren Emeritus Professor of History at Harvard University. He is writing an eight-volume biography of Franklin D. Roosevelt, four volumes of which have been published. Among his other books are *Our Country's Presidents, F. D. R. and the South, America in the Twentieth Century*, and the 1974 edition of the *Harvard Guide to American History*. He is past president of the Organization of American Historians and of the New England Historical Society. He has been Harmsworth Professor at Oxford and has lectured on five continents.

W. ELLIOT BROWNLEE is Professor of History at the University of California, Santa Barbara. He is a graduate of Harvard University, received his Ph.D. from the University of Wisconsin, and specializes in United States economic history. He has been awarded fellowships by the Haynes Foundation and the Charles Warren Center, Harvard University. His published works include *Progressivism and Economic Growth: The Wisconsin Income Tax, 1911–1929; Women in the American Economy: A Documentary History, 1675 to 1929;* and *Dynamics of Ascent: A History of the American Economy*. He is also the author of numerous articles and reviews.

A Note on the Type

The text of this book is set in CALEDONIA, a Linotype face designed by W. A. Dwiggins. It belongs to the family of printing types called "modern face" by printers — a term used to mark the change in style of type-letters that occurred about 1800. Caledonia borders on the general design of Scotch Modern, but is more freely drawn than that letter.